2003
The Supreme Court Review

2003
The

"Judges as persons, or courts as institutions, are entitled to
no greater immunity from criticism than other persons
or institutions . . . [J]udges must be kept mindful of their limitations and
of their ultimate public responsibility by a vigorous
stream of criticism expressed with candor however blunt."
—*Felix Frankfurter*

". . . while it is proper that people should find fault when
their judges fail, it is only reasonable that they should recognize the
difficulties. . . . Let them be severely brought to book,
when they go wrong, but by those who will take the trouble
to understand them."
—*Learned Hand*

THE LAW SCHOOL

THE UNIVERSITY OF CHICAGO

Supreme Court Review

EDITED BY

DENNIS J. HUTCHINSON
DAVID A. STRAUSS
AND GEOFFREY R. STONE

THE UNIVERSITY OF CHICAGO PRESS

CHICAGO AND LONDON

INTERNATIONAL STANDARD BOOK NUMBER: 0-226-36320-1

LIBRARY OF CONGRESS CATALOG CARD NUMBER: 60-14353

THE UNIVERSITY OF CHICAGO PRESS, CHICAGO 60637

THE UNIVERSITY OF CHICAGO PRESS, LTD., LONDON

The paper used in this publication meets the minimum requirements of American National Standard for Information Sciences–Permanence of Paper for Printed Library Materials, ANSI Z39.48-1984. ♾

TO J.S.H.

Love will abide, take things in stride . . .

CONTENTS

JOHN C. JEFFRIES, JR.

BAKKE REVISITED

In 1978, Lewis Powell saved affirmative action. By one vote—or perhaps only half a vote—he allowed the continued integration of elite institutions of higher education, despite persistent deficits in the academic qualifications of many minority applicants.

It is hard to imagine that integration could have had a more unlikely champion. A child of the Old South, Powell had lived most of his life, uncomplainingly, in racial segregation and educational apartheid. Like many southerners of his generation, Powell later found it incomprehensible that he had ever accepted the systematic subjugation of blacks, but accept it he had. Only after *Brown*,[1] and the massive challenge to legality that *Brown* provoked,[2] did the beliefs of his upbringing give way to the mandate of color-blindness before the law. Within a few years, he was asked to move beyond color-blindness, to which he had but newly been won, and embrace racial preference. This personal journey, which in some sense he never completed, led to Powell's opinion, for himself alone, in *Regents of the University of California v Allan Bakke*.[3]

That opinion was as conflicted as its author. On the one hand, Powell said that racial preferences in favor of minorities were con-

John C. Jeffries, Jr., is Emerson Spies Professor, Arnold H. Leon Professor, and Dean, the University of Virginia School of Law.

AUTHOR'S NOTE: Thanks go to Pam Karlan, Daryl Levinson, Dan Ortiz, Jim Ryan, Paul Stephan, Bill Stuntz, and Jay Wilkinson, all of whom read a draft of this paper and offered valuable comments. Thanks also go to my reseach assistant, Jamey Harris, who provided dedicated and cheerful research support, as well as useful criticism.

[1] *Brown v Board of Education*, 347 US 483 (1954).

[2] Powell's encounter with "massive resistance" and its purported justification in the doctrine of "interposition" is described in John C. Jeffries, Jr., *Justice Lewis F. Powell, Jr.*, 131–53 (Maxwell Macmillan, 1994) ("*Powell Biography*").

[3] 438 US 265 (1978).

stitutionally equivalent to discrimination against them and required the same judicial scrutiny. On the other hand, he denied the conclusion to which that doctrine led. He rejected the reasons for thinking "reverse" discrimination different from the traditional variety, yet he embraced that result. He dismissed the distinction between goals and quotas as "beside the point,"[4] but came to rest on precisely that ground. And throughout, his argument seemed devoid of any broad consistency that might be called principle. Indeed, the difference between the affirmative action plans that Powell found unconstitutional and those that he was prepared to uphold was not substantive, or even formalistic, but essentially aesthetic. Considered purely as a matter of craft—of consistency with precedent, coherency as doctrine, and clarity of result—Powell's *Bakke* opinion must be judged a failure.

Yet twenty-five years later, it carried the day. In *Grutter v Bollinger*,[5] the Supreme Court embraced not only Powell's result, but also his reasoning, in all its logic-chopping contradiction, embraced it not merely as a consequence of the need to count to five, but as a humane and hopeful response to an intractable problem. Unlike his contemporaries, Powell's successors found wisdom in his approach. Even dissenters had respectful things to say.[6] Despite years of strife and litigation, the constitutionality of affirmative action in higher education has now been determined, probably for a generation, along precisely the lines that Powell laid out in 1978.

The evolution of Powell's position from idiosyncratic outlier to received wisdom is one of the most interesting and unlikely stories in American constitutionalism. It tells us something about the risk of a priori reasoning in an imperfect world and about the Supreme Court's power to influence the course of public opinion to which, in the long run, the Court itself must respond. Ultimately, the history of Powell's opinion in *Bakke* also challenges the way many of us think about constitutional law.

---

[4] Id at 289 ("This semantic distinction is beside the point: the special admissions program is undeniably a classification based on race and ethnic background.").

[5] 123 S Ct 2325 (2003). Unless otherwise indicated, subsequent references are to *Grutter*. Occasional citations to its companion case, *Gratz v Bollinger*, 123 US 2411 (2003), are specifically identified.

[6] 123 S Ct at 2370 (Kennedy, J, dissenting) ("The opinion by Justice Powell, in my view, states the correct rule for resolving this case.").

I

Although affirmative action has remained durably controversial in the years since *Bakke*, the constitutional landscape has changed. At that time, there were essentially two positions. Each was intellectually coherent and well grounded in the rhetoric and decisions of the Supreme Court, and each laid claim to the moral conscience of the nation. Although partisans on each side underrated the other, both positions had substantial merit. But if the two positions were arguably equipollent, they were also utterly incompatible.

One view, pressed in *Bakke* and today, is that the Constitution requires color-blindness. Absent a specific remedial justification, the Constitution should be interpreted to forbid any governmental consideration of race or ethnicity. The rhetoric dates at least from the first Justice Harlan, who from the incomparable prestige of his *Plessy* dissent, declared that, "Our Constitution is color-blind."[7] The sentiment was echoed by Martin Luther King, Jr.,[8] by the early Thurgood Marshall,[9] and by a whole phalanx of law professors who, in the lead-up to *Brown*, insisted that, "Laws which give equal protection are those which make no *discrimination* because of race in the sense that they make no distinction because of race."[10] Racial classifications, they concluded, were "completely precluded" by the Constitution.[11]

No one defended color-blindness more eloquently than Alexander Bickel. In the interval between the Court's false start in *De-*

---

[7] *Plessy v Ferguson*, 163 US 537, 559 (1896) (Harlan, J, dissenting).

[8] Dr. King famously dreamed that "my four little children will one day live in a nation where they will not be judged by the color of their skin, but by the content of their character." Martin Luther King, Jr., *I Have a Dream*, in James Melvin Washington, ed, *A Testament of Hope: The Essential Writings and Speeches of Martin Luther King, Jr.* 217, 219 (1986). This line was later paraphrased as the title of an influential attack on affirmative action. See Shelby Steele, *The Content of Our Character: A New Vision of Race in America* (1990).

[9] See Brief for Appellants (No. 1) in *Brown v Board of Education*, 347 US 483 (1954), at 5 ("The State of Kansas has no power . . . to use race as a factor in affording educational opportunities to its citizens.").

[10] Brief of the Committee of Law Teachers Against Segregation in Legal Education in *Sweatt v Painter*, 339 US 629 (1950), at 8 (emphasis in original). The brief was written chiefly by Thomas I. Emerson of Yale and signed by 187 law professors.

[11] Id. But see David A. Strauss, *The Myth of Colorblindness*, 1986 Supreme Court Review 99 (arguing that Brown "is not rooted in colorblindness at all," but in a race-conscious nondiscrimination principle that is "logically continuous" with affirmative action).

Funis v Odegaard[12] and its return to the issue in *Bakke,* Bickel voiced the dismay that many felt at the threat to that ideal: "The lesson of the great decisions of the Supreme Court and the lesson of contemporary history have been the same for at least a generation: discrimination on the basis of race is illegal, immoral, unconstitutional, inherently wrong, and destructive of democratic society. Now this is to be unlearned and we are told that this is not a matter of fundamental principle but only a matter of whose ox is gored."[13]

Bickel's opponents argued that discrimination against minorities and discrimination in their favor were constitutionally different. After all, the "equal protection of the laws" guaranteed by the Fourteenth Amendment had been only recently and imperfectly achieved, and the fuller equality of which "the laws" gave promise remained a distant hope. Racial oppression required more than cessation; it required correction. It required more than a fastidious color-blindness, which did nothing to correct the legacy of a discrimination that had been neither fastidious nor color-blind. In short, wrong required remedy, and as the wrong had been racial, so too must be the remedy. For proponents of affirmative action, the immediate goal was not color-blindness but compensatory justice.[14]

This argument grounded in the social and historical context of racial preferences drew strength from political theory. At least since *Carolene Products,* constitutional lawyers had posited a special judicial role in the protection of "discrete and insular minorities."[15] In 1978, arguments drawn from political process theory were much in the air. The series of articles that John Hart Ely would collect and expand in *Democracy and Distrust* (1980) were beginning to appear,[16] and the idea of a "representation-reinforcing" approach

---

[12] 416 US 312 (1974) (dismissing a constitutional challenge to preferential admissions on grounds of mootness).

[13] Alexander M. Bickel, *The Morality of Consent* 132–33 (1975).

[14] Over three-fourths of the amici briefs in support of the University of California in *Bakke* supported affirmative action on this ground.

[15] *United States v Carolene Products Co.,* 304 US 144, 152 n 4 (1938) (raising the question whether "prejudice against discrete and insular minorities may be a special condition, which tends seriously to curtail the operation of those political processes ordinarily to be relied upon to protect minorities, and which may call for a correspondingly more searching judicial inquiry").

[16] See, for example, *Legislative and Administrative Motivation in Constitutional Law,* 79 Yale L J 1205 (1970); *The Wages of Crying Wolf: A Comment on Roe v. Wade,* 82 Yale L J 920 (1973); *The Constitutionality of Reverse Racial Discrimination,* 41 U Chi L Rev 713 (1974);

to constitutional law was gaining ground. Especially to the extent (much greater in 1978 than today) that racial preferences were seen as disadvantaging an undifferentiated population of "whites," political process theory had real bite. It countered the demand for the protection of *all* individuals with an argument against *judicial* intervention on behalf of majorities. The special judicial concern for those unable to compete in the political arena simply did not apply. Instead of the heightened scrutiny designed to look out for those who could not look out for themselves, benign discrimination should receive more relaxed review. The background rule of deference to majoritarian political decisions cut against strict judicial policing of affirmative action and in favor of permitting compensatory racial preferences approved or tolerated by the political branches.

Both of these positions made their way into the opinions in *Bakke*. Speaking for himself and three others, Justice Stevens insisted on color-blindness.[17] He based his decision on Title VI of the 1964 Civil Rights Act,[18] but since that statute had been (and still is) construed to follow the Equal Protection Clause, the opinion was read as a precursor of constitutional interpretation.[19] For Stevens, the case was governed by principles of "*individual* equality" and "*individual* fairness,"[20] principles that did not allow for efforts to do justice by groups or classes. On the other side, Justices Brennan, White, Marshall, and Blackmun rejected color-blindness and approved race-consciousness to remedy the effects of past dis-

---

Flag Desecration: A Case Study in the Roles of Categorization and Balancing in First Amendment Analysis, 88 Harv L Rev 1482 (1975); *Constitutional Interpretivism: Its Allure and Impossibility*, 53 Ind L J 399 (1978); *Toward a Representation-Reinforcing Mode of Judicial Review*, 37 Md L Rev 451 (1978); *Foreword: On Discovering Fundamental Values*, 92 Harv L Rev 5 (1978).

[17] 438 US at 418 (Stevens, J, with whom Burger, CJ, and Stewart and Rehnquist, JJ, joined, concurring in the judgment in part and dissenting in part).

[18] Title VI forbids racial discrimination by recipients of federal funding, a category that includes most private universities.

[19] For early decisions to this effect, see *Goodwin v Wyman*, 330 F Supp 1038, 1040 n 3 (SDNY 1971), aff'd (without opinion), 406 US 964 (1972) ("Essentially, the same showing is required to establish a violation of [Title VI] as is required to make out a racial discrimination violation of the Fourteenth Amendment's Equal Protection Clause."); *Gilliam v City of Omaha*, 388 F Supp 842, 847 (D Neb 1975) (following *Goodwin*). For subsequent decisions making the same point, see *United States v Fordice*, 505 US 717, 732 n 7 (1992) ("Our cases make clear . . . that the reach of Title VI's protection extends no further than the Fourteenth Amendment."); *Guardians Ass'n v Civil Service Comm'n of City of New York*, 463 US 582, 610 (1983) (Powell, J, concurring in the judgment) ("Title VI must be held to proscribe only those racial classifications that would violate the Equal Protection Clause or the Fifth Amendment").

[20] 438 US at 416 n 19 (emphasis in original).

crimination.[21] They relied on *Carolene Products* to justify less-than-strict scrutiny of remedial racial preferences[22] and announced a general readiness to uphold "benign" racial classifications in admissions decisions.

Faced with a choice between these views, Powell rejected both. He stubbornly refused to accept either of the coherent and readily defensible ways of thinking about affirmative action and sent his clerks to search for a middle way.[23] None of the intellectual or analytical difficulties they encountered turned him from his course. He knew precisely where he wanted to go and remained adamantly committed to getting there.

The motivation for Powell's resolve was largely negative. He recoiled from the consequences of both positions taken by his colleagues. On the one hand, he knew that rigorous adherence to color-blind admissions would very nearly eliminate African-Americans from elite institutions of higher education. The prospect of returning to all-white (or at least all non-black) medical schools, law schools, and colleges was repugnant. It would be bad for education and disastrous for race relations. At the very least, this was a step that the Supreme Court should not coerce. On the other hand, Powell also worried about the relaxed approach to racial preferences advocated by Brennan, White, Marshall, and Blackmun. Their approval of admissions quotas validated fixed commitments to various groups based on some metric of past discrimination. Powell feared that quotas would allow racial preferences to ripen into entitlements, to become entrenched as fixed percentages that could not readily be changed. He foresaw, in short, that admissions quotas would degenerate into a racial spoils system in higher education. Moreover, Powell saw little prospect that the compensatory rationale would place any meaningful limit on

---

[21] Id at 369 (opinion of Brennan, White, Marshall, and Blackmun, JJ, concurring in the judgment in part and dissenting in part) ("a state government may adopt race-conscious programs if the purpose of such programs is to remove the disparate racial impact its actions otherwise might have and if there is reason to believe that the disparate impact is itself the product of past discrimination, whether its own or that of society at large").

[22] Specifically, they borrowed from gender cases the formulation that has become known as "intermediate scrutiny." See 438 US at 359 ("racial classifications designed to further remedial purposes 'must serve important governmental objectives and must be substantially related to achievement of those objectives,'" quoting *Califano v Webster*, 430 US 313, 317 (1977) (quoting *Craig v Boren*, 429 US 190, 197 (1976))).

[23] See generally Jeffries, *Powell Biography* at 473–78 (cited in note 2).

the duration of such preferences. Powell thought of affirmative action as a transition, a short-term departure from the ideal of color-blindness justified only by pressing necessity. Allowing minority set-asides to continue until all effects of past societal discrimination had been eliminated might mean they would last forever.

Powell therefore crafted an approach designed both to permit affirmative action and to constrain it. He wanted to allow racial preferences in higher education while preserving the grounds for objecting to them, to permit race-conscious admissions under current conditions without conceding their long-term future. In short, he wanted to say "yes" now, while implying "no" later.

The components of Powell's mixed message are well known. On the one hand, he endorsed strict scrutiny. The use of this standard proclaimed that racial preferences were "in principle" unacceptable. It also assured a hospitable doctrinal ground for future attempts to curtail or limit affirmative action. On the other hand, Powell applied strict scrutiny with unexpected pliancy. As a result, racial preferences were allowed in fact, even as they were disapproved in theory. In specifying the compelling interest that justified that result, Powell avoided compensation and embraced diversity. Remedying the effects of past societal discrimination was a rationale that Powell thought justified too much and potentially for too long. Diversity was a softer and more fluid concept. It directed attention to participation rather than to compensation, to the importance of *some*, though not necessarily perfect, representation from all groups. Because diversity was a less ambitious goal, it could plausibly be the sooner achieved. Most important, diversity put the justification for racial preferences squarely on improving the educational experience of all students, rather than on helping a favored few. If, as educators insisted and Powell believed, racial, ethnic, and other kinds of diversity in the classroom enhanced the education of all students, then the search for minority representation could be seen as sound educational policy, not racial favoritism.

The trouble was that racial and ethnic diversity—which of course was the only sort that raised constitutional concerns—was most readily achieved through the kinds of admissions quotas that Powell had determined to strike down. He solved this problem by the intellectual equivalent of brute force. True diversity, he said, the diversity "that furthers a compelling state interest," encompasses qualifications and characteristics beyond race.[24] Quantification of racial preferences (for some unexplained reason) inhibited consideration of other factors. Therefore, setting aside a specified number of places for ethnic or racial minorities "would hinder rather than further attainment of genuine diversity."[25] In this way, the concept of "genuine" diversity acquired a plastic quality, justifying racial preferences insofar, and only insofar, as Powell did not find them offensive.

Time magazine summarized *Bakke* as, "Quotas No, Race Yes."[26] To communicate this ambivalence to the public at large, Powell hit upon a brilliant stratagem. Where the docket showed one case, Powell created two. He struck down the U.C. Davis admissions program with its strict numerical set-aside, but upheld the Harvard College admissions policy, which was not before the Court but which Powell nevertheless quoted at length.[27] "In such an admissions program," he said approvingly, "race or ethnic background may be deemed a 'plus' in a particular applicant's file, yet it does not insulate the individual from comparison with all other candidates for the available seats."[28] Having created two cases where there was in fact one, Powell then split his vote between them. At the suggestion of Justice Brennan, Powell styled his opinion not simply as affirming the decision below, which had struck down the Davis program, but as affirming in part and reversing in part.[29] As he announced from the bench on decision day: "Insofar as the California Supreme Court held that Bakke must be admitted to the Davis Medical School, we affirm. Insofar as the California Court prohibited Davis from considering race as a factor in admissions,

---

[24] 438 US at 315.

[25] Id.

[26] Time (July 10, 1978).

[27] 438 US at 316–17.

[28] Id at 317.

[29] The story of Brennan's intervention and Powell's response is told in Jeffries, *Powell Biography* at 486–87 (cited in note 2). Subsequently, Chief Justice Burger tried to persuade Powell to join a narrow opinion striking down the Davis admissions quota but leaving the acceptability of other affirmative action programs to another day. Powell rejected the overture and insisted on sticking with his bifurcated approach. See id at 488–89.

we reverse."[30] The invention of a split result broadcast to the nation in the clearest possible terms Powell's attempt at compromise.

The result reached by Powell in *Bakke* provoked mixed reactions, as would have been true of any outcome in that case, but many specifically approved the split decision. The *Washington Post* concluded that "everyone won,"[31] a sentiment echoed by Griffin Bell, who thought "the whole country ought to be pleased."[32] When attention turned from the result to the reasoning, reactions changed. Reviews of the intellectual craft of Powell's opinion were largely negative and sometimes scathing. Guido Calabresi found the decision "totally disappointing. In a deep sense, it settled nothing."[33] Vincent Blasi asked whether "Mr. Justice Powell Has a Theory?" and found "a disturbing failure . . . to give coherent, practical meaning to our most important constitutional ideals."[34] Harry Edwards gave the opinion "poor marks,"[35] and Ronald Dworkin found Powell's compromise "without sound intellectual foundation."[36] John Hart Ely thought Powell had forgotten that he was "not being asked to devise an affirmative action program but rather to rule on the constitutionality of the one the California officials have devised."[37] Critics from both the left and the right homed in on the difficulty of Powell's distinction between goals and quotas. As Laurence Tribe asked, "If it is not 'discriminatory' in some invidious or otherwise forbidden sense to prefer minorities on a case-by-case basis, why is it 'discriminatory' to do so more

---

[30] Quoted in Jeffries, *Powell Biography* at 494 (cited in note 2).

[31] *The Bakke Decision*, Washington Post (June 29, 1978), p A26.

[32] Quoted in *The Reaction: A Ruling for Every Group*, Washington Post (June 29, 1978), p A1. Other reactions, both favorable and unfavorable, are collected in Jeffries, *Powell Biography* at 496–98 (cited in note 2).

[33] Guido Calabresi, *Bakke as Pseudo-Tragedy*, 28 Cath U L Rev 427, 427 (1979).

[34] Vincent Blasi, *Bakke as Precedent: Does Mr. Justice Powell Have a Theory?* 67 Cal L Rev 21 (1979).

[35] Harry T. Edwards, *Preferential Remedies and Affirmative Action in Employment in the Wake of Bakke*, 1979 Wash U L Q 113, 114 (1979).

[36] Ronald Dworkin, *The Bakke Decision: Did It Decide Anything?* New York Review of Books (Aug 17, 1978), pp 20, 22.

[37] John Hart Ely, *Foreword: On Discovering Fundamental Values*, 92 Harv L Rev 5, 13 n 47 (1978).

mechanically and in gross?"[38] Robert Bork made the same point from the other direction: "[W]e have at bottom a statement that the Fourteenth Amendment allows some, but not too much, reverse discrimination. Yet that vision of the Constitution remains unexplained. . . . [It] must be seen as an uneasy compromise resting upon no constitutional footing of its own."[39] Antonin Scalia's comment was equally negative and characteristically colorful: "Justice Powell's opinion, which we must work with as the law of the land, strikes me as an excellent compromise between two committees of the American Bar Association on some insignificant legislative proposal. But it is thoroughly unconvincing as an honest, hard-minded, reasoned analysis of an important provision of the Constitution."[40]

What no one doubted was that Powell's opinion was, as Scalia put it, "the law of the land." Obviously, the four-one-four split robbed the decision of a clear majority position, but courts and commentators focused on Powell's fifth vote,[41] as did admissions departments across the country. The reason was simple. On any plausible reading of their opinion, Brennan, White, Marshall, and Blackmun were far more tolerant of racial preferences than Lewis Powell. This was evident in their reliance on remedial rationale, which had a broader reach and less flexibility than diversity, and in the "intermediate" standard of scrutiny. Powell's fifth vote rested on a narrower rationale and a more demanding standard of review. Even though no one shared Powell's position, it nevertheless ended up defining the kind of affirmative action that a majority of the Court was prepared to uphold.

II

Or at least, for a generation, so we thought. Eventually, anti-affirmative-action activists began to claim not merely that

---

[38] Laurence H. Tribe, *Perspectives on Bakke: Equal Protection, Procedural Fairness, or Structural Justice?* 92 Harv L Rev 864, 866 (1979).

[39] Robert H. Bork, *The Unpersuasive Bakke Decision*, Wall Street Journal (July 21, 1978), p 8.

[40] Antonin Scalia, *The Disease as Cure: "In Order to Get Beyond Racism, We Must First Take Account of Race,"* 1979 Wash U L Q 147, 148.

[41] See, for example, *UWM Post, Inc. v Bd of Regents of University of Wisconsin System*, 774 F Supp 1163, 1176 (ED Wis 1991) (citing Powell's opinion as authority for the proposition that "[i]ncreasing diversity is 'clearly a constitutionally permissible goal for an institution of higher education'"); *Davis v Halpern*, 768 F Supp 968, 975 (ED NY 1991) (finding that

Powell's position was ill-founded or illogical or unwise—all of which were eminently arguable—but that it was not the law. They sought to annul *Bakke* as precedent by arguing that the five Justices who approved race-conscious admissions had no common ground and therefore that their votes could not be summed up in favor of any position.[42] The basis for this surprising revisionism was a phrase in a Brennan footnote: "We also agree with Mr. Justice Powell that a plan like the 'Harvard' plan is constitutional under our approach, at least so long as the use of race to achieve an integrated student body is necessitated by the lingering effects of past discrimination."[43] Conceivably, in some other universe, the lingering effects of past discrimination might already have been resolved. If, therefore, one fixed on the phrase from the Brennan footnote and ignored the text to which that footnote was appended,[44] one could come up with an apparently straight-faced argument that Brennan et al. were in fact *more* restrictive of affirmative action than Powell and that Powell's position therefore did not command five votes. By this reasoning, anti-affirmative-action activists asked the lower courts to disregard *Bakke* as precedent and to strike down racial preferences without awaiting further

---

the "proper purposes" for which racial classifications have been upheld by the Supreme Court include "that of a university's obtaining the benefits which flow from enrolling an ethnically diverse student body"); *Uzzell v Friday*, 592 F Supp 1502, 1516 (MD NC 1984) (holding that "the opinion of Justice Powell [in *Bakke*] is the one which governs this case").

[42] See, for example, Brief for Petitioner in *Grutter v Bollinger*, 123 S Ct 2325 (2003), at 28–29 (declaring that "the opinions in *Bakke* leave unanswered the question of whether interests in academic freedom or diversity are compelling state interests justifying racial preferences in admissions"); Curt A. Levey, *Racial Preferences in Admissions: Myths, Harms, and Alternatives*, 66 Albany L Rev 489, 492 (2003) (arguing that the *Bakke* opinions had no "common denominator" and therefore could not be read together).

[43] 438 US 326 n 1 (opinion of Brennan, White, Marshall, and Blackmun, JJ) (citation omitted).

[44] Id at 326 (opinion of Brennan, White, Marshall, and Blackmun, JJ):

> We agree with Mr. Justice Powell . . . that the effect of the [California court's judgment] would be to prohibit the University from establishing in the future affirmative-action programs that take race into account. Since we conclude that the affirmative admissions program at the Davis Medical School is constitutional, we would reverse the judgment below in all respects. Mr. Justice Powell agrees that some uses of race in university admissions are permissible and, therefore, he joins with us to make five votes reversing the judgment below insofar as it prohibits the University from establishing race-conscious programs in the future.

To read this language as expressing reluctance to go *as far as* Powell in approving affirmative action requires at least one blind eye. Certainly, Powell himself suffered no confusion on whose was the broader and whose the narrower rationale. See 438 US at 294 n 34 (criticizing Brennan et al. for too readily finding justification for racial preferences).

word from the Supreme Court. And they succeeded. The Fifth Circuit professed itself unable to discern that *Bakke* had upheld racial preferences and declined to "read its fragmented opinions like tea leaves, attempting to divine what the Justices 'would have held'"[45] had they been willing to go *as far as* Powell. Instead, the Fifth Circuit chose to read the tea leaves of new appointments and to base its decision on a prediction—a quite plausible prediction—that color-blindness would carry the day on the Rehnquist Court.[46]

By the time the Michigan cases reached the Court, *Bakke*'s demise seemed almost certain. As Linda Greenhouse said, "*Bakke* had been dying an incremental and very public death for fifteen years, and it seemed most unlikely that either of the Michigan programs would survive. . . . Maybe, just maybe, the Court would be persuaded not to shut the door completely, but even that prospect seemed dubious."[47] Oral argument may have given a hint that *Bakke* was not quite dead, but the strength and clarity with which the Court embraced it took almost everyone by surprise.

What was not surprising was the Justices' dismissal of the debate over *Bakke* as precedent.[48] Faced with quibbling about how to count to five, they grandly waived the issue aside, saying that Powell's analysis in *Bakke*, whether previously controlling or not, from this day would be: "[T]oday we endorse Justice Powell's view that student body diversity is a compelling state interest that can justify the use of race in university admissions."[49] Speaking through Jus-

---

[45] *Hopwood v State of Texas*, 236 F3d 256, 275 n 66 (5th Cir 2000) (sometimes known as *Hopwood II*).

[46] It is a nice question whether the judges of the Fifth Circuit and others inclined to that view of the Constitution should have felt entitled to disregard *Bakke* on grounds of age and apparent infirmity, without resort to hypertechnical misinterpretation. My own inclination would be to regard considered rejection of Supreme Court precedent by the lower courts as acceptable in principle, though the Court has cautioned against that view. See, for example, *Agostini v Felton*, 521 US 203, 237–38 (1997) (reaffirming that, "[i]f a precedent of this Court has direct application in a case, yet appears to rest on reasons rejected in some other line of decisions, the Court of Appeals should follow the case which directly controls, leaving to this Court the prerogative of overruling its own decisions," quoting *Rodriguez de Quijas v Shearson/American Express, Inc.*, 400 US 477, 485 (1989)).

[47] Linda Greenhouse, *What Got Into the Court? What Happens Next?* (speech delivered at the University of Nebraska, Sept 15, 2003) (copy on file with the author).

[48] For an anguished recognition of the Supreme Court's take-it-or-leave-it attitude toward prior decisions, read Justice Scalia's account of his colleagues' willingness to accord stare decisis effect to *Roe v Wade* but not *Bowers v Hardwick* in *Lawrence v Texas*, 123 S Ct 2472, 2488–91 (2003).

[49] *Grutter*, 123 S Ct at 2337.

tice O'Connor, the Court then proceeded to recapitulate Powell's analysis and adopt his reasoning. The logical frailty that "genuine" diversity allowed individualized consideration of race but prohibited quantified advantage was enthusiastically embraced.[50] Powell's example of the Harvard admissions approach, which allowed race to be a (potentially decisive) "plus" factor in an applicant's file, was exhumed, restated, and reaffirmed.[51]

In fact the principal focus of debate among the Justices was not whether Powell's was the right approach—on which the agreement was surprisingly broad—but on whether the Michigan admissions programs sufficiently tracked his analysis. On one side, Justice Kennedy agreed with Powell's standard but dissented from the judgment upholding racial preferences on the ground that the Law School had gone too far.[52] On the other side, Justices Souter and Ginsburg dissented from the judgment striking down undergraduate racial preferences, taking the view that the undergraduate admissions program satisfied Powell's approach.[53] However one may characterize these variations on a theme, there seems to be a clear majority on the current Court for Powell's position from 1978.

In other respects as well, last term's affirmative action cases echoed *Bakke*. In a bit of brilliant lawyering, the University of

---

[50] 123 S Ct at 2342 ("As Justice Powell made clear in *Bakke*, truly individualized consideration demands that race be used in a flexible, nonmechanical way. It follows from this mandate that universities cannot establish quotas for members of certain racial groups or put members of those groups on separate admissions tracks.").

[51] Id at 2342–46.

[52] Id at 2370 (Kennedy, J, dissenting) ("The [*Bakke*] opinion by Justice Powell, in my view, states the correct rule for resolving this case. The Court, however, does not apply strict scrutiny.").

A similar characterization could be made, albeit less persuasively, of the dissenting opinion of Chief Justice Rehnquist. He cited and quoted Powell opinions in rejecting the Law School's admissions policies as not "narrowly tailored," see, for example, 123 S Ct at 2365 (Rehnquist, CJ, with whom Scalia, Kennedy, and Thomas, JJ, join, dissenting), but he gave less reason to think that any form of racial preference would survive his review. It may be better, therefore, to think of Rehnquist, along with Scalia and Thomas, as adhering to strict color-blindness, which of course is fundamentally at odds with Powell's opinion in *Bakke*. See 123 S Ct at 2350 (Scalia, J, with whom Thomas, J, joined, concurring in part and dissenting in part) ("The Constitution proscribes government discrimination on the basis of race, and state-provided education is no exception."); *Gratz*, 123 S Ct at 2433 (Thomas, J, concurring) ("I would hold that a State's use of racial discrimination in higher education admissions is categorically prohibited by the Equal Protection Clause.").

[53] *Gratz*, 123 S Ct at 2439–42 (opinion of Souter, J, joined in relevant part by Ginsburg, J, dissenting) (explaining at length why the undergraduate admissions program should be viewed as "closer to what *Grutter* approves than to what *Bakke* condemns").

Michigan litigated two lawsuits simultaneously and acquiesced in rushing the undergraduate admissions case to the Supreme Court by prejudgment certiorari.[54] This strategy gave the Justices something to strike down as well as something (it was hoped) to uphold,[55] thereby allowing the Court to replicate the bifurcated judgment that Powell reached in *Bakke*. The *Grutter* Court also echoed Powell's view, never made publicly explicit, that racial preferences should be temporary and transitional. At the *Bakke* conference, held on December 9, 1977, Powell agreed with Stevens that racial preferences might be acceptable temporarily but not as a permanent solution.[56] As the conversation veered toward common ground with the affirmative action supporters, Justice Marshall broke in to say that the need would last a hundred years. Marshall may have been right, but Powell recoiled at the prospect. Twenty-five years later, the Court gave a more sober estimate of the life of the preferences it upheld:

> It has been 25 years since Justice Powell first approved the use of race to further an interest in student body diversity in the context of public higher education. Since that time, the number of minority applicants with high grades and test scores has indeed improved. We expect that 25 years from now, the use of racial preferences will no longer be necessary to further the interest approved today.[57]

In one respect only did *Grutter* depart from *Bakke*, and that was not to confine or curtail Powell's reasoning but to broaden its focus and extend its reach. Justice O'Connor championed diversity not only in the classroom but beyond. After noting that higher education "must be accessible to all individuals regardless of race or ethnicity,"[58] she connected education to leadership: "Effective participation by members of all racial and ethnic groups in the civic life of

---

[54] Given that the university had won both cases below, it did not, of course, directly encourage Supreme Court review, but it did urge the Court to grant prejudgment certiorari in *Gratz* if it chose to hear *Grutter*. University of Michigan, Brief in Conditional Opposition to Certiorari Before Judgment in *Gratz v Bollinger*, 123 S Ct 2411 (2003), No 02-516 (filed October 29, 2002).

[55] In my view, the University of Michigan's defeat on the undergraduate admissions program was clearly foreseeable. That, at least, was the judgment reached several years ago when my university abandoned a very similar point system in its undergraduate admissions.

[56] This story is told in Jeffries, *Powell Biography* at 487–88 (cited in note 2).

[57] *Grutter*, 123 S Ct at 2346–47.

[58] Id at 2340.

our Nation is essential if the dream of one Nation, indivisible, is to be realized."[59] And again: "In order to cultivate a set of leaders with legitimacy in the eyes of the citizenry, it is necessary that the path to leadership be visibly open to talented and qualified individuals of every race and ethnicity."[60] It may be possible to confine these words to law schools (which, as O'Connor noted, produce a disproportionate share of public officials) or to higher education generally, but it may also be that diversity has now been writ large to include public institutions generally. The Court's emphasis on amici filings from American industry and the miliary reinforces that broad reading.[61] Just how far the Court meant to extend *Bakke* beyond the sphere of education will be the subject of future litigation. For now, it is enough to note that the debate has shifted from whether *Bakke* would be overruled to how far it will be extended.

In addition to the unapologetic embrace of Powell's opinion in *Bakke*, one other aspect of last term's decisions merits mention, and that is the scant attention paid to the misleading suggestion that racial integration of higher education can somehow be maintained without reference to race. Justice Thomas did mention the University of California at Berkeley, noting that Boalt Hall enrolled fourteen African-Americans (and thirty-six Hispanics) in the entering class in 2002, as compared to twenty African-Americans (and twenty-eight Hispanics) in the entering class in 1996, despite the intervention of Proposition 209 prohibiting all consideration of race.[62] What Thomas did not say is that in the year after Proposition 209, African-Americans at Berkeley dropped from twenty to

---

[59] Id at 2340–41.

[60] Id at 2341.

[61] See id at 2340 (citing and relying on amici briefs filed on behalf of "65 leading American Businesses," including Minnesota Mining & Manufacturing, Coca-Cola, Texaco, and Dow Chemical, and a group of "high-ranking officers and civilian leaders of the Army, Navy, Air Force, and Marine Corps, including former military-academy superintendents, Secretaries of Defense, and present and former members of the U.S. Senate").

[62] 123 S Ct at 2359 (Thomas, J, dissenting) (noting that "the sky has not fallen at Boalt Hall").

Proposition 209 is now Cal Const, Art 1, s 31(a), which provides:

The state shall not discriminate against, or grant preferential treatment to, any individual or group on the basis of race, sex, color, ethnicity, or national origin in the operation of public employment, public education, or public contracting.

one[63] and that the slow and partial rebound in African-American enrollment has been accompanied by the reemergence of a large gap in numerical qualifications. For the entering class in 2002, the median LSATs for whites and African-Americans at Boalt Hall were 166 and 157, respectively. This gap was the same as that in the same entering class at the University of Michigan, which openly took race into account and litigated to the hilt the necessity of doing so.[64] It is hard to suppress the doubt that Berkeley's admissions decisions are color-blind. One has only to imagine what would happen if the racial identifications were reversed. Suppose a university or an employer routinely preferred whites with *lower* numerical qualifications over African-Americans with *higher* numbers and claimed that this consistent and substantial disparity resulted wholly from individualized assessments having nothing to do with race. One need not pause long before predicting the outcome of that litigation.[65] I think it reasonable to conclude that if all consideration of race were barred from admissions decisions at elite educational institutions and *if that policy were enforced with the vigor and resourcefulness*

---

[63] The figures for the entering classes in 1996 through 2003 are as follows:

Fall Entering Class	African-Americans	Mexican-Americans and Other Hispanics
1996	20	28
1997	1	14
1998	8	23
1999	7	16
2000	7	18
2001	14	17
2002	14	36
2003	16	38

The data are available at http://www.ucop.edu/acadadv/datamgmt/lawdata/lawschol2.html.

[64] Daniel Golden, *Case Study: Schools Find Ways to Achieve Diversity Without Key Tool*, Wall Street Journal (June 20, 2003), p A1.

[65] The situation at UCLA is no more encouraging for those who claim to achieve racial diversity without reference to race. In the aftermath of Proposition 209, UCLA, which had the advantage of location in one of the nation's most diverse cities, made a concerted and sophisticated effort to recruit broadly through consideration of social and economic disadvantage. African-American enrollment fell to a low of three in 1999 and slowly rebounded to sixteen in the 2003 entering class. Data cited in note 63. Much of this improvement seems to have been due to programmatic admissions associated with an academic concentration in Critical Race Studies. Whether an admissions track for Critical Race Studies can fairly be termed color-blind is open to debate.

that anti-affirmative-action activists could bring to bear, the effect on African-American enrollment would be huge.[66]

Indeed, Thomas and Scalia implicitly concede the point in their remarks on "elite" education. If it were indeed true that racial diversity could somehow be achieved without reference to race, there would be no need to choose between racial diversity and admissions selectivity. Yet under current conditions, color-blindness would force exactly that choice. Thomas and Scalia recognized and confronted that dilemma. They were understandably reluctant to advocate resegregation, so instead they attacked academic selectivity. Thomas said that "Michigan has no compelling interest in having a law school at all, much less an elite one."[67] Scalia dismissed Michigan's desire to maintain a "prestige" law school, saying "[i]f that is a compelling state interest, everything is."[68] The full measure of their disdain for "elite" institutions became evident in their scorn for those who run them. For Thomas and Scalia, law school administrators are mere "aestheticists," unconcerned with students' "knowledge and skills," seeking only the "facade" of a class that "looks right, even if it does not perform right."[69]

In *Grutter*, the dissenters confined their contempt to elite *public* institutions,[70] leaving the implication that perhaps private universities could do as they pleased. Indeed, the rhetorical plausibility (if any) of their attack on elite public education derives from the unstated assumption that elite private universities would continue to

---

[66] It is interesting to speculate on why anti-affirmative-action activists in California have not tried to enforce Proposition 209 more rigorously. One possibility is that the reemergence of (unacknowledged) racial preferences has occurred gradually and recently, and opponents have not yet had time to mount another attack. Another possibility is that the anti-affirmative-action activists made a tactical decision not to press their victory in California until the Supreme Court ruled in the Michigan cases. Sharp reductions in minority enrollment, of the sort that occurred in the immediate aftermath of Proposition 209, would have hurt their cause in the Supreme Court. A third possibility is that the anti-affirmative-action activists, or at least some of them, care less about the actual practice than about the announced principle.

[67] 123 S Ct at 2354 (emphasis in original).

[68] Id at 2349.

[69] Id at 2354 (Thomas, J, with whom Scalia, J, joined (in relevant part), concurring in part and dissenting in part).

[70] Id (Thomas, J, with whom Scalia, J, joined (in relevant part), concurring in part and dissenting in part) ("there is no pressing public necessity in maintaining a public law school at all").

flourish. But if, as has been true to date, the constitutional standards of the Equal Protection Clause end up controlling Title VI, then private institutions would also have to choose between racial representation and academic selectivity. The effects of thoroughgoing color-blindness are therefore difficult to contemplate. The most prestigious, powerful, and enabling universities in the country would be forced either to enroll classes in which certain minorities would be largely absent or to overthrow the principles of selectivity and excellence on which the institutions were built. The willingness of Thomas and Scalia to confront that dilemma at least confirms their intellectual honesty. Whatever may have been said about the experience at Berkeley, they know full well that rigorous exclusion of race from admissions decisions would preclude meaningful racial diversity in the classrooms of all the nation's leading law schools.

III

This review of the Michigan decisions prompts three comments. All are personal, in the sense that they are matters of opinion, but the first is especially so.

I have come—slowly—to the view that Powell in *Bakke* was exactly right. He was right to allow racial preferences *and* also right to deploy the Constitution against their formalization and entrenchment. Moreover, the reasons for thinking Powell right in 2003 are essentially the same as those he would have given in 1978—namely, the unacceptability of the alternatives. If all consideration of race were squeezed out of admissions decisions, the prospects of white and Asian applicants would be marginally improved (owing to the impact of a few additional places on their greater numbers), but the prospects of African-American applicants (and certain other minorities) would be drastically reduced. A sharp cutback in African-American enrollment would hurt the law schools and hurt the nation. It would exacerbate a sense of grievance that already has more than adequate foundation. It would deprive the African-American community of a cadre of potential leaders. And it would make it that much harder for minorities to maintain a full commitment to our common future as Americans.

Additionally, rigorous color-blindness would deprive nonminority students of the personal, professional, and educational advantages of living and learning with minorities. This last point is sometimes dismissed by those who are far away from educational institutions, but I believe it is keenly felt by those who work and study in them. There are undoubtedly nonminority students eager for the "last" place in Michigan or Virginia (or Harvard or Yale, if Title VI were so read) and willing to accept that benefit under almost any circumstances, but there are many more students enrolled in those institutions who recognize that their experience would be impoverished by the absence of minorities. Under current conditions, strict color-blindness, if unambiguously adopted and rigorously enforced, would impair the quality of the education of all law students.

Perhaps less obviously, I think we would also have come to rue the more generous approach advocated by Brennan, White, Marshall, and Blackmun. Racial set-asides in higher education, which they were prepared to tolerate, would have been the most efficient way to achieve diversity in the classroom, but they would have proved corrosive. Any allocation of spaces on the basis of race or ethnicity would have been challenged as conditions changed, and those challenges would have been anything but edifying. Imagine the questions that would have been triggered by the growth of the Latino population. It seems obvious that the number of Latinos sought to be enrolled in California (and other) institutions would have increased, but on what calculation and by how many? Would the percentage of Latinos in the nation be the benchmark, or the percentage in California? Would gross population count, or only those over a certain age, or only those with certain minimum (English-language) test scores? And who would meet the ethnic definition? Would European-Americans be included simply because they had Hispanic surnames? Even if they didn't speak Spanish?

Most damaging of all would be the question of who pays for racial set-asides. If the number of Latino spaces increased, would the additions come from other ethnic minorities with their own claims for special treatment? From African-Americans? From capping the growing Asian population? Or would the category of undifferentiated "whites" become the universal donor for ever-increasing commitments elsewhere?

These are not pretty questions, and the debates occasioned by them could scarcely fail to divide and wound. Plausible arguments could and would be found to support different positions, which would then become the focus of coalitions organized around ethnic identity. Whatever allocations were made on day one would quickly come to feel like permanent entitlements to those who benefited from them, and whatever adjustments were not made on day two would as quickly become sources of grievance to those who did not prosper. The prospect of perpetual competition over racial and ethnic allocations is one that none should welcome, yet it is hard to see how approval of the Davis "quota" could have led anywhere else.

It is against this prospect that the uses of ambiguity come to the fore. As Paul Mishkin noted, *Bakke* "amounted to a proclamation of ambivalence that dramatically recognized and proclaimed the existence of legitimate moral and constitutional claims on both sides of the issue."[71] The refusal to give a clear answer had benefits that are practical and concrete, as well as rhetorical and symbolic. If the advantages accorded racial and ethnic minorities are not explicitly stated, they need not be explicitly undone. If adjustments are not announced and contested, a steady progression of divisive debates can perhaps be avoided. The burying of racial preferences in "plus" factors for certain individuals obscures and softens the sense of injury that even the most dedicated proponents of affirmative action must acknowledge will be felt by those who are disadvantaged for reasons they cannot control. Law schools will be better, happier, and more productive places if the lines separating the students who inhabit them are not harshly drawn.

This endorsement of Powell's position in *Bakke* does not depend, however, on ease of academic administration. On the contrary, I think it a virtue of Powell's compromise that it does not give law school (and other) administrators a perpetually free hand. Racial preferences in admissions may be justified, as I believe, by pressing necessity, but they are not something to which we should readily grow accustomed. They are desirable only in the limited sense that, under current conditions, living with them is better than living without them. As conditions change, we should be alert to the necessity to change with them and to curtail or eliminate racial "plus" factors as soon as possible. This inchoate future negative, the preservation of doctrinal objections and normative under-

---

[71] Paul J. Mishkin, *The Uses of Ambivalence: Reflections on the Supreme Court and the Constitutionality of Affirmative Action*, 131 U Pa L Rev 907, 917 (1983).

standings that call for racial preferences to end, is also part of Powell's legacy. It is as important—and as valuable—as his willingness to allow racial preferences in the interim.

A second observation prompted by the revivification of Powell's position in *Bakke* concerns the relationship between Court and country. History-minded scholars (and others) have challenged the notion that it is the business of the Supreme Court to lead the nation out of darkness. I think particularly of my colleague Michael Klarman, who has argued that even *Brown v Board of Education*, the most mythogenic and justifying of all modern decisions, was in fact more nearly a reflection of an emerging national consensus than a heroic attempt to uproot one.[72] The broad tides of social change sweep the Court along with the country, and rarely do the Justices stand long in the way. There is much to be said for this perspective, not least as a corrective to the extravagant judiciocentrism that pervades constitutional law classrooms, but there are also small acts of individual judgment or personality that profoundly affect the course of events. The division of opinion in *Bakke* shows that Lewis Powell's view of the matter was, at least among the Justices, idiosyncratic. If there was some broad movement propelling the country toward Powell's peculiar compromise, it seems to have bypassed his colleagues without noticeable effect. Had he not been there—and had the others not been evenly split—it is likely that the Court would have given the great question of affirmative action a clear answer, with the "sound intellectual foundation" that Ronald Dworkin so desired.[73] And the nation would have suffered for it. *Bakke*'s failure to achieve intellectual clarity—or, as I would prefer, its sacrifice of cogency for wisdom—resulted chiefly from the participation of one intransigent moderate who occupied ground he could not adequately defend, save by insisting that it lay between two alternatives he would not accept. Powell's compromise was uniquely his own.

---

[72] See generally Michael J. Klarman, *From Jim Crow to Civil Rights: The Supreme Court and the Struggle for Racial Equality*, chaps 6 and 7 (Oxford, 2004). For a more suggestive argument in the same direction, see John C. Jeffries, Jr. and James E. Ryan, *A Political History of the Establishment Clause*, 100 Mich L Rev 279 (2001) (analyzing modern Establishment Clause decisions "*as if they were* political" (emphasis in original)).

[73] See note 36. Compare Charles Fried, *Foreword: Revolutions*, 109 Harv L Rev 13, 48 (1995) (noting the contradictions in Powell's view but invoking "Aristotle's dictum that a wise man does not seek for greater precision than the subject allows").

With due allowance for the ultimate unknowability of historical "what-ifs," it is hard to believe that *Grutter* and *Gratz* would have come to rest on the same ground absent Powell in *Bakke*. Powell's opinion created space and opportunity for support to coalesce around his middle way. Without that opportunity, the Justices in 2003 would not have been confronted with prestigious testimonials for "plus-factor" diversity.[74] They would not have been reassured by a generation of qualified success. Most important, the frailty of reasoning that Powell's contemporary critics found so distressing would not have been shored up by experience. Leading scholars two decades later would not have been rhapsodizing about Powell's "vision of the unique democratic value of diversity in education" and his "powerful theory" of educational benefit,[75] much less defending his much-maligned distinction between quotas and goals.[76] *Bakke* bought time, and in that time a position that had once been perceived as eccentric came to seen as wise.

This is not to say, of course, that Powell's position prevailed in *Grutter* and *Gratz* entirely because of its merits, intellectual or otherwise. At least with the election of the second President Bush, if not before, proponents of affirmative action recognized Powell's compromise as the only game in town. The sometimes bitter criticism leveled against Powell from the left[77] faded in appreciation of the value of half a loaf. In part, therefore, the growth of support for Powell's position was tactical. That said, it is also true that Powell prevailed in part because of who and where he was. His position at the center of an equally divided Court meant that he spoke for the institution. In *Bakke*, Powell's view was decisive on the Court, and the prestige and authority of the institution gave his position weight and prominence that could never have been achieved by strength of reasoning. One need not believe that the Justices can permanently thwart popular conviction or force the nation where it will not go, in order to recognize that the Supreme

---

[74] See note 61.

[75] Akhil Reed Amar and Neal Kumar Katyal, *Bakke's Fate*, 43 UCLA L Rev 1745, 1773, 1751 (1996).

[76] Id at 1772–74 (arguing that using race "as one consideration among many" minimizes the costs and disadvantages of a more categorical approach).

[77] When *Bakke* was announced, Congressman Ronald V. Dellums pronounced himself "appalled" by the "racist decision," and Jesse Jackson called on blacks to "rebel." See Jeffries, *Powell Biography* at 496 (quoting and referencing these reactions) (cited in note 2).

Court has a voice in shaping public opinion. In *Bakke*, the exercise of that voice fell to Lewis Powell, and the results a quarter-century later reveal his impact.

Finally, it is startling to note how little either the insight or the impact of Powell's opinion in *Bakke* depended on his abilities as a lawyer. That is not to say that he lacked those abilities. Powell was a good lawyer and an uncommonly successful one. But his achievement in *Bakke* came *despite*, not because of, the constraints of legal reasoning. To the extent that the law as an intellectual craft influenced Powell in *Bakke*, it would have pushed him toward one of the "clear answers" provided by his colleagues. Either the Constitution required color-blindness, now and forever, as the Court itself had so often insisted, or racial preferences in favor of minorities were qualitatively different from discrimination against them and should be judged by a more tolerant constitutional standard. Neither argument is hard to write. What Powell did was to reject both arguments and to consign himself and his clerks to the frustrating and perhaps impossible task of finding an analytically presentable way of splitting the difference.[78] The resulting opinion is well written, admirably clear, anything but slapdash. But beneath the skillful prose and careful exposition lie difficulties that no artful phrasing can resolve. The lesser of those difficulties, at least in retrospect, is the watering-down of strict scrutiny. The notion of rigid tests with definite content has lost ground over the years, so that the departure from doctrine no longer seems as violent as it once did. The greater problem, of course, is the invention of "genuine" diversity as a concept that validated the end of racial preferences but disallowed the use of efficacious means to that end. Powell himself knew the weakness of his position, yet persisted in it. Yet if there was any special foresight in Powell's view, any gift of wisdom that justifies our later celebration of his position, it lies precisely in the analytic incongruity of "genuine" diversity. Without his willingness to embrace that contradiction—and to live with the criticism it provoked—Powell's compromise would have failed.

In short, *Bakke* provides a particularly telling example of constitutional adjudication as an appeal to the future. A generation ago,

---

[78] A narrative of the efforts of Powell's chambers to produce the *Bakke* opinion appears in Jeffries, *Powell Biography* at 468–78 (cited in note 2).

Alexander Bickel inveighed against the Supreme Court's "refusal, too often, to submit to the discipline of the analytically tenable distinction . . . ."[79] He insisted on "reason in the judicial process, on analytical coherence, and on principled judgment no matter now narrow its compass."[80] The problem, as he saw it, lay in the seductiveness of the "idea of progress" and in the Justices' (he spoke specifically of the Warren Court) willingness to seek vindication in future events rather than validation by contemporary reasoning.[81] In part, of course, Bickel was criticizing judicial triumphalism, and of that Powell—at least in *Bakke*—cannot fairly be accused. His position was not venturesome but fundamentally defensive, trying on the one hand to stave off a radical shift to strictly color-blind admissions while seeking on the other hand to preserve that ideal for future generations. He aimed less to remake the world by his lights than to ease the transition to a world we all agree is better for us all.

But if Powell in *Bakke* cannot fairly be charged with hubris, he does stand rightly accused of subordinating craft to outcome and of discharging the powers of his high office with a bet on the future. Whether such decisions are always unwise, or whether they are even avoidable, are more difficult questions.

Many years later, Richard Posner took a gentler view of such decisions in his defense of legal pragmatism.[82] "Everyday pragmatists," of whom Powell is surely an exemplar, are not, says Posner, indifferent to systemic concerns, but they are forward-looking, attentive to consequences, and empiricist.[83] Moreover, they are "hostile to the idea of using abstract moral and political theory to guide judicial decisionmaking."[84] This is as precisely applicable to Powell in *Bakke* as any general description could be. And in this view, Posner emphasizes, "there is no special analytical procedure that

---

[79] Alexander M. Bickel, *The Supreme Court and the Idea of Progress* 81 (1970).

[80] Id.

[81] Id at 11–12 ("Historians a generation or two hence . . . may barely note, and care little about, method, logic, or intellectual coherence, and may assess results in hindsight—only results, and by their future lights. . . . [O]ne sensed that this was what the Justices of the Warren Court expected, and that they were content to take their chances. They relied on events for vindication more than on the method of reason for contemporary validation.").

[82] Richard A. Posner, *Law, Pragmatism, and Democracy* (2003).

[83] Id at 59–60.

[84] Id.

distinguishes legal reasoning from other practical reasoning."[85] The two are "continuous," "so that no wide gulf separates judges from other decisionmakers, public and private."[86]

As a normative matter, this account of judging is deeply controversial. I have said enough to indicate where my sympathies lie, at least for the occasional great case where much is at stake and little is clear, but I do not wish to enter that debate in any general way. My purpose, rather, is to suggest that Posner's claim must be stronger and more controversial than he reveals, though surely not than he understands. It is not enough to say that "there is no special analytical procedure that distinguishes legal reasoning from other practical reasoning" nor any "wide gulf" between judges and political actors. As Bickel clearly saw and sharply regretted, sometimes the "special analytic procedure" of legal reasoning *thwarts* pragmatic decisions. Sometimes, there is indeed a "wide gulf" between legal reasoning and political wisdom. Sometimes, the gap between the conventional criteria of judging—what Bickel called "reason in the judicial process," "analytic coherence," and "principled judgment"—and a politically far-sighted decision is unbridgeably large. Where that is true, there is no easy melding of legal craft and political insight. The judge must choose between them.

Regents of the University of California v Allan Bakke was precisely such a case. The choice Powell faced there was not merely between two analytically coherent positions, but between analytical coherence on the one side and his hopes for the nation on the other. His reputation as a judge will stand or fall on the choice he made. So far, the returns look good.

---

[85] Id at 73.
[86] Id.

CASS R. SUNSTEIN

WHAT DID LAWRENCE HOLD?
OF AUTONOMY, DESUETUDE,
SEXUALITY, AND MARRIAGE

In 1900, Mr. Dooley famously said that "[n]o matter whether th' constitution follows th' flag or not, th' supreme court follows th' ilection returns."[1] The Court doesn't really do that. But members of the Supreme Court live in society, and they are inevitably influenced by what society appears to think.[2] My principal suggestion here is that the Court's remarkable decision in *Lawrence v Texas*[3] is best seen as a successor to *Griswold v Connecticut*:[4] judicial invalidation of a law that had become hopelessly out of touch with existing social convictions. So understood, *Lawrence*, like *Griswold*, reflects a distinctly American variation on the old English idea of desuetude. Put too simply, the basic idea is that when constitutionally important interests are at stake, due process principles requiring fair notice, and banning arbitrary action, are violated if criminal

Cass R. Sunstein is Karl N. Llewellyn Distinguished Service Professor, Law School and Department of Political Science, University of Chicago.

AUTHOR'S NOTE: I am grateful to Mary Anne Case, Elizabeth Emens, Carolyn Frantz, Richard A. Posner, Geoffrey Stone, and Adrian Vermeule for valuable comments; special thanks to Case, Frantz, and Vermeule for discussions. I am also grateful to Sarah A. Sulkowski for superb research assistance.

[1] Peter Dunne, *The Supreme Court's Decisions*, in *Mr. Dooley's Opinions* 26 (1900).

[2] Robert Dahl made this argument nearly a half-century ago, before much of the work of the Warren Court. Notwithstanding the passage of decades, his argument stands up well. See Robert Dahl, *Decision-Making in a Democracy: The Supreme Court as a National Policy-Maker*, 6 J Public L 279 (1957).

[3] 123 S Ct 2472 (2003).

[4] 381 US 479 (1965).

prosecution is brought on the basis of moral judgments lacking public support, as exemplified by exceedingly rare enforcement activity.[5] On this reading, *Lawrence* had a great deal to do with procedural due process, rather than the clause's substantive sibling.

In *Griswold*, it will be recalled, the Court invalidated a Connecticut law forbidding married people to use contraceptives—a law that was ludicrously inconsistent with public convictions in Connecticut and throughout the nation.[6] *Griswold* was decided in the midst of a substantial national rethinking of issues of sex and morality. Whatever the outcome of that rethinking, it was clear, by 1965, that reasonable people would no longer support bans on the use of contraceptives within marriage. In this respect, *Griswold* was quite similar to *Reed v Reed*.[7] There the Court struck down an Idaho statute giving a preference to men over women in the administration of estates of decedents who had died intestate—a law that was unquestionably a holdover from views about sex roles that were widely regarded as obsolete. *Reed* was decided in the midst of a substantial rethinking of gender roles; whatever the outcome of that rethinking, it was clear, by 1971, that a flat presumption in favor of men over women in employment would no longer be acceptable in principle.[8] *Lawrence* belongs in the same family. In

---

[5] I specify this brief statement below.

[6] 381 US 479 (1965).

[7] 404 US 71 (1971).

[8] The Court has shown special sensitivity to changing public convictions in the death penalty context. *Furman v Georgia*, 408 US 238 (1972), invalidated certain capital sentences, in a complex set of opinions that seemed to presage the end of capital punishment in the United States. At least in retrospect, *Furman* is best seen as a kind of "remand" to state legislatures, asking for a new assessment of whether capital punishment was consistent with contemporary values. The result of the "remand" was a new affirmation of public support for capital punishment, to which the Court subsequently deferred, see *Gregg v Georgia*, 428 US 153 (1976). In *Coker v Georgia*, 433 US 584 (1977), and *Enmund v Florida*, 458 US 782, 789–93 (1982), the Court relied heavily on contemporary practices in striking down death sentences for rape and for a defendant who did not take or intend to take life. More recently, the Court ruled that the Constitution forbids application to capital punishment to the mentally retarded, see *Atkins v Virginia*, 536 US 304 (2002); in so ruling, the Court relied heavily on what it saw as changing social values. In a theme echoed in *Lawrence*, the Court wrote, "A claim that punishment is excessive is judged not by the standards that prevailed in 1685 when Lord Jeffreys presided over the 'Bloody Assizes' or when the Bill of Rights was adopted, but rather by those that currently prevail." Id at 311. In a key passage, the Court suggested: "It is not so much the number of these States [abolishing the death penalty for the mentally retarded] that is significant, but the consistency of the direction of change. Given the well-known fact that anticrime legislation is far more popular than legislation providing protections for persons guilty of violent crime, the large number of States prohibiting the execution of mentally retarded persons (and the complete absence of States passing legislation reinstating the power to conduct such executions) provides

the area of sexual orientation, America is in the midst of a civil
rights revolution—one that has moved, in an extraordinarily short
time, toward delegitimating prejudice against and hatred for homosexuals. *Lawrence* was made possible by that revolution, of
which it is now a significant part.

In making this argument, my principal goal is not to evaluate
Lawrence, but instead to obtain an understanding of its scope and
of its relationship to other apparently dramatic decisions in the
Court's past. But even if my argument is correct, it must be acknowledged that the Court's remarkably opaque opinion has three
principal strands.[9] Each of those strands supports a different understanding of the Court's holding and the principle that supports it.

1. *Autonomy.* A tempting reading of *Lawrence* is straightforward:
*A criminal prohibition on sodomy is unconstitutional because it intrudes
on private sexual conduct that does not harm third parties.* On this
view, the Court has endorsed a quite general principle: *Without a
compelling justification, the state cannot interfere with consensual sexual
behavior, at least if that behavior is noncommercial.* On this view, consensual sexual behavior counts as a fundamental right for purposes
of the Due Process Clause. The state is forbidden to intrude into
the domain of consensual sexual behavior unless it can show that
its intrusion is the least restrictive means of achieving a compelling
state interest—a showing that will be impossible to make, at least
most of the time.

2. *Rational basis.* An alternative reading of *Lawrence*, also quite
broad, would take the Court to have held, not that sexual behavior
counts as a fundamental right requiring compelling justification,
but that *the criminal prohibition on sodomy is unconstitutional because
it is not supported by a legitimate state interest.* The principle here is
that *the government cannot interfere with consensual sexual behavior if
it is attempting to do so for only moral reasons, unaccompanied by a risk
of actual harm.* The implications of this reading are not so different

---

powerful evidence that today our society views mentally retarded offenders as categorically
less culpable than the average criminal." Id at 315. Note also that the Court emphasized
that even in states that authorized the death penalty to those with mental retardation, few
were actually willing to impose that punishment, an idea with clear links to the rationale
in *Lawrence*.

[9] In this respect, the decision is akin to *Plyler v Doe*, 457 US 202 (1982), in which the
Court struck down a law requiring children of illegal aliens to pay for public education;
there too the Court's opinion was an amalgam of considerations, without a clear doctrinal
foundation.

from those of the first; both are strongly Millian in nature.[10] But the two readings are nonetheless different, because the second depends not on the fundamental nature of the right to engage in sexual activity, but instead on the absence of even plausibly legitimate grounds for interfering with that right in the context of consensual sodomy. On this reading, *Lawrence* is rooted in an unusual form of "rational basis" review that would doom a great deal of legislation.

3. *Desuetude, American style.* A narrower reading of *Lawrence*, my emphasis here, would take the following form: *The criminal prohibition on sodomy is unconstitutional because it intrudes on private sexual conduct without having significant moral grounding in existing public commitments.* If this is the Court's holding, it is undergirded by a more general principle: *Without a strong justification, the state cannot bring the criminal law to bear on consensual sexual behavior if enforcement of the relevant law can no longer claim to have significant moral support in the enforcing state or the nation as a whole.* This aspect of the opinion is connected to the old idea of desuetude. It suggests that, at least in some circumstances, involving certain kinds of human interests, a criminal law cannot be enforced if it has lost public support.

It should be clear that while all three principles are potentially broad, the first and the second are the most far-reaching. And there is actually a fourth understanding of the opinion, one that cannot be characterized as the Court's holding, but one that is perhaps a subtext:

4. *Equality. Sodomy laws are unconstitutional because they demean the lives of gays and lesbians and thus offend the Constitution's equality principle.* The underlying principle is that at least as a general rule, *there is no legitimate basis for treating homosexuals differently from heterosexuals.* On this view, *Lawrence* is really a case about the social subordination of gays and lesbians, whatever the rhetoric about sexual freedom in general. *Lawrence*'s words sound in due process, but much of its music involves equal protection.

Each of the four ideas can be found in *Lawrence*, a claim that I hope to establish here. But I want to draw special attention to the third, which is, I believe, central to the Court's own analysis, and a key to the development of substantive due process over the past decades. In fact something like a desuetude principle is part and

---

[10] John Stuart Mill, *On Liberty* (Currin V. Shields, ed, Liberal Arts Press, 1956) (1859).

parcel of the *Lawrence* Court's treatment of the state's interest, showing why that interest counts as inadequate, and also of the Court's explanation of why the case cannot be distinguished from *Griswold* and its successors. When the Court asserts the absence of a "legitimate state interest which can justify its intrusion into the personal and private life of an individual,"[11] it is best understood to be saying that the moral claim that underlies the intrusion has become hopelessly anachronistic. And the anachronistic nature of that moral claim has everything to do with the Court's rejection, not of moral claims in general, but of the particular moral claim that underlies criminal prohibitions on same-sex sodomy.

Lawrence might be read broadly as an effort to enact some version of John Stuart Mill's *On Liberty*,[12] requiring respect for individual choices (at least with respect to sex) unless there is some kind of harm to others. But it is reasonable to understand the Court's decision more narrowly, as a ruling that forbids invocation of generally unenforced criminal law on the basis of a moral justification that has become anachronistic—at least when a constitutionally important interest is involved and when the absence of significant enforcement activity can be explained only by reference to the anachronistic nature of the relevant moral justification. This reading also helps clarify what made the decision possible and its fate. If I am correct, *Lawrence* was possible not because the Court reached, all on its own, an ambitious and novel view of the nature of constitutional liberty, or because it attempted to read a controversial view of autonomy into the Due Process Clause. The decision was possible only because of the ludicrously poor fit between the sodomy prohibition and the society in which the justices live. And if I am correct, *Lawrence* will have broad implications only if and to the extent that those broad implications receive general public support. For example, the Supreme Court may or may not read *Lawrence* to require states to recognize gay and lesbian marriages. But if and when it does so, it will be following public opinion, not leading it. Political and social change was a precondition for *Lawrence*, whose future reach will depend on the nature and extent of that change.

While I will spend most of my time on the Court's due process ruling, my own view is that the proper course in *Lawrence* was

---

[11] 123 S Ct at 2484.

[12] Mill, *On Liberty* (cited in note 10).

sketched by Justice O'Connor in her concurring opinion.[13] Rather than invalidating the Texas statute on grounds of substantive due process, the Court should have invoked the Equal Protection Clause to strike down, as irrational, the state's decision to ban homosexual sodomy but not heterosexual sodomy. In important respects, this approach would have been more cautious than the Court's own. It would have had the large advantage of making it unnecessary to overrule any precedent.[14] At the same time, an equal protection ruling would have recognized the fact, established by the Court's opinions, that the Equal Protection Clause does not build on long-standing traditions, but instead rejects them insofar as they attempt to devalue or humiliate certain social groups.[15] The problem in *Lawrence* is not adequately understood without reference to the social subordination of gays and lesbians, not least through the use of the criminal law. Hence Justice O'Connor's approach suggests, lightly to be sure, the plausibility of rationale (4) above, a rationale that seems to me essentially correct. And if states are required to punish heterosexual sodomy if they are attempting to punish homosexual sodomy, I believe that it is quite implausible to think that any form of sodomy would be subject to criminal prosecution; political safeguards are far too strong to permit significant numbers of arrests and prosecutions of heterosexuals for engaging in conduct that is quite widespread.

For all these reasons, invalidation on equal protection grounds would have been preferable to the substantive due process route. But if the Due Process Clause is to be invoked, the idea of desuetude provides a method for understanding, disciplining, and narrowing what the Court did. This reading of *Lawrence* prevents the opinion from being a simple invocation of "liberty"; it also helps explain what made the *Lawrence* decision conceivable from a gener-

---

[13] 123 S Ct at 2485 (O'Connor concurring).

[14] I do not engage here the debate over whether principles of stare decisis required the Court to refuse to overrule *Bowers v Hardwick*. My only suggestion is that the Court should not have overruled that decision when it was unnecessary to do so in order to decide *Lawrence*. A possible objection to the equal protection approach, one that I also cannot engage here, is that this approach is actually broader than that taken by the majority, above all because it would seem to require states to recognize same-sex marriages. It is true that an equal protection ruling would raise questions about bans on such marriages. But as we shall see, a due process ruling has the same effect.

[15] See, e.g., *City of Cleburne v Cleburne Living Center, Inc.*, 473 US 432 (1985); *Romer v Evans*, 517 US 620 (1996).

ally conservative Supreme Court. Best of all, it has considerable independent appeal.[16]

This article comes in four parts. The first explores the Court's dilemma in *Lawrence*—the state of pre-*Lawrence* law, the available options, and the difficulties with those options. The second discusses *Lawrence* itself, emphasizing the various strands to which I have referred. The third discusses possible readings of the decision and tries to unpack them. Here I draw attention to the more narrow reading of the opinion, suggesting that if understood in a way that emphasizes the anachronistic and almost never enforced nature of the Texas statute, the *Lawrence* decision can claim a strong foundation in both democratic values and the rule of law. The fourth explores the implications of the *Lawrence* decision for constitutional attacks on laws regulating sexual relationships, constitutional attacks on government discrimination against gays and lesbians, and constitutional attacks on laws refusing to recognize same-sex marriages.

I. The Court's Dilemma

The facts of *Lawrence* were exceedingly simple. Police officers in Houston, Texas, responded to a private report of a weapons disturbance in a private residence. They entered the residence, owned by John Geddes Lawrence. On entering, they did not see any weapons. But they did see Lawrence, engaging in a sexual act with Tyron Garner. Lawrence and Garner were arrested, held in custody, and convicted of the crime of "deviate sexual intercourse, namely anal sex, with a member of the same sex (man)."[17] They were each fined $200.[18] Deviate sexual intercourse is defined to include "any contact between any part of the genitals of one person and the mouth or anus of another person" or "the penetration of the genitals or the anus of another person with an object."[19] The

---

[16] See Guido Calabresi, *Foreword: Antidiscrimination and Constitutional Accountability (What the Bork-Brennan Debate Ignores)*, 105 Harv L Rev 80 (1991); Cass R. Sunstein, *One Case at a Time* (1999).

[17] 123 S Ct at 2475–76.

[18] 41 SW3d at 349.

[19] Id at 2476 (citing Tex Penal Code Ann § 21.01(1)).

Texas law was challenged on equal protection and due process grounds.[20]

The *Lawrence* Court had three options. It could have invalidated the Texas statute under the Equal Protection Clause. It could have invalidated the law on due process grounds. Or it could have upheld the law against both challenges. As we will see, the Court faced a serious difficulty in *Lawrence:* a majority believed, in my view correctly, that the Texas statute had to be invalidated—but any rationale for invalidation would inevitably raise serious doubts about practices, including the ban on same-sex marriages, that the majority did not want to question. For the majority, a central problem was to develop a rationale that would strike down the Texas statute without producing an unintended revolution in the law. Let us investigate the Court's options in light of preexisting law.

A. EQUAL PROTECTION

1. *Heightened scrutiny.* The Equal Protection Clause might have been used to strike down the Texas statute under decisions calling for "heightened scrutiny" of laws that discriminate against traditionally disadvantaged groups. The paradigm examples of such groups are, of course, African-Americans and women.[21] Perhaps laws discriminating against gays and lesbians should be subject to similarly skeptical judicial scrutiny.[22] To say the least, the Court has not laid down a clear test for deciding when such scrutiny will be applied; instead it has pointed to a series of considerations, including a history of discrimination, a circumstance of immutability, and political powerlessness.[23] Probably the best way of making sense of the doctrine is to say that heightened scrutiny is applied when the relevant discrimination is peculiarly likely to reflect prejudice and hostility rather than legitimate interests. In the context of race, for example, the problem is not that skin color is immutable, but that discrimination against African-Americans is usually based on illicit considerations; heightened scrutiny is a way of test-

---

[20] Id.

[21] See, e.g., *United States v Virginia*, 518 US 515 (1996); *Loving v Virginia*, 388 US 1 (1967).

[22] See David Richards, *Sexual Preference as a Suspect (Religious) Classification*, 55 Ohio St L J 491 (1994); Cass R. Sunstein, *Homosexuality and the Constitution*, 70 Ind L J 1, 8 (1994).

[23] See, e.g., *Frontiero v Richardson*, 411 US 677 (1973) (Brennan) (plurality).

ing whether other, legitimate, public-spirited justifications can actually be brought forward in defense of the relevant law. In principle, discrimination against homosexuals can easily be understood in analogous terms. Suppose, for example, that a school forbids homosexuals from becoming teachers,[24] or that a police department refuses to hire gay officers.[25] In both cases, prejudice is especially likely to be at work. If heightened scrutiny were applied, a ban on same-sex sodomy would be extremely difficult to defend.

As a matter of precedent, the problem is that the Court has never suggested that gays and lesbians are entitled to heightened scrutiny. In fact it has been extremely reluctant to expand the class of groups so entitled—ruling, for example, that rational basis review applies to discrimination against handicapped people[26] and elderly people.[27] These are not decisive problems, to be sure; a ruling that required heightened scrutiny is not foreclosed by existing decisions. But such a ruling would certainly be an innovation.

An alternative route to heightened scrutiny would be to contend that discrimination against homosexuals *is* a kind of discrimination on the basis of sex.[28] Here it might be suggested that if a law punishes same-sex sodomy, it is punishing people who would not be punished if their gender were different. But this view raises a number of complexities.[29] It would also seem to have broad implications, essentially treating all discrimination against gays and lesbians as indistinguishable from, because literally identical to, discrimination against women.[30]

2. *Rationality review.* When rational basis review is applied, statutes are almost always upheld under the Equal Protection Clause.[31] But three cases provided a plausible backdrop for the plaintiffs' challenge in *Lawrence*. Taken together, the three cases suggest that

---

[24] *Glover v Williamsburg Local School District Board of Education*, 20 F Supp2d 1160 (SD Ohio 1998).

[25] See, e.g., *Childers v Dallas Police Department*, 513 F Supp 134 (ND Tex 1981)

[26] *City of Cleburne v Cleburne Living Center, Inc.*, 473 US 432 (1985).

[27] *Massachusetts v Murgia*, 427 US 307 (1981).

[28] See Andrew Koppelman, *Why Discrimination Against Lesbians and Gay Men Is Sex Discrimination*, 69 NYU L Rev 197 (1994).

[29] See id for detailed discussion.

[30] See id; I essentially accept this claim in Sunstein, *One Case at a Time* (cited in note 16).

[31] See, e.g., id; *Lalli v Lalli*, 429 US 259 (1978).

a bare "desire to harm a politically unpopular group"[32] is constitutionally unacceptable. Texas's prohibition of homosexual sodomy, not affecting heterosexual sodomy, could be challenged as reflecting such a bare desire.

The problem in *United States Department of Agriculture v Moreno*[33] arose from Congress's decision to exclude from the food stamp program any household containing an individual who was unrelated to any other member of the household.[34] Thus the statute required that any household receiving food stamps must consist solely of "related" individuals.[35] The Court invalidated the statute. The Court noted that the legislative history suggested a congressional desire to exclude "hippies" and "hippie communes."[36] To this the Court said: "[I]f the constitutional conception of 'equal protection of the laws' means anything, it must at the very least mean that a bare congressional desire to harm a politically unpopular group cannot constitute a legitimate governmental interest. . . ."[37] This idea was extended in the *Cleburne* case, in which the plaintiffs challenged a city's denial of a special use permit for the operation of a group home for the mentally retarded.[38] Applying rational basis review, the Court admonished that "mere negative attitudes, or fear, unsubstantiated by factors which are properly cognizable in a zoning proceeding, are not permissible bases for"[39] unequal treatment. Thus the Court concluded that the discriminatory action under review was based "on an irrational prejudice."[40] And in *Romer v Evans*, the Court struck down a Colorado law forbidding localities from including gays and lesbians within the protection of laws prohibiting discrimination.[41] The Court held that the law violated rational basis review because it was based not on a legitimate public purpose but on a form of "animus"—with the apparent suggestion that statutes rooted in

[32] *United States Department of Agriculture v Moreno*, 413 US 528, 534 (1973).

[33] Id at 528.

[34] See id.

[35] Id at 530.

[36] Id at 534.

[37] Id.

[38] 473 US 432.

[39] Id at 448.

[40] Id at 450.

[41] 517 US 620 (1996).

"animus" represent core offenses of the equal protection guarantee. The Court said that the law stands (and falls) as "a status-based classification of persons undertaken for its own sake."[42]

An equal protection ruling in *Lawrence*, based on these cases, would have had a great deal of appeal. It would have made it unnecessary for the Court to reconsider *Bowers v Hardwick*.[43] It would have built carefully on *Romer v Evans*. In these ways, such a ruling would have been narrow, simply converting the *Moreno-Cleburne-Romer* trilogy into the *Moreno-Cleburne-Romer-Lawrence* quartet. On the other hand, it is not clear that such a ruling would have had more limited consequences than a due process ruling. An invalidation of the line between homosexual and heterosexual sodomy would have raised questions about a host of other discriminatory practices. Is the state permitted not to recognize gay marriages? To discriminate against homosexuals in its employment practices? Is the federal government permitted to maintain its "don't ask, don't tell" policy in the military context? If the Court wanted to cabin the reach of its ruling, and not to create anything like a revolution in the law, these were important (and difficult) questions to answer.

B. DUE PROCESS

The modern story of substantive due process begins in 1965, when the Court invalidated a Connecticut law forbidding the use of contraceptives by married people.[44] After that decision, the Court decided a set of cases protecting certain choices involving sex, reproduction, the family, and other areas that appeared to be intimate and private.[45] The cases turned out to be quite unruly, and there was no clear line between what was protected and what was not.[46]

A possible view would be that since *Bowers*, or at least since *Washington v Glucksberg*,[47] the Court has said something like this:

---

[42] Id at 621.

[43] 478 US 186 (1986) (holding that there is no fundamental right to engage in homosexual sodomy).

[44] *Griswold*, 381 US 479.

[45] See, e.g., *Eisenstadt v Baird*, 405 US 438 (1972); *Carey v Population Services International*, 431 US 678 (1977); *Roe v Wade*, 410 US 113 (1973).

[46] For a general discussion, see Cass R. Sunstein, *The Right to Die*, 106 Yale L J 1123 (1997).

[47] 521 US 702 (1997) (holding that there is no fundamental right to assistance in committing suicide).

"Thus far, but no further!" Since 1985, the Court has been extremely reluctant to use the idea of substantive due process to strike down legislation, and before *Lawrence*, the Court seemed unwilling to add to the list even if the logic of the prior cases suggested that it ought to do so.[48] On this view, the Court's refusal to overrule *Roe v Wade*[49] reflects not approval of that decision, and much less a willingness to extend its logic, but a kind of temporal dividing line between permissible and prohibited uses of substantive due process.[50] In other words, the continuing validity of *Roe* suggests not that the Court will try to follow the logic of the privacy cases, but that the Court will refuse to overrule its precedents while also failing to build on their logic.

If we sought to bring more principled order to the Court's decisions, we might invoke the Court's own words and insist that any asserted right must have a strong foundation in Anglo-American traditions. This was the limiting principle invoked in both *Bowers* and *Glucksberg*. In *Bowers*, the Court, quoting Justice Powell, emphasized the need to ask whether the relevant liberties "are 'deeply rooted in this Nation's history and tradition.'"[51] In *Glucksberg*, the Court said that "the development of this Court's substantive-due-process jurisprudence . . . has been . . . carefully refined by concrete examples involving fundamental rights found to be deeply rooted in our legal tradition."[52] The Court stressed that this historical test tended "to rein in the subjective elements"[53] and to avoid "the need for complex balancing of competing interests in every case."[54] The historical approach might have the advantage of disciplining judicial discretion, but it has the disadvantage of fitting extremely poorly with some of the cases. It is not at all clear, for example, that the right to choose abortion has a strong foundation in tradition. Nonetheless, it would hardly be implausible, before *Lawrence v Texas*, to argue that henceforth, the line between protected and unprotected interests would turn largely on history—

---

[48] The most obvious example here is *Glucksberg*, id.

[49] 410 US 113.

[50] See *Planned Parenthood of Southeastern Pa v Casey*, 505 US 833 (1992) (upholding some state restrictions on abortion).

[51] 478 US at 194.

[52] 521 US at 722.

[53] Id.

[54] Id.

and for that reason, *Lawrence* could well have been resolved favorably to the state.

II. WHAT THE COURT DID

A. SUBSTANTIVE DUE PROCESS REBORN

The heart of the Court's opinion in *Lawrence* began with a dramatic reading of precedent, stating, for the first time in the Court's history, that the Constitution recognizes a right to make sexual choices free from state control. Putting *Griswold* together with *Eisenstadt*, the Court said that "the right to make certain decisions regarding sexual conduct extends beyond the marital relationship."[55] Taken by itself, this statement equivocates between two readings: the state may not punish sexual activity through the particular *means* of threatening unwanted pregnancy;[56] or the state may not punish sexual activity at all. The first reading would fit with the Court's previous holdings. But the *Lawrence* Court clearly endorsed the broader reading. In speaking of homosexual activity in particular, the Court said that the government was seeking "to control a personal relationship that, whether or not entitled to formal recognition in the law, is within the liberty of persons to choose without being punished as criminals."[57] Thus the Court suggested that the state could not intrude on sexual liberty "absent injury to a person or abuse of an institution the law protects."[58] Here, then, is the foundation for a reading of *Lawrence* as rooted in a general principle of sexual autonomy.

The Court then turned from its precedents to an investigation of the suggestion in *Bowers* that prohibitions on same-sex sodomy "have ancient roots."[59] Rejecting that conclusion, the Court em-

---

[55] 123 S Ct at 2477.

[56] Thus it would have been possible to read the contraception cases as holding, not that the state may not punish consensual sexual activity, but that it cannot do so through the indirect and discriminatory means of threatening childbirth. The early privacy cases did not involve bans on sexual activity; instead they involved efforts to control such activity by prohibiting the use of contraception. A narrow reading of the cases would suggest that there is no right to immunity from state regulation of sex, but instead a right not to be subject to regulation through the indirect method of risking unwanted pregnancy. See Cass R. Sunstein, *Designing Democracy* (2002).

[57] 123 S Ct at 2478.

[58] Id.

[59] 478 US at 192.

phasized the complexity of American traditions on this count. In a lengthy discussion, the Court undermined the suggestion that there has been an unbroken path of hostility to same-sex sodomy. But the Court freely conceded that there is no history of accepting that practice; it did not contend that traditions affirmatively support a constitutional right to sexual freedom in that domain. On the contrary, and in a dramatic departure from both *Bowers* and *Glucksberg,* the Court said that long-standing traditions were not decisive. Current convictions were important, not old ones. "[W]e think that our laws and traditions in the past half century are of most relevance here."[60] Hence the Court stressed an "emerging recognition that liberty gives substantial protection to adult persons in deciding how to conduct their private lives in matters pertaining to sex."[61]

The emerging recognition could be seen in many places. First, the Model Penal Code did not endorse criminal penalties on consensual sexual activities conducted in private; and several states specifically changed their laws in response to the Model Penal Code.[62] Second, fewer than half the states (24) outlawed sodomy even in 1986, and the statutory prohibition went largely unenforced even in those states.[63] Third, the practices of Western nations have been increasingly opposed to the criminal punishment of homosexual conduct. Britain repealed its law forbidding homosexual conduct in 1967,[64] and the European Court of Human Rights concluded that laws banning consensual homosexual conduct are invalid under the European Convention on Human Rights.[65] Fourth, only thirteen states now forbid such conduct, and of these just four have laws that discriminate only against homosexual conduct.[66] "In those states where sodomy is still proscribed, whether for same-sex or heterosexual conduct, there is a pattern of nonenforcement with respect to consenting adults acting in private."[67]

---

[60] 123 S Ct at 2480.

[61] Id.

[62] Id at 2480–81.

[63] Id at 2481 (citing *Bowers,* 478 US at 192–93).

[64] Id (citing Sexual Offences Act, 1967, c 60, § 1).

[65] Id (citing *Dudgeon v United Kingdom,* 45 Eur Ct HR (1981)). The use of materials from other nations, for the interpretation of the U.S. Constitution, raises many complexities, which I cannot explore here.

[66] Id.

[67] Id.

The Court added that it had issued two decisions casting the holding of *Hardwick* "into even more doubt."[68] In *Casey*, the Court had reaffirmed not only *Roe* but also its commitment to substantive due process, emphasizing "that our laws and traditions afford constitutional protection to personal decisions relating to marriage, procreation, contraception, family relationships, child rearing, and education."[69] Thus the Court read *Casey* as an endorsement of the ideas underlying *Roe*, and not simply as a refusal to reject a decision on which the nation had come to rely. And in *Romer v Evans*, the Court struck down a law "born of animosity toward the class of persons affected."[70] These decisions made *Bowers* decreasingly plausible.

The Court acknowledged that the plaintiff's equal protection challenge, based on *Romer*, was "tenable."[71] But the Court said that "the instant case requires us to address whether *Bowers* itself has continuing validity."[72] (This is remarkable because the instant case "required" no such thing; it would have been fully possible to resolve the case without addressing *Bowers*.) The Court explained that if the Texas statute were invalidated on equal protection grounds, it would remain unclear whether a state could forbid both same-sex and different-sex sodomy.[73] The Court added that when "homosexual conduct is made criminal by the law of the State, that declaration in and of itself is an invitation to subject homosexual persons to discrimination both in the public and in the private spheres."[74] In the Court's view, the continued validity of *Bowers* "demeans the lives of homosexual persons."[75] Here the Court emphasized the stigma imposed by the law, coming not only from the fact that the act is a misdemeanor but also because of "all that imports for the dignity of the persons charged."[76] The collateral consequences of the criminal conviction could not be avoided.

At this point the Court emphasized that *Bowers* had been eroded

---

[68] Id.

[69] Id (citing *Casey*, 505 US at 851).

[70] Id at 2482 (quoting *Romer*, 517 US at 634).

[71] Id.

[72] Id.

[73] Id.

[74] Id.

[75] Id.

[76] Id.

not only by *Casey* and *Romer*, but also by independent sources. Academics had widely criticized the decision.[77] Five different state courts had refused to follow it in interpreting their own state constitutions.[78] The European Court of Human Rights, along with other nations, had rejected the *Bowers* approach, a relevant fact "to the extent that *Bowers* relied on values we share with a wider civilization."[79] Stare decisis was relevant but not conclusive, for the *Bowers* decision did not produce detrimental reliance "comparable to some instances where recognized individual rights are involved."[80] The Court concluded that "*Bowers* was not correct when it was decided, and it is not correct today."[81]

The Court was aware of the potential breadth of its ruling, and it took steps to clarify its scope. "The present case does not involve minors. It does not involve persons who might be injured or coerced or who are situated in relationships where consent might not easily be refused. It does not involve public conduct or prostitution. It does not involve whether the government must give formal recognition to any relationship that homosexual persons seek to enter."[82] What was involved instead was "full and mutual consent" to engage in "sexual practices common to a homosexual lifestyle. . . . The State cannot demean their existence or control their destiny by making their private sexual conduct a crime."[83] In a closing word, the Court said that the Texas law "furthers no legitimate state interest which can justify its intrusion into the personal and private life of the individual."[84]

B. OTHER VOICES

I will return to the complexities in the opinion shortly. For the moment, let us explore the views of the three other justices who wrote in *Lawrence*.

---

[77] Id at 2483 (citing C. Fried, *Order and Law: Arguing the Reagan Revolution—A Firsthand Account* 81–84 (1991); R. Posner, *Sex and Reason* 341–50 (1992)).

[78] Id (citing *Jegley v Picado*, 349 Ark 600 (2002); *Powell v State*, 270 Ga 327 (1998); *Gryczan v State*, 283 Mont 433 (1997); *Campbell v Sundquist*, 926 SW2d 250 (Tenn App 1996); *Commonwealth v Wasson*, 842 SW2d 487 (Ky 1992)).

[79] Id.

[80] Id.

[81] Id at 2484.

[82] Id.

[83] Id.

[84] Id.

1. *Equal protection and Justice O'Connor.* Justice O'Connor rejected the Court's due process holding and urged the equal protection route. Building on the *Moreno-Cleburne-Romer* trilogy, she contended that when a law is based on "a desire to harm a politically unpopular group," the Court has applied "a more searching form of rational basis review."[85] She added that invalidation, via rational basis review, is more likely when the challenged legislation "inhibits personal relationships."[86]

To be sure, Texas had justified its law as a means of promoting morality, and that kind of justification had been found sufficient in *Bowers*, which Justice O'Connor did not seek to disturb. But *Bowers* was decided under the Due Process Clause. *Lawrence* was different, because it presented the not-yet-decided question "whether, under the Equal Protection Clause, moral disapproval is a legitimate state interest to justify by itself a statute that bans homosexual sodomy, but not heterosexual sodomy."[87] She concluded that it is not. Under rational basis review, moral disapproval is not a sufficient basis for discriminating among groups of persons. "Texas' invocation of moral disapproval as a legitimate state interest proves nothing more than Texas' desire to criminalize homosexual sodomy."[88] And because the law is enforced so infrequently, "the law serves more as a statement of dislike and disapproval than as a tool to stop criminal behavior."[89]

Aware of the potentially broad implications of the equal protection argument, Justice O'Connor urged that her analysis would not doom all distinctions between homosexuals and heterosexuals. With her eye firmly on the military and on family law, she said that "Texas cannot assert any legitimate state interest here, such as national security or preserving the traditional institution of marriage."[90] In the latter context, "other reasons exist to promote the institution of marriage beyond mere moral disapproval of an excluded group."[91]

[85] Id at 2485 (O'Connor concurring).
[86] Id (O'Connor concurring).
[87] Id at 2486 (O'Connor concurring).
[88] Id (O'Connor concurring).
[89] Id (O'Connor concurring).
[90] Id at 2487–88 (O'Connor concurring).
[91] Id at 2488 (O'Connor concurring).

2. *Scalia, the slippery slope, and "a massive disruption of the current social order."* Justice Scalia's argument had three elements. First, he chastised the Court for what he saw as its palpable inconsistency on the issue of stare decisis. Invoking stare decisis, the Court had refused to overrule *Roe*, a nineteen-year-old ruling, in its *Casey* decision in 1992.[92] The same Court was now willing to overrule *Bowers*, decided seventeen years previously. Justice Scalia saw no justification for the differential treatment. Second, Justice Scalia urged that the Court's ruling would have extremely large implications. "State laws against bigamy, same-sex marriage, adult incest, prostitution, masturbation, adultery, fornication, bestiality, and obscenity" can be upheld "only in light of Bowers' validation of laws based on moral choices. Every single one of these laws is called into question by today's decision."[93] The Court's decision therefore entails "a massive disruption of the current social order"[94] (something that could not have been said about a decision to overrule *Roe*). Thus Justice Scalia urged that the Court's opinion "dismantles the structure of constitutional law that has permitted a distinction to be made between heterosexual and homosexual unions, insofar as formal recognition in marriage is concerned."[95]

Justice Scalia's third argument involved the proper interpretation of the Constitution in principle. After doubting that the Due Process Clause is a substantive safeguard at all, he urged that as it has developed, the idea of substantive due process has been disciplined by asking whether the relevant rights are "deeply rooted in this Nation's history and tradition."[96] Justice Scalia questioned the idea that there is an "emerging awareness"[97] that consensual homosexual activity should be protected; but his more basic objection was that any emerging awareness was irrelevant to the decision. "Constitutional entitlements do not spring into existence because some States choose to lessen or eliminate criminal sanctions on certain behavior."[98] Justice Scalia saw the Court as holding that

---

[92] Id (Scalia dissenting) (citing *Casey*, 505 US at 844).

[93] Id at 2490 (Scalia dissenting).

[94] Id at 2491 (Scalia dissenting).

[95] Id at 2498 (Scalia dissenting).

[96] Id at 2492 (Scalia dissenting).

[97] Id at 2494 (Scalia dissenting) (internal citation omitted).

[98] Id (Scalia dissenting).

the moral views underlying the Texas statute did not provide a legitimate basis for it. Here his objection was exceedingly simple: "This effectively decrees the end of all morals legislation."[99] With respect to equal protection, Justice Scalia urged that a rational basis was what was required, and that as for due process purposes, "the enforcement of traditional notions of sexual morality" provided the rational basis.[100]

3. *Thomas and the uncommonly silly law.* Justice Thomas's short dissenting opinion emphasizes that as a member of the Texas legislature, he would vote to repeal the relevant law. "Punishing someone for expressing his sexual preference through noncommercial consensual conduct with another adult does not appear to be a worthy way to expend valuable law enforcement resources."[101] Invoking Justice Stewart's concurrence in *Griswold*, he contended that the law is "uncommonly silly,"[102] but that nothing in the Constitution forbids it.[103]

III. INTERPRETIVE PUZZLES

I will suggest that *Lawrence* is best understood as responsive to what the Court saw as an emerging national awareness, reflected in a pattern of nonenforcement, that it is illegitimate to punish people because of homosexual conduct—and that the decision therefore embodies a kind of American-style desuetude. But to support this suggestion, it will be necessary to unpack the Court's opaque opinion, which raises a number of puzzles. Let us begin with the simplest.

A. A FUNDAMENTAL RIGHT OR RATIONAL BASIS REVIEW?

Was *Lawrence* based on rational basis review, or instead on something else? It is astonishing but true that this question is exceedingly difficult to answer.

---

[99] Id at 2495 (Scalia dissenting).

[100] Id at 2496 (Scalia dissenting).

[101] Id at 2498 (Thomas dissenting).

[102] Id (Thomas dissenting) (quoting *Griswold*, 381 US at 527 (Stewart concurring)).

[103] Id (Thomas dissenting).

If the Court had attempted to write a conventional due process opinion, it would have taken one of two routes. First, the Court might have said that the right to engage in consensual sexual activity qualifies as fundamental, so that the government may not interfere with that right unless it has a compelling justification.[104] Second, the Court might have said that whether or not the relevant right qualifies as fundamental, the state cannot interfere with it, simply because it lacks a legitimate reason to justify the interference. But the Court said neither, at least not in plain terms. The Court did not unambiguously identify any "fundamental interest" on the part of the plaintiffs that would support its ruling. In fact it did not use the "fundamental interest" formulation at any point in its analysis. Moreover, the Court did not say that the Texas statute lacked a "rational basis." In fact it did not use the "rational basis" formulation at any point in its analysis. Much of the opacity of the Court's opinion stems from its failure to specify what kind of review it was applying to the Texas statute. The conventional doctrinal categories and terms are simply missing.

To be sure, the Court did end its opinion with a reference to the absence of any "legitimate interest" on the state's part.[105] Justice Scalia seized on this point to urge that the Court issued a rational basis opinion after all[106]—a characterization to which the Court (revealingly?) does not specifically object. Thus Justice Scalia contends that much of the Court's opinion "has no relevance to its actual holding,"[107] which was that the statute failed rational basis review. Justice Scalia's reading cannot be said to be senseless; it is not demonstrably wrong. But I believe that it is incorrect, and that in the end the Court's opinion treats the underlying right as a fundamental one. Begin with the most relevant part of the Court's opinion:

> The petitioners are entitled to respect for their private lives. The State cannot demean their existence or control their destiny by making their private sexual conduct a crime. Their right to liberty under the Due Process Clause gives them the full right to engage in their conduct without intervention of the

---

[104] See, e.g., *Roe*, 410 US 113.

[105] 123 S Ct at 2484.

[106] Id at 2488 (Scalia dissenting).

[107] Id (Scalia dissenting).

government. "It is a promise of the Constitution that there is
a realm of personal liberty which the government may not enter." The Texas statute furthers no legitimate state interest
which can justify its intrusion into the personal and private life
of the individual.[108]

The Court immediately follows its reference to "no legitimate
state interest"[109] with the phrase, "which can justify its intrusion
into the personal and private life of the individual."[110] The Court's
emphasis on "respect for their private lives,"[111] on "control [of]
their destiny,"[112] and on "personal and private life"[113] suggests that
the interest involved is not an ordinary one—and that the Court
is demanding something more than a rational basis. The same
point is strongly suggested by the Court's reference, in this paragraph, to *Casey*,[114] which of course involved a fundamental right,
not a rational basis test.

But there is a more basic reason for seeing the Court's opinion
as finding the relevant interest to be fundamental. The Court begins with an effort to assimilate the issue in *Lawrence* to the issues
in *Griswold*, *Eisenstadt*, *Roe*, *Carey*, and *Casey*—all of which are now
taken, by the Court, to suggest a fundamental right in the domain
of sex and reproduction. Hence the Court refers to "the right to
make certain decisions regarding sexual conduct,"[115] to the individual's interest in making "certain fundamental decisions affecting
her destiny,"[116] and to the "emerging awareness that liberty gives
substantial protection to adult persons in deciding how to conduct
their private lives in matters pertaining to sex."[117] These statements
would be unintelligible if *Lawrence* were based solely on rational
basis review. Indeed, much of the Court's opinion would be dicta.
In the end, *Lawrence* is not plausibly a rational basis decision.

---

[108] Id at 2484 (quoting *Casey*, 505 US at 847) (internal citation omitted).

[109] Id.

[110] Id.

[111] Id.

[112] Id.

[113] Id.

[114] Id (citing *Casey*, 505 US at 847).

[115] Id at 2477.

[116] Id.

[117] Id at 2480.

An alternative reading is that the Court deliberately refused to specify its "tier" of analysis because it was rejecting the idea of tiers altogether. Perhaps the Court was signaling its adoption of a kind of sliding scale, matching the strength of the interest to the demand for state justification, without formally requiring identification of a fundamental right. And, indeed, some of the Court's decisions do suggest a partial collapse of the traditional tiers approach to judicial review.[118] For many years, Justice Marshall complained of the rigidity of the usual tiers, urging a more open-ended form of balancing.[119] Justice Marshall's views appeared to fall on deaf ears. But perhaps *Lawrence* reflects some appreciation of the difficulties in fitting all cases within the traditional framework. This is not a wholly implausible reading, but it would be quite surprising if the Court meant to adopt a sliding scale of analysis without saying so. The more natural interpretation is simpler: The Court's assimilation of the *Lawrence* problem to that in *Griswold* and its successors suggests that a fundamental right was involved.

B. AUTONOMY SIMPLICITER, OR DESUETUDE-INFORMED AUTONOMY?

But why, exactly, does the relevant interest count as a fundamental one? There are two possibilities. The first is that the right to engage in consensual sex counts, simply as a matter of principle, as part of the liberty that the Due Process Clause substantively protects. On this view, in *Lawrence* the Court accepted, to this extent, John Stuart Mill's view in *On Liberty*,[120] holding that the government may not interfere with (certain) private choices unless there is harm to others. The second and narrower idea is that this particular *kind* of sex—homosexual sex between consenting adults—counts as fundamental. It does so because of major changes in social values in the last half-century. On this view, *Lawrence* finds a fundamental right as a result of existing public convictions, with which the Texas statute cannot be squared, simply because sodomy prosecutions are so hopelessly out of step with them.

---

[118] See, e.g., the heightened approach to rational basis review in *Romer*, 517 US 620, and *Cleburne*, 473 US 432, and the softened approach to strict scrutiny in *Grutter v Bollinger*, 123 S Ct 2325 (2003).

[119] See *Dandridge v Williams*, 397 US 471 (1970) (Marshall dissenting); *San Antonio Independent School District v Rodriguez*, 411 US 1 (Marshall dissenting).

[120] See Mill, *On Liberty* (cited in note 10).

Lawrence could be read in either way. But the second interpretation is far more plausible. A simple autonomy reading would have
consequences that the Court did not likely intend. As Justice Scalia
suggests, it would raise, even more than the first, serious doubts
about prohibitions on adult incest, prostitution, adultery, fornication, bestiality, and obscenity.[121] (I do not mention his suggestion
that the Court has questioned laws forbidding masturbation,[122] for
one reason: There are no laws forbidding masturbation!) Now it
might be possible, even under the autonomy reading, to justify
most or all of those prohibitions on the ground that they counter-
act concrete harms, sufficient to support the intrusion on a presumptively protected right. (I return to this question below.) And
cases involving commercial activity probably must be analyzed in
a way that gives the government more room to maneuver. But it
would be surprising if *Lawrence* were understood to require a careful inquiry into the adequacy of government justifications for banning (say) adult incest and bestiality.

In any case, a simple autonomy reading would make the Court's
apparently pivotal discussion of "emerging awareness" into an ir-
relevancy. Recall that the Court rejected *Bowers* in large part by
pointing to a range of indications that bans on homosexual sodomy
have become out of step with existing values.[123] Hence two factors
were emphasized in the Court's ruling: only thirteen states prohibited sodomy; and the sodomy laws were rarely enforced, through
criminal prosecution, even in those states.[124] It does appear that
the Court was responding to, and requiring, an evolution in public
opinion—something like a broad consensus that the practice at
issue should not be punished.

These points suggest that the Court's decision was less about
sexual autonomy, as a freestanding idea, and closer to a kind of
due process variation on the old common law idea of desuetude.[125]
According to that concept, laws that are hardly ever enforced are

---

[121] 123 S Ct at 2490 (Scalia dissenting).

[122] Id (Scalia dissenting). There are of course laws forbidding public masturbation, but
that is a different matter. Nothing in *Lawrence* suggests that states are banned from regulating sexual conduct that occurs in public view.

[123] Id at 2479–82.

[124] Id at 2481.

[125] See, e.g., J. R. Philip, *Some Reflections on Desuetude*, 43 Jurid Rev 260 (1931); Linda
Rogers and William Rogers, *Desuetude as a Defense*, 52 Iowa L Rev 1 (1966).

said, by courts, to have lapsed, simply because they lack public support.[126] The rationale here is that unenforced laws lack support in public convictions, and they may not be brought to bear, in what will inevitably be an unpredictable and essentially arbitrary way, against private citizens.[127] Most American courts do not accept that idea in express terms.[128] But long ago, Alexander Bickel invoked the notion of desuetude to help account for *Griswold*.[129] The simple idea is that the ban on use of contraceptives by married people had become hopelessly out of touch with existing convictions—so much so that the ban could rarely if ever be invoked as a basis for actual prosecutions. The public would not accept a situation in which married people were actually convicted of that crime. In those circumstances, the statutory ban was a recipe for arbitrary and even discriminatory action, in a way that does violence to democratic ideals and even the rule of law. It does violence to democratic ideals because a law plainly lacking public support is nonetheless invoked to regulate private conduct. It violates the rule of law because a measure of this kind lacks, in practice, the kind of generality and predictability on which the rule of law depends.[130]

If anything, a ban on sodomy is even worse than the Connecticut law struck down in *Griswold*. Such a ban is used, not for frequent arrests or convictions, but for rare and unpredictable harassment by the police. An advantage of this reading is that it mutes the apparent roots of *Lawrence* in substantive due process. The idea of desuetude is, in a sense, a procedural one. There is a procedural problem: a lack of fair notice combined with denial of equal treatment, a problem that is inevitable in a system in which criminal prosecutions are rare and episodic. In fact, the idea of desuetude forbids criminal punishment not in spite of public values but in their service—a claim that the *Lawrence* Court makes explicitly.[131]

---

[126] Mortimer Kadish and Sanford Kadish, *Discretion to Disobey: A Study of Lawful Departures from Legal Rules* 129–31 (1973).

[127] *Poe v Ullman*, 367 US 497, 502 (1961) (quoting *Nashville, C. & St. LR Co. v Browning*, 310 US 362, 369 (1940)).

[128] For discussion, see Kadish and Kadish, *Discretion to Disobey* at 127–40 (cited in note 126); John Chipman Gray, *Desuetude of Statutes in the United States*, in *The Nature and Sources of Law* 189–97, 329–34 (2d ed 1921); Arthur E. Bonfield, *The Abrogation of Penal Statutes by Nonenforcement*, 49 Iowa L Rev 389 (1964).

[129] See Alexander Bickel, *The Least Dangerous Branch* 155 (1965).

[130] See Lon Fuller, *The Morality of Law* (1962).

[131] 123 S Ct at 2480.

Of course this interpretation of *Lawrence* raises its own problems; a desuetude-informed reading is far from simple and straightforward. The decision should not be read to say that each and every criminal statute becomes unenforceable if it is rarely enforced; that reading would be far too broad. (It could, for example, endanger laws forbidding domestic violence or marital rape in jurisdictions in which enforcement is rare.) At a minimum, it is also necessary to say that the rarity of enforcement is a product of the anachronistic nature of the moral judgment that underlies it. Building on this idea, the notion of desuetude might be applied whenever a criminal statute is rarely invoked *because* the public no longer supports the moral argument that lies behind it. Let us call this the broad version of the basic idea. But it is true that the Court is not well equipped to say when statutes are anachronistic, and any use of desuetude, under the Due Process Clause, is likely to be limited to certain interests that have a threshold of importance. Thus *Lawrence* must be understood as involving another, less ambitious version of the idea, suggesting that when those interests are implicated,[132] the state may not rely on a justification that has lost public support. Let us call this the narrow version of the idea.

Because of its modesty, the narrow version is obviously preferable; the Court should not be read to have gone as far as the broad version suggests. But there is an evident problem with the narrow version. For it to operate, we must have an antecedent way, to some extent independent of public convictions, to determine whether an interest has some kind of constitutional status. Without that independent way, the narrow version dissolves into the broader one: Any interest on which the public no longer wants to intrude becomes a fundamental one by definition. (Is this true of the right to use marijuana within the home? Of the right of sixteen-year-olds to drink alcohol within the home?) In the end, the *Lawrence* Court must have concluded that as a matter of principle, the right to engage in same-sex relations had a special status in light of the Court's precedents taken along with emerging public

---

[132] A freestanding desuetude argument would raise questions about many statutes, including those forbidding the private possession of marijuana. In the latter case, the ban does not affect a constitutionally fundamental interest, and hence a serious due process objection would be hard to mount.

convictions—and that the moral arguments that supported the ban were no longer sufficient to justify it.

In this sense, the "emerging public awareness" emphasized by the Court operated at two levels. First, it served to discredit the particular moral justification for the law, in a conventional use of the idea of desuetude. Second, it helped to inform the Court's judgment that the interest at stake could not be distinguished, in principle, from those involved in *Griswold, Eisenstadt, Carey*, and *Roe*. Hence some idea about autonomy is an inescapable part of the analysis. This second use of public convictions is not a use of the idea of desuetude; but it does belong in the same family. There are a number of complexities here, and I shall return to them shortly.

C. THE DOG THAT BARKED VERY QUIETLY: EQUAL PROTECTION

Lawrence was rooted in the Due Process Clause, not the Equal Protection Clause.[133] But it defies belief to say that it is not, in a sense, an equal protection ruling. Everyone knows that the case was about sexual orientation. When Justice Scalia urges that the Court "has largely signed on to the so-called homosexual agenda,"[134] he is correct in an important sense: The Court was not willing to legitimate, or to deem legitimate, "the moral opprobrium that has traditionally attached to homosexual conduct."[135] I have questioned Justice Scalia's broader suggestion that the Court meant to say that a moral position, unaccompanied by convincing evidence of tangible harm, is an illegitimate basis for law. The Court was concerned not to excise moral grounds from law, but instead to excise a *particular* moral ground, that is, the moral ground that underlies criminal prohibitions on same-sex relationships. The Court's judgment to this effect had a great deal to do with considerations of equality.

It is not hard to find support for this claim in the Court's opinion. In many places, the Court suggested that equality, and a particular sort of moral claim, were pivotal to the outcome. Consider this suggestion: "Persons in a homosexual relationship may seek

---

[133] Id at 2482.

[134] Id at 2496 (Scalia dissenting).

[135] Id (Scalia dissenting).

autonomy . . . just as heterosexual persons do."[136] Or this: "When
homosexual conduct is made criminal by the law of the State, that
declaration in and of itself is an invitation to subject homosexual
persons to discrimination in both the public and in the private
spheres."[137] Or this: "[A]dults may choose to enter upon this relationship . . . and still retain their dignity as free persons. . . . The
liberty protected by the Constitution allows homosexual persons
the right to make this choice."[138] Now delete, from the sentences
just quoted, the word "homosexual," and replace it with the word
"adulterous," or "bigamous," or "incestuous." Somehow the sentences do not work. The Court's due process decision was power-
fully influenced by a claim of equality.

D. WHAT LAWRENCE DID, WITH AN EVALUATION

If we emphasize the *Lawrence* Court's reliance on "emerging
awareness," we will see the decision as most closely analogous to
Griswold and *Reed*. When the Court held that married people could
not be prohibited from using contraceptives,[139] it was using the
Due Process Clause to forbid the invocation of a law that could
not be fit with current values. When the Court began to invalidate
sex discrimination of the most arbitrary kinds,[140] it was not making
a revolution on its own. *Lawrence* is in the same spirit. To the
extent that the *Lawrence* Court treated homosexual sodomy as
equivalent, in principle, to opposite-sex relationships, it was responding to the fact that with respect to the invocation of the
criminal law, the American public had come to the same conclusion. To the extent that the Court held that no legitimate state
interest justified the ban on same-sex relationships, it was acting
in the service of widely held convictions. Judges do not interpret
the Constitution to please majorities. But widespread social convictions are likely to influence anyone who lives in society. Judges
live in society. *Lawrence* is a testimonial to this process of influence.

If *Lawrence* is understood in these terms, should it be applauded

---

[136] Id at 2482.

[137] Id.

[138] Id at 2478.

[139] *Griswold*, 381 US 479.

[140] *Reed*, 404 US 71.

or deplored? I do not intend to answer that question fully here. An obvious issue is: Compared to what? I do believe that Justice O'Connor's equal protection approach would have been better and simpler—better because of its fit with precedent, simpler because it is analytically in the same line with *Moreno, Cleburne,* and *Romer.*[141] But what of the other alternatives? I have urged that if *Lawrence* is a kind of American-style desuetude, it can claim to be rooted in a form of procedural due process. A law of the sort that the Court invalidated is a violation of the rule of law; it does not provide fair notice; and it invites arbitrary and unpredictable enforcement, of just the sort that occurred in the case itself. Such a law also lacks a democratic pedigree. It is able to persist only because it is enforced so rarely.

1. *Specifying desuetude, American-style: National outliers or rare enforcement?* If a desuetude-type rationale is accepted, it is necessary to know when, exactly, it will be triggered. We can imagine many possibilities. The *Lawrence* Court emphasized two separate points: few states now forbid consensual sodomy; and even in states in which a ban is in place, prosecution is rare. The first point stresses the problem of states-as-outliers; the second is a more standard point about intrajurisdictional desuetude. In *Lawrence* itself, the two points marched hand-in-hand, but they could easily be pulled apart. A law might fit with existing social values in one state, but those values might be rejected in the rest of the union.[142] This would not be a simple case of desuetude, because the statute would, by hypothesis, receive support within the relevant state. By contrast, a state-specific analysis, based on more conventional ideas about desuetude, would emphasize the ideas of fair notice and arbitrariness and suggest that at least when certain interests are involved, a state may not bring the criminal law to bear when the values that underlie those laws are now anachronistic in that very state. Certainly the standard desuetude idea cannot be invoked in

---

[141] To say this is not to deny that Justice O'Connor's approach would raise complexities of its own. For example, it is not so easy to limit its reach; the approach would seem to raise doubts about bans on same-sex marriage, no less than the substantive due process approach. As I have suggested, one of the difficulties for the *Lawrence* Court was that any invalidation of the Texas law, which seemed constitutionally intolerable, would inevitably raise questions about practices that, whether or not constitutionally tolerable, the Court would not like to doubt for prudential reasons at least.

[142] The role of the Court in disciplining practices that are out of step with national values is stressed in Richard A. Posner, *Sex and Reason* 327–28 (1992).

a state in which the law in question is actively enforced. For the Supreme Court, the easiest cases are *Lawrence* and *Griswold:* those in which the relevant values lack support both in the enforcing state and in the nation as a whole. My emphasis here is not on national outliers, but on the fact that in Texas itself, the sodomy statute, hardly ever enforced, created problems of both unpredictability and arbitrariness.[143]

2. *Too little?* But for many defenders of the outcome in *Lawrence*, this interpretation will give the plaintiffs far too little. One obvious alternative is a more critical approach to conventional morality. Such an approach would not define liberty by identifying society's "emerging awareness" as if it were a kind of brute fact for judicial use, but would instead attempt to define the idea of liberty, and the legitimacy of intrusions on it, by reference to an evaluative account that is independent of whatever views now happen to prevail. For those who prefer this more critical approach, the problem with a desuetude-type interpretation is that it would allow states to have sodomy laws, or adultery laws, or fornication laws, so long as those laws are taken seriously and actually brought to bear against the citizenry. Wouldn't that situation be worse rather than better?

In fact it is possible to understand the Court's opinion in this more critical and evaluative way. Certainly the Court's use of the word "awareness" suggests that it believes the emerging view to be worth attention not merely because it is emerging but also because it is right. Consider too the Court's suggest that the framers "knew times can blind us to certain *truths* and later generations can see that laws once thought necessary and proper *in fact* serve only to oppress."[144] Perhaps we might build on the Court's reference to "truths" and what happens "in fact" to suggest its endorsement of a more independent and critical approach to public convictions.

---

[143] It should be noted that we do not quite know whether some kind of coherent pattern underlay enforcement of the law in Texas. The facts of *Lawrence* suggest one possibility: Perhaps prosecutors would not invade private domains to ferret out unlawful sodomy, but perhaps they would arrest people if the relevant acts were plainly visible. If so, one kind of arbitrariness would be avoided, for arrests would not be invidiously motivated or entirely random. But as the facts of *Lawrence* also show, a kind of randomness will be an inevitable result of this very policy. In any case, a problem of unpredictability exists even if the policy of arrest and prosecution follows some kind of pattern: The defendants in *Lawrence* had no reason to know that they would fall within that pattern.

[144] 123 S Ct at 2484 (emphases added).

But a more critical approach, from the Court, should not be accepted so readily. Let us agree that if the Court's judgments on the appropriate content of liberty were reliable, then a more critical approach would have much to be said in its favor. But even those who endorse that approach might agree that *Lawrence*, read in the way that I have suggested, has the advantage of comparative modesty—and that it does not foreclose use of the critical approach for the future. And for those who endorse the critical approach, there are reasons for caution. The first is the simple risk of judicial error. Unmoored from public convictions, there is a risk that the Court's conception of liberty will be confused or indefensible. (Recall *Dred Scott v Sandford*[145] and *Lochner v New York*.[146]) The second problem is the danger of unintended bad consequences. Even if the Court has the right conception of liberty, it may not do much good by insisting on it when the nation strongly disagrees. If the Court had held, in 1980, that the Due Process Clause requires states to recognize same-sex marriage, it would (in my view) have been responding to the right conception of liberty. But it would undoubtedly have produced a large-scale social backlash, and very likely a constitutional amendment, that would have made same-sex marriage impossible. The simple point is that judicial impositions may do little good and considerable harm, even from the standpoint of the causes that the Court hopes to promote. To be sure, these points are cautionary notes and no more. But at the very least, they suggest that where the Court is in a position to choose, a desuetude-type ruling, building on widespread convictions, has considerable advantages over a ruling that is based on the Court's own conception of autonomy.

3. *Too much?* Of course *Lawrence*, read in the way I have suggested, might be criticized from other directions. Perhaps a better alternative is Thayerism: An approach that would uphold any intrusion on liberty unless it lacks even a minimally rational basis.[147] This approach might be defended on the ground that a judicial judgment about emerging public convictions is not very reliable,

---

[145] 60 US 393 (1856) (holding that African-Americans were not citizens contemplated by the Constitution).

[146] 198 US 45 (1905) (holding unconstitutional a state statute establishing maximum working hours).

[147] See James Bradley Thayer, *The Origin and Scope of the American Doctrine of Constitutional Law*, 7 Harv L Rev 129 (1893).

and certainly less so than the evidence provided by actual legislation. If there is a serious risk in judicial efforts, why not require
people to resort to their political remedies? I believe that the idea
of desuetude provides a partial answer. If legislation is infrequently
enforced, most citizens can treat it as effectively dead. They have
nothing to worry about. At least in clear cases, it seems plausible,
and inoffensive to democratic values, to use the Due Process
Clause to forbid criminal prosecutions in cases of this kind. Both
Griswold and *Lawrence* are defining examples.

But perhaps the Court would have done better, in *Lawrence*, to
continue on the path marked out by *Bowers* and *Glucksberg*, and
hence to uphold any intrusion on liberty unless it runs afoul of
Anglo-American traditions. Due process traditionalism might be
supported on the ground that federal judges are not especially
good at evaluating our practices, and that if a practice has endured
there is good reason to support it, if only because many people
have endorsed it, or at least not seen fit to change it. When the
Court has urged that fundamental interests should be so defined
by reference to traditions, it has done so on the ground that traditionalism helps to cabin judicial discretion and to minimize the
risk of judicial error. Constitutional traditionalism therefore makes
decisions simpler at the same time that it makes them less likely
to go wrong. If economic terminology is thought to be helpful
here, the use of traditions by imperfect human beings might not
be perfect, but it is the best way to go because it minimizes both
"decision costs," taken as the burdens of deciding what to do, and
"error costs," taken as the problems introduced by making mistakes.

A central question is whether tradition-bound judges will make
more or fewer errors than judges who depart from traditions and
pay a great deal of attention to conventional morality. At least
some of those who are skeptical about substantive due process
might endorse traditionalism as a possible source of law, but also
conclude that it is proper for the Court to strike down statutes
that lack support in popular convictions. In other words, the desuetude-type approach of the *Lawrence* Court might be a modest,
cautious supplement to due process traditionalism, rooted in similar concerns. Indeed, a desuetude-type approach has the advantage
of underlining the procedural features of procedural due process.
As we have seen, a statute like that invalidated in *Lawrence* fails to

provide predictability, and it is a recipe for arbitrary enforcement. The Court's refusal to permit criminal convictions, under these circumstances, is not radically inconsistent with democratic ideals. In a sense, it helps to vindicate them.

4. *Coherence, optimal deterrence, and expressive condemnation.* Another response is possible, one that would raise questions about the coherence of any approach that draws on the idea of desuetude. For governments, there is a trade-off between the magnitude and the frequency of punishment. A government might decide to lessen the deterrent signal simply by scaling back enforcement. In the context of conduct that a state would like to deter, but not greatly, the sensible strategy might be to maintain a prohibition but to enforce it rarely. It is easy to imagine a city taking this approach with respect to nonflagrant speeding (driving, say, ten miles over the speed limit), or certain parking offenses (giving tickets rarely in certain places, for example), or certain alcohol or drug offenses (rarely arresting or convicting teenagers for use of alcohol, or infrequently arresting or convicting people for marijuana use). In fact countless prohibitions are rarely enforced. Is this situation unconstitutional? Why is a state banned from making this particular trade-off between severity and probability of sanction? If the desuetude idea is about absence of fair notice and discriminatory enforcement, shouldn't the Court strike down any statute that suffers from these defects, including those that not only have lost popularity, but also those that never had sufficient support to be a basis for frequent enforcement? In any case, the ex ante deterrent effect of a rarely enforced law, including the sodomy law in Texas, applies equally to all those subject to it. Isn't this ex ante equality a sufficient response to the objection of unpredictability?

To answer this objection, it is necessary to be more specific about the due process ruling in *Lawrence*. We could imagine many possible situations of rare or nonexistent enforcement, and these do not ordinarily raise constitutional problems. For example, the conduct might itself be unobjectionable, but prohibited to get at related conduct (as, perhaps, in the case of certain gambling, outlawed because it invites organized crime). Alternatively, the conduct might be mostly objectionable, but banned as a way of enforcing a prohibition on a subset of it (as in the case of sodomy laws used to punish nonconsensual sex). Or the conduct might be mostly objectionable, but a subset of it is unpunished, because it is close to the line (as in driving slightly over the speed limit). Or the conduct might be objectionable, but problems in obtaining witnesses and evidence are formidable (as, perhaps, in the cases of domestic violence and more obviously marital rape).

The problem with the Texas sodomy law was not only the fact that it was enforced rarely; infrequent enforcement stemmed from the particular fact that the moral claim that underlay it could no longer claim public support. The same cannot be said in the examples just described; in those cases, there is public ambivalence about arrest and conviction, but not because of a widespread belief that the prohibition is outmoded or rooted in values that no longer deserve support.[148] But *Lawrence* does not depend on this factor alone. It is also important that the interest at stake is similar, in principle, to those protected by earlier cases. In these circumstances, the state is required to produce, by way of justification, something other than a moral position that no longer fits with public convictions. To be sure, the effect of a rarely enforced law is similar to that of a lottery, and in that respect there is a degree of ex ante equality. But that's the problem. Criminal punishments should not operate like lotteries. People are punished ex post, not ex ante, and it is the ex post randomness that supports the Court's ruling, at least in the light of the particular interest involved.

Consider a final argument. One purpose of the criminal law is to impose expressive condemnation. For some conduct, the social judgment is in favor of expressive condemnation but opposed to much in the way of actual prosecution. As examples, consider laws forbidding adultery or the consumption of alcohol by sixteen-year-olds. Rare enforcement reflects a belief that the law, operating in conjunction with social norms, will deter misconduct optimally— and that criminal prosecution would be too heavy-handed, at least in most cases. Does it follow, from *Lawrence*, that states are forbidden from adopting the strategy of expressive condemnation with rare prosecution? Why isn't that strategy the most sensible one in some circumstances? The answer is that when certain interests are involved,[149] states are indeed forbidden from following that strat-

---

[148] It must be acknowledged, however, that in some of these cases, due process principles requiring fair notice and nonarbitrariness could be violated by criminal prosecutions.

[149] Consumption of liquor does not fall within the category of protected interests; on adultery, see below.

egy, and the reason has to do with the lack of fair notice and the inevitability of randomness. As I have emphasized, these are the conventional (procedural) concerns of the Due Process Clause.

IV. IMPLICATIONS

What are the implications of *Lawrence?* Because of the opacity of the Court's opinion, this is not an easy question to answer. In the fullness of time, it is imaginable that *Lawrence* will be a sport, a decision with no descendants, one in which the Court struck down a law that shocked its conscience but that proved unable to generate further doctrine. But it is no less imaginable that *Lawrence* will turn out to have broad consequences for regulation of sexual relationships, in a way that vindicates a quite general interest in sexual autonomy. *Bowers* had stopped a number of potential doctrinal innovations here; *Bowers* is no longer good law. And it is wholly imaginable that *Lawrence* will draw into question many forms of discrimination against gays and lesbians. If my basic argument is correct, the eventual path of the law will have a great deal to do with public convictions over time. My guess is that *Lawrence* will have some of the features of *Reed v Reed:* it will inaugurate a set of judgments, from lower courts and the Court itself, that go, in case-by-case fashion, toward eliminating the most arbitrary and senseless restrictions on liberty and equality. I am concerned in this section with the logic of the Court's opinion and with its bearing on issues that the Court did not resolve.[150]

A. SEX

Justice Scalia urged that *Lawrence* decrees an end to "morals" legislation,[151] and in the aftermath of the decision, it is natural to wonder about the constitutionality of laws forbidding sexual harassment, prostitution, adultery, fornication, obscenity, polygamy, and incest. Before *Lawrence*, such laws seemed quite secure. The Court had made clear that substantive due process would be used

---

[150] A more detailed treatment of the issues in this section appears in Cass R. Sunstein, *Liberty After Lawrence,* Ohio St L J (forthcoming 2004).

[151] 123 S Ct at 2495 (Scalia dissenting).

only to protect rights well recognized by tradition;[152] and in any event the privacy cases had originally been defined with close reference to reproduction and its control, not to sex itself.[153] But after *Lawrence*, it would be possible to contend that many statutory restrictions impose unconstitutional barriers to consensual sexual activity. And in each of these cases, it would be possible to urge both that the relevant right is a fundamental one and that the state lacks a legitimate basis for interfering with consensual activity. Let us see how the underlying issues might be assessed.

1. *Coercion.* The easiest cases involve coercion. In such cases, the predicate for *Lawrence*—consent—is absent. If consensual sex is not involved, there is no fundamental right that would require the state to provide a compelling justification. And for the same reason, the state has a perfectly legitimate, even compelling, reason to impose a restriction. In cases of sexual harassment, coercion of one or another sort is generally involved,[154] and hence a legal ban is perfectly acceptable. The same is true for many and indeed most cases involving incest, which involve minors unable to give legal consent.[155] The interest in preventing coerced sex is sufficient.

But somewhat harder cases are imaginable even here. Suppose, for example, that under a public university's sexual harassment policy, a teacher and a graduate student are banned from having a consensual relationship, even though the teacher is not (and will not be) in a supervisory position over the student. Or suppose that the incestuous relations are between adults—first cousins, let us say. In an "as applied" challenge, these would be genuinely difficult after *Lawrence*. If real consent is found in either case, a fundamental right might well be involved. But it would be possible to defend the broad sexual harassment prohibition as a way of reducing risks and introducing clarity for all. And it would be possible to defend

---

[152] This was the key point in lower court decisions rejecting constitutional challenges to decisions to punish (for example) adultery, see *Mercure v Van Buren Township*, 81 F Supp2d 814 (ED Mich 2000); *Commonwealth v Stowell*, 449 NE2d 357 (Mass 1983); *City of Sherman v Henry*, 928 SW2d 464 (Tex 1996); and incest, see *Smith v State*, 6 SW3d 512 (Tenn Crim App 1999); *State v Buck*, 757 P2d 861 (Or Ct App 1988).

[153] See, e.g., *Griswold*, 381 US 479; *Roe*, 410 US 113.

[154] See, e.g., *Franklin v Gwinnett County Public Schools*, 503 US 60 (1992).

[155] See, e.g., *Richardson v State*, 353 SE2d 342 (Ga 1987); *Commonwealth v Arnold*, 514 A2d 890 (Pa Super Ct 1986).

the ban on incest among adults as a way of eliminating certain psychological pressures and protecting any children who might result from medical risk.[156] In neither case can it be said that the prohibitions run afoul of some emerging national awareness. These are far weaker cases for invalidation than *Lawrence*, but some of the underlying logic of the case seems to raise doubts in imaginable applications.

2. *Commerce.* Other easy cases involve commerce. In the case of prostitution, it is hard to urge that a fundamental right is involved.[157] Under *Lawrence*, commercial sex is to be treated differently.[158] The outcome is easy; but the analysis is not. Why the sharp distinction between commercial and noncommercial sex? Why are sexual relations unprotected, or less protected, if dollars are exchanged? Books, after all, are protected, whether they are given away or sold. Part of the analysis here might be that commercial sex should not be treated more protectively than any other kind of commercial interaction, now subject to rational basis review.[159] But if sexual relationships have a special constitutional status, this distinction is far from obvious. The more basic claim must be that special constitutional status attaches to sexual intimacy, not to sexual relationships,[160] and that intimacy in the relevant sense is not involved when sex is exchanged for cash.[161] Hence no fundamental right is involved. To be sure, this argument is not entirely convincing. Many sexual relationships (including many that fall within the category protected by *Lawrence*) do not involve intimacy (except by definition). But perhaps the Court can be said to be suggesting that noncommercial sex involves intimacy frequently enough to justify protection of the overall class, whereas the opposite is true of sex-for-money.

But what justification does the state have for forbidding prostitu-

---

[156] See, e.g., *In re Tiffany Nicole M.*, 571 NW2d 872 (Wis Ct App 1997); but see *In re Termination of Parental Rights to Zachary B.*, 662 NW2d 360 (Wis Ct App 2003).

[157] See, e.g., *J.B.K., Inc. v Caron*, 600 F2d 710 (8th Cir 1979); *Morgan v Detroit*, 389 F Supp 922 (ED Mich 1975); *State v Allen*, 424 A2d 651 (Conn Super Ct 1980); *Blyther v United States*, 577 A2d 1154 (DC 1990).

[158] 123 S Ct at 2484.

[159] See, e.g., *Heart of Atlanta Motel, Inc. v United States*, 379 US 241 (1964).

[160] The case of bestiality should be understood similarly. It would be frivolous to argue that bans on bestiality eliminate the kind of intimate relationship protected by *Lawrence*.

[161] See *Commonwealth v Walter*, 446 NE2d 707, 710 (Mass 1983); *State v Price*, 446 NW2d 813, 818 (Iowa 1976).

tion? It is probably sufficient here to point to the adverse effects of prostitution on the lives of prostitutes; the risk of exploitation (and worse) is real and serious.[162] Nor are moral justifications, pointing to the corrosive effects of prostitution on sexuality and sex equality,[163] ruled off-limits by *Lawrence*. I am not taking a position on the complex and disputed question whether and how prostitution should be outlawed. My suggestion is only that under rational basis review, restrictions on prostitution are easily defensible. The ban on the sale of obscenity should be understood in similar terms;[164] the use of obscenity raises different issues, but here too *Lawrence* is best taken not to affect existing law.[165]

3. *Without coercion and without commerce.* For the state, the most serious problems, post-*Lawrence*, come in cases challenging restrictions on genuinely consensual and noncommercial practices. Begin with what might seem an intermediate case: bans on sexual devices.[166] Following the previous discussion, we should distinguish here between sale on the one hand and use on the other. On one view, the state could ban the sale itself, urging that it is attempting to regulate a commercial enterprise, and that it is permitted to do so in light of the commercial-noncommercial distinction just made. But even this is not entirely clear.[167] And could the state make it a crime for people to *use* such devices? The right to do

---

[162] See, e.g., *People v Mason*, 642 P2d 8, 12 (Colo 1982); *People v Johnson*, 376 NE2d 381, 386 (Ill App Ct 1978). Of course some of the risk stems from the very fact that prostitution is unlawful.

[163] See *Bell v United States*, 349 US 81, 84 (1955) (Minton dissenting); *People v Warren*, 535 NW2d 173, 177 (Mich 1995) (Levin dissenting); *State v Wright*, 561 A2d 659, 662 (NJ Super Ct App Div 1989).

[164] See, e.g., *Paris Adult Theatre I v Slayton*, 413 US 49, 58–59 (1973).

[165] The use can be banned under *Miller*, by reference to moral objections, though *Stanley v Georgia*, 394 US 557 (1969), protects the use of obscenity within the home. A different and in my view better analysis would point to actual harms, see Catharine MacKinnon, *Feminism Unmodified* (1986); Cass R. Sunstein, *Pornography and the First Amendment*, 35 Duke L J 589 (1986).

[166] See, e.g., *Williams v Pryor*, 240 F3d 944 (11th Cir 2001); *Pleasureland Museum, Inc. v Beutter*, 288 F3d 988 (7th Cir 2002) (remanding for consideration of whether a ban on sexual devices violated a fundamental right to privacy).

[167] Recall that the constitutional protection given to the use of contraceptives was extended to the sale of contraceptives. See *Carey* (cited in note 45). If a ban on the sale of contraceptives cannot be justified, it is not clear, after *Lawrence*, how the state can justify a ban on the sale of sexual devices. Before *Lawrence*, it might have been said that the privacy cases did not protect sexual activity as such, but merely banned the state from punishing that activity through the indirect and discriminatory means of risking unwanted pregnancy. But *Lawrence* forbids this narrow reading of the cases.

so might well fall within the protection of fundamental interests. In any case, what is the state's justification for banning such use? It is easy to imagine an as-applied challenge, in which a married couple (or for that matter an unmarried one, or for that matter a single person) attacks a ban on either the sale or the use of sexual devices with reference to *Griswold* itself.[168]

The difference is that in *Griswold*, the ban on use of contraceptives was an effort to prevent nonprocreative sex, whereas in the hypothetical case, the state is banning devices that are designed to increase sexual pleasure. But why, exactly, would it seek to do that? Is there something wrong with certain sources of sexual pleasure within constitutionally protected relationships? Perhaps the answer would be affirmative if real harms were involved, as for example through some (hardly all) sadomasochistic practices. Almost certainly the state could justify a prohibition on the public display of such devices. But we are not now speaking of these questions. At first glance, individuals have a fundamental interest here, and the state seems to lack a legitimate basis for intruding on that interest.

If there were laws forbidding masturbation, *Lawrence* would indeed raise extremely serious questions about them. But, as I have noted, there are no such laws.[169] What about laws forbidding fornication, understood to mean nonadulterous sex outside of marriage?[170] *Lawrence* creates serious doubts, simply because coercion and consent are not present. In any case, there seems to be an emerging social awareness that fornication is not a proper basis for criminal punishment.[171] And with respect to consenting adults, it is not easy to produce a legitimate ground for interfering with nonadulterous sex.[172] As I have noted, fully consensual incest is a

---

[168] See *Williams*, id at 952–53 (suggesting that an as-applied challenge is plausible).

[169] As I have noted, *Lawrence* raises no questions about laws forbidding public masturbation. The most plausible objection would be that mere offense is not a legitimate basis for regulating noncoercive sex; and indeed Justice Scalia seems to read the Court's opinion to have that implication. But the Court's rejection of the moral basis of the ban on sodomy should not be taken to forbid governments from protecting people from unwanted viewing of other people's sex lives.

[170] See, e.g., *Jarrett v Jarrett*, 449 US 927, 929 n 2 (citing Ill Rev Stat ch 38, § 11-8 (1977)).

[171] See, e.g., id; *In re J.M.*, 575 SE2d 441, 444 (Ga 2003); *State v Saunders*, 381 A2d 333, 339 (NJ 1977).

[172] Admittedly, rational basis review might be satisfied if, for example, the state urged that it was attempting to reduce the risks of unwanted pregnancy and venereal disease. But after *Lawrence*, rational basis review is unlikely to be applied here.

somewhat harder case. In the case of adult brothers and sisters, it might be urged that the goal is to prevent harms to any children who might result, or psychological difficulties that would predictably produce and accompany any such relationships. Certainly the ban on sexual relations within the family cannot be said to be anachronistic. There is no "emerging public awareness" that such relations should be accepted. But imagine, for example, that sex is banned among first cousins, in circumstances in which any harms are highly speculative. Rational basis review would be satisfied. But *Lawrence* does not apply rational basis review, and in some applications, the ruling would seem to throw legal prohibitions on incest into considerable doubt.

The most difficult cases involve laws forbidding adultery.[173] We could imagine actual adultery prosecutions;[174] we could also imagine cases in which government takes adverse employment action against those involved in adulterous relationships.[175] Here, as in other contexts, it would be possible to urge that a consensual relationship is involved, one with which the state may not interfere on purely moral grounds. On the other hand, it is possible to justify prohibitions on adultery by reference to harms to third parties: children, in many cases, and the betrayed spouse, in many more cases. The adultery laws can be seen as an effort to protect the marital relationship, involving persons and interests, including those of children, that are harmed if adultery occurs.[176] Marriage can and usually is understood as an exchange of commitments, which have individual and social value; and a prohibition on adultery, moral and legal, operates in the service of those commitments. If rational basis review is involved, prohibitions on adultery should certainly be acceptable—except, perhaps, in cases in which the married couple has agreed to nonexclusivity (in which case criminal prosecution would be especially surprising).

The difficulty here is that in the context of adultery, criminal prosecutions are extremely unusual, at least as rare as criminal prosecutions for sodomy. There is a good argument that criminal

---

[173] See *Marcum v MacWharter*, 308 US 635 (2002).

[174] See *Commonwealth v Stowell*, 449 NE2d 357 (Mass 1983).

[175] See *Oliverson v West Valley City*, 875 F Supp 1465 (D Utah 1995); *City of Sherman v Henry*, 928 SW2d 464 (Tex 1996).

[176] See *Oliverson*, id, at 1477.

prosecutions, in this context, are inconsistent with emerging social values. This is not because adultery is thought to be morally acceptable; it is not. It is because adultery is not thought to be a proper basis for the use of the criminal law. Perhaps it could be said that *Lawrence* turned at least in part on the Court's evident desire to ensure against practices that would "demean[] the lives of homosexual persons."[177] It is not plausible to say that the Court should take special steps to ensure against practices that would "demean the lives of" adulterers. But in the end, it is not so easy to distinguish an adultery prosecution from the sodomy prosecution forbidden in *Lawrence*.[178]

B. SEXUAL ORIENTATION, EMPLOYMENT, AND MARRIAGE

1. *Employment.* May a public employer discharge or punish an employee because of his sexual orientation or because of homosexual acts? Before *Lawrence*, the lower courts were divided on the issue.[179] The logic of *Bowers* supported the decisions upholding such discharges, at least against due process challenges. And it was possible to urge that because homosexual activity is not protected by the Constitution, government employees are permitted to discriminate against those who engage in that activity. At first glance, however, *Lawrence* resolves that question the other way. A public employer is not permitted to discharge an employee because she has exercised a constitutional right (an oversimplification to which

---

[177] 123 S Ct at 2482.

[178] Employment discrimination by the state against adulterers raises further complexities. On a standard analysis, protection against criminal prosecution, if it exists, is conclusive on the issue of public employment, forbidding discrimination against people who have engaged in constitutionally protected activity. One exception would apply when the government can invoke distinctive employment-related grounds for the discrimination. A public university's admissions office need not hire, as director of admissions, people who speak out in favor of race discrimination; perhaps discrimination against adulterers can, in some contexts, be similarly justified. In any case, everything turns on the reason for a due process ruling. If adultery prosecutions were banned on the basis of a rationale tied to the illegitimacy of using the criminal law, perhaps civil disabilities, as through employment discrimination, would be permissible. For details, see next note.

[179] See *DeSantis v Pacific Telephone & Telegraph Co., Inc.*, 608 F2d 327 (9th Cir 1979) (holding that homosexuals are not a protected class under Title VII); *Childers v Dallas Police Department*, 513 F Supp 134 (ND Tex 1981) (holding that a police department could refuse to hire a gay activist because of doubts about his character). Compare *Glover v Williamsburg Local Sch. Dist. Bd of Educ.*, 20 F Supp2d 1160 (SD Ohio 1998) (finding no rational basis for a decision not to renew the contract of a homosexual teacher); *Weaver v Nebo Sch. Dist.*, 29 F Supp2d 1279 (D Utah 1998) (to the same effect).

I shall return). If an employee has converted to Catholicism, or voted for a Republican, she may not be adversely affected for that reason. So too if an employee has exercised a right protected by the Due Process Clause. A state may not refuse to hire a secretary who has used contraception or had an abortion. Under *Lawrence*, government may not refuse to hire people who have engaged in same-sex relations. It could perhaps be argued that a criminal punishment is worse than a civil disability, and hence that the prohibition on criminal prosecution does not entail an equivalent prohibition on adverse employment actions. But the cases just described should be sufficient response to that argument.

Most cases of adverse employment action, prompted by homosexual activity, are easy after *Lawrence*. But there are some possible rejoinders. One would emphasize the reading I have stressed here: *Lawrence* turned not simply on a finding of a fundamental right, but more importantly on the Court's conclusion that the Texas criminal statute was no longer supported by public convictions. If desuetude is involved, then perhaps employment discrimination is permitted even if criminal prosecution is not. This argument is not at all implausible or incoherent. If we emphasize the idea of desuetude, then a moral judgment might be permissible for use in the employment context even if it cannot be invoked as a basis for criminal prosecution. A narrow reading of *Lawrence*, then, would suggest that the Due Process Clause forbids criminal punishment of sexual conduct not violative of existing moral convictions, but that there is no barrier to judgments, by government employers, that gays and lesbians should not be employed. But this approach reads *Lawrence* a bit too finely; it would be most surprising if the Court were to permit states not to hire, or to fire, people for engaging in the conduct that the Court held to be protected. The Court is best read to have found a fundamental interest, although desuetude-type ideas played a role in its judgment; and if so, states may not refuse to hire people who have engaged in the relevant behavior. In fact, a mild extension of the Court's own use of emerging convictions would suggest that the moral judgments that underlie the Texas statute may not be used for either criminal or civil disability.

Another response would emphasize that on occasion, the government may indeed refuse to hire people for engaging in constitutionally protected activity. The President is permitted to refuse to employ, as Secretary of State, someone who has publicly criticized his policies; so too, a public university is almost certainly allowed not to hire, or even to fire, an admissions officer who has said that women should not go to college, or that it is best for African-Americans to attend vocational school. In such cases, the university can claim, plausibly, that it is not trying to censor anyone, or to punish them for exercising a constitutional right, but instead to accomplish the substantive task that it has set for itself.[180] An admissions officer is not likely to be effective if he is on record as supporting race or sex discrimination. Might discrimination against gays and lesbians be similarly justified? This is not entirely unimaginable in some contexts, but in general, it is hard to see how the justification could be made convincing. Unless the state is to capitulate to private prejudice, as it is generally forbidden from doing,[181] it cannot easily invoke a distinct, employment-related reason to discriminate on the basis of sexual orientation.

It also follows that the "don't ask, don't tell" policy, in the military setting, is under new pressure. It is no longer possible to defend that policy simply by citing *Bowers*. If the policy is to be upheld, it is because courts should give great deference to military judgments, applying a form of rational basis review to them. I believe that federal courts are not likely to interfere with military judgments here, and that there is good reason for a general posture of deference to such judgments. In principle, however, it is extremely difficult to defend "don't ask, don't tell" against constitutional challenge, and this appears to be one of the exceedingly rare settings in which judicial interference with military judgments is probably justified.[182]

2. *Marriage*. Of course the largest issue is the fate of same-sex marriage. Under *Lawrence*, must states recognize such marriages? I have suggested that *Lawrence* is akin to *Griswold*; but *Griswold* led to *Roe*. Perhaps *Lawrence* will lead to its own *Roe*, in the form of a requirement that states allow gays and lesbians, not less than heterosexuals, to marry.

The issue is exceedingly complex. At first glance, *Lawrence* has nothing at all to do with same-sex marriage. It involved sodomy

---

[180] See *Pickering v Board of Education*, 391 US 563 (1968), for the basic framework.

[181] See *Palmore v Sidoti*, 466 US 429 (1984).

[182] For an argument to this effect before *Lawrence* was decided, see Cass R. Sunstein, *Designing Democracy* (2002).

prosecutions, brought under anachronistic laws, and the due process challenge to those prosecutions need not draw into doubt the still-universal practice of defining marriage to involve one man and one woman. In any case, the most natural challenge to laws rejecting such marriages is rooted in the Equal Protection Clause; and *Lawrence* said nothing about the Equal Protection Clause (perhaps because it sought to avoid the marriage issue). To the extent that the Court was emphasizing an "emerging awareness," its decision does not touch prohibitions on same-sex marriage—and will not do so unless and until such prohibitions seem as outmoded as bans on homosexual sodomy do today. Existing practice suggests universal opposition to same-sex marriage,[183] and polling evidence suggests that most Americans support existing practice.[184]

But under current law, the issue cannot be disposed of so readily. In *Loving v Virginia*,[185] the Court struck down a ban on racial intermarriage on two grounds. The first is the familiar equal protection ground, seeing that ban as a form of racial discrimination. But in a separate ruling, the Court also held that the ban violated the Due Process Clause. In the Court's words, "the freedom to marry has long been recognized as one of the vital personal rights essential to the orderly pursuit of happiness by free men."[186] It added that "[m]arriage is one of the 'basic civil rights of man,' fundamental to our very existence and survival."[187] The *Loving* Court's due process ruling was not free from ambiguity; the problem of racial discrimination played a large role. But subsequent cases confirm that the right to marry counts as fundamental for due process purposes—and is sufficient by itself to take the analysis into the domain of heightened scrutiny.

In *Zablocki v Redhail*, the Court struck down a Wisconsin law forbidding people under child support obligations to remarry unless they had obtained a judicial determination that they had met those obligations and that their children were not likely to become public charges.[188] The Court insisted that "the right to marry is

---

[183] Civil unions are a different matter, but they hardly can claim even strong minority support.

[184] See the summary at http://www.bpnews.org/bpnews.asp?ID=16337.

[185] 388 US 1 (1968).

[186] Id at 12.

[187] Id (quoting *Skinner v Oklahoma ex rel Williamson*, 316 US 535, 541 (1942)).

[188] 434 US 374 (1978).

of fundamental importance for all individuals,"[189] and that "the decision to marry has been placed on the same level of importance as decisions relating to procreation, childbirth, child rearing, and family relationships."[190] The Court said that it would uphold "reasonable regulations that do not significantly interfere with decisions to enter into the marital relationship."[191] But any direct and substantial interference with the right to marry would be strictly scrutinized. In a concurring opinion, Justice Stevens underlined the point, urging that the Constitution would cast serious doubt on any "classification which determines who may lawfully enter into the marriage relationship."[192]

In this light, a prohibition on same-sex marriage is not so easy to defend in the aftermath of *Lawrence*. Under the Court's decisions, a fundamental right does seem to be involved, one on which the state can intrude only by pointing to a countervailing interest that is not merely legitimate but also compelling. In the context of same-sex marriage, what might that interest be? What sorts of social harms would follow from recognizing marriages between people of the same sex? It is conventional to argue that the refusal to recognize same-sex marriage is a way of protecting the marital institution itself. But this is very puzzling; how do same-sex marriages threaten the institution of marriage? Or perhaps the state can legitimately reserve the idea of marriage to men and women for expressive reasons. Perhaps the state can urge that it does not want to give the same expressive support to same-sex unions as to opposite-sex unions. But why not? As compared to a ban on same-sex marriages, a prohibition on adultery seems easy to justify. Such a prohibition is likely, in numerous cases, to protect one or even both spouses, and to protect children besides. If, as I have suggested, *Lawrence* draws prohibitions on adultery into some doubt, it would seem to raise extremely serious questions about prohibitions on same-sex marriage.

But perhaps criminal punishment is special. Perhaps such punishment is quite different from, and to be assessed more skeptically than, a statute that confers the benefits of marriage on some but

[189] Id at 384.

[190] Id at 386.

[191] Id at 386–87 (citing *Califano v Jobst*, 434 US 47 (1977)).

[192] Id at 404.

not to all. Perhaps *Lawrence* forbids the state from using the heavy artillery of the criminal law—but without raising questions about civil rights and civil duties. It would not be at all implausible to say that the *Lawrence* Court was responsive to the assortment of disabilities associated with criminal punishment—a set of disabilities that might be thought unique. But *Loving* and *Zablocki* themselves raise questions for this kind of distinction. Neither case involved a criminal prohibition. Both applied careful judicial scrutiny to laws saying that certain people could not enter into the marital relationship.

Perhaps we should read *Loving* and *Zablocki* more narrowly.[193] Notwithstanding the Court's rhetoric, it is quite doubtful that the Court really meant to raise serious questions about *all* state laws dictating who may enter into a marital relationship. People are not permitted to marry dogs or cats or cars. They are banned from marrying their first cousins or their aunts. They cannot marry two people, or three, or twenty. Must these restrictions be justified by showing that they are the least restrictive means of achieving a compelling state interest? If so, at least some of them would be in serious trouble. Perhaps the ban on incestuous marriages could be defended by pointing to the risk of coercion and the danger to any children who would result. But as we have seen, it is easy to imagine some cases in which any such defense would be weak—as, for example, where the would-be spouses are both adults and do not plan to have children. Perhaps bans on polygamy could be defended by pointing to the risk of exploitation, especially of the women involved. But we might doubt whether *Loving* and *Zablocki* should be read to require a careful judicial inquiry into that question.

A possible opinion would urge that by deeming the right to marry fundamental, the Court did not mean to suggest that it would strictly scrutinize any law that departed from the traditional idea that a marriage is between (one) woman and (one) man. It meant only to say that when a man and a woman seek to marry, the state must have good reasons for putting significant barriers in their path. This rationale has the advantage of fitting with both

---

[193] It would also be possible to deny that the right to marry has a constitutional status—to urge that *Loving* and *Zablocki* were really equal protection cases. This view would have some appeal, especially to skeptics about substantive due process; but it does not fit with current law.

Loving and *Zablocki*. The problem is that it seems somewhat arbitrary and opportunistic. Why, exactly, should a marriage be defined in this way? Why, in any case, should the definition be such as to allow the state not to recognize same-sex marriages?

It is not at all easy to answer this question. True, the slippery slope problems are serious if it is said that the state must justify, in compelling terms, any limitation on the right to marry. For this reason the idea that there is any such right is deeply puzzling. But in my view, the major difference between *Lawrence* and a ban on same-sex marriage is that the sodomy law no longer fits with widespread public convictions, whereas the public does not (yet) support same-sex marriages. If we rely heavily on the desuetude-type passages of the Court's opinion, then it would be possible to sketch an opinion upholding the ban on same-sex marriages while also invalidating any state law that punishes consensual sodomy. Such an opinion would read *Loving* and *Zablocki* in the narrow way just suggested, with reference to slippery slope problems, and conclude that a rational basis is all that is required for a law that restricts the institution of marriage to one woman and one man. This opinion would certainly be plausible. The problem is a general one with any approach that relies on public convictions: they might not be principled. The public might have gone this far, and no further; but there may be no good reason for it not to have gone further. It is not easy to identify a principled distinction, aside from public convictions, between what the Court did in *Lawrence* and what a court would do in striking down a state's failure to recognize same-sex marriages.

Conclusion

The *Lawrence* decision is susceptible to two broad readings. The Court's ruling could easily be seen as a recognition of the constitutionally fundamental character of sexual liberty, disabling the state from controlling the acts of consenting adults without an extremely powerful justification. Alternatively, it could be seen as a rational basis holding with a strong Millian foundation—a holding that invalidates "morals" legislation, requiring harm to third parties whenever government is regulating private sexual conduct. In practice, these two readings would not be terribly far apart; they would use different doctrinal avenues to similar results.

I have suggested the possibility of a third and narrower reading, one that stresses, as the Court did, that a criminal ban on sodomy is hopelessly out of accord with contemporary convictions. Thus understood, the due process holding of *Lawrence* is genuinely procedural. It asserts a constitutional objection to statutes that are rarely enforced and that interfere with important human interests without anything like a justification in contemporary values. Such statutes are a recipe for unpredictable and discriminatory enforcement practices; they do violence to both democratic values and the rule of law. I have stressed the roots of *Lawrence* in a narrow, American-style version of the idea of desuetude—not because the broader readings are entirely implausible, but because the Court would have been extremely unlikely to rule as it did if not for its perception that the Texas law could not claim a plausible foundation in widely shared moral commitments. I believe that an equal protection ruling, of the sort sketched by Justice O'Connor, would have been preferable, not least because it would have emphasized what should be clear to all: The problem in *Lawrence* had everything to with the social subordination of gays and lesbians. But a due process ruling, understood in the relatively narrow terms outlined here, has considerable appeal.

What is the reach of *Lawrence?* Restrictions on sex that is nonconsensual or commercial are surely valid. By contrast, laws forbidding fornication (defined as extramarital but nonadulterous sex) are surely invalid. The Constitution probably forbids government from punishing, either criminally or civilly, those who have used sexual devices. The state is almost certainly banned from discriminating against those who have engaged in homosexual conduct, at least outside of certain specialized contexts (most notably the military). In some applications, bans on incest and adultery could be subject to serious constitutional challenge.

The hardest cases involve the failure to recognize same-sex marriages. If *Lawrence* is put together with *Loving* and *Zablocki*, it would seem plausible to say that the government would have to produce a compelling justification for refusing to recognize such marriages, and compelling justifications are not easy to find. If we emphasize an equality rationale, the subtext of *Lawrence*, then bans on same-sex marriages are in serious constitutional trouble. On the other hand, the ban on same-sex marriages cannot, at this point in time, be regarded as an anachronism, or as conspicuously out of touch with emerging social values; on the contrary, the ban on same-sex marriage continues to have widespread public support. In any case, there are strong prudential reasons for the Court to hesitate in this domain and to allow democratic processes much room to maneuver. The marriage issue, more than any other, will test the question whether *Lawrence* is this generation's *Griswold*— or the start of something far more ambitious.

MARY ANNE CASE

OF "THIS" AND "THAT" IN
LAWRENCE v TEXAS

In at least three different respects, this essay's title describes its
contents: First, rather than make a single overarching claim about
Lawrence, the essay makes a variety of different observations about
this and that aspect of the decision and its implications.[1] Second,
what follows is quite literally an essay about "this" and "that," as
well as "these" and "those" and related words of emphasis, direction, and identification in the opinion; one of the observations I
shall make is that a disproportionately high number of such words
have exceedingly ambiguous referents.[2] A lack of clarity concerning

Mary Anne Case is the Arnold I. Shure Professor of Law, University of Chicago Law
School.

AUTHOR'S NOTE: I am grateful for the comments of participants in the Northwestern Law
School Constitutional Theory Colloquium and the University of Chicago Law School
Work-in-Progress series, where this paper was presented; and for the help of Lisa Van
Alstyne, Steve Calabresi, George Chauncey, Anne Coughlin, Frank Easterbrook, Liz
Emens, Richard Epstein, Bill Eskridge, Chai Feldblum, Carolyn Frantz, Steve Giambroni,
Suzanne Goldberg, Bernard Harcourt, Dick Helmholtz, the late John Hersey, Nan Hunter,
John Jeffries, Andy Koppelman, Jim Leitzel, Jean Love, Jim Madigan, Randy Picker,
Nancy Polikoff, Todd Preuss, Gerry Rosenberg, Tana Ryan, Margaret Schilt, Bill Schwesig,
James Spindler, Bill Stuntz, Cass Sunstein, Larry Tribe, David Weisbach, Jim
Whitman, Rob Wintemute; John Jacob, custodian of the Powell archives at Washington &
Lee University for providing me with materials from the *Bowers v Hardwick* file; and my
research assistants Julie Mitchell, Corey Perry, and Tiffany Saltzman-Jones. Support for
this project came from the Frieda and Arnold Shure Research Fund of the University of
Chicago.

[1] While I understand that the best way to make this essay a success by legal academic
standards is to select one of the points I am making and stick with it, see Mary Anne
Case, *Atalanta's Apples: The Values of Multiplicity*, 19 Quinnipiac L Rev 243 (2000), the very
complexity and richness of the decision itself, even more than my own willingness to value
multiple claims in scholarship, prevented me from doing so.

[2] Although it may be commonplace to criticize Supreme Court opinions for being
obscure, the problem is rarely seen to be at the level of syntax. To test my sense that the
ambiguity of the prose in the *Lawrence* majority opinion was extraordinary and noteworthy,

antecedents in the opinion goes beyond the merely grammatical. More broadly, the language and reasoning of the opinion frequently point in a direction, but when the careful reader follows the text in that direction, it reverses itself or dissolves into ambiguity. The essay will thirdly explore only a few of many examples where the opinion starts its readers off with this and in the end may deliver that instead.

If, more than most cases, *Lawrence* "will be what we make of it,"[3] I hope we can make the most of it. But, if *Lawrence* is indeed "best interpret[ed] . . . as the opening bid in a conversation that the Court expects to hold with the American public,"[4] it behooves us to be sensitive to both what our conversation partner may have already said and what it may have hesitated to say. I will undertake a close textual reading of portions of the text and an expansion of the frame of reference for other portions, not for the purpose of fixing a meaning, let alone to fix a meaning I find normatively attractive, but in an effort to highlight precisely the ambiguities and evasions that make fixing a meaning difficult, yet may reveal underlying presumptions and hesitations. In focusing on the ambiguities and dangers I see in the majority opinion, my purpose is exactly the opposite of an attempt to generate a self-fulfilling prophecy of the potential limitations I identify, however.[5] The en-

---

I did not undertake a systematic comparative study, but I did informally search numerous comparable texts, including other Kennedy opinions and other opinions on particularly difficult or watershed issues, and found in them very few instances in which, at a purely syntactical level, referents were ambiguous, as compared with dozens of such instances in the text of the *Lawrence* majority opinion. I am not the only one to focus on the majority's word choice and ambiguous antecedents. See, for example, Richard Mohr, *The Shag-a-delic Supreme Court: "Anal Sex," "Mystery," "Destiny," and the "Transcendent,"* Cardozo L Rev (forthcoming 2004) (draft on file with author).

[3] As Evan Wolfson told those gathered for Lavender Law 2003.

[4] Robert C. Post, *Foreword: Fashioning the Legal Constitution: Culture, Courts and Law: "We must seek a conception of law which realism can accept as true,"* 117 Harv L Rev 4, 104 (2003).

[5] If, when seating people in the Supreme Court Bar section for the oral argument of *Lawrence* which I attended, the usher had asked, "Petitioner or Respondent?" in the way a wedding usher asks, "Bride or Groom?" I would unequivocally have answered, "Petitioner." But I am by orientation a pessimist who focuses on the flaw, to the extent that, in my days practicing law, my employers shrewdly observed they would get better work out of me if they lied to me about which side we were on. It is clear to me which side I am on here. To the extent I express some concern about the potential limits of *Lawrence* in this essay, I see what I say as the inverse of Scalia's dissent, which spoke in what from his perspective are apocalyptic terms about the broader implications of the decision: like Scalia, I don't want to bear gifts to the opposition so much as a cautionary tale to my side. My profound hope remains that much of what Scalia sees as a dark vision of *Lawrence*'s implications comes to pass while my own dark vision remains a phantasm that vanishes with the dawn.

terprise I see myself engaged in is akin to mapping a very dense terrain. Any effort to declare one aspect of the decision to be central and definitive would be premature given the multiple potential landmarks, some of which may turn out to be land mines.

The majority opinion's ambiguity of referents creates—and may be meant to create—a politics of possibility, but, it also, much less desirably, may be the result of discomfort with looking directly at and speaking directly about the subject.[6] The Justices may be doing what comes naturally to them, what well-brought-up people do when they are somewhat uncomfortable or uncertain—they turn awkwardly away and get caught up in circumlocutions.[7] Above all, the six Justices voting for Lawrence don't want to say something tacky or offensive, like Justices White and Burger did in *Bowers*.[8] And here I think they largely succeed—I was terrified the Court would say something wrong, bad, limiting, that would explicitly undercut the good the result would do. They appear to have avoided doing so, but the price paid is in clarity and precision of language. *Lawrence* is, as Cass Sunstein says, a "remarkably opaque" decision.[9]

Of course, transparency is not something we associate with polite discussions of sex.[10] The sex in *Griswold* could be hidden under

---

[6] The observations I make here are inspired by the tradition of revelatory close textual readings of *Bowers v Hardwick* such as Janet E. Halley, *Reasoning About Sodomy: Act and Identity In and After Bowers v Hardwick*, 79 Va L Rev 1721 (1993), and Kendall Thomas, *Corpus Juris (Hetero)Sexualis: Doctrine, Discourse and Desire in Bowers v Hardwick*, 1 GLQ 33 (1993). For another sort of suggestion that, as in *Bowers*, so in *Lawrence*, the sexual subject matter may have contributed to strategies of indirection by the Court, see the title of Laurence H. Tribe's forthcoming April 2004 Harv L Rev article, *Lawrence v Texas: The "Fundamental Right" That Dare Not Speak Its Name* (draft on file with author).

[7] The difficulty a legal system has with direct discussion of the sexual acts it regulates goes back at least to the penitentials. This difficulty has been particularly acute for sodomitical and homosexual acts. The U.S. Supreme Court itself twice upheld statutes prohibiting simply "the abominable and detestable crime against nature" against a vagueness challenge, notwithstanding substantial disagreement and variation among jurisdictions as to which acts were covered. See *Wainwright v Stone*, 414 US 21 (1973) (inter alia, alleged anal jail rape); *Rose v Locke*, 423 US 48 (1975) (forced heterosexual cunnilingus). The crime too horrible to be named among Christians transmogrified into "the Love that dare not speak its name" without ever being clearly and directly addressed. For further discussion, see, for example, Mary Anne Case, *Couples and Coupling in the Public Sphere: A Comment on the Legal History of Litigating for Lesbian and Gay Rights*, 79 Va L Rev 1643, 1680–93 (1993).

[8] *Bowers v Hardwick*, 478 US 183 (1986).

[9] Cass R. Sunstein, *What Did Lawrence Hold? Of Autonomy, Desuetude, Sexuality, and Marriage* 2003 Supreme Court Review (this volume).

[10] Indirection when the subject is sex is not new to the Court. In *Oncale v Sundowner Offshore Services, Inc.*, 523 US 75 (1998), where one can learn from the record that the male sexual harassment plaintiff alleged his male co-workers had made him the unwilling victim

the covers of the marital bed. It was never in fact observed, only implicated in the case. Even in *Bowers*, the act was shrouded, it had become *crimen illud horribile inter Christianos non nominandum*.[11] *Lawrence*'s sex is not quite right out in the open, but it is uncomfortably visible—the police "officers observed Lawrence and another man, Tyron Garner, engaging in a sexual act," an act the officers described, almost as flatly as they could, as "deviate sexual intercourse, namely anal sex, with a member of the same sex (man)."[12] In suggesting that the opacity of the majority's prose may be in part the result of discomfort, I do not mean to suggest that the Court shows evidence that it is particularly uncomfortable with anal sex, that it views this form of sex as particularly abject—the same problem might arise no matter what sex act Lawrence and Garner were caught doing. On one level it is simply something we were not meant to see or talk about.

But I also get the sense from all the vague referents that the Court may be averting its gaze because it does not know quite where to look—at the cock rings or the wedding rings, at the virulent homophobes or the nice nervous people, at the parade of horribles following in the wake of a substantive due process holding (Grand Marshal, Justice Scalia[13]), or at the even longer and potentially scarier one just around the corner behind an equal protection

---

of acts that could have violated Texas's Homosexual Conduct Law (e.g., by allegedly shoving a piece of soap into his rectum), Justice Scalia, author of the majority opinion, said little more of the facts alleged by Oncale than, "[t]he precise details are irrelevant to the legal point we must decide and in the interest of both brevity and dignity we shall describe them only generally." Id at 76.

[11] When and where exactly do we learn that the precise sex act for which Hardwick was arrested was what is commonly called 69 (i.e., mutual oral sex) with another man? Certainly not from the opinion. To find this out we may have to read journalistic accounts; see, for example, Joyce Murdoch and Deb Price, *Courting Justice: Gay Men and Lesbians v. the Supreme Court* 278 (Basic Books, 2001), or one of the many law review articles that, having named the act, make clear it is not classically a sodomitical one. See, for example, Anne B. Goldstein, *History, Homosexuality, and Political Values: Searching for the Hidden Determinants of Bowers v. Hardwick*, 97 Yale L J 1073, 1079 n 40 (1988).

[12] *Lawrence v Texas*, 123 S Ct 2472, 2475–76 (2003).

[13] Scalia's dissent tries several different orders of march for this parade. See, for example, *Lawrence*, 123 S Ct at 2490 ("State laws against bigamy, same-sex marriage, adult incest, prostitution, masturbation, adultery, fornication, bestiality, and obscenity are likewise only sustainable in light of *Bowers*'s validation of laws based on moral choices. Every single one of these laws is called into question by today's decision."). Many have ridiculed Scalia for including masturbation because they doubt the law prohibits it, but see, for example, *Rodgers v Ohio Dept of Rehab and Correction*, 632 NE2d 1355 (Ohio App 1993) (upholding prison prohibition on masturbation).

holding like Justice O'Connor's. Their gaze is forced back up or down wherever they look. On both a factual and an analytical level, the problem may be that no matter where the majority looks, it sees something it doesn't want to see. I will shortly give examples of places in the text where the majority may be led by an unwillingness to commit or a discomfort with implications to pursue a strategy of evasion.

Because some readers may already be impatient for a punch line, especially once I warn that underlying my approach to *Lawrence* is a pessimism that is the inverse of that in the Scalia dissent, let me preview some of my concerns here before proceeding to some close textual analysis. Ten years ago, in writing about the history of litigating for lesbian and gay rights, I described that history as "not . . . one of steady progress, more of one step forward, two steps back."[14] The intervening years may have improved the odds to two steps forward, one step back, but the trajectory is still far from simply onward and upward without serious reversals.[15] In just the last decade, Clinton's attempt to broaden possibilities for gays and lesbians in the military led to adverse Congressional action

---

[14] See Case, 79 Va L Rev at 1652 n 35 (cited in note 7).

[15] In addition to sounding a cautionary note about the future, this trajectory also casts some doubt on the historical claims made by the majority and by Sunstein's arguments in this volume for desuetude as the best account of *Lawrence*. Both Kennedy and Sunstein's arguments from recent history needs must take the form of a progress narrative to support their respective claims and, unfortunately, recent times, in addition to offering gays and lesbians examples of real gains in both law and popular opinion, have also generated some of the most virulent opposition in both realms. As the majority correctly noted in *Romer v Evans*, 517 US 620 (1996), Amendment 2 was, in its sweeping harshness, unprecedented in our jurisprudence. There is not even the clear evidence of a progress narrative for attitudes toward criminalization of consensual private homosexual conduct, of the sort Sunstein relies for his desuetude analysis. Consider the legislative history of the very Texas statute at issue in *Lawrence*, as described in Case, 79 Va L Rev at 1691–92:

> The statute originally prohibited both homo- and heterosexual acts; it was then amended to prohibit only homosexual acts and then further amended to prohibit an even broader variety of homosexual acts. . . . By a 1974 amendment, "Article 524 (Sodomy) was replaced with § 21.06 (Homosexual Conduct), which condemned only oral or anal sex between consenting adults of the same sex." The scanty legislative history indicates that a subcommittee "did seriously consider the decriminalization of the private homosexual acts of consenting adults, but . . . fear[ed] a backlash effect against the entire Penal Code should such acts be decriminalized."

(Prohibition on penetration with objects was added to the prohibited conduct in 1981.)
A time line such as this is particularly bad for the majority who, because it asserts that *Bowers v Hardwick* was "not correct when it was decided," cannot rely on evidence of increasing tolerance over the last eighteen years to the extent Sunstein can.

and more involuntary military discharges than ever; Boulder's anti-discrimination ordinance led to Amendment 2, which in turn led to *Romer*;[16] the Hawaii Supreme Court's same-sex marriage decision[17] led to the Defense of Marriage Act and a Hawaiian constitutional amendment reversing the decision,[18] but also to partnership rights from the Hawaiian legislature; and *Lawrence* itself seems to have sparked intensified interest in a federal constitutional amendment on same-sex marriage and a sharp decline of support in the polls for gay rights. Providing some support for Scalia's view that what he calls the "Kulturkampf"[19] over gay rights partakes of elements of class warfare, in almost every case, the more elite, less democratic actor (courts, the executive, a comparatively wealthy community) spearheaded the push in the pro-gay direction, the more populist (legislatures, the electorate generally) the backlash.

Now the Court has taken gay rights a step—perhaps a giant step—forward. But, though Lawrence and Garner prevailed, it remains to be seen how far into the public sphere and out of the now protected confines of their individual homes the *Lawrence* case, and the Court, will take them and others.

"A SMALL ROOM FOR PRIVACY"? OR, HOW FAR BEYOND THE CLOSET WILL LAWRENCE TAKE GAY RIGHTS?

It may be worth remembering that the first dictionary definition of closet is "an apartment or small room for privacy."[20] This apartment for "private and consensual" "adult" "Homosexual Conduct" is what the Court has now vouchsafed to John Geddes Lawrence.[21] But how much protection can gay men, lesbians, and bisexuals count on for activities beyond their own bedroom from a majority opinion that (1) uses the word private nearly two dozen

---

[16] *Romer v Evans*, 517 US 620 (1996).

[17] *Baehr v Lewin*, 852 P2d 44 (Hawaii 1993).

[18] Similarly, *Baker v Vermont*, 744 A2d 864 (Vt 1999), and resulting civil union law led to the "Take Back Vermont Campaign" and the electoral defeat of some moderate supporters.

[19] See *Romer*, 517 US at 636.

[20] *Webster's Seventh New Collegiate Dictionary* 156 (Merriam, 1971).

[21] Just as, nearly a quarter century earlier, the New York Court of Appeals, in striking down that state's sodomy laws in *People v Onofre*, 415 NE2d 936 (NY 1980), cert denied, 451 US 987 (1981), vouchsafed to those in New York the right to "noncommercial, cloistered" sex.

times to describe what it is protecting; (2) conspicuously does not take up the invitation pervading petitioners' briefs to recognize the collateral harms from the mere existence of the Homosexual Conduct Law on the employment and family law rights of gays and lesbians, but instead lists as collateral harms only those that follow from actual conviction, notwithstanding that much of the opinion is dedicated to showing how extraordinarily unlikely (and perhaps even unintended) actual conviction for private consensual adult conduct like Lawrence's is; and (3) cites with enthusiasm to the experience of Britain, where, whether or not the majority is aware of it, legislative decriminalization of private consensual adult sex between two persons of the same sex was followed by decades of (a) more virulent prosecution of public homosexual acts including, for example, "kissing and cuddling," (b) a very narrow definition of what was "private" and hence not criminal, and (c) no promo homo laws?[22]

Leave marriage and the military to the side for the moment. How confident can we be that, for example, (1) a replay of *Uplinger*[23] would result in vindication for a gay man extending to a stranger in a public place an explicit invitation to private sex; (2) a replay of *Shahar v Bowers*[24] would result in her reinstatement (after all, same-sex marriage is still against Georgia policy;[25] moreover, the state employers who have recently fired people for het-

---

[22] See discussion below. Given that the majority cites with enthusiasm only to the acts of decriminalization and that it is unclear whether any of its members are even aware of subsequent events, I certainly do not mean to suggest that there is anything in the text of the majority opinion that indicates an endorsement of these subsequent restrictions.

[23] *N.Y. v Uplinger*, 467 US 246 (1984), cert granted, 464 US 812 (1983), cert dismissed, 467 US 246 (1984), involved the criminalization of public solicitation for precisely the sort of private, consensual, noncommercial, adult sex acts at issue in *Lawrence* in a state in which the private sex acts themselves had already been granted constitutional protection and consequent immunity from criminalization by the *Onofre* decision. For further discussion see below.

[24] 114 F3d 1097 (11th Cir 1997) (en banc), cert denied, 522 US 1049 (1998) (allowing Georgia Attorney General to revoke offer of employment to lawyer because she had undergone a Jewish wedding ceremony with another woman).

[25] Indeed, Attorney General Bowers, possibly to avoid discovery into his own sodomous and adulterous activities, stipulated that his decision to withdraw Shahar's offer of employment "was based on no act of sexual conduct on Ms. Shahar's part," but only on her participation in a lesbian wedding, *Shahar v Bowers*, 120 F3d 211, 213 (11th Cir 1997), and the Eleventh Circuit en banc found that her marriage "could undermine confidence about the Attorney General's commitment to enforce the State's law against homosexual sodomy (or laws limiting marriage and marriage benefits to traditional marriages)." See 114 F3d at 1105 n 17.

erosexual sex such as adultery don't rely on the criminal law as much as unit cohesion, social policy, etc.); (3) a replay of *Bottoms*[26] or even a more conventional custody case wouldn't still lead to loss by the lesbian parent, at least as long as the purported basis for the decision was not homosexuality, per se, but homosexuality plus; (4) a replay of *Equality Foundation of Greater Cincinnati*[27] would strike down the charter amendment, reading *Romer* more expansively in light of *Lawrence*; (5) some case won't soon come along that will be the *Paris Adult Theatres*[28] to *Lawrence*'s *Stanley v Georgia*[29] or the *Powell v Texas*[30] to *Lawrence*'s *Robinson v California*[31]? What will be the Court's answer to Justice Rehnquist's question of *Lawrence*'s counsel at oral argument: "If you prevail, if this law is struck down, do you think that would also mean that a State could not prefer heterosexuals to homosexuals to teach kindergarten?"[32] I personally would like to think the Court has seen enough of the light to continue its protection of gays and lesbians even beyond the privacy of their homes and against threats short of the criminal law or Amendment 2, but there is enough ambiguity and hesitation in the opinion to worry me. Perhaps more to the point in the short term, there is enough ambiguity and hesitation in the opinion to allow those lower court judges disposed against gay rights claims to minimize or ignore the Supreme Court's new tone of respect and acceptance for such claims and rule, with a slight change in language, essentially as they would have before *Lawrence*

---

[26] *Bottoms v Bottoms*, 457 SE2d 102, 108 (Va 1995) (transferring custody of child from lesbian mother to maternal grandmother notwithstanding state supreme court holding that "a lesbian mother is not per se an unfit parent").

[27] *Equality Foundation of Greater Cincinnati v Cincinnati*, 128 F3d 289 (6th Cir 1997), cert denied, 525 US 943 (1998) (upholding, after remand by Supreme Court for reconsideration in light of *Romer*, city charter amendment precluding, inter alia, the adoption of "any policy which provides that homosexual, lesbian or bisexual orientation, status, conduct or relationship . . . entitles . . . a person . . . to have any claim of minority or protected status. . . .").

[28] *Paris Adult Theatres I v Slaton*, 413 US 49 (1973) (sustaining ban on exhibiting of obscene movies to consenting adults in a theater against a First Amendment challenge).

[29] 394 US 557 (1969) (protecting possession of obscene movies by individual in private home).

[30] 392 US 514 (1968) (upholding constitutionality of crime of public drunkenness).

[31] 370 US 660 (1962) (holding unconstitutional the criminalization of the status of being a drug addict).

[32] Transcript, *Lawrence v Texas*, 2003 US Trans LEXIS 30, *19 (Mar 26, 2003) ("Lawrence Transcript").

came down.[33] Although I hope I am wrong, I can imagine that, in the same way as *Bowers* turned out, in the opinion of at least some observers, in the end not to be as bad as was feared for the progress of gay rights, *Lawrence* may turn out not to be as good as many now hope.[34] I shall discuss the concerns enumerated above in detail below, but first, as promised:

LITERALLY OF "THIS" AND "THAT"

At least for strict grammarians, perhaps the most significant "that" in the entire majority opinion is the one that isn't there, in the sentence dissenting Justice Scalia describes as the opinion's "actual holding:"[35] "The Texas statute furthers no legitimate state interest which can justify its intrusions into the personal and private life of the individual."[36] Note, the majority says "which can justify . . ." rather than "that can justify. . . ." A classically trained

---

[33] Just before this article went to press, two lower court decisions that unfortunately lend strong support to this essay's pessimistic approach to *Lawrence* came down. The first, *Lofton v Secretary of Dept of Children and Family Services*, 2004 US App LEXIS 1383 (11th Cir 2004), upheld Florida's categorical ban on adoption by a gay man or lesbian, the only such ban among the fifty states. The second, *Kansas v Limon*, 2004 Kan App LEXIS 110, in which the young male defendant claimed that his punishment for the crime of consensual oral sex with an adolescent male could not constitutionally be orders of magnitude higher than the penalty would have been under the state's "Romeo and Juliet" exception had his sex partner been instead an adolescent female, had been remanded by the Supreme Court for reconsideration in light of *Lawrence*, but the appeals court, which had previously treated *Bowers* as dispositive of Limon's claims, once again ruled against him. The courts in both *Lofton* and *Limon* gave exceedingly short shrift to any claims that *Lawrence* should make a difference to the outcome or analysis of the cases before them.

[34] I do not mean to minimize the insult to gays, lesbians, and bisexuals of the language of the majority and Burger opinions in *Bowers* nor the value to them of the respectful language of the majority and O'Connor opinions in *Lawrence*. But, precisely the insult of the language of *Bowers* may have helped galvanize gays, lesbians, bisexuals, and their supporters while adding to the number of those supporters the many who were put off by what Justices White and Burger had to say. Additionally, of course, the language and holding of *Bowers* were used by numerous decision makers on and off the courts in the intervening years to the detriment of sexual minorities. I suspect, however, that if there had never been a *Bowers* decision at all (a different counterfactual than supposing that Blackmun's had been the majority opinion in *Bowers*), opponents of gays, lesbians, and bisexuals would simply have relied on different language and authority in taking essentially the same actions. Similarly, it remains to be seen how many minds and hearts *Lawrence* will change and how many decision makers will instead merely exploit or ignore its open-textured language as suits their purposes.

[35] *Lawrence*, 123 S Ct at 2488 (Scalia dissenting).

[36] Id at 2484.

grammarian would observe that this should signal the majority's intention for the clause to be a non-restrictive rather than a restrictive one (or, as Fowler puts it "non-defining" rather than "defining").[37] "Non-restrictive clauses are parenthetic. . . . A non-restrictive clause is one that does not serve to identify or define the antecedent noun."[38] Thus, if the majority opinion is careful about its grammar, the question of whether the opinion applies heightened or rational basis scrutiny can be answered by noting that, technically, the sentence can be shortened to "The Texas statute furthers no legitimate state interest" without altering its meaning. In other words, the statute fails the lowest level of scrutiny; no heightened scrutiny is required. Had the sentence continued with "that" rather than "which," it could correctly have been read to suggest instead that, while the Texas statute did "further a legitimate state interest," the interest was not one "that can justify its intrusion into the personal and private lives of individuals"; in other words, the majority would have been acknowledging a need to apply heightened scrutiny.[39]

Determining the significance of the ambiguity concerning the majority's level of scrutiny adds yet another level of ambiguity. If minimalism, in the sense of deciding only the minimum that has to be decided to determine the outcome of a particular case and leaving all else undecided, is an appropriate strategy for the Supreme Court,[40] then perhaps even the appropriate level of scrutiny

---

[37] Margaret Nicholson, *A Dictionary of American-English Usage Based on Fowler's Modern English Usage* 577 (Oxford, 1957).

[38] William Strunk, Jr. and E. B. White, *The Elements of Style* 3 (Macmillan, 2d ed 1972).

[39] The majority's use of "which" rather than "that" may be deliberately ambiguous or subconsciously motivated by ambivalence. Scalia, however, makes an unequivocal which-that error when he castigates the majority for "apply[ing] an unheard-of form of rational basis review that will have far-reaching implications beyond this case." 123 S Ct at 2488. Confused though he may claim to be by the majority, he surely is not claiming that it applied more than one unheard of form of rational basis review only one of which will have far-reaching implications. Clearly then, "which" rather than "that" should have introduced the clause following "unheard-of form of rational basis review"; the clause is not meant to be restrictive. In his assumption that rational basis review was in fact what the majority applied, Scalia may in part be relying on the which/that distinction, with which he is certainly familiar. See *Barnhart v Thomas*, 124 S Ct 376, 380–81 (2003), a case turning largely on the application of grammatical rules, in which Scalia sub silentio corrects the legislature's problematic use of "which" in the relevant statutory clause to a more correct and clear "that" in constructing an analogous example.

[40] In my own view minimalism is not generally an appropriate strategy for a court such as the U.S. Supreme Court, which takes only a tiny fraction of the cases presented to it, can go for decades before taking another case in a particular subject area, and is or ought to be in the business of providing guidance to lower courts which will be charged with

can occasionally fall under the heading of things to be left undecided. For example, if, as apparently was the case in *Lawrence*, a
particular statute lacked a rational basis, it does not necessarily follow that heightened scrutiny would not have been applied had a
rational basis not been lacking. The Court can be seen simply to
be applying the lowest level of scrutiny necessary to invalidate the
statute, while taking no position on whether, had a higher level
of scrutiny been necessary, it would have been appropriate to apply
it. Unfortunately, however, leaving this much unclear or undecided
risks giving far too little guidance to lower courts. Those lower
court judges simply interested in following the Supreme Court's
dictates may be hopelessly confused, whereas lower court judges
with an agenda of their own can pursue it relatively unconstrained.
In particular, just as some lower court judges read *Bowers* very
broadly to facilitate a ruling against gay rights litigants,[41] they can
now seek to read *Lawrence* very narrowly indeed to again reach
the same result.[42]

"Homosexual": "Group" or "Conduct"? "Us" or "Them"?

The majority is not the only opinion in *Lawrence* with
grammatical difficulties marked by ambiguity about referents.
Scalia's dissent drew criticism from William Safire[43] and a confes-

---

disposing of numerous cases the Supreme Court will not review. At least as, if not more,
dangerous to the orderly development of constitutional jurisprudence as is the much-criti-
cized quasi-legislative approach of cases such as *Roe v Wade* and *Miranda v Arizona* is the
opposite extreme of the Court's minimally disposing of the case before it while offering
no usable framework for the adjudication of countless similar or second-generation claims.

[41] See, for example, *Padula v Webster*, 822 F2d 97, 103 (DC Cir 1987) ("If the Court [in
Bowers v Hardwick] was unwilling to object to state laws that criminalize the behavior that
defines the class, it is hardly open to a lower court to conclude that state sponsored discrimination against the class is invidious.").

[42] See, for example, *Lofton*, 2004 US App 1383 at *29, 32–33 (acknowledging "Texas's
failure to offer a rational basis for [the] statute" struck down in *Lawrence*, but finding "[m]ost
significant, however, . . . the fact that the *Lawrence* Court never applied strict scrutiny, the
proper standard when fundamental rights are implicated, but instead invalidated the Texas
statute on rational basis grounds. . . ."). The *Lofton* court insisted that "the holding of
Lawrence does not control the present case. Apart from the shared homosexuality component, there are marked differences in the facts of the two cases. . . . Here the involved
actors are not only consenting adults, but minors as well. The relevant state action is not
criminal prohibition, but grant of a statutory privilege. And the asserted liberty interest is
not the negative right to engage in private conduct without facing criminal sanctions, but
the affirmative right to receive official and public recognition." Id at *33–34.

[43] William Safire, *The Way We Live Now: 10-19-03: On Lawrence: Flagellum Dei*, NY
Times Magazine 22 (Oct 19, 2003).

sion of grammatical error from Scalia himself. The dissent included the sentence: "Let me be clear that I have nothing against homosexuals, or any other group, promoting their agenda through normal democratic means." Questioned by Safire, Scalia confessed that he had "pondered for some time whether I should be perfectly grammatical and write 'I have nothing against homosexuals' or any other group's promoting their agenda,' etc. The object of the preposition 'against' after all, is not 'homosexuals who are promoting' but rather the promoting of (in the sense of by) homosexuals.'"

Several things are of note here. First, in an opinion in a line of opinions beginning with *Romer*[44] in which Scalia aligns himself with the democratic masses against the elite, Scalia surreptitiously avoids elite grammatical correctness, but, when caught out, explicitly abjures populism: "I decided to be ungrammatical instead of pedantic. . . . God—whom I believe to be a strict grammarian as well as an Englishman has punished me. . . . I am convinced that in this instance the A.P.[45] has been (unwittingly I am sure) the flagellum Dei to recall me from my populist illiterate wandering."[46] Second, there is technically no grammatical error in the sentence Scalia published; it is just a different sentence with a different

---

[44] See *Romer v Evans*, 517 US 620, 652 (1995) (Scalia dissenting) ("When the Court takes sides in the culture wars, it tends to be with the knights rather than the villeins—and more specifically with the Templars, reflecting the views and values of the lawyer class from which the Court's members are drawn."). For discussion of precisely how odd and revelatory the choice of Templars as combatants here is, see Mary Anne Case, *Deconstructing Scalia* (unpublished manuscript on file with the author).

[45] [Author's Note: According to Safire, the Associated Press had "quoted Scalia out of context as saying, 'I have nothing against homosexuals,' which seemed condescending." Safire, *Flagellum Dei* (cited in note 43)].

[46] Id. I. E. Nino's been a bad boy and must be punished. How much Scalia has come to love the whip—and how unerring his gift for saying exactly the wrong thing—is suggested by the fact that none of the parades of horribles he predicts in the wake of *Lawrence* (see above) includes S/M, despite prominent debates about its criminalization in Europe. See, for example, the so-called "Spanner case," *R v Brown*, 2 All ER 75 [1993] (House of Lords 1994), aff'd sub nom. *Laskey v UK*, 24 EHHR 39 (1997) (upholding conviction for various offenses including assault of members of a group of men engaged in hard core consensual sadomasochistic activities); Mark Lanler, *German Court Convicts Internet Cannibal of Manslaughter*, NY Times (Jan 31, 2004) (reporting on legal situation of Armin Meiwes, who advertised for and found a man "willing to be 'slaughtered'" whom he then killed with the victim's explicit consent in a videotaped "evening of sexual role-playing and violence"). See Case, *Deconstructing Scalia* (observing that "Scalia, as author, has a gift for saying exactly the wrong thing, for hitting a note so perfectly off key that its oscillations shatter the facade of his argument" and exploring examples). Compare *Barnes v Glenn Theaters*, 501 US 560, 575 (1991) (Scalia concurring) (listing among the activities Americans "have prohibited . . . not because they harm others but because they are considered . . . immoral . . . for example, sadomasochism, cockfighting, bestiality, suicide, drug use, prostitution, and sodomy").

object, producing a subtle shift in emphasis. No rule of grammar categorically prevents the object of the preposition "against" in Scalia's sentence from being "homosexuals" rather than any "agenda . . . promoting" they may do. Indeed, treating "homosexuals" as the object of "against" avoids another grammatical difficulty unmentioned by Safire or Scalia: "Group" is a singular, collective noun; a group promotes "its" agenda, not (if the agenda is its own) "their agenda."[47] Scalia's original sentence is a perfectly grammatical one, however, if the object of "against" is taken to be "homosexuals or any other group promoting [the homosexuals'] agenda." Consider, for example, the many groups from the ACLU to the Republican Unity Coalition who filed amicus briefs in support of Petitioner Lawrence. Or, more to the point when the author of the sentence is Justice Scalia, consider the Association of American Law Schools, condemned in Scalia's *Romer* and *Lawrence* dissents for "ha[ving] largely signed on to the so-called homosexual agenda"[48] by requiring its members to extract from recruiting employers "'assurance of . . . willingness' to hire homosexuals."[49]

It is these days a breach of manners, not of grammar, to say one is against homosexuals. But, for the anti-gay populace for whom Scalia claims to speak, homosexuals are indeed something to be against; even worse are "homosexual activists" promoting "the so-called homosexual agenda."[50] Scalia may have been more "clear" than he intended when he put the weight of his sentence, and hence of his disclaimed opposition, on "homosexuals."

The non-dissenting Justices also put the weight of their prose on "homosexuals" as a "group" rather than on the "conduct" in which they engage. This is clearest in O'Connor's equal protection concurrence, which crucially depends on "homosexuals" being a "group" targeted by the Homosexual Conduct Law, so as both to bring the case within the line of rational basis cases striking down

---

[47] At least in American English. God, being "an Englishman," would not have this difficulty, since in British English, collective nouns are plural.

[48] *Lawrence*, 123 S Ct at 2496. Scalia claims to mean by this phrase "the agenda promoted by some homosexual activists directed at eliminating the moral opprobrium that has traditionally attached to homosexual conduct." Id.

[49] *Romer*, 517 US at 653 (Scalia dissenting).

[50] Or maybe he does have something against their promoting that he hasn't got against them so long as they stay silent? Compare *Boy Scouts of America v Dale*, 530 US 640 (2000). Compare his discussion of "open" homosexuals below.

legislation whose objective was "a bare . . . desire to harm a politically unpopular group"[51] (the line on which the concurrence relies)[52] and to distinguish *Lawrence* from *Bowers,* which O'Connor would not overrule. It seems to matter to the majority as well that the petitioners were "engaged in sexual practices common to a homosexual lifestyle."[53] The majority's history is designed to show that the twentieth century brought an adverse singling out of homosexual persons and the "acts common to their lifestyle" and precisely this singling out is what the majority now sets its face against.[54] Like so much else in the move from *Bowers* to *Lawrence,* what Janet Halley described as the unstable elision between acts and identity has not disappeared in *Lawrence* so much as reversed its valence. *Bowers,* too, was a case about "this" and "that." In *Bowers* the majority unstably pointed to ambiguous referents to create "the double bind [by which Hardwick] was cinched."[55] Remember

---

[51] *Dept of Agriculture v Moreno,* 413 US 528, 534 (1973), quoted in *Lawrence,* 123 S Ct at 2485 (O'Connor concurrence).

[52] *Moreno, Cleburne, Eisenstadt, Romer.* Compare *Plessy v Ferguson,* 163 US 537, 550 (1896) ("[E]very exercise of the police power must be reasonable, and extend only to such laws as are enacted in good faith for the promotion of the public good, and not for the annoyance or oppression of a particular class.").

[53] *Lawrence,* 123 S Ct at 2484.

[54] See, for example, id at 2479 ("It was not until the 1970s that the state singled out same-sex relations."). I must say the argument the majority draws from this history of increased singling out strikes me as somewhat bizarre when viewed at any level of generality. Consider the following proposition: "The longstanding criminal prohibition of [sex with unmarried adolescent girls] . . . is as consistent with a general condemnation of non[marital] sex as it is with an established tradition of prosecuting acts because of [the age of the participants]." If true, does anyone think that it would give a convicted pedophile or statutory rapist a constitutional leg to stand on? The fact that their acts were "not thought of as a separate category from like conduct [with adult women]" but rather incorporated indistinguishably in a more general category that was more generally disapproved surely does not tell us enough about how to think about the prohibitions that remain once much of the category has been legalized. (Of course, the altered quotations immediately preceding are derived from the *Lawrence* majority. For the original unaltered version, substitute for the bracketed phrases above, respectively, "homosexual sodomy," "procreative," "their homosexual character," and "between heterosexual persons".)

Similarly, it is a commonplace of constitutional scholarship that regulation of expression purely because of its sexual explicitness was a comparative latecomer to Anglo-American law. See, for example, *Paris Adult Theatres v Slaton,* 413 US 49, 104 (1972) (Brennan dissenting). Indeed, in the United Kingdom, obscenity and blasphemy still are linked as grounds for censorship. See *Wingrove v UK,* 24 EHRR 1 (1996) (upholding blasphemy prosecution of sexually explicit video purportedly inspired by the writings of St. Teresa of Avila). No one that I know of has suggested that for this reason the singling out of obscenity for prosecution is somehow more problematic now that blasphemy is not merely legal, but constitutionally protected.

[55] Halley, 79 Va L Rev at 1749 (cited in note 6).

the *Bowers*'s majority's asserting that the question presented is whether the federal constitution "invalidates the laws of the many states that still make such conduct illegal"[56] and beginning its answer with the assertion that "[p]roscriptions of that conduct have ancient roots"?[57] As Halley asked, "What does the 'such' of 'such conduct' refer to? Sodomy generally or as inflected by the homosexuals who do it?"[58] It is no clearer in *Lawrence* what "that conduct" is, only that "that conduct" is now what gets protection rather than condemnation.

As the amici supporting Texas take pains to point out,[59] and as O'Connor acknowledges, the Texas law on its face targets "conduct," not "groups of persons" unlike, say, *Romer*'s Amendment 2.[60] And unlike, for example, the military's regulations, the Texas law does not "on [its] face discriminate against homosexuals on the basis of their sexual orientation."[61] On its face, the Texas law discriminates on the basis of sex, not orientation. Also unlike the military's "Don't ask/Don't tell" regulations—which treat differently homosexual acts homosexuals perform and those same homosexual acts performed by people who can demonstrate that they are not homosexual, just motivated by "immaturity, intoxication, . . . or a . . . desire to avoid military service"[62]—the Texas Homosexual Conduct Law seeks to punish alike any two men or any two women who violate it, whether the women are lesbians and the men gay[63] or not. Though the law clearly has an adverse disparate

---

[56] *Bowers*, 478 US at 190.

[57] Id at 192.

[58] Halley, 79 Va L Rev at 1749 (cited in note 6).

[59] Many of the briefs supporting respondents tried to make much of the fact that the laws apply to anyone, straight or gay, engaged in the prohibited acts with someone of the same sex.

[60] Amendment 2's text provided, inter alia, "[n]either the State of Colorado . . . nor any of its . . . political subdivisions . . . shall enact . . . any statute, regulation, ordinance or policy whereby homosexual, lesbian or bisexual orientation, conduct, practices or relationships shall constitute or otherwise be the basis of or entitle any person or class of persons to have or claim any minority status, quota preferences, protected status or claim of discrimination."

[61] *Watkins v U.S. Army*, 847 F2d 1329 (9th Cir 1988), cert denied, 498 US 957 (1990) (interpreting a predecessor of the "Don't ask/Don't tell" policy).

[62] Compare *Watkins*, 847 F2d at 1339 ("If a straight soldier and a gay soldier of the same sex engage in homosexual acts because they are drunk, immature or curious, the straight soldier may remain in the Army while the gay soldier is automatically terminated.").

[63] Whatever it may mean to be gay or lesbian. It is beyond the scope of this paper to say more about the much discussed definitional questions of who or what is a homosexual.

impact on homosexuals,[64] it does not quite measure up to Anatole France's famous example of disparate impact.[65] For, while the rich may have little if any desire to sleep under bridges or to beg, non-homosexuals ("drunk, immature or curious" or otherwise) might well, as the Army realizes, desire to engage in the conduct the Texas law prohibits.[66] Precisely these are the people for whom the penalty and stigma of a criminal law prohibiting Homosexual Conduct might be most likely to act as a successful deterrent.[67] While O'Connor may be right that "[t]hose harmed by this law are those who have a same sex sexual orientation,"[68] on the view of many of Respondent's amici those most benefited by the law are those without such an orientation who might otherwise be tempted. The assumption in briefs supporting the Respondent is that anyone can do these acts and anyone who does do them can be harmed by them.[69] Would a statute that is the inverse of "Don't ask/Don't

[64] For a discussion of the intriguing question of whether *Lawrence* breathes new life into constitutional disparate impact analysis, see Andrew Koppelman, *Lawrence's Penumbra*, Minn L Rev (forthcoming 2004). It does not seem to me that, on its face, the Supreme Court's decision to remand *Limon v Kansas*, 123 S Ct 2638 (2003), for reconsideration in light of *Lawrence* tells us much in this regard. Because the appeals court had treated *Bowers* as an obstacle to considering Limon's claim, and *Lawrence*, by overruling *Bowers*, removed the obstacle, it would have behooved the Supreme Court to remand for reconsideration even if neither *Bowers* nor *Lawrence* were actually relevant to Limon's claim. That is not to say I agree with the Kansas appeals court's opinion on remand, 2004 Kan App LEXIS 110. It is worthy of note that the "wider civilization" invoked by Justice Kennedy, and particularly the European Court of Human Rights whose *Dudgeon* decision Kennedy cited as a forerunner of *Lawrence*, recently issued a number of decisions vindicating claims that higher ages of consent for male homosexual acts violate the rights of gay youth and the men with whom they wish to have sex. See *SL v Austria*, [2003] ECHR 45330/99 (2003); *L and V v Austria*, [2003] ECHR 39392/98 (2003) and corresponding legislative initiatives. On the other hand, it may be worth remembering that the Supreme Court also remanded *Equality Foundation of Cincinnati* for reconsideration in light of *Romer*, but it then denied certiorari when the lower court nevertheless reaffirmed the constitutionality of the charter amendment. See note above.

[65] "The law, in its majestic equality, forbids the rich as well as the poor to sleep under bridges, to beg in the streets, and to steal bread." Anatole France, *Le Lys Rouge* (1894), in John Bartlett, *Familiar Quotations* 802 (Little, Brown, 14th ed 1968).

[66] See, for example, Alfred Kinsey et al, *Sexual Behavior in the Human Male* (1948), reprinted in William B. Rubenstein, *Cases and Materials on Sexual Orientation and the Law* 11 (West Pub, 2d ed 1997) (claiming that 37 percent of adult white males had had at least one adult homosexual encounter to the point of orgasm). In the context of "Don't ask/Don't tell," the military's willingness to accommodate someone who engages in occasional homosexual acts is often called the "queen for a day" exception.

[67] I am reminded of the reaction of one of my then employers, a partner at a large New York law firm and a married father, on the day *Bowers* came down. "This is a great decision," he insisted, "because we are all inherently bisexual and it saves us from ourselves."

[68] *Lawrence*, 123 S Ct at 2485.

[69] See, for example, Respondent's Brief, *Lawrence v Texas*, 2002 US Briefs LEXIS 102, *27 (filed Feb 17, 2003).

tell"—one that imposes no penalty on homosexual conduct by homosexuals[70] but fines straight people who engage in homosexual acts when "drunk, immature or curious"—pass muster with either the majority or O'Connor?[71] Or is the potential stigmatic effect of such a law enough to doom it as well?

More importantly, are we stopping "ourselves" or "them" in criminalizing the conduct at issue in the Texas law? At a formal level, the Texas law, no less than the Georgia law at issue in *Bowers*, describes the sort of conduct that might happen to anyone, although under Texas's formulation, even more than under Georgia's,[72] it is likely to happen much more often to homosexuals. Both Michael Hardwick and Laurence Tribe as his advocate[73] stressed the "us" part, but that backfired because of the Court majority's revulsion:[74] "We" are not "them," the Court appears to have said to itself.[75] Once again in *Lawrence*, advocates for the respondent (in *Lawrence*, Texas) stressed the "us" aspect, and once again this was not a winning strategy. Not only did the identity of the party stressing the universalizing as opposed to minoritizing aspect of the statute change, the valence of what it meant for the statute to be about "them" also changed. That Georgia's statute was seen to be about "the right [of] homosexuals to engage in sodomy"[76] caused five members of the

[70] Compare Elizabeth Emens, *Monogamy's Law: Compulsory Monogamy and Polyamorous Existence*, 29 NYU Rev Law & Soc Change 36 (forthcoming 2004) (suggesting the possibility of adultery laws distinguishing between persons in open marriages and those in marriages they agree will be monogamous).

[71] There is some indication from his handwritten notes after conference in *Bowers* that Justice Powell considered such an approach. Powell wrote, "I would not argue that *every person* has a fundamental right to engage in sodomy any time, any place. There are men who *can* gratify their sexual desire *only* with another man. Given this fact, I find it difficult lawfully to imprison such a person who confined his *abnormality* to a private setting with a consenting homo. . . . Possibly I could Remand to determine whether Hardwick suffers from this abnormality." Handwritten notes by Justice Powell, dated 4/3/86, from Powell archives *Bowers* file, Washington & Lee. Could we view homosexuals like drug addicts in the Netherlands, entitled to their fix once they can demonstrate they can't shake the habit? Or like prostitutes who can ply their trade once they register?

[72] Recall that the Georgia statute at issue in *Bowers*, unlike Texas's Homosexual Conduct Law, criminalized all penetrative oral and anal sex, even when the participants were a man and a woman, rather than two persons of the same sex.

[73] See, for example, Tribe, *The "Fundamental Right,"* Harv L Rev (forthcoming 2004); Case, *Couples and Coupling*, 79 Va L Rev at 1681 n 169.

[74] In *Couples and Coupling*, I associated this revulsion with Freud's notion of the narcissism of minor differences. Id at 1662.

[75] See, for example, Halley, 79 Va L Rev at 1769–70 (cited in note 6) (analyzing how "the Justices engage in masking their own potential status as sodomites even if they never stray from the class of heterosexuals.").

[76] *Bowers*, 478 US at 200.

court to uphold it in 1986; that Texas's statute was seen to target homosexuals caused six members of the Court, one of whom had joined and not repudiated Justice White's *Bowers* majority opinion, to strike it down in 2003. If there is a sea change, this might be it: gay people may not be "us" but they are fellow "citizens"[77] with a dignitary interest worthy of the Court's solicitude.

But what about that portion of "us" that still thinks being "them" is "immoral and destructive"?[78]

The Vanishing Reliance Interest

> Many Americans do not want persons who openly engage in homosexual conduct as partners in their business, as scoutmasters for their children, as teachers in their children's schools or as boarders in their home. They view this as protecting themselves and their families from a lifestyle that they believe to be immoral and destructive. The Court views it as "discrimination" which it is the function of our judgments to deter.[79]

One thing worth asking about these sentences is how much weight Scalia wants to place on "openly" in the first one. Is he suggesting that not "many Americans" object to accepting those who engage in homosexual conduct but do not do so "openly" (because they are either closeted or simply very private about their sex lives)? If so, he is giving ammunition to the majority: Lawrence and Garner's charged conduct was not "open."

I will come later to the question of openness. But for now let me ask why this passage is not in the section of Scalia's dissent dealing with the reliance interest in not overruling *Bowers,* nor do the people and interests mentioned in it come in for prominent attention when the subject is the comparative reliance placed on *Roe* and *Bowers* for stare decisis purposes. What about the reliance interests of opponents of tolerance for homosexual activity on the license *Bowers* may have given them to act on that intolerance? What about what, in *Romer,* Scalia in dissent described as "a modest attempt by seemingly [*sic*] tolerant Coloradans to preserve tra-

---

[77] *Lawrence,* 123 S Ct 2487, 2491 (O'Connor concurring).

[78] There remain plenty of such people, wishful thinking to the contrary notwithstanding. I wish it were otherwise, but I am not sure the evidence fully vindicates Sunstein's claim in this volume that "the public no longer supports the moral argument that lies behind" Texas's Homosexual Conduct Law. Sunstein, 2003 Supreme Court Review at 51 (cited in note 9).

[79] *Lawrence,* 123 S Ct at 2497 (Scalia dissenting)

ditional sexual mores"[80] and the State of Colorado described as its interest in "respect for other citizens' freedom of association, and in particular the liberties of landlords or employers who have personal or religious objections to homosexuality?" Why is this sort of reliance interest not discussed more in *Lawrence*, by either majority or dissent? Possibly because the authority of *Bowers* was often not necessary and sometimes not sufficient to give legal license to the disfavoring or exclusion of gays and lesbians. For example, the First Amendment principles of *Boy Scouts* and *Hurley* allow exclusion in the absence of an official Court position on the morality or legitimacy of the grounds for exclusion.[81] And *Bowers* did not suffice to save Amendment 2: no group, even of the most heinous felons convicted under the most unimpeachable of criminal laws, could constitutionally have the protection of the laws removed from them on so wholesale a basis as that found in Amendment 2. Possibly also because few if any of those who wish to discriminate against, disfavor, and condemn homosexuals actually rely on the Constitution for their authority to do so.[82] Unlike women and doctors affected by *Roe*, who may not rely on the Constitution to justify their abortion but surely do rely on its interpretation in *Roe* and its progeny to keep them out of jail for acting on their convictions, few if any opponents of tolerance for homosexuals or homosexual conduct depend directly on the state's attitude toward homosexuality to license either their own attitudes or their resulting behavior.[83] If polling data are any indication, most depend on religious conviction.[84]

---

[80] *Romer*, 517 US at 635.

[81] See *Boy Scouts of America v Dale*, 530 US 640, 660 (2000); *Hurley v Irish-American Gay, Lesbian and Bisexual Group of Boston*, 515 US 557 (1995).

[82] On another view, taking into account the reliance interests of homophobes is a little like providing reparation to slaveholders for freeing the slaves or for loss of white privilege to those who depended on segregation for a feeling of self-worth—the reliance interest is an interest not worth taking into account. N.B. the argument in favor of taking such claims seriously may have been stronger for slavery, which implicated property interests explicitly given constitutional protection.

[83] But see Kendall Thomas, *Beyond the Privacy Principle*, 92 Colum L Rev 1431 (1992) (suggesting that precisely the reliance gaybashers put in sodomy laws to license their private violence mandates striking down sodomy laws on constitutional grounds such as the Eighth Amendment). In *Lawrence*, Scalia has the *Bowers* ladder kicked out from under him. In *Romer*, he said *Bowers* provided the rational basis for Amendment 2. This reasoning seems to have doubled back on him as his brethren, perhaps moved by arguments like those Kendall Thomas made, may have realized that a decision that can be seen to license acts like Amendment 2 is constitutionally problematic.

[84] See, for example, *Religious Beliefs Underpin Opposition to Homosexuality*, Pew Research Center for the People and the Press (Nov 18, 2003), online at http://people- press.org/

The fact that the United States, unlike some other countries, does not seem full of "those who take their ideas of what is right and wrong from the law"[85] may be a double-edged sword for proponents of gay rights. On the one hand, it allows for some consensus on the lack of a serious reliance interest on the holding in *Bowers*. On the other, it makes it more likely that such convictions about the wrongness of "a homosexual lifestyle" as there now may be among the U.S. population will be resistant to change in the aftermath of *Lawrence*.

But how much worse off does *Lawrence* leave those who do not want openly gay or lesbian persons as teachers, tenants, etc.?

How Much State-Sponsored "Discrimination" Does the Lawrence Majority See It as Its "Function . . . to Deter"?

> The statutes [involved in *Bowers* and *Lawrence*] seek to control a personal relationship that, whether or not entitled to formal recognition in the law, is within the liberty of persons to choose without being punished as criminals.[86]

---

reports/display.php3?reportID=197 (last visited January 31, 2004). If this is so, a free-exercise claim may in most concrete circumstances offer more protection than *Bowers* would, although even it has already frequently been held insufficient. See, for example, *Hyman v Louisville*, 132 F Supp 2d 528 (WD Ky 2001) (rejecting claim of dentist to exemption from employment non-discrimination ordinance on grounds, inter alia, of his religious opposition to homosexuality); *Peterson v Hewlett-Packard* 2004 US App LEXIS 72 (9th Cir 2003) (upholding discharge and rejecting religious accommodation claim of employee fired for refusing to remove prominently posted Scripture verses condemning homosexuality from his work station).

[85] The phrase comes from British Home Secretary R. A. Butler's explanation of his Conservative "government's failure to act on the Wolfenden Committee's homosexuality recommendations." See Allan Horsfall, *Battling for Wolfenden in Radical Records: Thirty Years of Lesbian and Gay History* 17 (Bob Cant and Susan Hemmings, eds) (1988).

[86] *Lawrence*, 123 S Ct at 2478. The very next sentence is: "This, as a general rule, should counsel against attempts by the State, or a court, to define the meaning of the relationship or to set its boundaries absent injury to a person or abuse of an institution the law protects." It is quite unclear whether "This" is meant to refer to the preceding sentence or some larger portion of the preceding paragraph or even of the entirety of the opinion to this point. Although the sentence fits very nicely into my rubric of ambiguous referents, I shall not analyze it in depth here, but rather refer the reader to Richard Mohr's analysis of its "antecedentless 'This' which . . . points back to the fog of two evasions" including "a vacuous qualifier" in Mohr, *The Shag-a-delic Supreme Court* (cited in note 2). To experience similar doubts about referents, consider the majority's assertion that "the following considerations counsel against adopting the definitive conclusions upon which *Bowers* placed such reliance." *Lawrence*, 123 S Ct at 2478. How many of the remaining pages of the opinion embody the "following considerations"?

I will have more to say about entitlement to "formal recognition" later, but, for the moment, notice how wide a terrain there is between mandating recognition of a relationship and precluding the possibility of criminal punishment for it. Is this "a personal relationship that . . . is within the liberty of persons to choose without" (*a*) losing jobs as a result, at least when their employer is the state, or (*b*) losing custody of their children as a result, even when the competitor for custody has chosen a relationship "entitled to formal recognition in the law"?[87] The majority refuses to commit itself on that score. And it's not for want of having been prompted. The Petitioner's brief, in an effort to demonstrate that "the mere power of state legislatures to pass [facially nondiscriminatory sodomy laws] has been used to justify myriad forms of discrimination against gay and lesbian Americans as presumptive criminals," includes among its illustrative examples the following: "[S]odomy laws are often invoked to deny or restrict gay parents' custody of or visitation with their own children, to deny public employment to gay people, . . . to block protection of gay citizens under hate-crimes legislation." Additionally, the Texas law has been used "as a basis for preventing lesbians and gay men from serving as foster parents," and "to block the adoption of civil rights ordinances that would prohibit sexual orientation discrimination in employment and other core aspects of civil society."[88] The brief cites the state of Texas's own stipulation, in an earlier challenge to Sec. 21.06, that the law "brands lesbians and gay men as criminals and thereby legally sanctions discrimination against them in a variety of ways unrelated to the criminal law," including "in the context of employment, family issues, and housing."[89]

---

[87] See, for example, *J.B.F. v J.M.F.*, 730 S2d 1190, 1194 (Ala 1998) ("This is . . . not a custody case based solely on the mother's sexual conduct. . . . Rather, it is a custody case based on two distinct changes in the circumstances of the parties: (1) the change in the father's life, from single parenthood to marriage and the creation of a two-parent heterosexual home environment, and (2) the change in the mother's homosexual relationship, from a discreet affair to the creation of an openly homosexual home environment."). J.B.F., the mother who not only lost custody but also was prohibited from seeing her child in the presence of her partner, see *J.B.F. v J.M.F.*, 730 S2d 1197 (Ala App 1998), participated in a post-*Lawrence* challenge to the Alabama sodomy laws which was dismissed for lack of standing. See *Doe v Pryor*, 344 F3d 1282 (11th Cir 2003).

[88] Brief of Petitioner, *Lawrence v Texas*, 2002 US Briefs 102, *42–44 (filed Jan 16, 2003) (available online at LEXIS). Many of Petitioner's Amici raise similar points.

[89] Petitioner's brief at 43, citing *Texas v Morales*, 826 SW2d 201, 202, 203 (Tex App 1992).

O'Connor's concurrence uses some of this language from the Petitioner's brief almost verbatim, citing Texas's stipulation in *Morales* for the proposition that "the law 'legally sanctions discrimination against [homosexuals] in a variety of ways unrelated to the criminal law,' including in the areas of 'employment, family issues, and housing.'"[90] The majority, by contrast, cites *Morales* only for the proposition that the statute is rarely if ever enforced.[91] While it acknowledges that, "[w]hen homosexual conduct is made criminal by the law of the State, that declaration in and of itself is an invitation to subject homosexual persons to discrimination both in the public and in the private spheres,[92]" the majority opinion really discusses only two categories[93] of concrete collateral consequences from the Homosexual Conduct Law: first, the effects internal to the "personal relationship[s]"[94] of gays and lesbians, and second, those resulting from actual prosecution.

As to the former, the Court says that the "statutes [involved in *Bowers* and *Lawrence*] purport to do no more than prohibit a particular sexual act. Their penalties and purposes, though, have more far-reaching consequences, touching on the most private human conduct, sexual behavior, and in the most private of places, the home. The statutes do seek to control a personal relationship. . . ."[95] From a gay rights standpoint, the good news here is that, unlike the *Bowers* majority, the *Lawrence* majority is willing to connect the defendants' sex with a personal relationship and to weigh as a serious negative consequence the state's attempt to use the criminal law "to control [that] relationship."[96] But, the possible bad news

[90] See *Lawrence*, 123 S Ct at 2486 (O'Connor concurring) (citing *Morales*).

[91] See *Lawrence*, 123 S Ct at 2481.

[92] Id at 2482.

[93] Unless you count the citation in the historical section to the Model Penal Code commentary to the effect that such statutes "invited the danger of blackmail" from arbitrary enforcement. Id at 2480.

[94] Id at 2478, 2485.

[95] Id at 2478. The final sentence of this quote continues as quoted in text immediately above to speak about the relationship being "within the liberty of persons to choose without being punished as criminals."

[96] Compare Richard A. Posner, *Sex and Reason* at 349 (Harvard, 1992) ("Consensual sex in whatever form is . . . a method of cementing a relationship. . . . But the Supreme Court has made clear that it shares the dominant American preference for heterosexual relationships. . . . The Court does not want to facilitate the cementing of homosexual relationships, so it cannot be expected to view with sympathy the claim that anal intercourse is more important to homosexual relationships than to heterosexual ones because male homosexuals cannot have vaginal intercourse with each other.").

is that an emphasis on the connection of the relationship to the sex and the sex to the home does not in itself let gay people out of the closet: However much it may protect them from criminal prosecution[97] if they "choose to enter upon this relationship in the confines of their homes and their own private lives," these might be strict confines indeed. As suggested above and explored in further detail below, the "granting of marriage rights" may not be the only thing that "is not private enough to bring . . . within *Lawrence*'s purview."[98]

As to the latter, the majority says that, although but a Class C misdemeanor, the conduct:

> remains a criminal offense with all that imports for the dignity of the person *charged*. The petitioners will bear on their record the history of their criminal *convictions*. . . . We are advised that if Texas *convicted* a person for private, consensual homosexual conduct under the statute here in question the *convicted* person would come within the registration laws of at least four States were he or she to be subject to their jurisdiction. . . . This underscores the consequential nature of the *punishment* and the state-sponsored condemnation attendant to the criminal prohibition. Furthermore, the Texas criminal *conviction* carries with it the other collateral consequences always following a *conviction*, such as notations on job application forms, to mention but one example.[99]

This is the sum total of what the majority has to say about collateral consequences for gays and lesbians from the Homosexual Conduct Law, apart from occasional mention of stigmatic or dignitary harms such as the State's "demean[ing] their existence [and] control[ling] their destiny by making their private conduct a crime" or the problem that the statute's "stigma might remain even if it were not enforceable as drawn for equal protection reasons."[100] Nothing but a list of harms flowing from actual conviction, although the majority had spent the preceding historical section establishing at length (1) that the Texas

---

[97] In context, to "acknowledge that adults may choose to enter upon this relationship" and still "retain their dignity as free persons" appears to be roughly equivalent to the immediately preceding formulation of the relationship as "being within the liberty of persons to choose without being punished as criminals." That is to say, it appears to refer simply to a prohibition on criminal prosecutions. See below for discussion of the "dignity" of those implicated in the criminal justice system.

[98] Laurence Tribe, *The "Fundamental Right,"* Harv L Rev (forthcoming 2004).

[99] See *Lawrence*, 123 S Ct at 2482 (emphasis added).

[100] Id at 2484.

statute had rarely if ever been enforced before Lawrence and Garner's arrest; (2) that similar statutes in other jurisdictions, both in the present day and historically, were also rarely if ever enforced "against consenting adults in private"[101] (3) that this widespread "pattern of nonenforcement with respect to consenting adults acting in private" may well have been intentional.[102]

NOT "CRIMINALS": THE FRAMING EFFECT OF THE COURT'S CRIMINAL DOCKET

I can think of several reasons for the majority's avoidance of any mention of the many serious collateral consequences of criminalization raised in Petitioners' brief, reasons for the majority's focus on criminal law consequences of actual conviction to the exclusion of almost all other consequences: First, the majority may be focused on deciding precisely the case before it, which did, after all, involve an actual conviction, rare though such an event might be, and did, therefore, subject Petitioners to the consequences that follow from conviction.[103] They may simply have seen it as unnecessary to say more about other collateral consequences.

A second reason Kennedy and those who join him focus on the potential criminal law consequences of the Homosexual Conduct Law might be their participation in recent Supreme Court cases spelling out exactly what can happen to those arrested and convicted of crime, especially sex crime. Possibly the ability of the majority in general and Kennedy in particular to call readily to mind all the potentially awful things the Court has recently said we can do to sex offenders in particular and criminals in general has a framing effect on the *Lawrence* case.[104] Lawrence and Garner

---

[101] Id at 2479.

[102] Id at 2481.

[103] For a similar conclusion, see, for example, Nan Hunter, *Life After Lawrence: Notes on the Decision* (unpublished manuscript on file with the author) ("The Court . . . is also committed (in this field among many others) to deciding only what it must in each case, and foreclosing the fewest possible options for future decisions. This approach will give lower future federal courts great range in calibrating the extent to which the state can, in myriad ways short of criminal prohibition, prefer or discourage forms of sexual orientation").

[104] To the extent this is so, the *Lawrence* majority shares the concerns that led Justice Powell almost to be the fifth vote for Hardwick and, in the end, to write a concurrence suggesting that the Eighth Amendment prohibition on cruel and unusual punishment might foreclose "a prison sentence for such conduct—certainly a sentence of long duration." *Bowers*, 478 US at 197 (Powell concurring).

are not the sort of people the majority envisions being forced to register as sex offenders; being kept in a cell overnight, as Lawrence and Garner in fact were; or being subject to long sentences à la three strikes, to indefinite civil commitment as a repeat offender à la *Kansas v Hendricks* and its progeny, or to coercive attempts at rehabilitation à la the Kansas Sexual Abuse Treatment Program (SATP).[105]

As the author of the majority opinion in one of the Court's two recent Megan's law cases,[106] both of which upheld the sex offender registries, Kennedy had occasion to become quite familiar with what Lawrence and Garner might face were they to be subject to registration. He is willing to be more severe than a majority of his colleagues on sex offenses that, unlike those of Lawrence and Garner, "involv[e] minors[,] . . . persons who might be injured or co-erced or who are situated in relationships where consent might not easily be refused."[107] For example, he dissented in *Stogner*[108] from the majority's decision that the statute of limitations for acts of child sex abuse could not be resurrected legislatively once it had expired. And he wrote the majority in *McKune v Lile*,[109] upholding, against a self-incrimination challenge, the requirement of a sex of-fender rehabilitation program that participants, who were afforded prison privileges if they took part, disclose all the sexual offenses they have ever committed, even those for which they could still be prosecuted. He has shown concern, however, that civil con-finement under programs like Kansas's Sexually Violent Predator Act not use categories that are too imprecise or become a mecha-nism for imposing punishment.[110]

Kennedy and Souter were in the majority, but the rest of those voting for petitioner Lawrence were in the dissent, in *Atwater v*

---

[105] See *McKune v Lile*, 536 US 24 (2002).

[106] *Smith v Doe*, 538 US 84 (2003); the other was *Connecticut Dept of Public Safety v Doe*, 538 US 1 (2003).

[107] *Lawrence*, 123 S Ct at 2482. This coupling of the extension of protection to a newly respectable group with a more thoroughgoing willingness to fence out and treat harshly other groups still viewed as outcast is a common and much remarked on phenomenon. Compare, for example, *Plessy v Ferguson*, 163 US 537 (1896) (Harlan dissenting) (insisting that blacks cannot be made a separate caste while contrasting them with "the Chinese race . . . a race so different from our own that we do not permit those belonging to it to become citizens").

[108] *Stogner v California*, 123 S Ct 2446 (2003).

[109] 536 US 24 (2002).

[110] See *Kansas v Hendricks*, 521 US 346 (1997) (Kennedy concurring).

Lago Vista,[111] which authorized the police to lock up persons, who, like Lawrence and Garner, were arrested for crimes or misdemeanors whose maximum penalty is a small fine, not a jail sentence. Lawrence and Garner were in fact forced to spend the night in jail, before pleading guilty and paying a $200 fine,[112] the maximum penalty for the offense. Moreover, Kennedy was author of the majority opinion in a case argued the same day as *Lawrence*, in which the Court upheld the authority of a prison to limit the categories and numbers of those people who could visit a prisoner;[113] given the question the majority explicitly left open about the "formal recognition" a homosexual relationship may be entitled to, this case may have cast its shadow in reminding him of the potential disparate impact of prison on someone convicted of homosexual acts whose partner would not fit within the category of those authorized to visit. Finally, as discussed in greater detail below, Kennedy has recently called publicly for a criminal justice system that does not "degrade and demean" those caught up in it;[114] as author of the majority opinion in *Miller-El v Cockrell*,[115] Kennedy may have developed a particularly cautious attitude toward the state of Texas's criminal justice system.

In their particular emphasis on the injustice of bringing the mechanisms of the criminal law to bear on people like Lawrence and Garner, the Justices in the *Lawrence* majority may in a sense be the heirs of Justice Powell, who appears to have wrestled to find a way to "remove the fundamental unfairness of the statute"[116] in *Bowers* and who ultimately raised Eighth Amendment concerns in his concurrence. In what, if any, other respects could some of the Justices who voted for Lawrence be the heirs of Powell, who famously vacillated while the case was sub judice and ultimately repudiated his vote against Hardwick?

---

[111] 532 US 318 (2001).

[112] *Lawrence*, 123 S Ct at 2476.

[113] See *Overton v Bazzetta*, 539 US 126 (2003).

[114] See discussion below of Kennedy's endorsement of James Q. Whitman's *Harsh Justice*.

[115] 537 US 322 (2003) (remanding for post-conviction review of death row inmate's previously rejected *Batson* claim of race discrimination in jury selection).

[116] Unsigned, undated memo to Justice Powell in *Bowers* file, Powell archive, Washington & Lee.

EVIDENCE OF THE JUSTICES' OWN "EMERGING AWARENESS"

It may be wise not to forget a few other closely related decisions in which members of the *Lawrence* majority participated before joining the Court. Remember that in 1987 Souter signed on to the per curiam Opinion of the Justices, a New Hampshire Supreme Court advisory opinion on a then proposed legislative enactment "prohibiting homosexuals from adopting, being foster parents, or running a day care center." A majority of the Justices, including Souter, then held that, although it would violate the state constitution as applied to running a day-care center, the proposed categorical ban on homosexuals would be constitutional as applied to adoptive and foster parents, who would have more contact with the children in their charge.[117] With the majority of his New Hampshire Supreme Court colleagues, Souter appears to have accepted the legislature's assertion, in partial response to a request by the Justices for a "statement of factual findings about the nexus between homosexuality . . . and the unfitness of homosexuals as declared by the bill," that "[t]hese Statutory enactments . . . do not involve intrusion into the private lives of consenting adults, but rather further the public and governmental interest in providing for the health, safety, and proper training for children. . . ."[118] Souter did not join the dissenting opinion of Batchelder, who would have struck down the whole bill and instead required indi-

---

[117] *In Re Opinion of the Justices*, 530 A2d 21, 22 (NH 1987). The legislature proposed to define a "homosexual" as one who "performs or submits to any sexual act involving the sex organs of one person and the mouth or anus of another person of the same gender" (which is a subset of the conduct covered by the Texas law). The Justices insisted that the definition be revised so as to be limited to those who had recently, "voluntarily and knowingly" participated in such acts. Id at 24.

[118] Id at 22. The legislature went on to cite "the provision of a healthy environment and a role model for our children" and "the added social and psychological complexities a homosexual lifestyle could produce" as reason to "exclude homosexuals from participating in governmentally sanctioned programs of adoption, foster and day care." The Justices approved of these purposes as rationally related to the proposed categorical ban except with respect to day-care center operators, who, it found, would, as compared to adoptive or foster parents, have much less influence over, because less contact with, the children in their care. They relied in part on *Bowers* to find "no right to privacy or association infringed by the bill." Notwithstanding the Justices' Opinion as to the constitutionality of a New Hampshire ban, at present, gays and lesbians are permitted to adopt in that state. Florida is the only state with a categorical ban, which was again upheld by the Eleventh Circuit in the aftermath of *Lawrence*. See *Lofton*, 2004 US App LEXIS 1383.

vidualized assessment of an applicant's fitness, regardless of sexual orientation. (He almost certainly would not have been nominated to his present position if he had joined the dissent.)

And what about Justice Kennedy, author of the *Lawrence* majority? As a circuit judge, he participated in several cases on point, none of which bodes very well and one of which, were it to be indicative of anything like his current thinking would bode very badly indeed for a broader application of *Lawrence* beyond decriminalization of private consensual homosexual sex acts to protection of activities gay men and lesbians might wish to undertake beyond the confines of their apartment/closet. The most troubling case is among the earliest, and one in which Kennedy himself did not write, but rather joined the opinion written by District Judge W. J. Jameson, sitting as circuit judge by designation. That case, *Singer v U.S. Civil Service Commission*, was one of several to come before Kennedy involving challenges to the exclusion of gay persons from government opportunities.[119] The plaintiff, John Singer, had been fired from his job at the EEOC for "flaunting his homosexual way of life" by, for example, applying for a marriage license with another man,[120] speaking to the press about this attempt to be legally married, and embracing and kissing another man on the premises of his former employer. The Ninth Circuit panel on which Kennedy served upheld this discharge, saying:

> [A]ppellant's employment was not terminated because of his status as a homosexual or because of any private acts of sexual preference. . . . [T]he discharge was the result of the appellant's

---

[119] A month before *Singer* came down, Kennedy had participated in the per curiam opinion in *Society for Individual Rights v Hampton*, 528 F2d 905 (9th Cir 1975), involving a challenge to a policy of categorical exclusion of "all active homosexuals as unsuitable for government employment." By the time this case reached the Ninth Circuit, the Civil Service Commission, having lost in the District Court and in a similar case, *Norton v Macy*, 417 F2d 1161 (DC Cir 1969), had amended its policy accordingly to require, as those cases demanded, "a specific reason why the employee's homosexual activity made him unfit for the job in question." Hampton, 528 F2d at 906. The Ninth Circuit, asked only to rule on the availability of relief beyond an injunction, held that the district court's denial of such relief was proper given that the "court's rationale would invalidate discharge for homosexual activity only where such activity had no rational bearing on the individual's job performance [and t]hus the issue of liability would have to be separately litigated for each . . . class member." Id.

[120] Singer's litigation of Washington State's refusal to grant him and Paul Barwick a marriage license led to one of the earliest reported opinions concerning same-sex marriage, *Singer v Hara*, 522 P2d 1187 (1974) (rejecting claim that state ERA prevented denial of marriage license to a same-sex couple).

"openly and publicly flaunting his homosexual way of life and indicating further continuance of such activities," while identifying himself as a member of a federal agency. The Commission found that these activities were such that "general public knowledge thereof reflects discredit upon the Federal Government as his employer, impeding the efficiency of the service, by lessening public confidence in the fitness of the Government to conduct the public business. . . ." It is apparent from their statements that the Commission . . . officials appreciated the requirement of *Norton v. Macy* . . . that the discharge of a homosexual must be justified by a finding that his conduct affected the efficiency of the Service. . . . *Norton v. Macy* recognized that notorious conduct and open flaunting and careless display of unorthodox sexual conduct in public might be relevant to the efficiency of the service. . . . The Commission set forth in detail the specified conduct on which it relied in determining the appellant's unsuitability for continued employment. . . . We are able to discern "a rational basis" between the facts relied on and the conclusions drawn.[121]

When Singer petitioned for certiorari, then-Solicitor General Robert Bork supported the petition and, over the dissent of Burger, White, and Rehnquist, the Court did as Bork requested, vacating the Ninth Circuit ruling and remanding the case to the Civil Service Commission, whose policies on the employment of gays had liberalized since the date of Singer's discharge and who ultimately awarded him back pay.[122] Nevertheless, three central issues raised by John Singer's encounters with the legal system, all dismissed by the Ninth Circuit panel including Kennedy under the rubric of "open flaunting," remain somewhat open questions even in the aftermath of *Lawrence* nearly thirty years later: the question of legal marriage for same-sex couples,[123] the legal treatment of public displays of same-sex sexual interest and affection,[124] and the extent to which open homosexual conduct can be held against an individual by a governmental decision maker.[125]

---

[121] *Singer v United States Civil Service Commission*, 530 F2d 247, 255 (9th Cir 1976).

[122] For further discussion of Singer's case, including evidence of his flaunting not in the Supreme Court record, such as his adoption of the Yiddish name "Faygele" (slang for homosexual) and his "cross-dressing at work to further his understanding of sexism," and also evidence of his co-workers' unanimous support of the "educational and positive" experience of working with him, see Murdoch and Price, *Courting Justice* at 189–93 (cited in note 11).

[123] See discussion below.

[124] See discussion of solicitation laws below.

[125] See discussion below.

As Judge of the Court of Appeals, Kennedy authored other opinions ruling adversely to a gay plaintiff in cases implicating gay rights. The one that received the most attention during his nomination and confirmation process was a military discharge case, *Beller v Middendorf*,[126] in which Kennedy, although ruling against the gay and lesbian sailors, spoke sufficiently respectfully of them to raise the hopes of gay rights advocates and the fears of their opponents. His suggestion that some anti-gay discrimination might be unconstitutional and his favorable citation to the work of Laurence Tribe troubled senators like Jesse Helms and may have led to a delay in his nomination.[127] But, when Australian Anthony Corbett Sullivan sought to avoid deportation and remain in the United States with the male partner he had tried legally to marry, Kennedy rejected Sullivan's plea that for him to be deported "would result in 'extreme hardship' to himself and to his United States citizen male 'spouse' or 'life partner'. . . who would probably not qualify as an immigrant under Australian immigration laws."[128] Because "[d]eportation rarely occurs without personal distress and emotional hurt" and courts had previously upheld deportations that would separate family members, Kennedy held that the BIA was within its discretion in not finding Sullivan's case one of "extreme hardship."[129] Dissenting Judge Pregerson would have found extreme hardship, based on the cumulative burden of Sullivan's separation from "the person with whom he has lived and shared a close relationship for the past twelve years" and his forced return to Australia where, as a "highly publicized homosexual," he might suffer "employment difficulties and ostracism by his family and former friends."[130]

Of course, these decisions by Kennedy and Souter were issued a long time ago, and the Justices in the majority could well have included themselves personally when they described "an emerging awareness that liberty gives substantial protection to adult persons in deciding how to conduct their private lives in matters pertaining to sex."[131] I also would not underestimate the effect on the Justices

---

[126] 632 F2d 788 (9th Cir 1980), cert denied as *Beller v Lehman*, 452 US 905 (1981).

[127] See Murdoch and Price, *Courting Justice* at 377–79 (cited in note 11).

[128] *Sullivan v INS*, 772 F2d 609, 611 (1985).

[129] Id at 611.

[130] Id at 612.

[131] *Lawrence*, 123 S Ct at 2480. Compare *Boy Scouts*, 530 US at 699 n 30 (Stevens dissenting) (highlighting the evolution of Justice Blackmun's views on homosexuals from his

of having to deal with Colorado's Amendment 2, which seriously backfired on its proponents.[132] In atmospheric terms, what being confronted with Amendment 2 may have done for the Court in general and Justice Kennedy in particular is to cause them to think of gay rights in terms of a bashed gay person in Colorado potentially bleeding to death in the streets in front of a hospital that would not admit him and left with potentially no state recourse against the bigots who bashed him, the police who declined to stop them, and the hospital prepared to let him die.[133] This is a much better image for the future of litigation for the rights of gays, lesbians, and bisexuals than the image of Michael Hardwick in his bedroom with his one-night-stand's penis in his mouth.[134] Remember (1) how effective an image the little black girl at the schoolhouse door was for racial civil rights and (2) how effective an image the members of the Palm Beach County Board holding ballots up to the light to look for detached chads was in creating the image of standardless discretion producing at best chaos and at worst an election stolen by Democratic partisans in *Bush v Gore*.[135] From

joining in Rehnquist's *Ratchford* opinion comparing a gay student group to a group of measles sufferers spreading contagion and resisting quarantine to his "classic opinion in *Bowers*").

[132] As Scalia's dissent insisting that *Bowers* and *Romer* could not both stand backfired on Scalia. As I and others have noted, the deprivations Amendment 2 by its plain terms would have visited on gays, lesbians, and bisexuals in Colorado could not constitutionally have been visited on any group, even a group of felons. The *Romer* decision therefore did not logically entail overruling *Bowers*. But, with the Scalia dissent in *Romer* being, in effect, one more brief for Petitioner John Geddes Lawrence, the Justices in the majority in *Romer* were given, in the connection that dissent drew between *Bowers* and Amendment 2, a further reason to call the legitimacy of *Bowers* into question.

[133] I take this image fairly directly from the oral argument in *Romer* at which the questioning Justices, by means of examples much like this, struggled to understand the scope and implications of Amendment 2's sweeping language for the lives of gays, lesbians, and bisexuals in Colorado. See, for example, Transcript, *Romer v Evans*, 1995 US Trans LEXIS 120, *23–24 (Oct 10, 1995).

[134] I believe this statement to be true notwithstanding that I also believe that (1) sexual minorities should not have to be cast as abject victims in order to gain the Court's solicitude, and (2) former *Advocate* publisher David Goodstein had a point when he said, "Never forget one thing: What this movement is about is fucking." Dudley Clendinnen and Adam Nagourney, *Out for Good: The Struggle to Build a Gay Rights Movement in America* 466 (Simon & Schuster, 1999).

[135] See Mary Anne Case, *Are Plain Hamburgers Now Unconstitutional? The Equal Protection Holding of Bush v Gore as a Chapter in the History of Ideas About Law*, 70 U Chi L Rev 55 (2003) ("If I were to identify a single decisive moment in the oral argument of *Bush v. Gore*, it would be the moment when Justice Kennedy, putative author of the per curiam opinion, asked David Boies 'from the standpoint of equal protection clause, could each county give their own interpretation to what intent means, so long as they are in good faith and with some reasonable basis finding intent? . . . Could that vary from county to

what can be gauged from his opinions and public statements, Justice Kennedy more than most Justices is often motivated by a visceral sense of what is unjust. So, in a less rhetorically charged and fiery way, is the other likely swing voter on gay rights issues who also swung to Lawrence, Justice O'Connor. So one way for gays and lesbians to keep winning may be for them to be able vividly to present themselves as victims of injustice, not, in the future, necessarily as the abject outlaws Amendment 2 would have made them, but with the "dignity" the Court vouchsafed them in *Lawrence*.

That Kennedy has become more receptive to claims by gay people is shown by comparing the way in which he talks about them and the government's role in their lives in *Beller* and in *Lawrence*. In *Beller*, Kennedy dismissed the plaintiffs' claims that they suffered "the stigma of 'unfitness' for retention" in military service, saying, "[t]he real stigma imposed by the Navy's action . . . is the charge of homosexuality, not the fact of discharge. . . ."[136] It appears Kennedy has in the interim come to understand that the law is implicated in creating stigma, rather than stigma being just a social fact unrelated to the law. He has come to realize that the law does not merely embody or rely on, it creates and reinforces, social norms. It is this breakthrough that enables the conclusions that *Bowers*'s "continuance as precedent demeans the lives of homosexual persons"; "[t]he stigma th[e Homosexual Conduct] criminal statute imposes, moreover, is not trivial"; and the statute's "stigma might remain even if it were not enforceable as drawn for equal protection reasons."[137]

"IF THIS LAW IS STRUCK DOWN . . . WOULD [THAT] ALSO MEAN THAT A STATE COULD NOT PREFER HETEROSEXUALS. . . ?"[138]

The *Lawrence* majority's failure to mention collateral consequences of the criminal sodomy laws for those not arrested or con-

---

county?' . . . Justice Kennedy . . . sounded shocked [by David Boies's answer that it could]. . . . 'But here you have something objective,' Kennedy insisted. 'You are not just reading a person's mind. You are looking at a piece of paper, . . . this is susceptible of a uniform standard and yet you say it can vary from table to table within the same county.'").

[136] *Beller*, 632 F2d at 806. Kennedy was here trying to apply the theory articulated in Laurence Tribe, *Structural Due Process*, 10 Harv CR-CL L Rev 269, 282–83 n 42 (1975).

[137] *Lawrence*, 123 S Ct at 2482.

[138] See Transcript, *Lawrence v Texas*, 2003 US Trans LEXIS 30, *19.

victed is a bit like the *Romer* majority's failing to mention *Bowers*—in each case it is the elephant in the room. But the Court may want to wait until later to edge it out of the room more quietly and gradually rather than wrestle with it now and cause an unnecessary amount of eventually avoidable breakage as they try to force it too abruptly to the door. Therefore, just because the majority says nothing now doesn't mean they won't take action when the time comes.[139] On the other hand, according to Powell's biographer, John Jeffries, what may in the end have stopped Powell from being the fifth vote for Hardwick was

> Powell['s] wis[h] above all else, to avoid a broad declaration of a privacy right that would have consequences outside the field of criminal prosecution. . . . Powell feared that accepting Tribe's argument against criminal punishment for homosexual sodomy would entangle the Court in a continuing campaign to validate the gay "lifestyle" in a variety of other contexts. After all, if homosexuals had a right to engage in sex, would they not also have the right to object to any form of regulation or restriction disadvantaging them for having done so? Would gays have a right to serve in the military or the intelligence agencies? Would they have a right to teach in public schools or work in day care centers? Would there be a constitutional requirement that the laws allow homosexual adoption or same-sex marriage? This was not a revolution Powell was ready to lead. The eventualities down the road appalled him, but he could not see how they could be avoided if the Court were to declare a new fundamental right to engage in homosexual sodomy. . . .[140]

---

[139] There may be a slight disanalogy in that in *Romer* neither side had raised *Bowers*—the state had not relied on it and the respondents disclaimed a need to call it into question in order to win. But here, although petitioner did put collateral consequences in issue, it was by no mean necessary to reach them in order to decide the case. The absence of any discussion of such collateral consequences is disturbing only on a rhetorical, not a logical or doctrinal, level. (Similarly, I continue to believe, the absence of any mention of *Bowers* by the *Romer* majority may have been rhetorically, but was not at all doctrinally problematic.)

[140] John C. Jeffries, Jr., *Justice Lewis F. Powell, Jr.* 518 (Macmillan, 1994). If these were indeed Powell's concerns, there is a possibility Powell may have been influenced to worry about them by a memo written by his conservative Mormon clerk Mike Mosman arguing against Powell's own suggestion "that the Constitution might protect homosexual relationships that resemble marriage." Memo dated April 1, 1986, identified in Powell's hand as "Prepared for me by Mike after we had discussed this troublesome case," from Powell archives, *Bowers v Hardwick* file, Washington & Lee. Mosman warned that "once you conclude that homosexual and heterosexual 'marriages' are of equal Constitutional status, you would necessarily suggest that homosexuals have a right to adopt and raise children. Further, states would have great difficulty justifying other restrictions on homosexuality—such as no avowed homosexual public school teachers—since the Constitution would place homosexual and heterosexual relationships on a par with each other. These possibilities suggest that the 'marriage' idea has too many implications for other cases that you might want to

The more pessimistic reading of the difference in *Lawrence* between this (the collateral harms enumerated in Petitioners' brief) and that (the markedly different harms enumerated by the Court) is that the Court, like Powell, could still be "appalled [by] the eventualities down the road." Alternatively, one could note that although a majority is not willing yet to endorse Petitioners' broader claims, the good news is it may not be willing to foreclose them either. The ambiguity of the majority's silence leaves both doubt and possibilities.[141] That the Court would have been less able to avoid committing itself on this score is one reason why a due process holding is, unusually in this case, narrower and more limited than an equal protection holding and therefore possibly one reason why a majority of the Court opted against an equal protection rationale.[142]

---

decide differently." Id. Before this memo, most of the worries Powell articulated concerning the implications of a victory for Hardwick and the absence of a "limiting principle" concerned what I have characterized as the substantive due process parade of horribles, rather than implications sounding in equal protection. Both Powell's own notes worrying about the absence of a "limiting principle" and Mosman's earlier memo dated March 29, 1986, had repeatedly expressed concern that the result of the Court's ruling for Hardwick might be "unchecked sexual freedom, including prostitution because 'no limiting principle comes to mind.'" See Murdoch and Price, *Courting Justice* at 298 (observing that Powell's handwritten notes ask about a due process parade of horribles such as "Bigamy? Incest? Prostitution? Adultery?" and not an equal protection parade of horribles such as "Homosexual marriage? Homosexual teachers? Homosexual soldiers? Adoption by homosexuals?").

[141] For a similar conclusion, see Hunter, *Living with Lawrence*, Minn L Rev (forthcoming 2004) (noting that, given that the briefs had made much of the use of the sodomy laws to disadvantage gay people in family and employment law, "the omission of any reference to this body of case law in the majority opinion strongly suggests that all five Justices who joined the opinion were not ready to rule that homosexuality is irrelevant in all those contexts").

[142] Scholars and commentators have been saying for decades that a non-ideological doctrinalist playing connect the dots with *Griswold, Eisenstadt, Carey, Stanley v Georgia*, in short the whole line before *Bowers*, could only have concluded with a picture of something like a right to have private consensual sex—no other explanation makes good conventional doctrinal sense of the cases, especially when the rights at issue are taken at their most particular as Scalia ordinarily demands they be. See, for example, memo of law clerk Daniel Richman to Justice Thurgood Marshall concerning the *Bowers* case, quoted in Murdoch and Price, *Courting Justice* at 291 ("[T]his Court (though it would never phrase it this way) has essentially established a right to engage in recreational sex."). *Bowers* is the case that does not fit: leave it in place and there is no coherent conventional legal explanation for the lineup; remove it and you have a tidy, and what is more a pretty securely closed package. There's not much left further down on the slippery slope that isn't readily distinguishable; even Scalia's parade of horribles is pretty unimpressive. Not so with either an equal protection or desuetude holding—neither simply ties up loose ends, both open up a long list of not easily distinguishable next cases, with no logically decisive way of calling a halt to the parade. On the other hand, beyond the acts at issue in *Lawrence*, almost all activities potentially covered by a substantive due process holding in the *Griswold* line are either (a) already legal or (b) readily distinguishable because prohibited for reasons other than naked moral distaste.

In speaking of the *Romer* decision the year it came down, I said, "The opinion whose validity *Romer* calls most into question is not Justice White's in *Bowers v Hardwick*, but Judge Bork's in *Dronenberg v Zeck*."[143] That is to say, *Romer* called into question the premise articulated in that opinion that the mere fact of majoritarian disapproval of homosexuality is a sufficient warrant for legislation disadvantaging homosexuals.[144] Even now it seems to me that gays, lesbians, and bisexuals can more directly claim protections from adverse governmental consideration of their orientation in employment, family, and housing decisions by invoking *Romer*. Both the *Romer* majority and the O'Connor concurrence in *Lawrence* cite *Yick Wo*.[145] These days, we tend to look at that decision as a race discrimination decision. But the language of the opinion centers instead on the prohibition of any and all arbitrary discrimination. It just so happened that the arbitrariness of the discrimination became more visible when the Court focused on its racial impact. *Romer* revived an attention to arbitrariness that the O'Connor concurrence picks up.

For this reason, I argued long before the decision came down that the many scholars who predicted or endorsed an equal protection–based holding as a "narrower" ground of decision were too reflexively applying generally promising intuitions about constitutional law to this case without pausing to note that, due in part to the doctrinal peculiarities of the *Griswold* line, *Lawrence* may be an exception to the usual rules. By comparison, the potentially staggering and difficult to cabin breadth of an equal protection holding might have frightened the Justices in the majority.

For a similar conclusion, see Post, 117 Harv L Rev at 101 (cited in note 4) (arguing that an advantage of a due process over an equal protection holding is that it "enable[s] the Court to enter into the national debate about the status of homosexuality in a manner that stresses the positive value of nondiscrimination while preserving the Court's options in deciding how far it is willing to go in striking down legislation adversely affecting homosexuals.").

[143] Mary Anne Case, *Outlaws and Inlaws*, address delivered at the symposium, Gay Rights in Three Acts, NYU Law School (1996), transcript on file with the author, audiotape on file with the NYU J Law & Soc Change.

[144] See *Dronenburg v Zech*, 741 F2d 1388, 1397 (DC Cir 1984). Because Bork went on to find the military regulations at issue, which mandated discharge for homosexual conduct, had a rational basis beyond mere moral disapproval, the portion of the opinion concerning the presumptive validity of majoritarian choices is technically dicta. Compare *Dronenburg v Zech*, 746 F2d 1579, 1580 (DC Cir 1984) (dissent of Robinson, Wald, Mikva, and Edwards from denial of rehearing en banc) ("The panel's extravagant exegesis on the constitutional right to privacy was wholly unnecessary to decide the case before the court.").

[145] *Yick Wo v Hopkins*, 118 US 356 (1886), was a case in which a statute neutral on its face requiring anyone who wanted to operate a laundry within the geographic bounds of San Francisco to get approval from the authorities, a statute purportedly designed to prevent fire hazards, was enforced in such a way that virtually all people of Chinese descent who applied for licenses did not get them and virtually all Caucasians did.

Rehnquist's question of Lawrence's counsel, "If you prevail, if this law is struck down, do you think that would also mean that a State could not prefer heterosexuals to homosexuals to teach kindergarten?" is critical here.[146] Note the precise formulation of Rehnquist's question—the question is not can a State categorically ban homosexual teachers, but can it put a thumb on the scale, can it use sexual orientation as a tiebreaker, all other things being equal. The question is not one of categorical exclusion, as in the Opinion of the Justices of the New Hampshire Supreme Court or Society for Individual Rights.[147] It is probing the fault line between the Civil Service's pre-*Singer* per se policy and its post-*Singer* search for a nexus on a case-by-case basis. Under what circumstances, if any, can sexual orientation, in particular homosexual orientation, serve as a tiebreaker in governmental decision making?[148] Compare two bookending cases from the Court's docket that presented this question in the context of tiebreakers other than sexual orientation. *Reed v Reed* held that a State could not categorically prefer men to women as estate administrators for their deceased relatives.[149] But this past Term, the Court in the Michigan affir-

---

[146] *Lawrence v Texas*, 2003 US Trans LEXIS 30, *19. I am not suggesting Rehnquist himself was ever a gettable vote for Petitioner Lawrence (but see the discussion of the evolution of his vote on constitutional sex discrimination, below). After all, he's the one who compared a group of gay students to measles sufferers in need of quarantine in his dissent from the denial of certiorari in *Ratchford v Gay Lib*, 434 US 1080 (1978). But then, so long as we're talking about progress narratives and the evolution of members of the Court, recall that Blackmun, who wrote an eloquent dissent in *Bowers*, had joined the Rehnquist dissent in *Ratchford*.

[147] Although, with the prominent exception of miliary policies, categorical exclusions of gays, lesbians, and bisexuals from government opportunities is increasingly rare, and although they should be much harder to sustain than a nexus test, one of the few remaining such categorical exclusions, Florida's prohibition on gay or lesbian adoptive parents, was very recently upheld by the Eleventh Circuit in *Lofton*, 2004 US App LEXIS 1383, in an opinion that read *Lawrence* quite narrowly and dismissively.

[148] When the tiebreaker in question was race rather than orientation, the question was so charged that civil rights organizations paid off Sharon Taxman, the fired white teacher, rather than risk the Court answering, "It can never be used." See *Taxman v Piscatawy Township Board of Educ.*, 91 F3d 1547 (3d Cir 1996), cert granted, 521 US 1117 (1997), cert dismissed, 522 US 1010 (1997) (barring the use of race as a tiebreaker in determining which of two equally qualified teachers should be laid off). After certiorari was granted in this case, a settlement was reached, with the bulk of the funds used to pay Taxman coming from civil rights groups eager to avoid the creation of bad precedent. See, for example, Michael Booth, *Teacher's Libel Suit Rejected in Aftermath of Taxman Race Case*, Legal Intelligencer 4 (July 25, 2001).

[149] 404 US 71 (1971). This was not quite an all other things equal situation, the only thing being equal, virtually the only other factor the State statute took into consideration, was nearness of legal relationship to the decedent. This made it easier for the Court to call the preference for men arbitrary.

mative action cases said, in effect, that on occasion a state actor could even prefer blacks to whites, at least if it was an institution of higher learning seeking a critical mass of them.[150]

Ask the Rehnquist question about the other "groups" in the line of cases O'Connor relies on for her equal protection holding: Hippies? Unmarried heterosexuals? The mentally handicapped?[151] While categorical exclusion of such groups from teaching is unlikely to be permissible, it is equally unlikely that a court would hold that, for example, intelligence cannot be a tiebreaker in decisions about the hiring of teachers. Recent application of a nexus test when it comes to the sexual orientation of teachers has generally been favorable to gays, lesbians, and bisexuals.[152] On the other hand, anytime a per se standard is rejected, but a nexus would suffice, much virtually unreviewable discretion is given governmental decision makers.[153]

Would a majority of the Court chime in, even very softly, with the chant "2, 4, 6, 8, gay is just as good as straight," however ac-

---

[150] See *Grutter v Bollinger*, 123 S Ct 2325 (2003). I won't get into fears of the problem of quota preferences and affirmative action for gays lesbians and bisexuals that vexed the proponents of Amendment 2.

[151] How different is the attitude of swing Justices Kennedy and O'Connor to gays, lesbians, and bisexuals from their recently articulated views concerning Americans with disabilities, physical or mental? Compare *Board of Trustees of the University of Alabama v Garrett*, 531 US 356, 374 (2001) (Kennedy concurring, joined by O'Connor) ("Prejudice, we are beginning to understand, rises not from malice or hostile animus alone. It may result as well from insensitivity caused by simple want of careful, rational reflection or from some instinctive mechanism to guard against people who appear to be different in some respects from ourselves").

[152] See, for example, *Thompson v Wisconsin Dept of Public Instruction*, 541 NW2d 182 (Wis App 1995) (holding that, while criminal convictions for unconsented-to sexual touching of other men in cruising areas might be a sufficient basis for revocation of a pre-K-12 music teacher's license, "the superintendent must examine the offense and not the community reaction to it" and that relying on a role-model standard reflecting community attitudes to establish the required nexus between the conduct and the educational process was erroneous).

[153] This is particularly likely to be true in family law matters involving children, where the combination of an all-things-considered best-interests-of-the-child test and a dearth of reported opinions in comparison to the large number of cases decided leads to a lack of clarity as to the state of the applied law generally and as to the extent, in any given case, of a decision maker's reliance on any given factor. Compare the progress through the Virginia court system of the *Bottoms* case, in which the applicable standard was more demanding than best interests, but in which, despite insisting that lesbianism was not per se unfitness in a parent, the trial and state supreme court each found unfitness from different bits of evidence in the record, such as participation in oral sex and non-marital cohabitation for the trial court and heterosexual promiscuity and occasional careless parenting for the Supreme Court.

cepting most of the Justices now are of openly gay clerks and Court personnel? "3, 5, 7, 9, being gay is mighty fine," perhaps, but even this is not quite the same as moving all the way from endorsing the categorical exclusion of gay people from certain governmental opportunities[154] to imposing a categorical prohibition on treating sexual orientation as a relevant factor in any governmental decision. Although, unlike the majority, Justice O'Connor is willing explicitly to consider the collateral effects of Sec. 21 in areas unrelated to the criminal law, such as "employment, family issues, and housing," she does not specify what it would mean "for homosexuals to be treated in the same manner as everyone else." Moral disapproval, even in the absence of a criminal law backing up this disapproval, still plays a major role in many employment and family decisions.[155] Especially in Texas, where adultery and fornication (1) are not crimes, (2) are still subject to moral disapproval, according to Texas's counsel in *Lawrence*,[156] and (3) have fairly recently been used to deny public employment opportunities,[157] would treating homosexuals "like everyone else" mean that

---

[154] As the Supreme Court seemed willing to do in early immigration cases, see *Boutilier v INS*, 387 US 118 (1967), and as the Justices of the New Hampshire Supreme Court did in the 1987 *Opinion of the Justices* and as the Eleventh Circuit most recently did with respect to adoption, in *Lofton*, 2004 US App LEXIS 1383, discussed above.

[155] I am reminded of my first year in law school, with a classmate from the People's Republic of China. Repeatedly, our criminal law professor would ask this Chinese fellow student, "Is this a crime in China?" Repeatedly, she would answer, "No, you would not be criminally punished, but you would be morally condemned." Her tone left me with the distinct feeling criminal punishment could sometimes be the less harsh alternative.

[156] See *Lawrence v Texas*, 2003 US Trans LEXIS 30, *35 ("Q: Does Texas prohibit sexual intercourse between unmarried heterosexuals? Mr. Rosenthal: Well, it used to, it doesn't now, unless the sexual intimacy is in public. . . . Q: No, say, in a private situation like this. . . . Mr. Rosenthal: It does not criminalize it, it does not condone it. Q: What about adultery? . . . Mr. Rosenthal: Again, adultery is not penalized in Texas, but it is certainly not condoned in Texas. [Laughter.]"). The adulterers in the cases cited by Scalia as relying on *Bowers* to endorse their condemnation, far more than same-sex couples seeking admission to marriage, can fairly be said to be engaged in "abuse of an institution the law protects." This may distinguish them from gay people in some future case in which a state seeks to exercise its moral disapproval by some means other than criminal law. As Texas's attorney essentially conceded at oral argument, it is not necessary to wish to criminalize in order to wish to express disapproval.

[157] See, for example, *Sherman v Henry*, 928 SW2d 464 (Tex 1996), cert denied, 519 US 1156 (1997) (allowing police department to deny promotion to patrolman because of sexual affair with another officer's wife); *Shawgo v Spradlin*, 701 F2d 470 (5th Cir 1983), cert denied as *Whisenhunt v Spradlin*, 464 US 965 (1983) (upholding disciplinary action against cohabiting male and female couple of police officers); *Johnson v San Jacinto Junior College*, 498 F Supp 555 (S D Tex 1980) (upholding demotion of college registrar for adulterous affair found to violate policy requiring of faculty "high standards of moral, ethical and professional conduct"); compare, for example, *Childers v Dallas Police Dept*, 513 F Supp 134

a gay public school teacher or police officer has protection from adverse employment consequences or not? There are a host of cases
nationwide in which public employers bring termination proceedings
on the basis of the off-duty non-homosexual sexual conduct of employees, much of it perfectly legal and even arguably constitutionally
protected.[158] Usually these employees are teachers, police officers, or
others for whom a "conduct unbecoming" standard and the respect
of the community are seen to be particularly relevant.[159]

One lesson to be drawn from the unsettled state of the law concerning the scope of permissible public employment consequences
of heterosexual as well as homosexual conduct is that the issue of
employment discrimination against gays, lesbians, and bisexuals
may be difficult to settle in isolation. As persons on both sides of

---

(N D Tex 1981) (upholding police department's refusal to hire openly gay man as property
custodian). *Sherman* in particular is cited in Scalia's *Lawrence* dissent as having relied "on
Bowers in rejecting a claimed constitutional right to commit adultery." *Lawrence*, 123 S Ct
at 2490 (Scalia dissenting). It is far from clear, however, that the effect of overruling *Bowers*
will be to call the results of any of these cases sufficiently into question as to in future give
categorical constitutional protection to public employees' consensual adult sexual activities.

[158] See, for example, *Wishart v McDonald*, 500 F2d 1110 (1st Cir 1974) (upholding dismissal of teacher for having "carried in public view on his property in the town where he
taught, in a lewd and suggestive manner, a dress mannequin that he had dressed, undressed
and caressed"); *Potter v Murray City*, 760 F2d 1065 (10th Cir 1985) (upholding against free
exercise claim discharge of police officer for practicing polygamy); *Cronin v Amesbury*, 895
F Supp 375 (D Mass 1995) (upholding discharge of police chief who had written a sexually
explicit letter in response to an advertisement in a heterosexual pornographic magazine);
Pettit v Board of Educ., 513 P2d 889 (Ca 1973) (upholding dismissal of teacher for participating with her husband in swinger's club group sex parties); *Cook v South Carolina Dept of
Highways*, 420 SE2d 847 (SC 1992) (upholding discharge of highway patrolman in small
rural town for adulterous affair); *Borges v McGuire*, 487 NYS2d 737 (App Div, 1st Dept
1985) (denying NYPD authority to fire female officer for alleged offenses ranging from
unauthorized moonlighting to "bringing discredit on the Department" all arising out of
officer's posing for nude photos published in "girlie magazines" simply because this conduct
had taken place before officer's appointment); *Krout v Findlay*, 1985 Ohio App LEXIS 8493
(upholding discharge of husband and wife police department employees for allowing magazine to publish photographs of them nude); John Romano, *Publicity, Not Morals Miscues,
Tripped Up These Coaches*, St Petersburg Times (May 5, 2003) (reporting on the termination
of University of Alabama football coach Mike Price for visiting a Florida strip club and
inviting three strippers back to his hotel room); but see, for example, *Major v Hampton*,
413 F Supp 66 (E D La 1976) (holding IRS could not discharge agent for renting a New
Orleans apartment to which he and other men brought women for sex because this was
not the sort of off-duty conduct that could "rationally be said to be likely to bring the IRS
into disrepute"); compare *Shahar v Bowers*, 114 F3d 1097 (11th Cir 1997) (en banc) (upholding Georgia Attorney General's withdrawal of job offer from lawyer for participating in
Jewish lesbian wedding ceremony).

[159] But see *Carroll v Harrison Township Board of Trustees*, 2001 Ohio App LEXIS 5600
(upholding termination of road worker whose duties had been snow removal and patching
after guilty plea to federal charge of receipt of internet pornography, including four photos
of minors engaged in sexually explicit conduct).

the issue of the legitimacy of discrimination in employment on grounds of homosexual orientation have long insisted, it is difficult categorically to distinguish between this sort of discrimination and other arguably moral tastes employers may seek to vindicate in their hiring decisions. Compare, for example, Scalia's observation in *Romer* that the AALS, which precluded law firm interviewers from discriminating on grounds of sexual orientation, allowed them to "refuse to offer a job because the applicant is a Republican, . . . an adulterer, . . . went to the wrong prep school or . . . country club, . . . eats snails, . . . is a womanizer, . . . wears real animal fur or hates the Chicago Cubs" with gay rights pioneer Franklin Kameny's asking in a petition for certiorari, after noting that "some people consider dancing, liquor and even drinking coffee and tea immoral," "Will they next year, term as immoral left-handedness, red-headedness, a liking for horsemeat steaks, or membership in either political party or none at all?"[160] One increasingly proposed global solution takes the form of statutory protection of employees in both the public and private sector against discharge for legal off-duty conduct. Although smokers' advocates have been most prominent in lobbying for such protections, the statutory protections have been mobilized to defend those discharged for sexual conduct as well.[161]

It is worth noting that, whatever my own doubts about the extent to which the majority, without explicitly saying so, has set its face against collateral consequences to gays and lesbians in realms outside the criminal law, such as employment, Scalia seems to believe that it has.[162] Recall that immediately after the above-quoted

---

[160] See *Romer*, 517 US at 652–53 (Scalia dissenting); *Kameny v Brucker*, Petition for Writ of Certiorari at 27 (filed Jan 27, 1961) (challenging dismissal of astronomer from federal civil service job for being a homosexual and for having failed fully to disclose the reason for his arrest in a San Francisco men's room).

[161] Colorado had such a statute in place at the time of the Amendment 2 controversy. See Colo Rev Stat § 24-34-402.5 (Supp 1995).

[162] Scalia overplayed his hand in *Romer*, with the arguments in his dissent about the implications of striking down Amendment 2 going from his mouth in *Romer* to the majority's ear in *Lawrence*. So may it be again with the implications he enumerates in his *Lawrence* dissent. Remember, Colorado voluntarily abolished its sodomy law before passing Amendment 2, and though this Amendment was struck down, the courts ultimately upheld the Cincinnati charter amendment, with its slight difference in wording that eliminated the most extreme outlawry aspects, aspects which were probably not even quite intended by Amendment 2's drafters. One double bind the Court did not impose is the double bind of condemnation, which Scalia endorsed in *Romer* by saying that the very absence of a sodomy law, rather than indicate a tolerance for gay sex, could authorize other means of condemnation, like Amendment 2, to fill the void.

sentences about the "[m]any Americans who don't want to deal with homosexuals" whom they view as immoral, Scalia says, "The Court views [this] as 'discrimination' which it is the function of our judgments to deter."[163]

Of "Certain Truths" and Possible Relationships

An intriguing if not studied ambiguity pervades the choice of words in the rest of the opinion. Consider two examples, of dozens I could mention did time and space permit. First, consider this from the peroration in the penultimate paragraph of the majority, immediately before the judgment:

> [T]hose who drew and ratified the Due Process Clause of the Fifth Amendment or the Fourteenth Amendment . . . knew times can blind us to certain truths and later generations can see that laws once thought necessary and proper in fact only serve to oppress. As the Constitution endures, persons in every generation can invoke its principles in their own search for greater freedom.[164]

Are the "certain truths" to which the majority claims "times can blind us" only "particular" truths or are they also "certain" in the sense of fixed and unwavering, "dependable, indisputable, inevitable, objectively unquestionable"?[165] Saying, in effect, we "once [were] blind but now [we] see"[166] suggests that these truths are eternal verities, not contingent, variable, or socially constructed. This is a progress narrative with a vengeance and, according to the majority, the progress is to ever "greater freedom."[167] It also

---

[163] *Lawrence*, 123 S Ct at 2497.

[164] Id at 2484.

[165] See "certain" in *Webster's Seventh New Collegiate Dictionary* 254.

[166] Cf. *Amazing Grace*.

[167] It is also a bit unclear whether the majority has in mind each generation as a whole seeking greater freedom than its predecessor generation or, alternatively, that the "persons in each generation" whose "own search for greater freedom" (i.e., "their own search . . .") are e.g. racial minorities, women and now gays, lesbians and bisexuals—persons whose groups, as Richard Rorty put it, were "not yet the name[s] of a way of being human, but at most the name[s] of disabilit[ies]." Richard Rorty, *Feminism and Pragmatism: The Tanner Lecture*, 30 Mich Q Rev 231, 234 (1991). In either event, the logical result should be a freedom that increases from generation to generation (unless, of course, it does not increase absolutely because the freedom of groups is seen to have aspects of a zero sum game: for example, as slaves get one kind of freedom slaveholders lose another, as women in general and wives in particular get one kind of freedom, men and husbands lose another).

suggests that it would probably be a mistake to think the majority sense of history is thoroughgoingly social constructionist because of its adoption of something like a Foucauldian history of homosexuality. Consider first that the majority seems to think there really are homosexuals; as noted above, the opinion is about them almost as much as *Bowers* was, only the valence has changed. Second, compare *Casey*'s language about *Lochner* resting on "fundamentally false factual assumptions about the capacity of a relatively unregulated market."[168] No similar "false factual assumptions" can here be claimed, only false opinions of value.[169]

Moreover, in the majority's analysis of history, the due process and equal protection strains of the opinion, which elsewhere are in such perfect harmony, sound in somewhat discordant counterpoint.[170] As noted above,[171] every time I try to plot the historical events mentioned by the majority on a time line, I come up with a zigzag of ups and downs. Are things getting better or worse for homosexuals, for example, over the course of the "past half century" whose "laws and traditions" the majority identifies as "of most relevance here"?[172] Well, some of both. According to the majority, the last half century brought "an emerging awareness that liberty gives substantial protection to adult persons in deciding how to conduct their private lives in matters pertaining to sex."[173] (Zig.) But it also it also brought Amendment 2 and "[i]t was not until the 1970s that any State singled out same-sex relations for criminal prosecution."[174] (Zag.) This disharmony is understandable

---

[168] *Casey*, 505 US at 861–62.

[169] In this regard, I think George Chauncey is quite correct to suggest that the historical evidence from himself and others the majority in *Lawrence* relied on performed somewhat the same role as the social science evidence cited by the Court in *Brown v Board*. See George Chauncey, *Lawrence v Texas: Sexual Identity/Politics in the Twentieth Century*, University of Chicago Gender Studies Faculty Distinguished Lecture (Nov 5, 2003).

[170] Compare Sunstein, *What Did Lawrence Hold?* 2003 Supreme Court Review at 30 ("Lawrence's words sound in due process, but much of its music involves equal protection.").

[171] See note 15.

[172] *Lawrence*, 123 S Ct at 2480. In choosing fifty years as the relevant time period, the majority may have been taking a suggestion from Petitioner's reply brief at 3 (asserting that, in basing its "defense of the Homosexual Conduct Law against Petitioner's fundamental rights challenge . . . almost entirely on history long past, to the exclusion of all other considerations," Texas "distorts both the history Texas relies on and the last half-century's decisive rejection of state intrusion in this area."

[173] *Lawrence*, 123 S Ct at 2490 (internal quotations omitted).

[174] Id at 2479.

if we consider Sunstein's observation that the two clauses look at history from opposite directions, with the Due Process Clause providing a "safeguard[] against novel development brought about by temporary majorities who are insufficiently sensitive to the claims of history" and the Equal Protection Clause "an attempt to protect disadvantaged groups from discriminatory practices, however deeply engrained and long standing."[175] The disharmony may be hard to avoid if we examine the work the *Lawrence* majority is asking history to do, which involves both the progress narrative of equal protection and the due process narrative of increasing unwarranted limitations on liberty.

Second, consider the sentence that immediately follows the passage about the "statutes . . . seek[ing] to control a personal relationship" quoted above:

> When sexuality finds overt expression in intimate conduct with another person, the conduct can be but one element in a personal bond that is more enduring. The liberty protected by the Constitution allows homosexual persons the right to make that choice.[176]

Which choice exactly is "that choice," according to the majority? Is it the choice to "expres[s]" "sexuality" "overt[ly]" "in intimate conduct with another person,"[177] that is, the choice simply to have sex?[178] Is it the unweighted choice between casual sex and sex that is "but one element in a personal bond that is more enduring," such that not only casual sex itself, but the choice to keep it casual, has constitutional protection? Or is it only the choice to make "intimate conduct with another person . . . but one element in a personal bond that is more enduring," a choice the *Bowers* majority effectively denied to homosexuals when it infamously found, "No connection between, family, marriage or procreation on the one hand and homosexual activity on the other has been demonstrated. . . ."[179]

---

[175] Cass Sunstein, *Sexual Orientation and the Constitution: A Note on the Relationship Between Due Process and Equal Protection*, 55 U Chi L Rev 1161, 1163 (1988).

[176] *Lawrence*, 123 S Ct at 2478.

[177] Compare the conduct status distinction.

[178] Note how much contortion of Justice Kennedy's sentence was necessary to transform it into one in which the subject or agent is the choosing homosexual person he says the Constitution protects from a sentence in which the subject ("sexuality") is abstract and the verb ("finds overt expression") suggests more happenstance than active choice.

[179] *Bowers*, 478 US at 191.

This ambiguity is not new to that line of substantive due process cases from which *Lawrence* descends. *Eisenstadt*, too, left doubt as to whether the Court intended to endorse a right to copulate or only to protect copulation because of a link with pair bonding. Once again, grammatical choices heighten the ambiguity: The phrase "can be but one" wavers unsteadily between suggesting that it is merely possible (but hardly necessary) for sex to be subsumed in a more enduring personal bond and the suggestion that enduring personal bonds cemented by sex are what is being protected.[180]

In addition to ambiguity of referents in the grammatical sense, the majority, as many beginning with Scalia in dissent have noted, also is marked by an ambiguity of doctrinal referents. What, exactly, is the basis of the holding?[181] What exactly did the majority vouchsafe to Lawrence and Garner?

PRIVACY/LIBERTY/DIGNITY

As his earlier opinion in *Romer* makes clear, Kennedy has a habit of going back to first principles and to texts, disregarding the carefully erected tiers of scrutiny and three-part tests of constitutional common law.[182] To the extent that, as Fred Schauer claimed, constitutional law has taken on the texture of codification under the Internal Revenue Code,[183] Kennedy is doing the equiva-

---

[180] For a different suggested interpretation, deriving from what Mohr calls the "Catholic doctrine that a marriage unconsummated is not a marriage at all" and Kennedy's status as a Catholic the conclusion that the sentence is "just an oblique way of saying that sex is a necessary condition for whatever the 'enduring' homosexual 'bond' is," see Mohr, *Shag-a-delic Supreme Court*, Cardozo L Rev (forthcoming 2004).

[181] Because so many commentators, including Sunstein in this volume, have taken on this question, my own discussion of it will not, by and large, examine it with reference to the doctrinal categories others have focused on.

[182] To date this move has been criticized rather than respected by the textualist right, including Justice Scalia, himself only strategically a textualist. In both his *Lawrence* and his *Romer* dissent, Scalia complains about Kennedy's failure to adhere to conventional doctrinal terminology such as levels of scrutiny. If Scalia were true to the common law approach he employs when writing his own majority opinions, see, for example, *R.A.V. v City of St. Paul*, 505 US 377 (1992), and *Employment Division v Smith*, 494 US 872 (1990), the approach of leaving no case behind, he might realize that perhaps the only more precise and narrow description of the range of protected activities from Stanley's masturbation to the contracepted marital vaginal intercourse of Griswold's clients than as a right to have private consensual sex (see above note 142) might be the right to have and use devices in private consensual sex, a right which covers the films and the contraceptives both, as did the statutes that criminalized their use. See below.

[183] See Frederick Schauer, *Codifying the First Amendment: New York v Ferber*, 1982 Supreme Court Review 285.

lent of asking anew, "What is income?"[184] Thus, just as *Romer*'s majority opinion spoke in basic terms of removing the protection of the laws wholesale from gay men, lesbians, and bisexuals in Colorado, so *Lawrence*'s asks, what is liberty?[185]

The core of its answer, in what Scalia derided as the "sweet-mystery-of-life passage"[186] from *Casey*,[187] has a seldom recognized distinguished pedigree. Seeking, like his successors in *Casey*, to identify "the heart of liberty," the second Justice Harlan, in the *Poe v Ullman* dissent many see as a font of modern substantive due process, quoted what he said was "[p]erhaps the most comprehensive statement of the principle of liberty underlying these aspects of the Constitution."[188] This comprehensive statement, from Brandeis's dissent in *Olmstead*, begins in terms not far distant from the "sweet mystery of life":

> The makers of our Constitution undertook to secure conditions favorable to the pursuit of happiness. They recognized the significance of man's spiritual nature, of his feelings and of his intellect. They knew that only a part of the pain, pleasure and satisfactions of life are to be found in material things. They sought to protect Americans in their beliefs, their thoughts, their emotions and their sensations.[189]

It goes on, of course, more famously, to note that the Framers "conferred, as against the Government, the right to be let alone" and to declare the unconstitutionality of "every unjustifiable intru-

---

[184] Compare the trap of the narrow tailoring language in *Grutter*, see Post, 117 Harv L Rev at 46 (cited in note 4). One could say the inability to put things convincingly in conventional doctrinal terms is a weakness, but one could also note that these terms have become deracinated from the texts and purpose of the Constitutional provisions they interpret.

[185] Liberty is the first word of the *Lawrence* majority opinion, as it was of the *Casey* plurality. Justice Kennedy has long preferred "liberty" to "privacy" as a rubric for substantive due process cases. See, for example, David J. Garrow, *Liberty and Sexuality: The Right to Privacy and the Making of Roe v. Wade* 672 (Macmillan, 1994) (quoting Kennedy saying in response to questioning about *Griswold* at his Supreme Court confirmation hearings, "I think that the concept of liberty in the due process clause is quite expansive. . . . It is not clear to me that substituting the word 'privacy' is much of an advance over interpreting the word 'liberty' which is already in the Constitution.").

[186] *Lawrence*, 123 S Ct at 2489 (Scalia dissenting).

[187] "At the heart of liberty is the right to define one's own concept of existence, of meaning, of the universe, and of the mystery of human life." *Planned Parenthood of Southeastern Pennsylvania v Casey*, 505 US 833, 851 (1992), quoted in *Lawrence*, 123 S Ct at 2481.

[188] *Poe v Ullman*, 367 US 497, 550 (1961) (Harlan dissenting).

[189] *Olmstead v US*, 277 US 438, 478 (1928) (Brandeis dissenting), cited in *Poe v Ullman*, 367 US at 550.

sion by the government upon the privacy of the individual."[190] Nor was the *Olmstead* dissent Brandeis's first framing of liberty in these terms; much of the language of *Olmstead* quoted above is taken directly from the beginning of Warren and Brandeis's famous 1890 article "The Right to Privacy."[191]

As Jim Whitman has recently reminded us, Brandeis's conception of liberty and privacy has two strands, one the conventional Fourth Amendment "right to be let alone" and another a "continental-style dignity" strand that is central to the first several sentences of the *Olmstead* block quote in Harlan's *Poe* opinion, to the sweet-mystery-of-life passage in *Casey*, and even more clearly, to the *Lawrence* majority.[192] According to Robert Post, "Themes of respect and stigma are at the moral center of the *Lawrence* opinion, and they are entirely new to substantive due process doctrine."[193] They are not, however, new to the European conception of dignity, of which Justice Kennedy has been a conspicuous fan. Most recently and prominently, he devoted the better part of his speech to the American Bar Association Annual Meeting to an endorsement of Jim Whitman's indictment of the American criminal justice system by comparison with the continental European ideal of dignity for prisoners.[194] Said Justice Kennedy: "Professor Whitman concludes that the goal of the American corrections system is to degrade and demean the prisoner. . . . A purpose to degrade or demean individuals is not acceptable in a society founded on respect for the inalienable rights of the people."[195]

---

[190] Id.

[191] Samuel D. Warren and Louis D. Brandeis, *The Right to Privacy*, 4 Harv L Rev 193 (1890) ("[I]n very early times . . . liberty meant freedom from actual restraint. . . . Later, there came a recognition of man's spiritual nature, of his feelings and his intellect. Gradually the scope of these legal rights broadened; and now the right to life has come to mean the right to enjoy life,—the right to be let alone;—the right to liberty secures the exercise of extensive civil privileges. . . ."). Note that, in perhaps another instance of not knowing quite where to look, Brandeis, Esq. sought to locate in the right to life much of what Justices Brandeis, Harlan, and Kennedy would put at the heart of liberty.

[192] See James Q. Whitman, *The Two Western Cultures of Privacy: Dignity versus Liberty*, Yale L J (forthcoming 2004), available at http://papers.ssrn.com/abstract=476041 at 83–5.

[193] Post, 117 Harv L Rev at 97 (cited in note 4).

[194] See James Q. Whitman, *Harsh Justice: Criminal Punishment and the Widening Divide Between America and Europe* (Oxford, 2003).

[195] An Address by Anthony M. Kennedy, Associate Justice, Supreme Court of the United States, to the American Bar Association Annual Meeting (Aug 9, 2003), revised Aug 14, 2003, online at http://www.supremecourtus.gov/publicinfo/speeches/sp_08-09-03.html (last visited Jan 31, 2004).

The word "dignity" appears three times in *Lawrence*,[196] nearly as often as the word "privacy." In addition, the *Lawrence* majority opinion is rife with repeated use of words sounding in dignity, such as "respect," "stigma," and "demean." One who quickly peruses the prior uses of the word "dignity" in opinions of the U.S. Supreme Court gets the impression that the two sorts of litigants most likely to be seen to have a cognizable interest in dignity are prisoners and sovereign states.[197] *Lawrence* puts gays and lesbians one step away from the former toward the sovereignty of the latter. As noted above in the discussion of the need to frame *Lawrence* against the background of the Court's, and particularly Justice Kennedy's, recent criminal justice jurisprudence, a substantial driving force for the result in *Lawrence* may be that the majority and concurring Justices see people like Lawrence and Garner who engage in adult consensual homosexual conduct in private as precisely not the sort of people who should be spending the night in jail, or registering as sex offenders, or having done to them even any of the many things the Court has recently allowed to be done to those caught up by the criminal justice system, let alone what elements of that system may do without the Court's approval.

Is there a risk, though, that all gays and lesbians can be assured of from *Lawrence* is the substitution of the option of voluntary house arrest for the threat of prison? The word "privacy" may appear quite rarely in the majority opinion, each time in reference to or direct quotation from prior case law,[198] but the word "private" appears two dozen times,[199] about as often as the word "liberty."[200] "Private" can be a much more limiting word than "privacy," whose constitutional scope has infamously been extended to encompass

---

[196] It also makes appearances in Kennedy's *J.E.B.* concurrence, his *Carhart* dissent, and in Stevens's concurrence in *Bazzetta*, the prisoners' visitation case, argued the same day as *Lawrence*.

[197] Less frequently mentioned is the "dignity" of voters, people classified on forbidden grounds such as race and sex, the mentally ill, and would-be suicides.

[198] See Hunter, *Living with Lawrence*, Minn L Rev (forthcoming 2004) ("The only use of the word 'privacy' in the majority opinion outside of a quotation, is where the Court acknowledges that Griswold used that word to describe the relevant liberty interest.").

[199] For example, half a dozen variants of the phrase "consenting adults acting in private," ending with a final stress on "the very private nature of the conduct," appear in a mere two and a half paragraphs of the Court's discussion of enforcement practices. *Lawrence*, 123 S Ct at 2479.

[200] When near synonyms for each, such as "not public" and "freedom," are added into the mix, the ratio changes slightly in favor of liberty.

conduct that many see as anything but private. How much work is the oft-repeated word "private" doing in both assuring the result and limiting the reach of *Lawrence*? How far "[b]eyond the [p]rivacy principle"[201] will *Lawrence* go?

One place to look to investigate the possibilities is in a direction signaled by the majority, across the seas to Britain, in which the conduct for which Lawrence and Garner were arrested has not been a criminal offense for the last thirty-five years.

WHAT DOES IT MEAN TO POINT TO THE UNITED KINGDOM?

Among the "authorities pointing in an opposite direction"[202] from the one Chief Justice Burger attributed to "the history of Western Civilization,"[203] the *Lawrence* majority opinion mentions the 1957 Wolfenden Report of the Committee on Homosexual Offenses and Prostitution, Parliament's enactment of the Sexual Offences Act ten years later, and the 1981 ECHR decision in *Dudgeon v UK*. These are indeed important indicators of the "values we share with a wider civilization."[204] But to what extent can we decouple this set of legislative and judicial affirmations of tolerance for gay private life in the United Kingdom from the continuing and, in some respects, intensified, regulation of gay public life in Britain that followed them?

At least as much as in the United States, and for far longer, the history of the regulation of homosexuality in Britain has been

---

[201] Compare Thomas, 92 Colum L Rev 1431 (cited in note 83).

[202] See *Lawrence*, 123 S Ct at 2481.

[203] Id.

[204] *Lawrence*, 123 S Ct at 2483. Although the majority has been criticized, beginning with the Scalia dissent, id at 2495–96, for its invocation of non-U.S. sources of law and social norms, two things should be remembered here. First, it was not Justice Kennedy in *Lawrence*, but Justice Burger in *Bowers*, who first asserted the relevance of the legal treatment of "homosexual conduct . . . throughout the history of Western Civilization" to the question before the Court; Justice Kennedy's cites to European authorities simply show that the legal norms of "a wider civilization" have not for some time been as Justice Burger imagined. Second, invocation of foreign sources and trends is hardly new or out of fashion in substantive due process cases. See, for example, *Washington v Glucksberg*, 521 US 702, 711 n 8 and n 16 (1997) (citing Canadian case law and the legislative determinations of nations from Europe to the South Seas to establish the proposition that a "blanket prohibition on assisted suicide is the norm among Western democracies" and "[o]ther countries are embroiled in similar debates"); *Poe v Ullman*, 367 US 497, 555 n 16 (1961) (Harlan dissenting) (citing Western European and Canadian laws on contraception to contrast restrictive and "more permissive" legislation). To the extent that substantive due process cases citing to foreign sources are also criminal cases with an Eighth Amendment dimension, consider as well the (admittedly also criticized) use of foreign sources and trends in this area of law.

composed of alternating steps forward and back. With the limited exception of *Dudgeon*, affecting not Britain but only Northern Ireland, all the major decisional steps of advancement and retrogression in the United Kingdom were undertaken legislatively.[205] This should be noted by those who, drawing analogies to arguments made about abortion rights and desegregation, might be tempted to think that the obstacle to a steady advance of gay rights in the United States is an imperial judiciary stepping out ahead of public sentiments and that gradual legislative change would avoid backlash.

At the beginning of the nineteenth century in Britain, sodomy was a capital offense for which a record number of more than fifty men were executed in the first third of the century.[206] After several decades without executions, the 1861 Offenses Against the Person Act replaced the death penalty for buggery with sentences of from ten years to life.

> But in 1885 the famous Labouchère Amendment to the Criminal Law Amendment Act made all male homosexual activities (acts of "gross indecency") illegal, punishable by up to two years hard labor. And in 1898 the laws on importuning for "immoral purposes" were tightened up and effectively applied to male homosexuals. . . . Both were significant extensions of the legal controls on male homosexuality, whatever their origins or intentions. Though formally less severe than capital punishments for sodomy, the new legal situation is likely to have ground harder on a much wider circle of people, particularly as it was dramatized in a series of sensational scandals, culminating in the trials of Oscar Wilde, which had the function of drawing a sharp dividing line between permissible and tabooed forms of behaviour.[207]

The Labouchère Amendment was initially something close to an afterthought to a bill whose principal purpose was to deal with heterosexual offenses, notably the prostituting of adolescent girls as detailed in the outrage-inciting Maiden Tribute of Modern Babylon. The laws concerning consensual homosexuality and het-

---

[205] Although, as noted below, some of the most recent legislative steps forward were undertaken under judicial pressure from the European Court of Human Rights.

[206] A. D. Harvey, *Communications: Prosecutions for Sodomy in England at the Beginning of the Nineteenth Century*, 21 Historical J 939 (1978).

[207] Jeffrey Weeks, *Against Nature: Essays on History, Sexuality and Identity* 19 (Rivers Oram, 1991).

erosexual prostitution (this time of adult women) were again linked three-quarters of a century later, when the Wolfenden Committee was convened to investigate the possibility of their reform. The committee's famous 1957 report recommending decriminalization was the subject of the equally famous Hart-Devlin debates and of an endorsement in the London *Times* by many of the nation's cultural elite, including churchmen.[208] But its recommendations as to homosexual activity, unlike those concerning prostitution, were not supported by the government for another ten years. When Parliament finally moved to reform the laws concerning consensual homosexuality, it cut back on the report's recommendations. The 1967 Sexual Offenses Act, as recommended, exempted the military, set the age of consent for homosexual acts at 21 (as compared with 16 for heterosexual sex), and *raised* the penalty for an adult convicted of gross indecency with a young male of an age between 16 and 21. Additionally, however, it defined the phrase "in private" as narrowly as possible, for example making all consensual sexual activity involving three or more men illegal.[209]

Not until 2000, thanks to the European Court of Human Rights (ECHR)'s decision in *ADT v UK*, could three to five adult men safely have consensual sex anywhere in Britain, even in the privacy of one of their bedrooms, without risking prosecution for "gross indecency between men."[210] Not until 2003, after prompting from the ECHR, was the age of consent in Britain for homosexual

---

[208] Nicholas C. Edsall, *Toward Stonewall: Homosexuality and Society in the Modern Western World* 316 (Virginia, 2003). In 1952, the Church of England's Moral Welfare Council had preceded the Wolfenden Committee in issuing a report "carefully distinguishing between immoral and criminal conduct and calling for a reform of the law." Id at 315.

[209] See Edsall, *Toward Stonewall* at 321; Robert Wintemute, *Sexual Orientation and Gender Identity* 6 in Colin J. Harvey, *Human Rights in the Community* (Oxford, Hart, forthcoming 2004).

[210] See *ADT v UK*, 9 BCHR 112 (ECHR 2000) ("Gross indecency is not defined by statute. It appears, however, to cover any act involving sexual indecency between two male persons. If two male persons acting in concert behave in an indecent manner the offense is committed even if there is no physical contact. . . . From the police reports we have seen and the other evidence we have received it appears that the offence usually takes one of three forms[:] . . . mutual masturbation, intercrural contact; or oral-genital contact (with or without emission). . . . The applicant was involved in sexual activities with a restricted number of friends in circumstances in which it was most unlikely that others would become aware of what was going on. . . . The activities were therefore genuinely 'private' and . . . the court must . . . adopt the same narrow margin of appreciation it found applicable in other cases involving intimate aspects of private life."). For an explanation of the concept of the margin of appreciation through comparison to U.S. law, see Mary Anne Case, *Community Standards and the Margin of Appreciation*, Human Rights L J (forthcoming 2004).

and heterosexual sex equalized. Also after European prompting, this time from the Human Rights Act, the Sexual Offenses Act of 2003 substituted for the "men-only offense of 'solicit[ing] or importun[ing] in a public place for an immoral purpose' (which was applied mainly to male-male soliciting for non-commercial sexual activity) a gender neutral offense of soliciting for prostitution."[211] Sex in a public lavatory is now, for the first time, also prohibited on a gender neutral basis, as is "outraging public decency."[212] Indeed, all offenses "relating to public decency" must now be interpreted on a gender (and hence orientation) neutral basis, from prostitution to sadomasochism, obscenity and blasphemy to "insulting behavior."[213] Thus, convictions of two males for public displays of affection likely to be tolerated when engaged in by a heterosexual couple, such as the 1986 conviction of two men for "kissing and cuddling" at a central London bus stop at 2 in the morning,[214] should be a thing of the past.

But only time will tell how much "liberty" to pursue their "personal relationship[s] . . . without being punished as criminals" the 2003 Act will afford gay men, lesbians, and bisexuals in Britain. Consider that passage of the 1967 Act "scarcely affected" the number of persons prosecuted for buggery or attempted buggery, but in the decade after its passage the "recorded incidence of gross indecency between males . . . doubled, the number of persons prosecuted has trebled and the number of persons convicted has almost quadrupled."[215]

---

[211] Wintemute, *Sexual Orientation* at 7 (cited in note 209).

[212] Id at 8.

[213] Id at 9.

[214] See *Masterson v Holden*, 3 All ER 39 (QB Div [1986]). I might myself describe a small fraction of the enumerated conduct as fondling rather than cuddling, but that is not how the participants described it nor how it seems to be have been viewed by the court, who found them guilty on the complaint of a mixed-sex group of four passing heterosexuals apparently outraged by any gay public display of affection, however mild. Compare my *Couples and Coupling*, 79 Va L Rev at 1676–78, account of similarly unequal enforcement against public displays of affection in the U.S. gay bar cases of the 1950s. Note that this problem was addressed in the United States decades ago.

[215] See Roy Walmsley and Karen White, *Sexual Offences, Consent and Sentencing: A Home Office Research Report* 38–39 (1979). Although they consider alternate explanations such as changes in the prosecution rate and "changes in the attitude and behaviour towards homosexuals," Walmsley and White conclude that most likely "the Act itself is the source of the increase in statistics" because it "reaffirmed the unlawfulness of homosexual acts in public" and "introduced summary trials for gross indecency between males." Id at 40–41.

Nor was this the only negative backlash for gay rights in Britain over the course of the past half century. For example, in part to reign in what they saw as Labor-dominated local governments, in part in reaction to a perception of widespread classroom use of materials such as the European equivalent of *Heather Has Two Mommies*,[216] the Danish children's book *Jenny Lives with Eric and Martin*,[217] Prime Minister Margaret Thatcher's government added Section 28 to the Local Government Act of 1988. Section 28 provided, inter alia, that a "local authority shall not- (a) intentionally promote homosexuality or publish material with the intention of promoting homosexuality; (b) promote the teaching in any maintained school of the acceptability of homosexuality as a pretended family relationship."[218] Although there were periodic efforts at repeal, Section 28 remained in force in England until November 2003.[219]

---

[216] This book formed a prominent and controversial part of the New York City Schools Chancellor's proposed, and ultimately rejected, Children of the Rainbow curriculum, which was intended to teach tolerance and respect for a diversity of family forms but which provoked strong backlash. See, for example, Josh Barbanel, *Under "Rainbow" a War: When Politics, Morals and Learning Mix*, NY Times 34 (Dec 27, 1992).

[217] According to Wintemute, however, only one copy of the book was in fact available for use by London teachers. *Sexual Orientation* at 24 (cited in note 209).

[218] Available online at http://www.hmso.gov.uk/acts/acts1988/Ukpga_19880009_en_5.htm#mdiv28.

[219] See Local Government Act 2003, § 127(2). While a full comparison of British and American responses is beyond the scope of this article, it may be instructive to recall briefly some contrasting incidents of the history of no-promo homo legislation in the United States: In 1978 the infamous proposed Briggs Amendment to the California Constitution, which would have authorized the firing of any public school teacher found to have advocated homosexuality, failed to win a majority of the state electorate. Convinced that Ronald Reagan's opposition to its passage had been instrumental in the defeat of his amendment, Briggs himself told a reporter that for "Reagan to march to the drums of homosexuality has irrevocably damaged him nationally." See Clendinnen and Nagourney, *Out for Good* at 388 (cited in note 134). In 1985, an equally divided Supreme Court, 470 US 903 (1985), affirmed the lower court ruling in *National Gay Task Force v Board of Educ. of Oklahoma City*, 729 F2d 1270 (10th Cir 1984), striking down on First Amendment grounds prohibitions on teachers' "advocating, . . . encouraging or promoting" homosexuality embodied in a state statute modeled on the Briggs Initiative. A table in William N. Eskridge, Jr.'s *Gaylaw: Challenging the Apartheid of the Closet* 362–71, App B3 (Harvard, 1999), lists a handful of no-promo homo state statutes passed in the 1990s, most dealing with education, none comprehensive. In 1993, the commissioners of Cobb County, Georgia, adopted resolutions proclaiming, inter alia, "that 'the traditional family structure' is in accord with community standards, . . . that 'lifestyles advocated by the gay community are incompatible with those standards' . . . and that Cobb County would not fund 'activities which seek to contravene these existing community standards.'" Joel Achenbach, *A Report from the Front Line of the "Culture War."* Wash Post G01 (Sept 26, 1993). The ordinance was prompted by commissioners' objections to the subsidized production of Terrence McNally's *Lips Together, Teeth Apart*. It went unchallenged in court because it had no legal force—it was simply a declaration of principle. See, for example, Caroline Davies, *The Man Who Dared to Say No*, Mail

I do not mean to suggest that things are systematically worse
for gays, lesbians, and bisexuals in Britain than in the United
States. They have, to take just one small example, been able to
serve openly in the British military since 2000, again as a result
of prompting from the European Court of Human Rights.[220] Nor
do I mean to suggest that the experience Britain has had with decriminalization of private consensual homosexual acts in the past
is a necessary predictor of the American experience in the aftermath of *Lawrence*. Among other differences, the influence of the
First Amendment on American law and life may have already afforded greater protection for expressive activities by and on behalf
of gays, lesbians, and bisexuals in this country.

A more thorough comparison of the legal situation for gays, lesbians, and bisexuals in western Europe and the United States, which
is well beyond the scope of this article, might reveal more or less
systematic differences in protection and restrictions along a speech/
conduct axis and along a partnering/parenting axis. That is to say, in
general, European legal systems may be comparatively more likely to
have repealed criminal penalties for private consensual sex acts, more
likely to offer employment non-discrimination and recognition of gay
couples, and less likely to extend legal recognition to gays and lesbians
as parents; whereas the United States has been somewhat more likely
for a longer period of time to protect gays, lesbians, and bisexuals in
a variety of expressive activities with First Amendment dimensions
and to recognize them legally as parents of children.[221]

Against the comparative backdrop of the British experience over
the recent past, let me now turn to some analogies and implications in American law.

---

on Sunday 8 (Aug 22, 1993). More to the point, its principal identifiable concrete effect
was to penalize, not "the gay community," but Cobb County itself: the Olympic torch,
originally scheduled to travel through Cobb County, took a detour around it because the
Olympic organizers wished to distance themselves from the county's announced opposition
to "the gay community."

[220] See, for example, *Smith v UK* (2000), 29 EHRR 493 (Sept 27, 1999).

[221] For example, France has not criminalized consensual sodomy or other same-sex sexual
activity since the eighteenth century, and has offered recognition to registered same-sex
partnerships since 1999, but as recently as 2002 it and the European Court of Human
Rights, the same court that twenty years earlier had issued the *Dudgeon* decision praised
by Justice Kennedy, upheld the Paris Social Services Department's decision to deny a single
homosexual man authorization to adopt a child. See *Frette v France*, ECHR [2002] 36515/
97; see generally Nancy Polikoff, *Recognizing Partners but Not Parents/Recognizing Parents
but Not Partners: Gay and Lesbian Family Law in Europe and the United States*, 17 NY L Sch
J Hum Rts 711 (2000).

To What Extent Is "This . . . Controlled by Stanley"?

Perhaps the last time Court watchers had as much expectation that a decision protecting rights within the privacy of the home might soon lead to broader protection of those and related rights was when *Stanley v Georgia*[222] came down. Also without clearly specifying precisely how the protected right at issue fit within conventional doctrinal categories, the Court in *Stanley* held that criminal prosecution for the mere private possession in one's home of material concededly obscene would be unconstitutional.[223] It was in *Stanley* that Brandeis's passage on liberty made the full transition from academic writing, through dissent (*Olmstead* and *Poe*) and concurrence (Harlan's in *Griswold*, incorporating his *Poe* dissent by reference), to majority opinion.

In preparing for *Bowers v Hardwick* with his clerk, Justice Marshall "flatly stat[ed] 'This is controlled by *Stanley*.'"[224] Although there is much to be said for Marshall's claim, *Stanley* is not so much as cited by any opinion in *Lawrence*. This is almost certainly good news for gay rights: It indicates that at least six Justices see Lawrence and Garner's conduct as having so much more claim to dignity than Stanley's solitary use of obscene movies as to draw no analogy between them. The films in Stanley's possession were not protected because of their own intrinsic worth—after all, they were still themselves unprotected obscenity, and had the caption on the case been, not *Stanley v Georgia*, but *Georgia v "[T]hree reels of eight millimeter film*,"[225] Georgia would have prevailed. Instead their protection was a spillover from the protection of the home from government intrusion and the protection of ideas and the books and films that could provoke ideas. Unlike Stanley's films, however, Lawrence and Garner's anal sex is

---

[222] 394 US 557 (1969).

[223] The Court's later decision in *Osborne v Ohio*, 495 US 103 (1990), made clear that the right afforded in *Stanley* did not extend to the private possession of child pornography. The *Stanley* line's holdings concerning private possession of sexually explicit material thus track the distinction repeatedly drawn by the *Lawrence* majority between activity limited to consenting adults in private and that involving minors.

[224] Murdoch and Price, *Courting Justice* at 291 (cited in note 11). Marshall authored the majority opinion in *Stanley*. According to Justice Powell's conference notes from *Bowers v Hardwick*, now in the Powell archives at Washington & Lee, Marshall repeated at conference that "*Stanley* controls."

[225] 394 US 557, 559 (describing the obscene material found in Stanley's home). Compare a typical obscenity caption, such as, for example, *U.S. v 12 200 Ft. Reels of Film*, 413 US 123 (1973).

protected, not on a theory akin to overbreadth, that protection must be reluctantly extended to it in order to protect sex we really care about, like marital vaginal intercourse, but because their activities were sufficiently akin to those of a married couple as to be worthy of protection in their own right.[226]

The tone of *Lawrence* is not one evincing condescending disapproval of gay people. Nowhere does the Court suggest to Lawrence and Garner that "it may disapprove of what [they do], but . . . will defend to the death [their] right to [do] it." Recall that the last time the original formulation of this "remark attributed to Voltaire" made its way into a Supreme Court opinion, Justice Stevens announced in *Young v American Mini-Theatres*[227] that because "few of us would march our sons and daughters off to war to preserve the citizen's right to see 'Specified Sexual Activities' exhibited in the theaters of our choice," movies exhibiting such activities could "legitimately . . . [be placed] in a different classification" for regulatory purposes. Can gay people now? Much in the *Lawrence* opinions suggest not. At least to this extent, evidence supports Scalia's claim that the majority did indeed take sides in the culture wars, it did not just declare the private home neutral territory. But it may be wise to remember that the tone of *Stanley* also was not indicative of disapproval of the "man sitting alone in his house" watching obscene movies. Rather, the *Stanley* majority opinion helped itself to heroic platitudes about the impermissibility of the State's asserting "the right to control the moral content of a person's thoughts."[228] It is in other opinions involving obscenity and other sexually explicit speech, such as that of Stevens in *Young*, that a tone of distaste comes through more clearly. And these opinions followed soon after *Stanley*, foreclosing the hopes of those who saw in that case a portent of the Court's willingness to withdraw the government entirely from the policing of consenting adults' access to adult-themed obscene materials.

If *Lawrence* were indeed controlled by *Stanley*, its message might once again be, in effect, simply, "Get a room," keep it quite private

[226] "To say that the issue in *Bowers* was simply the right to engage in certain sexual conduct demeans the claim the individual put forward, just as it would demean a married couple were it to be said marriage is simply about the right to have sexual intercourse." *Lawrence*, 123 S Ct at 2478.

[227] 427 US 50, 70 (1976).

[228] *Stanley*, 557 US at 565.

if you want it protected. Obscenity law has not yet developed to the point that what can be "whispered in the closet shall be shouted from the housetops."[229] In the immediate aftermath of *Stanley*, some lower courts were prepared to extend its protections well beyond the four walls of a private home. As one district court reasoned, "If a rich Stanley can view a film . . . in his own home, a poorer Stanley should be free to visit a protected theatre. . . . We see no reason for saying he must go alone."[230] But in 1972, as part of a general reformulation of obscenity law,[231] the Supreme Court sharply limited the scope of access to obscene material, even when all viewers were consenting adults. The Paris Adult Theatres had "a conventional, inoffensive theater entrance, without any pictures" but with a sign warning, inter alia, that only adults were admitted and that "if viewing the nude body offends you, Please Do Not Enter." These safeguards "against exposure to juveniles and to passersby" were insufficient to foreclose the theaters being prosecuted for obscenity, according to the Supreme Court. Chief Justice Burger's majority opinion cited Alexander Bickel for the proposition that, "although a man may be entitled to read an obscene book in his room or expose himself indecently there, . . . if he demands a right to obtain the books and pictures he wants in the market and, to foregather in public places, discreet, if you will, but accessible to all—with others who share his tastes, then to grant him his right is to affect the world about the rest of us and to impinge on other privacies."[232]

The language of respect in both the *Lawrence* and *Stanley* opinions may not in the end be quite enough fully to vindicate what can still be perceived as low-value activity.[233] In the next two sections of this article, I shall consider the potential implications for two different sets

---

[229] Luke 12:3, quoted in Warren and Brandeis, 4 Harv L Rev at 195 (cited in note 191).

[230] *Karalexis v Byrne*, 306 F Supp 1363, 1367 (D Mass 1969), vacated and remanded, 401 US 216 (1971).

[231] *Miller v California*, 413 US 15 (1973), which articulated a three-part test for obscenity still in effect today, thereby ending the era of per curiam Supreme Court decisions summarily reversing obscenity convictions on the authority of *Redrup v New York*, 386 US 767 (1967), was issued on the same day as *Paris Adult Theatre*, discussed below. Both majority opinions were written by Chief Justice Burger.

[232] *Paris Adult Theatre I*, 413 US at 52, 58, 59 (1973).

[233] Compare *Note: The Constitutional Status of Sexual Orientation: Homosexuality as a Suspect Classification*, 98 Harv L Rev 1285, 1290, 1291 (1985) ("Withholding social recognition from the public aspects of gay personhood while 'heterosexual society revolves around its sexual orientation' is inherently unequal not only in its substantive restriction of gay liberties, but also in its imputation of stigma: homosexuality, like obscenity, may be tolerated only if quarantined.").

of criminal laws designed to hinder public acquisition of components of private, adult, consensual sex—the laws prohibiting the sale of sex aids and those criminalizing public solicitation even for private non-commercial homosexual sex. The solicitation cases may have this in common with successful obscenity prosecutions after *Stanley*: each presents the apparent paradox that constitutional protection is extended to activities in the home notwithstanding that acquiring from outside the home the means to these activities may be criminalized.[234] Thus, Stanley may have difficulty obtaining an obscene film for home viewing and Uplinger or Sawatzky[235] difficulty in acquiring a partner for private consensual homosexual sex without participating in a criminal act. Not only does the Alabama sex aids case, discussed in the next section, also present this issue, it also can be seen indirectly to call into question the assumption underlying obscenity laws that, to the extent obscene speech is designed simply to provoke sexual arousal, it is unworthy of constitutional protection.

THE GENDER OF AIDED ORGASM

The Alabama sex aids case, *Williams v Pryor*,[236] is now up before the Eleventh Circuit for the second time.[237] In lengthy and

[234] If the question, "Is geography destiny?" is central to the modern constitutional law of sexually explicit speech, from the community standards component of the *Miller* test for obscenity to the zoning questions of *Young, Renton*, and *Mt. Ephraim*, a third component of the geography of obscenity is the distinction between the home and all other places where sexually explicit speech may occur, even those populated entirely by consenting adults. It implicates the limits on the formation of voluntary special purpose communities, such as the 60,000 naked Hoosiers in the Hoosierdome imagined by Scalia in *Barnes v Glen Theaters*, 501 US 560 (1991), and the audience of the Paris Adult Theatre. And it also suggests that there is at least one safe place—his or her own home—for an outlier from community standards, for the person with Las Vegas tastes and sensibilities in Mississippi, to use the *Miller* formulation. But it more directly implicates the class issues also raised by the exemption of high art from the category of obscenity. Those who can comfortably stay in their private home may not only get greater access to sexually explicit speech, they may also more effectively shield themselves from it. Compare *FCC v Pacifica Found.*, 438 US 726 (1978), with *Erznoznik v Jacksonville*, 422 US 205 (1975). *Pacifica* restricted non-obscene sexually offensive expression that, through the airwaves, penetrated the home, but noted, citing *Erznoznik*, which protected such expression in a public place, that "outside the home, the balance between the offensive speaker and the unwilling listener may sometimes tip in favor of the speaker." For further discussion, see Mary Anne Case, *Community Standards and the Margin of Appreciation*, Hum Rts L J (forthcoming 2004).

[235] Petitioners before the Supreme Court in cases involving criminal prosecution of public solicitation for private consensual non-commercial sex, cited in note 23 above and discussed below.

[236] *Williams*, 220 F Supp 2d 1257 (2002).

[237] See *Williams v Pryor*, 240 F3d 944 (11th Cir 2001) for that court's earlier decision in the case.

sympathetic opinions, the lower court judge in that case has now twice struck down a portion of the Alabama obscenity law criminalizing sale of "any device designed or marketed as useful primarily for the stimulation of the human genital organs," first as lacking a rational basis and then, after reversal and remand, as an impermissible burden on plaintiffs' right to privacy. Accounts of the post-*Lawrence* oral argument in the Eleventh Circuit inclined toward predicting affirmance.[238]

The case goes beyond *Stanley* in involving sale (not just use) of sex aids like vibrators and dildos (somewhat more distant from the First Amendment umbrella that gave shelter to Stanley's "books . . . and . . . films"). Even Stanley may come out of the closet of the home with this Alabama case, led by at least two factors that make it appealing: First, to the extent the case starts with a conception of sex toys as marital aids and expands its protection out from there to encompass single individuals, it is like the *Griswold* and *Eisenstadt* of sex aids rolled into one. Second, its individual-user plaintiffs are not dirty old men seeking to buy inflatable dolls with functioning orifices so as to avoid human contact with actual women, but sympathetic female plaintiffs.

Everything about the case genders the use of sex aids as female and feminine: The "vendor plaintiffs" are women who appear to market their wares largely to other women, either at "in-house 'Tupperware' style parties . . . [for] sexual aids and novelties" or in retail stores featuring "romance enhancing products and novelties" such as "lingerie, . . . instructional videos . . . aromatherapy candles, romance novels and similar products," but no hard core porn, only "'soft porn' or 'R' rated videos."[239] Among the user plaintiffs are a married couple and another married woman "who uses sexual devices during intimate relations with her husband."[240] Even more extraordinarily, also among the user plaintiffs and the customers of the vendor plaintiffs and given a no less sympathetic hearing by the lower court are single women who "prefer to avoid sexual relations with others, due to prior negative relationships, or

---

[238] See http://appellateblog.blogspot.com/2003_09_01appellateblog_archive.html#106434 751461575612 (last visited Feb 14, 2004).

[239] *Williams*, 220 F Supp 2d at 1264 (2002); 41 F Supp 2d 1257, 1264 (1999).

[240] *Williams*, 220 F Supp 2d at 1265.

the risks of sexually transmitted diseases, or other risks associated with developing an intimate relationship."[241]

Without actually suggesting that this fact may amount to a violation of the plaintiffs' equal protection rights on grounds of sex, the district judge includes among the "undisputed facts" that, while prohibiting sale of the sorts of devices demonstrably effective at bringing women to sexual arousal and orgasm, Alabama imposes no similar prohibition on "ribbed and tickler condoms" and "[v]irility drugs, such as Viagra."[242] Given that the very statute at issue in *Eisenstadt* prohibited alike the distribution of any "article intended to be used for self-abuse, . . . the prevention of conception or for causing unlawful abortion,"[243] we may now come full circle if prescription of a vibrator, like prescription of birth control and abortion, is held, as a matter of constitutional law, to be between a woman and her doctor rather than a matter for the criminal law of the State.[244]

CAN LAWRENCE NOW INVITE GARNER HOME FOR ANAL SEX WITHOUT RISKING ARREST FOR SOLICITATION?

But what will happen when judicial intuitions about predatory male sexuality[245] are brought to the fore instead of gauzy visions of feminine sexuality? What will be the fate, in the aftermath of *Lawrence*, of state statutes criminalizing public solicitation even of private, consensual, non-commercial adult, homosexual

---

[241] Id.

[242] 41 F Supp 2d at 1265 (1999).

[243] *Eisenstadt v Baird*, 405 US 438, 442 n 2 (1972).

[244] Compare Rachel P. Maines, *The Technology of Orgasm: "Hysteria," the Vibrator, and Women's Sexual Satisfaction* (Johns Hopkins, 1999) (describing lengthy and extensive history of doctors therapeutically masturbating women to orgasm, manually at first, but with electrical devices as soon as they became available around the turn of the last century).

[245] Some evidence that Justices of the Supreme Court have in the past imagined gay men as sexual predators may be gleaned from the following anecdotes: When, in discussing *Bowers v Hardwick* with his colleagues, Lewis Powell remarked that he had never known a homosexual, Justice Blackmun responded, "But surely, Lewis, you were approached as a boy?" Murdoch and Price, *Courting Justice* at 307–8 (cited in note 11). According to Stuart Ross, the Clark clerk who drafted the *Boutillier* opinion, which allowed homosexual aliens to be excluded from the United States on grounds of "psychopathic personality," the Justices "probably thought a homosexual was somebody who tried to pick you up when you were hitchhiking." Id at 115–16.

sex?[246] In 1995, the Supreme Court denied certiorari in such a case, leaving in place the conviction of Kenneth Sawatzky for "offering to engage in an act of lewdness" with what turned out to be an undercover cop he encountered in a gay cruising area. In upholding the conviction, the lower court described the statute at issue as "designed to protect persons from being asked by others to engage in sexual activity." According to the court, "This case is neither about the regulation of conduct between consenting adults in the privacy of their bedrooms, nor the legal status to be provided to homosexual persons. Fundamentally, this case is about whether Oklahoma City may legally prohibit public solicitation for private, non-commercial acts of sodomy."[247] Oral sex was a criminal offense in Oklahoma in 1995. But several things should be noted here. First, the statute under which Sawatzky was convicted for soliciting oral sex also criminalized solicitation for many forms of lewdness not themselves criminal, such as "masturbation . . . or lascivious, lustful, or licentious conduct."[248] Second, the *Sawatzky* court opined that "reasonable prohibitions against soliciting sexual acts do not violate the First Amendment whether the underlying conduct is lawful or unlawful. Our view is based upon the unique status of sexual conduct in our culture. In our community, some form of overt sexual conduct, including the solicitation of some sexual acts, is simply not appropriate in public places."[249]

---

[246] A full survey of the state of the law concerning public solicitation for private sex acts immediately before *Lawrence* is beyond the scope of this essay, but it should be noted that there are a number of such laws still on the books and a number of recent reported cases enforcing them. Some provide disparate treatment to homosexual and heterosexual solicitations and, as discussed below, others have a likely disparate impact. The case in which the Kentucky sodomy law was struck down on state constitutional grounds, *Commonwealth v Wasson*, 842 SW2d 487 (Ky 1992), also involved solicitation, but under a statute that simply criminalized solicitation for the commission of any crime.

[247] *Sawatzky v Oklahoma City*, 906 P2d 785 (1995), cert denied, 517 US 1156 (1996). Compare the similar language from the Ninth Circuit's 1976 *Baker* opinion, joined by then Circuit Judge Anthony Kennedy and quoted above.

[248] *Sawatzky*, 906 P2d at 786 n 1.

[249] Id at 787 n 7. Compare sex in public places to smoking, another activity increasingly confined to private spaces out of concern for unconsenting others and restricted even among consenting adults in public or regulated spaces. Imagine treating littering with used condoms like littering with cigarette butts. Recall that drinking in public was what got Michael Hardwick arrested in the first place. See Art Harris, *The Unintended Battle of Michael Hardwick*, Washington Post C1 (Aug 21, 1986). See Petition for Certiorari in *Talley v California*, cert denied, 390 US 1031 (1968) (arguing that conviction of two men who kissed in a bar on New Year's Eve should not stand although some might find such conduct offensive, given that others might find it offensive "to watch others chewing gum, chewing or smoking tobacco, drinking alcoholic beverages . . . yet we certainly would not and should not attempt to proscribe these activities except by influence and example."), quoted in Murdoch and Price, *Courting Justice* at 145 (cited in note 11).

Two years before *Bowers v Hardwick*, the U.S. Supreme Court also had occasion to consider the constitutionality of statutes criminalizing solicitation of sexual activity. The case, *New York v Uplinger*,[250] came from a state whose highest court several years earlier, in the *Onofre* case which the Supreme Court had declined to review, had held on federal constitutional grounds that the underlying act of private adult noncommercial sodomy could not be criminalized.[251] When the New York Court of Appeals subsequently struck down a statute criminalizing loitering for the purpose of soliciting another to engage in deviate sexual intercourse, the U.S. Supreme Court initially took the case,[252] but then dismissed it as improvidently granted when a majority saw no way to untangle the holding as to solicitation from the underlying holding concerning the sex acts themselves, as to which it had not granted review.

How far has the Court come since *Uplinger*,[253] or even *Sawatzky?* Might the Court now be prepared to agree with gay rights pioneer Frank Kameny[254] that "we see no reason why a sexual invitation

---

[250] 467 US 246 (1984).

[251] See *Onofre*, 415 NE2d at 940–41 ("In light of th[e *Eisenstadt* and *Stanley*] decisions, protecting under the cloak of the right to privacy individual decisions as to indulgence in acts of sexual intimacy by unmarried persons and as to the satisfaction of sexual desires by resort to material condemned as obscene by community standards when done in a cloistered setting, no rational basis appears for excluding from the same protection decisions—such as those made by defendants before us [who were arrested for engaging in deviate sexual intercourse with other males]—to seek sexual gratification from what at least once was regarded as 'deviant' conduct, so long as the decisions are voluntarily made by adults in a noncommercial, private setting.").

[252] *N.Y. v Uplinger*, 447 NE2d 62 (1983).

[253] The oral argument of Uplinger included the following questions:

Q: [N]evertheless, if there is any right, as recognized in *Onofre*, and assuming for this purpose that there is, does that right extend to prohibiting the state from controlling attempts made in public? And why should the right to privacy to do things in private extend on to do the same or some portion of those things in public? ***

Q: The solicitation may be very private, very quiet, very polite, but nevertheless there is a person walking down the street who doesn't care to be solicited for a deviate sexual purpose and is very annoyed by it. Now may the state forbid that or not?

N.Y. v Uplinger, 1984 US Trans LEXIS 97 at 30, 32. Murdoch and Price attribute the first of these two quoted questions to Justice O'Connor. See Murdoch and Price, *Courting Justice* at 230 (cited in note 11).

[254] A former civil servant who dedicated the remainder of his life to the campaign for gay and lesbian equality after having lost his job when his homosexuality came to his employer's attention in the aftermath of an arrest for solicitation.

should really be placed in a different class from, say, an invitation to dinner,"[255] at least as regards the criminal law? Is it no longer thinkable that a Court majority might say, in a replay of *Sawatzky*, in a future case about solicitation or another public manifestation of homosexuality short of actual public oral or anal sex: "The state of [Oklahoma] thus has not sought to punish a mere status as [Colorado] did in [*Romer*]; nor has it attempted to regulate appellant's behavior in the privacy of his own home [as Texas did in *Lawrence*]?"[256] Would it matter if the solicitation were for bareback sex?

Like the laws at issue in *Lawrence*, solicitation laws raise issues of both liberty and equality. Perhaps the most straightforward equal protection issues arise when the statutory scheme provides explicit disparate treatment on grounds of sex,[257] but the most interesting questions of inequality arise with statutes having instead a predictable disparate impact by sex. Consider three variants of a prohibition on solicitation: (*a*) penalizing noncommercial solicitation more heavily than commercial, with the result that gay men are more likely to commit felonies and female prostitutes misdemeanors when soliciting;[258] (*b*) prohibiting solicitation for deviant (i.e., oral or anal) sex and not solicitation for vaginal intercourse; (*c*) criminalizing solicitation only when the solicitor knows or is reckless about the solicitation's offensiveness to the recipient. Solicitation

---

[255] Said while attacking the D.C. sodomy and solicitation laws at a press conference at the Pentagon while campaigning as an openly gay candidate for Congressional Delegate from D.C. in March 1971. Of the sodomy laws, Kameny said, "If you follow the advice given in most marriage manuals, . . . you could get ten years in jail and a $1000 fine, here in Washington." Clendinnen and Nagourney, *Out for Good* at 122 (cited in note 134).

[256] Compare *Powell v Texas*, 392 US 514, 532 (1968) ("The state of Texas thus has not sought to punish a mere status as California did in *Robinson;* nor has it attempted to regulate appellant's behavior in the privacy of his own home. Rather, it has imposed on appellant a criminal sanction for public behavior which may create substantial health and safety hazards, both for appellant and for members of the general public, and which offends the moral and esthetic sensibilities of a large segment of the community."). In *Powell*, the Court upheld a conviction for public drunkenness notwithstanding that a few years earlier, in *Robinson v California*, 370 US 660 (1962), criminal sanctions for status offenses had been held unconstitutional.

[257] As did the British prohibition on "importun[ing] in a public place for an immoral purpose," which, as discussed above, applied to importuning by males only until its reform in November 2003.

[258] See, for example, *Branche v Virginia*, 489 SE2d 692, 694 (Va App 1997) (rejecting claim that statutory scheme criminalizing solicitation violates equal protection because, in penalizing commercial solicitation less heavily that noncommercial, "it classifies those instances of oral sodomy that are typically engaged in by homosexual males as a felony where the same conduct undertaken by a female prostitute is classified as a misdemeanor."

statutes that make offensiveness to the hearer an element of the crime or treats solicitation as fighting words may, like fighting words doctrine generally, have a disparate impact by sex, protecting men more than women from unwelcome speech. The Supreme Court of Ohio, a state with a number of reported solicitation cases in the last decade, finally struck down on equal protection grounds the state statute which provided that "no person shall solicit a person of the same sex to engage in sexual activity with the offender when the offender knows such solicitation is offensive to the other person or is reckless in that regard."[259] Given that the overwhelming majority of the population is assumed to be heterosexual[260] and the differential social norms concerning male solicitation of females and of males, even when there is no explicit disparate treatment by sex, as there was in Ohio, statutes that make actual or potential offensiveness an element of the crime have the likely intent and effect of privileging straight men, who are more shielded from unwelcome approaches by other men than they are hampered in their attempts to solicit women.

Interestingly, of two very different forms of public declaration of one's interest in forming part of a homosexual couple, public solicitation and applying for a marriage license, perhaps the form of public recognition most under discussion in the aftermath of *Lawrence* is not solicitation, but marriage.

MARRIAGE

The question of marriage has been an undercurrent in gay rights activism and litigation for more decades than is generally acknowledged. The August 1953 issue of *ONE*, "The Homosexual Magazine," was held up by postal inspectors for three weeks, perhaps in part because the issue's cover posed the question, "Homosexual Marriage?" a question answered inside by an unabashed proponent of a double standard—marriage and monogamy for heterosexuals, continued freedom for homosexuals.[261] As discussed above, two of the

---

[259] *State v Thompson*, 767 NE2d 251, 267 (Ohio 2002).

[260] And, as a result, presumptively unreceptive to a homosexual advance.

[261] See *Reformer's Choice: Marriage License or Just License?* ONE 10 (August 1953) ("Imagine that the year is 2053 and homosexuality were accepted to the point of being of no importance. Now, is the deviate allowed to continue his pursuit of physical happiness without restraint as he attempts to do today? Or is he, in this Utopia, subject to marriage laws?"). Censorship of subsequent issues of the magazine ultimately led to the first gay

unsuccessful gay plaintiffs in gay rights cases before then Circuit Judge Anthony Kennedy, would-be immigrant Sullivan and fired civil servant Singer, had tried to be legally married to their male partners. In deliberating about *Bowers v Hardwick*, Justice Powell "raised the possibility that the Constitution might protect homosexual relationships that resemble marriage—stable monogamous relationships involving members of the same sex," but was talked out of this approach by his clerk, Mike Mosman.[262] "Coupling, in two senses of the word, is what is both defining and problematic for gay men and lesbians in this society. That is to say, 'coupling' as in 'forming a pair bond' and as in 'copulating' is exactly what gay men and lesbians may want to do and what troubles society when they try to do it."[263] Now that one kind of same-sex coupling has been protected in *Lawrence*, what sort of protection will others receive?

I agree with Laurence Tribe that the same-sex marriage "issue is the mirror image of"[264] *Boddie v Conn*,[265] but my mirror sends back a somewhat different reflection of that case than his. Central to the majority's holding in *Boddie* was the "conclusion . . . that, given the basic position of the marriage relationship in this soci-

---

rights victory in the Supreme Court, which summarily reversed an obscenity conviction first issued by a lower court judge who said, "The suggestion that homosexuals should be recognized as a segment of our people and accorded special privileges as a class is rejected" and then affirmed by the Ninth Circuit, who agreed that, "Social standards are fixed by and for the great majority and not by or for a hardened or weakened minority." See *ONE Inc., v Olesen*, 241 F2d 772 (9th Cir 1957), rev'd per curiam, 355 US 371 (1958); Murdoch and Price, *Courting Justice* at 33 (cited in note 11). As Justice Douglas's clerk had written in his bench memo, "The real question is . . . whether these people are entitled to express their thoughts and customs under the same standard that publishers of girly magazines operate." Id at 44. When told of his victory, *ONE*'s founder, Dale Jennings, says he responded, "Look, don't joke. The year 2000, yes. But not today." Murdoch and Price, *Courting Justice* at 47.

[262] See Memorandum from Mosman to Powell, April 1, 1986, in Powell archives, *Bowers* file. The hints that Powell might have been willing to protect homosexual relationships for which he himself appears to have used the term marriage, had he not been frightened by the implications the recognition "that homosexual and heterosexual 'marriages' are of equal constitutional status," id, might have for other aspects of gay equality, as discussed above, are a fascinating contrast to the conventional progress of debates on the subject, in which marriage is the very last thing to attract support, with many persons who favor employment non-discrimination and tolerate homosexual sexual conduct and gay and lesbian parenting still balking at recognition of gay couples. Compare Case, 79 Va L Rev at 1658–59 (cited in note 7).

[263] Case, 79 Va L Rev 1643 (cited in note 7).

[264] Tribe, *The "Fundamental Right,"* Harv L Rev (cited in note 6).

[265] 401 US 371 (1971) (holding it a violation of due process to deny divorce to those too poor to pay court fees).

ety's hierarchy of values and the concomitant state monopolization of the means for legally dissolving this relationship, due process does prohibit" denial of access to divorce to the poor.[266] By freeing the last component of the negative right from the restrictive threat of the criminal law, *Lawrence* seems to have removed the last nail from the coffin that previously locked couples interested in a conjugal relationship into the state-sponsored monopoly institution of marriage.[267] No longer quite sustainable is Harlan's claim in *Poe* that "[t]he laws regarding marriage which provide both when the sexual powers must be used and the legal and social context in which children are born and brought up, as well as laws forbidding adultery, fornication, and homosexual practices which express the negative of the proposition, confining sexuality to lawful marriage, form a pattern so deeply pressed into our social life that any Constitutional doctrine in this area must build on that basis."[268] After *Lawrence*, every constitutionally recognized aspect of liberty legal marriage formerly monopolized (sex, reproduction, parenting, etc.) seems, as a matter of constitutional right, no longer within the state's or marriage's monopoly control. To the extent that the so-called fundamental right to marry is, as is customary for fundamental rights under the U.S. Constitution, a negative liberty which establishes only a limit on state interference, *Lawrence*, at least as an analytical matter, may spell less the beginning than the end for same-sex couples of any claimed right of access to state-sponsored marriage rooted in substantive due process, rather than squarely in equal protection. To what extent is the U.S. Constitutional right to marry a positive right?

I have already argued at length[269] that under long-settled constitutional sex discrimination law, limiting marriage to a man and a woman is patently unconstitutional because it depends on "fixed notions concerning the roles and abilities of males and females"[270]

---

[266] *Boddie*, 401 US at 374.

[267] For further discussion, see Mary Anne Case, *What Stake Do Heterosexual Women Have in the Same-Sex Marriage, Civil Union, Domestic Partnership Debates* (unpublished manuscript on file with the author).

[268] *Poe v Ullman*, 367 US at 546.

[269] See, for example, Mary Anne Case, *"The Very Stereotype the Law Condemns": Constitutional Sex Discrimination as a Quest for Perfect Proxies*, 85 Cornell L Rev at 1447, 1486–90 (2000).

[270] *Mississippi University for Women v Hogan*, 458 US 718, 725 (1982).

of the sort the Court has struck down as impermissible sex stereotypes since the 1970s. On this theory, what may have brought a
federal constitutional right to same-sex marriage one step closer
is last Term's decision in *Hibbs*,[271] in which of all people Chief
Justice Rehnquist[272] reaffirmed that we have so strong and well-
established a constitutional orthodoxy on matters of sex and gender—an orthodoxy of no governmentally endorsed role differentiation in all matters including those related to family and child
rearing—that Congress has prophylactic Section 5 power to enforce it on the states.

Mind you, both my substantive due process and my sex discrimination claims here are analytic and textual, not at all a prediction about
the Court's likely views. When it comes down to it, a substantive due
process or sexual orientation discrimination basis for striking down
marriage's sex-respecting rules might seem more appealing than a sex
discrimination basis to some Justices, notably Kennedy, who dissented
in *Hibbs* and wrote the majority opinion in *Nguyen v INS*,[273] upholding a sex-respecting rule differentiating between mothers and fathers
despite the O'Connor dissent's assertion that the rule rested on impermissible sex-role stereotypes.

Contra to the way many others have read the text, I do not
take the *Lawrence* majority's reference to the continuing potential

---

[271] *Nevada Dept of Human Resources v Hibbs*, 538 US 721 (2003) (upholding enforcement
of the Family and Medical Leave Act).

[272] Rehnquist was notoriously a latecomer to acceptance of the current constitutional law
of sex discrimination's repudiation of distinctions between the roles of men and women.
While in the Office of Legal Counsel, he unsuccessfully urged the Nixon Administration
to oppose the ERA, accusing its supporters of "a virtually fanatical desire to obscure not
only legal differentiation between men and women but, as far as possible, physical distinctions between the sexes. I think there are overtones of dislike and distaste for the traditional
difference between men and women in the family unit, and in some cases very probably a
complete rejection of the woman's traditionally different role in this regard." See *Rehnquist:
ERA Would Threaten Family Unit*, Legal Times 4 (Sept 15, 1986). As an Associate Justice,
he regularly dissented from decisions striking down sex-respecting rules, although he did
concur in *Weinberger v Wiesenfeld*, 420 US 636 (1975), which, like *Hibbs*, concerned sex-
distinctions in the benefits offered parents of young children. As Chief, he accepted those
decisions as settled law in his *United States v Virginia* concurrence, 518 US 515 (1978),
while nevertheless seeking to retain a space for separate but equal treatment of the sexes.
For further discussion, see Case, 85 Cornell L Rev at 1462, 1475 (cited in note 269). *New
York Times* reporter Linda Greenhouse has suggested that Rehnquist's personal experience
as the father of a single working mother who occasionally when his daughter "had childcare problems . . . left work early to pick up his granddaughters from school" may have
influenced his change of position. See Linda Greenhouse, *Ideas and Trends: Evolving Opinions; Heartfelt Words from the Rehnquist Court*, NY Times 4-1 (July 6, 2003).

[273] 533 US 53 (2001).

legitimacy of the State's authority "to define the meaning of the relationship or define its boundaries" if there would otherwise be "abuse of an institution the law protects" to be intended to address the problem of same-sex marriage. Like so much of the rest of the majority's prose, this passage is admittedly obscure, but my best guess is that the reference is instead to something akin to the likely continuing validity of laws prohibiting bigamy and adultery, which can be seen as abuse of the institution of legal marriage even when extraordinary circumstances such as spousal consent allow the acts to take place "absent injury to a person."[274] Because of these negative externalities of adultery, the more interesting question about its future is not whether it will be unconstitutional to criminalize it after *Lawrence* (most likely not, since, as noted, it can cause harm to an institution the law protects), but rather, will legislatures, eager to strengthen traditional marriage and perhaps still interested in penalizing, condemning, or discouraging those engaged in homosexual conduct, now move to amend their adultery statutes so as to include within its definition homosexual conduct by a married person, either for purposes of the criminal law or related purposes, such as assessing fault in divorce or allowing actions for alienation of affection.[275]

CONCLUSION

Nearly a quarter century ago, Tom Grey wrote:

I expect that within a few years fornication and sodomy laws will be found unconstitutional, on something like the very dogma of the right of consenting adults to control their own sex lives that the Court has until now so rigorously avoided. But the real reasons for the decision will have little to do with any notion in the justices' minds that sexual freedom is essential to the pursuit of happiness. Rather the decisions will respond

---

[274] Compare *Lawrence v Texas*, 2003 US Trans LEXIS 30 at *15 ("Q: Why is this different from bigamy? Mr. Smith: . . . [B]igamy involves protection of an institution that the State creates for its own purposes and there are all sorts of potential justifications about the need to protect the institution. . . .").

[275] See *In re Blanchflower*, 834 A2d 1010 (NH 2003) (rejecting husband's plea to amend his divorce petition to include the fault-based ground of adultery and add his wife's lesbian lover as correspondent because the plain meaning of adultery required coitus (i.e., heterosexual vaginal intercourse) and rejecting the husband's sex- and orientation-based equal protection challenges on the ground that all non-coital acts, whether hetero- or homosexual, were excluded from the definition).

to the same demands of order and social stability that have produced the contraception and abortion decisions. . . . [T]he homosexual community is becoming an increasingly public sector of our society. For that community to be governed effectively, it must be recognized as legitimate. Perhaps something like marriage will have to be recognized for homosexual couples, not because *they* need it for their happiness (though they may), but because *society* needs it to avoid the insecurity and instability generated by the existence in its midst of a permanent and influential subculture outside the law. . . .[276] Some of the fierce conservatives in our midst will not see this conservative necessity, and their views will prevail in the legislatures of a few jurisdictions. The Supreme Court will then step in and play its traditional role as enlightened conservator of the social interest in ordered stability, and will strike down those laws, in the glorious name of the individual.[277]

At a much slower pace than Grey once predicted, the Supreme Court has taken the first steps, in *Romer* and in *Lawrence*, to rescue gays, lesbians, and bisexuals from outlaw status. At the moment, however, the legislatures of more than "a few jurisdictions" still resist what he long ago saw as the conservative necessity for recognizing "something like marriage . . . for homosexual couples." Will it take another twenty-five years for the once outlawed couples to become in-laws?

---

[276] [Author's note: Compare the O'Connor concurrence's citation of the language in Powell's *Plyler* concurrence concerning the constitutional impermissibility of a "legislative classification that threatens the creation of an underclass." *Lawrence*, 123 S Ct at 2487, citing *Plyler v Doe* 457 US 202, 239 (1982) (Powell concurring)].

[277] Thomas Grey, *Eros, Civilization and the Burger Court*, 43 L & Contemp Probs 83, 97 (1980).

RICHARD A. POSNER

THE CONSTITUTIONALITY OF THE COPYRIGHT TERM EXTENSION ACT: ECONOMICS, POLITICS, LAW, AND JUDICIAL TECHNIQUE IN ELDRED v ASHCROFT

In 1998, Congress in the Sonny Bono Copyright Term Extension Act added 20 years to the copyright term for both existing copyrighted works and copyrightable works not yet created. The Act was challenged by Eric Eldred and other publishers of public-domain works, represented by the redoubtable Stanford Law School professor and cyberspace guru, Lawrence Lessig (who conceived the case and shopped for clients[1]), as violating both the Copyright Clause and the Free-Speech Clause of the Constitution. But in *Eldred v Ashcroft*[2] the Supreme Court, in an opinion by Justice Ginsburg that six other Justices joined, upheld the Act's constitutionality. Justices Stevens and Breyer dissented, neither joining the other's opinion.[3]

Richard A. Posner is Judge, U.S. Court of Appeals for the Seventh Circuit, and senior lecturer, University of Chicago Law School.

AUTHOR'S NOTE: I thank Amanda Butler and Paul Clark for their very helpful research assistance, and Lawrence Lessig and William Patry for their very helpful comments on an earlier draft.

[1] See Steven Levy, *The Great Liberator*, Wired 140, 155 (Oct 2002).

[2] 123 S Ct 769 (2003).

[3] A deep mystery is why the Supreme Court agreed to review the case, the court of appeals having upheld the Act's constitutionality. Although it is a fascinating case, the outcome was foreordained, as I shall explain. Presumably Stevens and Breyer, who wanted to invalidate the Act, voted to grant certiorari, but it takes four votes to grant certiorari, and who might

The case presents interesting issues of intellectual property law and economics, and I shall begin with them and then move on to somewhat broader issues of constitutional policy and judicial method. But first some background.

The Constitution authorizes Congress "to promote the Progress of Science and useful Arts, by securing for limited Times to Authors and Inventors the exclusive Right to their respective Writing and Discoveries."[4] Despite the modern connotations of "science and useful arts," which would hardly extend to popular music, cartoon characters, spy movies, or even classic works of fiction, this language in its historical context appears to cover the whole range of literary and artistic works,[5] and so authorizes the grant of copyright protection to expressive works in a sense wide enough to encompass the products of modern popular culture.

Congress first exercised its authority under the Copyright Clause in 1790, granting a 14-year initial copyright term from date of publication with a right to renew for an additional 14 years. The initial term was extended by Congress to 28 years in 1831 and the renewal term was extended to 28 years in 1909 and (following various stopgap extensions beginning in 1962) to 47 years in the Copyright Act of 1976 and 67 years in the Sonny Bono Act in 1998. For works first published between January 1, 1923, and December 31, 1977 (the last effective date of the 1909 Act), the effect of the Sonny Bono Act was to create a 95-year term (the 28-year initial term plus the Act's 67-year renewal term). These term extensions were made applicable not only to new works but also to works under copyright when the extension was enacted,

---

the other two (or more) have been? A Machiavellian conjecture is that the other two liberal Justices on the Court, Souter and Ginsburg, voted to take the case hoping that a decision to uphold the constitutionality of the Sonny Bono Act would undermine the conservative Justices' jurisprudence of judicially enforced limits on Congress's enumerated powers, such as the power to regulate commerce. As we shall see, there is indeed a tension between that jurisprudence and the upholding of the constitutionality of the Sonny Bono Act against the claim that the Act exceeded the powers that the Copyright Clause of the Constitution grants Congress.

[4] US Const, Art I, § 8, cl 8.

[5] See *Burrow-Giles Lithographic Co. v Sarony*, 111 US 53, 58 (1884). The journal of the Convention for August 18, 1787, records that one of the purposes of the Patent and Copyright Clause was "to secure to *literary* authors their copy rights for a limited time." Quoted in Edward C. Walterschied, *Defining the Patent and Copyright Term: Term Limits and the Intellectual Property Clause*, 7 J Intellectual Property L 316, 352 (2000) (emphasis added). And "science" in eighteenth-century usage included "any art or species of knowledge," Samuel Johnson, *A Dictionary of the English Language* (1755).

though the 1831 extension was applicable to only those works under copyright that were in their initial copyright term. In 1976,
as required by the Berne Convention on copyright that the United
States was planning to (and eventually did) join, Congress substituted a nonrenewable term of the author's life plus 50 years for
the renewable 28-year term from date of publication, but the new
term was applicable only to future works, except for some unpublished works. The Sonny Bono Act made the term life plus 70
years, and granted the 20-year extension to existing as well as new
works. Under the 1976 Act, certain works, mainly works for hire
(that is, works in which the copyright is owned not by the person
who created the work but by his employer or other principal), had
been given a term of 75 years from publication or 100 years from
creation, whichever was shorter, and these periods were extended
to 95 and 120 years, respectively, by the Sonny Bono Act; these
extensions too were applied to existing copyright works as well as
new works. I shall ignore these refinements and focus on life plus
70 years.

The initial push for the legislation that eventuated in the Sonny
Bono Act had come years earlier from the children and grandchildren of Tin Pan Alley composers, who faced the prospect of
the loss of their lucrative royalties when the copyrights on their
parents' or grandparents' music expired (for example, the copyright on George Gershwin's composition *Rhapsody in Blue* was due
to expire in 2000), later joined by the Disney corporation, which
faced the imminent expiration of its copyright on its original
Steamboat Willie (Mickey Mouse) character, and by other owners
of lucrative copyrights soon to expire.[6] Indeed, anyone who owned
a copyright stood to benefit from the extension of the term, and
the closer the copyright was to expiration the greater the benefit
would be. Advocates of the extension pointed out that it would
improve the U.S. balance of trade because the United States is a
net exporter of copyrighted work, that it would conform the U.S.
term to the European term (European countries, which are more

---

[6] See Robert P. Merges, *One Hundred Years of Solitude: Intellectual Property Law, 1900–
2000*, 88 Cal L Rev 2187, 2236 n 219 (2000); Chris Sprigman, *The Mouse That Ate the
Public Domain: Disney, the Copyright Term Extension Act, and Eldred v. Ashcroft*, Findlaw's
Writ, <http://writ.news.findlaw.com/commentary/20020305_sprigman.html> (visited June
16, 2002); Daren Fonda, *Copyright's Crusader*, Boston Globe Magazine (Aug 29, 1999),
<http://www.boston.com/globe/magazine/8-29/featurestory1.shtml> (visited July 3, 2003).

protective of authors' rights than the United States, had already moved to life plus 70 years), that it would encourage efforts to preserve and restore old movies, and that, given increased longevity, it would increase the likelihood that descendants of authors would receive royalties. The advocates were aided by the fact that the extension was supported by popular celebrities from the world of entertainment and also that there was little opposition—and this for a reason illuminated by the theory of public choice, the theory that seeks to explain legislation in the hardheaded terms of rational self-interest. A copyright enables its owner to exclude competition from copiers, and so if there are no good substitutes for his work he will obtain a monopoly profit, of sorts, by being able to charge a price in excess of his marginal cost (the cost of making an additional copy). But a seller of public-domain work can expect only a competitive return, since anyone is free to sell the identical work in competition with him. So publishers of public-domain work like Eldred had a smaller stake in the size of the public domain (which term extension would shrink) than publishers of copyrighted work had in the propertized domain; the latter publishers thus had more to gain from enactment of term extension than Eldred and his confreres had to lose from that enactment, and so lobbied more vigorously for the extension than opponents lobbied against it.[7] Consumers were likely to be hurt by the shrinkage of the public domain, but consumers are diffuse and unorganized, and as a result carry relatively little weight in the political process (and foreign consumers none).

The legislation was, it is true, held up for years, but not because of opposition; rather, it was held hostage to the effort of the bar and restaurant industry to obtain relief from the royalties charged by copyright holders for playing background music. When Congress finally yielded to the industry's demand by including the re-

---

[7] Copyright owners were generous contributors to House and Senate sponsors and supporters of the Sonny Bono Act. According to the Center for Responsive Politics, in 1996 television, motion picture, and music interests donated $1,419,717 to six of the Act's eight sponsors and cosponsors—Spencer Abraham, Barbara Boxer, Dianne Feinstein, Orrin Hatch, Patrick Leahy, and Fred Thompson (information on donations to the other two, Howell Heflin and Alan Simpson, was not available). Disney, MCA, Viacom, Paramount Pictures, and Time Warner all donated conspicuously large amounts—for example, Disney gave $34,500 to Senator Leahy. See <http://www.opensecrets.org/politicians/candlist.asp?Sort=N&Cong=104> (visited July 3, 2003); see also Michael H. Davis, *Extending Copyright and the Constitution: Have I Stayed Too Long?* 52 Fla L Rev 989, 998–99 (2000).

lief sought in the term extension bill, the bill sailed through.[8] Partly because of the public-choice considerations that I have mentioned, and partly because Sonny Bono's untimely death and the support of the bill by entertainment celebrities and their children and even grandchildren[9] made it a sentimental favorite, the term extension act was a popular, or at least an uncontroversial, piece of legislation; the bearing of this on the constitutional issues is an important question that I take up later.

Professor Lessig limited so much of his attack on the Act as rested on the Constitution's Copyright Clause to the retroactive aspect of the Sonny Bono Act, that is, to the fact that it extended existing copyrights. The point he made was a simple but powerful one. The historic Anglo-American hostility to government grants of monopolies[10] caused the framers of the Constitution to authorize the granting of copyrights only for limited periods and only for the purpose of promoting intellectual and cultural progress by inducing the creation of expressive works. This is apparent from the wording of the Copyright Clause itself and has been repeated in numerous decisions of the Supreme Court.[11] If a work has already been created and copyrighted, extending its copyright term cannot be an inducement; the additional income enabled by the extension is a pure windfall.[12] In economic terms, which are the terms in which intellectual property is increasingly discussed, extending an existing copyright creates a deadweight loss with no offsetting incentive gains. The deadweight loss arises from the fact that the copyright holder will set a price higher than his marginal cost (which he can do because he is protected by the copyright from direct competition, though not from the competition of sub-

---

[8] The Act passed by voice vote.

[9] See Brief of Intellectual Property Law Professors as Amici Curiae Supporting Petitioners, *Eldred v Ashcroft*, 2001 US Briefs 618 (May 20, 2002); Hearings on S 483 before the Senate Committee on the Judiciary, 104th Cong, 1st Sess 26 (1997).

[10] See, for example, The Case of Monopolies (*Darcy v Allen*), 77 Eng Rep 1260 (KB 1602).

[11] See, for example, *Pennock v Dialogue*, 27 US 1, 19 (1829); Trade-Mark Cases, 100 US 82 (1879); *Butcher's Union Slaughter-House & Live-Stock Landing Co. v Crescent City Live-Stock Landing & Slaughter House Co.*, 111 US 746, 763 (1884); *Fox Film Corp. v Doyal*, 286 US 123, 127–28 (1932); *Brenner v Manson*, 383 US 519, 534 (1966); *Twentieth Century Music Corp. v Aiken*, 422 US 151, 156 (1975).

[12] This is not a new insight. See 24 *Annals* 1440–49 (1831) (remarks of Sen. William Bibb); David P. Currie, 2 *The Constitution in Congress* at 312 n 191 (2001).

stitutes), thus deflecting some consumers to works that cost a higher quality-adjusted amount to make but that seem cheaper because they are sold at a competitive price, a price equal to their marginal cost. The incentive purpose of copyright, which balances the deadweight cost by enabling the creator of an expressive work that may be very cheap to copy to recoup his initial investment in creating the work by being able to exclude copiers (the resulting deadweight cost is thus the price for encouraging the creation of new works), falls out of the analysis when one is speaking of expanding the copyright protection of a work that has already been created and copyrighted; obviously the existing copyright protection had sufficed to induce the creation of the work.

The argument is not airtight. William Landes and I have explained that copyright serves other valid economic purposes besides imparting incentives to create new expressive works,[13] consistent with the general proposition that commodification, or propertization, is efficient because it encourages careful exploitation of valuable resources. I need not dwell on these benefits here. As Landes and I explain, they argue not for slapping 20 years onto the existing copyright term but for the quite different system of copyright protection that we call "indefinite renewal," in which copyrights would be granted for a short initial term that could be renewed an indefinite number of times, but only for a stiff fee each time. The result would be to enlarge the public domain by clearing low-value copyrights (the vast majority) out of the propertized sector while allowing the handful of really valuable ones to remain owned in order that they might be exploited optimally. The Sonny Bono Act, in contrast, clogs the public domain by extending the copyrights on many old works whose copyright holders may be costly or even impossible to trace and negotiate with for a license, though this problem can be mitigated by an intelligent construal of the fair-use defense to copyright infringement or by modest statutory amendments.[14]

---

[13] See William M. Landes and Richard A. Posner, *Indefinitely Renewable Copyright*, 70 U Chi L Rev 471 (2003); Landes and Posner, *The Economic Structure of Intellectual Property Law*, ch 8 (2003); Richard A. Posner, *How Long Should a Copyright Last?* (J Copyright Soc, forthcoming).

[14] See William F. Patry and Richard A. Posner, *Fair Use and Statutory Reform in the Wake of Eldred* (Cal L Rev, forthcoming). 17 USC §§ 306(d) and (e) already go some way toward meeting this concern. They provide in essence that unless the Copyright Office is notified of the death of a copyright owner, it is conclusively presumed that he died at least 70 years ago and therefore that the copyright has lapsed. Surprisingly, these provisions were not mentioned in any of the opinions in *Eldred*.

So the Sonny Bono Act flunks a cost-benefit test, and its enactment was the product, in major part, of the asymmetrical structure of the costs and benefits—the costs diffused among U.S. and foreign consumers, the benefits concentrated in a small number of mainly U.S. corporate and private owners of lucrative copyrights. A popular law, but the asymmetry of support and opposition tarnishes its democratic credentials.

But what are the *constitutional* implications of the foregoing analysis? By confining his Copyright Clause challenge to the retroactive feature of the Sonny Bono Act, Lessig attacked the Act in its weakest spot. But he also opened himself to Justice Ginsburg's riposte, which occupies the first and most confident part of her opinion, that Congress has *always* made copyright extensions applicable to existing as well as new copyrights, so that Lessig's argument implies that every U.S. copyright statute, with the possible exception of the first, has been unconstitutional.[15] Yet if the Court had bought the argument, it would not have been the first time that the Court had upset centuries of unchallenged legislation—which anyway puts the case too strongly, since there were only two extensions (1831 and 1909) until 1962; and it is surprising that Justice Ginsburg, a liberal, would think the novelty of the challenge as great an obstacle to its succeeding as she seemed to think it. She quoted Holmes for the proposition that a page of history is worth a volume of logic, but it was Holmes also who warned against following a rule merely because it is old.[16] There is ancient folly as well as ancient wisdom; and it is telling that Ginsburg found nothing to say in favor of retroactivity except tradition and a vague sense of "fairness" (or, as a Congressman quoted approvingly by the Court, but without elaboration by either Congressman or Court, put it, "justice, policy, and equity alike"[17]). Someone who had obtained a copyright the day before the Sonny Bono Act became effective would have 20 years less protection than someone who obtained a copyright the next day. This discrepant treat-

---

[15] The first, as Justice Stevens explained in his dissent, 123 S Ct at 795–96, while it did apply to existing as well as new works, replaced for existing works the protection that those works enjoyed under state law. So it was a swap rather than the conferral of a windfall.

[16] O. W. Holmes, *The Path of the Law*, 10 Harv L Rev 457, 469 (1897) ("It is revolting to have no better reason for a rule of law than that it was laid down in the time of Henry IV.").

[17] 123 S Ct at 779.

ment, though inevitable whenever entitlements involve numerical criteria—think of the situation of someone whose copyright had expired the day before the Act became effective—is what was thought "unfair."

Actually there *is* an argument, though I am not aware that anyone has ever made it, in favor of retroactivity. It is that retroactivity focuses legislative and, in principle at least, public attention on copyright-term extensions in a way that a merely prospective extension would not. The effect of prospective extensions is so long deferred that it would be difficult to arouse anyone's ire over them. The effect on the public domain of extending the term of a work not yet created by 20 years is nil until 50 years after the author's death, and death plus 50 years might lie a century or more in the future. The Eldreds of this world might even lack standing to complain in court about their access to the public domain a century hence, let alone have an incentive to oppose the extension in Congress. By the same token, to the extent that there is anything to be said in favor of copyright-term extensions, the only people with an incentive to say it are people whose copyrights are about to expire; and so, in short, unless such extensions are retroactive, the absence of present consequences will preclude focused consideration of the merits of the extension.

This argument is quite different from Justice Ginsburg's claim, a makeweight, that "the consistent placement of existing copyright holders in parity with future holders" creates a reasonable expectation in the copyright holder that he will get the benefit of any legislative term extension enacted before his copyright expires.[18] It is unrealistic to suppose that such an expectation would affect an author's decision as to whether to compose another book, article, or other expressive work. Very weak, also, is Justice Ginsburg's claim that "the Framers guarded against the future accumulation of monopoly power in booksellers and publishers by authorizing Congress to vest copyrights only in 'Authors,'"[19] when as she knows copyrights are commonly assigned to publishers (or taken out in the publisher's name in the first place if it is a work for hire), and it would make no difference if the publisher instead of insisting on assignment took out the copyright in its own name from the start.

---

[18] Id at 786.

[19] Id at 779 n 6.

There is a further problem, this one analytical rather than tactical, with Lessig's decision to limit his attack on the Sonny Bono Act to its retroactive feature. The same argument against retroactivity—that the costs exceed the benefits because of the absence of incentive effects—is applicable in scarcely diminished form to the extension of the copyright term for new works as well. If the absence of such effects is decisive against retroactivity, either because such effects provide the only (or at least the main) economic argument for copyright or because they are the only basis upon which the Constitution allows Congress to grant copyright protection, then it is decisive against forward-looking extensions as well, owing to the combination of the existing very long term provided by the 1976 copyright statute with discounting to present value. If we suppose that the average minimum term of a copyright under the 1976 Act is 80 years (taking the average age of the authorship of a work as 40 and the average age of death as 70, so that a copyright term of life plus 50 years would give copyright protection to the work for 80 years), then under any realistic assumption about discount rates and depreciation rates (depreciation must be taken into account and not just discounting to present value because the income generated by most copyrighted works declines, and steeply too, with time), the present value of 20 years added to the copyright term is very slight. Suppose both rates are 5 percent, for a total of 10 percent (call this the net discount rate). Under a system of perpetual copyright, the present value of an infinite stream of income of $1 year would be $10 (= $1/r$, where r is the net discount rate). Under a limited copyright term (=t), the present value would be $(1 - e^{-rt})/r$. So if $t = 80$ and $r = .10$, the present value of $1 per year is $9.997, which is more than 99 percent of the present value of a perpetual copyright. Extending the term another 20 years would therefore have a wholly insignificant effect on authors' economic incentives. It would be an effect imperceptibly different from the zero effect on those incentives of extending the author's copyright after he has already produced the work. The logic of Lessig's argument therefore applies with essentially equal force to the Sonny Bono Act's extension of the copyright term for works created after the Act became effective.

But the logic doesn't stop there. It implies the unconstitutionality of *every* copyright-term extension, beginning with the 1831 copyright statute, which increased the initial term to 28 years while retaining the 14-year renewal, for a total of 42 years, up from 28 under the 1790 Act. For, using the same figures as above, it is easily shown that a 28-year term yields the author a present value that is 94 percent as great as that of a perpetual copyright, so that the increase in present value and therefore in authorial financial incentives brought about by extending the term another 14 years is slight. But this may be pressing logic too hard, as I'll explain shortly.

What is true, though unremarked by any of the Justices, is that although neither prospective nor retroactive copyright-term extensions beyond the 1790 term, let alone the 1976 term, yield incentive benefits, which are the only kind that the Copyright Clause of the Constitution contemplates, retroactive extensions are more pernicious in the following respect. To compare the present (negligible) benefits of a future extension with its deadweight costs, both sides of the balance must be discounted to present value, and when this is done the costs tend to disappear along with the benefits. But when an existing copyright is extended, the deadweight loss begins to accrue as soon as the copyright would have expired were it not for the extension, and so is much greater in present-value terms.[20] From an economic standpoint, therefore, retroactive extensions are even worse than prospective ones, but from a narrower legal standpoint that focuses on the fact that the encouragement of authorship is the only goal to which the Copyright Clause refers, the two types of extension are equally bad. The economic and legal approaches merge in the constitutional requirement of "limited Times." Perpetual copyright is not needed in order to provide authors with adequate incentives to invest in the creation of expressive works.

There is even a sense in which, from a narrowly legal perspective, prospective extensions are worse than retroactive ones rather than better as I just suggested. In an unusually sharp-tongued petition for rehearing (of course denied), Lessig upbraided the Court

---

[20] Though not as great as suggested by statistics quoted by Justice Breyer from a study which had found that the 2 percent or so of copyrights that still have commercial value after 55 to 74 years generate some $400 million a year in royalties; from this Justice Breyer inferred that "20 years of extra copyright protection will mean the transfer of several billion extra royalty dollars to holders of existing copyrights." Id at 804. Not that much, in all likelihood. The $400 million is a transfer payment, not a deadweight loss, which would be a substantially smaller amount (under the simplest assumption, one-half the amount); and discounting the reduced amount over 20 years would yield a figure closer to 1 billion than to several billion dollars. But this is a detail and Breyer was correct to emphasize the transaction costs involved in obtaining copyright permissions; these are an additional and quite substantial social loss from extending the copyright term.

for its failure to so much as cite, let alone attempt to distinguish, *United States v Lopez*,[21] the case in which the Court's conservative majority put teeth into the limitations that the Constitution's Commerce Clause imposes on Congress's regulatory power under that clause. Justice Ginsburg dissented in *Lopez*, so her ignoring the case was not a surprise. The petition for rehearing is plainly directed at the conservative Justices, and it makes a powerful doctrinal point. The Commerce Clause empowers Congress to regulate interstate and foreign commerce, but it does not define "interstate commerce," and until *Lopez* it had long been thought that Congress's regulatory power was plenary because in a modern economy there is virtually no transaction that is not linked in some way to interstate movements.[22] But the Court, seemingly out of a desire to limit federal power,[23] in *Lopez* and subsequent cases limited the commerce power, striking down federal laws that forbade carrying a gun within 1,000 feet of a school (the law involved in *Lopez* itself), that criminalized arson of an owner-occupied house, and that made violence against women a federal crime,[24] though in all these cases, especially the last, an effect on interstate commerce could readily be conjectured. Like interstate commerce, "limited Times" is a term of almost infinite elasticity, since in a literal sense any copyright term short of infinity would be limited. But just as deeming every transaction to be in commerce would be inconsistent with the intent of the framers of the Constitution to circumscribe Congress's power over the economy, so deeming every finite copyright term however long to be limited would be inconsistent with the framers' intent to limit Congress's power to create property rights in expressive works. Any attempt to impose a numerical limit on "limited Times" would be arbitrary, just as statutes of limitations and statutory enactment dates are arbitrary (remember the "fairness" argument for making copyright term extensions retroactive), but no more arbitrary than the lines the

---

[21] 514 US 549 (1995).

[22] This is the holding of *Wickard v Fillburn*, 317 US 111 (1942), and it was reaffirmed in *Lopez* and subsequent cases.

[23] See also *City of Boerne v Flores*, 521 US 507 (1997); *Kimel v Florida Board of Regents*, 528 US 62 (2000).

[24] *United States v Lopez*, 514 US 549 (1995); *Jones v United States*, 529 US 859 (2000); *United States v Morrison*, 529 US 598 (2000).

Supreme Court has been drawing in an effort to curb Congress's power to regulate commerce.[25]

The implications, however, of these analytically powerful arguments for putting teeth into the Copyright Clause are bizarre; and so we have the familiar tension between formalist and realist grounds of judicial decision. If every copyright that was issued more than 28 years ago is unenforceable because every extension of the copyright term after 1790 was unconstitutional (since the incentive effects of any further extension would have been as a practical matter nil), and if for the same reason no copyright issued from this time forward may constitutionally extend more than 28 years, the scope of intellectual property will have contracted remarkably and, at the federal level, irrevocably, barring a constitutional amendment or a Supreme Court change of heart, since the invalidation of longer terms would have been done by a constitutional interpretation. Not that this contraction would necessarily be a bad thing from an economic standpoint; but it would be surprising if either economic or legal-doctrinal analysis could persuade a majority of the Court to so radical a result in an area in which the Justices' powerful emotions are not engaged. Justice Breyer, who argued in his dissent that the Sonny Bono Act is unconstitutional whether applied to existing or new works, sought to cabin the implications of his position (a position difficult to limit to that Act) by pointing out that by signing on to the Berne Convention we committed ourselves to adopting a copyright term of life plus 50 years because that is one of the minimum requirements of copyright law that the Convention imposes on its signatories. But the treaty power cannot be used to override the Constitution.[26] Otherwise we could make a treaty with the Vatican whereby we agreed to make Roman Catholicism the official religion of the United States. Justice Breyer weakly added, "we are not here considering, and we need not consider, the constitutionality of other copyright statutes," and "this particular statute simply goes too far."[27] In so saying he was acknowledging that his test for the

---

[25] See, for example, the discussion of the Court's arson cases in *United States v Veysey*, 334 F3d 600 (7th Cir 2003).

[26] *Reid v Covert*, 354 US 1, 17 (1957); *Geofroy v Riggs*, 133 US 258 (1890).

[27] 123 S Ct at 813.

constitutionality of a copyright statute had no real bite, and advocating in effect ad hoc decision making.

There is another bizarre implication of the case against the Sonny Bono Act. It derives from further reflection on the *Lopez* case and its successor cases. Curtailing Congress's power over commerce creates space for state regulation. Curtailing its power over copyright would create a similar space—but a space that Lessig and his allies would hate to see filled. All Congress would have to do, to nullify the effect of the Supreme Court's invalidating the Sonny Bono Act and for that matter all predecessor copyright statutes back to 1831, would be to repeal the preemption clause in the copyright act, thus allowing states to issue copyrights. (This would not violate the Berne Convention provided all the states authorized copyrights that satisfied the Convention's minimum requirements; and anyway the United States can always withdraw from a treaty.[28]) Within days, California and New York would pass statutes creating perpetual copyright, unless the First Amendment would block such action, a question that I take up later—and answer in the negative.

All this is not to excuse, or even explain, the conservative Justices' failure to discuss the *Lopez* line of cases. It's not as if the cases had not been brought to their attention. Apart from their being cited in Lessig's brief, they were a focus of the oral argument, as well as of Judge Sentelle's dissent in the court of appeals.[29] But one must always remember that the Supreme Court is a political court, and its decisions, at least in major cases, cannot be expected to be, and are not, "principled" in any serious sense. The Court's conservative Justices are happy to give the states more elbow room when it comes to the employment conditions of state civil servants or the regulation of local business, but they don't want them messing with intellectual property law. Conservatives believe in property rights and do not distinguish sharply if at all between physical and intellectual property, even though the economics of the two types of property differ and near-total "commodification" of the

---

[28] Article 35.2 of the Berne Convention provides that any country may withdraw from the Convention simply by notice to the Director General of the bureau that the Convention creates to supervise compliance with the Convention's requirements.

[29] *Eldred v Reno*, 239 F3d 372, 380–83 (DC Cir 2001) (Sentelle, J, dissenting).

former (including rights of unlimited duration) makes a good deal more economic sense than near-total commodification of the latter.[30] Were Congress to respond to a decision invalidating the Sonny Bono Act (and perhaps the Copyright Act of 1976 as well) on constitutional grounds by repealing the Copyright Act's preemption clause and thus authorizing the states to grant copyrights (including perpetual copyrights—common law copyright, which states recognized until the 1976 Act preempted it almost entirely by dropping the publication requirement for obtaining federal copyright protection, is perpetual), chaos would ensue. But it could be averted by the Court's invalidating only retroactive extensions of copyright, leaving the bulk of federal copyright law intact—an "illogical" result but no more so than many pragmatic compromises made by judges.

Justice Ginsburg's main defense against the challenge to the Sonny Bono Act's validity under the Copyright Clause was that Congress can adopt any copyright law it wants, as long as the law is rational and does not violate any specific constitutional prohibition. So a copyright law that created perpetual copyrights, or that protected works that were not works of authorship,[31] or that allowed the government to copyright its documents and forbid quotation from them without governmental consent, or that allowed only white people to obtain copyrights, would be unconstitutional; but the length of the copyright term (short of infinite) and whether to extend it for existing as well as new works, not being issues addressed by specific constitutional language either in the Copyright Clause or elsewhere, are immune from judicial invalidation as long they are rational. That is an easy test, and one that the Sonny Bono Act passed. There was the mercantilist argument for the Act that I mentioned (we are a net exporter of copyrighted works); there is the fact that our international peers, the European nations, had adopted life plus 70 years; there is the long-unchallenged assumption that copyright-term extensions should apply equally to existing and new works; there is the "old-movies restoration" argument;[32]

---

[30] This is a principal theme of my book with Landes, *The Economic Structure of Intellectal Property Law* (cited in note 13).

[31] See *Feist Publications, Inc. v Rural Telephone Service Co.*, 499 US 340, 347–48 (1991).

[32] Films deteriorate; a firm that would have to incur substantial costs to transfer an aging film to a digital medium might not do so unless it had copyright protection, and the copyrights on a number of these old films were on the verge of expiration. See, for example, Hearings (cited in note 9 above) at 26 (testimony of Jack Valenti, president of the Motion

there is the essential arbitrariness of numerical limits, which makes courts reluctant, for example, to make up a limitations period for a law that does not specify a statute of limitations; there is the commodification argument (not mentioned by the Court—the argument I mentioned earlier that highly valuable properties, such as the Mickey Mouse character, will be exploited more efficiently if they are owned by someone[33]); and there is the further fact (also not mentioned by the Justices) that the longer the copyright term, the fewer the works that are affected by a further extension, because most copyrighted works lose their value after only a few years. These arguments vary considerably in strength, to be sure, and even when aggregated they don't amount to much. Justice Ginsburg laid great stress on one of the weakest—the interest in "harmonizing" our copyright law with that of Europe. She described as the "dominant reason" for the Sonny Bono Act the fact that Europe had gone to life plus 70,[34] but did not explain why that is a reason at all; on that ground one might argue that an author's moral rights should be protected by the Due Process Clause because European nations enforce such rights ("moral rights" are basically an author's rights not to have his work misattributed, or altered without his permission). She offered nary a hint as to *why* Europe had gone to life plus 70 years, and without knowing the reason how could one know whether it would be a good idea, or even a constitutionally valid idea, for the United States to follow suit? The reason for Europe's adopting life plus 70 years appears to be that as part of its efforts at unifying Europe economically, the European Union wanted to have a uniform copyright term; and for the same public-choice reasons that explain the Sonny Bono Act, it was politically more feasible to unify upward than downward.

Some of the other reasons for the Act that she threw into the stew are also makeweights, such as that the increase in the average age of parents when their children are born might, were it not for the

---

Picture Association of America). However, there is a contrary argument: that extending copyrights on movies impedes efforts to preserve "orphan works"—early films the copyrights on which are held by defunct studios or untraceable owners—because preservers would incur heavy expenses to identify and negotiate with the copyright owners. Id (testimony of Larry Urbanski). This is an example of the concerns that have led to the proposals made in my article with William Patry, cited in note 14 above.

[33] The "free Mickey Mouse" crowd has it backwards: if anyone can use the character for any purpose, Mickey is a slave.

[34] See 123 S Ct at 781 n 11.

lengthened copyright term, deprive them of the "pride and comfort in knowing that one's children—and perhaps their children—might also benefit from one's posthumous popularity," and that income from an author's past works finances his new works.[35] The second point is slight because even under the 1976 Act copyright does not expire before the author dies, although the longer the copyright term, the higher the price the author could get for selling his copyright.

Justice Breyer argued that the rationality test was too loose for a statute that regulated expression; and let me pause here to consider whether he was right that the First Amendment had a bearing on the constitutionality of the Sonny Bono Act. Justice Ginsburg thought not, for four reasons: (1) copyright law encourages expression; (2) copyright is limited to the expressive features of the copyrighted work and does not limit the copying of the ideas, opinions, or facts contained in the work; (3) "copyright law contains built-in First Amendment accommodations";[36] (4) the First Amendment "bears less heavily when speakers assert the right to make other people's speeches."[37] The first reason is beside the point, since whatever is true of copyright law in general, the Sonny Bono Act will have no tendency to increase the amount of expression, because it doesn't increase the incentives to create expressive works. The other reasons Ginsburg offers are sound, however, and the second[38] is especially powerful. Not only is copyright protection limited to the *form* of the copyrighted work, since the work can be paraphrased without risk of infringement; but almost all copyright owners want to disseminate rather than suppress their work. They do not want to disseminate it as broadly as they could in theory do, because that would require their charging a zero price; but they do want to disseminate it rather than to bottle it up. Disney is not trying to kill Mickey Mouse, and Gershwin's heirs do not wish to suppress *Porgy and Bess*. It is true, however, as Lessig's brief emphasizes, that to the extent that the costs of tracing and negotiating with the owners of copyrights of old works are frequently prohibitive, some of those works may simply disappear.[39]

---

[35] Id at 782 nn 14 and 15.

[36] Id at 788.

[37] Id at 789.

[38] Amplified in R. Polk Wagner, *Information Wants to Be Free: Intellectual Property and the Mythologies of Control*, 103 Colum L Rev 995 (2003).

[39] Again, see the discussion in Patry and Posner (cited in note 14).

It is also true that one can imagine changes in copyright law that would reduce freedom of expression significantly. Were there no fair-use defense to copyright infringement, for example, an author would be able to cripple his critics by forbidding them to quote from his work in a book review. Parodies, an important form of criticism, would be particularly hard hit, since often a parody must quote extensively from the parodied work in order to indicate what its target is. But fair use privileges parodies, and more broadly permits copying to the extent required by the very policy of free expression that animates the First Amendment. That is what Justice Ginsburg meant by built-in accommodations. The Sonny Bono Act does not cut into fair use or otherwise impede critical copying, though it does increase the cost of reproducing expressive works by reducing the size of the public domain. But this is where Justice Ginsburg's fourth point comes into play. What is limited when the size of the public domain shrinks is not new expression, but the reproduction of existing expression.

The point has less force than she gives it, however, and this for two reasons. First and obviously, free copying reduces the cost and hence increases the amount of dissemination of the copied work. Second, public-domain materials are an important input into new expressive works (few expressive works are completely new[40]), and so anything that diminishes them will increase the cost or reduce the quality of new expressive works. Justice Ginsburg's point about fair use is also weaker than it seems, because of the tendency of lower-court judges and particularly publishers to interpret the fair-use defense very narrowly.

But with due regard for the limitations of Justice Ginsburg's analysis, I share the Court's evident dubiety that bringing still *another* area of regulation (after pornography, and defamation, and commercial billboards, and campaign finance, and all the rest) under First Amendment scrutiny would be a step in the right direction. All other objections to one side, the project seems unmanageable. For consider Justice Breyer's suggested standard: a copyright statute, because it regulates speech and therefore must be more than minimally rational, "lacks the constitutionally necessary rational support

---

[40] "[P]oetry can only be made out of other poems; novels out of other novels." Northrup Frye, *Anatomy of Criticism* 97 (1957). See Landes and Posner, *The Economic Structure of Intellectual Property Law*, ch 2 (cited in note 13).

(1) if the significant benefits that it bestows are private, not public; (2) if it threatens seriously to undermine the expressive values that the Copyright Clause embodies; and (3) if it cannot find justification in any significant Clause-related objective."[41] When (1) is added to (3), we have a no-benefits case, so naturally the costs (2) dominate. But if the majority had agreed with Breyer's three points, it would have pronounced the statute irrational. There are only so many ways in which to say that if a statute has no redeeming virtues at all, it is irrational.

So let me return to the question whether, if in the wake of a hypothetical invalidation of the Sonny Bono Act, Congress were to repeal the copyright preemption clause and the leading intellectual-property states responded by legislating perpetual copyright, these new state laws would violate the First Amendment (which in modern times is thought to limit state as well as congressional regulation of speech, by virtue of the Due Process Clause of the Fourteenth Amendment). Maybe so, though for a reason that supports the majority opinion. Although from an incentive standpoint life plus 70 years is the equivalent of perpetual copyright, a person not imbued with economics would suppose them actually quite different. Shakespeare died in 1616. If the Sonny Bono Act had been in effect then, his works would have entered the public domain in 1686, and so the earliest of his works would have enjoyed copyright protection for almost a century. Yet from the perspective of 2003, a copyright term that expired in 1686 seems quite limited relative to perpetual copyright. Oddly, and I suppose irrelevantly, a finite copyright term of any length is 0 percent as long as the term of a perpetual copyright.

But one thing is clear: if as I believe the majority's First Amendment analysis is essentially correct, states after the copyright preemption clause was repealed could institute the Sonny Bono Act's term: and what then would Lessig, Breyer, and Stevens have achieved had they succeeded in persuading the Court to strike down the Act? Remember that the Act had very strong congressional support, suggesting that the Court might have faced retaliation in some form had it invalidated it on grounds hard to explain to the public at large. A wave of state copyright statutes might have been one of the upshots.

---

[41] 123 S Ct at 802.

All this said, had the Court wanted to invalidate the Act, either in toto or just as applied to existing copyrights, it could have done so in a professionally respectable opinion. Evidently it did not want to do so, probably because it had no sense that a great injustice was being perpetrated; and in the absence of such a sense there would be little motivation to invalidate a popular statute and perhaps precipitate the commotion suggested in the preceding paragraph. The personal views that I suspect motivated the Justices on both sides of the case are obscured by the imposing scholarly apparatus that the opinions deploy and that characteristically generate equally good or bad arguments for both sides.

Decisions later in the same Term dealing with affirmative action and with sodomy confirmed what every knowledgeable observer understands, that the Supreme Court is a political court, in the sense of dealing with cases that, since they are indeterminate on the basis of the canonical legal materials, such as constitutional text and previous decisions, can be decided only as an exercise of will (or, more politely, judgment), based on the temperament, ideology, emotions, and perspective of the individual Justices.[42] But it would be more accurate to say that the Court is both a political court *and* a "technical" court, and that the fact that it decides many cases that are not "political" in the ordinary sense helps to conceal from the public the degree to which the Court is a political body (though oddly, the general public seems less deceived on this score than the legal profession). The issue in *Eldred* would strike most observers as technical rather than political, yet the dissenting Justices, who had the stronger technical case, had the weaker overall case, primarily because a decision invalidating the Sonny Bono Act might well have opened a Pandora's Box out of which would fly federal amendments and state enactments that would create a worse situation, from the standpoint of a sensible copyright regime, than the Act did. Perhaps, then, despite the resolutely

---

[42] Anyone who doubts this should read the marvelous debate between a law professor and a journalist over the sodomy case: Jeffrey Rosen, *Kennedy Curse: Why the Court's Sodomy Ruling Was Worse Than Roe*, New Republic 15 (July 21, 2003); Andrew Sullivan, *Citizens: Why the Court's Sodomy Ruling Was Just Right*, id at 18. Rosen does a better job of arguing against the majority's position than the dissenting Justice, and Sullivan a better job of arguing for that position than the majority opinion; but so divergent are their premises and empirical hunches that, because there is no neutral ground for choosing between their premises and no empirical methodology for verifying or refuting their hunches, it is impossible to say which of them has the better of the argument, "objectively" speaking.

formalist character of most Supreme Court opinions nowadays, the decisions themselves, whether or not "political" in a familiar sense, are best understood as pragmatic, and thus as dictated by what the Justices consider best for society rather than by legal reasoning in some distinctive sense.

LILLIAN R. BEVIER

UNITED STATES v AMERICAN LIBRARY ASSOCIATION: WHITHER FIRST AMENDMENT DOCTRINE

In *United States v American Library* Association, Inc.[1] the Supreme Court sustained the Children's Internet Protection Act (CIPA),[2] which Congress enacted to address problems associated with the ready availability of Internet pornography to children in public libraries.[3] Considering whether to attempt a partial solution to the problem by encouraging libraries to use filtering software, Congress confronted a dilemma. Software filters exist that can block pornography, but they work imperfectly. For a variety of reasons, including technological constraints, limitations in human judgment, and the size and rate of growth of the Internet, currently available filtering software makes errors. Filters wrongly block some material, and wrongly fail to block other material. Thus filters designed to block "child pornography" will wrongly block much sexually explicit material that is not child pornography and

Lillian R. BeVier is John S. Shannon Distinguished Professor of Law and Class of 1963 Research Professor, University of Virginia School of Law.

Author's note: Thanks to Dan Bress, University of Virginia Class of 2005, for excellent research help.

[1] 123 S Ct 2297 (2003).

[2] 114 Stat 2763A-335, codified at 20 USC § 9134 (2000) and 47 USC § 254(h)(6) (2000).

[3] Ready availability of Internet pornography to children in public libraries is but one piece of the larger problem of Internet pornography, a subject about which citizens hold strong views and political debate is heated. For an excellent summary of the problem and its potential solutions, see Dick Thornburgh and Herbert S. Lin, eds, *Youth, Pornography and the Internet* (National Academy, 2002).

fail to block some that is. In CIPA Congress resolved the dilemma
presented by the phenomenon of overblocking by, first, providing
that a public library may not receive federal funding for Internet
access unless it "installs software to block images that constitute
obscenity or child pornography, and to prevent minors from obtaining access to material that is harmful to them"[4] and, second,
permitting a library to "disable" a filter "to enable access for bona
fide research or other lawful purpose."[5] A group of libraries, library
associations, library patrons, and Web site publishers brought a
facial challenge to CIPA in federal district court, claiming that requiring the filters violated the First Amendment because of their
technological incapacity to avoid overblocking. Observing that
"any public library that adheres to CIPA's conditions will necessarily restrict patrons' access to a substantial amount of protected
speech,"[6] and concluding that "[i]n providing its patrons with Internet access, a public library creates a forum for the facilitation
of speech,"[7] the district court subjected CIPA to strict scrutiny.
The court determined that the government has a compelling interest in preventing the dissemination of obscenity, child pornography, and, in the case of minors, material harmful to minors, and
it may have a similarly compelling interest in protecting unwilling
library staff and patrons from being exposed to patently offensive
sexually explicit material. Nevertheless, in a lengthy opinion by
Third Circuit Chief Judge Becker, the district court reasoned that,
on account of their acknowledged tendency to block protected
speech, Internet filters were an insufficiently narrowly tailored
means of achieving the government's interests and that less restrictive alternative means existed.[8]

---

[4] *American Library,* 123 S Ct at 2301 (Rehnquist) (plurality).

[5] 20 USC § 9134(f)(3); 47 USC § 254(h)(6)(D).

[6] 201 F Supp 2d 401, 411 (ED Pa 2002).

[7] Id at 464.

[8] The court found that:

> [L]ess restrictive alternatives exist . . . [t]o prevent patrons from accessing visual
> depictions that are obscene and child pornography, public libraries may enforce
> Internet use policies that make clear to patrons that the library's Internet terminals
> may not be used to access illegal speech. Libraries may then impose penalties on
> patrons who violate these policies, ranging from a warning to notification of law
> enforcement, in the appropriate case. Less restrictive alternatives to filtering that
> further libraries' interest in preventing minors from exposure to visual depictions
> that are harmful to minors include requiring parental consent to or presence dur-

By a vote of 6–3 the Supreme Court reversed. Chief Justice Rehnquist wrote a plurality opinion that Justices O'Connor, Scalia, and Thomas joined. The plurality determined that Internet access in public libraries constituted neither a traditional nor a designated public forum to which patrons had rights of access. Therefore, in requiring libraries to install filtering software as a condition for receiving federal funds, Congress had not induced them to engage in unconstitutional activity. Justices Kennedy and Breyer each concurred separately. Justice Stevens dissented, as did Justice Souter in an opinion joined by Justice Ginsburg. Thus there were five separate opinions.

A 6–3 decision with no majority opinion and four Justices writing separately is hardly unique for today's Court.[9] Often a multitude of opinions signals that a case has presented genuinely difficult issues about which the relevant precedents plausibly point to several different lines of analysis,[10] but *American Library* was not such a case. Instead it was a case in which the path to the Court's decision was marked with unusual clarity by well-established (if often contested) understandings of the First Amendment. The doctrinal choices were straightforward, familiar, and comparatively clear. Nevertheless, several members of the Court neither sought guidance from nor appeared willing to have their analyses constrained by either established law or customary methodologies of First Amendment decision making. For them, existing doctrine simply did not work. Though they did not argue explicitly that the Court ought to reconsider any of the obviously relevant precedents, these Justices simply ignored them. The disagreements that the opinions in *American Library* reflect, thus, do not appear to be

---

ing unfiltered access, or restricting minors' unfiltered access to terminals within view of library staff. Finally, optional filtering, privacy screens, recessed monitors, and placement of unfiltered Internet terminals outside of sight-lines provide less restrictive alternatives for libraries to prevent patrons from being unwillingly exposed to sexually explicit content on the Internet.

201 F Supp 2d at 410.

[9] See, for example, *Troxel v Granville*, 530 US 57 (2000) (6–3 plurality with five Justices writing separately); *Miller v Albright*, 523 US 420 (1998) (6–3 plurality with four Justices writing separately). See also Jed Handelsman Shugerman, *A Six-Three Rule: Reviving Consensus on the Supreme Court*, 37 Ga L Rev 893 (2003) (overview of increase in 5–4 decisions of Rehnquist Court).

[10] See *Virginia v Black*, 123 S Ct 1536 (2003) (holding that Virginia's ban on cross-burning with intent to intimidate does not violate the First Amendment).

a function of the inherent difficulty of the legal issues or even of any uncertainties in the meaning of the relevant precedents. Rather they seem to reflect fundamentally different understandings about the relevance of existing doctrine to the resolution of present controversies, as well as different conceptions of the Court's role in First Amendment cases.

In what follows I propose to defend the propositions that *American Library* was an easy case, that the decision was correct as an application of existing doctrine, and that the doctrine it applied is defensible and coherent. Part I offers a summary and analysis of the opinions. It calls attention to the variety of their approaches and demonstrates that they exemplify two troubling aspects of modern First Amendment jurisprudence, namely, the Justices' frequent failure to join analytical issue with one another and their surprising, seemingly unself-conscious willingness to propound what would amount to wholesale revisions of First Amendment doctrine without bothering to distinguish or explain the irrelevance of prior decisions. Part II argues that *American Library* was not a difficult case doctrinally, and that the result was correct. Turning briefly to the larger question of judicial methodology and the role of the Court in First Amendment cases, Part II suggests that Chief Justice Rehnquist's opinion reflects a different, and more restrained, view of the Court's role in the sort of First Amendment case represented by *American Library* than any of the separate opinions. Rehnquist's opinion and the precedents on which it relies rest on a relatively modest conception of judicial capacity with reference to the kind of statute that was here at issue —a statute that does not directly regulate or prohibit speech but that selectively subsidizes it and thus affects its quality and quantity.

I have previously described both the First Amendment model that Rehnquist's opinion reflects as well as that reflected in the separate opinions, and I have defended the relative merits of Rehnquist's approach.[11] Rather than rehearsing either the description or its defense at length, I will merely summarize them here. The view I embrace has not much support in the academy, where most commentators champion a more expansive conception of both the reach of the First Amendment and the capacity of judges to

---

[11] See, for example, Lillian R. BeVier, *Rehabilitating Public Forum Doctrine: In Defense of Categories*, 1992 Supreme Court Review 79.

instantiate it.[12] I hope nonetheless that it is a sufficiently justifiable and coherent view to merit another brief airing.

Though rule-based and categorical, thus implying confidence in the judicial capacity to identify the right rule and to fix and apply appropriate categorical boundaries, Chief Justice Rehnquist's opinion is the most self-effacing of the five opinions in *American Library* along another dimension: the categorical rules it applies lead the Court to subject CIPA to only rational basis review, thus giving substantial deference to the legislative judgment. In deferring to the political trade-offs embodied in CIPA, Rehnquist's opinion implicitly recognizes that, though the Court can craft rules that protect speakers from laws that punish or deter their speech, its ability more comprehensively to monitor the implementation of First Amendment "values" and actually to guarantee the "proper functioning" of the system of free expression is limited.

I. THE OPINIONS

CIPA stemmed from Congress's continuing efforts to protect minors from obscenity, child pornography, and other sexually explicit material thought to be harmful to them. These efforts have seemed increasingly urgent on account of the capabilities of modern technologies of dissemination, particularly the Internet. But despite the fact that the Court has repeatedly said that the interest in protecting minors is compelling, Congress's efforts to protect it have almost never passed First Amendment muster.[13] An interesting aspect of the opinions in *American Library*, however, is that no member of the Court treated the case as being centrally about the limits of Congress's power to protect minors from exposure to sexual content. Indeed, although the two dissenting opinions

---

[12] See, for example, Owen Fiss, *The Irony of Free Speech* 42 (Harvard, 1996) (proposing constitutional standard that would require courts to set aside allocations of government subsidies that "impoverish public debate by systematically disfavoring views the public needs for self-governance"); Robert C. Post, *Subsidized Speech*, 106 Yale L J 151, 194 (1996) (proposing that in subsidized speech cases courts must "locate subsidized speech in social space" and determine whether it is within public discourse or is within some other domain like that of management or professional speech; in addition it must determine whether the standards allocating government subsidies "should be understood as regulations of subsidized speech or instead as internal directives to state officials dispensing subsidies"). See also the tests proposed in the articles cited in note 44.

[13] For a summary of the cases, see text accompanying notes 110–20.

concede that the interest in protecting children is compelling, they pay only lip service to this concession. Instead, despite the fact that no Justice questioned either the fact or the legitimacy of Congress's motive to protect children, several Justices treated the case almost as though CIPA were aimed at the protected speech that might be overblocked.[14]

The central doctrinal choice that the Court confronted in *American Library* was whether the case concerned the limits of Congress's spending power or whether it raised the specter of an unconstitutional condition. The outcome under each doctrine pivoted on the standard of review its application dictated. If the case were characterized as involving Congress's spending power, the question was whether Congress had imposed a condition on libraries' receipt of federal funds that would "induce" them "to engage in activities that would themselves be unconstitutional."[15] This characterization assumes that the relevant First Amendment rights were those of library patrons and Web site operators. Under this approach, the Court would decide whether the provision of Internet access by public libraries constitutes a traditional or designated public forum, on the one hand, or a nonpublic forum on the other. If Internet access is a traditional or designated public forum, then libraries' denial of library patrons' rights of access or Web site operators' rights to communicate would be subject to strict scrutiny. If such Internet access is a nonpublic forum, then rational basis review would apply. Characterizing the case as an unconstitutional conditions case assumes that the relevant First Amendment rights were those of the libraries themselves. The claim would be that conditioning their receipt of federal funds on their installation of filtering software required them to relinquish their First Amendment rights. If this were the appropriate framework, and if the condition on the grant of federal assistance were deemed a penalty, the Court would apply strict scrutiny. A finding

---

[14] *American Library*, 123 S Ct at 2313 (Stevens dissenting) ("[T]he Children Internet Protection Act . . . operates as a blunt nationwide restraint on adult access to 'an enormous amount of valuable information . . .'"); id at 2320 (Souter dissenting) (noting that "the inevitable consequence" of the statute will be that "adults will be denied access to a substantial amount of nonobscene material harmful to children but lawful for adult examination, and a substantial quantity of text and pictures harmful to no one").

[15] *South Dakota v Dole*, 483 US 203, 206 (1987).

that the condition was merely a refusal to subsidize, however, would require only rational basis review.

A. CHIEF JUSTICE REHNQUIST

Chief Justice Rehnquist chose to frame the issue initially in terms of the proper limits on Congress's spending power, although to the extent that issue retains a federalism bite it was not the focal point of his analysis. His opinion takes as its analytical point of departure *South Dakota v Dole*,[16] in which the Court affirmed that, while Congress's ability to achieve national objectives through the use of the spending power and the conditional grant of federal funds is not limited by Article I's enumerations, it "may not be used to induce the States to engage in activities that would themselves be unconstitutional."[17] The issue is then whether public libraries could constitutionally decide on their own to install software filters that overblocked protected sexually explicit material. This in turn led to the question whether Internet access in public libraries is a traditional or designated public forum. If so, a library's use of overblocking software arguably would amount to a content-based restriction that would fail strict scrutiny unless it served a compelling state interest by the least restrictive means.[18]

Characterizing the "role of libraries in our society"[19] as being to "pursue the worthy missions of facilitating learning and cultural enrichment . . . [and] to provide materials 'that would be of the greatest direct benefit or interest to the community,'"[20] Chief Justice Rehnquist concluded that libraries were neither traditional nor designated public forums. They are not traditional public forums because unlike streets and parks they have not "'immemorially

---

[16] 483 US 203 (1987).

[17] Id at 210.

[18] One of the puzzles embedded in *American Library* is that of whose First Amendment rights are at stake. Implicit in a finding that libraries were public forums would be the conclusion either that Web site operators have First Amendment rights of access to libraries to communicate with library patrons or that library patrons have First Amendment rights of access to whatever protected speech is posted on the Internet—at least once the library had made the decision to provide Internet access. The opinions are surprisingly opaque on this point.

[19] *American Library*, 123 S Ct at 2303 (Rehnquist) (plurality).

[20] Id at 2303–04 (Rehnquist) (plurality).

been held in trust for the use of the public and, time out of mind, . . . been used for purposes of assembly, communication of thoughts between citizens, and discussing public questions,'"[21] and the Court had previously "rejected the view that traditional public forum status extends beyond its historic confines."[22] Nor would the provision of Internet access reflect libraries' "affirmative choice to open up [their] property for use as a public forum,"[23] a step which is required for designated public forum status. Libraries provide Internet access not "to 'encourage a diversity of views from private speakers,'"[24] such as Web publishers, but "to facilitate research, learning, and recreational pursuits by furnishing materials of requisite and appropriate quality."[25] The opinion's key sentence embodies Chief Justice Rehnquist's decision to eschew judicial second-guessing of libraries' decisions: "To fulfill their traditional missions, public libraries must have broad discretion to decide what material to provide to their patrons."[26]

Rehnquist identified two decisions which he described as similarly endorsing broad government discretion to decide what private speech to make available to the public. The first, *Arkansas Educational Television Commission v Forbes*,[27] sustained a public television station's right to make editorial judgments regarding inclusion and exclusion in candidate debates.[28] The other, *National Endowment for the Arts v Finley*,[29] which is usually categorized as an unconstitutional condition case, upheld Congress's power to require the NEA to use content-based criteria in making funding decisions.[30]

The discretion the plurality thought necessary in the library context included the discretion not merely to decide what books to acquire—the Court was unanimous on the need for discretion

---

[21] Id at 2305, citing *International Society for Krishna Consciousness, Inc. v Lee*, 505 US 672 (1992).

[22] *Arkansas Educational Television Commission v Forbes*, 523 US 666, 678 (1998).

[23] *American Library*, 123 S Ct at 2305 (Rehnquist) (plurality).

[24] Id (Rehnquist) (plurality).

[25] Id (Rehnquist) (plurality).

[26] Id at 2304 (Rehnquist) (plurality).

[27] 523 US 666 (1998).

[28] Id at 669, 683.

[29] 524 US 569 (1998).

[30] Id at 585–86.

at the acquisition stage[31]—but also to decide on what terms it would provide Internet access, to decide to use software filters to exclude all patrons from unprotected obscenity or child pornography, and to exclude minors from access to sexually explicit material deemed harmful to them, even if those filters might also exclude significant amounts of protected speech.[32] The plurality finessed the question whether the overblocking, considered alone, presented constitutional difficulties, concluding that any difficulties it presented were dispelled by the ease with which library patrons could have the software disabled. CIPA authorizes librarians to disable a filter "to enable access for bona fide research or other lawful purposes."[33] The plurality adopted the Solicitor General's representation at oral argument that, in order to have a site unblocked, a library patron would not "have to explain . . . why he was asking"[34]—a reading of the statute that seems rather strained, though perhaps not quite as illegitimate as Justice Souter suggests.[35] The district court had worried that requesting unblocking would be too embarrassing for some patrons, but the plurality dismissed this concern: "the Constitution does not guarantee the right to acquire information at a public library without any risk of embarrassment."[36]

The conclusion that public libraries could constitutionally install Internet filters that incidentally overblock sexually explicit protected material, at least if they made it easy for patrons to have the filters disabled, determined the legitimacy of CIPA as an exercise of the congressional spending power. The plurality then turned to the plaintiffs' alternative argument that the statute in-

---

[31] See *American Library*, 123 S Ct at 2306 (Rehnquist) (plurality); id at 2311 (Breyer concurring); id at 2312, 2315 (Stevens dissenting); id at 2320–21 (Souter dissenting).

[32] Significant in absolute terms; not perhaps significant in terms of the number of sites excluded relative to the total number of websites.

[33] 20 USC § 9134(f)(3) (disabling permitted for both adults and minors); 47 USC § 254(h)(6)(D) (disabling permitted for adults).

[34] *American Library*, 123 S Ct at 2307 (Rehnquist) (plurality) quoting Transcript of Oral Argument at 4.

[35] A library patron could simply be asked to affirm that his purpose is a lawful one. Such an inquiry would not require him to "explain . . . why he was asking" to have a filter unblocked, and it would appear to comport with the apparent statutory requirement that unblocking be "for research or other lawful purposes." The FCC has not issued additional regulations since *American Library* was decided. See *FCC Consumer Facts: Children's Internet Protection Act*, online at http://ftp.fcc.gov/cgb/consumerfactgs/cipa.html (Sept 17, 2003).

[36] *American Library*, 123 S Ct at 2307 (Rehnquist) (plurality).

fringed the First Amendment rights of the libraries because it imposed an unconstitutional condition on their receipt of federal
funds. Because public libraries are government entities, the argument that they have First Amendment rights of their own is
strained at best for they are themselves enjoined to respect the
First Amendment (and other constitutional) rights of citizens.[37] But
as the litigation in *American Library* makes clear, many public libraries do not want to install the filters CIPA required. Thus, they
argued that they possessed First Amendment rights of their own.[38]
The plurality finessed this argument too. Instead it assumed *ar-
guendo* that public libraries have First Amendment rights, and then
dismissed the unconstitutional conditions argument on its merits.
The plurality cited *Rust v Sullivan*[39] for the proposition that the
government in CIPA was not denying a benefit but "'simply insisting that public funds be spent for the purposes for which they
were authorized.'"[40] Moreover, invoking the conventional, if rather
opaque, categorical distinction familiar in unconstitutional conditions precedents, it concluded that CIPA did not impose a penalty
on libraries that chose not to install the filtering software. Instead,
the statute merely reflected Congress's permissible decision not to
subsidize such a choice. Finally, the plurality distinguished *Legal
Services Corp. v Velasquez*[41] on the ground that, unlike legal advocates for the poor, public libraries do not occupy a role that "pits
them against the Government."[42]

Chief Justice Rehnquist's opinion is in many ways a textbook
example of straightforward legal analysis. It is fair to criticize its
lack of nuance, to be sure, and it certainly makes no claim to rhetorical grandeur. Indeed, its tone is almost offhand. Moreover,
neither the precedents nor propositions on which he relies are

---

[37] See, for example, *Brown v Louisiana*, 383 US 131 (1966) (holding that protestors have
First Amendment right to sit in at public library to protest its discriminatory policies).

[38] The district court treated it with surprising sympathy, *American Library Association, Inc.
v United States*, 201 F Supp 2d 401, 491–92 (ED Pa 2002), and Justice Souter apparently
bought it, since he found that requiring the filters was an unconstitutional condition, *American Library*, 123 S Ct at 2318 (Souter dissenting).

[39] 500 US 173, 194 (1991).

[40] *American Library*, 123 S Ct at 2308 (Rehnquist) (plurality), quoting *Rust*, 500 US at
196.

[41] 531 US 533 (2001).

[42] *American Library*, 123 S Ct at 2309 (Rehnquist) (plurality).

altogether clear.[43] That is, the doctrines Chief Justice Rehnquist invokes are not models of coherence and they do not attract the uniform support of commentators.[44] In a closer case, the application of these doctrines would be far more problematic. In particular, in a closer case, Rehnquist's conclusory reading of the unconstitutional conditions precedents would require more explanation. But this was not a close case.

More importantly, Chief Justice Rehnquist's opinion has several decided virtues. It frames the First Amendment issue precisely. It locates the case squarely within the only proper doctrinal framework. It identifies the relevant precedents, specifies how they apply, and acknowledges and addresses—albeit for the most part in footnotes—the points on which the other Justices disagree.

The other opinions in *American Library*, on the other hand, leave one puzzled both about their doctrinal roots and about such seemingly basic questions as what and whose First Amendment rights

[43] For example, Chief Justice Rehnquist cited *Rust v Sullivan* for the proposition that it was constitutional for government simply to "insist . . . that public funds be spent for the purposes for which they were authorized." *American Library*, 123 S Ct at 2308 (Rehnquist) (plurality), quoting *Rust*, 500 US at 196. Subsequent cases have read *Rust* not to apply to cases in which the government "expends funds to encourage a diversity of views from private speakers." *Rosenburger v Rector and Visitors of the University of Virginia*, 515 US 819, 834 (1995). The answer to the question whether Internet access in libraries exists to encourage a diversity of views, or whether not funding library Internet services that fail to install pornography-blocking software is a means of spending funds for the purposes for which they were authorized is hardly susceptible to an uncontestable answer.

[44] The literature on both doctrines is extensive, and most of it reveals deep disagreement with the Court's approach. On the public forum doctrine, the classic is Harry Kalven, Jr., *The Concept of the Public Forum: Cox v. Louisiana*, 1965 Supreme Court Review 1, 11–12 (suggesting that "in an open democratic society the streets, the parks, and other public places are . . . a *public forum* that the citizen can commandeer"). See also Geoffrey R. Stone, *Fora Americana: Speech in Public Places*, 1974 Supreme Court Review 233, 253–54 (suggesting that "if we are to give content to the right to freedom of expression, we must seek a fair accommodation of the individual's interest in effective expression of that right, the public's interest in receiving the communication, and legitimate countervailing interests of the state"); BeVier, 1992 Supreme Court Review at 102–03 (cited in note 11) (defending Court's categorical approach to the public forum on ground that "the essential task of First Amendment rules is to restrain government from deliberately manipulating the content or outcome of public debate and to prohibit it from censoring, punishing, or selectively denying speech opportunities to disfavored views"). On the unconstitutional conditions doctrine, see Kathleen M. Sullivan, *Unconstitutional Conditions*, 102 Harv L Rev 1413, 1419 (1989) (suggesting that the function of unconstitutional conditions doctrine is to identify "a characteristic technique by which government appears not to, but in fact does burden [constitutional] liberties, triggering a demand for especially strong justification by the state"); Seth F. Kreimer, *Allocational Sanctions: The Problem of Negative Rights in a Positive State*, 132 U Pa L Rev 1293, 1300–01 (1984) (suggesting that, when they must resolve issues of subsidy and discrimination, "courts must distinguish between threats and offers . . . . The crucial task is to specify an appropriate baseline against which to determine whether the proposed allocation improves or worsens the citizen's situation").

are at stake—those of Web publishers to reach an audience, of library patrons to access the Web, or of libraries to decide what material to make available to their patrons. By focusing so intently on the fact that Internet filters incidentally block some protected speech, the separate opinions convey the impression that the First Amendment is not about protecting the speech rights of citizens from government punishment or manipulation of public debate but rather is about guaranteeing that speakers will be able to reach the maximum possible audience and that listeners will have access to the maximum possible speech. The view that the First Amendment charges the Court with the responsibility to maximize the *quantity* of speech to which citizens have access, and that this is the Court's function in government subsidy cases, is no doubt worthy of serious consideration, but it is not current First Amendment doctrine. First Amendment doctrine is almost exclusively a doctrine of negative rights, not one of positive rights. It is a doctrine not of entitlement but of protection from government.[45] If individual Justices want to reverse course on this very significant point, they should argue openly to that effect, and engage candidly the difficult issues the view presents. That, however, is not the course reflected in the separate opinions in *American Library*.

B. JUSTICE KENNEDY

Justice Kennedy's concurring opinion, for example, is enigmatic. Unlike the plurality, but without taking explicit note of his disagreement, he appears to suggest that Internet access in public libraries constitutes a public forum to which library patrons have First Amendment rights of access. But because that right was not "burdened in any significant degree"[46] in *American Library*, no facial challenge had been made out. Justice Kennedy clearly thinks the right exists, however, because he identifies several circumstances that would give rise to an as-applied challenge:

> If some libraries do not have the capacity to unblock specific Web sites or to disable the filter or if it is shown that an adult

---

[45] See, for example, David P. Currie, *Positive and Negative Constitutional Rights*, 53 U Chi L Rev 864 (1986) (general discussion of the differences between positive and negative rights, and argument that Constitution is principally a guarantor of negative rights).

[46] *American Library*, 123 S Ct at 2310 (Kennedy concurring).

user's election to view constitutionally protected Internet material is burdened in some other substantial way, that would be the subject for an as-applied challenge. . . .[47]

The implication is that "adult users" have a First Amendment right to view material in public libraries without any "substantial" burden. The opinion implies further that a library's decision to install a filter is subject to scrutiny substantially more intense than rational basis review, for Kennedy rejects the facial challenge not on the principle that libraries have discretion but on his own assessment of the degree to which the rights of adult library patrons are burdened by the law on its face, in light of the unblocking provision. Justice Kennedy does not explain why he thinks CIPA jeopardizes the rights of adult patrons.

Implicitly, Kennedy agrees with the plurality that *South Dakota v Dole* is the appropriate starting point. Thus the relevant question is whether a statute requiring libraries receiving federal funds to install software filters would "induce" them to engage in unconstitutional activity. It is not certain, however, that he also agrees that this question must be answered with reference to public forum analysis—though if he does he seems to disagree about the result that public forum analysis would dictate. This is surprising. Recall that the plurality held that libraries are not traditional public forums because, as Justice Kennedy himself wrote in *Forbes v Arkansas Educational Television Commission*,[48] "traditional public forum status" does not extend "beyond its historic confines."[49] The plurality also rejected the argument that libraries are designated public forums because they do "not acquire Internet terminals in order to create a public forum for Web publishers to express themselves."[50] Justice Kennedy, by contrast, seemed to think that the outcome of the facial challenge turned on the fact that overblocking did not impose a significant burden on a right of access to what he seems to have regarded as a designated public forum. But he did not explain why, or how, or on what theory this was such a forum.

---

[47] Id (Kennedy concurring).

[48] 523 US 666 (1998).

[49] Id at 678.

[50] *American Library*, 123 S Ct at 2305 (Rehnquist) (plurality) (emphasis added).

C. JUSTICE BREYER

Of all the opinions in *American Library*, Justice Breyer's concurrence exhibits the greatest indifference to existing First Amendment doctrine. Rejecting strict scrutiny as "too limiting and rigid,"[51] he also rejects rational basis review and the deference it accords to either the legislature or libraries. Instead he argues that the Court should "apply a form of heightened scrutiny, examining the statutory requirements in question with special care."[52] Citing an array of cases that arose in different contexts and applied doctrines unrelated either to public forum or unconstitutional conditions,[53] Breyer implicitly characterizes *American Library* as analogous to these decisions in that "complex, competing constitutional interests are potentially at issue or speech-related harm is potentially justified by unusually strong governmental interests."[54] In such cases, he asserts, the legislature has "less than ordinary leeway in light of the fact that constitutionally protected expression is at issue."[55] Though grounding his decision to engage in heightened scrutiny on the fact that "constitutionally protected expression is at issue," Breyer specifies neither whose constitutional rights are at stake nor whether his standard of review represents an application of *South Dakota v Dole*, or of unconstitutional conditions doctrine, or of something else entirely. The upshot of his approach is that, rather than deferring in principle to the legislative judgment, he implies that the Court has a clear comparative institutional advantage. Accordingly, he offers his own reconsideration of the statutory requirements and sustains them only because he is persuaded that the speech-related harm they cause is not disproportionate in relation to the Act's legitimate objectives.[56]

Justice Breyer exhibits his indifference to existing First Amendment doctrine in two ways. First, his handling of precedent ranges

---

[51] Id at 2311 (Breyer concurring).

[52] Id (Breyer concurring).

[53] Justice Breyer cites, for example, *Board of Trustees of State University of New York v Fox*, 492 US 469 (1989), which was a case having to do with a direct prohibition on commercial speech, and *Red Lion Broadcasting System, Inc. v FCC*, 395 US 367 (1969), a case that arose in and has been limited in its effect to the discrete context of regulation of broadcast regulation. *American Library*, 123 S Ct at 2311 (Breyer concurring).

[54] *American Library*, 123 S Ct at 2311 (Breyer concurring).

[55] Id at 2312 (Breyer concurring) (emphasis added).

[56] Id (Breyer concurring).

from cavalier to wildly acontextual. It is cavalier in that it fails to specify whether its point of reference is *South Dakota v Dole* or the unconstitutional conditions doctrine—or both, or neither. He purports to agree with the plurality that public forum doctrine is "inapplicable," but the plurality did not hold the doctrine inapplicable. Rather it found that, when applied, public forum doctrine did not require libraries to provide unblocked Web access. His handling of precedent is acontextual in that the cases on which he relies almost all arose in particular doctrinal categories that emerged from regulatory contexts quite different from the one that confronted the Court in *American Library*. For example, claiming to rely on "other contexts where circumstances call for heightened, but not 'strict,' scrutiny,"[57] and where he purports to find support for the proposition that "the key question in such instances is one of proper fit,"[58] Breyer cites several cases, only one of which actually involved the review of a government decision selectively to subsidize speech. Of the other three, one challenged a direct prohibition on commercial speech,[59] one challenged a regulation that directly compelled speech,[60] and one arose in the unique and idiosyncratic context of broadcast regulation.[61] These are, for good reasons, inapposite to *American Library*. In the context of subsidized speech the Court has always deployed public forum analysis and the unconstitutional conditions doctrine. This is so because the government is free to not subsidize *any* speech, and it has broad discretion to make policy decisions and implement them by spending public money. Thus its decisions selectively to subsidize speech pose First Amendment risks that are systematically different from those posed by direct regulation or selective criminal punishment of speech.[62]

---

[57] Id at 2311 (Breyer concurring).

[58] Id (Breyer concurring).

[59] *Board of Trustees of State University of New York v Fox*, 492 US 469 (1989).

[60] *Turner Broadcasting Systems, Inc. v FCC*, 520 US 180 (1997).

[61] *Red Lion Broadcasting Co. v FCC*, 395 US 367 (1969).

[62] Neither the public forum nor the unconstitutional conditions doctrines, nor the rules they supposedly generate, do a perfect job of mapping onto and "clarify[ing]" the constitutional values that matter to us." Post, 106 Yale L J at 195 (cited in note 12). Nonetheless, for better or worse in terms of their ability actually to guide the resolution of close cases, they serve the indispensable function of coordinating First Amendment decision making and they provide the analytical framework in terms of which lawyers cast their arguments and in accordance with which lower court judges make their decisions.

The second way in which Justice Breyer exhibits his indifference to First Amendment doctrine is that, though he implicitly claims to be merely reformulating or summarizing what the Court has always done, he posits what amounts to a wholesale revision of First Amendment doctrine. Characterizing CIPA as an Act that "directly restricts the public's receipt of information,"[63] Breyer implies that *whenever* "constitutionally protected expression is at issue"[64] the Court must apply a form of "heightened scrutiny." As he describes it, such scrutiny requires the Court to engage in a free-wheeling, multifactored, unanchored, ad hoc balancing inquiry:

> In such cases the Court has asked whether the harm to speech-related interests is disproportionate in light of both the justifications and the potential alternatives. It has considered the legitimacy of the statute's objective, the extent to which the statute will tend to achieve that objective, whether there are other, less restrictive ways of achieving that objective, and ultimately whether the statute works speech-related harm that, in relation to that objective, is out of proportion.[65]

There is a certain sense in which constitutionally protected speech is always at issue, since "all laws affect what gets said, by whom, to whom, and with what effect."[66] Surely, however, Justice Breyer is not proposing heightened scrutiny of all laws. With respect to the laws to which he would apply heightened scrutiny, however, the inquiry he would have the Court undertake amounts to a stunningly broad claim of judicial omniscience.[67] It implies that the Court possesses a metric with which to evaluate the absolute significance of a statute's objectives and to calibrate its relative significance in proportion to the harm it does to "speech-related interests." It suggests that the Court has the means to assess the ability of a particular statute to achieve its stated goal as well as

---

[63] *American Library*, 123 S Ct at 2310 (Breyer concurring).

[64] Id at 2312 (Breyer concurring) (emphasis added).

[65] Id at 2311 (Breyer concurring).

[66] Larry A. Alexander, *Trouble on Track Two: Incidental Regulations of Speech and Free Speech Theory*, 44 Hastings L J 921, 929 (1993).

[67] The claim of judicial omniscience implicit in Justice Breyer's formulation is apparently not born of any special solicitude for free expression. Of all the Justices, Justice Breyer has proved the least receptive to First Amendment claims. See Eugene Volokh, *How the Justices Voted in Free Speech Cases, 1994–2000*, 48 UCLA L Rev 1191 (2001).

to discern whether equally effective "less restrictive" means exist. Note, however, that Justice Breyer fails to specify the criteria by which the Court would make such judgments. Perhaps this lack of clarity is what *New York Times* Supreme Court reporter Linda Greenhouse referred to when she described Justice Breyer as a "Justice of minimalism"[68] who is in the habit of "leaving things undecided."[69] If so, then minimalism turns out to have significant costs. Eugene Volokh has trenchantly noted that there is no "physical device [that] can tell us whether some lump of government interest weighs more than some chunk of free speech right."[70] Justice Breyer's minimalism tenders no conceptual or theoretical help either, offering instead merely a verbal formula that, because it has the capacity neither to guide nor constrain judgment, casts the Court and those who must interpret or apply its decisions completely adrift.

D. JUSTICE STEVENS

Justice Stevens's dissent is the most difficult to parse because its doctrinal underpinnings are so obscure. He begins by asserting that it would be constitutionally permissible for local libraries to experiment with filtering and even to install filters on all their Internet terminals. He implies, in other words, that public libraries would not violate the First Amendment if they independently chose to install precisely the same filters upon which CIPA conditioned their receipt of federal funds. But Stevens does not confront the implications of this conclusion with respect to *South Dakota v Dole*, the linchpin of the plurality's analysis, nor does he attempt to refute Chief Justice Rehnquist's public forum analysis. Because he ignores *South Dakota v Dole* rather than explaining his disagreement with it, one can neither retrace nor evaluate the reasoning that presumably led him to conclude it was neither controlling nor even relevant.

Moreover, Stevens sends mixed signals on the question of whose First Amendment rights are at stake. Expressing concern with

---

[68] Linda Greenhouse, *Between Certainty and Doubt: States of Mind on the Supreme Court Today*, 6 Green Bag 2d 241, 243 (2003).

[69] Id at 242, quoting Cass R. Sunstein, *One Case at a Time: Judicial Minimalism on the Supreme Court* 3 (Harvard, 1999).

[70] Eugene Volokh, *Freedom of Speech, Shielding Children, and Transcending Balancing*, 1997 Supreme Court Review 141, 167–68.

CIPA's effect on local autonomy, for example, he asserts that the statute is unconstitutional because it operates as a "blunt nationwide restraint on adult access to 'an enormous amount of valuable information that individual librarians cannot possibly review.'"[71] To support his contention that CIPA is an overly broad restriction on adult access to protected speech, he relies on precedents that have nothing to do with conditional government spending. *Reno v ACLU*[72] and *Ashcroft v Free Speech Coalition*,[73] the cases on which he relies, invalidated direct bans that criminalized both protected and unprotected speech—indecent speech in *Reno* and virtual child pornography in *Ashcroft*. Justice Stevens also says that CIPA creates a "significant prior restraint"[74] on adult access to protected speech, which is by any measure an imprecise use of the term.[75] In what sense, one wonders, is this a prior restraint?

Finally, Justice Stevens concludes that CIPA is unconstitutional because it "impermissibly conditions the receipt of Government funding on the restriction of significant First Amendment rights."[76] Here he is apparently invoking the First Amendment rights of public libraries. He argues that libraries have such rights in a paragraph that offers not reasons but a series of disconnected, irrelevant platitudes. He begins by citing the plurality opinion for the proposition that "we have always assumed that libraries have discretion when making decisions regarding what to include in and exclude from their collections."[77] But he fails to acknowledge that the context for this assumption was the question whether the Court should apply strict scrutiny to libraries' judgments when they were challenged by *library patrons*, not whether libraries themselves have First Amendment rights vis-à-vis their funding sources. His next sentence analogizes library discretion to "'the business of

---

[71] *American Library*, 123 S Ct at 2313 (Stevens dissenting).

[72] 521 US 844 (1997).

[73] 535 US 234 (2002).

[74] *American Library*, 123 S Ct at 2315 (Stevens dissenting).

[75] See Mark S. Nadel, *The First Amendment's Limitation on the Use of Internet Filtering in Public and School Libraries: What Content Can Librarians Exclude?* 78 Tex L Rev 1117, 1130 (2000) ("No First Amendment scholar could seriously claim that [the action of a library in refraining from purchasing books] represents a 'prior restraint' of the unpurchased—and thus excluded—material.").

[76] *American Library*, 123 S Ct at 2315 (Stevens dissenting).

[77] Id (Stevens dissenting).

a university . . . to determine for itself what to teach,'"[78] citing
Justice Frankfurter's famous concurring opinion in *Sweezy v New
Hampshire*.[79] But *Sweezy* involved the limits of a state legislature's
inquiry into a teacher's political affiliations; it was decided on due
process, not First Amendment, grounds; and to the extent that
First Amendment rights were at issue, they were the rights of Professor Sweezy and not those of his public university employer. The
final sentence in this paragraph consists of a paean to "our Nation's
deep commitment 'to safeguarding academic freedom'" and to the
'robust exchange of ideas,'"[80] a citation to a decision involving the
First Amendment rights of teachers to refuse to sign loyalty oaths
at a state university,[81] and the concluding assertion—which is
nothing if not a non sequitur—that a "library's exercise of judgment with regard to its collection is entitled to First Amendment
protection."[82]

Justice Stevens asserts that a statute "penalizing a library for
failing to install filtering software . . . would unquestionably violate"[83] the First Amendment. It thus follows for him that the First
Amendment similarly protects public libraries from being denied
funds for failing to comply with such a directive. Stevens does
not explain the relevance of the cases he cites in support of this
proposition, which hold that government employment may not be
conditioned on the surrender of First Amendment rights. He acknowledges that *American Library* is not such a case. Instead, he
says, it is a case in which the government uses its treasury "to
impose controls on an important medium of expression."[84] Therefore it is governed by *Legal Services Corp. v Velasquez*,[85] which invites the question and compels the conclusion that "requiring the
filtering software on all Internet-accessible computers distorts" the

---

[78] Id (Stevens dissenting), quoting *Sweezy v New Hampshire*, 354 US 234, 263 (1957)
(Frankfurter concurring).

[79] 354 US 234, 263 (1957).

[80] *American Library*, 123 S Ct at 2316 (Stevens dissenting), quoting *Keyishian v Board of
Regents of University of State of New York*, 385 US 589, 603 (1967).

[81] *Keyishian v Board of Regents of University of State of New York*, 385 US 589, 603 (1967).

[82] *American Library*, 123 S Ct at 2316 (Stevens dissenting).

[83] Id (Stevens dissenting).

[84] Id (Stevens dissenting).

[85] 531 US 533 (2001).

medium because of the software's propensity to overblock and underblock.[86]

Justice Stevens disputes the plurality's reading of *Rust v Sullivan* on the plausible ground that later cases have confined its holding to situations in which the government seeks to communicate a specific message, which government is not trying to do with its conditional spending under CIPA.[87] He similarly discounts *Finley's* relevance, on the puzzling ground that in *Finley* it was not the NEA that challenged the restriction, whereas in *American Library* the libraries themselves were the challengers: "If this were a case in which library patrons had challenged a library's decision to install and use filtering software, it would be in the same posture as *Finley*. Because it is not, *Finley* does not control this case."[88] The question this distinction begs, of course, is whether *Finley* would have been decided differently had the NEA challenged the funding restriction, and if so, why.

E. JUSTICE SOUTER

Justice Souter's dissent begins by announcing his agreement with Justice Stevens on the unconstitutional conditions argument and his disagreement with the plurality that requiring the installation of blocking software mandates action by libraries that would be constitutional if they undertook it on their own. Souter disagrees with the assumption that "an adult library patron could, consistently with the Act, obtain an unblocked terminal simply for the asking."[89] For him, the case boils down to the question whether a local library could deny access to a "substantial amount of nonobscene material harmful to children but lawful for adult examination, and a substantial quantity of text and pictures harmful to no one."[90] This, after all, is the effect of overblocking software. Unconvinced by the analogy between decisions to install blocking software and decisions not to acquire material, Souter rejects rational basis review for the former. "[T]here is no preacquisition scar-

---

[86] *American Library*, 123 S Ct at 2317 (Stevens dissenting).

[87] Id at 2318 (Stevens dissenting).

[88] *American Library*, 123 S Ct at 2318 (Stevens dissenting), quoting *Rosenburger v Rector and Visitors of University of Virginia*, 515 US 819, 834 (1995).

[89] *American Library*, 123 S Ct at 2319 (Souter dissenting).

[90] Id at 2320 (Souter dissenting).

city rationale to save library Internet blocking from treatment as censorship, and no support for it in the historical development of library practice."[91]

Justice Souter fails both to confront the plurality's reliance on the relevant precedents and to link his analysis with any particular First Amendment doctrine. The two principal cases on which Justice Souter relies, *Bigelow v Virginia*[92] and *Board of Education, Island Trees Union Free School District No. 26 v Pico*,[93] seem hardly relevant. Neither involved conditional spending. *Bigelow* concerned a direct regulation of commercial speech, but from one of its sentences Justice Souter purports to derive support for his assertion that CIPA amounts to "censorship."[94] In *Island Trees* the Court was concerned with intentional decisions to eliminate books from school libraries because of disagreement with their *ideas*, a concern not present in *American Library*.[95] The overblocking that Internet filters cause does not raise the specter of official and deliberate suppression of particular disfavored ideas—indeed, it is the very randomness of the suppression that seemed to bother the dissenting Justices—nor was there in CIPA any hint that Congress harbored a "suspicious" motivation to suppress protected speech. The statutory directive regarding unblocking provides convincing evidence of this.

Instead of tying his analysis to First Amendment doctrine, Souter provides a historical exegesis on the "[i]nstitutional history of

---

[91] Id at 2324 (Souter dissenting).

[92] 421 US 809 (1975).

[93] 457 US 853 (1982).

[94] *American Library*, 123 S Ct at 2320 (Souter dissenting), quoting *Bigelow v Virginia*, 421 US 809, 829 (1975):

> The policy of the First Amendment favors dissemination of information and opinion, and the guarantees of freedom of speech and press were not designed to prevent the censorship of the press merely, but any action of the government by means of which it might prevent such free and general discussion of public matters as seems absolutely essential.

[95] The citation to *Board of Education, Island Trees Union Free School District No. 26 v Pico* is contextually inapt if not positively misleading. Justice Souter claims the case stands for the proposition that "removing classics from a school library in response to pressure from parents and school board members violates the Speech Clause." *American Library*, 123 S Ct at 2324. But the Court in *Island Trees* did not so hold. Rather, it held that whether the removal of books violated students' First Amendment rights depended upon "the motivation behind [the School Board's] actions." The plurality in *Island Trees* was concerned not merely with the fact that books had been removed "in response to pressure from parents." Its explicit concern was to prevent the official and deliberate suppression of ideas with which the School Board disagreed.

public libraries in America," which to him "discloses an evolution toward a general rule, now firmly rooted, that any adult entitled to use the library has access to any of its holdings."[96] Apparently Justice Souter is of the view that this "firmly rooted" general rule has acquired the status of a constitutional command, though he does not explain the process by which this came about.

II. American Library and First Amendment Doctrine: Justifying Judicial Deference

A. PUBLIC FORUM DOCTRINE

> If there is consensus on any aspect of contemporary First Amendment doctrine, it is that free speech jurisprudence is notorious for its flagrantly proliferating and contradictory rules, its profoundly chaotic collection of methods and theories.[97]

The separate opinions in *American Library* exacerbate this chaos. The concurring and dissenting Justices persistently fail to join issue with one another on crucial points. In addition, they disregard well-trodden doctrinal paths in favor of their own preferred, and often idiosyncratic, methodologies. This bespeaks indifference to the judicial craft and the rule of law, which are important constraints on the abuse of judicial power because they embody obligations of responsiveness to opposing arguments, attention to relevant precedents, and reasoned explanation.[98]

---

[96] *American Library*, 123 S Ct at 2322 (Souter dissenting).

[97] Robert Post, *Reconciling Theory and Doctrine in First Amendment Jurisprudence*, in Lee C. Bollinger and Geoffrey R. Stone, eds, *Eternally Vigilant: Free Speech in the Modern Era* 153 (Chicago, 2002).

[98] The rule of law, a complex concept, at the very least signifies "the constraint of arbitrariness in the exercise of government power . . . . [I]t means that the agencies of official coercion [which includes judges] should, to the extent feasible, be guided by rules. . . ." John Calvin Jeffries, Jr., *Legality, Vagueness, and the Construction of Penal Statutes*, 71 Va L Rev 189, 212 (1985). There exist few formal constraints on abuse of power by life-tenured federal judges, especially at the appellate level, see FRCP 52(a) (ensuring accountability of district court judges by requiring them to make "findings of fact and conclusions of law," and providing that "[f]indings of fact . . . shall not be set aside unless clearly erroneous . . ."), and certainly at the level of the Supreme Court. The Justices are subject to impeachment, US Const, Art II, § 4, but this is hardly a constraint on judicial abuse of power. See, for example, Linz Audain, *The Economics of Law-Related Labor V: Judicial Careers, Judicial Decisions, and an Agency Cost Model of the Judicial Function*, 42 Am U L Rev 115, 137 (1992) ("[W]hile Congress is responsible for monitoring the federal judiciary, the only monitoring tool Congress has to fulfill its task is the drastic remedy of judicial impeachment. That tool has been used with . . . rarity . . ."). The necessity of writing opinions represents an informal constraint on judicial power, for better than just outcomes, opinions permit the Court's constituency in the legal community—lawyers, judges, members of the legal acad-

The performance of these Justices is especially disappointing because *American Library* was such an easy case.[99] This is clear from a careful look at the public forum doctrine. Begin by considering the rights of library patrons, authors, even libraries themselves with respect to libraries' collections of print materials. All members of the Court agreed, as a matter of First Amendment law and practical necessity, that libraries must have substantial discretion over what materials to acquire and that rational basis review of their content-based acquisition decisions is therefore appropriate. This consensus is not surprising, since no court decision has ever "considered a First Amendment challenge to a library's decision not to purchase a book or to accept one as a donation."[100] Indeed, a "central, if not the principal, responsibility of libraries is making *managerial*, not ministerial, selection decisions."[101] It follows that, in their roles as providers and selectors of content, libraries are neither traditional nor designated public forums. This makes sense because libraries' acquisition decisions do not present a systematic discernible risk that government will deliberately manipulate the content of public debate, or attempt to distort its outcome, or censor, punish, or selectively deny speech opportunities to disfavored views.

Consider what this implies about whether public library patrons can in any meaningful sense be said to have First Amendment rights of access to particular works, or whether authors can be said to have First Amendment rights of access to library shelves. The conclusion that there are no rights of access to or for obscenity

---

emy—to monitor the Court's fidelity to the rule of law norms that supposedly constrain all government decision makers. In addition, they provide crucial guidance for other government officials, for ordinary citizens, for lawyers, and for lower court judges in future cases.

> [I]t is part of our understanding of judicial practice that judges' opinions should be reached by a process of 'reasoned elaboration,' and that judges should explain, justify, and give reasons for their decisions. . . . [I]t is part of our tradition that when courts issue judicial opinions . . . those opinions will provide professional readers with explanations for the results reached.

Frederick Schauer, *Opinions as Rules*, 62 U Chi L Rev 1455, 1465–66 (1995).

[99] A legitimate function of legal commentary is to notice when the Court, or various of the Justices, have failed to locate the cases before them in their appropriate doctrinal framework or, having decided to depart from or restructure that framework, have failed to justify the departure and explain its rationale. Thus the concern in this essay with the opinions in *American Library* and the attention to the issue of how they handle existing doctrine.

[100] Nadel, 78 Tex L Rev at 1124 (cited in note 75) (emphasis added).

[101] Id at 1134.

or child pornography is wholly unsurprising, as such materials are unprotected even from government punishment. Equally unsurprising, however, is the conclusion that there would be no rights of access to wholly protected speech, even to or for wholly protected speech of immense social or educational value.[102]

Another way to phrase the point is to say that citizens—whether library patrons or authors—have no right to require courts to scrutinize libraries' content-based acquisition decisions. It is important to note that this conclusion does not assume that the quantity of protected speech that libraries exclude is minimal. To the contrary, no library could possibly collect or even make available to its patrons every constitutionally protected work.[103] Nor does the conclusion assume that libraries' content-based decisions would survive strict scrutiny. Rather it reflects a judgment about comparative institutional advantage. Libraries' content-based acquisition decisions are a product of a complex interaction of professional judgments, patron preferences, and resource constraints that courts are ill-equipped to disentangle. It is worth remembering that the First Amendment is about *negative* rights. A library's decision not to purchase any particular material does not put at risk or threaten to punish any citizen for exercising First Amendment rights, nor does it require any citizen to forgo or to perform any action that the First Amendment protects from government interference.

The four concurring and dissenting opinions in *American Library* agree that libraries must have discretion over the acquisition of

---

[102] The single possible exception to this conclusion would arise in a case where a patron could prove that a library failed to purchase particular works because of disagreement with the viewpoint expressed therein. There are no such reported cases, however. Courts have occasionally been willing to consider and even to overrule libraries' removal decisions when they find them to be viewpoint discriminatory. See, for example, *Minarcini v Strongsville City School District*, 541 F2d 577 (6th Cir 1976); *Delcarpio v Saint Tammany Parish School Board*, 865 F Supp 350 (ED La 1994); *Roberts v Madigan*, 702 F Supp 1505 (D Colo 1989), aff'd, 921 F2d 1047 (10th Cir 1990); *Sheck v Baileysville School Committee*, 530 F Supp 679 (D Me 1982); *Salvail v Nashua Board of Education*, 469 F Supp 1269 (D NH 1979). It is plausible to conclude that they have done so, however, only because they feel confident that they can identify impermissible viewpoint discrimination in that context, but "when librarians decide what books to acquire, there is generally no way to know why any particular book was not selected. Nadel, 78 Tex L Rev at 1124 (cited in note 75).

[103] Id at 1129–30 ("[T]he First Amendment has been understood to permit a library to act to increase the likelihood that preferred content will be accessible to patrons, even when that entails effectively 'denying patrons access to the books it necessarily refrained from purchasing or discarded from its shelves. No First Amendment scholar could seriously claim that such action represents a 'prior restraint' of the unpurchased—and thus excluded—material.").

print materials. They do not agree that this judgment ought to control the constitutional analysis of CIPA. They regard the special characteristics of the Internet and the lack of precision of filtering software as moving the First Amendment boundary to the point where more stringent review is required. Several factors might be thought to justify this move, though none is ultimately persuasive. First, once a library decides to provide Internet access to its patrons, resource constraints appear to drop out of the picture as a possible justification for granting deference to the library's decision to deny access to particular works.[104] But this neglects "the cost of display terminals, Internet access links, and internal wires, modems, and servers, or the opportunity cost of using these terminals for disfavored uses."[105] Moreover, when it comes to protecting minors from child pornography and obscenity, deference to library discretion is justified not only by resource constraints but also by the fact that such material is unprotected, period. Even here resource constraints may enter the picture when libraries have to decide what means it will use to protect minors from such material. The "less restrictive alternatives" which Justice Stevens insists upon are in fact likely to be much more expensive than software filters.

Second, whereas the bases for most print media acquisition decisions usually remain below patrons' or judges' radar screens, the basis for requiring filters in CIPA was transparent, and the inevitability of overblocking was well understood. The inability of filters to avoid mistakes is a salient fact, as is the fact that such filters block—"suppress," if you will—a substantial amount of protected speech. But decisions not to purchase printed material also, and inevitably, "block"—suppress—a substantial amount of protected speech, and this fact has never been thought sufficient to bring strict scrutiny into play. Moreover, the purpose of the First Amendment is not to protect "speech as such."[106] Instead, the Court's aversion to regulation of speech "on account of its con-

---

[104] According to the district court in *Mainstream Loudoun v Board of Trustees of the Loudoun County Library*, 2 F Supp 2d 783, 793 (ED Va 1998), for example, "unlike an interlibrary loan or outright book purchase, no appreciable expenditure of library time or resources is required to make a particular Internet publication available to a library patron."

[105] Nadel, 78 Tex L Rev at 1129 (cited in note 75).

[106] Robert C. Post, *Recuperating First Amendment Doctrine*, 47 Stan L Rev 1249, 1250 (1995).

tent" reflects a prophylactic means of forestalling otherwise unde-
tectable, deliberate, government manipulation of public debate.[107]

Of course, even in nonpublic forums, government's decisions
must be "reasonable and not an effort to suppress expression
merely because public officials oppose the speaker's view."[108] A fair
reading of CIPA and the context in which it was enacted does not
support the inference that Congress intended to manipulate public
discourse or to handicap particular points of view—except to protect adults and minors from exposure to unprotected obscenity and
child pornography and to protect minors from exposure to sexually
explicit speech harmful to them. CIPA induces libraries to install
Internet filters pursuant to a transparent, constitutionally permissible, policy to protect adults from unprotected speech and minors
from speech unprotected for them, and no reason exists to doubt
the legislature's good faith in pursuing that policy. In addition,
Congress attempted to minimize the extent to which overblocking
would deny patrons access to protected speech. Though it is easy
to question its one-size-fits-all approach as a matter of policy,[109]
it is hard to find in that approach any evidence of discrimination
against particular points of view. In terms of their restrictiveness
and effectiveness, the means Congress adopted to achieve its compelling interests and the means that the district judge and the dissenters endorsed were different only in degree, and assessing them
required the kind of judgments about which judges possess no
comparative advantage and reasonable minds could plainly differ.
Moreover, implementation of the filter requirement "chills" no
speech—protected or unprotected—because CIPA neither punishes nor directly regulates speech. Finally, CIPA "suppresses"
speech only to the same extent that any library's inability to make
some material instantly available to its patrons suppresses speech.

---

[107] See generally Geoffrey R. Stone, *Content Regulation and the First Amendment*, 25 Wm &
Mary L Rev 217 (1983) (hostility to content-based regulation reflects concerns about treating categories of speech equally, about regulating speech on the basis of constitutionally
disfavored reasons, about preventing the communication of particular disfavored ideas, and
about improper governmental motivation).

[108] *Cornelius v NAACP Legal Education and Defense Fund*, 473 US 788, 800 (1985).

[109] See Laughlin, *Sex, Lies, and Library Cards: The First Amendment Implications of the Use
of Software Filters to Control Access to Internet Pornography in Public Libraries*, 51 Drake L
Rev 213, 279 (2003) (arguing persuasively that "[l]ocally designed solutions are likely to
best meet local circumstances. Local decision makers and library boards, responding to
local concerns and the prevalence of the problem in their own libraries, should decide if
minors' Internet access requires filters").

B. PROTECTING MINORS

Though the Court has always said that protecting minors from harmful sexually explicit material is a legitimate—even a compelling—interest, in recent years it has honored this interest almost exclusively in the breach. Whenever Congress has sought directly to control the content conveyed by modern technologies of communication—the telephone, cable television, the Internet—the Court has thwarted it. Indeed, the Court has become increasingly alert to patrol the First Amendment boundary between unprotected (obscenity, child pornography) and protected (other sexually explicit speech, such as indecent speech and virtual child pornography) speech, to make certain no protected speech—even protected speech of arguably negligible value—gets caught in a regulatory net cast at unprotected expression.

In *FCC v Pacifica Foundation*,[110] the Court sustained the FCC's authority to impose sanctions on broadcast licensees for broadcasting patently offensive but not obscene material—material that was merely "'vulgar,' 'offensive,' and 'shocking.'"[111] Justice Stevens wrote a plurality opinion in which he expressed the view that such material occupies a low rung in the hierarchy of First Amendment values and is "not entitled to absolute constitutional protection under all circumstances."[112] In addition, he reasoned that "the broadcast media have established a uniquely pervasive presence in the lives of all Americans"[113] and that "broadcasting is uniquely accessible to children."[114]

The Court has confined *Pacifica* to the broadcast media. It has found that the factors that supposedly justified greater regulation of the broadcast media do not obtain with respect to other technologies of communication, and no Justice—including Justice Stevens—currently embraces the notion that with respect to these other technologies the government can regulate the type of speech at issue in *Pacifica*. For example, the Court has struck down a statute prohibiting the interstate transmission of "indecent" commercial telephone

---

[110] 438 US 726 (1978).

[111] Id at 747 (Stevens) (plurality).

[112] Id (Stevens) (plurality).

[113] Id at 748 (Stevens) (plurality).

[114] Id at 749 (plurality opinion).

messages;[115] invalidated a statute permitting cable operators to seg-
regate indecent programming, block it from viewer access, and un-
block it only on a subscriber's request;[116] held unconstitutional a
statute authorizing cable operators operating public access channels
to prohibit the display of "sexually explicit conduct";[117] struck down
a law requiring cable operators who provide channels "primarily
dedicated to sexually oriented programming" either to scramble
them or to limit their transmission to between 10 P.M. and 6 A.M.;[118]
invalidated the provisions of the Communications Decency Act of
1996 criminalizing the "knowing" transmission to any person under eighteen of "indecent" messages or any messages that "in context depicts or describes, in terms patently offensive as measured
by contemporary community standards, sexual or excretory activities or organs";[119] and invalidated Congress's effort to ban virtual
child pornography.[120]

   In each of these cases the Court acknowledged the legitimacy
of Congress's interest in protecting children and purported to insist only that the government pursue this interest with less restrictive alternatives that are "at least as effective in achieving" it.[121]
And in each case the Court asserted that equally effective alternatives did, in fact, exist.[122] This assertion has been repeatedly and
persuasively debunked by dissenting Justices[123] and commenta-

---

[115] *Sable Communications, Inc. v FCC*, 492 US 115 (1989).

[116] *Denver Area Educational Telecommunications Consortium v FCC*, 518 US 727 (1996).

[117] Id.

[118] *United States v Playboy Entertainment Group*, 529 US 803 (2000).

[119] *Reno v ACLU*, 521 US 844 (1997).

[120] *Ashcroft v Free Speech Coalition*, 535 US 234 (2002).

[121] *Reno*, 521 US at 874. See also *Sable Communications*, 492 US at 126 ("Government
may . . . regulate the content of constitutionally protected speech in order to promote a
compelling interest [in shielding children] if it chooses the least restrictive means.").

[122] *Sable Communications, Inc.*, 492 US at 130–31; *Denver Area Educational Telecommunications Consortium*, 518 US at 755–57; *Playboy Entertainment Group*, 529 US at 816, 827; *Reno*,
521 US at 879; *Free Speech Coalition*, 535 US at 252–53.

[123] *Denver Area Educational Telecommunications Consortium*, 518 US at 835 (Thomas dissenting) (rejecting the majority's conclusion that the FCC's cable-blocking rules were not
the least restrictive means available); *Playboy Entertainment Group*, 529 US at 841 (Breyer
dissenting) (criticizing the majority's least restrictive means analysis and noting that "[w]ith-
out some empirical leeway the undoubted ability of lawyers and judges to imagine *some*
kind of slightly less drastic or restrictive an approach would make it impossible to write
laws that deal with the harm that called the statute into being").

tors.[124] The Court often prefaced its "search" for less restrictive alternatives by invoking *Butler v Michigan*,[125] a 1957 decision in which the Court, striking down a statute that banned *all* distribution in any medium of material deemed unsuitable for minors, said that the government may not "reduce the adult population to reading only what is fit for children."[126]

The statutes at issue in all these cases share two features absent from CIPA. Each was (1) a direct *regulation* of (2) *protected* speech because of its content. In other words, each of these cases involved a statute that expressly regulated or punished constitutionally protected speech in order to shield children. CIPA, by contrast, does not regulate or prohibit speech. Web site operators remain free to send, and individuals remain free to receive, every bit of content they were free to send and receive before the Act was adopted. Though overblocking filtering software does make some protected speech unavailable to library patrons *until they request unblocking*, the statute does not threaten to punish, and thus does not chill, any speech, whether protected or not. In addition, it is directed solely at speech that is not constitutionally protected. The overblocking is a random by-product of filtering software. It is not the exercise of a deliberate policy choice to deny anyone access to particular protected communications on the basis of either content or viewpoint. True, Congress's decision to rely on filtering software may not represent the "*least* restrictive" alternative. But in a situation like the one at issue in *American Library*, that is not, or should not be, required.[127]

Whether one regards the differences between CIPA and the other statutes that attempted to protect children as sufficient to justify the plurality's use of deferential review in *American Library*

---

[124] Volokh, 1997 Supreme Court Review at 149–56 (cited in note 70) (demonstrating that there were, in fact, no less restrictive alternatives that would have been as effective as the Communications Decency Act's total ban).

[125] 352 US 380 (1957).

[126] Id at 383. See, for example, *Reno* 521 US at 875 ("[T]he governmental interest in protecting children from harmful materials . . . does not justify an unnecessarily broad suppression of speech addressed to adults."); *Playboy Entertainment Group*, 529 US at 814 ("[T]he objective of shielding children does not suffice to support a blanket ban if the protection can be accomplished by a less restrictive alternative.").

[127] The plurality, claiming not to decide the issue, suggested reasons to be skeptical of the proposed alternatives. *American Library*, 123 S Ct at 2305 n 3 (Rehnquist) (plurality).

depends in large measure on whether one regards the different regulatory context of CIPA as warranting the conclusion that the statute presented different First Amendment risks than the other type of legislation. The answer turns on the Court's appropriate role in First Amendment cases.

C. THE COURT'S ROLE

In previous work I have argued that it is useful to view the divisions in the Court in public forum cases as reflecting a "tension between two models of the First Amendment which have competed . . . to supply the doctrine's underlying premise."[128] *American Library* reflects the same tension and presented the Court with the same choice between two First Amendment models. One I call the Enhancement Model. It reflects the notion that the Court's role in First Amendment cases is to craft rules that will affirmatively maximize the quantity and improve the quality of public debate. Under this model, any government action that has the discernible effect of restricting opportunities to engage in effective speech is presumptively suspect. This most especially includes government decisions to deny speakers access to publicly owned property dedicated to other uses and selectively to subsidize speech.[129] The premises of the Enhancement Model are the twin assumptions that ". . . the widest possible dissemination of information from diverse and antagonistic sources is essential to the welfare of the public"[130] and that the Court can and must develop legal rules to ensure that "the widest possible dissemination" becomes a reality. The model is more concerned with the quality and quantity of public debate than with the possibility of government abuse of power. It has profound but easily overlooked institutional implications, for not only does it in principle narrow the range of political judgment about what speech the government should support (either by providing a public forum or by directly subsidizing it) but it also implicitly claims that the Court has both a mandate and the capacity to assess, in a wide range of circumstances, the effects on the quality

---

[128] BeVier, 1992 Supreme Court Review at 101 (cited in note 11).

[129] Robert Post has persuasively argued that public forum and subsidized speech cases present the same range of issues. See generally Post, 106 Yale L J 151 (cited in note 12).

[130] *Associated Press v United States*, 326 US 1 (1944).

and quantity of public debate, the importance of the government's objectives, and the availability and efficacy of "less restrictive alternatives."

The competing model, the Distortion Model, presents the Court with a less ambitious agenda. In cases of denial of speech access or selective failure to subsidize, it eschews the effort systematically to assess the validity of government action in terms of its effects on the quality and quantity of public debate, the relative significance of the government's purpose, or the effectiveness of alternative means. "According to the Distortion Model, the essential task of First Amendment rules [in public forum and selective subsidy cases] is to restrain government from deliberately manipulating the content or outcome of public debate and to prohibit it from censoring, punishing, or selectively denying speech opportunities to disfavored views."[131] In such cases, the Distortion Model focuses exclusively on preventing government abuse of power and on detecting and forestalling deliberate governmental discrimination against disfavored viewpoints. It too has profound institutional implications. In the absence of discernible viewpoint discrimination or the systematic risk thereof, it rejects the Enhancement Model's claim to comparative institutional advantage at evaluating the appropriateness of political judgments regarding what speech the government should support. It embraces relatively bright-line and categorical rules, where outcomes turn on relatively few factors, rather than ad hoc decision making that claims to account for a multiplicity of variables. Where the effects of government decisions to pursue its policies by choosing the alternative of selectively subsidizing speech are in doubt—as they almost always are (and as they most certainly were in *American Library*)—the Distortion Model ordinarily gives the political branches the last word.

The Enhancement Model appears at first to be an artifact of an intensity of preference for robust public debate that the Distortion Model does not share, but this is not necessarily the case. Those who embrace the Distortion Model, rather, differ from those who support the Enhancement Model in the faith they are willing to repose in the judiciary not only to specify relevant constitutional norms but accurately to discern and assess all the factors relevant

---

[131] BeVier, 1992 Supreme Court Review at 103 (cited in note 11).

to an assessment of the effects of any particular decision. In particular, they do not regard the choice between the more open-ended Enhancement Model and the more categorical Distortion Model as being a straightforward one between the "precision of analysis"[132] that the Enhancement Model claims and "clarity of doctrine,"[133] because they question the very premise that "rigorous" judicial scrutiny generates either precise analysis or accurate results.[134]

Since the result in *American Library* is consistent with the Distortion Model, and since it was—or should have been—doctrinally a relatively easy case, there is considerable irony in the fact that the opinions in *American Library* give evidence that five members of the current Court embrace the more expansive conception of the Court's role that the Enhancement Model embodies. Only Chief Justice Rehnquist's plurality opinion exemplifies the Distortion Model, and it speaks for only four Justices. While acknowledging that the effect of CIPA may be to reduce somewhat the number of speakers who can reach audiences and of Internet users who can obtain access to certain Web sites, at least as compared to the situation that would obtain with federal subsidies without mandatory filters, the plurality perceived that the statute posed no threat either of deliberate government manipulation of public discourse or of purposeful discrimination by government against particular opinions. Absent such a threat, the selective subsidization of speech that CIPA effectuated did not present the kind of threat to First Amendment values that, according to the Distortion Model, the Court can effectively thwart. Absent such a threat, Congress ought to be free to make the judgment calls required in the choice to protect minors from obscenity and child pornography either by refusing to subsidize libraries that fail to install Internet filters (while allowing libraries to disconnect the filters at patrons' behest) or by refusing to subsidize only those that fail to take other steps.

Each of the separate opinions, on the other hand, including the concurrences, embraces the Enhancement Model. Each takes as its analytical point of departure the fact that current filtering tech-

---

[132] Stone, 25 Wm & Mary L Rev at 251 (cited in note 107).

[133] Id at 252.

[134] BeVier, 1992 Supreme Court Review at 115–19 (cited in note 11).

nology will inevitably block some protected speech and that therefore protected speech is, in Justice Breyer's phrase, "at issue." Each implicitly assumes that, despite the absence from CIPA of any threat of deliberate government manipulation of public debate or of any government effort to disfavor certain viewpoints, it is the Court's task to make the final normative and empirical judgments about the wisdom, the necessity, and the effectiveness of the various trade-offs that needed to be made if children were to be protected from sexually explicit images in public libraries. If the majority of the Court is prepared to undertake this task in future cases of selective subsidization of speech, it is at least to be hoped that they will deal more forthrightly than they did in *American Library* with the doctrinal residue they must then discard.

The recent pace of technological change can be disorienting, and the issue of how the law should react can seem daunting. The cyberlaw literature abounds with debate about whether the Internet ought to give rise to a whole new legal world or whether the better course is to adapt familiar principles and time-honored doctrines to the new frontier.[135] Thus it is easy to understand that some of the Justices might feel that a more ambitious approach is necessary. It might well seem that they can no longer keep their doctrinal bearings when they confront technologies or media different from the print media with regard to which most First Amendment doctrines were developed. If nothing else, the intellectual chaos evident in the array of opinions in *American Library* is profound and depressing evidence that their doctrinal bearings have, for the moment, been lost.

---

[135] Compare David R. Johnson and David Post, *Law and Borders—The Rise of Law in Cyberspace*, 48 Stan L Rev 1367 (1996) (championing cyberspace self-government) with Jack L. Goldsmith, *Against Cyberanarchy*, 65 U Chi L Rev 1199 (1998) (cyberspace should be treated no differently from real space for purposes of regulation and governance).

FREDERICK SCHAUER

INTENTIONS, CONVENTIONS, AND THE FIRST AMENDMENT: THE CASE OF CROSS-BURNING

In claiming that "even a dog distinguishes between being stumbled over and being kicked"[1] Justice Holmes demonstrated his limited knowledge of the canine world. But even if Holmes was wrong about dogs, he was right about the law, within which the distinction between what an agent intends and what actually occurs has spawned major lines of legal doctrine. In constitutional law, in torts, in contracts, and in criminal law, to name just the obvious examples, understanding law's resolution of the gap between the intended and the occurrent represents a large step toward understanding the most important doctrinal and theoretical problems.

This distinction between what someone intends and what in fact occurs is an important feature of law generally, but it also occupies a prominent position within those particular legal areas, most of which have nothing to do with the First Amendment, in which *words* are the instruments of operative legal consequences. The parol evidence rule gives pride of place to the "actual" (about which much more will be said presently) meaning of contract terms to the exclusion of what might have been intended by one

Frederick Schauer is Frank Stanton Professor of the First Amendment, John F. Kennedy School of Government, Harvard University.

AUTHOR'S NOTE: The research and writing of this article were supported by the Joan Shorenstein Center on the Press, Politics and Public Policy. Larry Alexander's comments on a draft of the article were extremely helpful, as was discussion with James Weinstein.

[1] Oliver Wendell Holmes, Jr., *The Common Law* 3 (Harvard/Belknap, 1963).

or even both of the contracting parties.[2] The debate between objective and subjective theories of contract is similar, again posing the issue whether the conventional meaning of contractual language, as opposed to the mental states of the parties, is (or is not) what defines the core of the contractual understanding.[3] Long before there was a *New York Times Co. v Sullivan*,[4] indeed, long before there was even a *New York Times*, the common law of libel wrestled with the question whether the ordinary meaning of allegedly defamatory language could produce liability even when the user of that language had no defamatory intent.[5] And for almost as long as there have been statutes and constitutions, questions of statutory and constitutional interpretation have focused on the question whether the plain meaning of statutory or constitutional language is superior or inferior to evidence of the outcomes actually intended by the legislators or drafters who wrote the words.[6]

The distinction between the intended meaning and conventional meaning has occasionally been an issue under the First Amendment, for it should come as no surprise that the distinction between what a word might mean to a particular speaker and what it might mean to the larger linguistic community sometimes tracks the distinction between what is and is not protected by the Constitution. Under the standard reading of *Brandenburg v Ohio*,[7] for example, speech advocating the use of force or unlawful activity may be punished only, inter alia, when the speech itself directly, or literally, urges violent or otherwise unlawful activity.[8] And even post-*Sullivan* defamation often makes liability turn on the distinction between what a speaker may have intended (or what a listener

---

[2] See Richard A. Lord, 11 *A Treatise on the Law of Contracts, by Samuel Williston* ch 33 (West, 4th ed 1999).

[3] Joseph M. Perillo, 1 *Corbin on Contracts* § 4.12 (West, rev ed 1993).

[4] 376 US 254 (1964).

[5] See *Restatement (Second) of Torts* § 563 (1977); Rodney A. Smolla, *Law of Defamation* § 4.2 at 4-6.1 (2d ed 2001).

[6] See Norman J. Singer, 2A *Sutherland Statutes and Statutory Construction* §§ 46.01–46.07 (5th ed 1992).

[7] 395 US 444 (1969) (per curiam). See Gerald Gunther, *Learned Hand and the Origins of Modern First Amendment Doctrine: Some Fragments of History*, 27 Stan L Rev 719 (1975); Hans Linde, *"Clear and Present Danger" Reexamined*, 22 Stan L Rev 1163 (1970).

[8] See *Masses Publishing Co. v Patten*, 244 Fed 535 (SDNY 1917) (L Hand, J).

or reader may have understood) and what the conventional meaning of the words actually is.[9]

Interestingly, the most direct manifestations of the distinction between a speaker's intentions and society's conventions of meaning arise when the speech is not linguistic, but rather, as it is said in the domains of the First Amendment, "symbolic."[10] And this should come as little surprise, because when people communicate their messages by means other than words the likelihood that the conventional meaning of the communication will be contested increases. This issue was precisely at the center of the various opinions in the Supreme Court's 2002 Term cross-burning decision, *Virginia v Black*,[11] for at the heart of the disagreement among the Justices was a deeper contest about the legal consequences that are to ensue under circumstances in which the message a communicator intends to send diverges from the message that a recipient of that message understands. It is not surprising that the Justices were confused on this issue, for questions about the relevance of speaker's intent, although pervasively important in free speech analysis, have rarely surfaced explicitly in either the case law or the literature.[12] *Virginia v Black* thus provides an excellent opportunity to examine more closely the question of speaker's intent and the resultant First Amendment significance of the potential divergence between what a speaker intended to communicate and what was in fact communicated by the conventional meaning of the words the speaker employed. Indeed, as we shall see, it may be that the widely accepted view that speaker's intent is an important component of First Amendment analysis is mistaken, and that First Amendment protection typically hinges on what a speaker *says* and not on what he or she intends to do with the speech. Moreover, because the First Amendment import of the divergence between

---

[9] See, for example, *Moldea v New York Times Co.*, 15 F3d 1137 (2d Cir 1993); *White v Fraternal Order of Police*, 909 F2d 512, 518 (DC Cir 1990); *Bertsch v Duemeland*, 639 NW2d 455, 461 (ND 2002); *Kelly v Arrington*, 624 So2d 546 (Ala 1993).

[10] See Melville Nimmer, *The Meaning of Symbolic Speech Under the First Amendment*, 21 UCLA L Rev 29 (1973).

[11] 123 S Ct 1536 (2003).

[12] The important exception is Larry Alexander, *Free Speech and Speaker's Intent*, 12 Const Comm 21 (1995), subsequently expanded in Larry Alexander, *Incitement and Freedom of Speech*, in David Kretzmer and Francine Kershman Hazan, eds, *Freedom of Speech and Incitement Against Democracy* 101 (Kluwer, 2000).

meaning and intent appears to be different to a majority of the *Black* Court when the message is nonlinguistic than when it is linguistic, the case also reveals something enduring but arguably mistaken about the Court's approach to the First Amendment dimensions of nonlinguistic communication.

I. Two Cases and Two Problems

Unlike most symbolic speech cases going back to *United States v O'Brien*,[13] *Virginia v Black* presented no issue about whether either the legislation in general or the particular prosecution under it was aimed at the communicative impact[14] of the targeted activity. There may in 1968 have been a (scarcely) plausible argument that the prosecution of David O'Brien for burning his draft card was not based on the communicative impact of his act,[15] and there was a much more plausible argument in 1984 that the prohibition on camping overnight in Lafayette Park in *Clark v Community for Creative Non-Violence*[16] was aimed not at the communicative impact of ideological sleeping but rather as much at those whose unlawful sleeping was a consequence of fatigue as it was at those who slept in order to send a message. Indeed, even

---

[13] 391 US 367 (1968).

[14] On the basic analytic structure distinguishing laws aimed at communicative impact from laws of general application with only an incidental effect on communication, see Laurence H. Tribe, *American Constitutional Law* § 12-1 (Foundation, 2d ed 1988); John Hart Ely, *Flag Desecration: A Case Study in the Roles of Categorization and Balancing in First Amendment Analysis*, 88 Harv L Rev 1482 (1975). For subsequent elaboration, see Larry A. Alexander, *Trouble on Track Two: Incidental Regulations of Speech and Free Speech Theory*, 44 Hastings L J 921 (1993). For a precursor, see Nimmer, 21 UCLA L Rev (cited in note 10).

[15] That the argument was scarcely plausible did not keep the Supreme Court from accepting it. Supported largely by a presumption against looking at actual legislative motive, a presumption that is much weaker now than it was in 1968, see *Church of the Lukumi Babalu Aye v City of Hialeah*, 508 US 520, 534 (1993); *Washington v Seattle School Dist. No. 1*, 458 US 457, 471 (1982); *Wallace v Jaffree*, 472 US 38 (1985); Laurence H. Tribe, *The Mystery of Motive, Private and Public: Some Notes Inspired by the Problems of Hate Crime and Animal Sacrifice*, 1993 Supreme Court Review 1 (1994), the Court in *O'Brien* analyzed the case under the plausible but actually untrue assumption that Congress prohibited the destruction of one's draft card in order to facilitate registration and immediate call-up and not to punish a particular form of dissent. Had the Court looked at the underlying legislative debates as closely in *O'Brien* as it came to do more frequently in later years, it would have had little trouble concluding that the actual motivations of Congress had little to do with registration efficiency and much to do with punishing anti-Vietnam protesters. See Dean Alfange, Jr., *Free Speech and Symbolic Conduct: The Draft-Card Burning Case*, 1968 Supreme Court Review 1, 15–16.

[16] 468 US 288 (1984).

some of the arguments in favor of the First Amendment permissibility of prohibitions on the desecration of the American flag[17] maintained, ultimately without success, that preserving the physical integrity of a national symbol was to be distinguished from prohibiting communication with a particular content from being transmitted.[18]

In the case of Virginia's prohibition on cross-burning, however, there was no dispute about the Commonwealth's aim. Virginia prohibited cross-burning precisely to prevent people from sending a message of a certain sort, and thus the case turned not on whether Virginia had targeted the communicative impact of cross-burning, for of course it had, but instead on whether this was one of the communicative impacts whose delivery the First Amendment did not protect. If the First Amendment allows prohibitions on genuine threats precisely because of their communicative impact, which it surely does,[19] then the question is transformed into the question of what it is that makes a communication a genuine threat, and it was on this question that the Court's focus on meaning and intention was centered.

Virginia v Black was in fact two cases and not one, and the difference between the two highlights the issue before the Court. Both of the cases arose under a Virginia statute that made it unlawful "for any person or persons, with the intent of intimidating any person or persons, to burn, or cause to be burned, a cross on the property of another, a highway or other public place."[20] The statute then went on to say that "[a]ny such burning of a cross shall be prima facie evidence of an intent to intimidate a person or group of persons."[21]

---

[17] See *United States v Eichman*, 496 US 310 (1990); *Texas v Johnson*, 491 US 397 (1989).

[18] See Kent Greenawalt, *O'er the Land of the Free: Flag Burning as Speech*, 37 UCLA L Rev 925 (1990); Frank I. Michelman, *Saving Old Glory: On Constitutional Iconography*, 42 Stan L Rev 1337 (1990); Geoffrey R. Stone, *Flag Burning and the Constitution*, 75 Iowa L Rev 111 (1989); Mark Tushnet, *The Flag-Burning Episode: An Essay on the Constitution*, 61 U Colo L Rev 39 (1990).

[19] *R.A.V. v City of St. Paul*, 505 US 377, 388 (1992); *Watts v United States*, 394 US 705, 708 (1969) (per curiam); *United States v Myers*, 104 F3d 76 (5th Cir 1997); *Lovell v Poway Unified School District*, 90 F3d 367 (9th Cir 1996); *United States v Himelwright*, 42 F3d 777 (3d Cir 1994); *United States v Kelner*, 534 F2d 1020 (2d Cir 1976); Note, *Threats and the First Amendment*, 125 U Pa L Rev 919 (1977).

[20] Va Code Ann § 18.2-423 (Michie 1996).

[21] Id.

In one of the two cases, the defendant Barry Black had been the leader of a Ku Klux Klan rally, on private property, which included a cross-burning that was visible to those on nearby property who were not part of the rally. There is no indication that intimidating such spectators or adjacent property occupiers was part of the rally's intent, or part of the leader's intent, but Black was nevertheless convicted under the statute largely because the statutory presumption—the "prima facie" component of the statute—allowed the jury to find an intent to intimidate from no evidence other than the evidence of the cross-burning itself. So although there appeared to be no intent to intimidate the particular people who were or might be observing the rally (which is not the same as saying there might not have been an intent to intimidate those nonviewing members of the community, especially African-Americans, who would become aware of the cross-burning and of the rally), the statutory presumption was sufficient to produce the conclusion that Black had the requisite statutory intent to intimidate.

In the companion case, however, there was little doubt about the existence of an intent to intimidate particular individuals. In that case, Richard Elliott, Jonathan O'Mara, and an unnamed third person attempted to burn a cross on the yard of Elliott's neighbor, James Jubilee. Although Jubilee was an African-American (unlike even the spectators and adjacent property owners in the *Black* case[22]), and although there appears little doubt that cross-burning, rather than some other technique of intimidation, was used precisely because of Jubilee's race, there is some indication that the original motivation to intimidate was not (or not entirely) racially based. Rather, the motivation behind the cross-burning involved, at least in part, Elliott's alcohol-assisted desire to retaliate against Jubilee for complaining to the authorities about the noise coming from shots fired in Elliott's back yard, the shots themselves apparently the result solely of Elliott's target-shooting hobby. Perhaps because of ample other evidence of an attempt to intimidate, therefore, the statutory presumption, unlike in Black's case, played no role in the convictions of Elliott and O'Mara.

The convictions of Black and of Elliott and O'Mara were reversed by the Supreme Court of Virginia, that court concluding,

---

[22] See Rodney A. Smolla, *Smolla and Nimmer on Freedom of Speech* § 3.10.50 at 3-23 n 11 (Matthew Bender, 2003).

substantially on the authority of *R.A.V. v City of St Paul*,[23] that the statutory prohibition on cross-burning, even apart from the presumption, was a constitutionally fatal exemplar of content-based and viewpoint-based discrimination against certain messages precisely because of the point of view the messages espoused. Because the Virginia court thus struck down the statute in its entirety on account of its alleged lack of viewpoint neutrality, the existence of the presumption played no essential role in the decision. Although the court concluded in dicta that the presumption was fatally overbroad, the statute's own focus on cross-burning and not on other forms of intimidation was what rendered it violative of the First Amendment, the Supreme Court of Virginia concluded, and its conclusions about the presumption were relegated to a comparatively minor role.

In the Supreme Court of the United States, however, the presumption loomed much larger. Writing for herself, Chief Justice Rehnquist, and Justices Stevens, Scalia, and Breyer, and reaching a result to which Justice Thomas also subscribed, Justice O'Connor upheld the core of the statute, rejecting the Virginia court's view that the case was controlled by *R.A.V.* Justice O'Connor followed the analytic structure of *R.A.V.* in allowing content-based distinctions within an area of nonprotection so long as the content distinction reflected the distinction and rationale for the initial nonprotection. The linchpin of the analysis for Justice O'Connor, therefore, was that cross-burning was simply a particularly virulent form of intimidation. Because intimidation remains unprotected by the First Amendment, she reasoned, it was permissible for Virginia to single out for special treatment those acts which lay along the same axis that produced First Amendment nonprotection in the first place. Thus, to use one of the examples from *R.A.V.*, if obscenity is unprotected in part because of its sexual explicitness and patent offensiveness, then it is not an impermissible form of content or viewpoint discrimination to single out especially explicit or

---

[23] 505 US 377 (1992). *R.A.V.* has produced a voluminous literature, of which some of the landmarks are Edward J. Cleary, *Beyond the Burning Cross: The First Amendment and the Landmark R.A.V. Case* (Random House, 1994); Akhil Reed Amar, Comment, *The Case of the Missing Amendments: R.A.V. v City of St. Paul*, 106 Harv L Rev 124 (1992); Elena Kagan, *Regulation of Hate Speech and Pornography After R.A.V.*, 60 U Chi L Rev 873 (1993); Elena Kagan, *The Changing Faces of First Amendment Neutrality: R.A.V. v St. Paul, Rust v Sullivan, and the Problem of Content-Based Underinclusion*, 1992 Supreme Court Review 29.

especially offensive obscenity for special treatment, even though it would violate the First Amendment to single out obscenity espousing a certain point of view for special treatment.[24] And because Justice O'Connor saw the Virginia statute as singling out not intimidation with a certain point of view but intimidation with special intimidating power, she concluded, over the dissent on this point of Justice Souter, joined by Justices Kennedy and Ginsburg, that the statute itself was a constitutionally permissible prohibition on unprotected intimidation.[25]

Not so, however, with the presumption. When the question turned from the validity of the cross-burning anti-intimidation statute itself to the validity of the presumption of an intent to intimidate from the act of cross-burning, a different majority emerged, and on this issue Justice O'Connor wrote for herself and a plurality, but over the dissents only of Justices Scalia and Thomas, in holding that the First Amendment was violated by the statutory presumption and by the inference, even if rebuttable, that any act of cross-burning manifested an underlying intent to intimidate. Because some acts of cross-burning were not intended to intimidate but were rather intended to communicate in less harmful and more First Amendment–worthy ways, Justice O'Connor reasoned, the presumption effectively imposed a penalty on protected speech that could not be permitted to stand.

II. Does R.A.V. Survive?

My goal here is to deal primarily with the issues of threats, intent, and nonlinguistic communication, and much less with the well-rehearsed issue of content-based and viewpoint-based distinc-

---

[24] After R.A.V., therefore, an obscenity law restricted to that subset of legally obscene materials (see Miller v California, 413 US 15 (1973)) that endorsed or promoted sexual violence would not survive constitutional scrutiny, because the viewpoint-based distinction between endorsing and condemning sexual violence (see American Booksellers Ass'n, Inc. v Hudnut, 771 F2d 323 (7th Cir 1985)) was not simply an extension of the reason why obscenity is not covered by the First Amendment. See Geoffrey R. Stone, Anti-Pornography Legislation as Viewpoint-Discrimination, 9 Harv J L & Pub Pol 461 (1986). For a pre-R.A.V. argument for narrowing obscenity law in just this way, see Frederick Schauer, Causation Theory and the Causes of Sexual Violence, 1987 Am Bar Found Res J 737.

[25] In a brief concurring opinion, Justice Stevens reiterated the substance of his opinion in R.A.V., and emphasized that a state may prohibit cross-burning with an intent to intimidate even if it does not prohibit other forms of threatening conduct. 123 S Ct at 1552 (Stevens concurring).

tions,[26] but any comprehensive analysis of *Virginia v Black* must at least acknowledge its treatment of *R.A.V.* and the question whether restrictions on cross-burning but not on other forms of intimidation are necessarily viewpoint-based.

In crucial respects, the Court's distinction, first set out in *R.A.V.* and then applied in *Black*, between what we might call cross-cutting and non-cross-cutting content-based distinctions is a sound and important one. We can start with the assumption that any distinction between speech covered by the First Amendment and speech not covered by the First Amendment is in some sense content-based.[27] The distinction between covered economic advocacy and uncovered price-fixing is content-based, as is the distinction between covered commercial advertising and uncovered advertising of securities, and as is the distinction between covered sexually explicit material and uncovered obscenity. But behind each of these distinctions is a rationale, and it is the insight of the Court's approach in *R.A.V.* and then in *Black* that distinctions drawn in pursuit of *those* rationales are best characterized as "more of the same," consequently not creating new or independent First Amendment problems. So if, to take another example, the distinction between covered foul language, like that protected in *Cohen v California*,[28] and uncovered fighting words is a matter of a confluence of lack of ideational content, harm to a targeted recipient, and likelihood of ensuing physical violence (and that is what *Chaplinsky v New Hampshire*[29] ap-

---

[26] On content and viewpoint discrimination, see generally David S. Day, *The Hybridization of the Content-Neutral Standards for the Free Speech Clause*, 19 Ariz St L J 195 (1987); Daniel A. Farber, *Content Regulation and the First Amendment: A Revisionist View*, 68 Georgetown L J 727 (1980); Martin H. Redish, *The Content Distinction in First Amendment Analysis*, 34 Stan L Rev 113 (1981); Steven H. Shiffrin, *Racist Speech, Outsider Jurisprudence, and the Meaning of America*, 80 Cornell L Rev 43 (1994); Paul B. Stephan, *The First Amendment and Content Discrimination*, 68 Va L Rev 103 (1982); Geoffrey R. Stone, *Content Regulation and the First Amendment*, 25 Wm & Mary L Rev 189 (1983); Geoffrey R. Stone, *Restrictions of Speech Because of Its Content: The Peculiar Case of Subject-Matter Restrictions*, 46 U Chi L Rev (1978); Susan H. Williams, *Content Discrimination and the First Amendment*, 139 U Pa L Rev 615 (1991).

[27] "In broadest terms, our entire First Amendment jurisprudence creates a regime based on the content of speech." *R.A.V.*, 505 US at 420 (Stevens concurring in the judgment). See also *Young v American Mini Theatres*, 427 US 50, 66–70 (1976) (Stevens for a plurality).

[28] 403 US 15 (1971).

[29] 315 US 568 (1942). Subsequent elaboration and narrowing of the category of fighting words came in *Lewis v New Orleans*, 415 US 130 (1974); *Gooding v Wilson*, 405 US 518 (1972); *Rosenfeld v New Jersey*, 408 US 901 (1972). See generally, Hadley Arkes, *Civility and the Restriction of Speech: Rediscovering the Defamation of Groups*, 1974 Supreme Court Review 281; R. Kent Greenawalt, *Insults and Epithets: Are They Protected Speech?* 42 Rutgers L Rev 298 (1991).

pears to suggest), then it would be permissible to draw a distinction (differential penalties, say, or prosecution of acts lying on one side of the distinction but not the other) that picked out for special legal attention a subclass of the class of fighting words based on particular lack of ideational content, particular likelihood of harm to a targeted recipient, and particular likelihood of causing physical violence, for these factors run with and not against the grain of the initial distinction between the covered and the uncovered speech.[30]

In contrast to such "more of the same" distinctions, other distinctions cut across rather than with the grain of the initial distinction between the covered and the uncovered. So, to take an extreme hypothetical example, if a statute were to prohibit Republican but not Democratic utterances of fighting words it would plainly fail, and, to take a real and not fanciful example, under *R.A.V.* it appears to be constitutionally impermissible to treat obscenity in the way the Supreme Court of Canada treated it,[31] by singling out within the class of obscenity only that obscenity that endorses or causes violence against women.[32] Because the distinction between endorsing and condemning violence against women is not part of the rationale for excluding obscenity from the coverage of the First Amendment,[33] this distinction cuts across rather

---

[30] I employ the language of "covered" and "uncovered" speech to distinguish those categories lying outside the scope of the First Amendment (fighting words (*Chaplinsky*), obscenity (*Paris Adult Theatre I v Slaton*, 413 US 49 (1973)), formerly defamation (*Beauharnais v Illinois*, 343 US 250 (1952)), formerly commercial advertising (*Valentine v Chrestensen*, 316 US 52 (1942)), and countless others that are so plainly outside the First Amendment as to have not even generated serious litigation) from the decision that certain instances of speech lying inside the First Amendment may wind up not being "protected" because their regulation on some occasion satisfies all the elements of a First-Amendment-inspired test. Thus, the regulation of verbal price-fixing is not covered by the First Amendment, but acts of explicit incitement to imminent political violence are unprotected by virtue of the operation of the *Brandenburg* test. For my own extensive elaboration of this distinction, see Frederick Schauer, *The Boundaries of the First Amendment: A Preliminary Exploration of Constitutional Salience*, 117 Harv L Rev (forthcoming 2004); Frederick Schauer, *Codifying the First Amendment: New York v Ferber*, 1982 Supreme Court Review 285; Frederick Schauer, *Categories and the First Amendment: A Play in Three Acts*, 34 Vand L Rev 265 (1981).

[31] *R v Butler*, [1992] 1 SCR 452.

[32] See note 15.

[33] Nor, in fact, and unlike *Chaplinsky*, is the noncoverage of obscenity a function of the harm it might be thought to produce, for the best understanding of the *Roth-Paris* approach is premised on the nonpossession of *Miller*-defined obscenity of First Amendment value, independent of any other value it might possess, and independent of the degree of harm it might be thought to be capable of producing. See Frederick Schauer, *Speech and "Speech"—Obscenity and "Obscenity": An Exercise in the Interpretation of Constitutional Language*, 67 Georgetown L J 899 (1979).

than with the grain of the rationale for noncoverage and would consequently be impermissible. Indeed, and contrary to how the Court understood the issue in *R.A.V.*, it is sounder to think of the distinctions in light of a First Amendment not that protects speech, but instead that prohibits certain reasons for restricting it.[34] From this perspective what is wrong with the cross-cutting distinctions is not so much that they are cross-cutting as that they are based on reasons and distinctions—between viewpoints, most notably—that the First Amendment simply cannot countenance, and that the distinctions that are not cross-cutting are acceptable because, by being based on distinctions that support the doctrinal structure itself, they reflect reasons the First Amendment does not deem impermissible.

As so recast, this understanding of why it can violate the First Amendment to restrict speech that the First Amendment does not value can be an important analytic tool, but its application in *Virginia v Black* rests on shakier foundations. For the majority, *R.A.V.* is explainable by the way in which the cross-burning prohibition there reflected the impermissible state motive to distinguish between, say, racial harmony and racial animosity, but the prohibition in *Black* rested on the constitutionally benign legislative judgment that cross-burning represented nothing more than a particularly virulent form of intimidation. And because excluding intimidating speech from the First Amendment rests on a permissible reason, the Court concludes, Virginia's motivations in targeting especially intimidating speech are constitutionally permissible.

A closer look at the dynamics of what causes cross-burning to be especially intimidating, however, makes the Court's distinction between *Black* and *R.A.V.* difficult to accept. What makes cross-burning more intimidating than, say, flag-burning or leaf-burning, or more intimidating than cross-bearing, is precisely the way in

---

[34] Although not usually expressed as it is in the text, the focus not on the protection of speech but on the exclusion of certain reasons for restricting it is consistent with the perspective of a large literature identifying the core of the free speech idea as preventing certain improper government motivations. See Larry A. Alexander, *Low Value Speech*, 83 Nw U L Rev 549 (1989); Elena Kagan, *Private Speech, Public Purpose: The Role of Government Motive in First Amendment Doctrine*, 63 U Chi L Rev 413 (1996); Jed Rubenfeld, *The First Amendment's Purpose*, 53 Stan L Rev 767 (2001); Frederick Schauer, *The Aim and the Target in First Amendment Methodology*, 83 Nw U L Rev 562 (1989); Frederick Schauer, *Cuban Cigars, Cuban Books, and the Problem of Incidental Restrictions on Communications*, 26 Wm & Mary L Rev 779 (1985).

which cross-burning's intimidating potential is a function of the racist but constitutionally protected point of view it embodies. Thus, Virginia's belief that burning a cross is especially intimidating is based solely on the viewpoint-based judgment that symbols with one point of view have effects that symbols with another point of view do not have. Cross-burning is indeed more intimidating than many other forms of intimidation, but the very fact that it is so much more intimidating to African-Americans than to others, as Justice Thomas's opinion makes so clear,[35] both explains its special horror and renders it difficult to reformulate its harm in viewpoint-neutral terms.

That the Court persuaded itself that cross-burning is simply a more virulent form of intimidation and not an example of cross-cutting viewpoint discrimination, however, is not surprising, for the Court's rationale here sounds in very much the same register as the frequently-discredited-by-everyone-except-the-Court secondary-effects doctrine.[36] In its secondary-effects cases, the Court has concluded that the First Amendment allows content-based restrictions on speech, so long as the restrictions are justified by harmful effects that are merely correlated with speech of a certain content and not caused by the message that the speech is communicating (neighborhoods whose theaters focus exclusively on Walt Disney movies are far less likely to be dangerous and to be the home to non-speech-related crimes than neighborhoods whose theaters feature "adult" fare). Similarly, the Court appears to believe that "intimidation," like crime in the vicinity of adult theaters, justifies drawing a distinction based on the fact that public displays of some content (flag-burnings) are less likely to be intimidating than public displays of some different content (cross-burnings). Under this rationale, however, even such First Amendment bedrocks as *Brandenburg v Ohio*[37] are open to challenge, because with not much reformulation we might define the harm at issue in

---

[35] 123 S Ct at 1552 (Thomas dissenting).

[36] *Erie v Pap's A.M.*, 529 US 277 (2000); *Barnes v Glen Theatre, Inc.*, 501 US 560, 593 (1991) (Souter concurring); *Ward v Rock Against Racism*, 491 US 781 (1989); *Boos v Barry*, 485 US 312 (1988); *Renton v Playtime Theatres, Inc.*, 475 US 41 (1986). For critique, see Geoffrey R. Stone, *Content-Neutral Restrictions*, 54 U Chi L Rev 46, 115–17 (1987); Philip J. Prygoski, *The Supreme Court's "Secondary Effects" Analysis in Free Speech Cases*, 61 Cooley L Rev 1 (1989).

[37] 395 US 444 (1969) (per curiam).

Brandenburg not as the prevention of syndicalism, as in the actual Ohio statute, but rather as the prevention of physical harm. If Clarence Brandenburg's call to "revengeance" against African-Americans had been understood by Ohio as creating a risk of physical violence, and had Brandenburg been prosecuted under a law aimed at decreasing the incidence of the "secondary effect" of physical violence, would the result have been different? And if not, as is almost certainly the case, then the use of the secondary-effects doctrine, whether in the adult theater cases or under different language in *Virginia v Black*, cannot do the work the Court expects of it.

That the Court's distinction between *Black* and *R.A.V.* is unsuccessful does not by itself answer the question whether *Black* is wrong and *R.A.V.* right, or vice versa. But the analytic failure of the Court's attempt to distinguish the two cases means that, hardly for the first time in American constitutional law,[38] there exist two mutually exclusive precedents with no clear indication that the latter supersedes the former. And under these circumstances, it remains for future cases to make the decision between them, and thus to determine whether it will be some version of the secondary effects doctrine that survives despite its analytical flaws, or whether instead the *Black* outcome will in the future be reformulated to make it clear that, *R.A.V.* and many other cases notwithstanding, the aversion to viewpoint-based regulation, at least in the area of racial intimidation, is not as unqualified as had previously been thought.[39]

---

[38] Everyone has his favorite example, but a good example from First Amendment doctrine is the inconsistency between *Amalgamated Food Employees Union v Logan Valley Plaza, Inc.*, 391 US 308 (1968), and *Lloyd Corp. v Tanner*, 407 US 551 (1972), an inconsistency not resolved until *Hudgens v NLRB*, 424 US 507 (1976).

[39] That racial intimidation is to the Court and to the Commonwealth of Virginia different from other forms of intimidation becomes more apparent when we focus carefully on the identity of the targets of the intimidation. As explored in the following section, the traditional understanding of the exclusion of threats, verbal harassment, and verbal intimidation from the coverage of the First Amendment is based largely on the face-to-face or otherwise individually targeted nature of the prototypical threat. Other forms of threats and intimidation are aimed at larger communities, however, and there is little doubt that the typical cross-burning is an attempt to intimidate an entire segment of the population. That cross-burning often has this aim and effect, however, does not resolve the First Amendment question, for this characterization seems to apply as well to Brandenburg's threats of "revengeance" against Blacks and Jews, and perhaps as well to Frank Collin's selection of Skokie as the planned locus for the march of the American Nazi Party. *Collin v Smith*, 578 F2d 1197 (7th Cir 1978), cert denied, 439 US 916 (1978). Perhaps an attempt to intimidate an entire community (even a local community) based on that community's race, religion,

III. Threats and the First Amendment

The distinction, if any, between *R.A.V.* and *Black* becomes an issue, however, only because of a logically prior one—the presumed exclusion of threats from the coverage of the First Amendment. In both cases the Court's analytic framework is premised on a venerable understanding that state and federal laws that are aimed at threats or intimidation may as a general proposition survive First Amendment attack.[40] The question, then, is whether that venerable understanding is sound, and, if so, whether the acts at issue in cases like *R.A.V.* and *Black* are the kinds of acts that count as threats or intimidation for First Amendment purposes.

That threats are not protected by the First Amendment seems so intuitively obvious that one searches in vain for a First Amendment case even raising the question whether the person who *says* "your money or your life" has a nonlaughable defense to a criminal prosecution.[41] Indeed, even when there is no quid pro quo, and thus no act that might better be described as "extortion"[42] than as a "threat," threats have long been understood to lie outside even the coverage of the First Amendment.[43] Numerous threats, and

---

ethnicity, or national origin ought to lie outside of the First Amendment, just as it lies outside the protection of freedom of expression in much of the rest of the democratic world, but reaching that conclusion in the United States, as the parallels with *Brandenburg* and Skokie demonstrate, would require major upheavals in existing First Amendment understandings and doctrines. We do not know whether eventually allowing the prosecution of group intimidation is what the Court had in mind in *Black*, but if it did not then the implications of *Black* remain even more mysterious.

[40] See generally C. Edwin Baker, *Human Liberty and Freedom of Speech* 54–69 (Oxford, 1989); G. Robert Blakey and Brian J. Murray, *Threats, Free Speech, and the Jurisprudence of the Federal Criminal Law*, 202 BYU L Rev 829 (2002); Stephen G. Gey, *The Nuremberg Files and the First Amendment Value of Threats*, 78 Tex L Rev 541 (2000); Kent Greenawalt, *Criminal Coercion and Freedom of Speech*, 78 Nw U L Rev 1081 (1984); Scott Hammack, *The Internet Loophole: Why Threatening Speech On-Line Requires a Modification of the Courts' Approach to True Threats and Incitement*, 36 Colum J L & Soc Probs 65 (2002); John Rothchild, *Menacing Speech and the First Amendment: A Functional Approach to Incitement That Threatens*, 8 Tex J Women & L 207 (1999); Recent Case, 111 Harv L Rev 1110 (1998).

[41] See Thomas M. Scanlon, *A Theory of Freedom of Expression*, 1 Phil & Pub Aff 203 (1971) (refusing to define "expression" to include "the communication between the average bank robber and the teller he confronts"). The statement in the text should be qualified by reference to the comprehensive discussion in *State v Robertson*, 649 P2d 569, 581–89 (Ore 1982).

[42] *State v Robertson*, 649 P2d 569, 581–89 (Ore 1982).

[43] See *Shackelford v Shirley*, 948 F2d 935, 938–39 (5th Cir 1991); *United States v Khorrami*, 895 F2d 1186, 1192 (7th Cir 1990); *United States v McDermott*, 822 F Supp 582, 591 (ND Iowa 1993).

not only the threats that one might make on the life of the President,[44] and not only the threats that one might make on an airplane to pilots and flight attendants,[45] are routinely subject to criminal sanctions without the intervention of the First Amendment. Sometimes we label this intimidation, sometimes we label it bullying, sometimes we label it harassment, and sometimes we label it a threat, but, regardless of the name, the typical case in which one person by his words makes another fear for his physical safety is one that has traditionally coexisted comfortably with even a strong First Amendment.[46]

The major exception to this principle, and even calling it an exception is likely a misnomer, has always been the threat that would not reasonably have been taken seriously. As exemplified by the overheated political rhetoric in *Watts v United States*,[47] involving a Vietnam protester who had publicly verbalized his wishes to have President Johnson "in my sights,"[48] the permissibility of sanctions for threats has for decades been qualified to exclude those rhetorical extravagances whose minimal likelihood of being taken seriously or literally distinguishes them from what the *Watts* Court referred to as "true" threats.[49]

It is one thing to say that the words in *Watts* did not constitute a true threat, but saying it does not tell us very much about the features that distinguish a true threat from a false one. So although *Watts* remains, *R.A.V.* and *Black* aside, the only Supreme Court case on threats and the First Amendment,[50] the case provides virtually no information on just what a threat *is* other than that that what Watts said was not one. And what makes the issue important is not only that First Amendment issues arising out of threats appear

---

[44] 18 USC § 871 (2000).

[45] 49 USC § 46318 (2000).

[46] See authorities cited in notes 36, 38, and 39.

[47] 394 US 705 (1969) (per curiam).

[48] Id at 706.

[49] Id at 708.

[50] The Court mentioned *Watts* in *N.A.A.C.P. v Claiborne Hardware Co.*, 458 US 886 (1982), and in so doing suggested once again that public political threats must be evaluated under *Brandenburg* standards. To the extent that that is the case, it is hard to imagine a constitutionally acceptable justification for prohibiting nontargeted public threats of unlawful action, and thus for prohibiting cross-burning, even with an intent to intimidate, that is not in some way focused on a discrete and moderately small number of individuals.

with increasing frequency[51] in the context both of hate speech and of attempts to intimidate abortion providers,[52] but also that the threatening feature of a true threat has frequently been misunderstood in the literature. Indeed, and perhaps as a result of the misunderstanding in the literature and in the earlier lower court cases, what makes a threat a threat for First Amendment purposes appears to have been misunderstood, *en passant*, by the Supreme Court in *Black*.

When we think of the archetypal threat, we imagine a threatener who actually intends to wreak physical (or perhaps financial or reputational[53]) harm on the target of the threat, and then uses words designed to convince the target that the threatener in fact has that intention. If the target is so convinced, if the target believes that the threatener intends to do him harm, then the target develops that array of unpleasant feelings that we tend to call "fear." But when the target has no reasonable belief in the likelihood that the threatener will carry out the acts literally encompassed by the words, the target will have no (or at least much less) reason to experience fear, and it would be fair to conclude that this is not a true threat.[54] Thus, when the words themselves promise harmful

---

[51] See *The Supreme Court—Leading Cases*, 117 Harv L Rev 226, 339 at pp 347–49.

[52] See *Planned Parenthood of the Columbia/Willamette, Inc. v American Coalition of Life Advocates*, 290 F3d 1058 (9th Cir 2002); *Planned Parenthood v American Coalition of Life Advocates*, 41 F Supp 2d 1130 (D Ore 1999); Blakey and Murray, 202 BYU L Rev (cited in note 40); Gey, 78 Tex L Rev (cited in note 40).

[53] Or emotional harm, which would be the best characterization of a threat to harm the target's friends or relatives.

[54] Part of what makes *Watts* confusing is the obvious fact that President Johnson was unaware of Watts's words and consequently did not have his fear level elevated by them. Where a threat is not communicated to the victim, neither fear nor intimidation are relevant. Unlike the more typical prohibition of threats, the prohibition on threats against the President and those in the line of presidential succession, 18 USC § 871 (2000), appears to rest on the view that intending to injure the President, unlike simply intending to do very much else, triggers extraordinary security measures that disrupt presidential activities solely by virtue of the existence of the threat. See *United States v Hanna*, 293 F2d 1080 (9th Cir 2002); *United States v Patillo*, 431 F2d 293 (4th Cir 1970); *Roy v United States*, 416 F2d 874 (9th Cir 1969); *United States v Adair*, 227 F Supp 2d 586 (WD Va 2002); Note, *Threatening the President: Protected Dissent or Political Assassination?* 57 Georgetown L J 553 (1969); Note, *Threats to Take the Life of the President*, 32 Harv L Rev 724 (1919). Had Watts been serious in his motivation, and had the likelihood of his putting the President in his sights been real, we would be better off thinking of his declared but noncommunicated (to the target) intentions not as a threat but as more akin to an attempt, or some other variety of preparatory offense, with the words constituting the overt act and the permissibility of very early intervention (we normally require that attempts be further along before official action is justified) based largely on the special circumstances of protecting the President. Nevertheless, it is the word "threat" that appears in various federal statutes, and not only

action but the likelihood of harmful action is perceived by the target as very low (as would have been the case even if Watts's words had in fact been heard by or conveyed to President Johnson), there is little or no fear and thus no threat. And that is why common schoolyard taunts of "I'll kill you" typically produce neither fear nor legal liability, and that is why as well that those who shout "Kill the umpire!" at a baseball stadium can ordinarily do so with legal impunity.

When the target is genuinely and reasonably afraid, however, there remains a question of why it is that placing someone in reasonable fear for his personal safety (or personal well-being in a larger sense) lies outside of the First Amendment. And perhaps the best explanation we can give might be that such an act brings together numerous reasons for nonapplication of the First Amendment, none of which by itself is a sufficient condition for nonapplication, but all of which, when combined, put the typical threat well beyond any plausible conception of the focus or rationale of the First Amendment.[55]

First, the typical threat is face-to-face and addressed to no audience larger than the immediate target. And although one-on-one or other face-to-face communications have a place in the theory and doctrine of the First Amendment,[56] much of importance about the First Amendment is captured in the utterance aimed at a larger and indeterminate audience. This is especially true when the subject of the speech is largely devoid, as is the typical threat, of political, ideological, or other normative content, and when the threat is delivered in order to serve the personal goals of the threatener rather than being aimed at larger social change or public good. Moreover, those threats that one reasonably may take seriously have the kind of immediate psychic effect that might fit within Greenawalt's category of "situation altering"[57] utterances, and that

---

those protecting the President, and one source of the confusion in the cases undoubtedly stems from the fact that the word "threat" tends to be used in such divergent ways.

[55] The pathbreaking work here is Kent Greenawalt, *Speech, Crime, and the Uses of Language* (Oxford, 1989). And see also Greenawalt's earlier *Speech and Crime*, 1980 Am Bar Found Res J 645.

[56] See Greenawalt, *Speech and Crime* at 676–77 (cited in note 55); Frederick Schauer, *"Private" Speech and the "Private" Forum: Givhan v Western Line School District*, 1979 Supreme Court Review 217; Steven Shiffrin, *Defamatory Non-Media Speech and First Amendment Methodology*, 25 UCLA L Rev 915, 932 (1978).

[57] Greenawalt, *Speech and Crime* at 680–83 (cited in note 55).

certainly come within what the Supreme Court has, in the context of one of the harms of fighting words, described as words that inflict injury by their very utterance.[58] Finally, the harm of the direct threat, unlike even the injury done by what the *Chaplinsky* court was likely imagining, is not ephemeral, and typically produces persistent rather than simply passing mental distress. Presumably the Court in *Chaplinsky* was thinking of a harm not dissimilar to the harm of hearing fingernails on a blackboard, or seeing a particularly gruesome picture, but such harms often end shortly after the stimulus itself is removed. In the case of the fear produced by a threat, however, the fear is caused not by the words themselves, but by the proposition that serious danger is likely, and the fear produced by hearing (and believing) such a proposition is not one that disappears quickly. In many instances, therefore, the harm produced by the kind of threat that involves a serious face-to-face (or equivalently targeted) announcement to the target that the announcer intends to harm the target is clear, present, and, for the target, substantial.

The foregoing account may help to explain why serious face-to-face or otherwise targeted threats are typically beyond the First Amendment's reach, but if this account is even close to a sound one, then it is noteworthy that it excludes any reference to whether the threatener actually intends to carry out the acts represented by the threat. There are occasional suggestions in both the case-law[59] and the literature[60] that threats are punishable consistent with the First Amendment only if there is some likelihood both that the threatener intends to carry out the threat and also that the threatener will in fact do so. And if we take *Watts* as of a piece with *Brandenburg v Ohio*,[61] not an unreasonable historical assump-

---

[58] *Chaplinsky*, 315 US at 572.

[59] See *Watts v United States*, 402 F2d 676, 691 (DC Cir 1968) (Wright dissenting), rev'd, 394 US 705 (1968). Indeed, the Supreme Court in *Watts* expressed "grave doubts" about whether an account other than that reflected in Judge Wright's dissent below could satisfy the demands of the First Amendment, 394 US at 708, and it is possible that this phrase has helped to produce the misconception I seek to remedy here. But it is unclear whether Judge Wright intended to require a showing of actual likelihood or merely an intent to carry out the threat, and the difference between a requirement of actual likelihood and a requirement of intent to follow through on the threat is the subject of the discussion here and in the opening part of the ensuing section.

[60] Gey, 78 Tex L Rev (cited in note 40); Note, *United States v Jake Baker: Revisiting Threats and the First Amendment*, 84 Va L Rev 287 (1998).

[61] 395 US 444 (1969) (per curiam).

tion given the timing of the two cases, such an interpretation of a constitutionally punishable threat is sound. To the extent that *Brandenburg* is best understood as embodying both a requirement of explicit and intentional incitement and a requirement of some likelihood that the inciter's audience will indeed act in accordance with the incited act—clear and present danger in modern clothing—then an incitement that does not make likely an ensuing unlawful act remains constitutionally protected.

Whether this account of the constitutional status of threats is sound, however, turns out to be a function of how we conceive of the harm that a threat does. If the harm of a threat is the harm of the threatened act, as the *R.A.V.* majority believed it, in part, to be,[62] then the likelihood of the threatened act occurring is properly part of the calculus. *Brandenburg* would then provide the proper analysis, such that threats that carry little likelihood of being carried out remain protected by the First Amendment. Moreover, to the extent that we remain in the thrall of the threats-against-the-President example, and take a threat against the President as a prototypical threat rather than an exigency-produced or historically-produced[63] unique example, we are again likely to see the core idea of a threat as located in the probability of the threat's consummation.

The probability of a threat's consummation, however, is a harm dramatically different from a harm located in the fear and distress of the listener and conceptualized in terms of the effect of the words on the target and not in terms of the probability of the occurrence of physical (or other) injury. If the harm of the threat is the fear and not the act, and this is consistent with seeing threats as of a piece with harassment and intimidation, then the threat of even an unlikely act would cause the requisite harm as long as the listener was unaware that the act was unlikely. When a listener has a reasonable belief that the threatened act will ensue, the fact that the reasonable belief is incorrect—the threatener had the intent but not the ability to carry out the threat, for example, or the threatener intended to scare or intimidate the listener but never

---

[62] 505 US at 388, concluding that one of the reasons that threats are unprotected by the First Amendment is that individuals need to be protected "from the possibility that the threatened violence will occur."

[63] See *Watts*, 394 US at 709 (Douglas concurring).

had any intention to follow through on the threat—is irrelevant, except perhaps as evidence in the initial determination whether the belief was reasonable. Our first conclusion, therefore, ought to be that if we properly understand the harm of the threat as coming from the effect on the target of the communication itself and not from the likelihood of the threatened act, then the actual likelihood of the threatened act occurring—the clear and present danger component of the *Brandenburg* test—is essentially beside the point. Unfortunately, the Court in *R.A.V.*, although recognizing that protecting the targets from fear was a primary purpose of the law of threats, also included the language about protecting against the possibility that the threatened act will in fact occur, and consequently *R.A.V.* itself contributes to the persistent confusion about the core of the problem of threats, and thus to the uncertainty about whether the probability of the threatened act occurring must be shown in order to support a constitutionally valid conviction.[64]

IV. Is Intent a First Amendment Requirement?

But even if the harm of a threat comes from its effect on the listener and not from the likelihood that the threatened act will occur, and even if it would therefore be mistaken to require

---

[64] Part of the confusion may stem from the apparent rigidity of *Brandenburg* itself. Consider an individual or organization who provides the names and addresses of abortion providers to those who wish to (and have the ability to) murder or otherwise harm those providers. This is the factual background for the "threat" and "intimidation" provisions of the Freedom of Access to Clinics Entrances Act, 18 USC § 248(a)(1)(2000), and also for the widely discussed (see Gey, 78 Tex L Rev (cited in note 40)) Nuremberg Files litigation. *Planned Parenthood v American Coalition of Life Activists*, 945 F Supp 1355 (D Ore 1996) (denying motion to dismiss), 23 F Supp 2d 1182 (D Ore 1999) (denying motion for summary judgment), 41 F Supp 2d 1130 (D Ore 1999) (granting injunction and affirming jury award of damages). If we take *Brandenburg* as requiring literal words of incitement rather than vague calls to action, and as requiring genuine immediacy of action (*Hess v Indiana*, 414 US 105 (1973)), and as encompassing the provision of factual information as well as the making of normative argument, then cases like the Nuremberg Files present a high likelihood of grave danger while also falling outside of the *Brandenburg* strictures. In other words, obliquely delivered information-laden calls for less-than-immediate concrete violent action addressed to sympathetic audiences appear to be extremely dangerous, yet appear as well to be protected under the standard understanding of *Brandenburg*. Faced with these alternatives, Congress and some courts appear to have chosen to describe these calls to action as threats rather than attempt to change or contextualize the holding in *Brandenburg*, despite the fact that the danger is better understood as coming from a call to concrete violent political action than as from a threat in the more precise sense. *Brandenburg* remains intact, therefore, largely at the cost of creating a new category of "threats" quite different from the category of threats as it has traditionally been understood in the criminal law and in parts of the law of the First Amendment.

a showing of actual likelihood (as opposed to perceived likelihood), two questions of intent remain. The first of these relates to the threatener's intent to carry out the threat itself, an issue that arises out of the suggestion in some lower court cases[65] and in the literature[66] that a threatener in order to fall outside the protection of the First Amendment must at least have intended to carry out the threat. Yet once we see that actual likelihood is itself no part of a threat's First Amendment status (or nonstatus, if you will), it is hard to see why an intent to follow through would be necessary. Perhaps, as seems to be suggested in the literature, such an intent requirement is a purely prophylactic measure designed to ensure that threats not likely to have been taken seriously will not be subject to legal liability, but such an approach seems rather an indirect way of achieving that end given the irrelevance except in an evidentiary way of the likelihood of the threatened act actually occurring. If we are concerned with erecting a buffer zone around the concept of a threat, there are ways of achieving those ends that are much less exercises in indirection, of which the most obvious is perhaps simply to have a more precise definition of what is to count as a threat in the first place.[67]

But even if the First Amendment does not impose a requirement of proof of intent to carry out the threat, we are not finished with intent, for it is plain that both the Commonwealth of Virginia and the *Black* majority (and, perhaps, the *Black* dissenters as well) believed that the First Amendment imposed upon Virginia a requirement that the threatener have specifically intended to intimidate. If there is no such First Amendment requirement, then Virginia's statutory presumption was superfluous to the requirements of the Constitution, and thus incapable of being unconstitutional in the way that the majority understood it. To put the issue more precisely, the Virginia statute prohibits not intimidation but inten-

---

[65] *United States v Watts*, 402 F2d 676, 691 (DC Cir 1968) (Wright dissenting).

[66] Note, *United States v Jake Baker*, 84 Va L Rev (cited in note 60).

[67] Moreover, the importance of a separate buffer zone is itself a function of whether a buffer zone is incorporated into the substantive rule itself. When the substantive rule is itself overprotective of First Amendment values in order to prevent those values from being underprotected in a nonideal world, as is plainly the case with defamation, for example, then adding an additional buffer zone is both a form of double counting, see *Calder v Jones*, 465 US 783 (1984), and an under-the-table way of slighting whatever may be the interests competing with the free speech interests. See Frederick Schauer, *Fear, Risk, and the First Amendment: Unraveling the "Chilling Effect*,*"* 58 BU L Rev 685 (1978).

tional intimidation, and the question is whether, apart from whatever mens rea requirement might be imposed by the criminal law generally, the First Amendment supplements this with a special First Amendment mens rea requirement, the import of which is that only by requiring a specific intent to intimidate could Virginia prosecute an intimidating act. That just this kind of intent was required by the First Amendment appears to have been assumed by the Virginia legislature, by the Virginia Supreme Court, and by the Supreme Court of the United States, but perhaps this assumption is unwarranted.

That the First Amendment does not impose an intent requirement may seem heretical, but let us examine the issue more closely. We start with the proposition that on frequent occasions a speech act is not protected by the First Amendment, and that this state of affairs is typically the consequence of that act being both less valuable (from a free speech perspective) and more harmful than the typical protected speech act. This is of course an egregious oversimplification of the architecture of the First Amendment, but it will do for present purposes. The question then is whether it is the character of the act itself or the nature of the speaker's intent that removes the case from First Amendment protection. And although it might be tempting to think, as both Virginia and the Court thought, that the speaker's intent is a necessary condition for nonprotection, it is hardly clear from the case law that this is so.

Consider first *Brandenburg*. Building on Learned Hand's opinion in *Masses Publishing Co. v Patten*,[68] *Brandenburg* requires not only a likelihood of a dangerous act actually ensuing (clear and present danger), but also a "direct" encouragement to that act. Typically we understand "direct" to refer to the literal or explicit meaning of the words of incitement, and that is why, to take one of the old chestnuts of *Brandenburg* analysis, Marc Anthony's oration over the body of Caesar would be immune from sanction,[69] but an explicit

---

[68] 244 Fed 535 (SDNY 1917). On the relationship between *Masses* and the *Brandenburg* test, see Gerald Gunther, *Learned Hand and the Origins of Modern First Amendment Doctrine: Some Fragments of History*, 27 Stan L Rev 719 (1975).

[69] See Gerald Gunther and Kathleen M. Sullivan, *Constitutional Law* 1049 (Foundation, 13th ed 1997). Understanding Marc Anthony's speech as not counting as "direct" for purposes of *Brandenburg* implies that his words were understood by his audience as vague or oblique, even if their general import was comprehended. If the audience understood his words as a literal code in which he was explicitly calling for specific action, the example collapses, and it is hard to imagine that Judge Hand in *Masses*, the Supreme Court in *Brandenburg*, or any of the subsequent commentators would exclude from the idea of a

call for immediate violent acts, assuming all of the other facets of *Brandenburg* were satisfied, would be subject to punishment. But although *Brandenburg* requires that specific words of incitement be used, and although a criminal prosecution would presumably necessitate proof that the speaker intended to use those words, nowhere does *Brandenburg* say anything about the speaker actually intending that what the words urge would in fact come to pass. So let us return to "Kill the umpire!" Suppose it is a moment of high drama late in a crucial baseball game between two traditional rivals, say the Yankees and the Red Sox. And suppose the Yankee left fielder, a man of Japanese origin and citizenship, having just hit the ninth inning home run that gives the Yankees the lead, returns to left field as the Red Sox are batting in the bottom of the ninth inning. When he arrives at his position, a Red Sox fan in the left field stands cries out, "Remember Pearl Harbor! Bomb the Jap with beer!" As a result of this encouragement, suppose then that a number of fans throw at the player whatever beer they have not yet consumed, some of it in full cans and plastic cups,[70] causing the player a serious head injury. The inciting fan is prosecuted for aiding and abetting a battery, or some such crime, and his defense is that he never intended that any of the fans actually do what he explicitly urged, any more than fans typically actually desire the homicide of the umpire whose calls have so displeased them. However reckless he may have been in not realizing that his words would be taken literally and acted upon, our left field fan insists that was not his intention, and therefore his words remain shielded by the First Amendment.[71]

"direct" incitement the use of Morse Code, semaphore signals, or code words whose specific meaning was well understood by both speaker and audience. Professor Alexander takes this to undercut the general view that literal incitement is required under *Brandenburg*, see Alexander, *Incitement and Freedom of Speech* (cited in note 12), but it seems more in the spirit of *Brandenburg* to maintain the literal incitement requirement, but with the qualification that one can literally incite by using language understood by the audience to refer in that context to highly specific acts of illegality, even if that language might depart from the dictionary meaning of that language.

[70] It is, of course, no longer actually possible to buy a full can of beer, in a can, at a baseball or football stadium, but the reason why this is now so makes it clear that my hypothetical is based on a long history of real events of just this sort.

[71] Those who are not baseball fans should feel free to substitute an example in which an angry crowd is milling around the gate agent at an airport under circumstances, again hardly fanciful, in which the flight is long delayed and the gate agent is providing either no information, or evasive information, or flat-out lies. One of the angry passengers cries out, "Get her away from that screen! We need to find out what the real story is!" whereupon another passenger throws the gate agent to the ground so he can see the computer screen. The

One possibility, of course, is that the fan's argument prevails, and that *Brandenburg*'s incitement component includes not only a requirement that explicit words of incitement be used, but also that the user of the words have intended or desired that the incited acts actually occur.[72] But if instead it may be right that the speaker can be prosecuted under the circumstances of our hypothetical example because he is as responsible for the ordinary meaning of his words as he is for the ordinary consequences of pulling the trigger on a gun ("I didn't know it was going to go off" is unlikely to be a good defense, even though guns sometimes misfire), then it may be that *Brandenburg* is best understood as saying what it said and not saying what it did not say. That is, *Brandenburg* may be best interpreted as not incorporating a distinct First Amendment–rooted intent requirement, although of course it will usually be the case that a person intends the ordinary meaning and natural consequences of the words he uses.

It is worthwhile noting here that the same issue appears to exist throughout the First Amendment. Although a person cannot be prosecuted for distributing obscene materials without proof that he knew the nature and character of the materials,[73] it is not necessary for the prosecution to show that the defendant intended for the purchaser to use the materials for prurient interest, even though some purchasers might have different goals for the material. In other words, although appeal to the prurient interest is, inter alia, the rationale for the noncoverage of obscenity by the First Amendment,[74] it is the materials in their ordinary and expected use that create the nonprotection, and not the distributor's mental state.

---

gate agent is injured, and the inciter is prosecuted. Assuming First Amendment coverage in the first instance (less clear than in the sports fan case), does the fact that the inciter may not have intended that his words be acted upon immunize him from prosecution?

[72] This is the understanding that one finds in the literature. See William W. Van Alstyne, *Interpretations of the First Amendment* 107–08 n 43 (Duke, 1984); Rodney A. Smolla, *Smolla and Nimmer on Freedom of Speech* § 10-22 (Michie, 1996); Frank Strong, *Fifty Years of Clear and Present Danger: From Schenck to Brandenburg and Beyond*, 1969 Supreme Court Review 41.

[73] *Hamling v United States*, 418 US 87 (1974); *Smith v California*, 361 US 147 (1959); Frederick F. Schauer, *The Law of Obscenity* 222–26 (1976); Note, *The Scienter Requirement in Criminal Obscenity Prosecutions*, 41 NYU L Rev 791 (1966).

[74] *Paris Adult Theatre I v Slaton*, 413 US 49 (1973); *Miller v California*, 413 US 15 (1973); *Roth v United States*, 354 US 476 (1957).

So too with defamation. Even putting aside the possibility that mere "reckless disregard" of falsity may generate liability consistent with the First Amendment,[75] even the degree of intentional falsity that goes by the name of "actual malice" in *New York Times Co. v Sullivan*[76] requires only that the defendant have known that the allegations were false but not that the defendant have intended that the allegations would cause harm.[77] And although less directly relevant because of the complex First Amendment status of commercial advertising, it is instructive that the status as commercial speech, a status that produces a lower level of First Amendment protection, is again a status that is determined by the content of the advertisements and not the intentions of the speaker.[78] That someone who advertises a product does not possess the profit-seeking motivation that partly justifies the lower level of protection does not change the approach that would be used to determine whether the material itself can be controlled, or whether the purveyor of the product may be sanctioned.

When we rehearse this litany of areas in which the First Amendment appears not to impose an intent requirement, we see that Virginia's intent requirement may have been superfluous, that the Court may have blundered by accepting it so easily, and that Justice Thomas, despite having relied on the long-discredited distinction between speech and conduct,[79] may nevertheless have accurately identified what lies at the heart of the issue in *Black*.

---

[75] I put this possibility aside largely because "reckless disregard" has been interpreted to require proof of "awareness of probable falsity," such that the publisher "in fact entertained serious doubts as to the truth of his publication." *St. Amant v Thompson*, 390 US 727, 731 (1968).

[76] 376 US 254 (1964).

[77] *Greenbelt Cooperative Publishing Ass'n v Bresler*, 389 US 6 (1970); *Beckley Newspapers Corp. v Hanks*, 389 US 81 (1967); *Garrison v Louisiana*, 379 US 64, 78–79 (1964).

[78] *Board of Trustees, State University of N.Y. v Fox*, 492 US 469 (1989); *Bolger v Youngs Drug Products Corp.*, 463 US 60 (1983). The point is underscored by the fact that commercial motivation does not lead to the withdrawal of what would otherwise be protection of the speech itself. *First National Bank of Boston v Bellotti*, 435 US 765 (1978); *Ginzburg v United States*, 383 US 463 (1966); *New York Times Co. v Sullivan*, 376 US 254 (1964).

[79] "[T]his statute prohibits only conduct, not expression." 123 S Ct at 1566 (Thomas dissenting). The classic defense of the importance of a speech-conduct (or expression-action) distinction is Thomas I. Emerson, *The System of Freedom of Expression* (Random House, 1970); Thomas I. Emerson, *Toward a General Theory of the First Amendment*, 72 Yale L J 877 (1963). The classic critique is Ely, *Flag Desecration* at 1494–96 (cited in note 14). See also C. Edwin Baker, *Human Liberty and Freedom of Speech* 70–73 (Oxford, 1989); Vincent Blasi, *The Pathological Perspective and the First Amendment*, 85 Colum L Rev 449, 471 (1985); John Yacavone, *Emerson's Distinction*, 6 Conn L Rev 49 (1973); G. Edward

Suppose that Virginia had simply omitted the intent requirement from the statute, and had prosecuted Black for intimidation.
That is, suppose, to take the clearest example, that Elliott and
O'Mara had burned a cross right on the line (on their property
but plainly visible from Jubilee's) between Elliott's house and that
of his African-American neighbor, and that Elliott and O'Mara
were then prosecuted for intimidating, or for threatening. At trial
the only evidence is the act of cross-burning, and the jury is asked
to conclude that the threatening dimensions of burning a cross are
as plain as the threatening dimensions of standing on the property
line and shouting the words "We will lynch you just like we
lynched your ancestors." Now if in the latter case no separate evidence of intent to intimidate or put in fear is necessary because
of the natural import of the words, and there is nothing in the
case law to indicate to the contrary, then it is clear that Virginia's
intent requirement is not something that would have been necessary in an ordinary case involving threatening words.

If this is so, then the Court may have been too quick to accept,
en passant, the necessity of the specific intent requirement. The
First Amendment does not of course prohibit Virginia from adding
such a constitutionally unnecessary but not constitutionally prohibited requirement, but if the requirement was unnecessary then
the presumption contained in it could not, except in a quite different kind of case, create nearly as much of a constitutional problem
as seven and perhaps even eight members of the Court imagined
it did. Alternatively, of course, seven to eight members of the
Court may have believed that such a requirement was constitutionally necessary, but if that is what they believe, then we still await
an explanation, in light of the existing case law, of why they believe
it, what First Amendment purposes it will serve,[80] and what this

---

White, *The First Amendment Comes of Age: The Emergence of Free Speech in Twentieth-Century
America*, 95 Mich L Rev 299, 358–60 (1996).

[80] Part of the issue is about the question whether the First Amendment protects speakers
primarily or merely instrumentally. If the First Amendment is the kind of deep-down individual right that treats speaker protection as an end in itself, as some theorists have advanced, see, for example, Ronald Dworkin, *Taking Rights Seriously* 190–98 (Harvard, 1977);
C. Edwin Baker, *Human Liberty and Freedom of Speech* (Oxford, 1989); Martin Redish, *The
Value of Free Speech*, 130 U Pa L Rev 591 (1982), then keying free speech protection to a
speaker having a certain kind of expressive or communicative intent may make some sense.
But if we protect speakers not foundationally but instrumentally to, for example, seeking
the truth, or correcting errors, or advancing knowledge, or preventing abuse of governmental power, then the speaker's state of mind has virtually no First Amendment import. Indeed, the fact that corporations have free speech rights, see, for example, *First National*

requirement does in, say, *Brandenburg* cases in which defendants claim simply that they were joking.

This line of analysis works, however, only if the communicative act of burning a cross is equivalent in important ways to the communicative act of uttering the words "We will lynch you just like we lynched your ancestors," and it may be on this issue that the *Black* case truly turns. In both Justice O'Connor's partly majority and partly plurality opinion, and in Justice Souter's partial dissent and partial concurrence in the judgment, much is made of the fact that cross-burning may serve what we can call "benign" purposes, such as affirming the solidarity of members of the Ku Klux Klan.[81] But of course various forms of language that standardly mean x may also on occasion mean something else. "We will lynch you just like we lynched your ancestors," for example, may be intended as a joke, hyperbole, metaphor, or irony, and we can imagine cases in which those who have used those words are, as in *Watts*, not taken seriously by anyone, and cases in which those words are taken seriously by a consequently terrified target, but in which the speaker subsequently claims he did not intend that they be taken seriously. Thus, it is clear that were the words both intended to intimidate and had the effect of intimidating, the First Amendment would not protect them. And it is equally clear that when the words are neither intended to intimidate nor understood as intimidating, *Watts* prohibits prosecution. The important case is the one in which there is an understanding of intimidation but no intent to intimidate, and it is here that the Court appears to have gone astray, at least if we conclude that the Court's conclusion and its overbreadth analysis would have been different in the case involving "We will lynch you just like we lynched your ancestors" than it was in the *Black* case itself.

It is possible that the Court focused so closely on nonstandard meanings of cross-burning as a consequence of an empirical dis-

---

Bank of Boston v Bellotti, 435 US 765 (1978), suggests that at the heart of American free speech understandings is an instrumental and not foundational focus on the speaker, for if we were concerned primarily with the speaker's self-expression it is not nearly so clear that we would protect corporate speech.

[81] There is of course nothing benign in the moral or political or sociological sense in something being used to affirm Klan solidarity, but as long as the evil of the Klan is irrelevant to the First Amendment, then using cross-burning to affirm Klan solidarity is no less benign under the First Amendment than is using flag-burning to affirm antiwar solidarity, or flag-waving to affirm pro-American solidarity.

agreement about the prevalence of the nonstandard meanings. Both the O'Connor and Souter opinions rely heavily on various secondary historical works, consistent with a recent and problematic trend on the Court to rely on secondary sources not cited by the parties to reach a conclusion about a genuinely contested factual issue that is central to the resolution of the case.[82] Based on their reading, Justices O'Connor and Souter appear to believe that cross-burnings that have neither intimidating intent nor intimidating effect occupy a large enough part of the universe of cross-burnings that reliance on the ordinary meaning of the act would be substantially overinclusive. By contrast, Justice Thomas, first in his widely reported questions from the bench during oral argument[83] and then in his dissenting opinion, appears to believe that cross-burning has essentially only one meaning, and that non-threatening (or nonintimidating) cross-burnings are about as frequent as nonthreatening utterances of the words "We will lynch you just like we lynched your ancestors." For this conclusion, Justice Thomas relies in part on his own collection of not-cited-in-the-briefs secondary sources, and in much larger part on his own perceptions from his own experiences and his own life.

The central question in *Black* thus turns out to be really three related questions. First is the factual question whether there is a sufficiently large domain of nonstandard uses of the communicative act of cross-burning to fault Virginia for scooping up the nonstandard and thus constitutionally protected uses within the ambit of a rule reaching the right result in the standard case. Second is the question of what resources the Court will draw on in answering the first question. And third is the question of whether it matters, and if so how much, that we are here dealing with the question of nonstandard uses of a nonlinguistic communicative act rather than a linguistic one. Having touched on the first two, it is now time to say something about the third.

V. Symbolic Speech Redux

Although it is hard to tell for sure, one suspects that the nonlinguistic aspect of the communication loomed larger for all

---

[82] For a lengthy commentary on this phenomenon, see Frederick Schauer, *The Dilemma of Ignorance: PGA Tour, Inc. v Casey Martin*, 2001 Supreme Court Review 267.

[83] See 2002 US Transcript LEXIS 74 (Dec 11, 2002).

of the Justices than might be justified. For Justice Thomas, whose First Amendment analysis was presented as an alternative to simply concluding that cross-burning is conduct and not speech, the analysis that first emerged in *United States v O'Brien*,[84] that was further developed in the flag-burning cases from *Spence v Washington*[85] through *United States v Eichman*,[86] and that has been embellished in cases like *Clark v Community for Creative Non-Violence*[87] as well as in the literature,[88] was beside the point. We do not know whether Justice Thomas wishes to discard the *O'Brien* approach, or whether instead he believes it is inapplicable as a threshold matter to cases of this type, but without his providing more elaboration this aspect of his opinion seems not terribly useful. It is true, as he says,[89] that the First Amendment is not applicable to someone who burns down a house and then claims he did it for political reasons, but it is not true that a statute prohibiting burning down houses for political reasons would be permissible. By collapsing the distinction between the communication-restricting aspects of laws of general application and the issue of laws aimed at the communicative impact of physical acts, this part of the Thomas opinion signals that the long-excoriated speech-conduct distinction may still have some life.

This aspect of Justice Thomas's opinion is important not because it signals the demise of the *O'Brien* approach, for Justice Thomas's potential vote on this issue is still only one out of nine. Rather, the importance lies in the way in which, although slightly more masked, the hold that a distinction between language and other forms of communication has on us pervades all of the other opinions, and pervades First Amendment thinking itself.[90]

In focusing on the nonstandard messages sent by acts of cross-burning, Justice O'Connor and Justice Souter both appear to reach conclusions different from the conclusions they would have reached

[84] 391 US 367 (1968).

[85] 418 US 405 (1974).

[86] 496 US 310 (1990).

[87] 468 US 288 (1984).

[88] See authorities cited in note 14 and also Keith Werhan, *The O'Briening of First Amendment Methodology*, 19 Ariz St L J 635 (1987).

[89] 123 S Ct at 1566.

[90] See Peter Meijes Tiersma, *Nonverbal Communication and Freedom of "Speech,"* 1993 Wis L Rev 1525.

had the case been about the words, "We will lynch you just like we lynched your ancestors." Although it is true that *Watts* likely prevents the state from punishing *all* uses of those words, for some might be as benign as the alleged threat in *Watts* itself, and although this fact presumably makes a *conclusive* statutory presumption of meaning (and not of intent) still constitutionally problematic, the tenor of both the O'Connor and Souter opinions signals that the worry about prohibiting or chilling nonstandard and First Amendment–protected uses of cross-burning is a large one. And that in turn seems to be a function of the resistance of Justices O'Connor and Souter to the idea that nonlinguistic communication can have the kind of tight distribution of possible meanings that we (or at least those of us who believe in plain meaning) associate with words and language. It is undoubtedly true that Justices O'Connor and Souter would acknowledge the similarity when we are dealing with nonverbal acts that have precise linguistic translations. The extended middle finger is the most obvious of these, but there are others as well, as when a band leader's drawing of his index finger horizontally across his neck is instantly understood by the musicians to mean "stop." In these and many other instances, the nonverbal communication seems akin to using semaphore flags to send a verbal message, and I doubt that any member of the current Court would propose treating any of these cases differently for virtually any purpose than they would treat a case involving words (or pictures) alone.

When there is no exact linguistic analogue, however, when there is nothing we would call a "translation," things get trickier, and one strongly suspects that one reason that both Justice O'Connor and Justice Souter focused so much on the nonstandard uses, and thus relied heavily on overbreadth analysis, is a background belief in the inherent imprecision of nonlinguistic communication. And although it is true that nonlinguistic communication that has some communicative content may still have multiple meanings and fuzzy edges—the Frenchman's shrug, for example—much the same can be said about language. It is of course rare for a speech-restricting statute to say exactly which language is prohibited, but one still wonders whether the focus on alternative and nonstandard meanings would have been as important had we been dealing with a case in which the issue was the potential nonstandard meaning of a verbal threat. If the Virginia statute had prohibited simply intimidation, or had prohibited the use of intimidating words, and if the prosecutor has presented evidence of the property-line use of "We will lynch you just like we lynched your ancestors," would the Court have been as concerned about a prosecution that treated this as a sufficient prima facie case as we suspect it would have been in an otherwise identical case involving cross-burning? And if not, then *Black* may be more about the Court's belief that "symbolic" speech is different from "real" speech than it may at first appear.

At the heart of the Thomas opinion, and to a considerable extent the Scalia opinion as well, is thus a position whose challenge remains unanswered in either the O'Connor or the Souter opinions. This is the view that for at least one nonlinguistic communicative act there is sufficient convergence of meaning such that it no more offends the First Amendment to use this meaning as a rebuttable indicator of these regulable consequences than it does to use the standard meaning of the words "Burn Down the Draft Board Now" as a rebuttable indicator of the communicative content that even *Brandenburg* allows to be punished. Although he does not put it this way, Justice Thomas appears to be claiming that cross-burning has a conventional meaning as firm as the conventional meaning of many words, and that the Court's analysis is deficient in failing to recognize that although convention is a necessary condition for linguistic meaning, it is also often a sufficient condition for meanings of other kinds. To note that cross-burning may have a conventional meaning with a moderately tight distribution around its central core is not necessarily to resolve the final issue in *Black*. After all, Justice Thomas may be wrong, as Justice O'Connor and Justice Souter think he is, for their opinions and their focus on other communicative uses of cross-burning are but a polite way of saying to Justice Thomas that his perceptions of the meaning of cross-burning, for understandable but no less mistaken reasons, are substantially narrower than are theirs. But whether Justice Thomas or Justices O'Connor and Souter are right about the meaning of cross-burning, it is clear that the Thomas opinion properly exposes the issue as one surrounding the content and the character of the conventional meaning of cross-burning.

What makes the issue even more important is the fact that the distinction between linguistic and nonlinguistic communication, or between traditional and nontraditional forms of protest, say, has doctrinal consequences in other parts of the First Amendment. Would the alleged balancing in *Clark v Community for Creative Non-Violence*[91] have had more bite if the communicators had been readers or writers or speakers rather than sleepers? Would *Texas v Johnson*[92] have been 9–0 rather than 5–4 had it involved a nationally important text (the Little Red Book in Mao's China comes to mind) rather than a nationally important symbol? Would *Robinson v Jacksonville Shipyards*,[93] taking seriously but ultimately rejecting a First Amendment defense to a sexual harassment claim, have even looked like a First Amendment case had it not been for the First Amendment associations of *Playboy* magazine, associations that come less easily to mind when the vehicle of the hostile environment is less characteristic of the First Amendment's traditions even if no less communicative? We do not know the answers to these questions, but we may suspect that *Virginia v Black* indicates that, even if not as overtly as in the opening portions of Justice Thomas's opinion, the distinction between language and other forms of communicative conduct has a greater pull on the development of First Amendment doctrine than we may imagine.

VI. Conclusion: Freedom of Speech and the Law of Speech

As the discussion in Part IV above has, I hope, shown, we know far less about the role of speaker's intent in First Amendment analysis than we have thought, and not necessarily because it is less important. The role of regulatory intent has been pervasively and importantly analyzed, but the role of a speaker's intent has been long neglected. Perhaps that neglect was justified, and speaker's intent is at best a minor wrinkle in free speech doctrine. But the confusion about the status of threats and the First Amendment, a confusion that neither *R.A.V* nor *Black* does much to dispel, suggests that the confusions about the role of speaker's intent would be better sorted out sooner than later.

To say this, however, is not necessarily to say that speaker's intent should in fact play a larger role than it plays now. Perhaps it

---

[91] 468 US 288 (1984).

[92] 491 US 387 (1989).

[93] 760 F Supp 1486 (MD Fla 1991).

should play a smaller role,[94] and perhaps understanding why this
is so would have kept Virginia from having gone down the wrong
path in its legislation, and would have prevented the Supreme
Court from following Virginia down the same false path. As it is,
the Court's unsatisfactory distinction between *R.A.V.* and *Black*
leaves open far more questions about hate speech and about threats
than it answers.

One reason the area of intent and the First Amendment remains
murky is that for too long we have treated First Amendment doctrine as entirely discontinuous from those other areas of law in
which the legal system has confronted the distinction between
what a speaker intends and what a speaker says. Because what it
is for a speaker to *mean* something varies with how this distinction
is negotiated, the questions that arise when there is a gap between
what a speaker intends the listener to understand and what the
listener in fact understands go to the heart of numerous different
areas of law. The First Amendment has learned little from debates
common in contract and defamation law, for example, or from debates about constitutional and statutory interpretation, but all of
these areas, like the First Amendment, involve the law of speech.
One need not think that the First Amendment can or should per-
vade very much of the law of speech to recognize nevertheless that
there are lessons from the laws's centuries-old confrontations with
language and meaning that could inform the First Amendment's
own special form of confrontation with speech. And one need not
think that the vast areas of regulation of communication now un-
encumbered by First Amendment thinking and doctrine should be
otherwise in order to appreciate that the law of language, whether
First Amendment constrained or not, could be refined for the better by understanding the role of intentions and conventions in the
operation of language. For although communication is at its core
conventional, and requires conventions in order to succeed, it is
not a necessary truth that the things we call "words" and "speech"
are the only types of conventions that make communication possible. When put this way, it seems obvious, but the obviousness of
the continuity between linguistic and nonlinguistic communication
remains to be fully grasped by the Supreme Court. Although Justice

---

[94] See note 80.

Thomas's conclusions in *Black* would require more repeal of existing First Amendment doctrine than many of us would be willing to accept, the special power of his observations about the conventional meaning of at least one item of nonlinguistic communication may nevertheless pave the way for finally giving the idea of "symbolic" speech the interment it so richly deserves.

SUZANNA SHERRY

THE UNMAKING OF A PRECEDENT

How far can you stretch precedent before it breaks? The 2002
Term suggests that some Justices seem to think that treating precedent like silly putty is preferable to acknowledging that it might
be in need of revision. But obvious inconsistencies in the application of precedent are a strong indication of underlying doctrinal
problems. In this article, I suggest that the majority's misuse of
precedent in *Nevada Department of Human Resources v Hibbs*[1] should
lead us to question the soundness of the Supreme Court's previous
cases defining the limits of Congress's authority under Section 5
of the Fourteenth Amendment. But the cloud that *Hibbs* casts over
precedent has a silver lining: the ways in which the Court misused
its own precedent point us to a better and more coherent reading
of Section 5.

Other scholars who have criticized the Court for its Section 5
doctrine have argued that the Court's jurisprudence is fundamentally mistaken because it misallocates authority between Congress
and the Court. I propose instead to take as a given that the Court
should police the boundaries of Congress's Section 5 power, and
that ultimately the Court rather than Congress must decide
whether a problem is sufficiently important to justify the congressional response, including the abrogation of state immunity from

Suzanna Sherry is the Cal Turner Professor of Law and Leadership, Vanderbilt University Law School.

AUTHOR'S NOTE: I thank Mark Brandon, Lisa Bressman, Paul Edelman, Daniel Farber,
Adam Samaha, and participants in the Harvard Conference on Constitutional Law for helpful comments on earlier drafts of this article. Charles Canter, Vanderbilt Law class of 2005,
provided excellent research assistance.

[1] 123 S Ct 1972 (2003).

suit. My suggested doctrinal revisions thus do not require a radical shift for a Court determined to limit congressional authority. I also remain agnostic on the soundness of particular outcomes. Whatever we might think of the decisions in recent Section 5 cases, this Court is unlikely to overrule them; the advantage of my approach is that it preserves most of the cases but makes them consistent with one another. Finally, my approach to Section 5 has the added benefit of forcing the Court to be more candid about the value choices that it inevitably makes. Note, then, that my purpose in this article is limited: I do not mean either to critique or to defend particular outcomes, but rather to make suggestions about the process by which the Court should decide cases—although process will inevitably have some effect on outcomes. Outcomes aside, however, improvements in the judicial decision-making process increase the Court's legitimacy, foster adherence to the rule of law, and diminish the opportunities for abuse of judicial authority.

I

A

Hibbs was decided against a rich background of recent federalism cases, many of them focusing on the contours of state sovereign immunity. Between 1999 and 2001, the Court invalidated five different congressional statutes that attempted to permit individual damage suits against states allegedly violating federal law. In each case, the Court relied on the confluence of two earlier precedents: *Seminole Tribe of Florida v Florida*,[2] which held that Congress is constitutionally permitted to abrogate state sovereign immunity only when it acts under the powers granted by Section 5 of the Fourteenth Amendment, and *City of Boerne v Flores*,[3] which limited the reach of Congress's Section 5 authority. The five subsequent cases held that in order to justify abrogating immunity, Congress must document a widespread pattern of unconstitutional action by states, and must enact only a congruent and proportional remedy. Among the federal statutes that failed this test were two that protected the aged and the disabled from discrimination.

---

[2] 517 US 44 (1996).
[3] 521 US 507 (1997).

During 2000 and 2001, eight United States Courts of Appeals applied this line of precedent to determine whether Congress had validly abrogated state immunity in the 1993 Family and Medical Leave Act (FMLA),[4] which, among other things, requires employers to provide unpaid leave for employees who are caring for an ill family member. Seven of the eight easily concluded that the FMLA could not constitutionally abrogate state sovereign immunity—and thus that individuals could not sue states for damages—because the FMLA was not a valid exercise of Congress's Section 5 powers as defined by the Supreme Court.[5] In 2002, the Supreme Court agreed to hear an FMLA abrogation case from the Ninth Circuit, the only appellate court that had upheld the abrogation.[6] Experts confidently predicted a reversal.

But in *Hibbs*, the Court affirmed the Ninth Circuit by a six to three vote, upholding Congress's abrogation of state immunity in the FMLA. The Court purported to rely entirely on existing precedent, holding that the FMLA met the requirements first elucidated in *City of Boerne* and elaborated in the subsequent cases. In the remainder of Part I of this essay, I argue that the seven presumably surprised Courts of Appeals were unequivocally right—and the Ninth Circuit and the Supreme Court wrong—in their application of precedent. Despite the Court's protestations to the contrary, under the precedents the FMLA is indistinguishable from the previously invalidated statutes. In Part II, I discuss the implications of this conclusion, and offer a revision of the Court's test of the scope of congressional power.

B

The Supreme Court's sovereign immunity jurisprudence is byzantine, and the precedents have been subject to much academic

---

[4] 29 USC §§ 2611–54.

[5] See *Laro v New Hampshire*, 259 F3d 1 (1st Cir 2001); *Lizzi v Alexander*, 255 F3d 128 (4th Cir 2001); *Townsel v Missouri*, 233 F3d 1094 (8th Cir 2000); *Chittister v Department of Community & Economic Development*, 226 F3d 223 (3d Cir 2000); *Kazmier v Widmann*, 225 F3d 519 (5th Cir 2000); *Sims v University of Cincinnati*, 219 F3d 559 (6th Cir 2000); *Hale v Mann*, 219 F3d 61 (2d Cir 2000).

[6] As it happens, the three judges on the panel were among the most liberal on the Ninth Circuit, all appointed by Democratic presidents: Reinhardt (Carter), Tashima (Clinton), and Berzon (Clinton).

criticism.[7] The basic doctrines, however, are fairly simple to state. The Eleventh Amendment, which provides that "[t]he judicial power of the United States shall not be construed to extend to any suit in law or equity, commenced or prosecuted against one of the United States by citizens of another State," means both more and less than it says. Despite its apparent limitation to "suits in law or equity" brought by "citizens of another state," it also prohibits suits in admiralty and suits brought by citizens of the defendant state.[8] Moreover, it embodies a principle that also protects unconsenting states from suits in their own courts.[9] On the other hand, "any suit" does not mean *any* suit; states are immune from suits seeking damages but not from suits that are nominally against state officials and seek purely prospective relief.[10]

By themselves, these doctrines—some of which date back to the turn of the last century—are quite protective of states. But the Rehnquist Court raised the federalism stakes even higher at the end of the twentieth century. Most of the earliest suits had involved cases arising under state law, or cases in which it was not clear that Congress intended federal law to permit suit against an unconsenting state. But what if Congress determined that states *should* be subject to suit for the violation of federal law? Could Congress abrogate the states' immunity, at least to the extent that that immunity was not dictated by the language of the Eleventh

---

[7] See, for example, Symposium, *State Sovereign Immunity and the Eleventh Amendment*, 75 Notre Dame L Rev 817 (2000); Edward A. Purcell, Jr., *The Particularly Dubious Case of Hans v. Louisiana: An Essay on Law, Race, History, and "Federal Courts,"* 81 NC L Rev 1927 (2003); James E. Pfander, *History and State Suability: An "Explanatory" Account of the Eleventh Amendment*, 83 Cornell L Rev 1269 (1998); Carlos Manuel Vazquez, *What Is Eleventh Amendment Immunity?* 106 Yale L J 1683 (1997); Herbert Hovenkamp, *Judicial Restraint and Constitutional Federalism: The Supreme Court's Lopez and Seminole Tribe Decisions*, 96 Colum L Rev 2213 (1996); Daniel Meltzer, *The Seminole Decision and State Sovereign Immunity*, 1996 Supreme Court Review 1; William A. Fletcher, *The Diversity Explanation of the Eleventh Amendment: A Reply to Critics*, 56 U Chi L Rev 1261 (1989); Vicki C. Jackson, *The Supreme Court, the Eleventh Amendment and State Sovereign Immunity*, 98 Yale L J 1 (1988); William A. Fletcher, *A Historical Interpretation of the Eleventh Amendment: A Narrow Construction of an Affirmative Grant of Jurisdiction Rather Than a Prohibition Against Jurisdiction*, 35 Stan L Rev 1033 (1983); John J. Gibbons, *The Eleventh Amendment and State Sovereign Immunity: A Reinterpretation*, 83 Colum L Rev 1889 (1983).

[8] *Ex parte New York*, 256 US 490 (1921) (admiralty); *Hans v Louisiana*, 134 US 1 (1890) (in-state citizens).

[9] *Alden v Maine*, 527 US 706 (1999).

[10] *Ex parte Young*, 209 US 123 (1908); *Edelman v Jordan*, 415 US 651 (1974).

Amendment? In two pre-1990 cases, the Court said yes: in *Fitzpatrick v Bitzer*[11] the Court held that states could be sued for damages under Title VII of the 1964 Civil Rights Act, and in *Pennsylvania v Union Gas Company*[12] the Court held that states could be sued for damages under the federal environmental statute CERCLA. In both cases, the plaintiff was a citizen of the defendant state, so that Congress was abrogating not the Eleventh Amendment itself but its extension by the Court.

The primary difference between *Fitzpatrick* and *Union Gas* was the source of Congress's power to enact the underlying statute. Title VII was enacted under Section 5 of the Fourteenth Amendment, which gives Congress the power to "enforce, by appropriate legislation" the substantive provisions of the amendment. CERCLA was enacted under the Commerce Clause. That difference became pivotal in 1996, when the Court overruled *Union Gas* in *Seminole Tribe of Florida v Florida*.[13] The *Seminole Tribe* case held that Congress has no power to abrogate state sovereign immunity unless it does so as a valid exercise of its Section 5 powers; the Commerce Clause gives Congress authority to enact laws, and to apply such laws to the states, but not to abrogate the states' immunity from suit.

By itself, *Seminole Tribe* might not have served to curtail federal power much. In 1996, established precedent gave Congress quite broad latitude in determining how to "enforce" the Fourteenth Amendment. But a year later, in a case that did not involve sovereign immunity, the Court sharply limited Congress's authority under Section 5. In *City of Boerne v Flores*,[14] the Court struck down the Religious Freedom Restoration Act (RFRA) as beyond Congress's authority under Section 5. The Court held that RFRA was an attempt to "enforce" an interest that was not actually protected by the Constitution under the Court's own precedent. "Congress," Justice Kennedy's majority opinion declared, "does not enforce a constitutional right by changing what the right is."[15]

---

[11] 427 US 445 (1976).

[12] 491 US 1 (1989).

[13] 517 US 44 (1996).

[14] 521 US 507 (1997).

[15] Id at 519.

Thus began a series of cases in which the primary question was whether, in abrogating state sovereign immunity, Congress was enforcing existing constitutional rights or was instead creating new rights. The former abrogations would be constitutional; the latter would not. The Court eventually refined the test to hold that, acting under Section 5, Congress could outlaw behavior beyond that prohibited by the Constitution itself only if the legislation was shown to be a "congruent and proportional" response to "a widespread pattern" of unconstitutional action by the states.[16] From 1997 until 2003, the Court did not uphold a single federal statute under this test. It struck down abrogations of immunity, as beyond the scope of Section 5, in the Age Discrimination in Employment Act (ADEA),[17] the Americans With Disabilities Act (ADA),[18] the Fair Labor Standards Act (FLSA),[19] the Lanham Act,[20] and the Patent and Plant Variety Protection Remedy Clarification Act.[21]

Then in *Hibbs* the Court upheld the abrogation of state immunity in the FMLA. So how is the FMLA different? Justice Rehnquist's majority opinion suggests two possibilities. First, because gender, unlike age or disability, is a suspect classification subject to intermediate scrutiny, Congress's power may be correspondingly broader when it seeks to remedy or prevent gender discrimination. Additionally or alternatively, Congress may have had sufficient evidence of a pattern of state constitutional violations when it enacted the FMLA. A close comparison between *Hibbs* and the earlier cases shows that neither distinction is sound.

---

[16] See *City of Boerne* 521 US at 520 ("congruence and proportionality"), 526 ("widespread and persisting deprivation of constitutional rights"), 531 ("widespread pattern"); *Florida Prepaid Postsecondary Educ Expense Bd v College Savings Bank*, 527 US 627, 639 ("congruence and proportionality"), 645 ("widespread and persisting deprivation of constitutional rights") (1999); *Kimel v Florida Board of Regents*, 528 US 62, 81 ("congruence and proportionality"), 82 ("widespread pattern"), 90 ("widespread pattern"), 91 ("widespread and unconstitutional . . . discrimination") (2000); *Board of Trustees of the University of Alabama v Garrett*, 531 US 356, 365 ("congruence and proportionality"), 368 ("history and pattern"), 372 ("congruence and proportionality"), 373 ("serious pattern"), 373 ("marked pattern"), 374 ("congruent and proportional") (2001).

[17] *Kimel v Florida Board of Regents*, 528 US 62 (2000).

[18] *Board of Trustees of the University of Alabama v Garrett*, 531 US 356 (2001).

[19] *Alden v Maine*, 527 US 706 (1999).

[20] *College Savings Bank v Fla Prepaid Postsecondary Educ Expense Bd*, 527 US 666 (1999).

[21] *Fla Prepaid Postsecondary Educ Expense Bd v College Savings Bank*, 527 US 627 (1999).

C

In *Hibbs*, the Court twice noted that gender classifications are subject to heightened scrutiny.[22] It explained that because age and disability discrimination are judged only under a rational basis test, "it was easier for Congress to show a pattern of state constitutional violations" in support of the FMLA than in support of the ADEA or the ADA.[23] But the doctrine of heightened scrutiny is of limited relevance in this context. It means only that the state must have a greater justification for discriminating on the basis of gender than for discriminating on the basis of other traits. That might mean that each individual *instance* of discrimination is more likely to be unconstitutional, but it is not, under the Court's precedents, a substitute for a congressional finding of a widespread pattern of unconstitutional discrimination.

Imagine, for example, that states impose additional requirements before granting driver's licenses to people over sixty-five and to women of all ages, on the basis of evidence that those groups are somewhat poorer drivers than the rest of the population. The additional requirements are rational, but probably not sufficiently important (or carefully enough tailored) to withstand intermediate scrutiny; thus the requirements are constitutional with regard to age but not with regard to gender. Evidence of such state behavior would therefore support a federal law designed to prevent gender discrimination, but not a federal law designed to prevent age discrimination. Nevertheless, if states (or most states) do *not* place these additional requirements on women seeking to obtain driver's licenses, the hypothetical federal law is not valid under Section 5 regardless of the level of scrutiny. The differing levels of scrutiny focus only on whether particular conduct is unconstitutional, not on whether the states have broadly engaged in the conduct.

In other words, under the requirement that Congress have evidence of a widespread pattern of unconstitutional state discrimination, the level of scrutiny affects only the *unconstitutional* portion of the test: there must still be *discrimination*, by *states*, sufficient to form a *widespread pattern*. Ultimately, then, the question is still reduced to whether there was more evidence of discrimination in

---

[22] 123 S Ct at 1978, 1982.

[23] Id at 1982.

Hibbs than in the earlier cases, and cannot be resolved by looking purely at the nature of the discrimination itself. As the next section shows, even assuming that all of the evidence before Congress involved gender discrimination that was not carefully tailored to achieve a sufficiently important state interest—and therefore would not survive heightened scrutiny—it still did not add up to any more of a pattern of unconstitutional action by states than did the evidence in the earlier cases.

D

In determining whether there is a widespread pattern of unconstitutional discrimination by states, the Court has carefully defined each of the relevant terms. In particular, in striking down the ADA's abrogation of immunity in *Board of Trustees of the University of Alabama v Garrett*[24] and the ADEA's abrogation in *Kimel v Florida Board of Regents*,[25] the Court made clear that three inquiries limit the type of evidence that can be used to justify a statute under Section 5. *Who*, *what*, and *how much* all matter. In *Hibbs*, however, the Court unquestioningly accepted the same type of evidence that it had previously found insufficient to support the ADA or the ADEA.

Discrimination by whom? In both *Kimel* and *Garrett*, the Court reiterated that Congress may not abrogate state sovereign immunity unless it finds a pattern of unconstitutional action *by the states*. It therefore rejected evidence of discrimination by private companies and by municipalities and other government entities. In *Kimel*, the Court explained that "the United States' argument that Congress found substantial age discrimination in the private sector . . . is beside the point."[26] In *Garrett*, the Court refused to credit a congressional finding that "society" had traditionally discriminated against the disabled, because "the great majority of" the incidents supporting that finding "[did] not deal with the activities of States."[27] The plaintiffs in *Garrett* also argued that evidence of discrimination by governmental actors other than states ought to count toward the

---

[24] 531 US 356 (2001).

[25] 528 US 62 (2000).

[26] Id at 90.

[27] 531 US at 369.

pattern of discrimination, because local governments, too, are subject to the Fourteenth Amendment. The Court explicitly rejected this argument, noting that because the Eleventh Amendment does not protect local governments, "[i]t would make no sense to consider constitutional violations on their part."[28]

Under the precedent, then, Congress should not be able to rely on evidence of discrimination by "society," by private parties, or by local governments, nor should it be allowed to extrapolate from such evidence to conclude that states must also be discriminating. But in *Hibbs*, the Court casually relied on just such evidence. The evidence cited by the Court included a 1990 Bureau of Labor Statistics study of private-sector employees and general testimony that the public and private sectors were similar.[29] The latter statements, however, were made not during hearings on the FMLA, but during 1986 hearings on a different bill, never enacted, which would have mandated parenting leave rather than leave to care for an ill family member. The Court cited no support for its bald declaration that evidence of parenting-leave discrimination was relevant to a finding on family-care leave because both "implicate the same stereotypes."[30] Nor did it explain why evidence from 1986 was sufficient to justify a different law enacted seven years later; this omission is particularly glaring in light of the fact that between 1986 and 1993 more than half the states had adopted some form of family-care leave.[31] Thus, the extrapolation from private-sector discrimination to public-sector discrimination was no more warranted when Congress passed the FMLA than when it enacted the ADEA or the ADA. Under the precedents, the Court should have demanded more direct evidence of state discrimination.

What kind of discrimination? The crux of *City of Boerne* was that the definition of the scope of constitutional protection—and thus of constitutional violations—was a task for the judiciary rather than the legislature. It was to guard against legislative redefinition of constitutional rights that the Court required Congress to document a widespread pattern of state transgressions against the Constitution. A showing of state behavior that Congress thinks repre-

---

[28] Id at 368.

[29] 123 S Ct at 1979 & n 3.

[30] Id at 1979 n 5.

[31] Id at 1989 (Kennedy dissenting).

hensible, but that is not unconstitutional, does not justify passage of legislation under Section 5. The Court has repeatedly emphasized, by word and deed, just how sharp this dividing line is.

In *City of Boerne* itself, the distinction between constitutional and statutory protection was the distinction between intentional religious discrimination and generally applicable policies with a disparate impact on religious observance. Shortly prior to the enactment of RFRA, the Court held in *Employment Division v Smith*[32] that, as a general rule, only statutes that intentionally target religious practices violate the Constitution. RFRA, on the other hand, required states to justify—by establishing a compelling interest—even neutral statutes with an incidental effect on religious practices. Congress heard evidence that many states had statutes and other policies with a disparate impact on religious practices. The Court, however, found such evidence insufficient to establish a pattern of constitutional violation: it demanded evidence that states were deliberately interfering with religious practices, whether by targeted statutes or by statutes whose generality was a mere pretext for religious hostility.[33] Evidence that states failed to exempt or accommodate religious believers who were affected by generally applicable laws was irrelevant because the failure to exempt or accommodate does not violate the Constitution.

City of Boerne is admittedly unusual: the enactment of RFRA was an obvious attempt by Congress to reverse the Supreme Court's holding in *Smith*. This threat to the Court's interpretive supremacy might have led it to overstate the limits on Section 5.[34] Subsequent cases, however, have continued to insist on the same narrow

---

[32] 494 US 872 (1990).

[33] 521 US at 530–31. The lack of evidence was an important factor in the Court's invalidation of RFRA. In *Boerne* the Court stated that the "lack of support in the legislative record . . . is not RFRA's most serious shortcoming," id at 532, and then focused on the lack of congruence and proportionality between the right and the remedy. By 2000, however, the Court had apparently refined its views of the nature of the *Boerne* requirements, noting that *Boerne* had rested on both grounds (without distinguishing between them in importance). *Kimel v Florida Board of Regents*, 528 US 62, 82 (2000). Later cases also tended to focus more on the question of congressional evidence of a pattern of state violations than on the issue of proportionality.

[34] Several commentators have noted that the Court seemed to view RFRA as deliberate defiance of the Court by Congress. See, for example, Robert C. Post and Reva B. Siegel, *Equal Protection by Law: Federal Antidiscrimination Legislation After Morrison and Kimel*, 110 Yale L J 441, 461 (2000); Michael C. Dorf and Barry Friedman, *Shared Constitutional Interpretation*, 2000 Supreme Court Review 61, 72.

reading of Congress's powers, even where Congress clearly meant no disrespect to the Court. Whether the Court would have developed the same rigid test had the Section 5 question first arisen in the context of an Eleventh Amendment case is a matter for speculation. But once the test was announced in *City of Boerne*, the Court apparently found no need to modify or relax it even in the absence of direct congressional challenges to the Court's authority.

Garrett, for example, provides confirmation that the difference between intentional discrimination and disparate impact is crucial in evaluating whether Congress has evidence of discrimination by the states. In concluding that the ADA would not be a proportional and congruent remedy even if Congress had found sufficient evidence of a pattern of unconstitutional discrimination against the disabled, the Court focused on the provision in the statute that forbids "'utilizing standards, criteria, or methods of administration' that disparately impact the disabled."[35] This provision, among others, was unwarranted in part because evidence of disparate impact "is insufficient [to establish a constitutional violation] even where the Fourteenth Amendment subjects state action to strict scrutiny."[36] Similarly, much of the evidence of state transgressions presented by Justice Breyer's dissent, but dismissed by the majority, involved state failures to make accommodations, a failure that essentially amounts to refusing to remedy a known disparate impact. Toleration of even a known disparate impact is insufficient to establish a constitutional violation, and thus cannot be used to support a congressional determination that states are violating the Constitution (unless Congress has evidence that the practice with a disparate impact was adopted *because of* rather than *in spite of* its impact—evidence that did not exist with regard to either the ADA or the FMLA).[37]

A somewhat different distinction between statutory and constitutional protection led to the invalidation of Congress's attempt to subject the states to suit for patent infringement. In *Florida Prepaid Postsecondary Education Expense Board v College Savings Bank*,[38] the Court adopted a narrow definition of what constitutes unconstitu-

---

[35] 531 US at 372.

[36] Id at 373.

[37] *Washington v Davis*, 426 US 229 (1976).

[38] 527 US 627 (1999).

tional state action with regard to patent infringement. The Court has long held that a patent is a form of property protected by the Fourteenth Amendment. But in *Florida Prepaid*, the Court focused more specifically on whether the mere act of infringement is a taking. It held that since the amendment prohibits states from taking property only if they do so without due process, Congress could not abrogate state immunity from patent infringement suits unless it had evidence that states did not themselves provide adequate remedies for infringement. In the absence of such evidence the Court invalidated the abrogation.[39]

These cases make clear that the Court's Section 5 jurisprudence demands a detailed and specific identification of the state's unconstitutional conduct. Conduct that is merely similar or related to unconstitutional conduct is insufficient, lest Congress slip over the line into defining rather than enforcing constitutional rights. But in *Hibbs*, the Court was not only vague about the exact nature of the states' unconstitutional conduct, it also relied explicitly on evidence of state behavior that the Court has previously held to be *constitutional*.

In prior cases, the Court demanded that Congress identify precisely the constitutional violation it was attempting to remedy: "the first step" in determining the constitutionality of an abrogation of immunity "is to identify with some precision the scope of the constitutional right at issue."[40] In *Hibbs*, however, even the Court seemed unable to pin down exactly why existing state family-leave policies were unconstitutional. It might be because such policies sometimes discriminated against men by allowing women but not men to take family leave;[41] it might be because states relied on "invalid gender stereotypes";[42] it might be because the policies "perpetuated" such stereotypes;[43] it might be because the absence of an affirmative, gender-neutral family-leave policy gives employers an incentive to discriminate in hiring and promotion;[44] it might

---

[39] Concededly, in *Florida Prepaid* there was little evidence of *any* patent infringement by states. The Court nevertheless carefully explained that evidence of mere infringement would not be enough in any case.

[40] *Garrett*, 531 US at 365.

[41] 123 S Ct at 1979.

[42] Id.

[43] Id at 1981 n 10.

[44] Id at 1982–83.

be simply because more women than men desire family leave;[45] or it might be because the stereotypes "created a self-fulfilling cycle" that led more women than men to desire family-care leave.[46] For each of these descriptions, the Court cited a small amount of empirical evidence in support. Although I argue later that even added together this evidence should have been insufficient to show a widespread pattern, the Court's jumbling of what might be called different theories of the nature of gender discrimination is in stark contrast to its rigid refusal to credit subtle forms of discrimination against the aged or the disabled.[47]

Justice Kennedy's concurrence in *Garrett*, which was joined by Justice O'Connor, highlights this contrast. Justice Kennedy sensitively described the type of discrimination that the ADA was designed to remedy:

> Prejudice, we are beginning to understand, arises not from malice or hostile animus alone. It may result as well from insensitivity caused by simple want of careful, rational reflection or from some instinctive mechanism to guard against people who appear to be different from ourselves. . . . There can be little doubt, then, that persons with mental or physical impairment are confronted with prejudice which can stem from indifference or insecurity as well as from malicious ill will.[48]

Despite this recognition that "discrimination" takes many forms, Justices Kennedy and O'Connor nevertheless joined the majority in holding that the ADA was not validly enacted under Section 5. The demands of state sovereignty impose a higher burden on Congress: "The failure of a State to revise policies now seen as incorrect . . . does not always constitute the purposeful and intentional action required to make out a violation of the Equal Protection Clause."[49] It is difficult to reconcile this insistence on a narrow definition of discrimination for Section 5 purposes—despite an awareness of its limitations—with the multiple descriptions of gen-

---

[45] Id at 1978 n 2, 1983.

[46] Id at 1982.

[47] One commentator finds "truly startling" the "extraordinarily generous account of the constitutional harm of sex discrimination" in *Hibbs*. Robert C. Post, *Foreword: Fashioning the Legal Constitution: Courts, Culture, and Law*, 117 Harv L Rev 4, 17 (2003).

[48] 531 US at 374–75 (Kennedy concurring).

[49] Id at 375.

der discrimination in *Hibbs*.[50] Indeed, Justice Kennedy himself apparently recognized the inconsistency, dissenting in *Hibbs* on the ground that the FMLA was no more justified under Section 5 than was the ADA. Justice O'Connor, however, joined both Justice Kennedy's concurring opinion in *Garrett* and Chief Justice Rehnquist's majority opinion in *Hibbs*, creating a conflict difficult to explain.

Even more difficult to understand is why the *Hibbs* Court found some of the evidence relevant at all. The Court has consistently held that state practices or policies that have a disparate impact on women or minorities are neither facially unconstitutional, nor subject to heightened scrutiny, unless they were adopted intentionally to discriminate.[51] And the Court made clear in *Geduldig v Aiello*[52] and *General Electric Company v Gilbert*[53] that distinctions based on child*bearing* ability are not intentionally discriminatory but merely have a disparate impact. Drawing a distinction between "pregnant women and nonpregnant persons" is not gender discrimination, according to precedent.[54] One would think, therefore, that state employment practices that have a disparate impact on women because of societal patterns in child*rearing* (or other family care) are similarly constitutional.

Nevertheless, in *Hibbs* the Court relied heavily on evidence that inadequate family-leave policies have a disparate impact on women. The Court cited approvingly the FMLA's own definition of the "gender-based discrimination" it was designed to remedy: "'due to the nature of the roles of men and women in our society, the primary responsibility for family caretaking often falls on women, and such responsibility affects the working lives of women more than it affects the working lives of men.'"[55] The Court also

---

[50] Compare Philip P. Frickey and Steven S. Smith, *Judicial Review, the Congressional Process, and the Federalism Cases: An Interdisciplinary Critique*, 111 Yale L J 1707, 1726 (2002) (suggesting that the Court in *Garrett* "applied to the legislative history a time-honored lawyerly shredding technique, the piecemeal critique, in which the evidence was examined in segmented fashion rather than for its cumulative impact").

[51] See *Washington v Davis*, 426 US 229 (1976); *Personnel Administrator of Massachusetts v Feeney*, 442 US 256 (1979).

[52] 417 US 484 (1974).

[53] 429 US 125 (1976).

[54] *Geduldig*, 417 US at 497 n 20.

[55] 123 S Ct at 1978, quoting 29 USC § 2601(a)(5).

pointed to evidence that "12 States provided their employees no family leave . . . to care for a seriously ill child or family member," and "many States provided no statutorily guaranteed right to family leave."[56] It explained that an apparently gender-neutral policy of providing leave to *neither* men nor women "would exclude far more women than men from the workplace," because "[t]wo-thirds of the nonprofessional caregivers for older, chronically ill or disabled persons are women."[57] All of this evidence establishes only that a number of states adopted policies with a disparate impact on women. The Court did not suggest that any of these policies were deliberately intended to discriminate. In establishing a pattern of state constitutional violations, then, this evidence should have been irrelevant in the same way that evidence of state refusals to accommodate religious practices or disabilities was irrelevant to the validity of RFRA or the ADA. Evidence of failure to remedy a disparate impact is simply not enough, under the precedents, to conclude that states are violating the Constitution by intentionally discriminating.

A second limit on the type of discrimination that constitutes evidence of a state pattern is that it must be exactly the conduct for which Congress seeks to impose liability on the states. In *Garrett*, the Court insisted that Congress identify a pattern of state discrimination in employment, and rejected evidence of state discrimination in other areas.[58] *Hibbs* again ignored this limit, justifying the FMLA's family-leave policy by interchangeably citing evidence of general employment discrimination against women, evidence of discrimination in the availability of parental leave, and evidence of the availability of postpregnancy medical leaves of different lengths.

Under the precedents, then, much of the evidence that the Court relied on to find a pattern of unconstitutional action by the states should have been excluded. With or without this evidence, however, taking the approach of the earlier cases would suggest

---

[56] Id at 1980–81. The Court includes statutory cites for only four states to support its statement that "many" states provided no guaranteed leave, id at 1981 n 8, and even this number is inflated because two of the states (Colorado and Kansas) were counted among the twelve that lacked any family-leave policies. Compare id at 1981 n 7 with id at 1981 n 8.

[57] Id at 1983.

[58] 531 US at 368, 372 n 7.

that there was insufficient evidence to find a *widespread pattern* of
state violations in any case. I conclude this section by contrasting
the amount of evidence found sufficient in *Hibbs* with the amount
of evidence found insufficient in *Garrett* and *Kimel*.

How much evidence of discrimination? The question of the amount
of evidence necessary to support a congressional exercise of power
under Section 5 raises several issues. Presumably, there is some
threshold below which the evidence does not support the finding
of a "widespread" pattern of state constitutional violations. As noted
above, there is also the question of which demonstrated instances
of classification or distinction should count as examples of unconstitutional behavior. But before even reaching these questions, we
must identify indicia of reliability sufficient to credit the evidence.
Thus, in previous cases the Court has also concerned itself with the
type of evidence heard by Congress.

The Court has consistently refused to accept "anecdotal" or
"isolated" statements as proof of discrimination.[59] In *Garrett*, the
Court dismissed "half a dozen examples" of arguably unconstitutional discrimination.[60] In *Florida Prepaid*, the Court found the
dearth of actual lawsuits prior to the enactment of the statute to
be evidence that states were not behaving unconstitutionally.[61] In
Hibbs, by contrast, the Court's finding of discrimination beyond
that documented by state law—discussed below—rested almost
entirely on isolated statements in testimony that ranged over several years.[62] As far as the Court was concerned, moreover, not a
single lawsuit challenging state policies was necessary to establish
that states were rampantly violating the Constitution.

The more important question, however, is whether the evidence
supports an inference of a "widespread pattern" of state violations.
Two examples of patent infringement suits against the states (and
eight such suits over 110 years) were insufficient to establish a pattern in *Florida Prepaid*.[63] Examples of arguably unconstitutional conduct in five states were insufficient in *Garrett*.[64] In *Kimel*, the Court

---

[59] See *City of Boerne*, 521 US at 531; *Kimel*, 528 US at 82, 89; *Garrett*, 531 US at 370.

[60] 531 US at 369. The Court then lists only five such examples, suggesting that "half a dozen" was a rough rounding.

[61] 527 US at 640.

[62] 123 S Ct at 1979–80.

[63] 527 US at 640.

[64] 531 US at 369–70.

held that proof of widespread unconstitutional action in California governmental agencies would not establish a pattern and thus "would have been insufficient to support Congress's 1974 extension of the ADEA to every State of the Union."[65] Similarly, in *City of Boerne* the Court made a point of contrasting the voting rights legislation upheld in *South Carolina v Katzenbach*,[66] which targeted only the limited number of jurisdictions in which constitutional violations "had been most flagrant."[67] At the time *Katzenbach* was decided, seven states and parts of four others were within the coverage of the statute.[68] The analysis in *City of Boerne* thus implies that violations by seven to eleven states are not sufficient to establish a widespread pattern justifying broad remedies, but only support limited congressional action targeted at the offending states.[69]

At the time the FMLA was adopted, somewhere between twenty-one and thirty states already had gender-neutral family-leave policies.[70] Of the remaining states, the *Hibbs* Court pointed to a total of fourteen that "provided their employees no family leave" and seven that had "childcare leave provisions that applied to women only."[71] As to the former, providing no family leave to either male or female employees, of course, is gender-neutral and constitutional, and so cannot provide evidence of a pattern of unconstitutional action by states. Of the seven that allegedly provided gender-based childcare leave, four in fact provided only *pregnancy disability* leave.[72] Providing leave for those who are disabled— whether by pregnancy and delivery or because of some other temporary medical condition—is not the same as providing childcare or family-care leave only to women; there is no suggestion that the four states failed to provide comparable leave to men who were temporarily disabled. Moreover, as noted earlier, the Court's own precedents hold that discrimination on the basis of pregnancy is

---

[65] 528 US at 90.

[66] 383 US 301 (1966).

[67] *City of Boerne*, 521 US at 532–33.

[68] See *Katzenbach*, 383 US at 318.

[69] Indeed, at least one article suggests that Congress will *never again* be able to amass the amount of evidence that it had when enacting the Voting Rights Act. Frickey and Smith, 111 Yale L J at 1723 (cited in note 50).

[70] See *Hibbs*, 123 S Ct at 1989 (Kennedy dissenting).

[71] Id at 1980–81 & nn 6–8 (majority).

[72] See id at 1980 n 6 (majority opinion), 1972 (Kennedy dissenting).

constitutionally permitted, so even if the four states had provided disability leave *only* to those employees whose temporary disability was caused by pregnancy, they cannot count toward the pattern of unconstitutional action.

That leaves exactly three states whose childcare-leave policies likely violated the Equal Protection Clause.[73] It is hard to see how constitutional transgressions by three states form a "widespread pattern" of unconstitutional state conduct, especially in light of the precedent and the large number of states with gender-neutral policies. Those three states, moreover, would not necessarily get a free ride. In addition to the possibility of direct constitutional challenges to their policies, *City of Boerne's* approval of *Katzenbach* shows that Congress could have imposed on the three offending states—but not on constitutionally innocent states—provisions identical to those of the FMLA. Even if we count official state policy more heavily than unsanctioned behavior by state actors— which the Court did not appear to do—three states is still a very small number. But it was enough for the *Hibbs* majority.

E

Some readers may remain unpersuaded that *Hibbs* cannot be reconciled with precedent. It is, one might contend, at the edge of the precedent but not beyond it.[74] Whether or not *Hibbs* is the case that stretches precedent to the breaking point hardly matters, however. The Court's rigid requirement that Congress find a widespread pattern of unconstitutional state action before exercising its powers under Section 5 will inevitably lead to a situation in which the Court upholds another statute that cannot possibly meet that test. Two possibilities are already working their way through the lower courts.

First, the Tenth Circuit has, since *Hibbs*, invalidated the congressional abrogation of immunity for suits brought under a different section of the FMLA. The court held that requiring employers to allow leave for an employee's own illness does not address gen-

---

[73] See id at 1980 n 6 (majority opinion), 1991 (Kennedy dissenting). As noted earlier, this still does not show that even these states discriminated, or were likely to discriminate, in the provision of family-care leave rather than parenting leave.

[74] An argument in favor of this position may be found in Post and Siegel, 112 Yale L J at 1972–80 (cited in note 34).

der discrimination and is therefore not a valid enactment under
Section 5.[75] It would be difficult to reach a contrary result under
the current doctrine, but allowing states to be sued for failing to
provide family-care leave while protecting them from suits for failing to provide medical leave is not likely to be a satisfactory result
for the Court that decided *Hibbs*.

Another abrogation, currently percolating through the federal
courts, is also likely to pose difficulties under current doctrine. Under Title VII, employers can be sued for employment practices
that have a disparate impact on racial minorities. Lower courts
have, so far, consistently allowed disparate-impact suits against
states despite claims of sovereign immunity.[76] Under the Court's
precedents, however, this is a problematic abrogation. Since disparate impact itself does not violate the Equal Protection Clause,
Congress would have needed evidence that states were using practices with a disparate impact as a pretext, in order to intentionally
discriminate. In 1973, when Congress extended Title VII to the
states, such evidence may or may not have existed; but even if it
did, Congress did not find it necessary to include such evidence
in the legislative record (in large part because, with *City of Boerne*
some twenty years in the future, it didn't know it had to).[77] As in
Hibbs, then, a Court resistant to immunizing states from Title VII
suits alleging disparate impact would have a difficult time finding
the requisite legislative justification. Nevertheless, it is hard to imagine that the Court would invalidate the abrogation: Title VII has
played a prominent role in mitigating the shameful history of race
relations in the United States, is popular with almost all segments
of the population, and is virtually sacrosanct. Striking down the
abrogation of immunity in that context would inevitably—and
intolerably—be read as a holding that the government is allowed
to discriminate on the basis of race. And given the Court's claim
in *Hibbs* that it was simply applying precedent—and the fact that

---

[75] *Brockman v Wyoming Dept of Family Servs*, 342 F3d 1159 (10th Cir 2003). This is the
first case to be decided after *Hibbs*, but other courts invalidated this abrogation prior to
Hibbs. See cases cited in id at 1165 & n 3.

[76] See *In re Employment Discrimination Litigation*, 198 F3d 1305 (11th Cir 1999); *Okrhulik
v University of Arkansas*, 255 F3d 615 (8th Cir 2000).

[77] The lower courts that have rejected sovereign immunity arguments in disparate-impact
cases point only to evidence that in 1973 states were using practices with a disparate impact,
not evidence that they were intentionally discriminating. See cases cited in note 76.

lower courts rejecting sovereign-immunity arguments in disparate-impact cases have unsurprisingly claimed to be following pre-*Hibbs* Supreme Court precedent—it is likely that a Supreme Court decision upholding the Title VII abrogation would treat precedent similarly.

The problem remains then: whether in *Hibbs* or in some future case, the evidence the Court finds sufficient to uphold an abrogation will be no stronger in quality or quantity from that which led it to invalidate other statutes. What are we to make of the Court's attempt to portray its decision as simply an unproblematic application of precedent? It is to that question that I now turn.

II

The result in *Hibbs* may be considered laudable, depending on whether we prefer to protect employees caring for ill family members or to protect sovereign states when the two interests conflict. So let us assume that the FMLA (including the abrogation of immunity) is a statute that should, indeed, have been upheld by the Supreme Court. The question is whether that assumption justifies the Court's decision. What *should* the Court do when the result that it believes correct is foreclosed by precedent? Three other cases from the Court's 2002 Term offer some illuminating guidance about different Justices' answers to that question. I begin by briefly examining those three cases, and then apply their lessons to the issue of congressional abrogation of state immunity.

A

In some ways, one could not imagine a case further from *Hibbs* than *Demore v Kim*.[78] In *Kim*, the five Justices often labeled as conservative upheld the detention of a deportable alien, pending his deportation hearing, despite the absence of any determination that he was either dangerous or posed a flight risk. This result would be neither surprising nor problematic but for a case two years earlier: in June 2001, the Court in *Zadvydas v Davis*[79] held that the government could not indefinitely detain an alien whose legally

---

[78] 123 S Ct 1708 (2003).

[79] 533 US 678 (2001).

mandated deportation was foiled by the unwillingness of any country to accept him. While the two cases are distinguishable on their facts, they are utterly inconsistent in tone and approach. In *Zadvydas*, Justice Breyer's majority opinion held that "the Due Process Clause applies to all 'persons' within the United States, including aliens."[80] It explicitly rejected the dissent's suggestion that removable aliens are entitled only "to be free from detention that is arbitrary and capricious."[81] In *Kim*, by contrast, the Court deferred to Congress's decision not to utilize individualized hearings on dangerousness or risk of flight, noting that "when the Government deals with deportable aliens, the Due Process Clause does not require it to employ the least burdensome means to accomplish its goal."[82] Chief Justice Rehnquist's majority opinion further stated that "this Court has firmly and repeatedly endorsed the proposition that Congress may make rules as to aliens that would be unacceptable if applied to citizens"—and cited in support Justice Kennedy's dissenting opinion in *Zadvydas*.[83] Indeed, the opinion in *Kim* cites Justice Kennedy's dissent in *Zadvydas* for legal support more than it cites the majority opinion. And, as with *Hibbs*, the Supreme Court's application of the precedent was unusual: four of the five Courts of Appeals that had reached the question had found the absence of a hearing for predeportation detention unconstitutional under *Zadvydas*; the only court upholding such detention had ruled before *Zadvydas* was decided.[84]

Does this mean that *Kim* was wrongly decided? No, no more than my critique of the opinion in *Hibbs* demonstrates that it was wrong. I simply suggest that *Kim* was a misapplication of precedent. The Court—in particular, Justice O'Connor, who was the only Justice to join the majority in both *Zadvydas* and *Kim*—had changed its mind about the scope of congressional authority over aliens. The reason for the change in views is not hard to fathom: between the June 2001 decision in *Zadvydas* and the January 2003

---

[80] Id at 693.

[81] Id at 694–95 (majority opinion), 721 (Kennedy dissenting).

[82] 123 S Ct at 1720.

[83] Id at 1717.

[84] See *Welch v Ashcroft*, 293 F3d 213 (4th Cir 2002); *Hoang v Comfort*, 282 F3d 1247 (10th Cir 2002); *Kim v Zigler*, 276 F3d 523 (9th Cir 2002), rev'd sub nom *Demore v Kim*, 123 S Ct 1708 (2003); *Patel v Zemski*, 287 F3d 299 (3d Cir 2001); but see *Parra v Perryman*, 172 F3d 954 (7th Cir 1999) (upholding detention before *Zadvydas*).

decision in *Kim*, America had become more sensitive to the dangers that aliens might pose. Nevertheless, the Court in *Kim* did not mention September 11, but instead pretended (as it had in *Hibbs*) that it was simply applying established precedent.

Like *Hibbs*, *Kim* illustrates the Court's misuse of precedent, but it does not offer any alternatives for a majority determined to reach a result foreclosed by precedent. In another case from the 2002 Term, Justice O'Connor's majority opinion exhibits the same problematic use of precedent as do *Hibbs* and *Kim*, but it can be contrasted with the opinions of several other Justices in the majority, hinting at an alternative approach to the question of what to do with unpleasant precedent.

In *Grutter v Bollinger*,[85] a slim majority upheld the University of Michigan Law School's affirmative action program. Purportedly applying strict scrutiny, the Court found that the program was narrowly tailored to accomplish a compelling state interest in obtaining a racially diverse law school class. While a detailed discussion of *Grutter* is beyond the scope of this article, even a cursory examination demonstrates that this is not the strict scrutiny that the Court has used in the past.

Justice O'Connor, in finding the program narrowly tailored, deferred to the law school's own determination of the benefits of a racially diverse student body, the lack of adequate alternative methods for obtaining a racially diverse student body, the detrimental effect alternative methods might have on the law school, and the temporary nature of the program.[86] Not since *Korematsu v United States*[87] has the Court upheld a racially discriminatory state policy under strict scrutiny, nor has it ever suggested that the challenged program is due any deference from the Court—instead it has always demanded that such programs be subjected to the most searching examination.[88]

The majority in *Grutter* also uncritically accepted the law school's representation that it was not seeking a fixed percentage

---

[85] 123 S Ct 2325.

[86] See id at 2338, 2339–40, 2345, 2346.

[87] 323 US 214 (1944).

[88] See, for example, *Adarand Constructors, Inc. v Pena*, 515 US 200 (1995); *City of Richmond v J.A. Croson Co.*, 488 US 469 (1989); *Wygant v Jackson Board of Education*, 476 US 267 (1986).

of minority students (i.e., an unconstitutional quota), but rather a "critical mass" that would prevent minority students from feeling isolated.[89] That "critical mass," however, varied by racial group: for Native Americans the critical mass ranged from 13 to 19 students, for Hispanics it was 47 to 56, and for African Americans it was between 91 and 108.[90] This "critical mass" of each group was, in almost every year (of a six-year period), within half a point of the percentage of applicants of that racial group.[91] Further, the admissions director consulted daily reports on the percentage of minority applicants admitted during the months-long admissions process.[92] This evidence at least raises the question whether the law school was candid in its assertion that it was not imposing racial quotas, but the majority did not probe that assertion.

Four other Justices—Justices Stevens, Souter, Ginsburg, and Breyer—joined Justice O'Connor's opinion in *Grutter*. Their views on the precedent, however, apparently differed from hers. Justice Ginsburg wrote a dissenting opinion in a companion case, *Gratz v Bollinger*[93] (which invalidated the University of Michigan's undergraduate affirmative action program). Joined in relevant part by Justices Souter and Breyer, Justice Ginsburg took issue with the majority's insistence "that the same standard of review controls judicial inspection of all official race classifications."[94] Instead, she suggested, "[a]ctions designed to burden groups long denied full citizenship stature are not sensibly ranked with measures taken to hasten the day when entrenched discrimination and its after effects have been extirpated."[95] Justice Stevens has long advocated a similar approach, suggesting that Equal Protection challenges be resolved by using a sliding scale rather than the current regime of three independent levels of scrutiny.[96] These Justices, then, joined Justice O'Con-

---

[89] 123 S Ct at 2339, 2343.

[90] Id at 2366 (Rehnquist dissenting).

[91] Id at 2368.

[92] Id at 2343 (majority opinion), 2372 (Kennedy dissenting).

[93] 123 S Ct at 2411 (2003).

[94] Id at 2442 (Ginsburg dissenting).

[95] Id at 2444.

[96] See, for example, *Craig v Boren*, 429 US 190, 211–12 (1976) (Stevens concurring):

There is only one Equal Protection Clause. It requires every State to govern impartially. It does not direct the courts to apply one standard of review in some cases and a different standard in other cases. I am inclined to believe that what has become known as the two-tiered analysis of equal protection claims does not

nor in finding the law school's program constitutional, but did not need to assert that the program should survive strict scrutiny—which, under the precedent, it most certainly should not have.[97]

An illuminating contrast to *Hibbs*, *Grutter*, and *Kim* may be found in another of the Court's decisions during the 2002 Term. In *Lawrence v Texas*,[98] six Justices voted to invalidate Texas's law prohibiting homosexual (but not heterosexual) sodomy. Like the outcome in *Hibbs*, this is a result that many applaud. But unlike *Hibbs*, only one Justice tried to pretend that the decision was consistent with earlier precedent. Justice Kennedy's majority opinion instead forthrightly overruled the inconsistent precedent of *Bowers v Hardwick*.[99] Only Justice O'Connor, concurring in the judgment, distinguished *Hardwick*. A brief examination of both cases demonstrates that Justice O'Connor's (mis)treatment of precedent in *Lawrence* is similar to the (mis)treatment of precedent in her *Grutter* opinion and in Chief Justice Rehnquist's opinion in *Hibbs* (which she joined).

In *Hardwick*, Justice White's opinion for the Court (which Justice O'Connor also joined) upheld a Georgia statute that criminalized sodomy between consenting adults. Those challenging the law suggested that it lacked a rational basis because it was based solely on the Georgia legislature's view that homosexual conduct was immoral. The Court explicitly rejected this argument that "majority sentiments about the morality of homosexual conduct should be declared inadequate" to provide a rational basis for the law.[100] Moreover, in *Hardwick* the Court framed the issue as "whether the Federal Constitution confers a fundamental right

---

describe a completely logical method of deciding cases, but rather is a method the Court has employed to explain decisions that actually apply a single standard in a reasonably consistent fashion.

See also *Adarand v Pena*, 515 US 200, 245–46 (1995) (Stevens dissenting) ("a single standard that purports to equate remedial preferences with invidious discrimination cannot be defended in the name of 'equal protection'").

[97] There is still the question why these four Justices joined Justice O'Connor's opinion rather than simply concurring in the result. The explanation is, I believe, institutional: a fractured case with no majority opinion would simply replicate *Regents of the University of California v Bakke*, 438 US 265 (1978), and all of the uncertainty it generated. However difficult to interpret and apply, Justice O'Connor's opinion in *Grutter* is at least an opinion for the Court.

[98] 123 S Ct 2472 (2003).

[99] 478 US 186 (1986), overruled in *Lawrence*, 123 S Ct at 2484.

[100] 478 US at 196.

upon *homosexuals* to engage in sodomy,"[101] suggesting that it focused on purely homosexual conduct despite the fact that the challenged Georgia statute prohibited all sodomy. Indeed, the Court
explicitly declined to decide the constitutionality of the statute as
applied to a married heterosexual couple.[102] Yet in *Lawrence*, Justice
O'Connor found that distinguishing between heterosexual and homosexual sodomy lacked a rational basis.[103] If a majority of Georgia
citizens can ban sodomy simply because they think homosexuality
is immoral, and the Court in upholding the ban does not care
whether it could constitutionally be applied to heterosexuals, it is
hard to see how a morality-based ban on homosexual sodomy lacks
a rational basis.

All eight of the other Justices agreed that adhering to *Hardwick*
would require the Court to uphold the Texas statute. So the five
Justices who found such a result intolerable under our Constitution
refused to hide behind false distinctions, and instead bluntly declared *Hardwick* to be flawed and overruled it. (The other three
dissented, and would have upheld the Texas statute.) Whether one
agrees with the overruling or not, at least it confronts the precedent rather than distorting it.

In *Hibbs* and these three other high-profile cases, then, some
Justices seemed determined to uphold precedent even when it required them to twist that precedent beyond recognition in order
to reach particular results. In two of the cases, other Justices who
reached the same results chose a different course, implicitly or explicitly rejecting the precedent. What might this phenomenon
teach us about the Court's Section 5 jurisprudence?

B

I draw two inferences from *Hibbs* and these additional illustrative
cases. The first is obvious: faced with uncomfortably constraining
precedent, the Court has a choice between dissembling or forthrightly admitting error. Too often, some current Justices seem to
prefer the former. This lack of candor is unfortunate for several
reasons. To begin with, it undermines the normative legitimacy

---

[101] Id at 190 (emphasis added).

[102] Id at 188 n 2.

[103] 123 S Ct at 2484.

of courts. It transforms the rule of law into the rule of men by allowing judges to reach their preferred results without confronting doctrinal inconsistencies. In a democratic regime, dissembling by government actors also deprives the citizenry of information necessary for deliberation and decision making. Lack of candor is particularly dangerous in unelected judges, because for them visible rationality is a substitute for democratic accountability. Distortion of precedent thus exacerbates the tension between popular democracy and constitutional democracy by disguising the reasons for judicial decisions. At a more practical level, it creates great uncertainty by freeing courts, especially lower courts, from any real constraints that might be imposed by precedent. Moreover, a lack of constraints can make more problematic the judiciary's counter-majoritarian aspect, and thus leave the courts more vulnerable to criticism.

The second inference from *Hibbs* is more subtle: the more apparent the dissembling—the easier it is to show that adherence to precedent demands a different result than that reached by the Court—the clearer the conclusion that the precedent itself is flawed. Every manifest distortion of precedent costs the Court in loss of legitimacy, and the expenditure is only justified when the course dictated by precedent is even more intolerable. If adherence to precedent demands an intolerable result, however, there must be something seriously wrong with the precedent.

Thus, what we learn from *Hibbs* is that the Court's sovereign immunity doctrine is a mistake. Combining the limits of *Seminole Tribe* and *City of Boerne* constrains Congress in ways that even some Justices most supportive of states' rights cannot stomach.

Two alternatives present themselves. The more radical is to overrule *Seminole Tribe*. The academic literature and the dissenting opinions in *Seminole Tribe* and *Alden v Maine* provide strong reasons in favor of that approach. Limiting Congress to its Section 5 powers in abrogating state sovereign immunity is a poor interpretation of the relevant constitutional provisions.[104] I have little to contribute here to that argument, although I think it is correct. However, it is an argument that has no chance of persuading the present Court.

---

[104] See *Alden v Maine*, 527 US 706, 762–808 (1999) (Souter dissenting); *Seminole Tribe of Florida v Florida*, 517 US 44, 101–85 (1996) (Souter dissenting); and literature cited in both cases.

If *Seminole Tribe* remains good law, then the alternative is to overrule or change current doctrine on Congress's Section 5 powers. Along those lines, others have criticized *City of Boerne* and its progeny. These critiques, however, are essentially all variants of one of two complaints: that the Court should not arrogate to itself the sole power to determine the meaning of the substantive provisions of the Fourteenth Amendment or that the Court should give more deference to Congress's determination that a particular law is necessary to prevent or remedy constitutional violations.[105] The persuasiveness of these critiques ultimately rests on one's view of judicial supremacy: to what extent should the Court be the final, authoritative, or sole interpreter of the Constitution, and when— if at all—should it defer to congressional judgments? Interesting as that debate may be, it appears to have had no effect on the Court itself; commentators have recently noted that the Court's self-aggrandizement actually appears to be increasing.[106]

I therefore propose instead to accept the premise that it is the Court's job, and not Congress's, to determine the boundaries of the substantive provisions of the Fourteenth Amendment (as well as of the rest of the Constitution), and that demanding close congruence between the perceived problem and the enacted remedy is the way to enforce that division of authority. But the *City of Boerne* test is not the only possible method of ensuring that Congress does not transgress constitutional bounds. The majority opinion in *Hibbs*, for all its flaws, can be used to craft a revised

---

[105] See, for example, John T. Noonan, Jr., *Narrowing the Nation's Power: The Supreme Court Sides with the States* (California, 2002); Post and Siegel, 112 Yale L J (cited in note 34); Robert C. Post and Reva B. Siegel, *Protecting the Constitution from the People: Juricentric Restrictions on Section Five Power*, 78 Ind L J 1 (2003); Susan Bandes, *Fear and Degradation in Alabama: The Emotional Subtext of University of Alabama v. Garrett*, 5 U Pa J Const L 520, 532–34 (2003); Frickey and Smith, 111 Yale L J (cited in note 50); William W. Buzbee and Robert A. Schapiro, *Legislative Record Review*, 54 Stan L Rev 87 (2001); Evan H. Caminker, *"Appropriate" Means-Ends Constraints on Section 5 Powers*, 53 Stan L Rev 1127 (2001); Ruth Colker and James J. Brudney, *Dissing Congress*, 100 Mich L Rev 80 (2001); Christopher Bryant and Timothy J. Simeone, *Remanding to Congress: The Supreme Court's New "On the Record" Constitutional Review of Federal Statutes*, 86 Cornell L Rev 328 (2001); Melissa Hart, *Conflating Scope of Right with Standard of Review: The Supreme Court's "Strict Scrutiny" of Congressional Efforts to Enforce the Fourteenth Amendment*, 46 Vill L Rev 1091 (2001). For a defense of the federalism principles underlying the Section 5 abrogation cases, see Lynn A. Baker and Ernest A. Young, *Federalism and the Double Standard of Judicial Review*, 51 Duke L J 75 (2001).

[106] See, for example, Larry D. Kramer, *Foreword: We the Court*, 115 Harv L Rev 5, 128–58 (2001).

test that keeps intact the results in the prior cases (with the possible partial exception of *Garrett*) but nevertheless upholds the FMLA as a valid exercise of Congress's Section 5 authority. Note again that the soundness of any of the decisions or of the underlying constitutional vision is beside the point; my quarrel with the Court here is not its results (or its interpretation of the Constitution) but its past and future use of precedent.

The key recognition lurking below the surface in *Hibbs* is that gender discrimination (and, by implication, race discrimination) is different from, and more invidious than, other types of discrimination.[107] The majority opinion dances around this question, and never quite admits that this distinction underlies its holding. The Court tries to use the fact that gender discrimination is subject to heightened scrutiny in order to shoehorn the FMLA into the structure established by the earlier cases without forcing its invalidation. As I argued above, this move fails. But the fact that gender discrimination is subject to heightened scrutiny also suggests that it is more problematic than other types of discrimination. The Court—rightly or wrongly—perceives age discrimination and disability discrimination, like practices with a disparate impact on minorities, women, or religious observers, as somehow not "real" problems.[108] Perhaps the cause for the different perceptions is the recentness of the American recognition that age or disability discrimination is a problem at all; perhaps it is that there is still controversy about the extent of the problem; perhaps it is that age and, especially, disability discrimination are more complex, in part because they are intertwined with questions of accommodation and allocation of resources rather than always arising from stereotypes

---

[107] See also Post and Siegel, 112 Yale L J at 1979–80 (cited in note 34) (predicting, prior to the decision in *Hibbs*, that "it is possible that the Court will decide the case on the basis of its attitude toward the substantive civil rights agenda advanced by the FMLA"); Bandes, 5 U Pa J Const L at 521 (cited in note 105) (characterizing *Garrett* as "animated by empathy for some actors and lack of empathy toward others"); Jed Rubenfeld, *The Anti-Antidiscrimination Agenda*, 111 Yale L J 1141 (2002) (suggesting that Court views "traditional" antidiscrimination law as more justifiable than recent extensions); compare Richard H. Fallon, Jr., *The "Conservative" Paths of the Rehnquist Court's Federalism Decisions*, 69 U Chi L Rev 429 (2002) (suggesting that inconsistencies in the Court's federalism doctrines are driven by an underlying conservative substantive agenda).

[108] I argue elsewhere that the Court has taken a similarly unconcerned approach to sexual orientation discrimination. See Suzanna Sherry, *Warning: Labeling Constitutions May Be Hazardous to Your Regime*, 67 L & Contemp Probs (forthcoming 2004).

or simple prejudice.[109] Whatever the source, the distortion of precedent in *Hibbs* reflects a different attitude toward gender discrimination than toward (some) other types of discrimination.[110]

But what if we were to take this insight and use it to revise the precedent rather than simply to drive results? *If* gender discrimination is worse than age discrimination, then we should be more willing to sacrifice the states' immunity from suit in the service of eradicating gender discrimination. This in turn implies that the Court should abandon its current rigid stance of requiring that *every* exercise of Congress's power under Section 5 be supported by a fixed quantum of evidence of particular state behaviors, and instead adopt a more flexible balancing test. The scope of Congress's Section 5 power should turn on some unquantifiable relationship between the need for the legislation and the harm it causes to states.[111] Where the Court finds that Congress is trampling on the states for little reason, it should invalidate the abrogation. Where the importance of the federal statute outweighs its detrimental effect on states, the abrogation should be upheld.[112]

---

[109] For a wonderful exploration of the interaction between the Court and American culture as it plays out in the context of gender discrimination, see Post, 117 Harv L Rev at 11–41 (cited in note 47).

[110] Suggesting that the Court implicitly views gender discrimination as more problematic —particularly in the context of Section 5—raises questions about *United States v Morrison*, 529 US 598 (2000), in which the Court struck down a portion of the federal Violence Against Women Act (VAWA). The Court found that creating a federal civil remedy for gender-motivated violence exceeded Congress's authority under both the Commerce Clause and Section 5. But the puzzle is more apparent than real: the question in *Morrison* was whether Congress could regulate individual behavior—rather than state behavior—under Section 5; resolution of that question need not depend on how abhorrent the Court finds the individual behavior. Alternatively, one might speculate that the Court envisions a continuum of invidiousness, so that race discrimination justifies even greater congressional authority than does gender discrimination. This latter approach has the further advantage of reconciling *Morrison* with the apparently contrary result in *United States v Guest*, 383 US 745 (1966).

[111] One might argue that Justice Kennedy adopted such a test in his dissent in *Hibbs* by framing the question as whether "subjecting States and their treasuries to monetary liability at the insistence of private litigants is a congruent and proportional response to a demonstrated pattern of unconstitutional conduct by the States." 123 S Ct at 1986. See Post, Harv L Rev at 23 n 105 (cited in note 47).

[112] Although I suggest that such a flexible test should be applied to Congress's exercise of its Section 5 powers, an alternative argument might propose it as a measure of Congress's overall ability to abrogate state sovereign immunity, whether under Section 5 or under Article I. Such a reframing of my argument, however, would directly confront the holding in *Seminole Tribe*, which seems (especially after *Hibbs*) less vulnerable than *City of Boerne* and its progeny.

For those readers who blanch at the prospect of such an unconstrained approach, let me make two admissions and then point to
an area in which just such a test has worked tolerably well. First,
my test will predictably produce more unpredictable results than
the Court's current test. But the Court's (mis)application of the
current test managed to produce the surprising result in *Hibbs;* the
only difference between the Court's approach and mine is that
mine could produce the result in *Hibbs* without mangling the test
itself. Second, to the extent that one disagrees with the Court's
assessment of the problem Congress is addressing—that is, finds
a particular kind of discrimination to be more or less problematic
than the Court does—one will not be happy with the Court's decisions under my test. For readers afraid of that eventuality, let me
ask you: are you happy now? Liberals are appalled by *Kimel* and
Garrett, conservatives think *Hibbs* is a disaster, and, as far as I can
tell, almost everybody dislikes *City of Boerne.*[113] So why not have
the Court admit that it is drawing distinctions among types of discrimination and put its weighting of the interests out in the open?

In an analogous area, this kind of open-ended approach has
worked very well. Of all the cases that come before the Supreme
Court, the cases most similar to those raising federalism issues are
those raising separation-of-powers questions.[114] Both separation of
powers and federalism implicate basic structure, and both serve to
balance power and check potential abuses. We recognize this af-
finity when we teach federalism and separation of powers in one
course and individual rights in another. Indeed, sometimes is it
difficult to tell the difference between a separation-of-powers question and a federalism question. The Section 5 cases are a good
example of this overlap: *City of Boerne* was primarily about the allocation of authority between Congress and the courts, but in the

---

[113] But see Marci A. Hamilton and David Schoenbrod, *The Reaffirmation of Proportionality
Analysis Under Section 5 of the Fourteenth Amendment,* 21 Cardozo L Rev 469 (1999) (defense
of *City of Boerne* by one of the City's attorneys); Ronald D. Rotunda, *The Powers of Congress
Under Section 5 of the Fourteenth Amendment After City of Boerne v. Flores,* 32 Ind L Rev 163
(1998) (defending *City of Boerne*); Ira C. Lupu, *Why the Congress Was Wrong and the Court
Was Right: Reflections on City of Boerne v. Flores,* 39 Wm & Mary L Rev 793 (1998) (partial
defense of *City of Boerne*); William P. Marshall, *The Religious Freedom Restoration Act: Establishment, Equal Protection, and Free Speech Concerns,* 56 Mont L Rev 227 (1995) (expressing
doubts about RFRA's constitutionality before *City of Boerne*).

[114] Others have noted the relationship, especially in the context of congressional abrogation of state sovereign immunity. See, for example, Colker and Brudney, 100 Mich L Rev
(cited in note 105).

context of abrogation of sovereign immunity the Section 5 jurisprudence serves mostly to protect the states from congressional
overreaching.[115]

Thus, in searching for an alternative approach to defining the
scope of congressional powers under Section 5, we might look to
separation-of-powers cases. In particular, the Supreme Court has
long struggled to determine what powers of adjudication Congress
can confer on courts that do not meet the requirements of Article
III. These courts, whose judges are not life-tenured, are sometimes
called legislative courts. Examples include military courts, territo-
rial courts and local courts for the District of Columbia, and most
administrative agencies. Under what circumstances can an agency
or other specialized body resolve disputes that might otherwise be
decided by an Article III court? After briefly flirting with a rigid
rule prohibiting legislative courts from deciding *any* matter that
would be within the constitutional jurisdiction of Article III courts,
the Supreme Court recognized that the jurisdiction of Article III
courts and legislative courts might overlap.[116] The question then
became defining the limits of legislative courts' jurisdiction.

Like determining the scope of congressional power under Section 5, defining the jurisdiction of legislative courts raises questions
about how to allow Congress sufficient flexibility without abandoning judicially enforced constraints. Too few limits will allow
Congress to undermine the independence of the judiciary or the
sovereignty of states; too many limits will prevent Congress from
enacting needed legislation. Facing such a situation in the context
of legislative courts, the Court expressly eschewed bright-line
rules: "Although such rules might lend a greater degree of coherence to this area of the law, they might also unduly constrict Congress's ability to take needed and innovative action pursuant to its
Article I powers."[117] Instead, the Court has considered a number
of factors, always with an eye to determining whether the danger

---

[115] Scholars vary in whether they treat the abrogation cases as raising primarily federalism
questions or primarily separation-of-powers questions. Compare, for example, Fallon, 69
U Chi L Rev (cited in note 107) (federalism) with Post and Siegel, 112 Yale L J (cited in
note 34) (separation of powers).

[116] See *Williams v United States*, 289 US 553 (1933) (no overlap permitted); *Glidden Co.
v Zdanok*, 370 US 530 (1962) (overlap permitted); *Palmore v United States*, 411 US 389
(1973) (flexible test adopted).

[117] *Commodities Futures Trading Commission v Schor*, 478 US 833, 851 (1986).

of subverting judicial independence outweighs Congress's practical need to resort to a legislative court. In *Commodities Futures Trading Commission v Schor*,[118] for example, the Court upheld the allocation of a state-law counterclaim to a legislative court, but noted that Congress could not create "a phalanx of non-Article III tribunals equipped to handle the entire business of the Article III courts . . . without evidence of valid and specific legislative necessities."[119] The danger of such a scheme, the Court recognized, was that Congress might be "'transfer[ing] jurisdiction [to non-Article III tribunals] for the purpose of emasculating' constitutional courts."[120] Ironically, Justice O'Connor—who has recently been applying rigid precedent in flexible ways—authored the majority opinion in *Schor*.

This flexible approach, ultimately policed by Article III courts, has allowed Congress to create myriad administrative agencies, local courts for the District of Columbia,[121] non-Article III courts with specialized subject matter jurisdiction,[122] and provisions that require certain disputes to be resolved by binding arbitration.[123] But the Court drew the line and invalidated Congress's attempt to confer on a set of non-Article III courts jurisdiction to decide *all* civil claims related to a bankruptcy proceeding, including the power to preside over jury trials and the authority to issue declaratory judgments, writs of habeas corpus, and any other order necessary for enforcement of their own judgments.[124]

Adopting a test used to define the boundaries of jurisdiction is especially apt in light of the Court's stated mission in its Section 5 cases. As many scholars have noted, the Court's careful scrutiny of congressional enactments under Section 5 is a way of ensuring that Congress does not use its enforcement powers as a pretext to surreptitiously redefine the substantive meaning of the Fourteenth

---

[118] 478 US 833 (1986).

[119] Id at 855.

[120] Id at 850, quoting Chief Justice Vinson's dissenting opinion in *National Mutual Insurance Co. v Tidewater Co.*, 337 US 582, 644 (1949).

[121] *Palmore v United States*, 411 US 389 (1973).

[122] *Ex parte Bakelite Corp.*, 279 US 438 (1929).

[123] *Thomas v Union Carbide Agricultural Products Co.*, 473 US 568 (1985).

[124] *Northern Pipeline Construction Co. v Marathon Pipe Line Co.*, 458 US 50 (1982).

Amendment.[125] While such an illicit motive was arguably apparent on the surface of RFRA and its legislative history, it will not always be easy to tell the difference between an honest congressional attempt at prophylaxis and a statute passed to expand rather than enforce constitutional mandates. In evaluating Section 5 legislation, demanding a sufficient reason for congressional action serves to guard against hard-to-detect illicit motives. The balancing test used in the context of legislative courts serves an analogous purpose: it guards against intentional subversions of judicial independence masquerading as mere administrative rearranging.[126] To the extent that Congress assigns to non-Article III courts a broader range of cases than is practically necessary, we might suspect that it is doing so because it wishes to control the body making the decisions. And to the extent that Congress fashions an overinclusive statutory remedy to an underdocumented constitutional problem, we might suspect that Congress is more interested in creating rights than in enforcing them.[127]

An open-ended balancing approach would allow the Court to place as much weight as it wished on the need to protect states from suit, while still permitting Congress to abrogate immunity in the service of what the Court considers important goals. Evidence of unconstitutional state behavior would be one relevant factor but would not be dispositive. Additional factors could in-

---

[125] See, for example, Post, 117 Harv L Rev at 12 (cited in note 47); Buzbee and Schapiro, 54 Stan L Rev at 136–39 (cited in note 105); Vicki C. Jackson, *Federalism and the Court: Congress as the Audience?* 574 Annals (AAPSS) 145, 150–51 (2001); Dorf and Friedman, 2000 Supreme Court Review at 93 (cited in note 34); Richard H. Fallon, Jr., *Foreword: Implementing the Constitution,* 111 Harv L Rev 54, 131–32 (1997); but see Caminker, 53 Stan L Rev at 1166–68 (cited in note 105).

[126] The alternative approach to smoking out illicit motives—bright-line tests that purport to measure mechanically the congruence between means and ends—is reflected not only in the Section 5 cases but also in long-established equal protection doctrine. My argument in text is that separation-of-powers cases provide a better model than do individual-rights cases when, as in the Section 5 context, the Court is policing federalism and interbranch relations. For a critique of the Court's apparent equating of states to individual rights-holders, see Suzanna Sherry, *States Are People Too,* 75 Notre Dame L Rev 1121 (2000).

[127] There is, of course, still the question of whether the Court *ought* to distrust congressional motives in this context. For a variety of views on this question, see, for example, Suzanna Sherry, *Irresponsibility Breeds Contempt,* 6 Green Bag 2d 47 (2002); Colker and Brudney, 100 Mich L Rev (cited in note 105); Buzbee and Schapiro, 54 Stan L Rev. at 141–43 (cited in note 105); Caminker, 53 Stan L Rev at 1182–83 (cited in note 105); Neal Devins, *Congress as Culprit: How Lawmakers Spurred on the Court's Anti-Congress Crusade,* 51 Duke L J 435 (2001).

clude the breadth of the statute (currently encompassed by the "congruence and proportionality" part of the test) and the Court's own judgment about the importance of the statutory goal. But in contrast to the Court's decision in *Hibbs*, which tried to disguise the Court's valuation of the goal as the mechanical measuring of the quantum of evidence, under a balancing test the Court would have to discuss candidly the reasons it found the intrusion on state sovereignty more or less warranted than in prior cases.[128]

That candor, moreover, might have a salutary effect on the decisions themselves. A Court forced to confront head-on the clash between state sovereignty and the interests of the disabled, for example, could no longer hide behind a pretense that the ADA's flaws lie in the congressional record. Instead, the Court would have to choose between openly admitting that it finds discrimination against the disabled more tolerable than race or gender discrimination, or engaging in a more sensitive and nuanced discussion of the burdens that the ADA puts on states. One possible result of this more careful analysis might be a distinction between the pure antidiscrimination provisions and the accommodation provisions of the ADA, with abrogation upheld for the former but not the latter. Such a distinction makes sense on several levels. It recognizes the difference between prejudice and less invidious reasons underlying discrimination. It takes into account the greater burdens that accommodation requirements place on employers. It distinguishes between intentional discrimination and failure to remedy a known disparate impact. And, finally, it is pragmatically defensible under current Eleventh Amendment doctrines: individuals in need of an accommodation could still prevail by suing a state official for prospective relief, while individuals harmed by intentional discrimination would no longer be barred from obtaining back pay or other retrospective relief. But such a sensible scheme is virtually impossible under the Court's current rigid approach to Section 5.

Although a balancing test might thus lead to a partial overruling of *Garrett*, it is unlikely to affect the Court's other Eleventh

---

[128] For a similar plea for candor about a statute's actual impact on federalism, see Post and Siegel, 112 Yale L J at 2048–58 (cited in note 34). For an analogous argument in the context of administrative agencies, see Lisa Schultz Bressman, *Beyond Accountability: Arbitrariness and Legitimacy in the Administrative State*, 78 NYU L Rev 461 (2003).

Amendment precedents. Even a candid Court is likely to be willing to hold that the property interests at stake in patent or trademark cases, or the need to protect individuals over forty from discrimination by their (often older) employers, or even a desire to compensate overtime work at a higher rate, do not outweigh state sovereignty concerns.

Here, then, is the bottom line. The primary advantage of a bright-line rule, such as the one the Court purports to follow in its Section 5 cases, is that it is supposed to constrain the discretion of judges. The decision in *Hibbs*, however, shows that at least *this* bright-line rule is not a constraint. If the rule does not serve its intended purpose, and adherence to the rule demands an intolerable level of precedential manipulation, then it is time to abandon the rule. Indeed, in the context of the scope of Congress's Section 5 authority, *no* bright-line rule will work, because the balance of power among Congress, the Court, and the states is too complex and fluid. Only a test that gives the Court flexibility but forces it to justify its choices has any hope of succeeding.[129]

C

There is one last notable aspect of my discussion of the interrelationships among precedent, candor, and the choice between bright-line rules and flexible balancing tests: Justice O'Connor appears to play a pivotal role. Her application of precedent was unique in all the cases other than *Hibbs*, and was shared only by Chief Justice Rehnquist in *Hibbs* itself. She authored the majority opinion in *Grutter*, and was one of only two Justices (the other was Justice Breyer) in the majority in both *Grutter* and *Gratz*. Even more intriguing, she was the primary modern architect of the balancing test used in the legislative courts context, and has previously exhibited a distaste for bright-line rules.[130]

---

[129] There is, of course, a lively literature on whether this is true beyond Section 5: constitutional scholars debate endlessly the relative virtues of rules and standards, categorization and balancing, and theory-driven and pragmatist judging. This article is not the place to rehash that debate, although it is intended as a (minor) contribution to it.

[130] Besides the legislative courts cases, there are other indications the Justice O'Connor favors multifactor balancing tests over bright lines. Her concurrence in *Employment Division v Smith* argued that the same result could be reached by using a balancing test. 494 US 872, 903–07. See also Suzanna Sherry, *Civic Virtue and the Feminine Voice in Constitutional Adjudication*, 72 Va L Rev 543, 604–13 (1986).

Based on my analysis, one might argue that recently Justice O'Connor seems to be professing an adherence to mechanical rules but actually applying the more flexible standards she has traditionally favored. This article has suggested that both *Hibbs* and *Grutter* exhibit this pattern. Her votes in *Grutter* and *Gratz* are even more interesting at a deeper level. The primary difference between the affirmative action program upheld in *Grutter* and the one invalidated in *Gratz* was that the latter applied a rigid formula while the former required individualized consideration of all applicants. One might therefore argue that Justice O'Connor is instructing universities to use her preferred method of decision making.[131]

But the legislative courts cases—as well as others—suggest that sometimes Justice O'Connor has been open about her application of more flexible tests. Why not last Term? Resolving that puzzle is beyond the scope of this article, but I offer a few possibilities. Perhaps she is afraid that candor in cases involving some type of discrimination might have adverse consequences. Perhaps she has been influenced by Justice Scalia, who has argued at various times for rigid rules, visible constraints, and judicial lack of candor.[132] Perhaps long tenure, especially during times of political change or turmoil, affects judges' outlook. Whatever the reason, the consequences are troubling.

CONCLUSION

Despite some appearances to the contrary, precedent is not infinitely malleable. In this article, I have tried to identify the most egregious distortions of precedent from the 2002 Term, and conclude that this Court—especially Justice O'Connor—seems particularly inclined to maintain a facade of adhering to precedent rather than straightforwardly acknowledging its limitations or weaknesses. Nowhere is that more apparent than in the Court's evalua-

---

[131] A final irony, however, is that the likely effect of the two affirmative action cases will be to force universities with large applicant pools to disguise the use of rigid mechanical formulae, pretending that they are instead engaged in individualized consideration. Universities will thus be engaging in the same dissembling that characterizes Justice O'Connor's recent decisions—but in reverse.

[132] See Daniel A. Farber and Suzanna Sherry, *Desperately Seeking Certainty: The Misguided Search for Constitutional Foundations* 29–54 (Chicago, 2002).

tion of the constitutionality of federal statutes enacted under Section 5 of the Fourteenth Amendment. The Court's need to distort precedent to uphold the FMLA in *Nevada Department of Human Services v Hibbs* illustrates the weaknesses of the Court's current Section 5 doctrine. My proposed replacement for that doctrine builds on *Hibbs* and has the added benefit of forcing the Court to confront openly the issues that led it to distort precedent. Thus, while my test may produce results that are neither better nor more predictable than the results under the Court's test, it will at least produce greater candor.

This Term, Justice Scalia accused the majority of playing fast and loose with stare decisis.[133] But a candid overruling is still better than pretending that the Court is following precedent when it is not. Ultimately, then, the decision in *Hibbs* tells us a great deal more about the integrity of the Court and the soundness of current doctrine than it does about the constitutionality of the FMLA.

---

[133] *Lawrence v Texas*, 123 S Ct 2472, 2487–91 (2003) (Scalia dissenting).

CAROLYN J. FRANTZ

CHAVEZ v MARTINEZ'S CONSTITUTIONAL DIVISION OF LABOR

Somewhere in the midst of overruling *Bowers v Hardwick*[1] and allowing educational affirmative action,[2] the Court last Term also managed to reconceptualize the Fifth Amendment's privilege against compelled self-incrimination. *Chavez v Martinez*[3] posed what turned out to be a rather significant question: whether, in the context of a custodial interrogation, § 1983 damages for a violation of the privilege against compelled self-incrimination are available after an incriminating statement has been compelled, but before any attempt has been made to use testimony thus obtained at trial. The Court held that the privilege protects against only the use of compelled incriminating statements against the witness at a criminal trial, not the act of compulsion itself.

Carolyn J. Frantz is Assistant Professor, University of Chicago Law School.

AUTHOR'S NOTE: For comments, thanks to: Al Alschuler, Rick Bierschbach, Michelle Friedland, Don Herzog, Bernie Meltzer, Geof Stone, David Strauss, Cass Sunstein, Nelson Tebbe, and Adrian Vermeule. Particular thanks are due to David Benner, who provided research assistance as well as substantive insights.

I clerked on the Supreme Court for Justice Sandra Day O'Connor in the OT 2001 Term, during which time cert was granted in *Chavez v Martinez* and *McKune v Lile* was argued and decided on the merits. This article discloses no Court confidences to which I may have been privy during my time there.

[1] *Lawrence v Texas*, 123 S Ct 2472 (2003) (overruling *Bowers v Hardwick*, 478 US 186 (1986)).

[2] *Grutter v Bollinger*, 124 S Ct 35 (2003).

[3] *Chavez v Martinez*, 123 S Ct 1994 (2003).

Chavez, however, left open the possibility of recovery under substantive due process for at least some of those who are denied recovery under the privilege. In so holding, *Chavez* essentially accomplished a constitutional division of labor between the privilege and substantive due process. After *Chavez,* concerns that apply only to the conduct of the criminal trial are reflected in the privilege, while concerns about compulsion itself (the propriety of government attempts to obtain testimony) are left to due process. This conclusion was by no means a necessary one (and is in fact in tension with the Court's existing precedents), and thus *Chavez* requires a new look at both the privilege and due process. This article explores the implications of the Court's new approach.

I. Chavez Itself

A. THE OPINION

The facts of the case are as follows: Ben Chavez, a California police patrol supervisor, questioned Oliverio Martinez in a hospital emergency room after Martinez had been shot in the head by police officers during an altercation.[4] A transcript of the tape of the questioning shows that Martinez was never given his *Miranda* warnings, that the questioning continued even after he told Chavez that he didn't want to talk about the incident, and that he repeatedly stated that he was dying and wanted to be treated rather than questioned.[5] Despite his injuries, Martinez survived, but no criminal charges were ever brought against him. He filed a civil suit, seeking § 1983 damages from Chavez for violation of his Fifth Amendment privilege against compelled self-incrimination (made applicable to the states through the Fourteenth Amendment) and his Fourteenth Amendment right to substantive due process. In a divided set of opinions, the Court denied Martinez relief on his self-incrimination claim and remanded his substantive due process claim for further consideration.

The Court's decision is complicated: it produced six separate opinions and a slew of partial joinings. Justice Thomas wrote the lead opinion, joined in full by the Chief Justice and practically in

---

[4] Id at 1999.

[5] Id at 2010 (Stevens, J, dissenting).

full by Justice Scalia.[6] Justice O'Connor also joined the part of Justice Thomas's opinion discussing Martinez's privilege claim, making a four-Justice plurality for Thomas's views on that question.

Rejecting Martinez's privilege claim, Thomas reasoned that the text of the Fifth Amendment—"[n]o person . . . shall be compelled in any criminal case to be a witness against himself"[7]—indicates that some attempt to use information in a criminal case is an essential element of any violation of the privilege.[8] Moreover, Thomas argued, doctrine favors the use view; in particular, the immunity rule. If a person can be compelled to incriminate himself if granted use immunity, Thomas reasoned, "mere coercion" of incriminating testimony cannot be constitutionally prohibited.[9] He acknowledged that the Court had held that the privilege "can be asserted in any proceeding, civil or criminal, administrative or judicial, investigatory or adjudicatory . . . ," but declared these cases to be merely prophylaxis to protect the right in a future criminal trial. Such rules, he reasoned, are necessary because they remove the temptation to use compelled statements inappropriately and preserve the accused's right to object to their later introduction at trial.[10]

In a part of his opinion Justice O'Connor did not join, Thomas argued further that Martinez's substantive due process rights had not been violated, because Chavez's behavior did not "shock the conscience."[11] Characterizing Chavez's questioning as not motivated by a desire to harm Martinez, and noting the need to gather evidence from a suspect who seemed about to die, Thomas pressed for a narrow understanding of due process in the context of such police interrogations.

Justice Souter, joined by Justice Breyer, concurred in Thomas's conclusion, though not his reasoning, as to Martinez's privilege

---

[6] Justice Scalia declined to join Justice Thomas's one-paragraph conclusion ordering a remand, a disagreement he himself described as being of "little consequence" given that both he and Justice Thomas agreed that Martinez should not succeed on his substantive due process claim. Id at 2009 (Scalia, J, concurring in part in the judgment).

[7] US Const, Amend V.

[8] *Chavez*, 123 S Ct at 2000.

[9] Id at 2001–02.

[10] Id at 2003.

[11] Id at 2005 (citing *Rochin v California*, 342 US 165, 172, 174 (1952)).

claim. Souter agreed that the privilege's purpose was to protect against the use of compelled statements at trial, but he refused to say that, in principle, the privilege could never be the basis of § 1983 liability when no attempt at use is made. Even though he agreed that Martinez's claim was "well outside the core of Fifth Amendment protection," Souter argued that "'extension[s]' of the bare guarantee may be warranted if clearly shown to be desirable means to protect the basic right against the invasive pressures of contemporary society."[12] Along the lines suggested by Justice Thomas, Souter justified the Court's precedents seemingly allowing the privilege to be raised and decided at the moment of compulsion as prophylactic. In Martinez's case, however, Souter concluded that there was no showing of the necessity for prophylaxis, nor any basis for distinguishing Martinez's case from the myriad of other violations of the privilege and the prophylactic rules (like *Miranda*) designed to implement it.[13]

Justice Souter also wrote a one-sentence opinion for the Court (for himself, Breyer, Ginsburg, Stevens, and Kennedy) on the substantive due process question, ordering a remand to the Ninth Circuit.[14] In describing Martinez's substantive due process claim, Souter also used the language of "shock the conscience" to guide determination of the due process question.[15]

Justice Scalia wrote separately to reiterate his view that § 1983 does not provide a remedy for violations of prophylactic rights, such as *Miranda*, and to disagree pointedly with Justice Souter that the statute created a remedy for purposes of effectively implementing a right, its function being only to remedy actual rights *violations*. He added his view that Martinez had waived any right to bring a substantive due process claim by failing to raise it in his brief to the Ninth Circuit.

The remaining three Justices dissented on the privilege question. Justice Stevens wrote for himself alone, excerpting a portion of the transcript of the questioning in order to emphasize the dis-

---

[12] Id at 2007 (citations omitted).

[13] Id at 2007.

[14] Id at 2008. Those interested in nose-counting will note that, joining neither Thomas's nor Souter's opinion on substantive due process, Justice O'Connor did not vote at all on that issue.

[15] Id.

tressing nature of the facts.[16] Stevens also characterized the due process question as broader than simply whether government behavior "shocks the conscience." Violations of constitutional rights "implicit in the concept of ordered liberty," he maintained, are protected by due process. Stevens noted that the privilege was itself incorporated against the states through the Due Process Clause because it was implicit in the concept of ordered liberty. Thus, Stevens argued, Martinez's privilege claim was also a due process claim.[17]

The main dissent on the privilege question was written by Justice Kennedy. Stevens joined Kennedy's opinion in its entirety, and Justice Ginsburg joined almost in full. She disagreed with the other two privilege dissenters only on the relevance of the fact that Martinez had not been read his *Miranda* rights—Justices Kennedy and Stevens conceded that exclusion would be a sufficient remedy for the *Miranda* violation. Justice Ginsburg declined to take a stand on that issue.

Kennedy spoke for all three in arguing that Martinez's privilege against compelled self-incrimination was violated at the moment the police officer "exploit[ed] his pain and suffering with the purpose and intent of securing an incriminating statement."[18] "Our cases and our legal tradition," he wrote, "establish that the Self-Incrimination Clause is a substantive constraint on the conduct of the government, not merely an evidentiary rule governing the work of the courts."[19] In particular, Kennedy relied on an array of cases in which the privilege issue was resolved at the moment of compulsion, including the previous Term's *McKune v Lile*.[20]

Justice Kennedy did acknowledge that "many questions about

---

[16] Id at 2010–13, 2012 n 3 (Stevens, J, dissenting in part and concurring in part).

[17] Id at 2011–12.

[18] Id at 2017. That said, Justice Kennedy's opinion is at least a bit unclear about the distinction. At points in his opinion, he seems to limit his view that the privilege against compelled incrimination protects against compulsion to instances where the compulsion is "severe" or when it causes "severe . . . pain" or the compulsion is "direct and commanding." 123 S Ct at 2013. Justice Ginsburg also uses the word "severe." Id at 2018. Since Kennedy's most formal presentation of his view omits the word "severe" ("In my view the Self-Incrimination Clause is applicable at the time and place police use compulsion to extract a statement from a suspect"), I will assume the other uses are simply rhetoric. Id at 2016.

[19] Id at 2014.

[20] 536 US 24 (2002) (holding that threatened loss of privileges for a prisoner who refused to incriminate himself as part of a treatment program for sex offenders did not violate the privilege).

the meaning and extent of the Clause are [not] simple of resolution, and [some of] the cited cases are [difficult to] reconcile."[21] But he identified no precedents in need of overruling. In particular, he found a way to justify the most troubling precedents for his view: those based on the immunity rule. To Thomas's claim that because incriminating testimony can be constitutionally compelled with immunity, the privilege does not protect against compulsion, Kennedy responded that this proves only that "the right is not absolute."[22] Kennedy added that due process might address some of his concerns, even in light of the majority's view of the privilege, because the "larger definition of liberty under the Due Process Clause" protects against "use of torture or its equivalent in an attempt to induce a statement."

Rounding out the six opinions, Justice Ginsburg wrote separately to emphasize the similarity of the facts of the case to those in *Mincey v Arizona*,[23] in which the Court had held that due process required the suppression of involuntary statements made during an in-hospital interrogation.[24] Ginsburg also noted the potential of due process to fill the gap left after *Chavez*.

B. THE DIVISION OF LABOR

Somewhere in this array, it is possible to distill two holdings: first, that Martinez had shown no privilege violation because no attempt had been made to use his statement against him at a criminal trial, and second, that his substantive due process claim needed to be evaluated on remand. As I will show, these holdings establish a constitutional division of labor between the privilege and due process based on the following distinction: concerns about use of compelled testimony in a criminal trial will be dealt with through the privilege, whereas concerns about the propriety of obtaining such confessions fall under due process.

1. *The Fourth Amendment/Fifth Amendment contrast.* To see this more clearly, consider the contrast between *Chavez* and the Court's seminal decision in *Bivens v Six Unknown Named Agents of*

---

[21] 123 S Ct at 2015.

[22] Id at 2015.

[23] 437 US 385 (1978).

[24] 123 S Ct at 2018.

the Federal Bureau of Narcotics.[25] In *Bivens,* the Court authorized the award of money damages for a Fourth Amendment violation, an illegal search and seizure, which yielded no incriminating evidence. Justice Harlan's concurrence argued that if no monetary recovery were provided, the privacy intended to be protected by the Fourth Amendment would go unprotected: the government could invade citizens' homes and persons virtually without limit.[26] The Fourth Amendment's exclusionary rule was adopted to provide extra deterrence against these privacy violations; in the Fourth Amendment context, there is no independent constitutional problem with the *use* of the illegally obtained evidence, only with the means used to obtain them.[27]

Chavez treats the Fifth Amendment privilege almost as the opposite of the Fourth Amendment—it is the exclusionary rule that implements the privilege's guarantee.[28] Assuming Justice Souter's opinion controls, money damages may be available, but only (like the exclusionary rule in the Fourth Amendment context) if the need for extra protection for the right against use at trial can be shown.[29]

---

[25] *Bivens v Six Unknown Named Agents of Federal Bureau of Narcotics,* 403 US 388 (1971). *Bivens* is technically not a § 1983 case (because § 1983 only applies to actions taken under color of state, not federal, law), though the analysis is similar. *Harlow v Fitzgerald,* 475 US 335, 342 (1986). When state officials are involved, § 1983 damages are available for Fourth Amendment violations.

[26] 403 US at 408–09.

[27] *Mapp v Ohio,* 367 US 643 (1961). Interestingly, much like *Bivens,* where no incriminating evidence was found, the dissenters appear to advocate for § 1983 recovery even if the coercion does not actually give rise to a confession. This explains why no mention is made in the opinion of whether Chavez actually said anything incriminating.

[28] See Geoffrey Stone, *The Miranda Doctrine in the Burger Court,* 1977 Supreme Court Review 99, 139 n 214 ("[I]f the sole concern of [privilege] cases was with the use of evidence, it would be sufficient simply to allow the defendant to move to suppress if and when that problem arises."); *United States v Balsys,* 524 US 666 (noting that unlike the Fourth Amendment, which considers "breaches of privacy complete at the moment of illicit intrusion, whatever use may or may not be made of their fruits . . . [t]he Fifth Amendment . . . offers no such degree of protection.").

[29] The lack of § 1983 damages is telling for the scope of the privilege violation itself. Section 1983 is by no means an unlimited source of damages for constitutional violations—various immunities and things like the *Parratt* doctrine limit recovery under that section. But nothing particular to § 1983 provides any reason to generally exclude damages for the class of privilege violations denied in *Chavez,* absent a conclusion that no violation of the privilege has occurred in Martinez's case. For instance, one could imagine an argument that the suppression remedy is adequate to deter privilege violations, so § 1983 damages are not necessary to implement the right. But even if true, this would not be a reason to deny § 1983 damages—nothing limits them to instances where they are necessary. More importantly, merely limiting § 1983 is not what the Court had in mind—all of the Justices'

This distinction between the Fourth and Fifth Amendments intersects interestingly with the constitutional history of co-interpretation of the provisions. In *Boyd v United States*, the Court had presented the view that, so similar are the purposes of the Fifth Amendment privilege and the Fourth Amendment's prohibition on unreasonable searches and seizures, the two run "almost into each other."[30] It was not clear in *Boyd*, however, if those similar concerns were related to privacy (what now seems to be the province of the Fourth) or the conduct of the criminal trial (the province of the Fifth) or some hybrid of the two.[31] *Boyd* was a complex case, in any event, involving the suppression of compelled documents—an issue which, at the time, was thought to raise more serious Fifth Amendment problems than at present.[32]

The issue of incorporation raised the issue again. Although the Fourth Amendment's protection against unreasonable searches and seizures was incorporated against the states via due process in *Wolf v Colorado*,[33] the Court did not at that time consider due process to require the exclusionary rule. The reasoning of *Wolf* characterized the exclusionary rule as a subsidiary remedy.[34] There was no mention of the privilege, and no suggestion (not even in dissent) that the exclusionary rule might be necessary because the Fourth

---

opinions frame the issue as the scope of the right itself, not simply as the appropriate remedy to enforce it.

[30] 116 US 616, 630 (1886).

[31] Id at 630 ("It is not the breaking of his doors, and the rummaging of his drawers, that constitutes the essence of the offense; but it is the invasion of his indefeasible right of personal security, personal liberty, and private property, where that right has never been forfeited by his conviction of some public offense,—it is the invasion of this sacred right which underlies and constitutes the essence of Lord Camden's judgment. Breaking into a house and opening boxes and drawers are circumstances of aggravation; but any forcible and compulsory extortion of a man's own testimony, or of his private papers to be used as evidence to convict him of crime, or to forfeit his goods, is within the condemnation of that judgment. In this regard the fourth and fifth amendments run almost into each other.").

[32] See Richard A. Nagareda, *Compulsion "To Be a Witness" and the Resurrection of Boyd*, 74 NYU L Rev 1575 (1999) (describing the interaction of the Fourth and Fifth Amendments in the context of the production of incriminating documents).

[33] 338 US 25, 28 (1949).

[34] Id at ("[W]e have no hesitation in saying that were a State affirmatively to sanction such police incursion into privacy it would run counter to the guaranty of the Fourteenth Amendment. But the ways of enforcing such a basic right raise questions of a different order. How such arbitrary conduct should be checked, what remedies against it should be afforded, the means by which the right should be made effective, are all questions that are not to be so dogmatically answered as to preclude the varying solutions which spring from an allowable range of judgment on issues not susceptible of quantitative solution.").

Amendment also protects against conviction based on improperly seized evidence.

When the Court finally incorporated the exclusionary rule, in *Mapp v Ohio*,[35] it emphasized the need for the exclusionary rule as a protection of the underlying privacy right. It nodded, however, to the possibility that the Fourth Amendment's exclusionary rule might also have something to do with trial-related rights, and also with the privilege. The Court wrote in *Mapp*:

> we find that, as to the Federal Government, the Fourth and Fifth Amendments and, as to the States, the freedom from un-conscionable invasions of privacy and the freedom from convic-tions based on coerced confessions do enjoy an "intimate rela-tion". . . . The philosophy of each Amendment and of each freedom is complementary to, although not dependant upon, that of the other in its sphere of influence—the very least that together they assure in either sphere is that no man is to be convicted on unconstitutional evidence.[36]

This cryptic statement muddied the conceptual relationship be-tween the two Amendments, leaving confusion as to the purpose of each.

The relationship of the Fourth and Fifth Amendments was soon to arise again, however, when the privilege was finally incorporated against the States. In *Malloy v Hogan*,[37] the Court incorporated the privilege, focusing on concerns about the nature and fairness of the use of compelled statements as evidence in a criminal trial. In doing so, however, it noted that its incorporation of the privilege was "fortified by [the] recent decision" in *Mapp*, reaffirming *Boyd's* suggestion that the privilege and the Fourth Amendment's prohi-bition on unreasonable searches and seizures share a similar justi-fication and scope.[38] The dissenters in *Malloy* took exception to this characterization, arguing that *Mapp's* suggested "intimate rela-tionship" could not be an identity[39] because the concerns of the two Amendments are distinct.

Since *Malloy*, questions about the relationship between the Fourth and Fifth Amendments have largely faded into the consti-

---

[35] 367 US 643 (1961).

[36] *Mapp v Ohio*, 367 US 643, 657 (1961).

[37] 378 US 1 (1964).

[38] Id at 8–9.

[39] Id at 20–21 (Harlan, J, dissenting).

tutional background. Almost forty years later, however, *Chavez* has now vindicated the *Malloy* dissenters, at least on the interrelationship between the Fourth and Fifth Amendments (though not necessarily on the question of whether the Fifth Amendment privilege ought to have been incorporated on its own terms). After *Chavez*, the prohibition on unreasonable searches and seizures looks very different from the privilege—the Fourth Amendment is about privacy and the Fifth Amendment about trials. *Chavez* provides that to the extent privacy or other nontrial concerns do arise in privilege-like, rather than search-and-seizure-like, contexts, due process is the appropriate mechanism for evaluating them.

2. *Graham v Connor*. Before turning to the more concrete implications of *Chavez*, I should note the impact of the rule in *Graham v Connor*.[40] The Court in *Graham* held that, where police behavior potentially violates both the Fourth Amendment and the substantive due process prohibition of conscience-shocking behavior, the claim ought to be analyzed under the Fourth Amendment.[41] *Graham* suggested a critical constraint on constitutional divisions of labor—where a more specific provision of the Constitution governs the relevant conduct, substantive due process may not be used as a ground for recovery.

Graham explains why the majority analyzed Martinez's privilege claim first. Had the privilege been held to apply, *Graham* would have precluded substantive due process recovery on the same facts.[42] Justice Thomas's footnote discussing *Graham* chides Justice Kennedy for suggesting that substantive due process can provide extra recovery for particularly egregious forms of compulsion (such as torture) while the privilege provides recovery for compulsion generally.[43] Thomas seems right on this: to be consistent with *Graham*, the remand on the substantive due process question makes sense only given the Court's holding that Martinez had no privilege claim. The Court made clear in *Sacramento v Lewis*[44] that *Graham* does not create a bar to substantive due process recovery where the other relevant constitutional provision does not

---

[40] 490 US 386 (1989), cited in 123 S Ct at 2004 n 5.

[41] Id.

[42] 123 S Ct at 2004 n 5.

[43] Id.

[44] 523 US 833 (1998).

"apply."[45] It is the Court's conclusion that the privilege did not apply that freed it to remand the substantive due process question.[46]

But the existence of *Graham* also underscores the significance of *Chavez*'s characterization of the privilege. If the Court is committed to *Graham*, the division of labor between the privilege and substantive due process cannot merely be discretionary; it must be necessary. That is, *Chavez* could not simply allocate a task that could be accomplished through the privilege to substantive due process—*Graham* precludes such a move. Instead, its conclusion must rest upon a more fundamental conclusion about the privilege: that the concerns left to substantive due process can be dealt with *only* in that way.

II. What Chavez Does to the Privilege

By focusing the privilege on the use at trial of compelled statements at trial, *Chavez* has a potentially significant impact on

---

[45] Id at 843–44.

[46] This is at least a little more complicated than I've described it. The Court has never settled on a test for determining whether a constitutional provision "applies." Some sitting Justices think *Graham* is only implicated where there would otherwise be duplicative recovery. *Albright v Oliver*, 510 US 266, 289 n 2 (Souter, J, concurring in the judgment); id at 305 (Stevens, J, joined by Blackmun, J, dissenting). But *Graham* itself seems to be in tension with that view. Categorizing Graham's case under the Fourth Amendment rather than substantive due process at least potentially had real bite for petitioner Graham, who had been kept away from treatment for a diabetic reaction by police officers who suspected him of a crime. As the *Graham* Court noted, analysis under the Fourth Amendment requires only an objective inquiry into the officers' motives, while the "shocks the conscience" test takes into account the officers' subjective motivations. 490 US 386, 390–93 (1989) (describing test for "shocks the conscience" due process claim as including consideration of good faith of officers). In other words, it is possible Graham might have recovered under one provision and not another. See also Peter J. Rubin, *Square Pegs and Round Holes: Substantive Due Process, Procedural Due Process, and the Bill of Rights*, 103 Colum L Rev 853 (2003) (noting that, had the Court merely been concerned that Graham's Fourth Amendment claims and substantive due process claims were duplicative, it would not have remanded for consideration under the former).

Lewis was an easy case. In that case, the Court found that *Graham* did not bar consideration under substantive due process of a "shocks the conscience" due process claim arising out of a high-speed police chase that ended in the motorcyclist's death before police capture. Because the motorcyclist had never been "seized" by the police, the Fourth Amendment had never been applicable, and therefore did not supersede the substantive due process claim. What makes *Lewis* easy is that there was no factual overlap between the elements of Lewis's Fourth Amendment and substantive due process claims. The elements of Martinez's two claims, by contrast, do overlap significantly (as did Graham's). Allowing a remand on Martinez's substantive due process claim consistent with *Graham* thus requires drawing a finer distinction than is presently in doctrine about what it means for a constitutional protection to "apply."

the privilege. Though both Justice Thomas and Justice Souter acted as though the decision was dictated by precedent, *Chavez* enunciates a new approach with real implications for the future.

A. THE PRIVILEGE PRECEDENTS

The Court's holding that the privilege is violated only by the use at trial of compelled testimony (and that suppression of the compelled statement and its fruits[47] is the basic remedy) is in tension with a robust line of privilege precedents. In *Maness v Meyers*,[48] for instance, the Court overturned the contempt conviction of an attorney sanctioned for advising his client not to produce potentially incriminating evidence (pornographic magazines) in a civil proceeding. The Court focused on the harm to the client of *releasing* the information, denying that a motion to suppress would solve the privilege problem. It is not possible to "unring the bell," the Court said, once the information is out.[49] If suppression were the only remedy, and compulsion at the civil proceeding was allowed, the Court explained, Maness "would be compelled to surrender the very protection which the privilege is designed to guarantee."[50]

Maness was not an outlier: it tapped into a long tradition of decisions allowing the privilege to be asserted in noncriminal actions, such as bankruptcy proceedings,[51] disbarment hearings,[52] congressional investigations,[53] and other administrative actions,[54] even though later use of the testimony at a criminal trial was uncertain. "Pleading the Fifth" has become a staple feature of noncriminal proceedings, allowing witnesses to remain silent rather than incriminating themselves and later seeking suppression when their statements are offered against them in a criminal trial.

As recently as 1998, all of the current Justices save Ginsburg and Breyer have signed onto dicta quoting *Maness*'s statement

---

[47] See *Kastigar v United States*, 406 US 441, 461–62 (1972).

[48] 419 US 449 (1975).

[49] Id at 460.

[50] Id at 462.

[51] *McCarthy v Arndstein*, 266 US 34 (1924).

[52] *Spevack v Klein*, 385 US 511 (1967).

[53] *Quinn v United States*, 75 S Ct 668 (1955).

[54] *Petition of Groban*, 352 US 330, 333 (1957) ("privilege applies to interrogations as well as in prosecutions.").

about the insufficiency of the suppression remedy.[55] Indeed, only a year before *Chavez*, the Court decided another compulsion-based privilege case, *McKune v Lile*, in a way that is inconsistent with *Chavez*'s view of the privilege.[56] A prisoner, Lile, objected to being ordered, on pain of transfer to a level within the prison with fewer privileges and greater security restrictions, to participate in a sex offender rehabilitation program that required him to admit to the crimes for which he had been incarcerated as well as to any other sexual crimes he may have committed. The Court dismissed his complaint, with a four-Justice plurality concluding that, within the prison context, only the threat of an "atypical and significant hardship" can form the basis for a privilege action.[57] Justice O'Connor concurred in the judgment on the ground that, even in a nonprison context, the disadvantages Lile faced were not so great as to be compulsive.[58]

According to the majority's reasoning in *Chavez*, however, there was a much more serious problem with Lile's claim: the privilege poses no bar to compelling Lile to admit to his crimes, only to using the admissions in a later criminal action. That is, if *Chavez* is right, the question the Court addressed in *McKune* ought not even to have been an issue. In fact, under the majority's reasoning, Lile clearly lacked a cause of action.

Thus, both Thomas and Souter faced a serious challenge from the Court's precedents to the use requirement they endorsed in *Chavez*. Rather than admitting the difficulties and overruling (or reconceptualizing) these decisions, the Justices in the majority attempted to salvage them. They recharacterized these decisions as mere prophylactic protections for the privilege, rather than as applications of the privilege itself.

This strategy ought to seem surprising. The Court's recent opinion in *Dickerson*,[59] rejecting a congressional attempt to supplant the *Miranda* warnings, was authored by Chief Justice

---

[55] *United States v Balsys*, 524 US 666, 683 n 8 (1998) (holding that the privilege does not protect against use in a foreign prosecution). Ginsburg and Breyer dissented on other grounds.

[56] The *Chavez* dissenters noted the tension with *McKune*. *Chavez*, 123 S Ct at 2015.

[57] 536 US at 37–38.

[58] Id at 48 (O'Connor, J, concurring in the judgment).

[59] *Dickerson v United States*, 530 US 428 (2000).

Rehnquist, a member of the *Chavez* majority. That opinion assiduously avoided the language of prophylaxis to describe *Miranda*.[60] It is strange to find Rehnquist joining an opinion, a mere three years later, that expressly invokes prophylaxis in the privilege context to explain *Miranda* and a host of other privilege rules. It is even more surprising that the *Dickerson* dissenters—Justices Thomas and Scalia—authored and joined (respectively) this prophylactic rules-based approach to the privilege.[61] Thomas's *Chavez* opinion does not suggest that these privilege-based prophylactic rules are constitutionally compelled—and hence Thomas and Scalia presumably think Congress could legislatively abolish them, posing no square conflict with their analysis in *Dickerson*. But this is mere technical consistency. Their *Dickerson* opinion referred to even the nonconstitutional prophylactic *Miranda* rule as a "lawless practice," and an "extraordinary . . . mistake."[62] But it is a mistake, apparently, they are now willing to embrace, and indeed, expand.

Justice Souter's *Chavez* opinion (joined by Justice Breyer) lists several categories of prophylactic privilege rules, including *Miranda* itself, "barring compulsion to give testimonial evidence in a civil proceeding,"[63] "requiring a grant of immunity in advance of any testimonial proffer,"[64] and "precluding threats or impositions of penalties that would undermine the right to immunity."[65] Souter's second example is probably the most important for these purposes: the right to "up-front" immunity. The suggestion that a person facing compulsion has a right to obtain immunity *before* testifying is by no means novel. In *Lefkowitz v Turley*, the Court stated:

> [A] witness rightly protected by the privilege may rightfully refuse to answer unless and until he is protected at least against the use of his compelled answers and evidence derived therefrom in any subsequent case in which he is a defendant.[66]

---

[60] See generally Susan R. Klein, *Identifying and (Re)Formulating Prophylactic Rules, Safe Harbors, and Incidental Rights in Constitutional Criminal Procedure*, 99 Mich L Rev 1030 (2001).

[61] 530 US at 446.

[62] Id at 428.

[63] 123 S Ct at 2007 (citing *McCarthy v Arndstein*, 266 US 34 (1924)).

[64] 123 S Ct at 2007 (citing *Kastigar v United States*, 406 US 441 (1972)).

[65] 123 S Ct at 2007.

[66] *Lefkowitz v Turley*, 414 US 70, 78 (1973).

On the majority's view that the privilege protects only against the use of evidence at trial, such an immunity requirement can only be prophylactic: it is a way of stopping a potential *later* privilege violation.

Justice Thomas suggests two explanations for this kind of prophylaxis. The first is seemingly based on the fear that, once the cat is out of the bag, there will be no way the government can stop itself from using the information against the individual. Thomas quotes *Michigan v Tucker*:[67] "Testimony obtained in civil suits, or before administrative or legislative committees, could [absent a grant of immunity] prove so incriminating that a person compelled to give such testimony might readily be convicted on the basis of those disclosures in a subsequent criminal proceeding."

But why cannot the suppression remedy handle this problem? The statement in *Tucker* was not intended to suggest that a later suppression remedy would be ineffective; its point was only that this testimony, if introduced in a later criminal trial, could incriminate.[68] And although there may be a temptation to ignore the demands of a constitutional rule requiring suppression, Thomas's endorsement of this rationale is awkward at best. In the contexts in which Thomas's rule would remove the temptation to admit compelled statements—contexts like congressional investigations where up-front immunity is at least potentially available—it should be relatively easy to separate the compelled from the non-compelled.[69]

The real impact of Thomas's concern ought to be on the large portion of confessions obtained in the police interrogation room, where there is no meaningful opportunity for up-front immunity. Judgments about whether those statements were obtained in unconstitutionally compulsive circumstances are more difficult, and

---

[67] 123 S Ct at 2003 (quoting *Michigan v Tucker*, 417 US 433, 440 (1974)).

[68] 417 US at 440.

[69] Application of a subpoena and other threats of contempt are simply compulsive. Although a few new types of contexts may arise where the actual degree of compulsiveness inherent in the threat is unclear—consider Justice O'Connor's view in *McKune v Lile* that the changes in prison conditions were not serious enough to be compulsive—by and large, in most circumstances where a grant of up-front immunity is possible, the necessity of suppression is clear enough as to remove the temptation not to suppress confessions obtained in those circumstances (and what little temptation there is occurs in the form of the application of the "voluntariness" doctrine, Thomas's second basis for prophylaxis in this context).

the propriety of suppression must be decided at a moment when the content of the testimony is in fact already known.

If Thomas is right that the incriminating nature of testimony so jeopardizes courts' judgments that they cannot adequately enforce the suppression requirement, it would seem he must endorse a prophylactic rule far broader than what he suggests: a rule requiring the prophylactic suppression of *all* confessions made during interrogations (on the theory that we cannot trust ourselves accurately to sort out the proper from the improper once we see the content of the confession). At the very least, Thomas would logically have to embrace a requirement of present counsel for all interrogations (on the theory that this, like up-front immunity, would stop improper disclosures before they come out). Thomas clearly does not mean to go this far, casting serious doubt on his endorsement of prophylactic rules in a context that least requires them.

Thomas's second reason why prophylaxis requires an up-front grant of immunity is based on the issue of voluntariness:

> Because the failure to assert the privilege will often forfeit the right to exclude the evidence in a subsequent "criminal case," it is necessary to allow assertion of the privilege prior to the commencement of the "criminal case" to safeguard the Fifth Amendment trial right. If the privilege could not be asserted in such situations, testimony in those judicial proceedings would be deemed "voluntary"; hence, insistence on a prior grant of immunity is essential to memorialize the fact that the testimony had really been compelled.[70]

The voluntariness principle is little used. The idea seems to be that some people who were subjected to compulsion have acted in ways that suggest they would have been willing to cooperate voluntarily.[71] Concerns about voluntariness, however, require only that the witness *raise* the privilege at the moment of compulsion, not that the court *resolve* it. This is not to say that it is always necessary to raise the objection—we do not require the suspect to raise the objection in the interrogation context, for instance, where

---

[70] 123 S Ct at 2003 (citations omitted).

[71] See, e.g., *Garner v United States*, 424 US 648, 650 (failure to claim privilege waived later objection); *United States v Kordel*, 397 US 1, 7 (1970) (same); *Rogers v United States*, 340 US 367, 371 (1951) (same).

the suspect cannot be expected to be aware of the need to ob-ject[72]—or even that it would be sufficient. But it would at least negate the suggestion that the witness had no objection to testi-fying.

Consider *Lefkowitz v Turley*, which gave support to the up-front immunity rule. In his opinion, Justice White contemplated a very practical solution to the problem of raising the privilege in a pro-ceeding in which it did not apply. In such a circumstance, a person potentially compelled to incriminate himself may invoke the privi-lege and seek immunity. If the request for immunity is denied, and "he is nevertheless compelled to answer, [assuming the other requirements of the privilege are met] his answers are inadmissible against him in a later criminal proceeding."[73] He has made clear that his answers are not voluntary without necessitating that the constitutional question be actually resolved at that time. This is precisely what happened in *Garrity v New Jersey*[74]—police officers were compelled, by threat of losing their jobs, to answer questions in an Attorney General's investigation of an alleged parking-ticket-fixing scheme. They objected,[75] and when the government sought to use against them in a criminal prosecution their compelled an-swers, they were suppressed.[76] This later suppression motion pro-vides what has been called "informal use immunity."[77] Under the majority's understanding of the privilege, informal use immunity ought to be sufficient to avoid the voluntariness problem.

It was precisely on this basis that Justice White dissented in *Spevack v Klein*,[78] which held that a lawyer could remain silent without penalty in a disbarment proceeding on the basis of the

---

[72] Peter Westen and Stewart Mandell, *To Talk, to Balk, or to Lie: The Emerging Fifth Amendment Doctrine of the "Preferred Response,"* 19 Am Crim L Rev 521, 536–37 (1982). Only in voluntariness cases like those cited by Justice Thomas—*Garner, Korbel,* and *Rogers,* where the witnesses had ample opportunity to consider their options and act accordingly—has the Court insisted on an objection at the moment of compulsion.

[73] 414 US at 78–79.

[74] 385 US 493 (1967).

[75] In fact, in *Garrity* defendants did not even object at the time the statements were taken; at least according to the dissent's characterization of the facts (which the majority does not seriously dispute), they complied seemingly willingly. Id at 502 (Harlan, J, dissenting).

[76] Id.

[77] Larry J. Ritchie, *Compulsion That Violates the Fifth Amendment: The Burger Court's Defi-nition,* 61 Minn L Rev 383, 389 (1976–77).

[78] 385 US 511 (1967).

potential use of his statements against him at a later criminal trial.[79] White queried why such a holding was necessary in the face of *Turley's* procedure for claiming the privilege—since the testimony would be suppressed at any future criminal trial, there is "little legal or practical basis, in terms of the privilege . . . for preventing the discharge of a public employee or the disbarment of a lawyer who refuses to talk about the performance of his public duty."[80] White made a similar point in his *Maness* concurrence. Concerns about voluntariness do not require up-front immunity.

There thus appears no reason for the prophylactic rule requiring up-front immunity on the majority's view of the privilege. It is therefore difficult to see any justification for Justice Souter's suggested prophylactic rule against threats or penalties that burden the (nonexistent) right. Similarly, it is difficult to see any justification for Souter's prophylactic rule against self-incrimination in civil proceedings—so long as the exclusionary rule excludes admissions compelled in civil proceedings from use in subsequent criminal proceedings. Under the view of the privilege in *Chavez*, there should be no problem with compelled testimony in that setting.

Prophylactic explanations thus fail to explain privilege cases where the right could be raised and decided before any use in a criminal trial. Prophylaxis is not, however, the only possibility for salvaging at least some parts of privilege doctrine. Justice Thomas gives another sort of explanation for one particular subset of cases where the privilege is raised and decided early: those involving litigants who are compelled not only to incriminate themselves without a grant of formal immunity, but also to affirmatively waive their right to later seek suppression should the matter come before trial. This was true of the sanitation workers and the police officer facing termination of government employment in *Uniformed Sanitation Men Association v Commissioner of Sanitation of the City of New York*[81] and *Gardner v Broderick*,[82] as well as the attorney threatened

---

[79] Id at 531 (White, J, dissenting) (citation omitted). See also Westen and Mandell, 19 Am Crim L Rev at 524–25 (cited in note 72) (arguing that holding off on a privilege challenge until the evidence is sought to be used at trial would satisfy the demands of the constitutional provision).

[80] 419 US 449, 472 (1973).

[81] 392 US 280 (1968).

[82] Id at 273 (1968).

with divestment of his political party leadership in *Lefkowitz v Cunningham*.[83] Justice Thomas suggests in *Chavez* that these cases do not require a prophylactic justification—they can instead be treated as something akin to unconstitutional conditions cases. He says: "A waiver of immunity is therefore a prospective waiver of the core self-incrimination right in any subsequent criminal proceeding, and States cannot condition public employment or other benefits of that sort on the waiver of constitutional rights."[84]

But Thomas's statement makes little sense.[85] If, as the cases have held, government employment cannot be conditioned on the waiver of the privilege, such waivers would be invalid under the privilege itself, without any help from the doctrine of unconstitutional conditions. So long as the employee suitably objects to signing the waiver, its invalidity could be determined later, at the moment the evidence is sought to be introduced. It is hard to see why the doctrine of unconstitutional conditions would push that review up to an earlier time. In fact, the architects facing loss of government contracts were asked to sign a waiver in *Lefkowitz v Turley*,[86] the case I have already relied on for an endorsement of an object now/suppress later approach to the privilege. The timing even of the waiver cases, therefore, also seems to be off.

The majority's view of the privilege in *Chavez* therefore necessitates overruling (or at least rewriting) a dizzying array of privilege precedents. In addition to the waiver cases, the reasoning (though not the outcome) of *McKune* is an obvious loser, as is *Spevack*, the disbarment case.[87] *Maness* also appears to have gotten its analysis

---

[83] 341 US 801 (1977).

[84] 123 S Ct at 2002 n 2.

[85] And for that matter, so do most efforts to concoct a general theory of unconstitutional conditions. See, e.g., Frederick Schauer, *Too Hard: Unconstitutional Conditions and the Chimera of Constitutional Consistency*, 72 Denver U L Rev 989 (1995); Larry Alexander, *Impossible*, 72 Denver U L Rev 1007 (1995); Cass Sunstein, *Why the Unconstitutional Conditions Doctrine is an Anachronism (With Particular Reference to Religion, Speech, and Abortion)*, 70 BU L Rev 593, 606–07 (1990) (arguing that the doctrine requires an analysis of the appropriateness of government pressure in particular substantive constitutional areas). But see Richard A. Epstein, *Bargaining with the State* (1993) (characterizing the unconstitutional conditions doctrine as avoiding inefficient negotiations between the government and private individuals).

[86] 414 US 70 (1973).

[87] See Steven D. Clymer, *Are Police Free to Disregard Miranda?* 112 Yale L J 447, 469 (2002) (suggesting that, without doing so explicitly, the Court quickly backtracked on *Spevack*).

wrong,[88] in that there was no reason why Maness should not have been required, after he made clear his objection, to submit his pornographic magazines in the civil proceedings and to seek suppression if they were used against him in a subsequent criminal prosecution. More importantly, a range of cases allowing the privilege question to be decided in noncriminal cases, such as the bankruptcy and the congressional investigation cases, have got to go: this includes *McCarthy*, *Quinn*, and a number of others.[89]

Given this, *Chavez*'s view of the privilege ought to change practice in at least in one very significant respect: the Court ought to allow testimony to be compelled in noncriminal proceedings, and wait to use the suppression remedy to address whatever problems arise in the criminal trial. This change of practice would alter the privilege's role in a variety of contexts. Essentially, government actors could compel individuals to make incriminating statements, so long as they were willing to risk having to forgo use of that evidence and its fruits in a subsequent criminal trial. Of course, they may do this now, but only if they explicitly grant up-front immunity. The new understanding of the privilege would seem to remove that requirement.

Given the need to suppress not only compelled statements themselves, but also the fruits of those statements, courts may bristle at the thought of waiting until the criminal trial to resolve privilege questions. Later privilege determinations may result in more complex, and frequent, questions about what constitutes the fruits of improper testimony.[90] This potential annoyance does not, however, justify reviewing a potential violation before it occurs. And it brings up an interesting possibility: prosecutors might themselves have a reason to keep effectively giving immunity, even if courts cannot compel it. Prosecutors sometimes build firewalls around evidence that may later be suppressed, in order to be sure that valuable related evidence is not treated as improper fruit of the compelled statement that must itself be suppressed.[91] Given

---

[88] The conclusion in *Maness* might have been supportable on other grounds, since the contempt citation was against his lawyer, who arguably was providing good faith legal advice. See *Maness*, 419 US 449, 473 (White, J, concurring).

[89] See, e.g., *McCarthy v Arndstein*, 266 US 34 (1924); *Quinn v United States*, 75 S Ct 668 (1955); *Bram v United States*, 168 US 532 (1897); *Counselman v Hitchcock*, 142 US 547 (1892).

[90] See *Kastigar v United States*, 406 US 441, 461–62 (1972).

[91] See Westen and Mandell, 19 Am Crim L Rev at 531 (cited in note 72); Nagareda, 74 NYU L Rev at 1637 (cited in note 32) (describing advantages to the government of resolving privilege questions early in the process).

prosecutors' interests in up-front determination of which evidence is likely to be admissible and which is not, defendants may effectively be informed of the status of their testimony by the prosecutor's actions. But the choice to officially or even unofficially immunize, after *Chavez*, ought to remain in the hands of the prosecutor.

B. JUSTIFICATIONS FOR THE PRIVILEGE

If the privilege is merely this kind of trial right, what justifies it? Finding any justification for the privilege (at least one that even roughly tracks the doctrine) is a difficult, perhaps impossible, task.[92] Figures as prominent as Jeremy Bentham and Henry Friendly[93] considered the privilege indefensible, and modern attempts to justify it have found no more receptive audiences. As William Stuntz has recently written, "It is probably fair to say that most people familiar with the doctrine surrounding the privilege against self-incrimination believe that it cannot be squared with any rational theory."[94]

Construing the privilege as simply a trial right both helps and hinders the inquiry. By limiting the range of justifications that can be advanced, it focuses the question, but also takes off the table some of what might be considered the more compelling reasons. The list of possible justifications for the privilege was most comprehensively set out by the Court in *Murphy v Waterfront Commission*:[95]

> [The privilege] reflects many of our fundamental values and most noble aspirations: our unwillingness to subject those suspected of crime to the cruel trilemma of self-accusation, perjury, or contempt; our preference for an accusatorial rather than an inquisitorial system of criminal justice; our fear that self-incriminating statements will be elicited by inhumane treatment and abuses; our sense of fair play . . . , our respect

---

[92] See, e.g., 5 *Jeremy Bentham, Rationale of Judicial Evidence*, bk IX, pt IV, ch III, § III; David Dolinko, *Is There a Rationale for the Privilege Against Self-Incrimination?* 333 UCLA L Rev 1063 (1986) (answering the question posed by the title: "no"); William Stuntz, *Self-Incrimination and Excuse*, 88 Colum L Rev 1227, 1228 (1988); Akhil Reed Amar and Renee B. Lettow, *Fifth Amendment First Principles: The Self-Incrimination Clause*, 93 Mich L Rev 857, 857 (1995) ("The Self-Incrimination Clause of the Fifth Amendment is an unsolved riddle of vast proportions.").

[93] Henry J. Friendly, *Benchmarks* 266–84 (1967).

[94] Stuntz, 88 Colum L Rev at 1228 (cited in note 92).

[95] 378 US 52, 55 (1964).

for the inviolability of the human personality and of the right of each individual to a "private enclave where he may lead a private life"; our distrust of self-deprecatory statements; and our realization that the privilege, while sometimes "a shelter to the guilty," is often a "protection to the innocent."

After *Chavez*, many of these justifications are no longer viable. "Respect for the inviolability of the human personality"—that it is inconsistent with human dignity to force a person to malign herself[96]—and the individual's right to a "private enclave" would seem to be violated whenever an individual is compelled to disclose self-incriminating information, whether or not it is later used in a criminal trial. If legal protection for these concerns exists anywhere after *Chavez*, it is in substantive due process, not the privilege.

Similarly, concerns about testimony elicited by inhumane treatment and the "cruel trilemma" cannot animate the privilege as construed by the *Chavez* Court. Because both of these theories focus on the particular cruelty of the process of obtaining testimony,[97] they would seem to be implicated regardless of use at trial.

So what's left? Evidentiary reliability is one possibility: concerns about reliability and the protection of the innocent, for instance, arise only when compelled statements are actually used at trial. But as Akhil Amar and Rachel Lettow have argued, if evidentiary reliability is the justification for the privilege, at least one major feature of present privilege doctrine would have to be abandoned: the rule that the fruits of compelled testimony, as well as the testimony itself, must be suppressed.[98] Moreover, serious consideration would have to be given to the actual reliability of statements made in various contexts. Confessions made under the threat of the rack and screw are more likely to be unreliable, as are confessions obtained under psychological pressure during interrogation,[99] than confessions made in the context of, say, civil proceedings.[100]

---

[96] Robert Gerstein, *Privacy and Self-Incrimination*, 80 Ethics 87, 88 (1970).

[97] This may not seem intuitively true about the cruel trilemma. For more in-depth discussion, see text accompanying notes 118–21.

[98] Amar and Lettow, 93 Mich L Rev at 899–90, 922–23 (cited in note 92).

[99] Why innocent people would confess to avoid physical torture is obvious. For a discussion of why innocent people might falsely confess under different sorts of pressures, see generally Saul M. Kassin and Katherine L. Kiechel, *The Social Psychology of False Confessions: Compliance, Internalization, and Confabulation*, 7 Psychol Sci 125 (1996).

[100] See text accompanying note 129.

The choice of an accusatorial system over an inquisitorial one and the concept of "fair play" in the courtroom battle remain potential justifications of the privilege as a trial right. But these justifications are circular. Why is the use of compelled self-incriminatory statements "unfair"? Why shouldn't "fairness" focus on evidentiary reliability rather than balance of power?[101] Why does an accusatorial system require this particular rule?

III. Due Process After Chavez

Confining the privilege to the conduct of the trial shifts to due process many of the troubling questions associated with the privilege: what restrictions does the Constitution place on governmental gathering of information from individuals? *Chavez*'s division of labor requires us to look at these questions in a new way: a way that is separate from the specific prohibition against compelled self-incrimination.

A. THE PRIVILEGE'S DUE PROCESS HERITAGE

As Justice Stevens was careful to note, it is not possible to separate the privilege completely from due process: they have always significantly overlapped. Before the privilege was incorporated against the states, the Court relied on due process—in particular, due process voluntariness—to suppress testimony obtained by improper police methods.[102] And the decision to incorporate the privilege signaled that it was required by due process. In *Malloy v Hogan*, the Court reached beyond the sort of physical and psychological torture that had characterized the due process voluntariness cases: Indeed, *Malloy* involved testimony compelled by the threat of contempt in a formal investigation, rather than by physically or psychologically torturous interrogation.[103]

Even after the privilege was incorporated, the standards established by the due process voluntariness cases continued to inform determinations of whether particular confessions had been com-

---

[101] See Dolinko, 333 UCLA L Rev at 1076 (cited in note 92) (presenting and critiquing the "fair fight" view).

[102] See generally Catherine Hancock, *Due Process Before Miranda*, 70 Tulane L Rev 2195 (1996).

[103] 378 US 1 (1964).

pelled within the meaning of the privilege.[104] Then came *Miranda*, which shifted the focus in cases involving custodial interrogation from ex post analysis of voluntariness to an ex ante avoidance of coercive interrogation. But some aspects of the due process voluntariness standard survived *Miranda*—some evidence obtained in *Mirandized* interrogations still could, in theory, be problematic under the privilege.[105] And the exceptions to *Miranda*'s exclusionary rule—for instance, that non-*Mirandized* confessions can be used for impeachment—do not apply where due process requires suppression. Particularly relevant here is Justice Ginsburg's focus in *Chavez* on *Mincey v Arizona*, a due process case arising in a factual setting similar to *Chavez*. In *Mincey*, the Court held that due process required suppression of a statement obtained in circumstances where an exception to *Miranda* would otherwise apply.

Due process therefore clearly plays some role in relation to the privilege. The difficulty is identifying which aspects of the this role are attributable to concerns about the conduct of criminal trials (now largely governed by the privilege[106]), and which are attributable to concerns about government compulsion, which are now subject to separate due process consideration. If, after *Chavez*, due process must take responsibility for a role that previously belonged to the privilege—defining the propriety of government attempts to elicit information from individuals—what does that role look like?

B. NARROW DUE PROCESS

The Court in *Chavez* remanded Martinez's substantive due process claim for damages. Most of the Justices referred to this as a "shock the conscience" claim. Presumably, some form of recovery under this standard is available for some failed privilege claimants. The difficult question after *Chavez* is how narrowly that category should be defined.

---

[104] See generally Hancock, 70 Tulane L Rev (cited in note 102).

[105] See, e.g., *Berkemer v McCarty*, 468 US 420, 433 n 20 (1984) (acknowledging the limited role of due process voluntariness after *Miranda*).

[106] The Court has previously decided that due process does not forbid comment on defendant's failure to testify, as required under the privilege in *Griffin v California*, 380 US 609 (1965). See id at 619 (Harlan, J, concurring) (citing *Twining v New Jersey*, 211 US 78, and *Adamson v California*, 332 US 46).

"Shock the conscience" due process claims belong in a line of cases, most famously including *Rochin v California*,[107] where the Court held that convictions based on evidence obtained in a conscience-shocking manner violate due process, and that evidence obtained in such a way must therefore be suppressed.[108] More generally, however, "shock the conscience" due process claims often focus on concerns outside the courtroom. As noted in *Sacramento v Lewis*,[109] the "shock the conscience" test has come to serve as a general standard for claims of bad behavior against government officers, such as the police. Section 1983 damages—as well as suppression in suitable instances—are available for successful "shock the conscience" claimants.[110]

The narrowest construction of "shock the conscience" due process focuses on the propriety of government conduct without reference to self-incrimination. That is, in a case of self-incrimination compelled through physical force, the due process inquiry focuses on whether the force was conscience-shocking, *not* on whether employing force in order to obtain a confession shocks the conscience. In Martinez's case, such a claim would turn on the allegation that the police interfered with Martinez's health care—which was, in fact, Justice Thomas's focus in *Chavez*.[111] It would make no difference whether the police were trying to coerce a self-incriminatory statement or information that might incriminate someone else. On this understanding, the distinctive privilege-like aspects of the situation would be irrelevant.[112]

---

[107] 342 US 165 (1952).

[108] *United States v Salerno* describes two separate types of substantive due process violations against the states: those that interfere with fundamental rights (the incorporation test) and those that shock the conscience. 481 US 739 (1987). Peter Rubin has usefully articulated the conscience-shocking standard as itself "defining a fundamental right: the right against conscience-shocking governmental behavior." Rubin, 103 Colum L Rev at 833, 846 (cited in note 46).

[109] 523 US 833 (1998).

[110] Id at 846–47.

[111] 123 S Ct 1994, 2005 (Thomas, J, concurring) ("Here, there is no evidence that Chavez acted with a purpose to harm Martinez by intentionally interfering with his medical treatment. . . . Nor is there evidence that Chavez's conduct exacerbated Martinez's injuries or prolonged his stay in the hospital.").

[112] This is not to say that *all* factors relating to subjective motivation would be ignored under this understanding of shock the conscience—motive is typically relevant to such inquiries, see note 106—only that the particular motivation to compel self-incriminating information would not contribute to the conscience-shocking nature of any particular behavior. On the narrow view, seeking to compel incriminating information would not be wrong except insofar as it is specifically prohibited by the privilege.

If due process is defined in this way, there would be a significant gap between the two guarantees: many people who are within the privilege's protection for purposes of suppressing compelled testimony at trial would not receive due process protection for the compulsion used to elicit the confession.[113] The privilege requires suppression in contexts where the government's behavior is not independently unconstitutional.

To help see this point, imagine another hypothetical litigant, Jones. Jones is an employee of the police department, suspected of criminal misfeasance in the workplace. She is approached by her superiors and threatened with termination if she refuses to answer their questions—the threat of termination is typically sufficient compulsion for privilege purposes.[114] To avoid termination, she provides self-incriminatory information. The implication of *Chavez* is that this information would be suppressed in a future criminal proceeding against her, but she would not receive § 1983 damages for the method used to draw out her testimony. Separated from its incrimination-focused goal, there is nothing conscience-shocking about firing a government employee suspected of misfeasance for refusing to answer questions. Similarly, the government's use of a subpoena to compel self-incriminatory information is within the heart of the privilege,[115] but is not per se conscience-shocking. After *Chavez*, and assuming this conception of due process, evidence obtained in this manner would be suppressed in a criminal trial, but damages would not be recoverable under the due process clause.

C. POTENTIAL EXPANSIONS

One impact of *Chavez* may be to signal an expanded view of the due process inquiry beyond the question whether government

---

[113] Arnold H. Loewy, *Police-Obtained Evidence and the Constitution: Distinguishing Unconstitutionally Obtained Evidence from Unconstitutionally Used Evidence*, 87 Mich L Rev 907, 934 (1989) (noting that some, though not necessarily all, coerced confessions are also obtained through unconstitutional means, giving rise to a separate action).

[114] The facts of this hypothetical somewhat resemble those in *Cleversy v Perry Township*, 1991 US Dist LEXIS 19801, where a police officer was asked to resign after invoking his privilege in an interrogation about on-the-job misfeasance. It is unclear from the Court's opinion, however, whether Cleversy was told that he would be terminated from his government employment had he refused to resign, and whether the termination/resignation followed upon his invocation of the privilege, rather than the allegation of misfeasance itself. In any event, Cleversy was denied § 1983 relief.

[115] *United States v Mandujano*, 425 US 564, 566 (1976).

conduct shocks the conscience. There are two possible expansions after *Chavez*, one based on privacy, which seems implausible, and one based on cruelty, which seems more promising.

1. *Privacy*. One possibility would be to argue that *any* government compulsion of self-incriminating testimony violates due process. This view—essentially a privacy-based notion that individuals have a right to keep "nasty" information about themselves to themselves—would require due process damages whenever an individual was compelled to disclose self-incriminating information.[116]

This seems unlikely. Such a rule would give due process a role far more extensive than the privilege pre-*Chavez*. Given the immunity rule, the privilege could not plausibly be seen as protecting people from *ever* having to make public incriminating information about themselves. How can this violation of one's privacy be constitutionally problematic, if compelled disclosure is permitted if the witness is granted immunity?[117] Under this view, all witnesses granted immunity would have a § 1983 action for damages. This is implausible.

Indeed, the immunity cases have explicitly rejected such a basis for the privilege. In *Brown v Walker*, the Court described the justification for the immunity rule thus:

> the fact that the testimony may tend to degrade the witness in public estimation does not exempt him from the duty of disclosure. A person who commits a criminal act is bound to contemplate the consequences of exposure to his good name and reputation, and ought not to call upon the courts to protect that which he has himself esteemed to be of such little value. . . . The design of the constitutional privilege is not to aid the witness in vindicating his character, but to protect him against being compelled to furnish evidence to convict him of a criminal charge.[118]

Justice Kennedy attempts to make more plausible a privacy-oriented view of the privilege by recasting the immunity cases as suggesting that the privilege is not absolute. But this is not convincing: It would

---

[116] For a discussion of defenses of this "privacy" argument, see Dolinko, 333 UCLA L Rev at 1107–37 (cited in note 92).

[117] 123 S Ct at 2001–02.

[118] *Brown v Walker*, 161 US 591, 605–06 (1896).

be one thing if the privilege were qualified so that it applied only in the absence of a strong government interest in compelling testimony.[119] That sort of qualification would indicate what Justice Kennedy suggests: that there is a constitutional protection against compulsion of incriminating information itself, but that it is not absolute, giving way in the face of competing government interests. But it is not possible to conceptualize immunity this way. The immunity rule allows the government to compel incriminating information whenever it wishes, so long as it provides assurance in advance that the evidence will never be used in a criminal trial against the individual. The government need show no particular interest in the testimony—only a willingness to provide use immunity. This suggests, not a compromise between the privilege and competing government interests, but a conception of the privilege that assumes no "privacy" interest in nondisclosure.[120]

2. *Cruelty.* A more promising suggestion is that due process after *Chavez* might protect not only against improper government behavior to elicit a confession, but also against certain features of the pressure to confess. The claim that there is something (unconstitutionally) cruel about forcing someone to incriminate herself has a long pedigree. This notion is most commonly encapsulated in the suggestion that the privilege protects against the "cruel trilemma." As recognized in *Murphy v Waterfront Commission*, this is the choice between facing criminal punishment for confessing to a crime, perjury prosecution for lying, or contempt for remaining silent.[121] Not all choices that implicate the privilege look like this: for instance, custodial interrogations pose more of a cruel dilemma —confess and be convicted or continue to face the pressure of the

---

[119] It is at least possible that it is qualified in this way. *Baltimore City Department of Social Services v Bouknight*, 493 US 549 (1990).

[120] To see the point, consider what would happen to the right of trial by jury in the face of a Court decision that no jury trial is required whenever the government chooses to assemble a panel of six judges to adjudicate the case. Such a ruling (implausible, of course) would not suggest that the jury right was qualified (whereas a right to dispense with jury trials in times of national emergency would), but would rather suggest a different understanding of the right altogether: that its purpose is to protect against the potential arbitrariness of the decision of one adjudicator, rather than provide the accused with the potentially ameliorating influence of laypeople in the criminal justice process.

[121] Albert W. Alschuler, *A Peculiar Privilege in Historical Perspective: The Right to Remain Silent*, 94 Mich L Rev 2625, 2645 (1996).

interrogation room.[122] This is not unique to interrogation. Lile, for instance, had only two choices, to admit guilt or lose his privileges.[123]

Even under the Court's characterization of the privilege in *Chavez*, both types of cruelty are, in a sense, avoided. If a compelled confession is suppressed, the individual never faces either the trilemma or the dilemma. But if cruelty is the focus, this may not be what matters. Perhaps what is cruel about these dilemmas and trilemmas is the uncertainty of having to make the choice in what seems like a no-win situation. Without up-front immunity, witnesses have no way of knowing for sure whether their confessions will lead to conviction.

The idea that such uncertainty is itself unconstitutionally cruel has some support in historical practice.[124] Moreover, the desire to protect against the uncertainty makes sense of many of the pre-*Chavez* precedents. This view of the privilege precedents borrows from Stephen Clymer's defense of *Spevack v Klein*. Though in a post-*Chavez* world, Spevack, the lawyer, would be forced to wait until the government attempted to use his testimony against him at a criminal trial, if the concern of the privilege is avoiding the cruel trilemma, earlier resolution might be required. As Clymer notes, Spevack had no way aside from asking the Court to require a grant of immunity of knowing that he would not be convicted on the basis of his testimony. If that uncertainty is cruel, up-front immunity would be the best way to avoid it.

Clymer argues, however, that actual immunity is not necessary. A clear precedent establishing the suppression of compelled testimony would also avoid the cruel trilemma. Thus, Clymer argues

---

[122] Peter Westen and Stewart Mandell have classified at least three cruel choices protected by the Fifth Amendment—the classic cruel trilemma, where a witness faces prosecution for perjury, prosecution for truthfully admitting the crime, or punishment for failure to testify; the special situation of the defendant whose punishment for failure to testify is the cost of pleading his privilege on the witness stand; and the interrogated suspect, who must choose between telling police what they wish to hear and continuing with burdensome interrogation. Even though all three are slightly different, Westen and Mandell note, they "share a common value: All are designed to protect persons from having to choose between serving as the instruments of their own criminal condemnation or suffering alternative sanctions for refusing to do so." Westen and Mandell, 19 Am Crim L Rev at 521–22 (cited in note 72).

[123] *Bankes v Simmons*, 963 P2d 412, 412 (Kan 1998).

[124] See generally Alschuler (note 121).

that, because *Garrity* had not been decided at the time the question was put to Spevack, he could not be punished for his silence in the face of uncertainty about whether his testimony would later be suppressed.[125] Later Spevacks, however, would not need immunity. This might also account for *Maness*, based on the Court's recognition that there was no obvious means under Texas law for obtaining immunity for compelled testimony in a civil proceeding.[126] Indeed, because there is little reason for the Court to hear a case if the answer to the privilege question is clear, Clymer's requirement might well justify the early hearing of all trilemma cases to have come before the Court.

Although this argument seems to explain many privilege precedents, the Court did not press this view of the privilege. Justice Thomas's opinion explicitly denies the relevance of a witness's certainty of suppression, and no other Justice argues for it.[127] But despite its apparent rejection as an aspect of the privilege, might it survive as an aspect of due process? Might we, after *Chavez*, conclude that those subject to the cruel trilemma ought to receive damages for the situation in which they have been put? One potential advantage of such a rule is that it would enable a requirement of up-front immunity, albeit based on due process rather than the privilege.[128] Due process would then fill many of the gaps between

---

[125] See Clymer, 112 Yale L J at 470 n 99 (cited in note 87) (citing *The Supreme Court, 1967 Term,* 82 Harv L Rev 93, 206–10 (1968)).

[126] See *Maness,* 419 US at 462 n 9; cf. Ritchie, 61 Minn L Rev at 389 n 39 (cited in note 77).

[127] 123 S Ct at 2002.

[128] Avoiding such uncertainty on whichever basis would also serve the government's purposes–the government has an interest in having the issue resolved at the moment of compulsion rather than at the criminal trial. Westen and Mandell, 19 Am Crim L Rev at 524–26 (cited in note 72). As Westen and Mandell have noted, waiting until the criminal trial to raise the privilege question puts the government in a "decidedly worse position"— under existing doctrine, the prosecution is precluded from using what appear to be fruits from the compelled statement in the trial unless it can meet the "heavy burden" of proving that they had an independent source. Id at 531. If the issue is raised at the time of compulsion, by contrast, the government could choose to remove the threat and forgo the testimony altogether, freeing itself to introduce potentially related evidence without having to prove its source. As Westen and Mandell argue, this may in fact be the basis of rules about voluntariness—the government's interest may justify a requirement for bringing the privilege claim to the attention of the prosecution, which can then decide whether forcing testimony through immunity is worth it. Similarly, the government would surely like to know early whether a Court is going to find a particular context compulsive so that it can adjust the preparation of its case accordingly. It would no longer have to worry about giving immunity—might as well wait and see if it's necessary later, at the suppression hearing— but it still has an interest in knowing what's going to occur at that hearing. Given that not only improperly obtained confessions, but also their fruits, would be excluded, the govern-

the privilege as construed by *Chavez*, and privilege doctrine as previously understood.

Viewed through the lens of due process, however, protection against the cruel trilemma seems more nuanced. It is easy to understand why physical and some kinds of psychological pressure are cruel, and cruel to all who are compelled to encounter them. But what exactly is cruel—and unconstitutionally so—about having to make a difficult choice in the face of possible conviction for a crime of which you are accused? Considering such a choice unconstitutionally cruel to those who are actually *guilty* seems perverse. After all, it is the fact of guilt that is the cause of the problem. Would we think the position of a bank robber who must choose between killing a witness and getting caught is cruel? Of course not. If it were not for the privilege's presence in the Constitution, would we even imagine that putting the guilty in such a bind violated due process? But to the extent that it is not only the guilty, but also the *innocent*, who face such a choice, constitutional concerns seem more plausible.

Figuring out who the choice is likely to affect, and how, depends on a closer reading of context. As the cruel trilemma is conceived—as a choice between conviction for perjury, contempt, or the underlying crime, usually in the context of in-court testimony or other official investigation—it seems as though it ought to affect only the guilty. After all, the innocent cannot always tell the truth and avoid sanction. But it is not so simple. One worry that animates concerns about cruelty in this context is the possibility that the innocent will not be able to prevail due to the clever tactics of the questioner or the confusion of the courtroom.[129] Thus, even the innocent might fear imprisonment on the basis of the trilemma, and that fear itself may be cruel. The best claim for a due-process-based rule allowing silence even at congressional hearings or civil proceedings is the fear that innocent witnesses may experience not knowing whether their testimony will be suppressed at a later criminal trial, and not know-

---

ment would need to build firewalls around confessions that would later be suppressed—a not insignificant effort it would assuredly like to avoid wherever necessary. The government's interest in certainty thus resembles that of the individual witness, who would like to make her choice in possession of as many facts as possible about the risks involved.

[129] Bernard Meltzer, *The Privilege Against Self-Incrimination*, New Republic (Mar 14, 1955), at 18.

ing how their testimony might be construed if admitted at that trial. I suspect that this problem is, in fact, significant. The challenge of *Chavez* is for the Court to decide how, and in what contexts, due process ought to deal with this problem. Perhaps this problem alone would justify a due process rule requiring up-front determinations of immunity.

The calculus is somewhat different when dealing with the cruel dilemma. Because someone in Martinez's position must either admit guilt or continue with the interrogation, the solution of truthfully protesting innocence is unlikely to be successful. Only an admission of guilt, true or false, would have stopped the interrogation. And those who face custodial police interrogation are, if anything, less likely to be aware of the possibility of suppression than those facing the "cruel trilemma" in a civil proceeding or congressional investigation.[130] The fears of, and actual risks to, the innocent are thus considerably greater in these contexts. Focusing on due process after *Chavez* might, in fact, open up a new debate about police interrogation.

CONCLUSION

If anything privilege-related is unconstitutionally cruel in violation of due process after *Chavez*, it is what may have happened to Martinez. He may have felt he had to choose between admitting guilt and exposing himself to conviction for fighting with police officers and receiving life-sustaining medical treatment, in a circumstance where he could not have been expected to know that suppression of his statement would protect him. If any cruelty associated with the pressure to incriminate oneself violates due process, this would seem to be the best candidate. Thus, it is telling that Justices Thomas, Scalia, and Rehnquist voted to deny Martinez any due process relief. If, ultimately, the Court rules this way, the implications of *Chavez* are vast.

But the Court left open the possibility that substantive due process will fill some of the roles previously played by the privilege. Constitutional protection against government attempts to

---

[130] See Susan R. Klein, *No Time for Silence*, 81 Tex L Rev 1337, 1346 (a suspect under interrogation has no knowledge of whether or not his statements will later be used against him at trial).

secure incriminating information will surely, after *Chavez*, have to be rethought, and rethought in a way that requires consideration of the general demands of due process rather than the privilege. But it is at least an open question what the Court will do.

GEORGE RUTHERGLEN

THE IMPROBABLE HISTORY OF
SECTION 1981: CLIO STILL BEMUSED
AND CONFUSED

Everyone knows that the Equal Protection Clause applies only to state action. What is not generally appreciated is that Congress seemingly repealed this requirement in the Civil Rights Act of 1991.[1] That act amended section 1981, a general prohibition against racial discrimination, to make clear that it "protected against impairment by nongovernmental discrimination and impairment under color of State law."[2] Among the rights protected by section 1981 are those "to the full and equal benefit of all laws and proceedings for the security of persons and property as is enjoyed by white citizens."[3] This provision is the acknowledged, if often neglected, predecessor of the Equal Protection Clause. The "full and equal benefit" clause of section 1981, like the rest

George Rutherglen is John Barbee Minor Distinguished Professor of Law, University of Virginia.

AUTHOR'S NOTE: I would like to thank Vince Blasi, Gerhard Casper, Michael Collins, Barry Cushman, Earl Dudley, Risa Goluboff, John Harrison, John Jeffries, Pam Karlan, Mike Klarman, Daryl Levinson, Chuck McCurdy, Caleb Nelson, Dan Ortiz, Jim Ryan, Ted White, and Ann Woolhandler for comments on an earlier draft of this article. I am also grateful to the participants at a summer workshop at the University of Virginia for their comments and to Kate McCune, Karen Francis, Derek Bentsen, and Francesca Fornari for their work as research assistants. This article was made possible through financial support from the Earle K. Shawe Professorship in Employment Law and the Class of 1957 Summer Research Grant.

[1] Pub L No 102-166, 105 Stat 1071 (1991).

[2] 42 USC § 1981(c) (2000).

[3] 42 USC § 1981(a) (2000).

of section 1981, was initially enacted under the Thirteenth Amendment.[4] As the *Civil Rights Cases* first recognized,[5] this amendment, unlike the Fourteenth Amendment, applies to private action as well as to state action. It prohibits all forms of slavery, whether established by private contract or by public law. Despite this broad constitutional prohibition against slavery, and the intended role of section 1981 in enforcing it, doubts about the constitutionality of the statute were raised soon after its enactment. In response, Congress approved and secured ratification of the Fourteenth Amendment, partly to incorporate some provisions of section 1981 in the Constitution and partly to assure that its remaining provisions were themselves constitutional. Congress then reenacted section 1981 under the powers newly granted by the Fourteenth Amendment.[6]

The dual enactment of section 1981 has created uncertainty and ambiguity, not only over its origins, but over its scope: whether it reaches all forms of private racial discrimination, as the Thirteenth Amendment reaches all forms of involuntary servitude; or whether it is limited to discrimination in the form of state action, just like the Fourteenth Amendment. In the Civil Rights Act of 1991, Congress tried to resolve these questions by firmly resting its authority to enact the statute under the Thirteenth Amendment, and accordingly, amending the statute explicitly to cover all forms of private racial discrimination. But in the process, Congress seems to have inadvertently removed a cornerstone of constitutional law by making the "full and equal benefit" clause, the statutory predecessor to the Equal Protection Clause, applicable to private action. This consequence hardly seems likely, although the circuits are now split on this issue.[7] Resolving this conflict will require, if not a decision of the Supreme Court, at least an appreciation of section 1981 and its convoluted history.

---

[4] Civil Rights Act of 1866, 14 Stat 27. This act is quoted in relevant part in the Appendix.

[5] 109 US 3, 20, 23 (1883).

[6] Enforcement Act of 1870, 16 Stat 140. This act is quoted in relevant part in the Appendix.

[7] For cases requiring state action under the "full and equal benefit" clause of section 1981, see *Youngblood v Hy-Vee Food Stores, Inc.*, 266 F3d 851, 855 (3d Cir 2001); *Brown v Philip Morris, Inc.*, 250 F3d 789, 799 (3d Cir 2001) (dictum). For cases not requiring state action, see *Phillip v University of Rochester*, 316 F3d 291, 294–98 (2d Cir 2003); *Chapman v Higbee Co.*, 319 F3d 825, 829–33 (6th Cir 2003) (en banc).

The enactment and reenactment of section 1981 during Reconstruction formed part of an intricate series of legislative maneuvers that coincided with congressional consideration of the Reconstruction amendments, as well as other civil rights legislation. Congressional debates over all these different enactments confounded several separate issues, not the least of which were the origins and scope of section 1981. These purely statutory issues may not have been significant in and of themselves, but they figured prominently in the debates over the Fourteenth Amendment and, in particular, over the deep and enduring question of what constitutes equality under the Equal Protection Clause. Questions about the coverage of the clause—why it was limited to state action—were merged with questions about the kind of equality that it protected— whether it was civil, political, or social. Civil rights were the subject both of section 1981 and the Fourteenth Amendment,[8] while political rights were addressed by the Fifteenth Amendment. Social rights, as even Justice Harlan asserted in his famous dissent in *Plessy v Ferguson*,[9] were entirely outside the protection of the law. If the great virtue of equality as a legal concept is its variable content depending upon the baseline from which equality is judged, its corresponding defect is that it means different things to different people. During the debates over the Fourteenth Amendment, the meaning of section 1981 was inevitably drawn into the controversies—to this day not fully resolved—over the meaning of the Equal Protection Clause.

For this reason, section 1981 was soon completely overshadowed by the Fourteenth Amendment and fell into a long period of disuse in which it had virtually no independent significance. It received some attention in the first half of the twentieth century and then was spectacularly revived in one of the last decisions of the Warren Court, *Jones v Alfred H. Mayer Co.*[10] That decision interpreted a companion statute, section 1982, in a fashion that radically extended it beyond the Fourteenth Amendment, by discarding any limitation on the statute to state action. The Burger and Rehnquist

---

[8] More precisely, the Privileges or Immunities Clause and the Equal Protection Clause in section 1 of the Fourteenth Amendment. John Harrison, *Reconstructing the Privileges or Immunities Clause*, 101 Yale L J 1385, 1410–51 (1992).

[9] *Plessy v Ferguson*, 163 US 537, 559–61 (1896) (Harlan, J, dissenting).

[10] 392 US 409 (1968) (hereafter *Jones v Mayer*).

Courts endorsed this decision, but later expressed reservations about it, leading Congress eventually to amend section 1981 in the Civil Rights Act of 1991. In doing so, Congress ratified the broad interpretation that the statute had received in *Jones v Mayer*.

The core of section 1981 is now codified in subsection (a) of the statute, which reads as follows:

> All persons within the jurisdiction of the United States shall have the same right in every State and Territory to make and enforce contracts, to sue, be parties, give evidence, and to the full and equal benefit of all laws and proceedings for the security of persons and property as is enjoyed by white citizens, and shall be subject to like punishment, pains, penalties, taxes, licenses, and exactions of every kind, and to no other.[11]

The remaining subsections of the statute were added by the Civil Rights Act of 1991 and address issues raised by judicial decisions. Subsection (b) provides a gloss on the phrase "make and enforce contracts," applying it to all aspects of a contractual relationship from formation through termination. Subsection (c) makes clear that the statute extends from state action to private discrimination. This last is the most celebrated and hotly contested issue under section 1981, forming the core of the Supreme Court's decision in *Jones v Mayer*.

How the statute achieved its present form is a complicated story of decisiveness, neglect, and reconsideration. Much of this story has been told before, most insightfully by Gerhard Casper, who offered the first and most balanced account of section 1981 in his article, "Jones v Mayer: Clio Bemused and Confused Muse."[12] He avoided the extreme positions taken in that case, and in much subsequent commentary, that interpreted the statute as applying to all forms of private discrimination or to none. For the moment, that issue has been resolved by the addition of subsection (c) to the statute, a provision whose consequences nevertheless have yet to be fully appreciated. As it currently reads, section 1981 prohibits racial discrimination in all forms of contracting, no matter how minor or personal. The literal terms of the statute now cover all market transactions and much else besides, reaching most forms of public and private discrimination on the basis of race. Whether

---

[11] 42 USC § 1981(a) (2000). The full text of section 1981 appears in the Appendix.

[12] 1968 Supreme Court Review 89.

Congress has the power to go so far, however, remains an open question, reviving the need for the middle course first outlined by Professor Casper.

This article takes a similar approach, seeking to explain how an otherwise obscure statute evolved into a broad and almost limitless prohibition against racial discrimination. Despite its nearly universal coverage, section 1981 has been unjustly neglected as a source of protection for civil rights. Throughout its history, the statute has grown up in the shadow of the Fourteenth Amendment, which itself is a curious development since the statute was enacted under the Thirteenth Amendment. Nevertheless, in the first century of its existence the statute's scope was limited almost entirely to that of the Fourteenth Amendment. Part I recounts the history of enactment that supports this conclusion and Part II recounts the judicial decisions that accepted it, from Reconstruction to the eve of *Jones v Mayer*. This decision is the fulcrum on which the history of section 1981 turns, transforming questions about how the statute was limited by the Fourteenth Amendment into questions about how far it went beyond it. This decision, and the deliberately truncated view it took of the statute's structure and history, are analyzed in Part III. Part IV examines the implications of *Jones v Mayer*, the consequences of congressional ratification of this decision in the Civil Rights Act of 1991, and the constitutional questions raised by the current scope of the statute.

I. Reconstruction

Section 1981 originated as part of the Civil Rights Act of 1866, at the beginning of the great wave of civil rights legislation and constitutional amendments enacted during Reconstruction. The act's history has been intensively—not to say exhaustively—examined and contested for two distinct purposes: to determine the scope of the act itself; and, in addition, to interpret the Fourteenth Amendment, whose section 1 overlaps in large part with section 1 of the act. Partisans of different positions in these debates have emphasized different passages in the legislative history, perhaps confirming the adage that relying on legislative history is like "looking into a crowd and seeing your friends."[13] The significance

---

[13] Harold Leventhal, *Some Observations on the Use of Legislative History in the 1981 Supreme Court Term*, 68 Iowa L Rev 195, 214 (1983).

of this evidence, however, depends upon the relationship between the act and the amendment. For this reason, the history of the act subsequent to its passage deserves as much attention as the legislative debates that preceded its enactment.

Most of the controversy over the Civil Rights Act of 1866 has concerned the state action issue: whether the act prohibits only discrimination by state officials or whether it also prohibits discrimination by private individuals. This way of putting the question tends to exaggerate the contrast between these alternatives, forcing the statute into the mold of debates over state action that arose in the latter half of the twentieth century rather than the issues Congress confronted in the middle of the nineteenth century. As will subsequently appear, Congress embraced neither of these alternatives in passing the 1866 act, most likely because neither was clearly presented to it. It did not choose between all-or-nothing interpretations of the act: that it applied only to state action or that it applied to all forms of private discrimination. Instead, Congress adopted an interpretation that gradually emerged as a compromise between these two extremes: a prohibition against private violations of public rights. This compromise explains two features of the act's development: first, the significance of the provisions for enforcing the act, both as originally enacted and in subsequent legislation; and second, the overlap in coverage between the act and the Fourteenth Amendment. We begin with a brief summary of the act's provisions, aims, and legislative history.

A. ENACTMENT OF THE CIVIL RIGHTS ACT OF 1866

The debate over the Civil Rights Act of 1866 primarily concerned a single question, posed in a variety of different ways: whether the act exceeded the powers granted to Congress under the recently ratified Thirteenth Amendment.[14] Section 2 of that amendment gives Congress the power to enforce the prohibition against slavery and involuntary servitude found in section 1. Opponents of the 1866 Act raised doubts about the power of Congress to confer rights of equal citizenship upon the newly freed slaves, rather than just to remove the immediate consequences of slavery

---

[14] Charles Fairman, 6 *History of the Supreme Court of the United States: Reconstruction and Reunion, Part One* 1172–1204 (Macmillan, 1971).

itself. Congressional power to invalidate state laws denying equal citizenship was crucial to the effectiveness of the act because it was aimed at the "Black Codes," passed in several southern states immediately after ratification of the Thirteenth Amendment.[15] These codes imposed severe legal disabilities on the newly freed slaves and sought to return them to a legal status practically equivalent to slavery, but formally in conformity with the Thirteenth Amendment. The Freedmen's Bureau Bill, which was under consideration by Congress at the same time, conferred similar protection upon the newly freed slaves, but by its own terms, expired when the former Confederate states were restored to their full status in the Union.[16] As even opponents of the state action interpretation concede,[17] the 1866 Act was principally directed against the Black Codes. It follows that it was aimed primarily at state action.

This conclusion is borne out by an examination of section 1 of the act, which is quoted in full in the Appendix.[18] Section 1 confers three separate rights: first, it makes "all persons born in the United States and not subject to any foreign power, excluding Indians not taxed," citizens of the United States; second, it confers on these citizens a list of specific legal capacities, including the right "to make and enforce contracts"; and third, it grants these citizens the right "to full and equal benefit of all laws and proceedings for the security of persons and property" and to "be subject to like punishment, pains, and penalties, and to none other." Both the legal capacities and the right to equal protection are subject to the further baseline requirement of racial equality: that the rights conferred by section 1 be the "same . . . as is enjoyed by white citizens." Taken together, all of these provisions directly contradicted the denial of rights attempted by the Black Codes. The preemption clause of section 1 made this clear, making the rights conferred by the act effective despite "any law, statute, ordinance, regulation, or custom to the contrary notwithstanding."

---

[15] Fairman emphasizes this aim to the exclusion of all others, in terms that are perhaps more vociferous than persuasive. Id at 1226–27.

[16] Id at 1163–68, 1249–53; Casper, 1968 Supreme Court Review at 102–05 (cited in note 12).

[17] Robert J. Kaczorowski, *The Nationalization of Civil Rights: Constitutional Theory and Practice in a Racist Society 1866–1883* 56 (Garland, 1987) ("Nevertheless, the primary focus of Bill was on the states.").

[18] Act of April 9, 1866, § 1, 14 Stat 27.

The remainder of the act specified the remedies and procedures for enforcing the rights conferred by section 1, creating a criminal prohibition in section 2, now codified as section 242 of the Federal Criminal Code. This section makes it a crime for "any person who, under color of any law, statute, ordinance, regulation or custom" deprives anyone of the rights granted by section 1.[19] Much of the debate over the act focused on its enforcement provisions in section 2, which seemed to single out state officers for criminal prosecution simply because they acted in compliance with state law. This is not our concern today with the state action doctrine, but more nearly the opposite: where we are concerned about extending constitutional prohibitions to private discrimination, the members of the Thirty-Ninth Congress were concerned with creating federal remedies directed against state officers. As we shall see in the next section, Congress addressed the latter fear by incorporating parts of the act in the Fourteenth Amendment and then by reenacting the entire 1866 Act under the new powers granted by that amendment.

When the act was under consideration, however, its opponents did not speak in terms that sharply distinguished between coverage of private individuals and coverage of state officers, but blurred the two together. In their view, the act was objectionable both because it applied directly to private conduct and because it imposed liability on state officers.[20] Supporters of the act responded in kind, defending it in terms that can only be puzzling on a state action interpretation. Senator Trumbull, the author of the act, responded to the question whether section 2 of the act punished state officers with the following observation: "Not State officers especially, but everybody who violates the law. It is the intention to punish everybody who violates the law."[21] He evidently meant that private individuals could be prosecuted for acting according to a law or custom that authorized racial discrimination. The same point emerges again in debates over section 1983, enacted in the

---

[19] Id § 2. The full text of this section appears in the Appendix.

[20] Robert J. Kaczorowski, *The Enforcement Provisions of the Civil Rights Act of 1866: A Legislative History in Light of Runyon v McCrary*, 98 Yale L J 565, 570–71 (1989). For a summary of the debates on this issue, see Harrison, 101 Yale L J at 1402–04 (cited in note 8).

[21] Cong Globe, 39th Cong, 1st Sess 500 (1866). For references to other statements like this, see Kaczorowski, 98 Yale L J at 585–86 & n 98 (cited in note 20).

Civil Rights Act of 1871, which was intended to provide a civil remedy analogous to the criminal prohibition in section 2 of the 1866 Act.[22]

Senator Trumbull's statement offers a possible interpretation of the "under color of" clause in section 2 of the Civil Rights Act of 1866 only by extending the clause beyond the state action doctrine as we now understand it. The clause makes private discrimination authorized by state law equivalent to the action of state officials and it also reaches private action not authorized by any official state enactment but in conformity with established customs. Advocates of the state action interpretation have sought a way out of this dilemma by emphasizing that "custom" at the time meant customary law.[23] Thus Senator Trumbull's reference to private individuals violating the act would refer to private action that was authorized either by state legislation or customary law. This response, however, preserves the state action interpretation of the act only by creating problems for the state action doctrine under the Constitution. Private action authorized by customary law, on this interpretation, would constitute state action, seemingly expanding the scope of state action far beyond the holding of *Shelley v Kraemer*.[24] This interpretation raises a multitude of questions about the extent of state action involved in laws permitting private discrimination.

We cannot expect Congress to have clearly resolved such questions in the Civil Rights Act of 1866. Especially in the circumstances of Reconstruction, custom played a larger role as a source of law than it does today, having the authority of authors like Blackstone firmly behind it.[25] Alternative sources of law were also less prominent because government in general was much smaller, and in the unreconstructed states of the South, either hostile to the newly freed slaves or based on antebellum law and custom that,

---

[22] Eric H. Zagrans, *"Under Color of" What Law: A Reconstructed Model of Section 1983 Liability*, 71 Va L Rev 499, 540–89 (1985); Alfred Avins, *The Ku Klux Klan Act of 1871: Some Reflected Light on State Action and the Fourteenth Amendment*, 11 SLU L Rev 331 (1967).

[23] See, e.g., Fairman, 6 *History of the Supreme Court* at 1238–44 (cited in note 14).

[24] 334 US 1 (1948).

[25] Blackstone has an elaborate discussion of particular customs as a source of law. William Blackstone, 1 *Commentaries on the Laws of England* 74–79 (1776). In a separate article, I have examined the issues raised by custom as a source of law in greater detail. *Custom and Usage as Action Under Color of State Law: An Essay on the Forgotten Terms of Section 1983*, 89 Va L Rev 925 (2003).

in fact, treated them as slaves. In these circumstances, traditional forms of discrimination could have operated as law, without even raising the question whether they were law.[26] Against this background, we should not expect members of Congress to draw a sharp distinction between state action and private action. It is surprising, not that the distinction was blurred, but that it was drawn at all. When it was, as in Senator Trumbull's remarks quoted earlier, it was only to emphasize the possibility of private individuals acting under color of state law. Congress took up this suggested connection between private conduct and public discrimination in subsequent legislation.

B. THE FOURTEENTH AMENDMENT AND THE CIVIL RIGHTS ACT
   OF 1866

Congress began debate over the Fourteenth Amendment just as it concluded debate over the 1866 Act and addressed one issue crucial to understanding both sources of law: whether the act exceeded the powers of Congress under the Thirteenth Amendment. Objections to the act on this ground were met by statements in the debates over the Fourteenth Amendment that Congress would receive new enforcement powers that would remedy any defect in the act as originally passed. In particular, section 5 of the amendment would give Congress the power to enforce the rights to equal citizenship granted by section 1.[27] These rights were modeled on those granted by the act, and by entrenching them in the Constitution, Congress rendered them immune from attack as unconstitutional and, just as significantly, from repeal by subsequent Congresses.[28] After ratification of the Fourteenth Amendment, and while they still had a majority, the Republicans promptly reenacted the Civil Rights Act of 1866 in the Enforcement Act of 1870.[29]

---

[26] For citations to the debates over the Civil Rights Act of 1866 using custom in this sense, see Casper, 1968 Supreme Court Review at 116–19 (cited in note 12).

[27] See id at 1270–83 (recounting drafting of originally proposed section of the amendment and debates in the House of Representatives).

[28] See id at 1290–98 (recounting debates over Privileges or Immunities Clause in the Senate); Harrison, 101 Yale L J at 1408–10 (cited in note 8). Sections 2 and 3 of the amendment also sought to preserve Republican majorities in Congress by denying southern states full representation in the House if they failed to grant freedmen the right to vote and by denying eligibility for public office to former adherents of the Confederacy.

[29] Act of May 31, 1870, 16 Stat 140. The full text of the relevant provisions of this act appears in the Appendix.

A comparison of the act and the amendment confirms the extent to which their provisions overlap. As recounted earlier, section 1 of the act granted three separate rights: to equal citizenship, to a variety of specific legal capacities, and to equal treatment under law. These rights are strikingly similar to those conferred by section 1 of the amendment. The first sentence of the amendment confers state and national citizenship on "[a]ll persons born or naturalized in the United States and subject to the jurisdiction thereof." The second sentence then denies the states any power to abridge "the privileges or immunities of citizens of the United States" which, as we shall see, can be taken as a compendious way of referring to the specific capacities listed in the act. The Equal Protection Clause then follows at the end of this sentence. Section 1 of the amendment therefore begins and ends in the same place as section 1 of the act: by conferring citizenship on all persons within the jurisdiction of the United States and by guaranteeing the equal protection of the laws.

The meaning of the Privileges or Immunities Clause admittedly has remained obscure, but recent scholarship reveals that it was intended to cover at least the capacities listed in the Civil Rights Act of 1866.[30] The more general, if more cryptic, language of "privileges or immunities" would have appeared more suitable for a constitutional provision, partly because it used the terminology of privileges and immunities already used in Article IV to identify the incidents of state citizenship.[31] The *Slaughter-House Cases*[32] later exploited the ambiguity in this language to give the Privileges or Immunities Clause a narrow interpretation, limiting it to rights explicitly identified in the Constitution, such as the right to petition the federal government, and to a narrow range of implied rights, such as those with respect to navigable waterways. Yet the common goals and structure of section 1 of the Fourteenth Amendment and section 1 of the Civil Rights Act of 1866 remain undeniable.

The most that can be said for the decision in the *Slaughter-House Cases* is that it presupposes (but then exaggerates) the genuine differences between section 1 of the amendment and section 1 of the

---

[30] Harrison, 101 Yale L J at 1410–33 (cited in note 8).

[31] US Const, Art IV, § 2.

[32] *Slaughter-House Cases*, 83 US 36, 73–80 (1873).

act. An obvious difference, although one that has not figured in interpretation of the act, is the absence of any statutory provision analogous to the Due Process Clause. A further disparity, however, has been crucial to the development of the act: the absence of any explicit reference to state law in section 1. The rights granted by that section are not, like those granted by the amendment, explicitly limited by the state action doctrine. "No State" and "nor shall any State" are the phrases that preface and limit the duties imposed by the Privileges or Immunities and Equal Protection Clauses. But no such language appears in the corresponding clauses in the act.

The preemption clause in section 1 of the act might be thought to incorporate a state action requirement through its reference to "any law, statute, ordinance, regulation, or custom, to the contrary notwithstanding." This clause, however, does not import a state action requirement. It refers, first of all, to "any law," including federal law, indicating that its purpose was to override all sources of law inconsistent with the act.[33] This purpose could be accomplished independently of the act's coverage and, arguably, became more important if the act covered private discrimination, requiring a wider range of preemption of inconsistent laws. The significance of the preemption clause, however, has been diminished by its subsequent deletion from codified versions of the act,[34] probably on the ground that its function was already served by the Supremacy Clause of the Constitution.[35]

Section 2 of the act, as noted earlier, contains a similar clause, making it a crime for "any person who, under color of any law, statute, ordinance, regulation or custom" violates the rights granted by section 1 of the act. According to advocates of the state action interpretation, this phrase limits the coverage of the entire act. It makes the rights granted by that section enforceable only against individuals acting under the authority of those sources of law. Moreover, a nearly identical "under color of clause" appears in section 1983,[36] which itself was modeled on section 2 of the act

---

[33] Caleb Nelson, *Preemption*, 86 Va L Rev 225, 238 (2000).

[34] The preemption clause was deleted when the act was codified in sections 1977 and 1978 of the Revised Statutes of 1874. This deletion was made without any explanation by the revisers. Insofar as the clause operated against preexisting federal law, it was made unnecessary by the revision, whose sole purpose was to render all of the revised provisions consistent.

[35] US Const, Art VI.

[36] 42 USC § 1983 (2000).

in a provision enacted in the Civil Rights Act of 1871.[37] In a long line of cases, section 1983 has been limited to state action.[38] Although both section 2 and section 1983 cover "any person," and so seemingly apply to actions by private individuals, the real limitation on both statutes, according to advocates of the state action interpretation, is from the sources of law under which individuals act. On their view, the troublesome phrase, "any person," must be confined to the limiting context of persons acting under color of state law.

These arguments, however, for all their force, lose sight of the central fact about the enactment of section 1981: that it was initially enacted under the Thirteenth Amendment, which has always been understood to apply to private action. This understanding was usually expressed as the "primary and direct" operation of the amendment, and of the legislation enforcing it, on private individuals.[39] State action was a limit on congressional power under the Fourteenth Amendment, but not the Thirteenth Amendment. In the debates over both amendments, and over the 1866 Act, Congress was concerned to limit federal power, but it did so in different ways. The Thirteenth Amendment and the 1866 Act were aimed at "the obliteration and prevention of slavery with all its badges and incidents."[40] The Fourteenth Amendment was aimed at state action. Important as this latter limitation is, it cannot simply be read back into a statute which Congress had already passed under another source of constitutional authority.

A state action interpretation of the statute is anachronistic for a deeper reason as well. The Civil Rights Act of 1866 may have been passed only a few months before congressional approval of the Fourteenth Amendment,[41] but it was enacted well before the state

---

[37] Act of April 20, 1871, § 1, 17 Stat 13. For further discussion of this act, see Part I.C.

[38] *Adickes v Kress & Co.*, 398 US 144, 162–69 (1970).

[39] *Civil Rights Cases*, 109 US 3, 20 (1883). The quoted statement was dictum in the *Civil Rights Cases*, but it became a holding in *Clyatt v United States*, 197 US 207, 216–18 (1905). For a history of enforcement of the Thirteenth Amendment against private forms of peonage, see Risa Goluboff, *The Thirteenth Amendment and the Lost Origins of Civil Rights*, 50 Duke L J 1609 (2001).

[40] *Civil Rights Cases*, 109 US at 20–21.

[41] The act itself was passed just as the Joint Committee on Reconstruction began its deliberations over how to frame the amendment and its requirement of state action. See Fairman, 6 *History of the Supreme Court* at 1260–61, 1270–74 (cited in note 14) (giving chronology of drafting and debates over the Fourteenth Amendment).

action doctrine crystallized as a clear limit on federal power in subsequent judicial decisions. Some might question whether it has ever
been clarified at all. In its most abstract form, the doctrine tends
to obscure as much as it illuminates. It focuses debate on the extent
of state involvement in disputed activity—which usually can be
found in some form—rather than on the ultimate question whether
the state's activity conforms to the Constitution. Even private violations of individual rights, when they are not prohibited by state law,
almost always have been authorized, endorsed, or otherwise permitted by some form of state action. The ultimate question is not
whether such action is present, but whether it is consistent with the
Constitution. The assessment of the state action doctrine offered
by Professor Charles Black some time ago still holds true today:
"the truth is that eight decades of metaphysical writing around the
'state action' doctrine have made it the paragon of unclarity."[42]

The doctrine certainly was no clearer to those who drafted and
debated the Fourteenth Amendment. The historical record reveals
no single, accepted meaning for the clauses subject to the state
action requirement—the Privileges or Immunities Clause, the Due
Process Clause, and the Equal Protection Clauses.[43] The inherently contested meaning of these clauses, both then and now, suggests that Congress had no single overriding purpose in mind in
framing and approving them. As with other Reconstruction
amendments and legislation, Congress had multiple independent
objectives, which were to some degree incompatible. The two
most prominent that emerge from the debates are obviously at
odds with one another: achieving a degree of equality for the newly
freed slaves, yet preserving a limited form of Federal Government.

In fact, in the debates over the Civil Rights Act of 1866, doubts
about its constitutionality were framed in terms that blurred the
distinction between private action and state action. Supporters of
the act repeatedly expressed concern over pervasive discrimination
in the South, both public and private.[44] These passages do not establish that the act was aimed at all forms of private discrimination,

---

[42] Charles L. Black, Jr., *Foreword: "State Action," Equal Protection, and California's Proposition 14*, 81 Harv L Rev 69, 89 (1967).

[43] William E. Nelson, *The Fourteenth Amendment: From Political Principle to Judicial Doctrine* 60–61 (Harvard, 1988).

[44] Kaczorowski, *The Nationalization of Civil Rights* at 53–57 (cited in note 17).

just as the relationship between the act and the Fourteenth Amendment does not establish that it was aimed only at state action. Both the problems that Congress faced and its objectives in addressing them were far too ambiguous to support either of these extreme positions. Congress was not confronted with a situation in the South in which state officials took one position toward the newly freed slaves and private individuals took another. It was confronted with concerted resistance to Reconstruction from both sources, including legislation such as the Black Codes, that formally complied with federal law but that permitted continued denial of federal rights.

C. SUBSEQUENT CIVIL RIGHTS ACTS

In the Enforcement Act of 1870,[45] passed after ratification of both the Fourteenth and the Fifteenth Amendments, Congress reenacted the Civil Rights Act of 1866. Actually, it did so in two different forms: first, by passing an abbreviated version of section 1 of the earlier act (along with an abbreviated version of the criminal prohibition in section 2); and second, by reenacting the entire act by reference.[46] The point of reenacting the 1866 Act was to take advantage of the additional powers conferred by section 5 of the Fourteenth Amendment. The point of doing so twice, however, has been lost to history, as it may have been to some of the senators who voted for it. At least one protested that he voted for the legislation without any awareness that it contained any of the reenacting provisions.[47]

The focus of the 1870 Act was on protection of the right to vote under the newly ratified Fifteenth Amendment. Although the literal terms of the amendment refer only to denial or abridgement of the right to vote "by the United States or by any State," it was initially interpreted to support congressional power to prohibit private interference with the right to vote.[48] The 1870 Act con-

---

[45] Act of May 31, 1870, 16 Stat 140. This statute is also sometimes called the Voting Rights Act of 1870. *Runyon v McCrary*, 427 US 160, 195 (1976) (White, J, dissenting).

[46] Act of May 31, 1870, §§ 16–18, 16 Stat 144. The full text of these sections of the act appears in the Appendix.

[47] Casper, 1968 Supreme Court Review at 123 n 164 (cited in note 12).

[48] For a discussion of these decisions, see Michael Les Benedict, *Preserving Federalism: Reconstruction and the Waite Court*, 1978 Supreme Court Review 39, 71–75; Michael G. Collins, *Justice Bradley's Civil Rights Odyssey Revisited*, 76 Tulane L Rev 1979 (1996).

tained such prohibitions, against private attempts to obstruct the right to vote,[49] but it also contained similar prohibitions against the private denial of other federal rights. In addition to reenacting section 2 of the 1866 Act, the 1870 Act prohibited private conspiracies to deny federal rights to equal treatment, including federal statutory rights.[50]

Both of these criminal prohibitions were later augmented by the Civil Rights Act of 1871, also known as the Ku Klux Klan Act. As this name implies, this act was addressed to widespread violence, both public and private, against the freedmen and their supporters in the South. This act created civil remedies corresponding to section 2 of the 1866 Act, in what is now codified as section 1983, and to the conspiracy provisions of the 1870 Act, in what is now codified as section 1985(3).[51] The first of these provisions, as noted earlier,[52] created a cause of action for deprivation of federal rights "under color of any statute, ordinance, regulation, custom, or usage, of any State" and the second created a cause of action for conspiracies to deny federal rights to equal treatment.

The interrelationship among all these provisions is a complicated question, but it illustrates two points: first, that Congress recognized the need for enhanced remedies for the denial of federal rights; and second, that in creating these remedies, Congress

---

[49] §§ 4, 5, 19, 20, 16 Stat 141, 144. Some of these provisions were held unconstitutional because they were not limited to discrimination on the basis of race, while others were upheld because they were limited to federal elections. It was not until several decades after Reconstruction had ended that any of these provisions was struck down because it applied to private action. See Benedict, 1978 Supreme Court Review at 71–75, 78 (cited in note 48).

[50] Act of May 31, 1870, § 6, 16 Stat 14. This provision was first codified as section 5508 of the Revised Statutes of 1874 and eventually became 18 USC § 241 (2000). It has had a checkered history in the courts. In dictum, it was applied to private action infringing the right to vote in *United States v Cruikshank*, 92 US 542, 555–56 (1875), but it was later narrowly interpreted in *Hodges v United States*, 203 US 1, 16–20 (1906). An intervening decision, *United States v Harris*, 106 US 629, 632, 635–44 (1883), had held unconstitutional another criminal prohibition derived from section 2 of the Civil Rights Act of 1871, but *Hodges* itself was later overruled to the extent it was inconsistent with the constitutional holding in *Jones v Mayer*, 392 US at 441–43 n 78. Modern decisions have found no constitutional defect in applying section 241 to private action. See *United States v Guest*, 383 US 745, 754 (1965).

[51] 42 USC §§ 1983, 1985(3) (2000), originally enacted in the act of April 20, 1871, §§ 1, 2, 17 Stat 13. This act is also known as the Ku Klux Act or the Ku Klux Klan Act, *Monroe v Pape*, 365 US 167, 171 (1961). I have discussed these provisions more fully in Rutherglen, 89 Va L Rev 925 (cited in note 25).

[52] See notes 36–37 and accompanying text.

did not distinguish between purely private action and state action, at least not in the way that we do now. The need for additional enforcement provisions was plain enough, based on the increasing resistance to Reconstruction from state officials in the South and from terrorist organizations like the Ku Klux Klan.[53] The prevalence of both forms of resistance led Congress to enact remedies that applied to private as well as public actions that denied civil rights. This position is clearest in the remedies for conspiracies to deny federal rights, in the criminal prohibition enacted in the 1870 Act and in the civil remedy in section 1985(3). It also reappears in the enactment of section 1983 to create a civil action analogous to section 2 of the 1866 Act.[54]

In the century since these statutes were first enacted, their interpretation has evolved along sharply different lines. The received view today is that section 1981 applies to private action, while section 1983 applies only to state action. Section 1985(3) remains something of a hybrid: its literal terms apply to private action, but the underlying rights that it protects usually involve state action.[55] This understanding of the statutes establishes a parallel between the coverage of the main statutes, section 1981 and section 1983, and the coverage of the corresponding constitutional provisions under which each was enacted: the Thirteenth Amendment for section 1981, and the Fourteenth Amendment for section 1983. This attractive symmetry between statutes and sources of congressional authority in the Constitution nevertheless quickly breaks down.

In all of the enforcement provisions enacted during Reconstruction, Congress addressed the general problem of widespread resistance in the South. Finely parsing the remedies that Congress enacted to address discrete forms of resistance, using powers conferred on it by a single amendment, does not reflect the scale or the nature of the problem that Congress confronted. Thus, as noted earlier, section 1981 was originally enacted under the Thir-

---

[53] See Eric Foner, *Reconstruction: America's Unfinished Revolution, 1863–67* 412–59 (Perennial Library, 1988) (discussing the background and enactment of these acts).

[54] Fairman, 6 *History of the Supreme Court Part Two* at 151–52 (cited in note 14).

[55] *Griffin v Breckenridge*, 403 US 88, 95–101 (1971). The criminal prohibitions in section 241 and section 242 are treated like their civil analogues, respectively, in section 1985(3) and section 1983. *United States v Guest*, 383 US 745, 782 (1966) (§ 241); *Screws v United States*, 325 US 91 (1945) (§ 242); *Monroe v Pape*, 365 US 167 (1961) (§ 1983).

teenth Amendment but was reenacted under the Fourteenth Amendment. Likewise, section 1983 was enacted to augment remedies already provided by the Civil Rights Act of 1866. It might be a useful shorthand to say that section 1983 was passed under the power of Congress to enforce the Fourteenth Amendment, but as the preamble to the act itself says, it was enacted "for other Purposes" as well.[56] Among those was providing a remedy in section 1983 for denial of rights secured "by the Constitution," not just by the Fourteenth Amendment.

Section 1981 now applies to all forms of private discrimination and section 1983 applies to none, when both sections were addressed to the problem of both public and private discrimination on the basis of race. The compartmentalized treatment of these statutes makes each one of them easier to administer, dispensing with the need in most cases to inquire into what constitutes a "custom" or "usage" of discrimination. As discussed in Part III, this separate treatment of different statutes can be justified for that reason, but it does not reflect their common and ambiguous origins. These origins indicate that these statutes covered some forms of private discrimination, but not all. It was the opponents, not the supporters of the civil rights laws, who protested that these laws would amount to comprehensive federal regulation of private conduct.[57] Limiting federal regulation to private violations of public rights avoided this problem. It limited federal law to prohibiting only private action that amounted to a custom of continued discrimination or that directly interfered with the exercise of federal rights. This is not to say that Congress had a precise idea of exactly which forms of private action were prohibited. No one did, as subsequent decisions about the scope and validity of these new federal laws revealed.[58]

Despite such uncertainties, when Congress did enact legislation generally prohibiting private discrimination, it plainly presupposed that the legislation that it had already passed was more limited in scope. In the Civil Rights Act of 1875,[59] Congress prohibited private discrimination in public accommodations, such as inns and

---

[56] Act of April 20, 1871, 17 Stat 13.

[57] See Harrison, 101 Yale L J at 1403–04 (cited in note 8); Zagrans, 71 Va L Rev at 544–47 (cited in note 22).

[58] See note 50 (*Cruikshank, Hodges, Harris*).

[59] 18 Stat 335 (1875).

railroads. Rights to participate in public life, not necessarily to be treated as an equal by every other private citizen, were at the limit of what Congress thought to be within its powers in 1875. This later legislation would have been entirely unnecessary if earlier legislation already reached all forms of private discrimination in contracting. Under the 1866 Act, only the more limited rights, simply to participate in public economic life, were protected: the rights to be a person generally recognized as capable of entering into contracts and holding property. These rights could not be violated by isolated acts of discrimination, but only by concerted refusals to deal with an entire class of individuals. The reference to "custom" in the 1866 Act captures the collective nature of the denial of rights that could be actionable, even if it does not precisely delineate its scope.

The most plausible account of the problems that Congress faced during Reconstruction provides the most compelling interpretation of what it did: it sought to prevent the most widespread forms of public and private discrimination without, however, transforming federal power into a form of general government that threatened to take over all of state law. The coexistence of these opposed concerns can be found throughout the intricate history of Reconstruction. As Alexander Bickel was the first to emphasize, the entire period revealed a marked disparity between the visionary ends of racial equality that Congress avowed, often only after heated debate, and the immediate effects of the legislation and constitutional amendments that it approved.[60] This disparity has bedeviled commentators who, since Bickel, have tried to reconcile *Brown v Board of Education*[61] with the pervasive acceptance of segregated schools, in the North as well as in the South, when the Fourteenth Amendment was adopted. Usually they have given priority to the abstract goals of racial equality avowed by Republican legislators, minimizing the exigencies of Reconstruction politics that led many of the same Republicans to tolerate a variety of specific forms of discrimination.

The historical evidence may—or may not—support this preference for abstract principles over concrete controversies, but it does

---

[60] Alexander M. Bickel, *The Original Understanding and the Segregation Decision*, 69 Harv L Rev 1, 61–65 (1955).

[61] 347 US 483 (1954).

indicate that Congress was aware of the disparity between its stated goals and its chosen means. Certainly, Congress recognized the inadequacy of the means that it initially chose to end discrimination, even if those means were limited only to the South. From the original enactment of the Civil Rights Act of 1866 through the passage of the Civil Rights Act of 1875, Congress sought in each step that it took to remedy the inadequacies of what it had done before. Freeing the slaves in the Thirteenth Amendment was not enough, nor guaranteeing the capacities of citizenship in the Civil Rights Act of 1866, nor constitutionalizing the equal protection of the laws in the Fourteenth Amendment, nor protecting the right to vote in the Fifteenth Amendment, nor enforcing all of these rights in the Enforcement Act of 1870 and the Civil Rights Act of 1871. These enactments, and many others during Reconstruction, were revolutionary for their times, but they did not produce racial equality. With the end of Reconstruction, this failure became all too apparent, as the Civil Rights Act of 1866 fell into a long period of neglect, along with all the other civil rights legislation passed during this period.

II. Enforcement, Interpretation, and Neglect

Despite the controversy that attended the enactment and reenactment of the Civil Rights Act of 1866, its subsequent fate as an independent source of law was anticlimactic. Even during Reconstruction, the enforcement of the act was closely tied to the Fourteenth Amendment, raising issues that were addressed almost entirely in constitutional terms. And after Reconstruction, as the Fourteenth Amendment lost significance as a prohibition against racial discrimination, so also did the act. By the time the act was suddenly revived in *Jones v Mayer*, it was treated simply as an addendum to claims based directly on the Constitution. The triumph of the state action interpretation of the act was so complete that it was taken for granted. In the era of Jim Crow, the effectiveness of the act almost exactly tracked that of the Fourteenth Amendment, waning with it as segregation increased and then gradually regaining force in the decisions leading up to *Brown v Board of Education*.

A. RECONSTRUCTION DECISIONS

Even with the broadest possible interpretation, the Civil Rights Act of 1866 would not have provided an effective remedy for racial discrimination if it only created a private right of action. The newly freed slaves were in no position to go to court to assert their rights, and their white supporters, assuming they could assert claims on their behalf, would have had to bring them in state courts almost uniformly hostile to Reconstruction. Both the military and the Freedmen's Bureau provided the federal officials needed to ensure that the act was obeyed. Hence the initial enforcement of the act was by military commissions and by courts established in the Freedman's Bureau, and later by government actions, both civil and criminal, in the federal courts.[62] Government prosecution in a sympathetic federal forum was crucial to the success of the act.

For this reason, the first decisions under the act to reach the Supreme Court concerned its jurisdictional provisions, and in particular, those authorizing removal of cases from state court to federal court. One such case was *Blyew v United States*,[63] involving a prosecution of a white man for murdering an African-American woman. The state courts were alleged to be inadequate to try this case because they did not admit the testimony of African-American witnesses, in violation of both the Fourteenth Amendment and the 1866 Act. Under section 3 of the act, the federal courts had jurisdiction over "all causes, civil and criminal affecting persons who are denied" rights under the act, including cases removed from state court on this ground. The Supreme Court narrowly interpreted the term "affecting" to apply only to the parties to the case, excluding both the victim of the crime and the witnesses to it as persons who could support federal jurisdiction. The reasoning of the decision is at best dubious—because the murder victim's interests were effectively aligned with those of the prosecution—but its general implications for protecting the safety of the freedmen and their supporters were truly alarming. The whole point of section 3 was to vindicate the rights of those who could not obtain

---

[62] Kaczorowski, *The Nationalization of Civil Rights* at 125–55 (cited in note 17); Foner, *Reconstruction* at 148–50 (cited in note 53).

[63] 80 US 581 (1871).

redress in the state courts, including victims of private, racially motivated violence who sought equal enforcement of the criminal law on their behalf.

This narrow and formalistic interpretation of the statute was confirmed in a series of cases decided together after Reconstruction had ended. The best known of these is *Strauder v West Virginia*,[64] whose holding under the Equal Protection Clause has overshadowed its interpretation of the 1866 Act. This case concerned a state statute that explicitly disqualified African Americans from serving on juries. The defendant, also an African American, sought to remove the case from state court on this ground, and the Court both upheld removal and then found the state statute unconstitutional. These holdings reveal how interpretation of the act followed interpretation of the Constitution—allowing constitutional rights to be vindicated through statutory procedures—but they did not result in a broad interpretation of the act itself. On the contrary, in the companion case of *Virginia v Rives*,[65] the Court held that removal was not allowed when blacks were excluded from the jury under a facially neutral state law discriminatorily applied by state officials.[66] As this case illustrates, questions of jurisdiction and removal effectively determined the extent to which federal law displaced the ordinary operation of the state courts in civil rights cases. The focus of these decisions on issues of jurisdiction in criminal cases—as opposed to substantive law in civil cases—reveals how far the concerns of that period are from those of recent years.[67] They soon crystallized in the limits on federal power established by the *Civil Rights Cases*.[68]

---

[64] 100 US 303 (1879).

[65] Id at 313 (1879).

[66] To further complicate the historical record, a third case decided at the same time, *Ex parte Virginia*, 100 US 339 (1879), held that a state judge who excluded blacks from the jury could be prosecuted under the Civil Rights Act of 1875, which contained a provision, unlike the Civil Rights Act of 1866, specifically prohibiting discrimination in the selection of juries. Taken together, all three of these cases made the remedy under federal law depend upon the precise way in which state or federal law was framed.

[67] The cases decided by the Supreme Court during and immediately after Reconstruction were representative of the criminal cases decided by the lower federal courts under the Reconstruction civil rights acts. Fairman, 6 *History of the Supreme Court Part Two* at 188–92, 199–220 (cited in note 14).

[68] 109 US 3 (1883).

B. THE CIVIL RIGHTS CASES

The *Civil Rights Cases* did not directly address the constitutionality of the 1866 Act, but drastically narrowed its scope nevertheless. These cases held unconstitutional the provisions in the Civil Rights Act of 1875 prohibiting racial discrimination in public accommodations, defined as "inns, public conveyances on land or water, theaters, and other places of public amusement."[69] Such facilities were public only in the sense that they were open to the general public, not that they were operated by the state. Because they did not involve any state action, the Supreme Court held that they were beyond the power of Congress under section 5 of the Fourteenth Amendment. In reaching this conclusion, the Court noted that the 1866 Act was similarly restricted to state action, specifically in its provisions for criminal enforcement in section 2.[70] This statement, although dictum in the *Civil Rights Cases*, was confirmed a decade later by a decision holding that the jurisdictional provisions of the 1866 Act did not apply to contracts of common carriage, similar to those for public accommodations covered by the 1875 Act.[71]

In the *Civil Rights Cases*, the Court also held that the 1875 Act exceeded the power of Congress under the Thirteenth Amendment, and it is this holding that bears most directly on the interpretation of the 1866 Act. The Court reasoned that private discrimination did not constitute a "badge of slavery" that could be remedied by the exercise of congressional power under section 2

---

[69] Civil Rights Act of 1875, § 1, 18 Stat 335 (1875). Sections 2 and 3 of the act provided for the enforcement of section 1 and were held unconstitutional along with that section. Section 4 independently prohibited racial discrimination in the selection of jurors and had already been held to be constitutional in *Ex parte Virginia*, 100 US 339 (1880). See *Civil Rights Cases*, 109 US at 15 (acknowledging this point).

[70] Id at 16–17. The Court's citations actually are to the version of the act codified in the Revised Statutes of 1874, discussed more fully in the next section of this article.

In the earlier decision in *Hall v DeCuir*, 95 US 485 (1877), Justice Clifford took an even narrower view of the act, at least as it applied to action under color of federal law. Speaking only for himself, he found the act ineffective to alter the terms of navigation licenses granted under previously enacted federal statutes. Id at 508–09 (Clifford, J, concurring in the judgment). The licenses therefore preempted state law that *required* integration on river boats in interstate commerce. Id at 490–91; id at 498–99 (Clifford, J, concurring in the judgment). What is surprising about his statement is that it concerned racial integration in exactly the opposite situation from that presented in *Plessy v Ferguson*, 163 US 537 (1896), in which state law required segregation.

[71] *Bowman v Chicago & Northwestern Ry.*, 115 US 611, 615–16 (1885).

of the Thirteenth Amendment.[72] This limitation on congressional power applied equally to all of the civil rights acts, seemingly preventing Congress from enacting any general prohibition against private discrimination. The narrow interpretation of the 1866 Act offered as dictum in one part of the Court's opinion was virtually compelled by its holding in another. Although the Court recognized that the Thirteenth Amendment reached private action beyond the scope of the Fourteenth Amendment,[73] the Court was unwilling to recognize either that Congress did—or even that it could—prohibit all forms of private discrimination.

Surprisingly, Justice Harlan, the sole dissenter in the *Civil Rights Cases*, agreed with the majority on this proposition. Although he would have held that Congress had the power to prohibit private discrimination under both the Thirteenth and the Fourteenth Amendments, he recognized that these amendments stopped short of protecting "social rights" to racial equality.[74] Under section 5 of the Fourteenth Amendment, he reasoned that Congress had the power to regulate public accommodations because state action was involved in conferring authority on the owners of these facilities to serve the general public.[75] Under section 2 of the Thirteenth Amendment, his reasoning is more equivocal, finding that Congress had the power "at least, of protecting the liberated race against discrimination, in respect of legal rights belonging to freemen, where such discrimination is based on race."[76] He seemingly left open the question whether Congress had any greater power. Even so, he limited the 1866 Act to alleviating the "burdens and disabilities which constitute badges of slavery and servitude."[77] Consistent with this reasoning, he would have broadly upheld prohibitions against private discrimination that denied the legal rights of full citizenship,[78] but he stopped well short of upholding a general prohibition against private discrimination.

The goal of equal citizenship was not what divided the Supreme

---

[72] 109 US at 23–25.

[73] Id at 20.

[74] Id at 59–60 (Harlan, J, dissenting).

[75] Id at 58–59.

[76] Id at 37.

[77] Id at 35.

[78] Id at 54 (Harlan, J, dissenting).

Court, but the means necessary to achieve it. As Justice Harlan said in his dissent, "The one underlying purpose of congressional legislation has been to enable the black race to take the rank of mere citizens."[79] The majority did not disagree, but asserted that this goal had been largely achieved.[80] Justice Harlan was more pessimistic both about achieving this goal and about the means necessary to do so. In his view, legislation to safeguard the basic rights of citizenship necessarily included prohibitions against denial of those rights by private individuals. For him, a state action interpretation of the act was not problematic because he favored a broad interpretation of the state action doctrine under the Fourteenth Amendment. In *Jones v Mayer*, as will appear in Part III, a private interpretation of the act was acceptable for exactly the opposite reason: because a holding that state action reached private discrimination would have had unacceptably broad consequences for the Fourteenth Amendment. That decision accordingly compartmentalized the interpretation of the act so that it had no state action requirement at all.

C. REDUNDANCY AND NEGLECT

The *Civil Rights Cases* themselves were a harbinger of how narrow the constitutional and statutory decisions would be. In fact, until the middle of the twentieth century, the Civil Rights Act of 1866 appeared on the docket of the Supreme Court entirely in a supporting role. As early as the *Slaughter-House Cases*,[81] the Supreme Court recognized that the Fourteenth Amendment was aimed at eliminating the Black Codes, the same immediate aim as the Civil Rights Act of 1866.[82] Subsequent decisions simply took the overlap between the act and the amendment for granted. Thus, the celebrated case of *Yick Wo v Hopkins*,[83] which protected aliens from covert racial discrimination, cited the act as having coverage

---

[79] Id at 61.

[80] Id at 25.

[81] 83 US 36 (1873).

[82] Id at 70. The same reasoning was used to limit the scope of civil rights legislation. *Hodges v United States*, 203 US 1, 4 (1906) (criminal enforcement provisions in civil rights acts do not apply to crimes against nonblacks); *Kentucky v Powers*, 201 US 1, 35 (1906) (no removal under civil rights laws available to white defendant); *Snowden v Hughes*, 321 US 1, 5 n 1 (1944) (section 1981 applies only to claims of racial discrimination).

[83] 118 US 356, 369 (1886).

coextensive with the amendment. And conversely, where the Fourteenth Amendment did not prohibit discrimination, neither did the act. Thus in *Pace v Alabama*,[84] the Court upheld a state antimiscegenation law against arguments that it violated both the amendment and the act. Cases over this entire period accepted the presumed equivalence of constitutional and statutory law in three different kinds of cases: those concerned with removal, already discussed in a previous section;[85] those involving claims by aliens, like *Yick Wo v Hopkins*;[86] and those involving rights to property, culminating in a companion case to *Shelley v Kraemer*.[87] This last line of cases led the way to *Jones v Mayer*.

These cases did not, strictly speaking, concern section 1981, but the companion statute, section 1982, which also originated in the Civil Rights Act of 1866. Section 1982 codifies the provisions in section 1 of the Act concerned with property rights. The first decision of the Supreme Court to interpret these provisions was *Buchanan v Warley*,[88] which held unconstitutional an ordinance preventing blacks from living on any block with a majority of whites. The ordinance also imposed a corresponding disability upon whites, but was struck down because it interfered with the property rights of blacks and whites alike. The Court rested its holding on the Fourteenth Amendment, finding a deprivation of property without due process,[89] but in reaching this conclusion, the Court relied on the right to purchase property under the 1866 Act.[90] The Court expressed the same equivalence, but with the opposite effect, in *Corrigan v Buckley*,[91] holding that neither the act nor the amendment prohibited private discrimination through a racially restrictive

---

[84] 106 US 583, 585 (1883). This decision was overruled in the Warren Court by *Loving v Virginia*, 388 US 1, 11–12 (1967).

[85] See Part II.B.

[86] For other decisions concerned with aliens, see *Takahashi v Fish & Game Comm'n*, 334 US 410, 419 (1948) (state law making "alien Japanese" ineligible for fishing licenses invalid); *Perkins v Elg*, 307 US 325, 328–29 (1939) (citizenship conferred by birth in the United States under both the Fourteenth Amendment and the Civil Rights Act of 1866); *United States v Wong Kim Ark*, 169 US 649 (1898) (same).

[87] 334 US 1 (1948).

[88] 245 US 60 (1917).

[89] Id at 82.

[90] Id at 78–79.

[91] 271 US 323 (1926).

covenant.[92] Technically, the case concerned federal action under the Fifth Amendment instead of state action under the Fourteenth Amendment because it arose in the District of Columbia, but the Court found no claim under either amendment sufficient to support federal jurisdiction.[93] The Court reached the same conclusion with respect to the claim under section 1982, but also expressed doubts about whether it had been properly raised in the pleadings.[94]

The holding in *Corrigan*, regardless of its basis, was effectively overruled in *Shelley v Kraemer*,[95] which held the same kind of racially restrictive covenant unconstitutional. *Shelley* concerned property in Missouri, while its companion case, *Hurd v Hodge*,[96] concerned property, as in *Corrigan*, in the District of Columbia. In *Shelley*, the Court distinguished *Corrigan* on the ground that the earlier decision considered only the constitutionality of private agreements, wholly apart from efforts to enforce them in the courts,[97] and in *Hurd*, the Court relied on section 1982 rather than the Fifth Amendment as the ground for its decision.[98] In neither case did the Court have to contradict the precise holding in *Corrigan*, although much of its reasoning was plainly inconsistent with that decision. In *Shelley*, the Court famously ignored the fact that judicial enforcement is always the ultimate issue in any concrete case, implying that state (or federal) action could be found virtually everywhere; and in *Hurd*, the Court again equated the scope of section 1982 with the constitutional prohibition against discrimination, making its statutory decision as fully dependent upon its interpretation of the Constitution as any explicit constitutional holding.[99] Only with *Jones v Mayer* was the equivalence between the 1866 Act and the Constitution broken. No sooner was it bro-

---

[92] Id at 330–31.

[93] Id at 330–32. The Court also found no substantial claim under the Thirteenth Amendment. Id.

[94] Id at 330–31.

[95] 334 US 1 (1948).

[96] Id at 24 (1948).

[97] Id at 8–9.

[98] Id at 28–30.

[99] Id at 31–33. The lower courts were in conflict on the question whether the assistance of state officers in enforcing private acts of discrimination amounted to action under color of state law. Compare *Valle v Stengel*, 176 F2d 697 (3d Cir 1949) (finding such action) with *Watkins v Oaklawn Jockey Club*, 86 F Supp 1006 (WD Ark 1949) (finding none).

ken, however, than it was replaced by an even stronger connection with other, statutory sources of civil rights law.

III. Jones v Alfred H. Mayer Co.

After nearly a century of virtually complete neglect, sections 1981 and 1982 suddenly came back to life in *Jones v Mayer*. The plaintiffs in that case alleged that a private developer had discriminated against them by refusing to sell them a home in a recently completed subdivision. The plaintiffs brought their main claim under section 1982, alleging that they had been denied the right to buy real property because they were black. The plaintiffs also alleged that the developer was engaged in state action, by taking over the functions of a municipality in constructing and maintaining the subdivision, but no participation by the state was otherwise apparent. The case thus squarely presented the question whether section 1982 created a claim for purely private discrimination beyond the scope of the Fourteenth Amendment. The Court held that it did, relying principally on statements in the congressional debates over the Civil Rights Act of 1866 that recounted the pervasive discrimination, both public and private, against the newly freed slaves in the South.

The Court also emphasized the breadth of the language in section 1982, guaranteeing all citizens "the same right . . . as is enjoyed by white citizens . . . to inherit, purchase, lease, sell, hold, and convey real and personal property." Yet, as Justice Harlan pointed out in his dissent, the literal terms of the statute are ambiguous as between a right to be free of public discrimination in the capacity to hold property and the right to be free of private discrimination in the exercise that capacity. What, after all, was the right already "enjoyed by white citizens" that the statute extended to all citizens? Before 1866, whites had the capacity to hold property, but not the right to be free of racial discrimination in exercising that capacity. The capacity itself could only be conferred or denied by the state, not by instances of private discrimination. Indeed, interpreted as a statute concerned with legal capacity, the entire 1866 Act presupposed that the exercise of these capacities would not always culminate in a completed transaction. If whites and blacks had equal capacity to hold, sell, and buy property, they also had the capacity to refuse to do so.

The legislative history, as noted earlier,[100] is just as ambiguous as the text of the act, leading both the majority and the dissent in *Jones v Mayer* to draw equal and opposite inferences from the same passages in the congressional debates. Should the statements of the act's supporters be read as protecting only the legal capacity of the newly freed slaves to hold property? Or as protecting them from private discrimination that systematically frustrated their attempts to hold property? Thus, Senator Trumbull, the sponsor of the act, said that its purpose was to protect fundamental rights, such as "the right to acquire property, the right to go and come at pleasure, the right to enforce rights in the courts, to make contracts, and to inherit and dispose of property."[101] The majority interpreted this statement to mean that the act would do more than simply dismantle the Black Codes that had denied legal capacity to blacks. It would also protect them from private discrimination.[102] The dissent, however, cited precisely the same speech for the conclusion that the act was aimed solely at the Black Codes and similar forms of state action.[103]

These arguments over the legislative history, however, tell less than half the story. The key to determining whether the 1866 Act prohibited private discrimination lies less in how it was debated before its passage than in what happened afterward. As discussed earlier,[104] Congress both reenacted the statute and passed several other statutes, in particular, sections 1983 and 1985(3) that created civil remedies for denial of federal rights. Section 1983 was modeled on the criminal prohibition in section 2 of the 1866 Act, and section 1985(3) was modeled on another criminal prohibition, which had been enacted in the Enforcement Act of 1870, which also reenacted the 1866 Act. Like sections 1981 and 1982, these provisions were rescued from nearly a century of neglect by the Warren Court and applied against private

---

[100] See Part I.A.

[101] Cong Globe, 39th Cong, 1st Sess 475 (1866).

[102] 392 US at 432.

[103] Id at 458 (Harlan, J, dissenting).

[104] See Part I.C.

individuals.[105] Yet this enforcement legislation was emphasized in neither the majority opinion nor the dissent in *Jones v Mayer*.[106]

The justices neglected these statutes apparently because they were more concerned with preserving a narrow holding—applicable only to sections 1981 and 1982—than with preserving a narrow interpretation of these statutes. An interpretation of section 1982 alone would have been surprisingly narrow, as Justice Harlan pointed out in his dissent.[107] It added only modestly to the prohibition against discrimination in real estate transactions enacted by the Civil Rights Act of 1968, which had been passed while the case was pending.[108] The extension of the majority's interpretation of section 1981 to section 1982, which was all but inevitable given their common source in the 1866 Act, resulted in the coverage of all private contracts. This consequence of the decision is broad enough, but in the contracts most likely to give rise to litigation, in employment and in public accommodations, section 1981 simply supplements the Civil Rights Act of 1964.[109] By contrast, the implications of any decision expanding the state action doctrine to reach the claim in *Jones v Mayer* would have been startling, transforming a wide range of conduct previously thought to be entirely private into state action subject to the Fourteenth Amendment.

The majority opinion, of course, avoided any such implication by holding that state action was unnecessary to make out a claim under section 1982. But it could reach this conclusion only by severing the connection between the rights granted in section 1982 and the provisions passed by Congress to enforce those rights. The majority made section 1982 (and, by implication, section 1981) into a freestanding source of both rights and remedies for private racial discrimination. Justice Harlan, in dissent, was unwilling to take this step and instead reasoned that both the rights and the remedies created by the 1866 Act were limited to state action. In

---

[105] *Monroe v Pape*, 365 US 167 (1961) (§ 1983); *Adickes v S. H. Kress & Co.*, 398 US 144, 162–69 (1970) (§ 1983); *Griffin v Breckinridge*, 403 US 88 (1971) (§ 1985(3)); *United States v Guest*, 383 US 745 (1971) (§ 241).

[106] It was mentioned only in passing in the majority opinion. 392 US at 436.

[107] Id at 477–79.

[108] Pub L No 90-284, 82 Stat 73, codified as 42 USC §§ 3601–19 (2000).

[109] Pub L No 88-352, Titles II, VI, 78 Stat 241, 243–46, 253–66, codified as 42 USC §§ 2000a to a-6, 2000e to e-17 (2000).

contrast to the majority, he tied the scope of section 1 of the act to the criminal prohibition in section 2, which is limited to action "under color of any law, statute, ordinance, regulation, or custom." He argued that the reference to custom in this clause meant only customary law that amounts to state action.[110]

For reasons discussed earlier, Justice Harlan's reasoning is not wholly satisfactory. Even if "custom" meant "customary law" in 1866, the distinction between the two terms was more permeable then than it is now.[111] This term appealed to Congress because it solved the main problem that it faced during Reconstruction: how to enforce federal rights in the South without establishing a national government that could entirely displace state law. "Custom" reached concerted private action to deny federal rights but did not regulate all action, private or public, that might result in isolated acts of discrimination. A similar compromise was adopted in the criminal prohibition in section 2 and in the corresponding civil remedy in section 1983. The remedy created by section 1985(3) solved the same problem by making much the same compromise: by providing a remedy for conspiracies to deny federal rights, but without creating a general federal tort law.

Plausible as it is, however, the implications of such reasoning in *Jones v Mayer* would have been startling. A decision on this ground would have had the same disturbing ramifications as a finding of state action. Earlier decisions had already established that the "under color of" clause in section 1983 was coextensive with the state action doctrine. Yet its "under color of" clause was derived from the "under color of" clause in section 2 of the 1866 Act. A broad interpretation of these statutory clauses would have resulted in a broad interpretation of the state action doctrine under the Fourteenth Amendment. State action as a limitation on constitutional rights and duties would have become almost no limitation at all. A broad interpretation of section 1 of the 1866 Act could not be allowed to spread to section 2, where it would automatically apply to section 1983 and then to the Fourteenth Amendment.

In fact, the plaintiffs alleged a claim based directly on the Four-

---

[110] 392 US at 457, 461–62, 475. Justice Harlan addressed these questions again, and was equally circumspect about answering them, in a case directly concerned with section 1983. *Adickes v Kress & Co.*, 398 US 144, 162–69 (1970).

[111] See Part I.A.

teenth Amendment, which the Supreme Court did not address in light of its holding under section 1982.[112] Having avoided a direct holding on the constitutional issue, the majority had no reason to adopt a line of reasoning with constitutional implications. The majority opinion accordingly took care to distinguish the rights against private discrimination created by section 1 from the criminal prohibition in section 2. For similar reasons, the majority also avoided any discussion of the relationship between section 1 and the enforcement provisions of subsequent civil rights acts. Broad as the implications of *Jones v Mayer* actually have been, they would have been immeasurably broader if they had reached as far as section 1983.

The plaintiffs in *Jones v Mayer* also had good reason to overlook the compromises embodied in these enforcement provisions. These required proof of action under color of state law or custom under section 1983 or of a conspiracy to deny equal rights under section 1985(3). Neither of these elements would have been easily established, as evidenced by the plaintiffs' refusal even to argue that they were victims of a custom of discrimination.[113] They wanted instead an easily proved claim for private discrimination, not an intricate remedy that would have moved the entire focus of the litigation back toward satisfying the requirements of sections 1983 and 1985(3). The Supreme Court was confronted with the stark choice of requiring proof of state action or finding a prohibition against all forms of private discrimination.

More fundamentally, a compromise that was plausible and necessary during Reconstruction had become outdated and superfluous over the century that intervened. By the time *Jones v Mayer* was decided, the balance had shifted in favor of the civil rights

---

[112] 392 US at 413 n 5. Justice Douglas's conference notes indicate that a majority of Justices initially embraced this ground for the decision, analogizing the real estate development in *Jones v Mayer* to the "company town" in *Marsh v Alabama*, 326 US 501 (1946). Papers of William O. Douglas, Box 1423, Jones v Alfred H. Mayer Co., Nos. 107–08 (Conference of April 5, 1968). This ground for the decision, even if it had been ultimately accepted, would not have amounted to a holding that private discrimination in property and contracts amounted to state action, but in Justice Douglas's own words, would have involved "fly specking" the case to find other aspects of state involvement. Id. There is no indication that the Court would have expanded the holding in *Shelley v Kraemer*, 334 US 1 (1948), to make all private transactions enforceable under state law into state action.

I am grateful to Mike Klarman for calling these entries in the Douglas papers to my attention.

[113] 392 US at 475 n 65 (Harlan, J, dissenting).

laws over protecting federalism. This shift was nowhere more pronounced than in the modern civil rights legislation that provided the immediate context for the decision in *Jones v Mayer*. While the case was pending in the Supreme Court, Congress enacted federal fair housing legislation in the Civil Rights Act of 1968. Because the act was not retroactive, the plaintiffs had no claim under the new legislation.[114] Yet it generally provided the same remedies that they sought for racial discrimination in housing. The only difference between the new law and section 1982 is the now familiar one of coverage. Section 1982 covers all transactions concerned with property, while the Civil Rights Act of 1968 had an exception for some single-family dwellings and owner-occupied apartment houses.[115] The sweep of section 1981 is even broader, embracing all contracts regardless of who makes them, what they concern, or how much they are worth. The seemingly universal coverage of sections 1981 and 1982 remained inconsequential, so long as these statutes were interpreted to be coextensive with the Fourteenth Amendment and its state action requirement. The holding in *Jones v Mayer* changed all that, giving them the broadest possible scope in regulating nearly all transactions in a market economy.

Despite this breathtaking increase in coverage, these newly expanded prohibitions against racial discrimination could hardly be found inconsistent with the balance of federal and state power in the new civil rights legislation. The Civil Rights Act of 1968 applied federal law to a broad range of transactions in property, historically governed by state law, and the Civil Rights Act of 1964 went even further in prohibiting discrimination in public accommodations and employment, also areas traditionally regulated by the states. In the abstract, the expanded coverage of sections 1981 and 1982 was dramatic, even alarming. In practice, it absorbed only a few exceptions in the new legislation and covered only a scattering of other cases,[116] none of which was likely to result in

---

[114] Id at 417–18 n 21.

[115] 42 USC § 3603 (2000).

[116] For cases involving property, see *Pinchback v Armistead Homes Corp.*, 907 F2d 1447 (4th Cir 1990) (discrimination in leasing); *Jiminez v Southridge Co-op*, 626 F Supp 732 (ED NY 1985) (alleged discrimination in purchase of apartment); *Dale v City of Chicago Heights*, 672 F Supp 330 (ND Ill 1987) (alleged retaliation by city officials against landlords who rented to black tenants). For those involving public accommodations, see *Perry v Command Performance*, 913 F2d 99 (3d Cir 1990) (refusal to serve black customer at beauty parlor);

litigation. This pattern has continued to this day, despite the amendment of section 1981 to cover all forms of private discrimination. Ironically, the expanded coverage of the statute has been acceptable because it has been so insignificant.

The modern civil rights laws also figured in the constitutional holding in *Jones v Mayer*. The Civil Rights Acts of 1964 and 1968 took up where the Civil Rights Act of 1875 left off, extending the constitutional prohibition against discrimination to private action. Congress enacted the modern statutes, however, under its power over interstate commerce, in order to avoid the holding in the *Civil Rights Cases* limiting its powers under the Thirteenth and Fourteenth Amendments. In *Jones v Mayer*, the Court largely ignored these limits on congressional power, finding the analysis in the *Civil Rights Cases* "academic" in light of decisions upholding the constitutionality of the Civil Rights Act of 1964.[117] Freed from this precedent, the Court could broadly interpret the Thirteenth Amendment to authorize Congress to remedy "the badges and incidents of slavery"[118] by any appropriate means.[119] Where the *Civil Rights Cases* found that it "would be running the slavery argument into the ground to make it apply to every act of discrimination,"[120] *Jones v Mayer* found a prohibition against private discrimination simply to be an appropriate means of reaching the legitimate end of abolishing the last vestiges of slavery.

Like the writer whose work creates his own precursors out of previously unrelated authors,[121] *Jones v Mayer* created its own authority out of statutes enacted almost a century apart. By abandoning the Fourteenth Amendment as the model for interpreting sections 1981 and 1982, the Court necessarily adopted the modern civil rights laws as a substitute. Although the Court was careful to

---

Wyatt v Security Inn Food & Beverage, Inc., 819 F2d 69 (4th Cir 1987) (discrimination by hotel lounge to limit number of black patrons); *Hernandez v Erlenbusch*, 363 F Supp 752 (D Ore 1973) (discrimination by tavern against Spanish-speaking customers); *Bobbitt by Bobbitt v Rage Inc.*, 19 F Supp 2d 512 (WD NC 1998) (discrimination by restaurant in requiring black customers to prepay pizza order).

[117] 392 US at 441 n 78.

[118] Id at 439.

[119] Typically, the Court framed its argument in terms of a quotation from the legislative history. Id at 443–44.

[120] 109 US at 24.

[121] Jorge Luis Borges, *Kafka and His Precursors*, in *Selected Nonfictions* 363, 365 (Penguin, 1999).

cite these laws only to minimize the significance of its decision,[122] they actually furnished the political support essential for acceptance of a broad prohibition against private discrimination. The recent enactment of similar prohibitions by Congress put the Court in the position of agreeing with what Congress had already done, instead of appearing to act entirely on its own. A more modest extension of sections 1981 and 1982 to private discrimination could have been accomplished by relying on civil rights acts passed closer in time to the original enactment of these sections and more closely tied to them by explicit textual references. If relying on older laws provided a stronger justification for interpreting sections 1981 and 1982 to reach narrower forms of private discrimination, relying on more modern laws provided a better explanation for the Court's actual decision. A decision that modestly expanded on recent civil rights legislation met "the felt necessities of the time" better than an endorsement of compromises reached during Reconstruction.[123] Whether or not updating statutes in this manner is a legitimate method of interpretation,[124] it is one vindicated by the subsequent course of judicial decisions and congressional action in response to *Jones v Mayer*. The next part turns to these developments.

IV. Consolidation and Implications

The decisions immediately after *Jones v Mayer* reaffirmed and extended its holding, initially from section 1982, concerned only with property, to section 1981, concerned with contracts. Only later did the Supreme Court have second thoughts about these decisions and only when they threatened to go beyond the bounds set by modern civil rights legislation. Even then, only one genuinely limiting decision was handed down, and it was soon superseded by Congress.

---

[122] 392 US at 413–17. Congress itself, in passing the Civil Rights Act of 1968, remained completely agnostic on the effect, if any, that this act would have on the pending decision in *Jones v Mayer*. Id at 415–16.

[123] Oliver Wendell Holmes, Jr., *The Common Law* 5 (Belknap Press, Harvard, 1968).

[124] Guido Calabresi, *A Common Law for the Age of Statutes* 129–31 (Harvard, 1982); William Eskridge, *Dynamic Statutory Interpretation* 258–59 (Harvard, 1994).

A. DECISIONS EXTENDING JONES V MAYER

The process of consolidation began, naturally enough, with decisions reaffirming *Jones* as applied to real estate transactions. In *Sullivan v Little Hunting Park, Inc.*,[125] the Court applied section 1982 to a lease of property within a development whose recreational facilities were operated by a private corporation. In *Tillman v Wheaton-Haven Recreation Association*,[126] the Court took this process one step further and applied both section 1981 and section 1982 to membership in a residentially based swimming club. The decisions in both cases alluded to defenses based on freedom of association, but found that the organizations in question were not private clubs because they were open to all residents of the relevant community.[127] The constitutional right to freedom of association continues to haunt a broad interpretation of section 1981, but these early decisions brushed off such concerns about regulating transactions between private individuals.[128] The Court, instead, pursued and extended the logic of *Jones v Mayer*: first, to provide a general damage remedy,[129] and second, to prohibit private discrimination in contracting.[130] The latter holding, in particular, gave these statutes nearly universal coverage.

This understanding was confirmed in *Johnson v Railway Express Agency, Inc.*,[131] a case involving claims of employment discrimination under both section 1981 and Title VII. Although the Court eventually dismissed the plaintiff's claim under section 1981 as time barred, it assumed that section 1981 covered the full range of employment contracts, even those of small employers exempt from Title VII.[132] In this respect the decision resembled *Jones v Mayer*; it modestly extended the coverage of a modern civil rights statute by recognizing a claim under the Civil Rights Act of 1866.

---

[125] 396 US 229 (1969).

[126] 410 US 431 (1973).

[127] *Sullivan*, 396 US at 236; *Tillman*, 432 US at 438.

[128] See also *Memphis v Greene*, 451 US 100, 120–24 (1981) (reasoning that § 1982 applied to all forms of racial discrimination that resulted in an impairment of a property interest, but finding no evidence of such an impairment).

[129] *Sullivan*, 396 US at 239–40.

[130] *Tillman*, 432 US at 439–40.

[131] 421 US 454 (1975).

[132] Id at 460–61 (remedies under § 1981 are "separate, distinct, and independent" of those under Title VII).

And, as in *Jones v Mayer*, the modern legislation was passed without any attempt to affect claims under the earlier act.[133]

The decision in *Johnson* also added to the remedies available under Title VII in another way: following *Sullivan*, the Court approved the award of damages for violation of section 1981.[134] This seemingly minor innovation actually transformed the litigation of employment discrimination claims. At the time, Title VII authorized only equitable relief, which included only a limited monetary recovery in the form of back pay.[135] With larger monetary stakes in the form of damages, plaintiffs had more reason to sue and attorneys more reason to represent them. Plaintiff's attorneys in these cases usually obtain compensation through awards of attorney's fees or through contingent fees, both of which are correlated with the plaintiff's success on the merits, including the amount of money recovered.[136] The Court's approval of damages as a remedy under section 1981 also had important and unforeseen implications for Title VII, which was eventually amended to provide a similar remedy to plaintiffs who did not have claims under section 1981. These plaintiffs, mainly in sex discrimination cases, are now entitled to recover damages up to a ceiling determined by the size of the employer.[137] In a manner typical of section 1981, the routine doctrinal elaboration of its provisions in *Johnson* had profound consequences that extended far beyond the case itself.

The consequences of section 1981 remained largely unchallenged so long as they found at least analogous support in statutes recently passed by Congress. When they went further, they were immediately challenged, as was evident in *Runyon v McCrary*,[138] a case alleging racial discrimination in private schools. As a purely doctrinal matter, *Runyon* was an easy case. Attendance at a private school requires a contractual relationship between the parties. It follows that a school that refused to accept black applicants, as the schools in *Runyon* did, violated section 1981's prohibition against private discrimination in contracting. The case was difficult only because Con-

---

[133] Id at 459.

[134] Id at 460.

[135] 42 USC § 2000e-5(g) (2000); *Albemarle Paper Co. v Moody*, 422 US 405, 421 (1975).

[136] *Hensley v Eckerhart*, 461 US 424, 436 (1983); *Venegas v Mitchell*, 495 US 82 (1990).

[137] 42 USC § 1981a (2000).

[138] 427 US 160 (1976).

gress had not legislated on the subject of segregated private schools, probably because such "white academies" had multiplied in response to court-ordered busing to desegregate the public schools. Congress had little reason to expose itself to further controversy on this issue by expanding the scope of desegregation decrees.

The real question in *Runyon* was whether *Jones v Mayer* could be taken at face value: whether section 1981 (like section 1982) really applied to all private transactions. Several complications and qualifications to the decision only returned to this central question. Justice White filed a dissenting opinion that advanced a novel interpretation of the act's codification in the Revised Statutes of 1874. He would have held that section 1981, but not section 1982, was limited to state action under the Fourteenth Amendment.[139] His argument for this conclusion rests on the status of the Revised Statutes as the official codification of the federal civil rights laws. Title 42 of the United States Code, which is the modern codification of the civil rights laws, only provides evidence of laws whose authoritative source is the Revised Statutes, as amended by the Statutes at Large.[140]

The Revised Statutes split section 1 of the Civil Rights Act of 1866 into two parts: section 1981, concerned with most of the rights protected under the original act; and section 1982, concerned with only the rights to property.[141] The version of section 1981 in the Revised Statutes is accompanied by annotations indicating that it was drawn from the Enforcement Act of 1870, while those accompanying section 1982 indicate that it was drawn from the Civil Rights Act of 1866. These annotations led Justice White to conclude that section 1981 applied only to state action because it was enacted solely under the Fourteenth Amendment, which was ratified in the interval between the 1866 Act and 1870 Act. This conclusion gave him a convenient way to distinguish section 1982, whose official version could be traced back to the 1866 Act and ultimately to congressional power to prohibit private discrimination under the Thirteenth Amendment.

---

[139] Id at 195–205 (White, J, dissenting).

[140] See USC (2000) at III (indicating enacted titles of USC). Sections 1981 and 1982 were first placed in Title 42 in the 1952 edition of the United States Code. They previously appeared as 8 USC §§ 41, 42 beginning with the 1928 edition.

[141] Section 1977 of the Revised Statues is the official version of section 1981. Section 1978 of the Revised Statutes is the official version of section 1982. The full text of these sections of the Revised Statutes appears in the Appendix.

This argument perhaps is too contrived to be taken entirely seriously, but even on its own terms, it has two overriding defects. The first is Justice White's supposition that the reenactment of the Civil Rights Act of 1866 in the Enforcement Act of 1870 involved only the exercise of powers under the Fourteenth Amendment. In fact, the 1870 Act was not passed entirely, or even mainly, under the Fourteenth Amendment. As its formal title states, it is "An Act to enforce the Right of Citizens of the United States to vote in the several States of this Union, and for other purposes." This purpose invokes the *Fifteenth* Amendment, but even this source of authority is not exclusive. The "other purposes" also listed in the title include reenacting the 1866 Act, whose provisions did not concern the right to vote. On White's own argument, therefore, the "other purposes" of the 1870 Act involve congressional authority under the Fourteenth Amendment. But having gone this far, the reenactment could equally well involve congressional authority under the Thirteenth Amendment. Indeed, it had to do so, because these "other purposes" included protecting the constitutionality of the 1866 Act.

This point leads to the second, and more severe, defect in Justice White's argument. It supposes that Congress, in codifying federal law in 1874, intended to undo all of its work only four years earlier, in 1870, in reenacting the 1866 Act. The whole purpose of the reenactment was to put the 1866 Act on a more secure constitutional footing. According to Justice White, sections 1981 and 1982 in their codified form would be more—not less—vulnerable to arguments that each exceeded the power of Congress. On his view, each section depended only on the powers of Congress under the single amendment under which it was enacted. Section 1981, being enacted only under the Fourteenth Amendment, would have had no support in congressional power under the Thirteenth Amendment; and conversely, section 1982 would have had no support under the Fourteenth Amendment. It is implausible that Congress in enacting a codification in 1874 would have silently undermined the entire point of reenacting both sections in 1870.[142]

---

[142] The different annotations to sections 1981 and 1982 in the Revised Statutes probably concern an entirely different issue, involving the different coverage of each of these sections. Section 1981 (section 1977 of the Revised Statutes) applies to all "persons," while section 1982 (section 1978 of the Revised Statutes) applies only to "citizens." The coverage of persons in section 1981, including aliens, was added by section 16 of the Enforcement Act of 1870, while the coverage only of citizens in section 1982 reflects the original terms of

Justice White also alluded to a less desperate, but also less drastic, limit on the coverage of section 1981, based on the constitutional right to freedom of association.[143] On the record in *Runyon*,
however, no defense could be made out on this ground because,
as in the earlier homeowner's association cases, the segregated
schools were in fact open to the general public, so long as the
racial restrictions on admission were met.[144] Nevertheless, the very
breadth of section 1981 assures that, at some point, it will come
into collision with the right to freedom of association. Recent decisions of the Supreme Court have revitalized this right.[145] Modern
civil rights laws also recognize the force of claims of freedom of
association by allowing exceptions for small employers or for similar situations in which the parties to a transaction come into close
contact with one another.

In raising these arguments in dissent, Justice White seemed to
be motivated less by their intrinsic merit than by his view, already
expressed as a dissenter in *Jones v Mayer*, that the extension of the
1866 Act to private discrimination was generally a bad idea.[146] Yet,
instead of directly addressing the precedential force of that decision, he gave it only cursory treatment, as did the majority opinion.
That opinion was by Justice Stewart, who had also written the
majority opinion in *Jones v Mayer*. Only the concurring opinion,
by Justice Stevens, treated the issue at any length.[147] He prefaced
his opinion with the assumption that *Jones v Mayer* was wrongly
decided, but he nevertheless concluded that the decision remained
binding because it followed the principles of equality embodied in
modern civil rights legislation. The interpretation of section 1981
to reach private discrimination, of course, went beyond those

---

section 1 of the Civil Rights Act of 1866. The effect of these differences in coverage was
to restrict the right to hold property to citizens, following state common law that typically
contained such restrictions. The Revised Statutes, like the original civil rights acts, pre-
served this feature of existing law. Having separated the rights originally granted by the
1866 Act into two separate sections, the revisers probably wanted to explain why they took
this step.

[143] *Runyon*, 427 US at 212.

[144] Id at 175–76. Defenses based on the constitutional right to parental control over education and to privacy also failed. Id at 176–78; id at 187–89 (Powell, J, concurring).

[145] *Boy Scouts of America v Dale*, 530 US 640, 653–61 (2000); *Roberts v United States Jaycees*,
468 US 609, 617–29 (1984); *Board of Directors of Rotary Int'l v Rotary Club of Duarte*, 481
US 537, 544–49 (1987); *New York State Club Ass'n v New York*, 487 US 1, 10–15 (1988).

[146] 427 US at 193–95, 208–09 n 13.

[147] Id at 189–92 (Stevens, J, concurring).

statutes in coverage and remedies, but it followed the same basic principle of prohibiting racial discrimination in private transactions. How far these principles could be applied beyond the actual scope of the modern statutes was the question that animated the decisions after *Runyon*.

B. DECISIONS LIMITING JONES V MAYER

In the aftermath of *Runyon*, theoretical questions about the soundness of *Jones v Mayer* became practical questions about the scope of section 1981, and in particular, about how far it could be expanded in light of modern civil rights laws. Taken as a whole, the decisions after *Runyon* answered, "not much," although different approaches were taken in different cases. The expansive decisions, such as they were, tended to be on issues on which the Constitution and the modern civil rights acts agreed. Thus, section 1981 was interpreted to support claims by whites as well as blacks,[148] and to support claims on the basis of national origin as well as race.[149] In both of these instances, restricting the statute to claims only by racial minorities would have introduced a discrepancy with constitutional law which would, in fact, have raised questions about the constitutionality of the act as so interpreted. Modern constitutional decisions have required strict scrutiny of all classifications on the basis of race and national origin,[150] and the modern civil rights acts have broadly prohibited almost all classifications on these grounds.[151] The restrictive decisions, with one exception, were on issues on which the Constitution and the modern statutes diverged. Section 1981 was accordingly limited to claims of intentional discrimination, as opposed to claims of disparate impact or discriminatory effects,[152] and it was further limited, as ap-

---

[148] *McDonald v Santa Fe Trail Transp. Co.*, 427 US 273, 285–96 (1976).

[149] *Saint Francis College v Al-Khazraji*, 481 US 604, 609–13 (1987). A companion case reached the same conclusion under section 1982. *Shaare Tefila Congregation v Cobb*, 481 US 615, 617–18 (1987).

[150] *Adarand Contractors, Inc. v Pena*, 515 US 200, 235–36 (1995) (opinion of O'Connor, J); id at 239 (Scalia, J, concurring in part and concurring in the judgment).

[151] As in Title VII of the Civil Rights Act of 1964, 42 USC § 2000e-2(i), (j), (m) (2000); see *United Steelworkers v Weber*, 443 US 193, 208 (1979) (allowing affirmative action in employment in carefully defined circumstances).

[152] *General Bldg. Contractors Ass'n v Pennsylvania*, 458 US 375, 391 (1982).

plied to state officials, by the defenses available to claims for constitutional torts under section 1983.[153]

This pattern fits the cases only roughly, and in any event, cannot explain the decision in *Patterson v McLean Credit Union*,[154] which held that section 1981 does not cover claims of discrimination in the performance of contracts, as opposed to their formation.[155] *Patterson* involved a claim of racial harassment in employment, otherwise covered by Title VII of the Civil Rights Act of 1964, which prohibits discrimination in all aspects of the employment relationship. *Patterson* held that section 1981 did not reach so far, protecting only the right "to make and enforce contracts," not the right to have them performed.

The artificiality of this distinction, despite its basis in the text of section 1981, illustrates the general difficulty of developing a coherent account of the decisions in this period. *Patterson* seems to have limited the scope of the statute because of doubts about the validity of *Jones v Mayer*, while other decisions in this period accepted *Jones v Mayer* without any qualifications. Any one of these decisions might depend on a variety of different arguments, from the effect of modern civil rights statutes to the dictionary definition of "race" in the nineteenth century. With so many arguments to choose from, and so many shifting coalitions of justices who could choose among them, the absence of any regular pattern of decisions should come as no surprise.

In the end, the consequence of the decisions nevertheless was plain enough: congressional intervention to resolve the principal questions about the scope and application of section 1981. In the Civil Rights Act of 1991, Congress amended the statute specifically to overrule *Patterson*, and because that decision also called the validity of *Jones v Mayer* into question, to codify the application of section 1981 to private discrimination.

C. RATIFICATION AND RECODIFICATION

In explicitly extending section 1981 to cover private discrimination, the Civil Rights Act of 1991 completed the process, begun in

---

[153] *Jett v Dallas Indep. School Dist.*, 491 US 701, 731–36 (1989).

[154] 491 US 164 (1989).

[155] Id at 175–78.

Jones v Mayer, of inverting the relationship between the statute and the Fourteenth Amendment. Where the amendment's state action requirement used to operate as a ceiling on the act's coverage, now the rights granted by the amendment created only a floor for the statute's prohibition against private discrimination. With the exception only of the Due Process Clause, all of the rights protected by section 1 are now protected by section 1981 from private discrimination. These statutory protections cannot be freed entirely from the restraining influence of the Fourteenth Amendment, since in some circumstances the coverage of the amended statute depends upon the exercise of congressional power to enforce that amendment. These cases are perhaps few and far between, because Congress retains broad power to prohibit private discrimination on the basis of race under the Commerce Clause and under the Thirteenth Amendment. Yet these cases raise the question, which is even more pressing simply as a matter of statutory interpretation, of how far the coverage of section 1981 now extends.

A consideration of that question must begin with what the Civil Rights Act of 1991 sought to accomplish. The act made a variety of changes in the federal laws against employment discrimination, most of them united only by the common purpose of addressing issues already raised by judicial decisions interpreting those laws. The act endorsed and consolidated the trends established by liberal decisions on civil rights, limiting or overruling several restrictive decisions and clarifying or extending others. The amendments to section 1981, in this respect, are altogether typical. By adding new subsections (b) and (c) to the statute, Congress overruled *Patterson v McLean Credit Union* and codified *Jones v Mayer*. To civil rights advocates, this pervasive theme represented a cause for hope, especially in an era in which they have seen only fitful and infrequent progress. For their opponents, however, the act was hardly a defeat, for reasons that reveal the underlying dynamics of the act's passage and reception. In the first place, few groups today want to be seen as opponents of civil rights legislation. Political conservatives, who often are taken to be opponents of such legislation, prefer to portray themselves as advocates of the original goals of the civil rights movement, usually framed in terms of a "colorblind" conception of racial equality. They are opposed to practices that explicitly discriminate against racial and ethnic minorities, but they are also opposed to programs of affirmative action that explicitly grant preferences to such groups.

For all these reasons, the principal item on the agenda in the Civil Rights Act of 1991 was not section 1981, but the theory of disparate impact under Title VII, imposing liability on employers for neutral practices with discriminatory effects and thereby encouraging them to engage in affirmative action. The act became controversial only over the extent to which it was, as conservatives characterized it, a "quota bill."[156] Once they obtained assurances that it was not, they acquiesced in passage of the act and it was signed, after an earlier version had been vetoed, by the first President Bush. Abstracting from details of the compromise that made passage of the act possible, the overall posture adopted by Congress was one of qualified endorsement of the gains made by civil rights advocates. Section 1981 figured in that endorsement. Since it did not raise any controversial questions of affirmative action, the broad interpretation of the statute and its extension to additional claims of discrimination could not be opposed on that ground. Just as much as the judicial decisions interpreting the statute to reach private discrimination, the codification and expansion of those decisions in the Civil Rights Act of 1991 rested on the modern consensus about the appropriate scope of civil rights laws. Opposition to effective remedies for private discrimination could not be based on principle, only on the relative costs and benefits of different remedies. These might be of great concern to employers, the defendants in almost all of the cases under section 1981, but their opposition to expanded liability could not rest on a general hostility to civil rights. The restraints inherent in such qualified opposition are reflected in the terms in which these sections were amended or enacted.

The narrowest of these changes was the addition of subsection (b) to section 1981, which specifically overruled *Patterson*. This new subsection defines the term "make and enforce contracts" to encompass all aspects of the contractual relationship, effectively making the coverage of section 1981 in employment cases as broad as Title VII.[157] Of course, the overall coverage of section 1981 goes

---

[156] 136 Cong Rec S 1522 (Feb 2, 1990) (remarks of Sen. Hatch).

[157] The phrase "make and enforce contracts" now includes "the making, performance, modification, and termination of contracts, and the enjoyment of all benefits, privileges, terms and conditions of the contractual relationship." 42 USC § 1981(b) (2000). By way

far beyond such cases, embracing any kind of contract whatsoever. Nevertheless, its coverage of all contractual relationships was not enlarged by the addition of subsection (b). That aspect of its coverage was only indirectly called into question by *Patterson* and only to the extent that it was motivated, like other decisions restricting section 1981, by the aim of preventing *Jones v Mayer* from being carried to its logical conclusion. In adding subsection (b) to the statute, Congress rejected one such limiting strategy.

In subsection (c), Congress addressed the more general question of the validity of *Jones v Mayer*. As noted earlier, this provision laid to rest any lingering doubts about that decision, but in terms with surprisingly broad implications. In stating that "[t]he rights protected by this section are protected against impairment by non-governmental discrimination," this subsection created a claim for private discrimination involving any of the rights granted by section 1981. These go beyond the right "to make and enforce contracts" and include the right to equal protection of the laws, in the statute's language, the right "to the full and equal benefit of all laws and proceedings for the security of persons and property" and to "be subject to like punishment, pains, penalties, taxes, licenses, and exactions of every kind, and to no other." Although subsection (b) does not address the nature of this underlying right, and in particular, whether it retains a state action component, it plainly goes beyond the Equal Protection Clause of the Fourteenth Amendment. The latter protects only against denial of equal protection by "any State." Subsection (c) seemingly abrogates this aspect of the state action doctrine.

Whether this abrogation is effective, and to what extent, are open questions. Congress did not focus on this consequence of subsection (c), but instead, in the two committee reports on the Civil Rights Act of 1991, identified this subsection only as a provision reaffirming the holding in the private school desegregation case, *Runyon v McCrary*.[158] Perhaps Congress could be saved from itself by taking the state action requirement and reading it back

---

of comparison, Title VII prohibits discrimination against any individual in hiring and discharge and "with respect to his compensation, terms, conditions, or privileges of employment" and it prohibits segregation or classification "which would deprive or tend to deprive any individual of employment opportunities or otherwise adversely affect his status as an employee." Id § 2000e-2(a)(1), (2) (2000).

[158] HR Rep No 102-40, 102d Cong, 1st Sess, pt I, at 92 (1991); id, pt II, at 37.

into the rights that are protected. This strategy will not work with respect to the right "to make and enforce contracts" because that would completely frustrate Congress's stated intent to ratify the result in *Runyon*. But it might be more successful with respect to the right to equal protection. All of the components of this right listed in the statute refer either explicitly to "laws and proceedings" or implicitly to government action in the form of "punishment, pains, penalties, taxes, licenses, and exactions of every kind."[159] Taking this step would limit subsection (c) in much the same way that the Supreme Court has already limited section 1985(3), insofar as it applies to private conspiracies to deny equal rights by making those rights a matter of state action.[160]

The result of this reasoning is less disturbing than the need to engage in it at all. It raises, albeit in slightly different form, all the arguments over private discrimination and state action that figured in *Jones v Mayer*. Subsection (c) was intended to endorse the reasoning in that case, although it is no small irony that it fails to endorse the holding, which concerns section 1982, whose provisions were left untouched by the Civil Rights Act of 1991. On the most probable reading of both statutes, they now have the following effect: section 1981 reaches private action with respect to contracts, but not with respect to other rights that have a "state action" component, despite the coverage of all forms of private discrimination in subsection (c); but section 1982, which contains no provision corresponding to subsection (c), reaches all forms of private discrimination with respect to property. The literal terms of the statutes do not quite add up and neither does the reasoning that supports their most plausible interpretation. The private nature of the rights protected is either selectively emphasized or completely ignored. Sections 1981 and 1982 are not the first statutes that fail to achieve overall coherence. Legislatures, after all, have more freedom to reach expedient compromises than do courts. Yet the interpretation of these statutes in their current form has the disconcerting feeling of "déjà vu all over again."

---

[159] One of the decisions applying the equal protection component of section 1981 to private discrimination has taken this approach. *Chapman v Higbee Co.*, 319 F3d 825, 832–33 (6th Cir 2003) (en banc).

[160] 42 USC § 1985(3) (2000). The corresponding criminal prohibition, originating in the Enforcement Act of 1870, is 18 USC § 241 (2000). See note 50.

This concern is not wholly theoretical. The right to free association has already been mentioned and it has been reaffirmed by recent decisions of the Supreme Court. Another line of recent decisions limits the power of Congress under section 5 of the Fourteenth Amendment, raising the same questions about the broad scope of civil rights legislation that were raised in the aftermath of Reconstruction.[161] The recent decisions have not considered limitations on congressional power to remedy racial discrimination, either by eliminating "badges of slavery" under the Thirteenth Amendment or by regulating economic activity under the Commerce Clause. If these questions, as applied to section 1981, have been only indirectly addressed by the Supreme Court, they have not been addressed at all by Congress. In amending the statute, Congress focused only on the particular decisions that it intended to confirm or overrule, neglecting other consequences of the new subsections that it added to the statute.[162] This development—or, more precisely, the absence of one—suggests that section 1981 has always remained hostage to the immediate problems that have led to its enactment, interpretation, or amendment.

Returning to the statute's original focus upon private violations of public rights provides a way to interpret it narrowly to avoid constitutional issues raised by the scope of its current coverage. Where it is most subject to constitutional challenge, it also has the least support in its historic purpose: to provide opportunities to participate in public life regardless of race. As originally enacted, section 1981 was intended to protect public rights, although it provided for enforcement against private as well as public infringement. In the modern civil rights acts, Congress has extended the principle against discrimination further, reaching a wide range of private conduct in housing, employment, and public accommodations. All of these activities have a public dimension as well, even if they do not involve the government, because they affect an individual's ability to participate in a broad range of transactions and

---

[161] *City of Boerne v Flores*, 521 US 507 (1997); *United States v Morrison*, 529 US 598 (2000).

[162] Congress did not explicitly invoke particular constitutional powers in the statement of purposes at the beginning of the Civil Rights Act of 1991, but it identified as one purpose of the act "expanding the scope of relevant civil rights statutes," among them section 1981 and Title VII of the Civil Rights Act of 1964. Pub L No 102-166, § 3(4), 105 Stat 1071 (1991). All of these statutes were passed, or were previously amended, under some combination of the Thirteenth and Fourteenth Amendments and the Commerce Clause.

relationships with other members of the general public. Yet some contracts do not involve public life even in this extended sense. This is most apparent with respect to contracts involving matters of privacy and free association. To the extent that contracts pose a genuine threat to these rights, they fall outside the goals of Congress either in the Reconstruction civil rights acts or in their modern counterparts. Contracts with individuals creating close personal relationships do not plausibly implicate "badges of slavery" and have only a remote impact on interstate commerce. Individual decisions, for instance, about hiring a private nurse involve the exercise of the capacity to contract on both sides of the transaction. They do not involve a denial of the capacity or general ability of one side or the other to make this decision.[163] Whether by statutory interpretation or constitutional decision, the actual coverage of section 1981 is likely to fall short of its literal terms.

Outside the core area of employment discrimination, section 1981 remains a statute whose theoretical coverage vastly exceeds its actual application. Obvious targets for litigation, such as racially segregated private clubs, do not generate very many decisions, and when they do, they involve clubs that are not genuinely private.[164] Other, novel applications of the statute, to claims of discrimination in service contracts or in retail purchases, are even more infrequent.[165] The force of the statute in extending the principle of discrimination to new fields has, for the moment, been suspended.

---

[163] As Professor Black put the point, "Law does not, in our legal culture, commonly deal with dinner invitations and the choice of children's back-yard playmates." Black, 81 Harv L Rev at 102 (cited in note 42). Justice Powell made the same point in his separate opinion in *Runyon v McCrary*, 427 US 160, 187–89 (1976) (Powell, J, concurring). Private clubs which create opportunities for public advancement, through contacts and status, raise different issues, on which the lower federal courts have been divided.

[164] *Wright v Salisbury Club, Ltd.*, 632 F2d 309 (4th Cir 1980) (exclusion from club violates section 1981 because club is not truly private); *Durham v Red Lake Fishing and Hunting Club, Inc.*, 666 F Supp 954 (WD Tex 1987) (same); *Watson v Fraternal Order of Eagles*, 915 F2d 235 (6th Cir 1990) (removal of black partygoers at private party at private club states claim under section 1981); *Olzman v Lake Hills Swim Club, Inc.*, 495 F2d 1333 (2d Cir 1974) (allegations of racially discriminatory operation of swimming club states claim under section 1981).

[165] *Scott v Eversole Mortuary*, 522 F2d 1110 (9th Cir 1975) (refusal to provide mortuary services to Native Americans); *Bagley v Lumbermens Mut. Cas. Co.*, 100 F Supp 2d 879 (ND Ill 2000) (refusing to enter into loan agreement on grounds of race); *Howard Sec. Services, Inc. v Johns Hopkins Hospital*, 516 F Supp 508 (D Md 1981) (refusal of hospital to enter into contract with corporation owned and operated by black president).

Its current role is to augment the remedies for previously recognized forms of discrimination.

V. Conclusion

Even in its current, supplementary role, section 1981 offers an accurate reflection of civil rights law. Its central purpose has always been to protect the right to participate in public life, regardless of race, and to provide remedies for both public and private violations of that right. The visionary principles that find expression in section 1981 have never been—and perhaps could never be—implemented in a manner that entirely fulfilled their promise of equality. Since the statute's enactment during Reconstruction, each era has taken its own attitude toward the problems of discrimination that it faced. And even when laws have been enacted and effectively enforced against the forms of discrimination prevalent in one era, new practices have arisen to take their place and to raise issues of discrimination to be confronted later. The modern civil rights statutes have proved to be more effective in eliminating discrimination in episodic rather than continuous fashion, through concentrated efforts over a few years rather than routine enforcement over several decades.[166] This conclusion certainly is borne out by the history of section 1981, enmeshed as it is in most of the deep and enduring controversies over civil rights law.

The parallel development of section 1981 with the Fourteenth Amendment might lead one to suspect that the statute represents only the statutory penumbra of constitutional developments. At strategic points in its evolution, section 1981 has received legislative support, if only by analogy, through other civil rights laws, but these too have depended on constitutional developments. Such skepticism about the independent significance of section 1981, whatever else might be said for or against it, stands much of the current criticism of judicial review on its head. It presumes that constitutional decisions determine the interpretation of statutes, and through them, the content of legislation. At their most extreme, the current critics of constitutionalism either deny that con-

---

[166] John J. Donohue III and James J. Heckman, *Continuous vs. Episodic Change: The Impact of Civil Rights Policy on the Economic Status of Blacks*, 29 J Econ Lit 1603 (1991).

stitutional decisions have any lasting effects at all[167] or assert that these effects are deleterious.[168] The history of section 1981 establishes that these decisions exercise a far more profound and pervasive influence over all of federal law, by articulating principles that find expression in judicial interpretation of statutes and in their enactment and amendment by Congress.

The current scope of section 1981 has resulted less from an accident of judicial interpretation, later ratified by congressional amendment, than from the tendency of one generation's disputes over the statute's coverage to become the next generation's unquestioned assumptions about its purpose and effect. *Jones v Mayer* may not have been entirely correct, but neither was it wholly wrong. It recognized the need, perceived from the statute's very beginnings in the Civil Rights Act of 1866, to provide comprehensive enforcement against the private, as well as public, denial of equal rights. How far such enforcement should extend, or whether it should be reversed, has now been addressed mainly by Congress in the modern civil rights statutes, to which section 1981 serves as a necessary supplement. Whether the statute continues in this role, as part of the uneven but expanding remedies for discrimination, necessarily remains an open question. The statute's history suggests that periods of relative neglect and quiescence have not determined its ultimate significance. We might fruitfully take section 1981 as a reflection of our nation's simultaneous allegiance and ambivalence toward principles of equality: the avowal at our founding that all of us are created equal and the fitful attempts over our history to make good on this promise. In this respect, the complicated evolution of section 1981 tells us as much about ourselves as about our law.

STATUTORY APPENDIX

42 USC § 1981 (2000). Equal rights under the law

(a) Statement of equal rights.
    All persons within the jurisdiction of the United States shall

---

[167] Gerald N. Rosenberg, *The Hollow Hope: Can Courts Bring About Social Change?* 336–43 (Chicago, 1991).

[168] Larry Kramer, *The Supreme Court, 2000 Term, Foreword: We the Court*, 115 Harv L Rev 4, 158–69 (2001). For a more nuanced account of the effect of constitutional decisions

have the same right in every State and Territory to make and enforce contracts, to sue, be parties, give evidence, and to the full and equal benefit of all laws and proceedings for the security of persons and property as is enjoyed by white citizens, and shall be subject to like punishment, pains, penalties, taxes, licenses, and exactions of every kind, and to no other.

(b) "Make and enforce contracts" defined.

For purposes of this section, the term "make and enforce contracts" includes the making, performance, modification, and termination of contracts, and the enjoyment of all benefits, privileges, terms, and conditions of the contractual relationship.

(c) Protection against impairment.

The rights protected by this section are protected against impairment by nongovernmental discrimination and impairment under color of State law.

42 USC § 1982 (2000). Property rights of citizens

All citizens of the United States shall have the same right, in every State and Territory, as is enjoyed by white citizens thereof to inherit, purchase, lease, sell, hold, and convey real and personal property.

Civil Rights Act of 1866, 14 Stat 27.

Be it enacted by the Senate and House of Representatives of the United States of America in Congress assembled, That all persons born in the United States and not subject to any foreign power, excluding Indians not taxed, are hereby declared to be citizens of the United States; and such citizens, of every race and color, without regard to any previous condition of slavery or involuntary servitude, except as a punishment for crime whereof the party shall have been duly convicted, shall have the same right, in every State and Territory in the United States, to make and enforce contracts, to sue, be parties, and give evidence, to inherit, purchase, lease, sell, hold, and convey real and personal property, and to full and equal benefit of all laws and proceedings for the security of person and property, as is enjoyed by white citizens, and shall be subject to like punishment, pains, and penalties, and to none other, any law, statute, ordinance, regulation, or custom, to the contrary notwithstanding.

---

on legislation, see Michael J. Klarman, *Brown, Racial Change, and the Civil Rights Movement,* 80 Va L Rev 7, 141–50 (2000).

Sec. 2. *And be it further enacted*, That any person who, under color of any law, statute, ordinance, regulation, or custom, shall subject, or cause to be subjected, any inhabitant of any State or Territory to the deprivation of any right secured or protected by this act, or to different punishment, pains, or penalties on account of such person having at any time been held in condition of slavery or involuntary servitude, except as a punishment for crime whereof the party shall have been duly convicted, or by reason of his color or race, than is prescribed for the punishment of white persons, shall be deemed guilty of a misdemeanor, and, on conviction, shall be punished by fine not exceeding one thousand dollars, or imprisonment not exceeding one year, or both, in the discretion of the court.

Enforcement Act of 1870, 16 Stat 140.

Sec. 16. *And be it further enacted*, That all persons within the jurisdiction of the United States shall have the same right in every State and Territory in the United States to make and enforce contracts, to sue, be parties, give evidence, and to the full and equal benefit of all laws and proceedings for the security of person and property as is enjoyed by white citizens, and shall be subject to like punishment, pains, penalties, taxes, licenses, and exactions of every kind, and none other, any law, statute, ordinance, regulation, or custom to the contrary notwithstanding. No tax or charge shall be imposed or enforced by any State upon any person immigrating thereto from a foreign country which is not equally imposed and enforced upon every person immigrating to such State from any other foreign country; and any law of any State in conflict with this provision is hereby declared null and void.

Sec. 17. *And be it further enacted*, That any person who, under color of any law, statute, ordinance, regulation, or custom, shall subject, or cause to be subjected, any inhabitant of any State or Territory to the deprivation of any right secured or protected by the last preceding section of this act, or to different punishment, pains, or penalties on account of such person being an alien, or by reason of his color or race, than is prescribed for the punishment of citizens, shall be deemed guilty of a misdemeanor, and, on conviction, shall be punished by fine not exceeding one thousand dollars, or imprisonment not exceeding one year, or both, in the discretion of the court.

Sec. 18. *And be it further enacted*, That the act to protect all persons in the United States in their civil rights, and furnish the means of their vindication, passed April nine, eighteen hundred and sixty-six, is hereby re-enacted; and sections sixteen and seventeen hereof shall be enforced according to the provisions of said act.

Revised Statutes of 1874.

Sec. 1977. All persons within the jurisdiction of the United States shall have the same right in every State and Territory to make and enforce contracts, to sue, be parties, give evidence, and to the full and equal benefit of all laws and proceedings for the security of persons and property as is enjoyed by white citizens, and shall be subject to like punishment, pains, penalties, taxes, licenses, and exactions of every kind and no other.

Sec. 1978. All citizens of the United States shall have the same right in every State and Territory, as is enjoyed by white citizens thereof to inherit, purchase, lease, sell, hold, and convey real and personal property.

KENNETH L. KARST

JUSTICE O'CONNOR AND THE
SUBSTANCE OF EQUAL CITIZENSHIP

Throughout her twenty-two Terms of service on the Supreme
Court, Justice Sandra Day O'Connor has been subjected to labeling,
and the labels form a pattern. She has been called a pragmatist;[1]
a centrist;[2] a positivist[3] who tends to defend the established legal
order;[4] a moderate conservative who typically favors a modest judicial role in lawmaking;[5] a judge whose view of the structure of government emphasizes the defense of state sovereignty against undue
intrusions of federal (judicial or legislative) power;[6] a one-case-at-a-
time "minimalist" who seeks middle paths to decision and to doctrinal statement, and who prefers incremental movement to sweeping

---

Kenneth L. Karst is David G. Price and Dallas P. Price Professor of Law Emeritus,
University of California, Los Angeles.

Author's note: My thanks to Alison Anderson, Devon Carbado, William Rubenstein,
David Sklansky, Jonathan Varat, and Adam Winkler for their careful and sympathetic readings of a draft of this article. Four other UCLA colleagues would have been excellent
sources, for they served as clerks for Justice O'Connor. I have deliberately steered clear of
consulting them, or even showing them a draft of this article. At several points in the article
I indulge in unbridled speculation, and I want to avoid any possible inference that a clerk
has told tales out of school. I am grateful for the assistance of our law school's splendid
research librarians, especially Jennifer Lentz and Kevin Gerson.

[1] Robert W. Van Sickel, *Not a Particularly Different Voice: The Jurisprudence of Sandra Day
O'Connor* 132 (Peter Lang, 1998).

[2] Gene Sperling, *Justice in the Middle*, Atlantic Monthly 26 (March 1988).

[3] Van Sickel, *Not a Particularly Different Voice* at 57–59 (cited in note 1).

[4] Stephen E. Gottlieb, *Three Justices in Search of a Character: The Moral Agendas of Justices
O'Connor, Scalia, and Kennedy*, 49 Rutgers L Rev 219, 232 (1996).

[5] Van Sickel, *Not a Particularly Different Voice* at 54–55, 66–68 and passim (cited in note 1).

[6] Nancy Maveety, *Justice Sandra Day O'Connor: Strategist on the Supreme Court* 21–22,
42–43 (1996).

change;[7] one who shuns bright-line rules in favor of "balancing" doctrines that focus attention on factual contexts;[8] a successful builder of coalitions with other Justices.[9] The pattern of labeling is plain, centering on institutional and structural concerns. Largely ignored by these labels are Justice O'Connor's attitudes toward substantive justice and her contributions to the development of substantive law.

In this article I explore Justice O'Connor's decisions and opinions in the substantive areas of sex discrimination, abortion choice, religious freedom, racial discrimination, and discrimination based on sexual orientation.[10] All these subjects inhabit doctrinal arenas where the courts shape the right of equal citizenship under the Fourteenth Amendment. To personalize the matter, all these subjects offer a Justice repeated opportunities for contributing to a more inclusive community. I begin by introducing the substantive themes in an overview of Justice O'Connor's first five Terms—which were the last five Terms of the Burger Court. Then, turning to more recent decisions, a more detailed second section deals separately with the subjects of religion, race, and gender roles. In these fields, she has confronted a recurrent difficulty: how to preserve the ideal of inclusion when the ideal itself is opposed by the exclusionary pressures of group status politics. A third section briefly examines some tensions between Justice O'Connor's strong commitment to state sovereignty and the protection of equal citizenship.

Justice O'Connor's contributions to these fields of law are impressive. She has played a notable role in preserving some doctrinal

---

[7] Cass R. Sunstein, *One Case at a Time: Judicial Minimalism on the Supreme Court* 9, 62, 124 (Harvard, 1999). See also Van Sickel, *Not a Particularly Different Voice* at 5, 45–46, 175–76 (cited in note 1) ("marginalist"); Maveety, *Justice Sandra Day O'Connor* at 3–4, 25–73 (cited in note 6) ("accommodationist").

[8] Kathleen M. Sullivan, *The Supreme Court, 1991 Term—Foreword: The Justices of Rules and Standards*, 106 Harv L Rev 22, 58–62, 78–80, 91–93, 100–07 (1992).

[9] Maveety, *Justice Sandra Day O'Connor* at 3–7, 53–56, 133–35 (cited in note 6).

[10] I recognize that "storytelling, like the Sun in the sky, obscures as much as it reveals." Timothy Ferris, *Seeing in the Dark* xvi (Simon & Schuster, 2002). I have left out some fields of law in which Justice O'Connor has well developed views and has made important contributions to the development of the law. Two major examples are the fields of criminal justice and federal jurisdiction, both of which can bear on the vindication of equal citizenship. For a critical view, emphasizing these themes, see Herman Schwartz, *Lady Day* (Book Review), The Nation 34 (Aug 4, 2003). On Justice O'Connor, race, and police searches, see Devon Carbado, *(E)Racing the Fourth Amendment*, 100 Mich L Rev 946, 974–89, 1005–12 (2000). One day, surely, a judicial biography will treat these subjects, along with the topics discussed here.

forms vital to equal citizenship (in the law of sex discrimination, abortion choice, and affirmative action) and bringing another such form to the forefront of the law's attention (concern for religious outsiders). Even in the field of sexual orientation, after an early missed opportunity, she has participated in the Supreme Court's more recent turn toward protection of lesbians and gay men as full members of the society and polity. In the aggregate this record is remarkable; it is worthy of particularized examination. Each of the discussions proceeds chronologically, not in an attempt to write history, but to highlight Justice O'Connor's continuing role in developing the substantive law of equal citizenship. Proceeding in this way, perhaps we shall see that a Justice and the law she serves can evolve in a symbiotic process.

I. Prologue: The Burger Court Years

When Justice O'Connor joined the Court in 1981, replacing Justice Potter Stewart, her very status as the first woman Justice prompted expectations, hopes, fears. It was widely known that Justice O'Connor, an honors graduate of Stanford Law School in 1952, had been unable to find law firm employment in San Francisco or Los Angeles. Of course she could not fail to be sensitive to claims that women were systematically denied inclusion in the public world, including the world of work. Would her views on "women's issues" set her apart from the other Justices? Would she bring a distinctively feminine point of view to decision making?[11] President Reagan, who had appointed her to the Court, was a prominent opponent of any claim to abortion rights, but at her confirmation hearing she deflected questions about *Roe v Wade*,[12] and she generally came across as a moderate conservative.[13]

In Justice O'Connor's very first Term, the Court faced a major sex discrimination case, *Mississippi University for Women v Hogan*.[14]

---

[11] The classic here is Suzanna Sherry, *Civic Virtue and the Feminine Voice in Constitutional Adjudication*, 72 Va L Rev 543 (1986). See also Maveety, *Justice Sandra Day O'Connor* at 19–22, 25–26 (cited in note 6); Van Sickel, *Not a Particularly Different Voice* at 111–60 and passim (cited in note 1).

[12] 410 US 113 (1973).

[13] A few of her votes in the Arizona state senate had seemed to some right-to-life activists to betray a pro-choice attitude, but those votes might also rest on grounds unrelated to such an attitude. Maveety, *Justice Sandra Day O'Connor* at 16–19 (cited in note 6).

[14] 458 US 718 (1982).

Or, to put it more carefully, the Court faced a case that would become "major" because of Justice O'Connor's opinion. Joe Hogan wanted to attend nursing school near his home, but he was turned down when he applied for admission at the local state university (Mississippi University for Women, or MUW), for enrollment was limited to women, and Hogan lacked that qualification. MUW's admissions policy had been adopted during an era when nursing was seen as "women's work"; the question was whether the policy might now be justified by something other than sex-role stereotyping. This setting—a man raising the issue of discrimination—had characterized several of the Supreme Court's early decisions on the subject, notably including *Craig v Boren*[15] in 1976. In that case the Court had adopted a formula for heightened judicial scrutiny in cases of governmental sex discrimination. To pass this scrutiny, the *Craig* Court held, the state must show that its policy of sex discrimination is "substantially related" to an "important" governmental interest.[16]

In applying the *Craig* standard, the courts generally have concluded that the state interests are "important"; the real potency of the standard lies in its exacting scrutiny of sex discrimination as a "substantially related" means to achieve those interests. But, in the Term preceding Justice O'Connor's arrival on the scene, Justice William H. Rehnquist, a dissenter in *Craig*, had led a counterattack on heightened scrutiny in such cases. He wrote opinions of the Court in two cases. *Michael M. v Superior Court*[17] upheld a state law that, in a case of unmarried sexual intercourse involving young people under eighteen, made the young man, but not the woman, guilty of statutory rape. And *Rostker v Goldberg*[18] upheld an act of Congress requiring men, but not women, to register for a potential military draft. In both cases, Justice Rehnquist's equal protection formulation effectively displaced the *Craig* standard's demanding means scrutiny, substituting a much softer formula: that there is no constitutional violation in treating men and women differently

---

[15] 429 US 190 (1976). The Court invalidated a law that allowed women over 18 to buy 3.2 beer, but allowed men to buy the same beer only when they reached the age of 21.

[16] As every law student learns, this standard was designed to be "intermediate"—between the mere "rationality" that sufficed to sustain economic regulations and the "strict scrutiny" that amounted to a strong presumption of invalidity in cases of racial discrimination.

[17] 450 US 464 (1981) (5–4).

[18] 453 US 57 (1981) (6–3).

if men and women are not "similarly situated."[19] Precisely because
generations of sex-role stereotyping have retained considerable acculturating influence, a judge who is looking to find a difference
between men and women can always find one.[20] Justice Rehnquist
was—and he did.

Enter Justice O'Connor, replacing the Justice who had invented
the "similarly situated" formula.[21] With the Court thus reconsti-
tuted, a 5–4 majority concluded that MUW had violated Joe
Hogan's equal protection rights by excluding him. If this decision
turned out to be momentous, a little of the credit should go to
Justice William J. Brennan, Jr. Because Chief Justice Warren
Burger was in dissent, it fell to Justice Brennan, as the senior Justice in the majority, to assign the writing of the Court's opinion—
and he assigned it to Justice O'Connor. Her resulting opinion
not only reconfirmed the *Craig* standard, but characterized it
as demanding an "exceedingly persuasive justification" for explicit sex discrimination by any government instrumentality.[22]
Justice O'Connor rejected the dissenters' argument that MUW's
women-only policy was designed to expand women's educational
choices, pointing out that the sex discrimination here certainly
was not based on any showing that women lacked opportunities
for nursing training. Rather, the policy tended to "perpetuate
the stereotyped view of nursing as an exclusively women's job."[23]
The constitutional protection against sex discrimination regained
its vigor, and—except for one doctrinal area—has retained it ever
since.[24] In other words, in her very first Term Justice O'Connor
made a crucial contribution to the substantive right of equal citizen-

---

[19] *Michael M.*, 450 US at 471; *Rostker*, 453 US at 79.

[20] The most illuminating discussion of these two cases, in my judgment, is Wendy W.
Williams, *The Equality Crisis: Some Reflections on Culture, Courts and Feminism*, 7 Women's
Rts L Rep 175 (1982).

[21] *Schlesinger v Ballard*, 419 US 498, 508 (1975) (Stewart, J, for the Court). Justice Stewart
had joined Justice Rehnquist's opinions of the Court in the two 1981 cases that threatened
the demise of intermediate scrutiny of official sex discrimination.

[22] This expression, ironically, had been coined in an opinion by Justice Stewart—an opinion denying a claim of sex discrimination, saying the discrimination was neither explicit in
the law nor intended by the legislature. *Personnel Adm'r of Massachusetts v Feeney*, 442 US
256, 273 (1979).

[23] *Mississippi University for Women v Hogan*, 458 US at 29.

[24] The exceptional cases lie in the area of congressional power over immigration and
nationality. A recent—and dismaying—example is *Nguyen v INS*, 533 US 53 (2001), discussed in the text at note 195.

ship, and to women's inclusion in the public life of the national community.

At the time of Justice O'Connor's nomination to the Court, her views in a different subject area had led to another sort of prediction about her judicial future. During her seven years as a state judge, her most noteworthy extrajudicial writing had been an article that, in its most significant passages, applauded the Burger Court's recent efforts to rein in federal courts' jurisdiction—particularly their habeas corpus jurisdiction over state criminal convictions, but more generally their jurisdiction over issues of state law.[25] These recent developments in the Supreme Court had been led by her long-time friend, Justice Rehnquist, with whom she would soon be allied in the defense of state prerogatives.

Her enlistment in that cause came early—also in her first Term, just a month before the *Hogan* decision. The occasion was *FERC v Mississippi*,[26] perhaps the most important case in the sequence that led from *National League of Cities v Usery*[27] to *García v San Antonio Metropolitan Transit Authority*[28] and beyond.[29] In *FERC*, the Court upheld a provision in an act of Congress that directed state public utilities commissions to consider adopting specified federal standards for regulating utility rates and other conduct. The opinion of the Court was written by Justice Harry A. Blackmun, who would dissent in *Hogan*, a decision announced a few weeks later. Justice O'Connor dissented from the chief holding in *FERC*, arguing that Congress could not constitutionally "conscript state utility commissions into the national bureaucratic army."[30] This dissent led Justice Blackmun to characterize Justice O'Connor's arguments in language that was, to put it mildly, intemperate. A few tidbits are illustrative: He referred to one "rhetorical assertion" as "demonstrably incorrect," called various statements "exercises in the art of *ipse dixit*," and suggested that others were "absurd"

---

[25] Sandra Day O'Connor, *Trends in the Relationship Between the Federal and State Courts from the Perspective of a State Court Judge*, 22 Wm & Mary L Rev 801 (1981).

[26] 456 US 742 (1982).

[27] 426 US 833 (1976).

[28] 469 US 528 (1985).

[29] The culminating decision in this sequence on federal "commandeering" of state government officers went Justice O'Connor's way, and she wrote for the Court. *New York v United States*, 505 US 144 (1992).

[30] *FERC v Mississippi*, 456 US 742, at 775 (1982).

or "peculiar." In summary, he said, "While these rhetorical devices make for absorbing reading, they unfortunately are substituted for useful constitutional analysis." Thus did Justice Blackmun welcome his new colleague to the Court. Justice O'Connor responded in kind twice—her words were "absurdity" and "disingenuous"—but largely she resisted temptation.

Surely the dispute over state sovereignty remained in the Justices' consciousness when, a year later, the Supreme Court decided *Akron v Akron Center for Reproductive Health, Inc.*[31] This case was Justice O'Connor's first occasion to consider the constitutionality of state or local regulations of abortion choice. In an opinion by Justice Lewis F. Powell, the Court struck down a city council's legislative package of restrictions requiring, among other things, that a second-trimester abortion be performed in a hospital, and that various steps be taken "supposedly" (Powell's word) to insure the patient's informed consent.[32] The parties had not argued that *Roe v Wade* should be overruled, but the majority nonetheless reaffirmed *Roe*, applying its "trimester" approach to invalidate the abortion regulations before the Court.[33] Justice O'Connor dissented, in a strongly worded opinion; she was joined by Justices White and Rehnquist, who had dissented in *Roe* a decade earlier. Calling *Roe*'s trimester formula "unworkable,"[34] she maintained that a state had an important interest in protecting both potential life and women's health throughout the term of pregnancy. She argued that a regulation should be valid so long as it was not

---

[31] 462 US 416 (1983).

[32] Justice Powell's distrust of the Akron council's good faith is evident throughout his opinion. The law required a doctor to give the woman a packet of information about the condition of the fetus, the risks attendant on abortion, and the like—all plainly designed, in the view of Justice Powell for the majority, not to inform the woman but to dissuade her from ending her pregnancy. The law also imposed a 24-hour waiting period between the woman's signature on a consent form and the abortion.

[33] For those few readers who may be new to this subject: In *Roe* the Court had interpreted "liberty," in the Fourteenth Amendment's Due Process Clause, to give the woman discretion to choose to have an abortion during roughly the first third of the normal term of pregnancy. After that time, the Court ruled, the state had a "compelling" interest that justified regulations to protect the woman's health. After the fetus became "viable," roughly two-thirds of the way through the normal term of pregnancy, the state could forbid abortions altogether, or otherwise regulate for the protection of potential human life, except in a case where an abortion was necessary to protect the woman's life or health.

[34] In an early draft she also called the trimester framework "unprincipled," but she eliminated this word before releasing her opinion. Maveety, *Justice Sandra Day O'Connor* at 95, 104 n 2 (cited in note 6).

unduly burdensome on a woman's freedom to choose an abortion. If a regulation were adjudged to create such an "undue burden," she said, then and only then should it be subjected to strict judicial scrutiny. In a footnote, she maintained that "legislatures, with their superior fact-finding capabilities, are certainly better able to make the necessary judgments [about good medical practice] than are Courts."[35] For Justice O'Connor, nothing in Akron's entire legislative package—specifically including a second-trimester hospital requirement and a mandatory twenty-four-hour delay—unduly burdened the woman's choice whether to have an abortion. That the law increased the cost of an abortion was not enough, in her judgment, to constitute an undue burden.

It may be amusing, for those who like to think about the Supreme Court as a small community, to note that in the *Akron* dissent Justice O'Connor gave Justice Blackmun's handiwork in *Roe v Wade* much the same treatment he had given her dissent in *FERC* the previous year. But my own assessment places Justice O'Connor's *Akron* dissent in another frame. *Roe v Wade* was and remains the most famous modern instance of the application of federal judicial power to displace state and local legislative policy in an area of traditional state concern, that is, the protection of life and health. All the Court's decisions invalidating state abortion regulations, from *Roe* to *Akron*, had been rested on substantive applications of the Due Process Clause of the Fourteenth Amendment. In 1977, in a factual setting distant from abortion rights, Justice White had objected to a policy of open-ended deployment of substantive due process to invalidate state laws:

> The Judiciary, including this Court, is the most vulnerable and comes nearest to illegitimacy when it deals with judge-made constitutional law having little or no cognizable roots in the language or even design of the Constitution. . . . [T]he Court should be extremely reluctant to breathe still further substantive content into the Due Process Clause so as to strike down legislation adopted by a State or city to promote its welfare. Whenever the Judiciary does so, it unavoidably pre-empts for itself another part of the governance of the country without express constitutional authority.[36]

---

[35] 462 US 456 n 4.

[36] *Moore v East Cleveland, Ohio,* 431 US 494, at 544 (1977) (White, J, dissenting).

It seems likely that Justice O'Connor saw *Akron* primarily in the light of this principle of judicial self-restraint. Yet, for her—we may speculate—a second consideration may have played its own part. For her, in 1983, the attitude of the *Akron* majority may have seemed analogous to the attitude of the *FERC* majority in approving an assertion of federal power that displaced state legislative sovereignty.[37]

Three years after *Akron*, the Court decided *Thornburgh v American College of Obstetricians and Gynecologists*,[38] holding invalid a similar set of restrictions on abortion choice, similarly adopted as a package by the Pennsylvania legislature. Now the vote was 5–4, with Chief Justice Burger joining the *Akron* dissenters. Justice White's *Thornburgh* dissent included a passage reiterating his 1977 concerns, just quoted, about the judiciary's vulnerability when it strikes down laws in the name of "fundamental" liberties "nowhere mentioned in the Constitution."[39] In *Thornburgh* Justice O'Connor wrote a separate dissenting opinion, restating the main points of her *Akron* dissent. In her summary, she manifested her concern about the arrogance of federal power. The Court, she said, had made bad law by fastening a "straitjacket" on the fifty states.[40]

The *Thornburgh* case had been argued in November 1985; *Bowers v Hardwick*[41] came on for argument in March 1986; the two cases were both decided in June 1986. No doubt the draft opinions in *Thornburgh* had been circulating when *Hardwick* was argued. In *Hardwick*, a 5–4 majority of the Court, including Justice O'Connor, upheld Georgia's sodomy law in application to homosexual sodomy. Justice White, assigned to write for the Court, took the occasion to produce an opinion that was callous and dismissive, utterly insensitive to the consequences of criminalizing expressions of homosexual intimacy—the central point of Justice Blackmun's dissent. This case might have been an occasion for Justice O'Connor to write a concurrence that explored questions of real-world context. But if we see her vote as centered on due process doctrine,

---

[37] Justice White, ever a believer in strong congressional power, had joined the majority in *FERC*.

[38] 476 US 747 (1986).

[39] Id at 790.

[40] Id at 828, 833. Justice O'Connor also dissented on procedural grounds.

[41] 478 US 186 (1986).

it is explainable. Justice White now had an opportunity to translate his former dissents into constitutional law.[42] To demonstrate that the case was properly bracketed with *Thornburgh*, Justice White repeated, almost verbatim, the main strictures in his 1977 dissent, quoted above.

I believe Justice O'Connor, like Justice White, saw *Hardwick* and *Thornburgh* in the same institutional light, and that she was not focusing on either case as an occasion for dealing with substantive issues of equality and inclusion.[43] Indeed, *Hardwick* had been argued for the challenger to the law as a case presenting a due-process "liberty" claim, applicable alike to the bedroom behavior of heterosexual couples. The text of the law had invited just that argument,[44] which downplayed the state's discriminatory policy. One wonders what Justices Powell and O'Connor might have made of

---

[42] Famous as Justice O'Connor may be for writing separate concurrences in big cases, here she merely joined the opinion of the Court.

[43] Here I follow the conventional readings of the opinions in *Hardwick*, but those are by no means the only reasonable readings. Marc Spindelman has offered a close analysis of Justice White's majority opinion that emphasizes the importance of social context as a guide to interpretations of constitutional "liberty." In this view, that opinion can be read as holding that, in 1986, the historical consensus that gay sex violated important social norms had not yet—repeat, *yet*—been displaced by a consensus around the norms of tolerance and inclusion. Spindelman analogizes the distance between prevailing social norms at the time of *Hardwick* and norms at the time of *Romer v Evans*, discussed in the text at note 309, to the social-norms distance between *Naim v Naim*, 350 US 985 (1956), when the Court fudged to avoid deciding on the validity of a miscegenation law, and *Loving v Virginia*, 388 US 1 (1967), when the Court unanimously held such a law invalid. Marc S. Spindelman, *Reorienting Bowers v Hardwick*, 79 NC L Rev 359, 384–402, 446–62 (2001). The Spindelman article will reward a careful reading, even if you are inclined to take Justice White's doctrinal explanation in the conventional manner.

[44] The Georgia law was not, in terms, limited to homosexual sodomy. At the oral argument, however, Georgia's counsel said the law would not be applied to heterosexual sodomy. This concession raised a serious constitutional challenge founded on the Equal Protection Clause, but the majority dealt with the resulting advocacy quandary by evading the question altogether—and this despite the dissent of Justice John Paul Stevens, 478 US at 214–20, explicitly raising the equality issue.

Spindelman, 79 NC L Rev at 468–71 (cited in note 43), recalls a question that Justice O'Connor asked at the oral argument in *Hardwick*, a question that might have arisen from concerns that a decision invalidating the Georgia sodomy law could heighten the national panic about AIDS, just then reaching its zenith. It was not beyond reason to imagine that an intensified panic would produce an antigay backlash with grave consequences for lesbian and gay Americans. We just can't know the degree to which that concern may have contributed to the majority votes in *Hardwick*. We can say that concern about a decision's possible contribution to backlash politics would not appear to the Justices as a new idea. See, for example, *Brown v Board of Education* 349 US 294 (1955) (Brown II, "all deliberate speed"). And see the discussion of Justice O'Connor's concurrence in *Lynch v Donnelly*, in the text immediately following and at note 94.

the case if antigay discrimination had been in the forefront of the briefs and oral argument.[45]

If *Hardwick* was a missed opportunity for advancing the idea of a broadly inclusive polity, the latter years of the Burger Court offered similar opportunities in other doctrinal settings. To round out this survey of Justice O'Connor's first five Terms, we turn to the subjects of religion and race, both of which can test a Justice's devotion to the principle of equal citizenship.

Justice O'Connor is widely known for her concurring opinions.[46] One of her best known and most influential concurrences placed the idea of a broadly inclusive public world at the center of her concerns. The case was *Lynch v Donnelly*,[47] decided midway in her third Term. The City of Pawtucket, Rhode Island, at city expense, had erected a city-owned Nativity scene (crèche) as part of a Christmas season display in a park. When some local citizens brought a lawsuit to enjoin the city from continuing this display, the mayor of Pawtucket seized this heaven-sent opportunity to score points. He held a televised news conference at the scene of the crèche to say the opponents were trying to "take Christ out of Christmas."[48] The federal district court held that the city's display was official sponsorship of religion, and thus a violation of the Establishment Clause. The Supreme Court reversed, 5–4, in an opinion by Chief Justice Burger that set a modern record for consecutive conclusory assertions. The city wasn't sponsoring Christian doctrine, because . . . well, because government officials had been giving symbolic support to religion from the nation's earliest days, and this particular official symbol of one of the two central miracles of Christianity didn't seem to him to be an establishment of religion any more than did the earlier forms.[49] Not

---

[45] Having wondered, I doubt that such an emphasis on inequality would have changed either Justice's vote. Discrimination, after all, was vividly brought to the Court's attention, for it was the central point in Justice Stevens's dissent. In 2003, however, inequality was Justice O'Connor's ground for voting to hold the Texas sodomy law invalid. *Lawrence v Texas*, 123 S Ct 2472, 2484 (2003) (discussed in the text at note 322).

[46] See, for example, Alexander Wohl, *O'Connor, J, Concurring*, ABA J 42 (Dec 1989).

[47] 465 US 668 (1984).

[48] *Donnelly v Lynch*, 525 F Supp 1150, 1158–59 (DRI 1981), rev'd, *Lynch v Donnelly*, 465 US 668 (1984).

[49] For trenchant analysis of this "any more than" test, see William W. Van Alstyne, *Trends in the Supreme Court: Mr. Jefferson's Crumbling Wall—A Comment on Lynch v Donnelly*, 1984 Duke L J 770.

surprisingly, the Chief Justice's list of historical symbolic supports consists almost entirely of supports for Christianity, with a couple of nods to Judaism.[50] Here we have an illustration of a principle of general application: When we attune the interpretation of constitutional rights to historical traditions, we tend to favor the cultural Haves. For the cultural Have-nots, the same history is a nightmare from which they are trying to awake.[51]

The *Lemon* test, the Establishment Clause's prevailing doctrinal formula, has invited question-begging for three decades, but has not been abandoned.[52] In *Lynch* Justice O'Connor—not for the first time and certainly not the last—joined the opinion of the Court but added her own "clarification" of the *Lemon* test, placing the question of governmental endorsement or disapproval of religion at the center of inquiry. Is the purpose of the government support for religion to provide endorsement (or disapproval) of religion?[53] Does the support, in the view of a "reasonable observer," "have the effect of communicating a message of government endorsement or disapproval of religion"?[54] As a number of commentators have suggested, this concern for dignitary harms bears a strong family resemblance to the concerns of modern equal protection doctrine as applied to discrimination against "outsiders" in other categories of self-identity, such as race or sex or sexual orientation.[55]

---

[50] 465 US at 674–78.

[51] My apology to James Joyce.

[52] In *Lemon v Kurtzman*, 403 US 602 (1971), the Court (per Burger, CJ) held that governmental support for religion would satisfy the Establishment Clause provided that it (i) had a secular legislative purpose, (ii) had a principal effect that neither advanced nor inhibited religion, and (iii) avoided excessive "entanglement" of government with religion.

[53] 475 US at 689.

[54] Id at 692.

[55] See, for example, Arnold H. Loewy, *Rethinking Government Neutrality Towards Religion Under the Establishment Clause: The Untapped Potential of Justice O'Connor's Insight*, 64 NC L Rev 1049, 1057 (1986). Among many good discussions along these lines, an especially enlightening one is Alan E. Brownstein, *Harmonizing the Heavenly and Earthly Spheres: The Fragmentation and Synthesis of Religion, Equality, and Speech in the Constitution*, 51 Ohio St L J 89, 102–12, 142–54 and passim (1990). For elaboration and an update, specifically addressed to Justice O'Connor's votes and opinions, see Alan E. Brownstein, *A Decent Respect for Religious Liberty and Religious Equality: Justice O'Connor's Interpretation of the Religion Clauses of the First Amendment*, 32 McGeorge L Rev 837, 845–62 (2001) ("*A Decent Respect*").

While we are giving credit, let us note that John Garvey, three years before *Lynch*, suggested that "the Establishment Clause, no less than the Equal Protection Clause, is worried about the psychic and moral affront from discrimination." John H. Garvey, *Freedom and Equality in the Religion Clauses*, 1981 Supreme Court Review 193, 212 (citing, inter alia, the early school prayer cases).

Justice O'Connor's endorsement principle has been criticized as too indefinite, as a pathway to judicial subjectivity, and the like.[56] Those concerns are real enough,[57] and in some types of cases— notably, when government has provided material aid to religious schools—reasonable judges are likely to reach differing conclusions on the issue of endorsement.[58] In other cases, however—notably those in which government officially displays the symbols of religion—the endorsement principle's difficulties of application may not disappear, but they do recede. One case that remains easy is officially sponsored public school prayer, which is unconstitutional and surely will remain so.[59]

Even "easy cases" of officially sponsored religious expression may not seem easy to all judges. *Lynch* itself is a case in point. The dissenters readily agreed that official endorsements of religion

---

[56] An early thoughtful criticism along these lines is Steven D. Smith, *Symbols, Perceptions, and Doctrinal Illusions: Establishment Neutrality and the "No Endorsement" Test*, 86 Mich L Rev 266, 283–91 and passim (1987). For a recent criticism, with supporting analyses of decisions in the last two decades, see Jesse H. Choper, *The Endorsement Test: Its Status and Desirability*, 18 J L & Pol 499 (2002).

[57] A decade ago I discussed these criticisms in detail and concluded that the endorsement principle, although far from crisp, had set judges on the right path—that is, toward recognizing that the problem of exclusion is the central concern of the Establishment Clause. Kenneth L. Karst, *The First Amendment, the Politics of Religion and the Symbols of Government*, 27 Harv CR-CL L Rev 503, 512–25 (1992). For more recent confirmation, see the discussion in the text at note 94.

[58] A good illustration is *Agostini v Felton*, 521 US 203 (1997), in which the Supreme Court upheld, 5–4, the deployment of public school teachers to provide remedial education on the grounds of religious schools. Justice David Souter, for the four dissenters, condemned this form of aid as an unconstitutional governmental endorsement of religion. The majority explicitly concluded otherwise—in an opinion by Justice O'Connor, perhaps not the sole proprietor of the "endorsement" test, but undoubtedly a respected authority on the subject. For a persuasive critique of efforts to make the endorsement principle do the same service in public funding cases that it does in cases of official displays of religious symbols, see Brownstein, 32 McGeorge L Rev at 862–65 (cited in note 55). Brownstein says Justice O'Connor needs to do more explaining if she is to "convince the polity that these decisions [on government funding of religious institutions] reflect accepted constitutional values." Id at 865. In this season of American politics, I wonder whether the polity cares. Another sort of case promises similar difficulties for the endorsement principle: the case in which the legislature accommodates free exercise values by allowing a religious exception to a regulatory law. Still, as a huge (and growing) literature attests, no other doctrinal formula does any better than the endorsement principle in resolving these accommodation cases.

[59] A plan for a school-sponsored student chaplain's prayer at football games came under constitutional attack before it was put into effect. The absence of a showing of actual effects was central to the argument of the three Justices who dissented from the Supreme Court's decision in *Santa Fe Ind. School Dist. v Doe*, 530 US 290 (2000), holding the plan unconstitutional. Although this seems an easy case to me, I concede that one might argue that prayers offered by students merely accommodate their free exercise concerns, and are neither intended nor perceived as carrying the school's endorsement.

created a risk of alienating effects on religious outsiders—and they saw precisely that in Pawtucket's crèche. I agree with the dissenters; the mayor's statement, obviously intended to polarize the local electorate, lends special force to their point. The abstraction of the "reasonable observer," in this case, seems not to have given much weight to the view of religious outsiders. Given Justice O'Connor's clearly expressed concern for those very people, it seems fair to wonder: what was she thinking? Viewed as an exercise in doctrine-oriented strategy, this opinion, like many another concurring opinion, might be seen as a way to win support (perhaps now, perhaps in the future) from members of the majority, who might be more receptive to the endorsement principle if they saw that it left some leeway for upholding static displays. From another perspective we might recall that this decision came in Justice O'Connor's third year as a Justice. In those early days, when the Supreme Court was divided on "judgment calls,"[60] she was likely to be aligned, more often than not, with the Chief Justice and with Justices White, Powell, and Rehnquist.

Justice O'Connor's vote notwithstanding, her concurrence in *Lynch* remains notable for two vital insights, one of which I outline here:[61] When government's expression assigns an individual or a group to an outsider status, the state has committed a serious status harm, in violation of the Fourteenth Amendment's principle of equal citizenship. Every generation of law students since 1954 has read *Brown v Board of Education*,[62] where the Court famously made the point in the context of race. Justice O'Connor's explicit recognition of the principle's force in the context of religion is a milestone in our jurisprudence: "The Establishment Clause prohibits government from making adherence to a religion relevant in any way to a person's standing in the political community."[63] For her,

---

[60] This term comes from a 1996 lecture by Justice O'Connor in Belfast. She explained in that lecture why governmental endorsement of religion was harmful to individuals and to the political community, and she went on to say, "The line-drawing process can be an agonising one . . . . To achieve mutual respect and equality among religions with differing beliefs, one has to make judgment calls about which accommodations are essential to prove that society is taking an individual's religious beliefs seriously, and which accommodations will leave those of other faiths feeling shunned and excluded." Sandra Day O'Connor, *Religious Freedom: America's Quest for Principles*, 48 No Ireland Legal Q 1, 8 (1997).

[61] See the discussion of the second one in the text at note 94.

[62] 347 US 483 (1954).

[63] 465 US at 687.

one's standing in the political community is not simply a matter of access to the vote, or free speech, or other civil liberties.[64] Rather she is saying that the government's message of exclusion is itself a stigmatic harm, and an unconstitutional denial of full membership in the community.

The subject of racial discrimination had been a perennial on the Supreme Court's docket when Justice O'Connor took her place, and the parade of cases has not stopped. Some questions about race seemed fairly well settled in 1981. Official racial discrimination had to pass the strictest form of judicial scrutiny, but the concept of discrimination, in constitutional cases, required a showing of purpose. A law that was racially neutral on its face would not be struck down merely because it had disparately harsh effects on members of a racial minority.[65] On the other hand, a racially disparate effect of conduct by a private employer (or landlord, etc.) might, under some federal civil rights acts, be enough to establish a presumptive case of violation of law, shifting to the employer (etc.) the burden of proving that the practice in question (such as a qualification for hiring) served a legitimate purpose.[66] Some forms of affirmative action, both state and federal, had found limited approval, but by fragmented Courts.[67] Right after she joined the Court, Justice O'Connor confronted several cases that presented new questions, calling for refinements in the existing doctrine governing racial discrimination.

The first major case in this group added a dimension to the Court's jurisprudence of racially discriminatory "purpose." As early as *Washington v Davis*,[68] Justice Stevens had made clear in his concurrence that one part of the evidence of legislative purpose would always be a law's racially disparate effects.[69] The Court gave life to this prediction in *Rogers v Lodge*,[70] decided in Justice O'Connor's

---

[64] Here I am disagreeing with the narrower interpretation of Justice O'Connor's reference to political standing suggested by Steven Smith, 86 Mich L Rev at 307–08 (cited in note 56).

[65] *Washington v Davis*, 426 US 229 (1976), is still the leading citation for this proposition.

[66] The leading decision interpreting the employment discrimination title (Title VII) of the Civil Rights Act of 1964 is *Griggs v Duke Power Co.*, 401 US 424 (1971).

[67] The decisions were *Regents of University of California v Bakke*, 438 US 265 (1978), and *Fullilove v Klutznick*, 448 US 448 (1980).

[68] 426 US 229 (cited in note 65).

[69] Id at 253–54. The majority opinion also alluded to this point. Id at 242.

[70] 458 US 613 (1982) (6–3).

first Term. In 1911 a rural county in Georgia had adopted a system of county-wide, at-large voting for electing the five members of its board of commissioners. Although more than half of the county's population was black in 1980, and its registered voters were 38 percent black, no black commissioner had ever been elected. If the county were divided into districts, then—given the prevalence of racial bloc voting and the residential concentration of black voters—one would expect that at least one black commissioner would be elected. Past discrimination in Georgia (and the county), both in voting mechanisms and in education, had contributed to the relatively low voter registration of black citizens, according to the district court. That court also found that the county board had been unresponsive to black citizens' concerns about road paving, school segregation, and the contribution of county money to private white "segregation academies." So, in addition to the racially disparate results of the at-large elections, other indicators of purposive governmental discrimination could be found, despite the absence of evidence of particular acts of discrimination by particular officials. The state of this record closely resembled the record in an earlier case, where a plurality of the Court, in an opinion by Justice Stewart, had rejected similar circumstantial evidence as insufficient, insisting on proof of improper purpose by factors that were more "objective."[71] But in *Rogers*, a 6–3 Supreme Court concluded that strong evidence of this kind was sufficient to show a discriminatory purpose in maintaining the at-large electoral system.

In joining the Court's turnaround, Justice O'Connor set a course from which she has not wavered. The judiciary, in her view, properly lends its weight to the dismantling of formal structures of racial subordination, and to the inclusion of all citizens as full participants in the political community. What strikes me here is her willingness, at this early date, to take the context of a politics

---

[71] *Mobile v Bolden*, 446 US 55 (1980) (6–3). In *Mobile*, Justices Marshall and Brennan dissented. So did Justice White—who, as the author of *Washington v Davis*, ought to know a discriminatory purpose when he saw one, and who saw such a purpose here. Justice Stevens concurred in the judgment. Justice Blackmun, concurring, agreed with Justice White that a wrongful purpose had been shown, but thought the remedy of dismantling an at-large system was too severe. Justice O'Connor replaced Justice Stewart just one year after the *Mobile* decision. In *Rogers*, 458 US 613, Justice White wrote the opinion of the Court. He was joined by the other *Mobile* dissenters, along with Chief Justice Burger (who had been part of Justice Stewart's *Mobile* plurality), Justice Blackmun, and Justice O'Connor.

of group status domination as a reason for distrust of legislative motives. This insight, together with her concerns in *Lynch* about the tendency of group status politics toward exclusion of groups from equal citizenship, can do important service in a variety of modern settings, including intrusions on the right of abortion choice and discrimination based on sexual orientation.

When government seeks to redress the effects of past racial discrimination by adopting race-conscious remedial programs (what we now call affirmative action), even the most enthusiastic supporters—the Brennans and the Marshalls—have agreed that the courts must take a careful look at the government's asserted justifications. Justice O'Connor first addressed this problem in 1986, in *Wygant v Jackson Board of Education.*[72] A local school board had been charged, in a complaint before the state's civil rights commission, with racial discrimination in the hiring of teachers. In settlement of this complaint, the board promised to take affirmative steps to hire and keep minority teachers. One means of maintaining a significant number of minority teachers was written into the board's contract with the teachers' union: In the event that the board's budget should require layoffs, the seniority system would be respected, but the percentage of minority teachers laid off would not exceed the overall percentage of those teachers in the system. Thus some recently hired minority teachers would be kept on the job, while some more senior white teachers would be laid off. The budget crunch did come, and some white teachers with seniority brought an action to enjoin the board from laying them off in order to protect minority teachers with less time in service. The lower courts upheld the board's action, but the Supreme Court reversed, 5–4. Justice O'Connor, who joined in most of Justice Powell's plurality opinion, added a concurring opinion of her own.

Wygant, in one dimension, took up where the 1978 *Bakke* decision[73] had left off. In *Bakke,* a 5–4 Supreme Court had held invalid a state university medical school's racial quota for admissions,[74] but a different 5–4 majority had held that the university could consider

---

[72] 476 US 267 (1986).

[73] *Regents of University of California v Bakke,* 438 US 265 (cited in note 67).

[74] Justice Stevens, writing for four Justices, did not reach the constitutional question, but said that the quota violated Title VI of the 1964 Civil Rights Act. Justice Powell concluded that the quota violated both the constitutional guarantee of equal protection and Title VI.

race, among other factors, in an admissions program designed to diversify the student body. Justice Powell was the only Justice to concur in both of those determinations; for many years, however, shorthand references to *Bakke* generally have been understood to refer to his separate opinion.[75] Not surprisingly, *Wygant* also fragmented the Court—on the immediate result, on the question of the appropriate standard of review for "remedial" affirmative action, and on the conditions that would justify remedial action. Justice Powell's opinion in *Wygant* spoke for a plurality of three Justices; as in *Bakke*, he applied a strict scrutiny standard of review. He concluded that the only "compelling" state interest in sight was the school board's compensation for its own prior discrimination. As he had said in *Bakke*, compensating for past societal discrimination was not such a compelling interest; nor was the preservation of minority teacher "role models" for students. In the record below, he said, the board had not sufficiently demonstrated past racial discrimination that would justify present compensatory action. The plurality would neither consider "nonrecord materials" nor remand the case for amplification of the record. Justice Powell did, however, remark that some valid efforts to remedy the effects of prior discrimination necessarily would impose burdens on innocent persons (that is, persons who had not themselves been shown to engage in discrimination); such a burden, he said, would be permissible.[76]

One might make an argument founded on a close look at the context of this particular affirmative action program—indeed, Justice Stevens did argue in dissent—that an inclusionary, remedial purpose for race-based affirmative action set it apart from invidious governmental support for racial subordination.[77] In this first encounter with affirmative action, however, Justice O'Connor rejected such a contextual argument. Her concurring opinion agreed with Justice Powell on the result, on the need for strict scrutiny

---

[75] The opinion of Justices Brennan, White, Blackmun, and Marshall did join Justice Powell's opinion in its affirmation that race could be used constitutionally as one factor in a "diversity" admissions program. That part of the Powell opinion, then, was an opinion of the Court.

[76] Justice White added a short opinion, concurring only in the judgment. While hiring preferences might sometimes be justified, he said, discharges of white teachers to make room for black teachers was unconstitutional. 476 US at 294.

[77] Id at 313.

of race-based affirmative action, and on the insufficiency of the lower courts' asserted justifications for the school board's race-based layoffs—that is, remedying societal discrimination, or providing role models for the students. But her opinion was notable for its effort to find common ground among the Justices.[78] As to the standard of review, for example, she suggested that there was not a great deal of difference between a "compelling" state interest and one that was merely "important"[79] She also made clear that her concurrence was conditioned on a principle that would allow a considerable scope for race-conscious mechanisms to remedy the effects of past discrimination. Thus, it would not be necessary for the school board to make a specific finding of its own prior discrimination in order to justify remedial action; requiring such a finding "would severely undermine public employers' incentive to meet voluntarily their civil rights obligations." Nor need a government employer's affirmative action program be "limited to the remedying of specific instances of identified discrimination" in order to satisfy the requirement of "narrow tailoring" to the remedial goal.[80]

Making unmistakable her receptiveness to significant forms of affirmative action, Justice O'Connor went so far as to suggest that a statistical disparity between the percentage of qualified black teachers on a school's teaching staff and the percentage of qualified black teachers in the local teacher employment pool—the kind sufficient to support a "pattern or practice" claim of discrimination under Title VII of the 1964 Civil Rights Act—would constitute a "compelling" interest justifying the school board in establishing a voluntary affirmative action hiring plan.[81] She even wrote, tantalizingly for our recent interests, that compensation for past discrimination should not be taken to be the only justification for affirmative action. At this point she specifically mentioned that Justice Powell's *Bakke* opinion had considered the promotion of racial

[78] On Justice O'Connor's contributions to the deliberations of the conference, see Maveety, *Justice Sandra Day O'Connor* at 110–11 (cited in note 6). During these deliberations, she seems to have changed her vote in the case, thus changing the result. Id.

[79] The dissenters in *Wygant*, following the opinion of the "Brennan four" in *Bakke*, would deploy the intermediate standard of review used in *Craig v Boren*, 425 US 190 (cited in note 15).

[80] 476 US at 287.

[81] Id at 292.

diversity among students in a state university as a "compelling" interest passing the test of strict scrutiny—and here she even cited the *Wygant* dissents of Justices Marshall and Stevens as further supporting authority.[82] Plainly, Justice O'Connor appreciated, even at this early date, the responsibility of government to contribute to a greater degree of racial inclusiveness, at the very least in government's own institutions. The *Wygant* concurrence, particularly in its encouragement of various forms of affirmative action of the "right" sort, set Justice O'Connor on the beginning of a long path, on which she would soon become the Supreme Court's most important doctrinal voice on the subject of affirmative action.[83]

In the Burger Court years, several aspects of Justice O'Connor's decisions warrant highlighting. First, when government engages in a constitutionally disfavored form of discrimination, either explicitly (as in *Hogan*) or tacitly but in a context suggesting an inference of purpose (as in *Rogers v Lodge*), she is ready to hold that behavior unconstitutional, and in so doing to defend the right of equal citizenship and the claims of an inclusive polity. Second, on some occasions when others (I include myself) might consider that inclusion and equal citizenship were at stake, she appears not to have seen the cases in that light, but to have viewed them instead through prisms of institutional concern about judicial modesty, or states' prerogatives, or both (as in the early abortion cases, or in *Hardwick*). Third, on still other early occasions, she clearly articulates the principle of equal citizenship, but finds the specific claims to inclusion before her insufficient to attract her vote (as in *Lynch*, or in *Wygant*). In the remainder of this article I shall argue that, in the years of the Rehnquist Court, Justice O'Connor generally has been increasingly attentive to issues of inclusion, increasingly skeptical of legislators who practice exclusionary identity politics, increasingly ready to identify cases as implicating claims to equal citizenship—and, crucially, increasingly likely to put her vote behind such claims.

II. Toward an Inclusive Public World

In the opinion of the Court in *Mississippi University for Women v Hogan*,[84] we hear the voice that Justice O'Connor has

---

[82] Id at 286.

[83] See text at notes 129–74.

[84] 458 US 718 (cited in note 14).

consistently sounded in the field of sex discrimination. Out of her own early experience with law firms that defined "lawyer" as male, she knew the meaning of exclusion from the public world she had been trained to serve.[85] Read once more these words from the *Hogan* opinion. If you say them aloud to yourself, you will hear the voice I have identified:

> . . . MUW's policy of excluding males from admission to the School of Nursing tends to perpetuate the stereotyped view of nursing as an exclusively woman's job. . . . [This] policy lends credibility to the old view that women, not men, should become nurses, and makes the assumption that nursing is a field for women a self-fulfilling prophecy.[86]

The core principle in this pronouncement is capable of wider application. In the pages that follow, we shall see how Justice O'Connor has elaborated on this theme, staking the nation's claim to a community public life that is inclusive of every individual.

In the years since Chief Justice Burger's retirement, the Supreme Court repeatedly has confronted cases raising issues of inclusion. The political context for many of these decisions has been the form of backlash politics I have called cultural counterrevolution.[87] This political development found its early energy in opposition to the Supreme Court's decisions in the 1960s on school desegregation, criminal justice, and school prayers. Appeals to this opposition served the "Southern strategy" that has converted what was once a Democratic "solid South" into the Republican Party's

---

[85] From the many sources that could be cited here, I have selected these passages from her recent book, part memoir and part essay:

When I went to law school in the middle of the last century, there was only a handful of women students in the major law schools around the country. Women's work was still thought to be largely at home or, for some, as schoolteachers or nurses. . . . I graduated near the top of my class from one of the better law schools in the country [Stanford]. My male classmates had no trouble finding jobs. I interviewed with several firms in California but received no job offer—other than [a] job as a legal secretary.

Sandra Day O'Connor, *The Majesty of the Law: Reflections of a Supreme Court Justice* 152, 199 (Random House, 2003).

[86] 458 US at 729–30.

[87] See Kenneth L. Karst, *Religion, Sex, and Politics: Cultural Counterrevolution in Constitutional Perspective*, 24 UC Davis L Rev 677 (1991) ("*Cultural Counterrevolution*"); Karst, *Law's Promise, Law's Expression: Visions of Power in the Politics of Race, Gender, and Religion* 31–66 and passim (Yale, 1993) ("*Law's Promise*").

regional core.[88] Race is one wedge issue that has served this purpose.[89] Others have been religion and "family values." Long before
the 1960s, the South's "culture-Protestantism" tended to reflect
conservative religious orthodoxy on questions of "sex, divorce,
abortion, equal rights for women, pornography, drugs, alcohol, education, child-rearing, parental authority, and general behavior."[90]
By the end of the 1970s, the white Southerners who shared these
views were joined by a great many other Americans in support of
what came to be called the Social Issues Agenda, a campaign plan
centered on defense of an older social order in matters of religion,
race, and gender roles. This form of politics played with great success in the presidential elections of the 1980s.[91] The agenda's intended audience consisted mainly of voters who felt left out as
they watched what they saw as the upheavals of the 1960s (the
secularization of the state, the civil rights movement) and the
1970s (the women's movement, the gay rights movement). These
changes could be seen as a threat, not just to their worldviews but
to their senses of self. Their concerns have blended moral umbrage
with grief for the loss of much of their former status dominance,
and fear for further losses.[92]

Political operatives who would appeal to the constituency for
cultural counterrevolution understand that government is a huge
reservoir of symbols, and that law itself serves expressive purposes
as a set of authoritative pronouncements about right and wrong.
Since around 1980, especially when the Supreme Court has come
to consider the validity of legislation touching religion and "family

---

[88] The strategy was prominent in Senator Barry Goldwater's presidential campaign in
1964, but took hold in 1968 when Richard Nixon swept the South, except for the four
states that went to Governor George Wallace.

[89] The Southern strategy attacked not only school desegregation, but also Congress's civil
rights legislation. When President Lyndon B. Johnson signed the Civil Rights Act of 1964
into law, he said to an aide, "I think we just delivered the South to the Republican Party
for a long time." Bill Moyers, *What a Real President Was Like*, Wash Post C5 (Nov 13,
1988).

[90] Charles P. Roland, *The Ever-Vanishing South*, in Patrick Gerster and Nicholas Cords,
eds, 2 *Myth and Southern History* 155, 162–63 (2d ed 1989), reprinted from 48 J Southern
Legal Hist 3 (1982).

[91] See Nathan Glazer, *The Social Issues Agenda*, in John L. Palmer, ed, *Perspectives on the
Reagan Years* at 5 (Urban Institute, 1986).

[92] On the latter, see J. M. Balkin, *The Constitution of Status*, 106 Yale L J 2313 (1997),
and citations in note 87.

values," the laws before them have been enacted in furtherance of the Social Issues Agenda, and in response to the constituency for cultural counterrevolution. One need not be a cynic to notice that success in presidential elections brings with it the power to influence judicial appointments, and—to a considerable extent, but by no means always—the Social Issues Agenda has prospered in court.

In this section we renew our exploration of Justice O'Connor's votes and opinions in the areas of substantive constitutional law we previously visited. The section proceeds in three parts. The first deals with the protection of religious freedom promised by the First Amendment's Establishment Clause. Next comes racial equality, and in particular affirmative action. The section concludes with a look at issues of sex and gender equality, including not only cases of discrimination on the basis of sex or sexual orientation, but also cases involving claims to reproductive freedom.

In all these discussions, our focus is the theme of inclusion— or, in its constitutional dimension, the principle of equal citizenship. Under that principle, every individual is presumptively entitled to "the dignity of full membership in the society, . . . [treatment as] one who is worthy of respect, one who 'belongs.' Stated negatively, the principle presumptively forbids the organized society to treat an individual either as a member of an inferior or dependent caste or as a nonparticipant."[93] An abiding problem for those who would promote an inclusive society in America is the practice of a politics of group status domination, in which political operatives mobilize constituencies by fanning hostilities against other groups. When the courts deal with issues concerning race, religion, sex roles, or sexual orientation, they are—in spite of themselves—enmeshed in this form of identity politics. A persistent conundrum in all these fields—one that Justice O'Connor has often confronted and sometimes articulated specifically—is this: How can we keep constitutional rights focused on individual claimants, when the world of politics persistently lumps individuals into groups labeled Us and Them?

---

[93] Here I have quoted myself: Kenneth L. Karst, *The Supreme Court, 1976 Term— Foreword: Equal Citizenship Under the Fourteenth Amendment*, 91 Harv L Rev 1, 5–6 (1977) ("*Equal Citizenship*"). For a fuller treatment, see Kenneth L. Karst, *Belonging to America: Equal Citizenship Under the Constitution* (Yale, 1989).

A. RELIGION AND THE POLITICS OF EXCLUSION

In *Lynch v Donnelly*,[94] we saw that Justice O'Connor's concurring opinion recognized the potential for serious status harms to individuals and groups when government officially endorses religion. A second crucial insight in that opinion is that the government's religious expression carries the danger of dividing a community's politics along religious lines. Justice O'Connor was careful not to make the existence of political divisiveness a new element of the *Lemon* formula—that is, an independent ground for holding that governmental support religion is unconstitutional.[95] But she properly identified political division along religious lines as "an evil addressed by the Establishment Clause," and noted that this kind of divisiveness may be some evidence of excessive entanglement, or of government endorsement of religion.[96] Because religion is, for many of us, a core element of personal identity, religious division has often played a polarizing role in American society. As Justice O'Connor remarked in 1996, "Religious convictions are generally too strong" to be contained in the usual forms of politics, which feature compromise and manage to preserve community harmony through the shifting of majorities on different issues.[97]

Although there is wisdom in Justice O'Connor's comment that "religious harmony is more likely to arise from keeping religion and politics apart as much as possible,"[98] the separation is difficult to obtain—because the politicians will not cooperate. They often find it useful to mobilize constituencies by inflaming religious hostility, and they know how to make use of those constituencies on behalf of clients whose interests are centered more on the accumulation of wealth and power than on the spread of The Word. For a political operative who would turn the local scene into a battle between Us and Them, religious division is a tried-and-true wedge.[99] And the operative knows that a symbol's power lies in its diffuse, whole-picture effect. Where a discourse on the meanings

---

[94] 465 US 668 (cited in note 47).

[95] *Lynch*, 465 US at 869.

[96] Id.

[97] O'Connor, 48 No Ireland Legal Q at 2 (cited in note 60).

[98] Id.

[99] I have discussed the modern versions of this sort of politics in Karst, *Law's Promise* (cited in note 87). Specifically on religion, see id at 21–22, 27–29, 37–40, 147–60.

of America can induce yawning, a flag touches the emotions. So with religious symbols: a Nativity scene touches the sense of human connection in a way that lies beyond the power of any verbal description of this central miracle of Christianity. So, if the endorsement principle seeks to protect a religious outsider's sense of belonging, the government's display of a religious symbol is an ideal context for applying the principle. Justice O'Connor, by insisting on awareness of the potential political abuses of the symbols of religion, has kept before us the vision of a more inclusive society and polity.

The endorsement principle has not found favor with all the Justices. In the Supreme Court's next encounter with officially sponsored religious symbols, two separate religious holiday displays in Pittsburgh came under challenge as violations of the Establishment Clause. Since 1981, a Christian Nativity scene (crèche),[100] donated by the Holy Name Society (as a sign indicated), had been placed on the grand staircase of the Allegheny County Courthouse, next to some poinsettia plants and evergreens. The crèche included an angel holding a banner saying "Gloria in Excelsis Deo" (Glory to God in the Highest). Just outside the City-County Building, next to the city's official forty-five-foot Christmas tree, was an eighteen-foot menorah (candelabrum), donated by Chabad, a Jewish group, but stored and erected each year since 1982 by the city. At the foot of the tree was a sign bearing the mayor's name and declaring the city's "salute to liberty." The local chapter of the American Civil Liberties Union, along with some religious leaders and other individuals, sued to enjoin continued display of these official symbols. The federal district court, citing *Lynch v Donnelly*, upheld the constitutionality of the displays, but a divided court of appeals reversed, holding that the displays "tacitly endorsed Christianity and Judaism" and thus violated the Establishment Clause.[101]

In the Supreme Court these cases produced a three-part division. Justices Brennan, Marshall, and Stevens would have held both displays unconstitutional. Chief Justice Rehnquist, and Justices

---

[100] Including the Holy Family, wise men, shepherds, angels, and farm animals.

[101] *ACLU v Allegheny County*, 842 F2d 655, 662 (3d Cir 1988) (2–1). The dissenting judge began his opinion with these words: "It is unfortunate that plaintiffs have succeeded in stifling governmental commemoration of two miracles which occurred about one hundred-fifty years apart in time, but so few miles in distance—and muffling the message of peace and understanding that pervades the joint observance." 842 F2d at 663.

White, Scalia, and Kennedy, would have upheld both displays. Justices Blackmun and O'Connor agreed that the crèche violated the Establishment Clause, but concluded that the menorah and Christmas tree were unobjectionable. So, the tree and menorah won, 6–3, and the crèche lost, 5–4.[102] In the latter case, the five majority Justices embraced the endorsement principle and found that the crèche did endorse Christianity. Justices Blackmun and O'Connor, however, found no endorsement of religion in the "salute to liberty" display of the menorah and Christmas tree. Justice O'Connor concurred separately, in an opinion devoted almost entirely to applying and defending the endorsement principle. In this opinion she elaborated on her *Lynch* concurrence, emphasizing again that the question whether government has endorsed religion should be viewed through the eyes of a hypothetical "reasonable observer" who sees the governmental action in its context. Such a test, she conceded, "requires careful and often difficult line-drawing and is highly context specific," but it does capture "the essential mandate of the Establishment Clause," and warrants continued judicial refinement.[103] In this light, she saw the crèche, in context, as a symbol of government endorsement of Christian belief, but saw the menorah and Christmas tree, again in context, as offering a message of pluralism—or, as we might put it, inclusion.

Justice Anthony M. Kennedy, writing for the four Justices who found no violation of the Establishment Clause in either of these "purely passive symbols of religious holidays,"[104] made a special point of rejecting the endorsement principle in its entirety. He complained of a "jurisprudence of minutiae"[105] that would distinguish the Pittsburgh crèche from the Pawtucket crèche on the basis of the latter's physical location near secular symbols. More broadly, he called the endorsement principle "flawed in its fundamentals and unworkable in practice."[106] Absent a showing of coercion, or of "an obvious [governmental] effort to proselytize on behalf of a particular religion,"[107] he would uphold the two governments' recognitions of

---

[102] *Allegheny County v ACLU*, 492 US 573 (1989).

[103] 492 US at 630–31.

[104] Id at 664.

[105] Id at 674.

[106] Id at 669.

[107] Id at 661. His example of the latter type of violation was the permanent erection of a large Latin cross on the roof of city hall.

the holiday season. He did define coercion broadly enough to include, for example, the "indirect" coercion of classroom prayer.[108] As for protecting religious outsiders against a sense of exclusion, he equated the Court's decision on the Nativity scene with a conclusion "that the First Amendment creates classes of religions based on the relative numbers of their adherents. Those religions enjoying the largest following must be consigned to the status of least-favored faiths so as to avoid any possible risk of offending members of minority religions."[109]

With this outpouring of sympathy for the cultural Haves ringing in our ears, let us turn to *Lee v Weisman*,[110] in which Justice Kennedy wrote the opinion of the Court in holding unconstitutional a public middle school's sponsorship of prayers of invocation and benediction at its graduation ceremony. He concluded that, because the graduation ceremony is typically an important event in the life of students and their families, attendance was in a practical sense compulsory. So, government was, in effect, coercing students to participate in a religious exercise. For that reason, said Justice Kennedy, the case did not require the Court to "revisit the difficult questions dividing us in recent cases"—prominently citing the *Allegheny* case.[111] For our purposes the most interesting features of Justice Kennedy's opinion were (1) its emphasis on the pressures on adolescents to conform to the expectations of their peers or the school—that is, their reluctance to appear to be outsiders, and (2) its persistent reference to the "reasonable perception" of "the nonbeliever or dissenter," one who does not share the religious point of view being expressed in the graduation prayers. These concerns are, to put it mildly, similar to those expressed by Justice O'Connor when she has pointed up the harms inflicted on outsiders by official endorsement of religion.

The latest count of the Justices on the application of the endorsement principle to religious symbols has been 5–4 in favor,[112] and it is not clear that this majority will survive the next few years'

---

[108] Id at 661 n 1, citing with approval *Engel v Vitale*, 370 US 421 (1962).

[109] Id at 677.

[110] 505 US 577 (1992).

[111] Id at 586–87.

[112] This is made clear when one peruses the six opinions in *Capitol Square Review and Advisory Board v Pinette*, 515 US 753 (1995).

changes in the Court's personnel.[113] But it matters little whether the word "endorsement" survives as a doctrinal talisman; the important point is that the inclusion, material and symbolic, of religious outsiders in public institutions is taken seriously as a constitutional claim. At least in the school context, *Lee v Weisman* assures us that a standard based on coercion and proselytizing offers substantial protection to the interests of religious outsiders in equal participation in the school community. This assurance was strengthened when six Justices saw coercion and proselytizing in the context of school-sponsored prayer at a public high school football game.[114] What is clear is that Justice O'Connor, in her interpretation of the Establishment Clause, has made a lasting contribution to our understanding of the ideal of inclusion as the heart of the principle of equal citizenship. Indeed, her insights about the interplay of law and the politics of group status domination offer analogies worthy of translation to other areas of constitutional doctrine, from race-conscious affirmative action to the right of reproductive choice.

B. RACE, POLITICS, AND THE STAYING POWER OF CASTE

If Justice O'Connor found a ready audience for her concerns about the exclusionary effects of official religious symbols, surely one reason is that she was addressing a generation that took *Brown v Board of Education*[115] for granted. The nation's realization of the principle of equal citizenship begins in the abolition of caste. For the organized community to treat an individual as a member of a subordinate caste—as a nonparticipant in public life—is a violation of the Fourteenth Amendment.[116] The most obvious case for applying this principle, in the years since *Brown*, has been the case of explicit or intentional governmental racial discrimination in the fashion of the Jim Crow laws. For some observers, including some

---

[113] Here we might note that the appointing authority said, during the 2000 election campaign, that his models for judicial appointments would be Justices Scalia and Thomas. Since that time there has been no evidence of a change in the President's inclination.

[114] *Santa Fe Ind. School Dist. v Doe*, 530 US 290 (cited in note 59). Writing for the Court in an opinion joined by the entire majority, Justice Stevens also noted that "an objective Santa Fe High School student will unquestionably perceive the inevitable pregame prayer as stamped with her school's seal of approval." Id at 308.

[115] 347 US 483 (1954).

[116] See note 93 and accompanying text.

Justices, racial equality under law not only begins in this application but ends there. In these observers' view, racial equality means
the formal neutrality of government.[117]

In this model of formal racial neutrality, three preferences are
salient: (1) a preference for limited governmental responsibility,
with government's duty limited to avoiding its own deliberate discrimination; (2) a preference for private ordering, and avoidance
of government intrusion on private decisions; (3) a preference for
individualized remedies in the fashion of the common law, in
which (i) allowable claims are limited to persons who can prove
they are the direct victims of specifically identified acts of discrimination, and (ii) the burden of remedy can be imposed only on those
who have deliberately engaged in those acts or those who have
directly benefited from them. Every arguably discriminatory act,
in other words, is evaluated without reference to its societal and
historical context, as if history were a blank page. The racial status
quo is taken as equilibrium.[118] In this tunnel vision a race-conscious
remedy—one aimed at redressing the myriad corruptions of public
life produced by the stigma of caste—is itself a transgression of
formal neutrality, for it alters the equilibrium of the status quo.
In other words, the model of formal racial neutrality, much in
vogue during the years of the Rehnquist Court, is a recipe for civil
rights deregulation.

Justice O'Connor's opinions in the field of racial equality show
that she can take this model or leave it alone. In the discussion
that follows, I emphasize her opinions concerning racial equality
in the workplace and in higher education—two arenas of our public life where concerns about inclusion are unquestionably legitimate, and race-conscious remedies have been under attack.

The relation of decent work to citizenship is plain enough.
Work is a source of independence, of family security, of personal
achievement, of a respected social status—in our society, a major
source of an individual's sense of his or her own worth.[119]

---

[117] In this passage I have borrowed from the substance and some of the rhetoric in a
1989 article, Kenneth L. Karst, *Private Discrimination and Public Responsibility: Patterson in
Context*, 1989 Supreme Court Review 1 ("*Private Discrimination*").

[118] On status quo neutrality, see Cass R. Sunstein, *The Partial Constitution* 3–7, 68–81,
328–32 and passim (Harvard, 1993).

[119] I take this statement to be self-evident to readers of this journal. For those who want
elaboration, I suggest Judith Shklar, *American Citizenship: The Quest for Inclusion* 63–101
(Harvard, 1991); William E. Forbath, *Caste, Class, and Equal Citizenship*, 98 Mich L Rev

Throughout the era of slavery and the era of Jim Crow, the social meanings of work played a crucial role in the definitions of race in American society, and they still do.[120] The concern for individual fairness came together with a concern for integration of the workforce in the adoption of Title VII (the employment discrimination title) of the Civil Rights Act of 1964. This dual concern bears emphasis. Work is not just a means by which an individual earns an income. It is an arena of our public life in which people can come to know one another, not just as abstractions bearing labels such as race or sex or disability, but as whole persons. The integration of the workplace is an educational experience of no little importance for social relations—indeed, social peace. One of the most important contributions of the armed services to American life is their day-to-day teaching, to large numbers of our citizens—to servicemembers, and through them to their families and friends— that men and women are much more than their labels, and that they are to be valued for who they are as whole persons. Workforce integration benefits not only individual workers, but the whole society. In this perspective, one aim of Title VII is to avoid perpetuating the effects of past systematic racial discrimination in employment. It is both a reflection of our national aspiration to "ensure that equality defines all citizens' daily experience and opportunities as well as the protection afforded to them under the law,"[121] and a crucially important means to that end.

This conclusion is foreign to the model of formal racial neutrality. In a rigorous application of that model, Title VII would be limited severely, by analogy to the law of intentional torts. The only suitable defendants would be wrongdoers with evil hearts— employers who deliberately harm minority or women workers. Remedies would be strictly limited to those who can prove that they, individually, have been directly harmed by this wrongdoing. A decade before Justice O'Connor joined the Supreme Court, the Burger Court had rejected this model in *Griggs v Duke Power Co.*,[122] holding unanimously that, when an employer's job require-

---

1 (1999); Kenneth L. Karst, *The Coming Crisis of Work in Constitutional Perspective*, 82 Cornell L Rev 523, 530–38 (1997).

[120] Id at 538–48. Indeed, access to decent work has always played an important role in constituting our sense of nationhood. See id at 548–53.

[121] O'Connor, J, dissenting in *Metro Broadcasting, Inc. v FCC*, 497 US 547, 611 (1990).

[122] 401 US 424 (1971).

ment of a high school diploma had a racially disproportionate disqualifying effect on black job applicants, this showing gave such
an applicant a prima facie case of racial discrimination under Title
VII. The proof of a prima facie case by a showing of statistical
racial disparity did suggest a group concern that deserved a remedy, but it did not press the employer to adopt a racial version of
"proportionate representation" in hiring and promotions. In one
aspect, the Court accommodated formal equality's preference for
private autonomy: the employer could preserve the job requirement by showing that it was a necessary qualification for the work
in question.

The *Griggs* formula admonished employers to take responsibility
for minimizing the race-based harms of their practices. By en-
listing employers throughout the nation in an effort to diminish
the segregation of workplaces, *Griggs* responded to a larger concern about the public effects of private racial discrimination. And,
in another wider perspective, *Griggs* recognized that racism
often—perhaps typically—operates at the margins of consciousness, affecting beliefs and behavior without taking the form of purposeful harm based on race.[123] The decision managed to achieve
major social gains through a classic lawyer's instrument, the allocation of the burden of proof.

These gains are not cost-free, as Justice O'Connor realized. One
way to avoid "disparate impact" liability under Title VII would
be for an employer to engage in race-conscious affirmative action
hiring—a practice the Supreme Court had approved, rejecting a
Title VII challenge to the employer's remedial action.[124] Some employers then began to argue that the disparate impact theory of a
prima facie case should be discarded, at least in cases where supervisors were making subjective evaluations of employee performance. Because it would be hard to validate supervisors' individual
subjective evaluations as business necessities, they argued, the disparate impact theory was pressing them into "quota hiring," and

---

[123] See Linda Hamilton Krieger, *The Content of Our Categories: A Cognitive Bias Approach
to Discrimination and Equal Employment Opportunity*, 47 Stan L Rev 1161, 1199–1211 and
passim (1995); Charles R. Lawrence III, *The Id, the Ego, and Equal Protection: Reckoning with
Unconscious Racism*, 39 Stan L Rev 317 (1987). See also Linda Hamilton Krieger, *Civil Rights
Perestroika: Intergroup Relations After Affirmative Action*, 86 Calif L Rev 1251, 1276–91 and
passim (1998).

[124] *United Steelworkers v Weber*, 443 US 109 (1979),

so should be abandoned in such cases. In 1988 Justice O'Connor resisted that argument, but did support giving the employers a major gain in return. In *Watson v Fort Worth Bank and Trust*,[125] she wrote for the Court in confirming the applicability of the disparate impact theory to subjective evaluation cases, and then, writing for a plurality of four Justices, concluded that, when a statistical racial disparity is used to establish a prima facie case of discriminatory impact (not just in cases of subjective evaluation), the plaintiff must identify a specific employment practice and prove that this practice was the cause of the disparate impact. These are huge hurdles for the employee, but even if she clears them, she is not home free; the employer need only produce some evidence of a business justification (not "necessity"), at which point the employee has the burden of demonstrating that the practice does not significantly serve a legitimate business interest. The very next year, with the recently appointed Justice Kennedy as the fifth vote, a majority wrote this restructuring of burdens of proof into Title VII in *Wards Cove Packing Co., Inc. v Atonio*.[126] The employers' victory was short-lived; in 1991 Congress amended Title VII to restore the *Griggs* approach in its fullness, in a law pointedly entitled the Civil Rights Restoration Act.[127]

In one view, Justice O'Connor's position in *Watson* and *Wards Cove* has been taken to indicate that she saw the *Griggs* (statistical disparity) method of proving disparate impact as a cousin of the "societal discrimination" that, in *Wygant*, had been insufficient as a basis for affirmative action by a government employer. That, coupled with a concern that *Griggs* might be pressing employers to solve their problems by surreptitious quota hiring—so the argument goes—may have persuaded her that *Griggs* needed major surgery. Such a line of reasoning has been suggested and, I think, convincingly criticized.[128] But the suggestion about Justice O'Connor's view needs to be reconsidered in the light of her opinions

---

[125] 487 US 977 (1988).

[126] 490 US 642 (1989) (White, J, writing for the Court). *Wards Cove* had a broader application; it was not a case involving subjective evaluation.

[127] Pub L No 102-166, 105 Stat 1071, 42 USC § 2000e (1991). Speaking of politics, Alaska's legislators in Congress obtained a provision that effectively ruled out protection for the cannery workers at Wards Cove.

[128] Alfred W. Blumrosen, *Society in Transition III: Justice O'Connor and the Destabilization of the Griggs Principle of Employment Discrimination*, 14 Women's Rts L Rep 315 (1992).

on race-conscious affirmative action in the field of employment. We have seen her position on this subject when government is the employer; that was the *Wygant* case, where she said that the right kind of statistical disparity would, indeed, justify voluntary affirmative action hiring. It remains to examine her views on affirmative action programs mandated by government for its contractors.

In 1989, in this *Review*,[129] I said that Justice O'Connor's opinions on affirmative action could be seen (as could Justice Powell's opinions) to represent several important aims: (1) avoiding "a politics of racial hostility";[130] (2) affirming the necessity for an affirmative action program to pass the test of strict judicial scrutiny; (3) preserving some latitude for affirmative action in response to "both the practice and the lingering effects of racial discrimination against minority groups in this country";[131] and (4) specifying in some detail how a governmental body could pass the demanding test of strict scrutiny. That assessment still seems justified.

Let us begin with racial politics. In the *Croson* case, with Justice O'Connor writing the Court's opinion, the Supreme Court held unconstitutional an ordinance of the city of Richmond, Virginia, requiring contractors with the city to set aside 30 percent of their subcontracting business for subcontractors owned by members of specified racial or ethnic minorities.[132] A majority of the Richmond city council were black, and in one view the set-aside could be seen as an instance in which "a racial group [had] the political strength to negotiate 'a piece of the action' for its members"—as Justice Stevens had said on an earlier occasion.[133] Justice O'Connor did not make such a charge in her *Croson* opinion, but she did advert to the possibility that such a racial classification of benefi-

---

[129] Karst, *Private Discrimination* at 39–46 (cited in note 117).

[130] O'Connor, J, writing the opinion of the Court in *Richmond v J.A. Croson Co.*, 488 US 469, 493 (1989).

[131] The quoted words are from Justice O'Connor's opinion of the Court in *Adarand Constructors, Inc. v Peña*, 515 US 200, 237 (1995), written six years after the article from which I have drawn this paragraph, but they parallel one point made in that article.

[132] *Croson*, 488 US 469 (cited in note 130). Justice O'Connor reaffirmed the Court's rejection of the contextual argument that affirmative action could be justified as a remedy for Jim Crow's large-scale effects—here, including a drastic limit on the numbers of minority subcontractors, and a similar limit on opportunities for those minority subcontractors who managed to stay in business. Such "societal" discrimination would not do here, any more than it did in *Wygant*, 476 US 267 (cited in note 72).

[133] *Fullilove v Klutznick*, 448 US 448, 539 (1980) (Stevens, J, dissenting).

ciaries of government action might rest on "simple racial politics," and might "lead to a politics of racial hostility."[134]

Racial hostility has, indeed, intruded into recent American politics. Perhaps the lowest point was reached in a television ad in support of Senator Jesse Helms's bid for reelection in 1990. In the video image, a white man's hands held a letter, and then crumpled it. An announcer's voice indicated that this was a rejection letter; the employer had given preference for the job to a minority applicant. Not coincidentally, the Democratic candidate was Harvey Gantt, an African American man who was looking more and more like a winner. Helms won the election, and political operatives all over the country got their own message. So, is this episode Exhibit A for the proposition that affirmative action means ugly racial politics?

Surely no black North Carolinian would see 1990 as the dawn of racial politics in the state. The Fifteenth Amendment was adopted in 1870, but—once the heady days of Reconstruction had ended—the "black vote" in North Carolina was reduced to negligible proportions by a resurgent white supremacy movement led by the (old) Democratic Party,[135] and did not again reach weighty proportions until the Voting Rights Act of 1965 took hold.[136] Throughout the era of Jim Crow, race was at the heart of politics. Putting to one side the *ultima ratio* of lynching,[137] the Supreme Court itself provided a capsule catalogue of the electoral features of this politics of racial hostility, recalling such features as white primary elections, and taking special note of a variety of mechanisms for enforcing literacy requirements against black citizens but not against whites: "grandfather clauses, property qualifications, 'good character' tests, and the requirement that registrants 'understand' or 'interpret' certain matter."[138] As every black citizen in

---

[134] 488 US at 493.

[135] Michael Perlman, *Struggle for Mastery: Disenfranchisement in the South, 1888–1908* 171–72 (North Carolina, 2001) (black disenfranchisement in North Carolina, 1898–1900).

[136] In North Carolina in 1948, some 13 percent of black citizens were registered to vote. In 1966, a year after the enactment of the Voting Rights Act, the number surpassed 50 percent. J. Morgan Kousser, *Colorblind Injustice: Minority Voting Rights and the Undoing of the Second Reconstruction* 245 (North Carolina, 1990). Kousser's chapter, id at 243–76, is entitled "A Century of Electoral Discrimination in North Carolina."

[137] I owe this arresting term to Charles L. Black, Jr., who used to refer to lynching as the *ultima ratio*, the force of last resort that stood behind the Jim Crow system.

[138] *South Carolina v Katzenbach*, 383 US 301, 311 (1965).

North Carolina would understand in 1990, the TV ad about affirmative action was simply a convenient way to tap into the emotions of white voters who had lived through the generation of status changes that allowed a black man to present a serious challenge to Senator Helms.[139] The civil rights movement, like the women's movement, has been an unremitting claim of status equality, and such a claim always produces a backlash among those who fear the loss of their status dominance. It would be a shame of constitutional dimension if the Supreme Court were to stifle remedial racial politics while ignoring backlash racial politics.[140]

There is power in the suggestion that "The moral imperative of racial neutrality is the driving force of the Equal Protection Clause."[141] If we were starting today to create a new desert-island society, unquestionably that morality should be written into law, and obeyed strictly. The problem, as Justice O'Connor has more recently noted, is not just that a strict rule forbidding race-conscious remedies would require a departure from the Court's line of precedents. It is that an earlier politics of racial hostility was so effective for so long (and not just in the South) that it produced myriad deformations of opportunities to realize the benefits of equal citizenship. A rigorous insistence on formal racial neutrality today would leave in place the "unhappy persistence of both the practice and the lingering effects of racial discrimination against minority groups in this country." That persistence, she said, "is an unfortunate reality, and government is not disqualified from acting in response to it."[142]

---

[139] These were the status changes that made race a "wedge issue" for Senator Helms's party, given the prominence of Democratic presidents and congressional majorities in enacting civil rights laws.

[140] I do not discuss the subject of race and electoral districting. One reason is that it is far from clear that creating "safe" minority districts is more advantageous to minority interests than creating a larger number of districts in which minority constituents have considerable weight. (For reasons that most readers will find obvious, the Republican Party generally has favored concentrating minority voters in a few districts.) A second reason is that I ought to leave this subject to those who are better qualified to discuss it. See, e.g., Pamela S. Karlan, *Easing the Spring: Strict Scrutiny and Affirmative Action After the Redistricting Cases*, 43 Wm & Mary L Rev 1569 (2002); Vikram David Amar, *Of Hobgoblins and Justice: O'Connor's Jurisprudence of Equality*, 32 McGeorge L Rev 823, 831–35 (2001).

[141] So Justice Kennedy declared, in *Croson*, 488 US at 518 (cited in note 130). But he immediately added that a rule of automatic invalidity of race-conscious remedies would be a significant break with precedent, and should not be undertaken "at this point." 488 US at 519.

[142] *Adarand Constructors, Inc. v Peña*, 515 US at 237 (cited in note 131).

Even so, a race-conscious remedy must pass the test of strict judicial scrutiny. Since the *Adarand* decision, such a remedy in an act of Congress is also to be subjected to this skeptical standard.[143] Yet, Justice O'Connor once again made sure that the door remained open for some forms of affirmative action. Writing for the Court, she left undecided the question whether the courts might be justified in paying some special deference to the judgments of Congress, as a coequal branch of the national government, that some interests might be sufficiently compelling to justify affirmative action, and that some race-conscious means might be necessary (and narrowly tailored) to achieve those interests.[144] In other words, although the change in context from state to congressional legislation did not take affirmative action out from under the requirement of strict judicial scrutiny, that contextual change might well influence the interpretation of that standard's requirements. Prominent in Justice O'Connor's *Adarand* opinion is the theme that, even when strict scrutiny is in order, circumstances alter cases; courts must be prepared, she says, to take "relevant differences into account—indeed, that is [strict scrutiny's] fundamental purpose."[145] (This sort of attention to context is, of course, a trademark of her opinions in many areas of constitutional doctrine.) Specifically referring to affirmative action, she went out of her way to make clear that a governmental goal of inclusion was entitled to serious judicial respect. Strict scrutiny, she let it be understood, does not imply an inability to distinguish "between a 'No Trespassing' sign and a welcome mat."[146] Justice Ginsburg, dissenting, remarked on these comments in Justice O'Connor's opinion as indicating agreement between the two Justices that, within the "strict scrutiny" formula, the Court's affirmative action doctrine would allow for doctrinal evolution, "informed by and responsive to

---

[143] Id. This decision struck down a congressional subcontracting set-aside for minority businesses. Where Justice O'Connor in *Croson* had suggested that more judicial deference might be paid to a congressional affirmative action program than to a city program, in *Adarand* she concluded that strict scrutiny was appropriate for an act of Congress, too.

[144] 515 US at 228–31, 236–37. She dropped a hint that even the *Fullilove* precedent, 448 US 448 (cited in note 133), sustaining a similar congressional set-aside, might be reconfirmed. 515 US at 234.

[145] Id at 228.

[146] Id at 229. Here she was quoting Justice Stevens in his dissent, who said the Court's opinion ignored this difference. She said, "It does nothing of the kind." Id.

changing conditions."[147] In hindsight, with last Term's decisions in mind, this characterization seems apt.

Previously, in her *Croson* opinion, Justice O'Connor had gone to considerable lengths to spell out how a governmental body might justify a race-conscious remedy for public or private employment discrimination. First, the discrimination must be specifically identified. One means of proving this element, she made clear, was statistical: she cited twice, with approval, a court of appeals decision that had allowed Ohio to show prior discrimination by comparing the percentage of minority businesses in the state with the percentage of state purchases from minority firms.[148] Second, the race-conscious remedy must be narrowly tailored to the discrimination in question, and used only after race-neutral remedies were found wanting. This tailoring would require (*a*) that any set-aside for minority contractors bear a clear relation to the percentage of qualified minority businesses in the area;[149] (*b*) a time limit, after which the program would be reevaluated; and (*c*) provision for waivers on the model of the law involved in *Fullilove*.[150] These specifications are demanding, but not beyond the power of a city or state to satisfy.[151]

---

[147] Id at 276.

[148] The decision was *Ohio Contractors Ass'n v Keip*, 713 F2d 167 (6th Cir 1983), cited by Justice O'Connor, *Croson*, 488 US at 502 and 503. It appears that lower courts will have a considerable say in future applications of *Croson*'s standards. In Ohio, the contractors returned to court, found some new judges, and obtained a ruling that the very same law now failed *Croson*'s requirements of findings of specified discrimination and narrow tailoring. A new Sixth Circuit panel deployed a far more demanding statistical analysis than its predecessor panel had used, and the Supreme Court declined to review the decision. *Associated Gen. Contractors of Ohio, Inc. v Drabik*, 214 F3d 730 (6th Cir 2000), cert denied sub nom. *Johnson v Associated Gen Contractors of Ohio, Inc.*, 531 US 1148 (2001). Justice O'Connor did not dissent from this denial of review, but neither did anyone else. See also the decisions cited in note 151.

[149] In *Croson* itself, only .67 percent of subcontracts in the Richmond area in 1978–83 had gone to minority businesses, and the Richmond population was around 50 percent African American. This is a dramatic statistical disparity, but Justice O'Connor said that the city's 30 percent quota was not shown to relate to the proportion of minority subcontractors in the area. That the Jim Crow era had left a paucity of minority contracting businesses was not sufficient for her—to Justice Marshall's astonishment.

[150] In that law, a waiver was allowed when the minority business's higher bid was not explainable by reference to the effects of past discrimination. 488 US at 508.

[151] The City of San Francisco, for example, went back to the drawing board and came up with an affirmative action plan that survived a constitutional challenge. *Associated General Contractors v Coalition for Economic Equity*, 950 F2d 1401 (9th Cir 1991), cert denied, 503 US 985 (1992). For the mayor's report, see Mayor Willie Brown, *Breaking the Status Quo: San Francisco's Attempt to Ensure Fairness in Public Contracting*, 10 Stan L & Pol'y Rev 227 (1999). This success, however, did not end the story. The Pacific Legal Foundation has

When we turn to higher education, last Term's decisions in the *Grutter* and *Gratz* cases[152] make unmistakably clear that Justice O'Connor means what she has been saying all along: Race-based affirmative action by a governmental body requires strict scrutiny, but the meaning of strict scrutiny must be adapted to the contexts before the courts, and some forms of affirmative action are valid.[153] Two such programs governing admission to the University of Michigan came to the Supreme Court; in *Grutter*, the Court (5–4) upheld the law school's program, and in *Gratz* the Court (6–3, with Justice O'Connor concurring) held the undergraduate admissions program unconstitutional. Because our focus here is Justice O'Connor, the center of the discussion that follows is her opinion for the Court in *Grutter*. By any test, this is an opinion of immense importance. Coming as it does after the series of decisions we have just seen, where Justice O'Connor led the Court's resistance to one after another affirmative action plan in other settings, this opinion is all the more striking for its commitment to the goal of an inclusive public world and the constitutional principle of equal citizenship.

The structure of the opinion is easily summarized; in its first two parts, it follows Justice Powell's opinion in the 1978 *Bakke* case:[154] (1) The law school's race-conscious program must pass the

brought a series of lawsuits in the state courts, challenging the city's program under Proposition 209, a measure adopted by California voters in 1996, designed to do away with government use of race in employment, contracting, and education. The courts thus far have rejected these suits without reaching the merits. See, e.g., *S.F. Wins Prop. 209 Case in Court of Appeal*, San Fran Chronicle A25 (April 15, 2000); *Contracting Law Survives Challenge*, San Fran Chronicle A14 (Sept 28, 2002).

Denver's affirmative action program has similarly been upheld, under the *Croson* standards. *Concrete Works of Colorado, Inc. v City and County of Denver*, 321 F3d 950 (10th Cir 2003). However, the Eleventh Circuit struck down Dade County's program, concluding that the district court's "findings" (the issues plainly are not merely factual, but highly evaluative) on past discrimination and narrow tailoring should be accepted unless they were "clearly erroneous." *Engineering Contractors Ass'n of South Florida v Metropolitan Dade County*, 122 F3d 895 (11th Cir 1997).

In sustaining a post-*Croson* challenge to a Washington county's affirmative action program (for want of narrow tailoring), the Ninth Circuit provided a useful how-to-do-it guide for local governments. *Coral Construction Co. v King County*, 941 F2d 910 (9th Cir 1991) (outlining the uses of statistical and anecdotal evidence of past discrimination, and the various elements of narrow tailoring).

[152] *Grutter v Bollinger*, 123 S Ct 2325 (2003); *Gratz v Bollinger*, 123 S Ct 2411 (2003).

[153] For a painstaking earlier analysis of Justice O'Connor's opinions on affirmative action in other contexts, and their likely application to diversity admissions to universities—an analysis that turned out to be an accurate prediction—see Akhil Reed Amar and Neal Kumar Katyal, *Bakke's Fate*, 43 UCLA L Rev 1745 (1996).

[154] 438 US 265 (cited in note 67).

test of strict judicial scrutiny. (2) Diversification of the student body, including racial diversity, serves compelling state interests in shaping an effective educational process. (3) The Michigan law school program, as a means to diversification, is sufficiently narrowly tailored to pass constitutional muster. Justice Kennedy explicitly agreed as to (1) and (2), making the vote 6–3 on the question of diversity as a compelling state interest. But he dissented sharply from (3). The Chief Justice, joined by Justices Scalia, Kennedy, and Thomas, wrote a dissenting opinion; he agreed with (1), but—assuming for argument that (2) was appropriate—dissented at length as to (3). The main dispute, then, went to the question of a narrowly tailored means. I deal with that question first, and then return to Justice O'Connor's articulation of the values of diversity in higher education.

In concluding that the law school plan was narrowly tailored to the diversity goal, Justice O'Connor begins with a context-conscious point, saying the inquiry "must be calibrated to fit the distinct issues raised by the use of race to achieve student body diversity in public higher education."[155] This seemingly innocent sentence is, in fact, what all the fuss is about in *Grutter*. Both the Chief Justice and Justice Kennedy reject Justice O'Connor's view that the institutional context shapes the contours of strict judicial scrutiny. For the Chief Justice, here as always, every racial classification must surmount the same extremely high burden of justification—and in all his experience with affirmative action he has never met a justification he didn't dislike. For the Chief Justice, remember, affirmative action is, like Jim Crow, "a creator of castes"[156]—and never mind that a subordinated caste of Americans of European ancestry is nowhere to be seen. Justice Kennedy, striking a harsher note, says the majority's strict scrutiny is "manipulated to distort its real and accepted meaning,"[157] and insists on a "scrutiny that is real, not feigned,"[158] of the narrow tailoring of the program. In applying their versions of True Strict Scrutiny, the dissenters say that the law school's professed goal of a "critical mass" is belied by its failure to tailor its use of race narrowly to achieve the goal of diversity. The basis for both dissent-

---

[155] 123 S Ct at 2341.

[156] *United Steelworkers v Weber*, 443 US 109, 254 (1979) (Rehnquist, J, dissenting).

[157] 123 S Ct at 2370.

[158] Id at 2373.

ers' distrust lies in the school's admissions statistics. Minority admission offers and enrollments had fluctuated insufficiently from year to year to convince them that the school had anything other than a quota in mind. Finally, the law school had not adopted a termination date for affirmative action.

I repeat: the dispute in the opinions in *Grutter* was all about the question whether strict scrutiny had a single meaning for all forms of affirmative action in all institutional contexts. Justice O'Connor, having been careful to negate any such position in *Adarand*,[159] is no more receptive to it here. At this point in her opinion, she sets out the factors leading to her conclusion that the law school's program is narrowly tailored: the absence of a fixed quota or separate track for admission, the individualized assessment of candidates,[160] the weight given to nonracial considerations in the diversity component of that assessment, and the significant overlap of the distributions of LSAT scores and grades for minority admitees with those for other admitees. Then she rejects the idea that narrow tailoring implies that the school must pursue all conceivable nonracial alternatives in its quest for diversity. At the end of the Court's opinion, Justice O'Connor notes that twenty-five years have elapsed since *Bakke*, and says the Justices in the majority "expect" that after another twenty-five years the need for racial preferences will have passed.[161]

This analysis leaves implicit a point that deserves explicit statement, in the interest of clarifying the main difference between the

---

[159] See text at note 145.

[160] In *Gratz*, Justice O'Connor joined the Chief Justice's opinion of the Court, which held invalid the affirmative action ingredient in the university's freshman admissions program. Taking as given *Grutter*'s acceptance of student body diversity as a compelling state interest, the Court concluded that the program's automatic assignment of 20 points (out of the 100 points that would guarantee admission) to a minority applicant, in practice, admitted all qualified minority applicants, without any individualized evaluation. The opinion also included a disquisition on prior affirmative action decisions. Justice O'Connor joined in the opinion of the Court, but added a short concurrence of her own, briefly describing the freshman admissions affirmative action program and calling it a "nonindividualized, mechanical one." 123 S Ct at 2433. Justice Breyer joined this opinion except for its concurrence in the opinion of the Court—presumably to avoid associating himself with some of the Chief Justice's larger-scale remarks. The University of Michigan has already changed its undergraduate admissions program to assure the individualized determinations prescribed in *Gratz*. Greg Winter, *U. of Michigan Alters Admissions Uses of Race*, NY Times A12 (Aug 29, 2003).

[161] Justice Thomas calls his *Grutter* dissent a partial concurrence; he "agrees" that after 25 years all racial preferences will be unconstitutional. 123 S Ct at 2363–65. Justice Ginsburg, concurring, registers her view that this statement in the Court's opinion is not a limit imposed by the Fourteenth Amendment, but a hope. 123 S Ct at 2347–48.

majority and the two dissents I have discussed. Ever since *Bakke* there has been a tension between the acceptance of student diversity as a goal and the requirements of strict scrutiny in its strictest sense.[162] The tension becomes more evident when one reads the Court's more recent opinions striking down programs of affirmative action in other contexts, such as government contracting.[163] Consider the question of narrow tailoring. In those cases, the state's interest looks backward to compensating for specific past discrimination. The fashioning of a narrowly tailored remedy is, therefore, a task readily defined. A city's racially preferential hiring plan for its contractors' choices of subcontractors, for example, must set a percentage for the preference that bears a close relation to the percentage of qualified minority subcontractors in the immediate region. Waivers must be available if local minority subcontractors cannot be found. The city must try race-neutral methods of assuring participation by minority subcontractors, if they are available (e.g., relaxation of bonding requirements or other barriers to entry into subcontracting). And such a plan must be subjected to periodic review, to assure that racial preferences last no longer than is necessary to remedy the past discrimination.[164]

Once the achievement of a diverse student body is accepted as a compelling interest, the question of narrow tailoring necessarily looks to the future. Now the design of a narrowly tailored race-conscious admissions system is focused on the goal of diversity. (This contextual difference, which seems obvious enough, is something the *Grutter* dissenters either reject or minimize.) Token representation of a minority group is entirely antithetical to the educational goals of diversity. I say this on the basis of my own law school teaching experience since the late 1950s, two decades before *Bakke* was decided. So, the idea of a "critical mass" is not an artifice or a "mask," but is implicit in the goal of diversity.[165] And, as a

---

[162] See, for example, Kenneth L. Karst and Harold W. Horowitz, *The Bakke Opinions and Equal Protection Doctrine*, 14 Harv CR-CL L Rev 7, 7–20 (1979).

[163] The *Croson* case, 488 US 469 (cited in note 130), and the *Adarand* case, 515 US 200 (cited in note 131).

[164] See text following note 149.

[165] Reaching a critical mass without affirmative action is next to impossible. True, the UCLA law faculty has added Critical Race Studies to its growing list of fields of concentration, and this program surely has contributed to an increased yield of minority students enrolled—increased, that is, from the post-1996 nadir, when potential minority applicants saw California's Proposition 209 as a "No Trespassing" sign. (Who would apply to a school in order to be the only African American in a classroom of 80 students?) For a richer

onetime practitioner of diversity admissions,[166] I can understand why the administration of a program intended to produce a critical mass tends to regress to a mean, staying in a fairly narrow range from year to year. Surely there is some (roughly set) minimum number of students in a critical mass, a minimum that does not vary from one year to the next. Surely, too, at some point (also roughly set), enough special effort to secure diversity is enough. Neither of these is capable of precise specification—and if they were to be made rigid, they would be decried as an unconstitutional quota. Justice Powell anticipated just such adjustments in his *Bakke* opinion: "[T]he weight attributed to a particular quality [e.g., race] may vary from year to year depending on the 'mix' both of the student body and the applicants for the incoming class."[167] To infer bad faith from efforts to assure the critical mass, or from the lack of great variation in the numbers of minority applicants offered admission or enrolled, is simply unwarranted.

There is another important difference between diversity admissions to a law school and an affirmative action program for government contractors, as a remedy for past discrimination. The latter type of program calls for a specified time limit, or at least periodic review, to assure that the minority preference in hiring is limited to its remedial purpose. In the case of race-conscious admissions to diversify a student body, however, something like a time limit is built into the diversity goal itself. At some point, when the law school admissions officer looks at the student body (or the candidates accepted in recent years), it may be clear that other criteria (including grades and LSAT scores) will produce what the school

---

analysis of the UCLA experience, see Cheryl I. Harris, *What the Supreme Court Did Not Hear in the Grutter and Gratz Cases*, 51 Drake L Rev 697, 705–07 (2003).

[166] I should disclose here that I was the chair of the UCLA law faculty committee that devised a diversity admissions program in 1978, following the *Bakke* decision. We made clear that many nonracial considerations were relevant to diversifying our admissions; examples would be work experience, or age, or parenthood, or demonstrated leadership, or talent in the arts, or foreign travel—these are merely suggestive. And, a whole-person evaluation was made by a faculty subcommittee in every single case of diversity admission. We were not engaging in a surreptitious preference for race, not sneaking a quota into the system, not doing one thing while pretending to do another. I should not be surprised to learn that some law teachers and administrators in Ann Arbor took offense at the accusations by the *Grutter* dissenters, and at recently published insinuations, by law scholars elsewhere, that diversity is no more than a rationale of convenience with the real goal of producing a quota.

[167] 438 US at 317–18.

sees as a critical mass of minority students.[168] From that time on, the school has no need for—nor any interest in—further action to diversify with respect to race. In *Grutter*, Justice O'Connor is prepared to trust the law school faculty's judgment as to that point. The dissenters express their distrust, no doubt because they think the present program is a quota in disguise. But, if the point of considering race in an affirmative action program is racial diversity, and racial diversity is attained at some future time without a special program so aimed, why would any law faculty want to continue to give a "plus" for race?

Now let us return to the initial point in Justice O'Connor's *Grutter* opinion: the characterization of the Michigan law school's interest in achieving a diverse student body as "compelling." One important feature of the case is that the majority (joined as to this point by Justice Kennedy) embraces the position that was Justice Powell's alone in *Bakke*, and makes it into a full-scale doctrinal precedent. Here Justice O'Connor does invoke Justice Powell's rather conclusory discussion of diversity's contribution to a university's educational quality, but she goes far more deeply into the reasons why diversity in the student body of a major law school is important. The district court had made findings about diversity as a means to "cross-cultural understanding" and more spirited classroom discussions. (Cross-cultural understanding does not equal sweetness and light; sometimes the understanding conveyed will accentuate conflict in perspectives and in material interests.)

Justice O'Connor takes the matter even further. She emphasizes the need to prepare students for success in a working population that becomes more diverse every year, and in enterprises doing business worldwide; here she refers to arguments made by the numerous businesses that took the trouble to make these points in briefs amici curiae.[169] She also cites an amicus brief, much discussed in the *Grutter* oral argument, spelling out the armed forces' need for diverse leadership—and thus the need of service academies and university ROTC programs for diverse student bodies. She finds further support for the same general argument in the

---

[168] Presumably because K–12 education and college education are now combining to produce a diversified pool of applicants across the full ranges of grades and test scores.

[169] In particular, the brief of General Motors Corp., and the brief of 65 major companies with global interests. Briefs amici curiae were also filed on behalf of numerous media companies.

amicus brief of General Motors Corporation: the nation's well-being requires "racial and ethnic diversity in the senior leadership of the corporate world" to avoid the productivity losses from a stratified workforce, with minorities dominant in the labor corps and whites in the higher levels of management.[170]

With this transitional discussion, Justice O'Connor moves beyond the successful operation of classroom education to the world outside the walls of academe. The universities, and law schools in particular,

> represent the training ground for a large number of our Nation's leaders. . . . In order to cultivate a set of leaders with legitimacy in the eyes of the citizenry, it is necessary that the path to leadership be visibly open to talented and qualified individuals of every race and ethnicity. All members of our heterogeneous society must have confidence in the openness and integrity of the educational institutions that provide this training. . . . Access to legal education (and thus the legal profession) must be inclusive of talented and qualified individuals of every race and ethnicity, so that all members of our heterogeneous society may participate in the educational institutions that provide the training and education necessary to succeed in America.[171]

The goal of diversity in a law school's student body is of compelling importance, then, not only because it serves to improve the school's educational product, but more generally because it advances minorities' educational opportunities, and thus makes possible the integration of leadership in America's institutions. So, not only is the Court's "narrow tailoring" discussion forward-looking; its conclusion that diversity is a compelling interest also looks to the future, in two senses. First, the day-to-day experience of law students in a diversified school teaches them—not just those admitted in the diversity program, but other students who may need the lesson even more—that it is natural for the professional world, and more broadly the middle class, to be multicultural. Second,

---

[170] Brief amicus curiae of General Motors Corp., *Grutter*, 123 S Ct 2325, at 22–26. Significantly, labor agrees. The AFL-CIO, citing impressive social science evidence, argued that university graduates with experience in diversified student bodies are significantly less likely than other graduates to retain negative racial stereotypes that translate into practices of employment discrimination. Brief amicus curiae of American Federation of Labor and Congress of Industrial Organizations, *Grutter*, 123 S Ct 2325 at 21–28 and passim.

[171] 123 S Ct at 2341.

the law school produces graduates who will populate the nation's most influential institutions, public and private.

The integration of American institutions is, indeed, a goal that deserves recognition as a compelling interest, justifying race-conscious governmental action toward that end. Before *Bakke* was decided—that is, before strict scrutiny of affirmative action had begun to develop into a complex term of art—this point was being made.[172] If it has been muffled in more recent times, one reason surely is the emphasis in judicial opinions on affirmative action (in contexts of employment) as a remedy for specifically defined wrongdoing. Concern over today's racial stratification of status positions fits awkwardly into that theory of justification, for the stratification is the legacy of myriad beliefs and actions that add up to racial subordination. In the words of the legal philosopher Elizabeth Anderson, "The kind of affirmative action practiced by selective schools should be viewed more as a forward-looking remedy for segregation than as a backward-looking remedy for discrimination."[173] The segregation cited here is not Jim Crow, but racial isolation from social networks caused by the historical (and not yet eradicated) association of the races with rankings in the status order. The nation didn't even begin to dismantle this structure of advantage until the mid-twentieth century.

In *Bakke*, Justice Powell rejected the claim that a compelling justification for affirmative action could be found in remedying the societal discrimination of the past. The *Grutter* opinion does not retreat from that position. But, for the building of a future-oriented doctrine that will recognize the vital importance of integrating America's institutions, the opinion offers a point of beginning.[174] Justice O'Connor, once again, has trained a beacon of light on the constitutional dimensions of the goal of achieving an inclusive national society. A landmark opinion, indeed.

---

[172] For example, Kenneth L. Karst and Harold W. Horowitz, *Affirmative Action and Equal Protection*, 60 Va L Rev 955, 963–66 (1974) (part of a symposium on *DeFunis v Odegaard*, 416 US 312 (1974)).

[173] Elizabeth S. Anderson, *From Normative to Empirical Sociology in the Affirmative Action Debate: Bowen and Bok's The Shape of the River*, 50 J Legal Educ 284, 303 (2000). For a much fuller analysis, see Elizabeth S. Anderson, *Integration, Affirmative Action, and Strict Scrutiny*, 77 NYU L Rev 1195 (2002).

[174] See Kenneth L. Karst, *The Revival of Forward-Looking Affirmative Action*, 104 Colum L Rev 60 (2004).

C. CITIZENSHIP AND THE POLITICS OF GENDER ROLES

In the pages that follow I consider Justice O'Connor's contributions, during the years of the Rehnquist Court, on the subjects of sex discrimination, abortion choice, and sexual orientation. The theme that unites these three topics is politics, specifically, the politics of gender roles within the Social Issues Agenda for cultural counterrevolution.[175] Politicians have found—and fostered—constituencies centered on these issues of gender. As we have seen, this is backlash politics.[176] The message may be: Vote for Our candidate, who will bring the law to bear on those miscreants who reject the allocation of gender roles central to Our way of life. The law thus enacted may never be enforced. Yet, it can be portrayed as an authoritative statement of the moral order, and a symbol of the status order indicating that Our group is in charge. An analogy from another field of constitutional doctrine would be the expression of a religious group's status dominance through the government's symbolic endorsement. For that matter, religious views have been prominent in the modern politics of gender roles.

During the same 1990 campaign that featured the "white hands" television ad, Senator Jesse Helms brought together the themes of gendered sex roles, abortion choice, and sexual orientation in a single paragraph of a political speech. Notice especially his references to law. Although the U.S. Senate has little to do with some of these issues, his main job in this speech is not to specify a legislative program, but to let his listeners know he is on their side:

> Think about it. Homosexuals and lesbians, disgusting people marching in our streets demanding all sorts of things, including the right to marry each other. How do you like them apples? Isn't our obligation, yours and mine, to get up and do some demanding on our own? What about the rights of human beings, born and unborn? What about the rights of women who want to stay in the home doing the most important job there is—raising our children?[177]

In the rhetoric attending this brand of politics, men must be men, women must be women, each must be seen to behave according

---

[175] See text at note 87.

[176] See text at note 87. On the political-social response to the women's movement, see Susan Faludi, *Backlash: The Undeclared War Against American Women* (1991).

[177] Edward A. Gargan, *Will Jesse Rise Again?* LA Times (Magazine) 14, 18 (Oct 28, 1990).

to traditional expectations, and any blurring of the gender line is intolerable.[178] Given the destabilization of gender relations that has helped to rouse this constituency into being, one way to make political hay is to promise a new stability, deploying law to police the gender line.[179] The law in question is the law governing sex discrimination, abortion choice, and sexual orientation. On all three counts, Justice O'Connor's recent record has been a disappointment to the constituency for cultural counterrevolution.

1. *Sex discrimination.* Like racial discrimination, sex discrimination has both a statutory and a constitutional aspect. Two opinions by Justice O'Connor in the field of employment discrimination are worth mentioning here, not so much for their doctrinal importance as for what they tell us about Justice O'Connor's views on inclusion as an essential of equal citizenship—that is, full participation in the society and polity. Just a year after the *Wygant* decision, the Supreme Court faced a statutory challenge to a California county's voluntary affirmative action plan in the field of employment.[180] The plan set flexible short-term goals for selecting women and minority applicants for jobs in categories where those groups were significantly underrepresented. Partly influenced by the plan's "plus factor" for women, the county's transportation agency had promoted Diane Joyce to be a road dispatcher, in preference to a male applicant whose qualifications were otherwise similar.[181] A majority of the Court upheld the agency's hiring; Justice O'Connor, concurring only in the judgment, provided a sixth vote in support of the decision. Her opinion followed the strict-scrutiny pattern of

---

[178] On the "frightening malleability of gender," see Ann Snitow, *Retrenchments v. Transformation: The Politics of the Antipornography Movement,* in *Caught Looking: Feminism, Pornography & Censorship* 10, 11 (F.a.c.t. Book Committee, Kate Ellis, 1988).

[179] The power of law to deliver on this promise of stability is distinctly limited. For some examples, see Kenneth L. Karst, *Law, Cultural Conflict, and the Socialization of Children,* 91 Cal L Rev 967 (2003) (*"Socialization of Children"*).

[180] *Johnson v Transportation Agency, Santa Clara County, California,* 480 US 616 (1987). The challenge to the affirmative action plan was brought under Title VII, the employment discrimination title of the Civil Rights Act of 1964, which prohibits sex discrimination as well as racial discrimination. A constitutional challenge, such as prevailed in *Wygant,* might have been possible, but had not been raised by the plaintiff.

[181] The man had narrowly outscored her in a first interview; the second interview group, which recommended the man for promotion, consisted of three men, one of whom had been the target of a sexual harassment charge Diane Joyce had filed, and another who had previously called her a "rebel-rousing, skirt wearing person." 480 US at 624. To the reader: Ask your friends—Is it worse to rouse a rabble, or to rouse rebels?

the Powell and O'Connor opinions in *Wygant*, closely examining the factual context (1) to be sure that the public employer had a basis for its voluntary remedial action (a statistical basis would suffice[182]), and (2) to be sure that the particular hiring decision did not result from a quota-like automatic preference for women, but rather from a whole-person evaluation of candidates. As to the county's justification for an affirmative action remedy, Justice O'Connor noted that, prior to this promotion, the agency had never employed a woman road dispatcher, and had no women in any skilled craft job—not a single one among the agency's 238 skilled craft positions. As for the county's particular decision to award the promotion, she concluded from a careful review of the record that Joyce did not get her new job from some automatic preference. Rather, she was highly qualified—and, in the county's evaluation, sex was "only one element of a number of considerations" in the promotion.[183] Reading this opinion, one can hear overtones of Justice O'Connor's opinion for the Court in the *Hogan* case five years before.

In another prominent case involving the statutory ban on sex discrimination in employment, Justice O'Connor also wrote a separate opinion.[184] The plaintiff, Ann Hopkins, claimed that a local office of the accounting firm Price Waterhouse had denied her a partnership in violation of Title VII. The evidence indicated that some partners were generally opposed to partnerships for women, and plainly showed that other partners strongly asserted that her behavior was not sufficiently "feminine." At the same time, more legitimate motives probably played some role in the decision—for example, a concern that the plaintiff might be deficient in interpersonal skills. Confronted with such a "mixed motives" case, the Supreme Court concluded that sex stereotyping in partnership promotion decisions was, indeed, a violation of Title VII, and went on to hold that Price Waterhouse could prevail only if it could show by a preponderance of the evidence that a legitimate motive, standing alone, would have produced the same decision.[185] Justice

---

[182] This approach followed from her view in *Wygant*, 476 US 267 (cited in note 72), and foreshadowed her opinion in *Croson*, 488 US 469 (discussed in the text at note 132).

[183] 480 US at 656.

[184] *Price Waterhouse v Hopkins*, 490 US 228, at 261 (1988).

[185] This interpretation was analogous to decisions in mixed-motive cases under the Equal Protection Clause. For example, *Arlington Heights v Metropolitan Housing Development Corp.*, 429 US 252 (1977); *Hunter v Underwood*, 471 US 222 (1985). The main issue in *Price Waterhouse* concerned the burden of proof. The dissenters thought that, in a mixed-motives

O'Connor's concurring opinion is noteworthy for her recognition that, in mixed-motives cases, assigning plaintiffs the burden of proving that the illicit motive was a "but for" cause of employers' actions would seriously undercut Title VII's purposes to deter intentional discrimination and to compensate for injuries caused by that discrimination. In making this point, Justice O'Connor observed that the plaintiff had proved that sex stereotyping had been a substantial factor in the decision to pass over Hopkins's application. She went on:

> It is as if Ann Hopkins were sitting in the hall outside the room where partnership decisions were being made. As the partners filed in to consider her candidacy, she heard several of them make sexist remarks in discussing her suitability for partnership. As the decisionmakers exited the room, she was *told* by one of those privy to the decisionmaking process that her gender was a major reason for the rejection of her partnership bid.[186]

Under those circumstances, Justice O'Connor did not think it unfair to shift the burden to the employer "to convince the factfinder that, despite the smoke, there is no fire."[187]

In these two cases, women were seeking access to what had long been considered "man's work." In Santa Clara County's affirmative action plan, Diane Joyce found a welcome mat; in the Price Waterhouse firm, Ann Hopkins found a "No Trespassing" sign.[188] Justice O'Connor understood the difference, because she could put herself in the position of each of these women. (In *Price Waterhouse*, she even invited readers of her opinion to view the case through the eyes of Ann Hopkins.) There is a general lesson here, and it is important. Empathy—the capacity and inclination to see a situation through the eyes of another—is a quality much to be desired in judges who are considering the claims to inclusion that lie at the heart of equal citizenship.

---

case, the burden should remain on the plaintiff to prove an illicit ground for the employment discrimination. This case was under consideration by the Court at the same time as the *Wards Cove* case, discussed in the text at note 126. The Civil Rights Restoration Act of 1991 makes clear that, in a mixed-motives case, the employer bears the burden of showing that it would have taken the same action even if sex (race, etc.) were not a motivating factor. See *Desert Palace, Inc. v Costa*, 123 S Ct 2148 (2003).

[186] 490 US at 272–73 (emphasis in original).

[187] Id at 266.

[188] See text at note 146.

The most important recent constitutional decision on explicit sex discrimination by government is *United States v Virginia*,[189] in which the Supreme Court, 7–1, held that Virginia Military Institute (VMI), a state college, could not constitutionally exclude women. Justice Ruth Bader Ginsburg wrote the opinion of the Court, which Justice O'Connor joined. That opinion made heavy use of *Hogan*, not just the decision as a precedent, but also the strong language of Justice O'Connor's opinion. To justify denying women an opportunity that is open to men, Justice Ginsburg repeatedly said, the state must satisfy the intermediate standard of *Craig v Boren*,[190] as understood in *Hogan* to require an "exceedingly persuasive justification." Against this standard, the generalizations about women's capacities or interests offered by the state, and accepted by the lower courts in this case, would not do.

One could see all this coming—not just the result, but the Court's explanation. During the oral argument, there was a revealing colloquy between Justice O'Connor and Paul Bender (who argued for the United States that VMI's exclusion of women violated the Equal Protection Clause). I quote from the *Law Week* summary:

> Justice O'Connor asked Bender if strict scrutiny is needed for the analysis, or if intermediate scrutiny could be used.
> Bender acknowledged that intermediate scrutiny could be used.
> Then why urge a different standard? O'Connor questioned.
> The government expected the issue to come up, and it's an open question what standard to apply.
> O'Connor disagreed with that assessment and suggested that Bender look at *Hogan*.[191]

Only Justice Scalia dissented, but he was in his usual form.[192] Chief Justice Rehnquist concurred in the judgment, but dissociated himself from Justice Ginsburg's emphasis on the need for "exceedingly persuasive justification." He preferred the milder locution for intermediate scrutiny used in *Craig v Boren*,[193] to which, he said, "We

---

[189] 518 US 515 (1996).

[190] 429 US 190 (cited in note 15).

[191] *Arguments Before the Court*, 64 US L Week 3493, at 3494 (1996).

[192] Justice Thomas did not participate; his son was attending VMI. I have discussed the Court's opinion, and Justice Scalia's dissent, in Kenneth L. Karst, *"The Way Women Are": Some Notes in the Margin for Ruth Bader Ginsburg*, 20 U Hawaii L Rev 619 (1998).

[193] 429 US 190 (cited in note 15).

have adhered . . . ever since."[194] This "We" was in the corporate-We tradition. In *Craig* itself, and throughout the twenty years until this case, the Chief Justice had persistently opposed (or undermined) heightened scrutiny for official sex discrimination. Score one for Justice Ginsburg—and one for Justice O'Connor.

Any precedent is pliable to a degree, and that goes for the phrase "exceedingly persuasive." Five years after the VMI case, the Supreme Court decided *Nguyen v INS*,[195] another in a series of cases testing the immigration and nationality laws against the equal protection guarantee found in the Fifth Amendment's Due Process Clause. By a 1940 act of Congress, a nonmarital child born to one citizen parent and one noncitizen parent is automatically a U.S. citizen if the mother is the citizen-parent. If it is the father who is a citizen, however, the child becomes a U.S. citizen only if (i) a blood relationship is established by clear and convincing evidence, (ii) the father promises in writing to support the child financially, and (iii) the father's paternity is formally recognized before the child's eighteenth birthday.[196] In this case the first two statutory requirements were met; DNA testing had established the father's paternity with a 99.98 percent probability, and the father had raised and supported the child in the United States since he was six years old. However, the father had not obtained a formal declaration of parentage from the state court until the child was twenty-eight, and so it was the 1940 statute's third condition that was challenged in this case. The father had joined in the child's petition for recognition of U.S. citizenship, but the Immigration and Naturalization Service (INS) denied the petition. The Court upheld this statutory sex discrimination, 5–4.[197]

Justice Kennedy, writing the opinion of the Court, recited the facts just stated, and recited *Craig v Boren*'s requirements of heightened judicial scrutiny.[198] But, with this recitation, the majority's

---

[194] *Virginia*, 518 US 558.

[195] 533 US 53 (2001).

[196] Paternity is formally recognized, under this statute, by a legitimation under state law, a sworn declaration of paternity by the father, or a court order declaring his paternity.

[197] The effect of the decision was to make the child (now an adult), who had committed some serious crimes, eligible as an alien for immediate deportation. Nguyen's case surely was not helped by his testimony in his deportation hearing that he was a citizen of Vietnam, not the United States.

[198] See the text at note 15.

interest in heightened scrutiny ended. Justice Kennedy hypothesized two justifications for the law: first, the need to assure that the child really is biologically related to the father, and, second, the need to assure that the child has an opportunity during his or her minority to develop a connection to the father, and to the United States. These were "important" interests, he said, and the law's third requirement of a formal legitimation was "substantially related" to achieving them. "The difference between men and women in relation to the birth process is a real one."[199] So, fathers and mothers "are not similarly situated with regard to the proof of biological parenthood," and all that equal protection demands is "that all persons similarly situated should be treated alike."[200] If this language sounds familiar, one reason may be that it was the very language deployed by then-Justice Rehnquist in the 1981 *Michael M.* case, when he set out to undermine the serious means scrutiny demanded by *Craig v Boren*.[201] So, says Justice Kennedy, the 1940 law's third requirement—formal legitimation—aims "to ensure an acceptable documentation of paternity."[202]

Remarkably, Justice Kennedy went on to say that the relation of this required formality to his two hypothesized purposes amounted to "exceedingly persuasive" justification for the law's requirement that a father (but not a mother) engage in this formality.[203] With respect, this declaration fails the straight-face test. The majority opinion does not employ even mildly heightened scrutiny, let alone require an "exceedingly persuasive justification." As for scrutiny of the law's purposes: When heightened scrutiny is taken seriously, purposes later imagined by government lawyers or Justices will not do, and there was no evidence that Congress in 1940

---

[199] 533 US at 73.

[200] Id at 63.

[201] See the discussion of the 1981 cases in the text at notes 17–18.

[202] 533 US at 63.

[203] Id at 70. Justice Kennedy remarked at this point that in the VMI case the Court had said that a justification was "exceedingly persuasive" when it was substantially related to an important governmental interest (the *Craig* standard). Turnabout is fair play. After all, in *Hogan* and in the VMI case, the Court had said that the *Craig* standard (substantial relation to important interest) meant "exceedingly persuasive justification." But—and this is a crucial "but"—ever since *Craig* in 1976, just about everyone has said that sex discrimination implied *some* significant heightening of judicial scrutiny. This opinion talks the talk of heightened scrutiny, but does not walk the walk.

had the hypothesized purposes in mind.[204] As for means scrutiny—that is, the need for sex discrimination in the law's third requirement of formal recognition: The facts of *Nguyen* had provided both kinds of assurance called for in the majority's imagined purposes. In other words, there was no need to go outside *the record in this very case* to demonstrate the availability of alternative means to serve the government's (hypothesized) purposes without engaging in sex discrimination. Under any seriously heightened scrutiny, the law would be in trouble. But, of course, the majority had no intention of really applying the demanding standard of review that *Craig v Boren* had applied to sex discrimination.

Justice O'Connor, writing for the four dissenters, went through every single step of the majority opinion, demolishing unsupported assumptions and exposing gaps in the argument. It must have been particularly galling for her to see the standard of review she had rescued in *Hogan* subjected to such manipulation. If I were writing about anyone but Justice O'Connor, I might use the term "cold fury" to describe this dissent. In the end, she made unmistakably clear that the majority had not subjected the law to heightened scrutiny, but had waved it through with no serious scrutiny at all. The Court's flaccid receptivity in 2001 to 1940-style sex discrimination is not exonerated by the disclaimer in the majority opinion's coda, with its surprisingly uninformed assumption that the only problem with sex-role stereotypes lies in "misconception and prejudice," and its Tartuffian assertion that the statute does not "show disrespect" for fathers or mothers.[205]

Reading Justice Kennedy's strictures in his recent *Grutter* dissent about fidelity to a "real, not feigned" standard of strictness,[206] one may be reminded of the *Nguyen* case, and his relaxed version of an "exceedingly persuasive justification" for sex discrimination. Justice O'Connor's attitude in *Nguyen* toward what seems to her (and to me) to be a watering down of the standard of review can be matched against Justice Kennedy's attitude in *Grutter*. In *Nguyen*,

---

[204] In 1940, surely sex-role stereotypes were embedded in the worldview of the (overwhelmingly male) members of Congress. Of course, they would say, nonmarital children—they would say illegitimates—would be brought up by their mothers, while the fathers would disappear.

[205] 533 US at 73.

[206] See text at note 158.

of course, Justice Kennedy is persuaded that the law's requirement of a formal legal proceeding to establish paternity adds something important, even though both paternity and connection to the United States are undisputed. Justice O'Connor, in contrast, is acutely aware of the sex stereotyping just below the surface of the statute, and of the silliness of insisting on a formality to prove points clearly established by the evidence in the case. In *Grutter*, she is convinced that diversity in law school admissions really is of compelling importance. Justice Kennedy states his agreement with that proposition in the abstract, but seems to differ on the meaning of diversity, which for the majority implies keeping track of numbers (as Justice Powell's *Bakke* opinion had noted, quoting Harvard's affirmative action plan).[207] As *Grutter* and *Nguyen* illustrate, both the invocation and the application of a standard of review always imply something about the judge's estimate of the importance of the interests at stake in the case. This is not A Bad Thing. After all, you can't take the judgment out of judging.

Given so cursory a bow toward heightened scrutiny in *Nguyen*, it behooves us to search for a more material explanation. Two possible solutions come to mind. First, some Justices might have seen this as an "aliens case" or a "foreign relations case." In this view, when the Court confronts an equal protection challenge to a congressional regulation of aliens or immigration or nationality, all bets are off. One version of this position is adopted by Justice Scalia in his concurring opinion, which renews his previous argument that the Court simply has no constitutional power to confer citizenship on a basis other than Congress prescribes, irrespective of any equal protection violation.[208] In 1976 Justice Stevens had written for the Court in concluding that, "given Congress's broad power over immigration," congressional regulation of aliens was entitled to the greatest possible judicial deference—indeed, virtually presented a political question.[209] The problem with this "aliens/immigration/nationality" explanation is that the majority opinion in *Nguyen* takes note of an analogous 1977 decision along

---

[207] If Justice Kennedy agrees with the majority's definition of diversity, why say that strict scrutiny is designed to force the school "to seriously explore race-neutral alternatives"? 123 S Ct at 2374. It should be noted here that most state university law schools around the country have explored such alternatives to the point of faculty exhaustion, without success.

[208] 533 US at 73–74. Justice Thomas joined in this opinion.

[209] *Mathews v Díaz*, 426 US 67, 81–82 (1976).

these lines,[210] but declines to reach the issue. Perhaps some Justices in the majority were reluctant to announce a broad deference to Congress, for fear of inviting further congressional excess in the field of citizenship. But at least such a ground would not pollute the jurisprudence of sex discrimination.

Alternatively, the Court might have seen this as an "unwed fathers case," following some decisions in which putative fathers have been unsuccessful in blocking adoption of a nonmarital child[211] or suing for a nonmarital child's wrongful death,[212] even though the mothers of nonmarital children did not encounter the same legal disabilities. At this point, a legal realist might notice that Justice Stevens also played a crucial role in those decisions—and had foreshadowed one of them in a dissent in another case.[213] Justice Stevens's vote was necessary to make a majority in *Nguyen*, and his prior opinions on unwed fathers are liberally cited by Justice Kennedy. Yet the *Nguyen* majority opinion does not make them a main foundation for the decision. The precedents, after all, are in some tension with the Court's more recent adoption of a demanding standard of review for laws restricting actions to establish paternity of nonmarital children.[214] It seems doubtful that Justice Stevens really favors a general relaxation of standards of review in sex discrimination cases, and perhaps that is why Justice O'Connor was moved to say, at the end of her *Nguyen* dissent, "I trust that the depth and vitality of these precedents [requiring heightened scrutiny for official sex discrimination] will ensure that today's error remains an aberration."[215] The fruition of her hope,

---

[210] *Fiallo v Bell*, 430 US 787 (1977). The Court upheld a restriction on the immigration law's conferral of preferred status in cases involving the parent-child relationship. A mother's relation to a nonmarital child was allowed the preference, but a father's relation to a nonmarital child was not.

[211] *Lehr v Robertson*, 463 US 248 (1983) (opinion of the Court by Stevens, J, distinguishing *Caban v Mohammed*, 441 US 380 (cited in note 213)).

[212] *Parham v Hughes*, 441 US 347 (1979).

[213] *Caban v Mohammed*, 441 US 380, at 401 (1979) (Stevens, J, dissenting), decided the same day as *Parham*, 441 US 347 (cited in note 212).

[214] Justice O'Connor had pointed the way in her concurrence in *Mills v Hableutzel*, 456 US 91, 102 (1982). The cases culminated in *Clark v Jeter*, 486 US 456 (1986), in which Justice O'Connor wrote for a unanimous Court, adopting the intermediate standard of review used in sex discrimination cases. Could Justice Stevens have considered those cases as presenting a "woman's issue," while seeing *Nguyen* as presenting a "man's issue"? The year 2001 would seem to be a quarter century late for such a distinction.

[215] 533 US at 97.

it would appear, lies in the presidential election returns, where the politics of cultural counterrevolution can be expected to carry considerable weight in the immediate future.[216]

2. *Abortion choice*. I have said that the backlash politics of gender roles brings together, in a single package, three constitutional subjects that appear in casebooks under different doctrinal names: sex discrimination, abortion choice, and sexual orientation. Lest we forget this political reality, here is a list of moral evils offered by the head of the National Christian Action Coalition in a Family Issues Voting Index:

> planned parenthood, the pill, no-fault divorce, open marriages, gay rights, palimony, test-tube babies, women's liberation, children's liberation, unisex, day-care centers, child advocates, and abortion on demand. A man is no longer responsible for his family. God has been kicked out, and humanism enthroned.[217]

The interconnection of these subjects in modern American politics is a datum worth consideration when judges come to deal with one of them in apparent isolation. From the 1970s to the present day, the politics of abortion choice has been central to the larger cultural conflict over women's roles.[218] No examination of women's status in American life would be complete without a treatment of their constitutional right to control their own sexuality and maternity. To put the matter in a nutshell, the most important "women's equality" opinion in Justice O'Connor's career is not the *Hogan* opinion but her co-authored plurality opinion in *Planned Parenthood of Southeastern Pennsylvania v Casey*.[219]

---

[216] See note 113.

[217] The Index was a 1980 report card on legislators circulated by Rev. Robert Billings, quoted in Erling Jorstad, *The Politics of Moralism: The New Christian Right in American Life* 83 (Augsburg, 1981). A more recent coupling of two of these issues was made by Virginia Thomas, whose husband is a Justice. She took time out from her duties as director of the Heritage Foundation's liaison with the Bush (II) White House to write a public letter protesting opposition to Judge Charles Pickering's candidacy for promotion to the Fifth Circuit. The opponents' agenda, she said, was "all about abortion and homosexuality." Virginia Thomas, *To Judge Pickering: They Can't Take Away Your Honor*, Wall St J A18 (Mar 14, 2002).

[218] See generally Kristin Luker, *Abortion and the Politics of Motherhood* (1984); Rosalind Pollack Petchesky, *Abortion and Woman's Choice: The State, Sexuality, and Reproductive Freedom* 241–76 (Northeastern, rev ed 1990).

[219] 505 US 833 (1992).

When we last saw Justice O'Connor at work in this doctrinal setting,[220] however, she was criticizing the trimester approach in the opinion in *Roe v Wade*, and arguing that state regulations of abortion should be subjected to strict scrutiny if (but only if) they unduly burdened a woman's choice to have an abortion. As I have suggested, those opinions give no indication that she was focusing on abortion choice as an issue bound up with the roles allowed to women. Rather, the opinions emphasize due process liberty as a doctrinal arena where courts were in need of greater self-restraint. This perspective is not surprising, for both the *Roe* opinion and its detractors portrayed the claim to a right of abortion choice as a claim of liberty: a woman's freedom to control her body.[221] Even on the pro-choice side of the constitutional argument, there was remarkably little mention of a concern that today is seen as central: Women need control over their sexuality and maternity if they are to have opportunities to participate in the public world, including the world of work—that is, if they are to be equal citizens. It is worth two paragraphs to recall why this is so.[222]

For the moment, put aside the legal barriers that excluded women from positions of responsibility in the public world, and focus instead on the private world of women's intimate relations with men. From the earliest recorded civilizations up to the mid-twentieth century, male power over women's sexuality and maternity restricted them to a passive role, permitting them to control conception and childbirth only by a strategy of denial. One who sees herself as receptive rather than active in this central aspect of her life could easily be led into a pattern of hesitant behavior and diminished self-confidence—in other words, a reenactment of the

---

[220] See text at note 34.

[221] See Reva B. Siegel, *Reasoning from the Body: A Historical Perspective on Abortion Regulation and Questions of Equal Protection*, 44 Stan L Rev 261, 348–49 (1992).

[222] I have been on this particular soapbox since 1976. Much in the following two paragraphs is adapted from these writings, listed in the order of publication: Kenneth L. Karst, *Book Review* (of Gerald Gunther, *Cases and Materials on Constitutional Law*, 9th ed), 89 Harv L Rev 1028 (1976); Karst, *Equal Citizenship* (cited in note 93); Kenneth L. Karst, *The Freedom of Intimate Association*, 89 Yale L J 624, 659–64 (1980); Kenneth L. Karst, *Woman's Constitution*, 1984 Duke L J 447, 472–80 ("*Woman's Constitution*"); Karst, *Cultural Counterrevolution* (cited in note 87). I claim no property right in this idea. Important early articulations include Sylvia A. Law, *Rethinking Sex and the Constitution*, 132 U Pa L Rev 955 (1984); Ruth Bader Ginsburg, *Some Thoughts on Autonomy and Equality in Relation to Roe v Wade*, 63 NC L Rev 375 (1985). The most complete exposition of the theme—a "must" for anyone who would understand it—is Siegel, 44 Stan L Rev at 222 (cited in note 221).

stereotype of weakness, through retreat into dependence and domesticity. When abortion was first made a statutory crime in the nineteenth century,[223] the legislation was sold to the public with a number of arguments, but the most powerful was the idea that women were destined to be mothers, and that abortion and birth control were selfish "derogations of maternal duty."[224] (That is to say, Senator Helms[225] was singing an old song.)

The prevailing pattern of gender roles was self-reinforcing, and had its own effects on public life, where women were discouraged from seeking employment outside the zone of "nurture" (nurse, teacher, secretarial assistant). Under the influence of this pattern— some political operatives still call the pattern "family values"— women were largely excluded from the public sphere and kept under male tutelage at home. The experience of many women in the workplace during World War II, followed by the advent of the birth control pill, dramatically changed this structure of opportunity, and—even more fundamentally—worked a positive influence on a great many women's self-perception. An unwanted pregnancy, absent the power of abortion choice, threatened a woman's ability to continue in college, or take a job. But control over one's own sexuality and maternity was not just necessary for women to respond to new opportunities or advantages. It offered a path to self-realization.

My untutored guess is that Justice O'Connor's view of the abortion choice issue had begun to take seriously the doctrinal implications of these considerations at least as early as 1989, when the Supreme Court decided *Webster v Reproductive Health Services*.[226] President Reagan, still an opponent of abortion rights, had made two more appointments to the Court, and those who hoped that *Roe* would be overruled took heart. Former Solicitor General Charles Fried presented to the Court the Bush (I) administration's

---

[223] Until this time, the common law treated abortion as completely within the control of the pregnant woman up to the point of "quickening," the sensation of movement of the fetus. Siegel, 44 Stan L Rev at 281–82 (cited in note 221).

[224] Id at 301–04. Siegel quotes one rhetorical question, asked of a hypothetical woman considering abortion, "Have you the right to choose an indolent, selfish life, neglecting the work God has appointed you to perform?" Id at 303, quoting Augustus K. Gardner, *Conjugal Sins Against the Laws of Life and Health* 225 (1870) (Arno photo reprint, 1974).

[225] Quoted in text at note 179.

[226] 492 US 490 (1989). Certainly the tone of her *Webster* concurrence, 492 US at 522, differs markedly from the tone of her *Akron* dissent.

view that favored overruling *Roe*. In *Webster* the Court stepped to
the brink, but did not take the leap.[227] Missouri's law required a
doctor performing an abortion on a fetus of twenty weeks of gestation to perform weight and lung maturity tests to determine
whether the fetus was viable.[228] Chief Justice Rehnquist, joined by
Justices White and Kennedy, concluded that this requirement
would violate the *Roe* trimester framework, but upheld it nonetheless. Justice Scalia called for an express overruling of *Roe*. Justice
O'Connor provided the fifth vote to uphold the law, but she said
it satisfied *Roe*'s requirements; thus there was no need to reach the
broader issue. She added: "when the constitutional invalidity of a
State's abortion statute actually turns on the constitutional validity
of *Roe v Wade*, there will be time enough to reexamine *Roe*. And
to do so carefully."[229]

Well, now. Justice Blackmun, dissenting, said the majority had
"silently" overruled *Roe*, and women's groups all over the country
sounded the alarm. Their lobbying produced a political irony. Following the *Webster* decision, bills to restrict abortion choice were
introduced in dozens of state legislatures; only a few states adopted
such laws. Elections in which abortion choice restrictions were
highlighted took a swing toward the pro-choice candidates, and a
number of prominent politicians announced their pro-choice
views.[230]

Part of the fallout from *Webster* was a spate of law review arti-
cles, including a collection of five in the *University of Pennsylvania
Law Review*. The central theme was the "meaning" of *Webster*, of
necessity a predictive enterprise. One article, by Susan Estrich and
Kathleen Sullivan, must have been of interest to Justice O'Connor.
Its title was "Abortion Politics: Writing for an Audience of
One,"[231] and it was as candid a piece of advocacy as you will ever

---

[227] On the "blizzard of draft opinions" circulated by the Justices before *Webster* was decided, see Peter Irons, *Brennan v Rehnquist: The Battle for the Constitution* 317 (1994).

[228] The law also forbade public employees to perform abortions in public hospitals. The
majority upheld this provision, citing earlier decisions sustaining state and federal refusals
to fund abortions.

[229] 492 US at 526.

[230] See Laurence H. Tribe, *Abortion: The Clash of Absolutes* 177–91 (1990); Lisa A. Klop-
penburg, *Measured Constitutional Steps*, 71 Ind L J 297, 318–22 (1996); Barry Friedman,
Dialogue and Judicial Review, 91 Mich L Rev 577, 665–67 (1993).

[231] 138 U Pa L Rev 119 (1989). The other articles in the colloquy were: Walter Dellinger
and Gene B. Sperling, *Abortion and the Supreme Court: The Retreat from Roe v Wade*, 138
U Pa L Rev 83 (1989) (the retreat is bad news); James Bopp, Jr. and Richard E. Coleson,

see in a law review. Whatever *Webster* might mean, the authors said, "eight men may read our briefs, but the real audience is one woman. Sandra Day O'Connor . . . is in the position single-handedly to decide the future of abortion rights. [This article] is nothing more or less than our best try, using whatever legal and persuasive talents we have, to convince an audience of one to stand up to those who are turning their backs on women."[232]

After a brief introduction, the authors got right to the point. Reproductive choice was essential to a woman's control of her future; leaving to the state the power to make such a momentous decision means allowing politics to run individual women's lives. After a thoughtful exploration of Justice O'Connor's "undue burden" analyses in *Akron* and *Thornburgh*, and her critique of *Roe's* trimester approach, the authors took up some particularized questions suggested by those early opinions, notably the questions of a hospitalization requirement and a twenty-four-hour waiting period—both of which made the authors nervous. But, they correctly said, "Justice O'Connor's motives in this regard hardly appear punitive."[233] They argued, as Justice Powell had strongly suggested in *Akron*, that laws such as these were intended less to protect pregnant women than to place obstacles in their paths when they sought to exercise their right of choice. The political process, the authors said, cannot be trusted to protect women's interests in controlling their maternity. (I return to this theme later.[234]) Here they were especially eloquent:

> Only women get pregnant. Only women have abortions. Only women will endure unwanted pregnancies and adverse health consequences if states restrict abortions. Only women will suffer dangerous, illegal abortions where legal ones are unavailable. Yet every restrictive abortion law has been passed by a legislature in which men constitute a numerical majority. And every restrictive abortion law, by definition, contains an unwritten clause exempting all men from its strictures.[235]

What Does Webster Mean? 138 U Pa L Rev 157 (1989) (*Roe* is doomed, and that is good news); Dawn Johnson, *From Driving to Drugs: Governmental Regulation of Pregnant Women's Lives after Webster*, 138 U Pa L Rev 179 (1989) (*Webster* has implications outside the abortion context); and Leonard A. Cole, *The End of the Abortion Debate*, 138 U Pa L Rev 217 (1989) (the abortion pill RU486 will make it all moot).

[232] 138 U Pa L Rev at 122–23.

[233] Id at 150.

[234] See text at notes 255–61.

[235] 138 U Pa L Rev at 151.

They concluded their powerful discussion of abortion politics with a call for help:

> That's why politics should not dictate constitutional rights. That's why women need Justice Sandra Day O'Connor so badly.[236]

Two more years would pass before *Planned Parenthood v Casey* would come before the Supreme Court. In the interim, however, the Court dealt with three other cases involving choice issues, and in all three cases Justice O'Connor supported protections for women who were seeking to exercise their rights of choice. A cursory treatment of these cases will suffice here. In the wisdom of hindsight, they can be seen as steps on the road to her *Casey* opinion.

Hodgson v Minnesota.[237] In the spring of 1990 the Court held invalid a Minnesota law requiring notice to both parents before a minor could obtain an abortion, but upheld a "backup" law allowing, as an alternative to two-parent notice, a "judicial bypass" in which a court could approve a minor's abortion. (Such bypass decisions are typically sought by the minor along with one parent.) As to each law, the vote was 5–4, and Justice O'Connor's vote was decisive. She joined Justice Stevens's plurality opinion striking down the unadorned two-parent notification requirement. Justice Stevens elaborately explained the potential for a parent's violent response to the news that his daughter was pregnant.[238] I say "his" advisedly. Justice O'Connor surely knew which parent usually goes to court with the daughter. In a separate opinion she remarked that only half of American children live with both parents, and made clear the inadequacy of the statute's exception for a young woman who has been abused in her family—because reporting the abuse involved notifying the abusive parent.[239] In this opinion she also joined Justice Kennedy in upholding the bypass system, believing it adequately protected the minor's right of choice.

---

[236] Id at 155.

[237] 497 US 417 (1990).

[238] The empirical support for this conclusion was impressive. See Justice Stevens's summary of the district court's findings on the question. Id at 438–44.

[239] See Twila L. Perry, *Justice O'Connor and Children and the Law*, 13 Women's Rts L Rep 81, 83 (1991), commending Justice O'Connor for her sensitivity to these realities of young women's lives.

Rust v Sullivan.[240] In the spring of 1991, the Court upheld a "gag rule" regulation of the Secretary of Health and Human Services (HHS) that prohibited family planning agencies funded under a 1970 act of Congress from (i) providing counseling (or referral) on abortion as a method of family planning, (ii) encouraging or advocating abortion as a method of family planning, or (iii) providing counseling in any facility that was not physically and financially separate from any facility engaging in prohibited activities. Some federal grantees and some doctors challenged the regulation as unauthorized under the 1970 act, and as a violation of agencies' First Amendment rights and of agency clients' rights of reproductive choice. The vote was 5–4, with three Justices dissenting on constitutional grounds. Justice O'Connor, dissenting separately, said, "One may well conclude, as Justice Blackmun does [in his dissent], that the regulations are unconstitutional [under the First Amendment]." But she did not join either that portion of his dissent or the portion resting on *Roe v Wade;* rather, she would follow "the time-honored practice of not reaching constitutional questions unnecessarily." She concluded that the HHS regulations were not justified under any persuasive reading of the act of Congress, and that they raised "serious First Amendment concerns." Accordingly, the regulations should be invalidated.[241]

Bray v Alexandria Women's Health Clinic.[242] The third case was decided in the fall of 1991, at the outset of the Term in which *Casey* would be decided. Operation Rescue was a national association that organized massive anti-abortion demonstrations, physically blocking access to clinics at which abortions were performed. The large numbers of demonstrators frequently overwhelmed the capacity of local police to contain them. Some birth control clinics in the Washington, D.C. metropolitan area sued in federal court to enjoin Operation Rescue from trespassing on clinic grounds and obstructing access to the clinics. The suit was based on the modern version of part of the Civil Rights Act of 1871 (the Ku Klux Klan

---

[240] 500 US 173 (1991).

[241] Id at 223–35. Shortly after this decision, the "gag rule" regulations were challenged in court, where a preliminary injunction held up enforcement until President William J. Clinton rescinded them immediately after taking office in January 1993.

[242] 506 US 263 (1991).

Act), authorizing injunctive relief against a conspiracy to deprive persons of the equal protection of the laws. They succeeded in the lower courts, but lost in the Supreme Court, 6–3.[243] The majority, per Justice Scalia, interpreted the law to require showings that the conspiracy in question (i) be founded on some class-based discriminatory animus, and (ii) be aimed at interfering with rights protected against private encroachment. The action failed on both grounds, the majority held. Justice O'Connor, dissenting, would read the 1871 act broadly to protect all classes seeking to exercise their rights in unprotected circumstances similar to the victims of the Klan's violence. The class in *Bray*, she said, consisted of women, victims of a conspiracy "whose motivation is directly related to characteristics unique" to their status as women—that is, "their ability to become pregnant and their ability to terminate their pregnancies."[244] She did say, "This case is not about abortion."[245] Still, on reading her opinion I recalled the words of Estrich and Sullivan about women's crucial interests in control over their maternity. Randall Terry, the founder of Operation Rescue, made his own connection between abortion choice and the domestic roles that women were supposed to play. Just five days after the *Bray* case was decided in the Supreme Court, an interview with Terry appeared in *Time* magazine. He referred to the National Organization of Women's program as an exemplar of a "put-your-kids-in-day-care-and-go-out-and-pursue-a-career, proabortion mentality."[246]

Three months later, the Supreme Court agreed to hear *Planned Parenthood v Casey*. Pennsylvania is one of the states that has pro-

---

[243] Justice Souter was one of the six who concurred in the judgment, but he dissented from the case's disposition. He would have remanded the case for further proceedings under a second part of the statute, prohibiting conspiracy to prevent or hinder state officers from enforcing the equal protection clause.

[244] 506 US at 348–50. As to the majority's second point, Justice O'Connor concluded that no specific intent need be shown under the act's second prohibition, mentioned in the text just above, and said that Operation Rescue was just such a conspiracy.

[245] Id at 354. Her point was that it is a case about a private conspiracy to deprive members of a protected class of their legally protected interests, and whether the 1871 act covers such a conspiracy.

[246] Richard Lacayo, *Crusading Against the Pro-Choice Movement* (interview of Randall Terry), Time 26 (Oct 21, 1991). In the same interview Terry pictured the abortion issue as one battlefield in "a cultural civil war" pitting "Satan's agenda" against God's "moral absolutes."

duced a large volume of anti-abortion-choice legislation in the years since *Roe v Wade*,[247] and *Casey* presented a challenge to several provisions in yet another anti-abortion-choice package.[248] Two were the most significant restrictions on abortion choice: (1) An "informed consent" condition (*a*) requiring the doctor to inform the patient of various health risks and of the probable gestational age of "the unborn child," and to make available to the woman a packet of state-produced "pro-life" information on various aspects of the abortion decision; and (*b*) requiring a twenty-four-hour delay from the time of delivery of this information to the performance of the abortion procedure. (2) A requirement that a married woman state in writing that she has informed her husband that she is about to undergo an abortion.[249] The Third Circuit court of appeals, prominently citing Justice O'Connor's opinions in *Webster* and *Hodgson*, held that under the Supreme Court's recent decisions, the strict scrutiny standard of *Roe* no longer applied to all abortion choice regulations. Specifically, the court would not follow the lead of *Akron* and *Thornburgh*, which would have implied invalidating the regulations here. Rather the court adopted the "undue burden" standard that Justice O'Connor had been advocating ever since *Akron* in 1983. Strict scrutiny would be deployed only when a regulation imposed an undue burden on the right of choice; absent such a burden, a regulation need only pass the standard of rationality. Following this path, the court used the rational basis standard for all the regulations except the husband-notification requirement, which in the court's view did impose an undue burden and thus merited strict scrutiny. In the end the court invalidated the husband-notification requirement and upheld all the others. Rachael Pine and Sylvia Law, commenting after the court of appeals decision came down, said the Supreme Court was "certain to confirm the Third Circuit's predictions

---

[247] The *Thornburgh* case, 476 US 747 (cited in note 38), dealt with Pennsylvania's earlier package of laws restricting abortion choice.

[248] The law was one of the few anti-abortion-choice laws passed in the period just after the *Webster* decision. See note 226 and accompanying text.

[249] The statute also (*a*) required one parent's informed consent for an abortion on a young woman under 18, but made provision for a judicial bypass; (*b*) required the doctor to report on various aspects of an abortion procedure; and (*c*) waived its requirements in a medical emergency. The court of appeals had interpreted the latter provision broadly, to permit the doctor to take action in any case of a significant threat to the life or health of the woman. All these provisions were upheld by the Supreme Court, 7–2.

and interpretations by either explicitly or implicitly overruling *Roe.*"[250]

The oral argument in the Supreme Court followed a familiar pattern, with the state (and Solicitor General Kenneth Starr, presenting the views of the Bush (I) administration) arguing that the *Roe* standard should be replaced with across-the-board rationality review of abortion choice regulations, and counsel for the challenging clinics arguing that across-the-board strict scrutiny was essential to protect women's right of choice. Justices O'Connor and Kennedy asked questions indicating an inclination to adopt a case-by-case approach to the validity of such regulations.[251]

In the event, the Court upheld (7–2) the "informed consent" requirement, including the twenty-four-hour waiting period, and held invalid (5–4) the requirement of husband notification.[252] But the path to this result was not direct.[253] At the conference two days following the oral argument, five Justices voted to uphold all the regulations. There were four votes to overrule *Roe* explicitly,[254] but although Justice Kennedy thought the laws before the Court were valid, he was not ready to take that doctrinal step. Justice O'Connor, sticking to an "undue burden" standard, would uphold all but the husband-notification requirement. As for that one, she expressed great concern for abused and battered wives. Besides, when did government get the power to tell married couples what they must decide? Justice Souter would retain the *Roe* precedent. Several weeks later, Justice Kennedy told Justices O'Connor and Souter he would join them in reaffirming the core holding of *Roe*, and those three decided to issue the joint opinion that proved decisive in the case. In the allocation of responsibility for initial drafting,

---

[250] Rachael N. Pine and Sylvia A. Law, *Envisioning a Future for Reproductive Liberty: Strategies for Making the Rights Real*, 27 Harv CR-CL L Rev 407, 411 (1992).

[251] *Arguments Before the Court*, 60 US L Week 3727–29 (1992).

[252] *Planned Parenthood of Southeastern Pennsylvania v Casey*, 505 US 833 (1992). The other regulations, cited in note 249, were upheld on the basis of recent precedent and without elaborate discussion.

[253] The following account, apparently based on interviews with some Justices, comes from David G. Savage, LA Times (Dec 13, 1992), A1, reprinted in William Cohen and David J. Danielski, *Constitutional Law: Civil Liberty and Individual Rights* at 920–21 (Foundation, 5th ed 2002).

[254] Chief Justice Rehnquist and Justice White (the two dissenters in *Roe*), along with Justices Scalia and Thomas. Justice Blackmun (author of *Roe*) and Justice Stevens would use strict scrutiny and invalidate all the regulations.

Justice Souter would write about precedent, Justice Kennedy would write on the meaning of due process "liberty," and Justice O'Connor, emphasizing women's right of choice, would set out the "undue burden" standard of review for abortion choice regulations as applied to the laws before the Court. They would, essentially, affirm the results reached by the court of appeals, upholding all the regulations except for the husband-notification requirement.

The *Casey* joint opinion, I have said, is Justice O'Connor's most important contribution to women's equal citizenship.[255] But all three authors of the joint opinion made clear their concern for women's status as equal citizens. Justice Souter, speaking of the *Roe* precedent, said:

> [F]or two decades of economic and social developments, people have organized intimate relationships and made choices that define their views of themselves and their places in society, in reliance on the availability of abortion in the event that contraception should fail. The ability of women to participate equally in the economic and social life of the Nation has been facilitated by their ability to control their reproductive lives.[256]

Justice Souter was not making the point, trivialized in the Chief Justice's dissent, that people had "grown accustomed to the *Roe* decision."[257] Rather he was making a substantive argument about women's equal citizenship. Women came to understand, after *Roe*, that they, and not men (at home or in government offices), had control over their own maternity, and thus over their destinies. *Roe* was an acculturating influence, important not only to individual women but generally to the equal status of women in American society.

Justice Kennedy posed the issue of due process liberty as a question about the state's power to define morality in legislation so that, in practical terms, "a woman lacks all choice in the matter" of abortion choice.[258] He went on to describe the sacrifices imposed by pregnancy and motherhood, and to say that the woman's

---

[255] I mean here to give Justice O'Connor credit, not only for her own writing, but for the more important contribution of preparing the way, in her statements to the conference, for what became the joint opinion and, in several vital parts, the opinion of the Court.

[256] Id at 856.

[257] Id at 957.

[258] Id at 850.

suffering is too intimate and personal for the State to insist, without more, upon its own vision of the woman's role, however dominant that vision has been in the course of our history and our culture. The destiny of the woman must be shaped to a large extent on her own conception of her spiritual imperatives and her place in society.[259]

These two quotations from the joint opinion are momentous. In *Casey*, for the first time, a majority of the Supreme Court[260]—in company with Randall Terry, of all people—articulates the right of reproductive choice as essential to women's control over their social roles and their status as equal citizens.[261]

We come now to Justice O'Connor's own portion of the joint opinion. In setting out the "undue burden" standard, she modifies what she said in *Akron* (and what the court of appeals applied in *Casey*), substituting a new version considerably more protective of the right of choice. Now the conclusion that a law imposes an undue burden on women's right of abortion choice is not merely a preliminary to the application of strict scrutiny; the undue burden, by itself, invalidates the law. A law creates an undue burden, Justice O'Connor elaborates, when it imposes a substantial obstacle to the exercise of the right of choice. The Pennsylvania law, absent a medical emergency, required a married woman seeking an abortion to sign a statement that she had informed her husband of the intended procedure. At this point, Justice O'Connor reviews in great detail the findings of the district court, and the conclusions of a large body of social science studies of domestic violence, about the likely effects of such a required notice on wives who do not want to tell their husbands about their abortions. The district court concluded that in such cases there is a distressingly high probability that a compelled notification will lead to abuse by the husband—not just of the wife, but of their children.

---

[259] 505 US at 852.

[260] Justices Blackmun and Stevens joined the parts of the joint opinion that I have just quoted, making them part of the opinion of the Court.

[261] True, the Court rested decision on due process liberty, not on the Equal Protection Clause. But the guarantee of equal citizenship derives from the Fourteenth Amendment as a whole. See Karst, *Equal Citizenship* at 42–46 and passim (cited in note 93). For an astute analysis comparing due process and equal protection claims as instruments in subordinated groups' quests for equal citizenship, see William N. Eskridge, Jr., *Destabilizing Due Process and Evolutive Equal Protection*, 47 UCLA L Rev 1183 (2000).

Counsel for the state sought to minimize this burden by pointing out that only 20 percent of women seeking abortions are married, and some 95 percent of those (19 out of 20) will voluntarily tell their husbands. Here Justice O'Connor makes an important point for future cases: "Legislation is measured for consistency with the Constitution by its impact on those whose conduct it affects. . . . The proper focus of constitutional inquiry is the group for whom the law is a restriction, not the group for whom the law is irrelevant."[262] For those women who have reason to fear abuse (of themselves or their children), "a spousal notice requirement enables the husband to wield an effective veto over his wife's decision."[263] We might add that the risk of abuse is triggered, not only by the news of an intended abortion, but also by the news that the wife is pregnant, perhaps (in the husband's mind) by another man. In closing this discussion, Justice O'Connor has this to say:

> A State may not give to a man the kind of dominion over his wife that parents exercise over their children. [The husband-notice law] embodies a view of marriage consonant with the common-law status of married women but is repugnant to our present understanding of marriage and of the nature of rights secured by the Constitution. Women do not lose their constitutionally protected liberty when they marry.[264]

Do the words of Susan Estrich and Kathleen Sullivan echo in the background?

Then, what about the twenty-four-hour delay, which Justice O'Connor concludes is valid? (I put aside the provision requiring the doctor to inform the woman about the status of the fetus, and to let her know about the state's anti-abortion literature. The burden of that requirement is far from trivial, but it pales by comparison to the burden imposed by the twenty-four-hour wait.) My own view is that a rigorous application of the undue-burden analysis, the very kind employed for the spousal-notice law, ought to produce a similar conclusion of invalidity. Even the court of appeals agreed with the district court that the burdens of this delay—on a woman who has limited means, or lives out of town, or fears abuse if her husband finds out—might be highly significant. But

---

[262] 505 US at 894.

[263] Id at 897.

[264] Id at 898.

that court seemed to be trying to "psych out" Justice O'Connor's views, as expressed in *Akron*, where she voted to uphold just this sort of delay, and in *Hodgson*, where the delay implicit in a judicial bypass did not trouble her much. As for *Hodgson:* in her *Casey* discussion of the spousal-notice law, Justice O'Connor distinguished decisions similar to *Hodgson*, saying that they rested "on the quite reasonable assumption that minors will benefit from consultation with their parents and that children will often not realize that their parents have their best interests at heart. We cannot adopt a parallel assumption about adult women."[265] As for *Akron:* well, perhaps Justice O'Connor in 1992 was not quite the same person who wrote that dissent in 1983.

Here let me venture a speculation. We know that, in the discussion with Justices O'Connor and Souter that led to the joint opinion, Justice Kennedy—who had initially said he would uphold all the Pennsylvania laws—agreed to join Justice O'Connor in voting to invalidate the spousal-notice law. That law surely presented the women's-rights aspect of the case in its strongest light. Suppose, however, that Justice Kennedy still had no inclination toward holding any of the other laws invalid. Given the importance of cementing Justice Kennedy's agreement with the "undue burden" approach, and the importance of a united front—why else write a joint opinion?—perhaps it would be prudent to uphold the twenty-four-hour delay for lack of sufficient evidence of the burden in this particular case. That course of action would leave open the possibility of a new challenge to such a law—perhaps even this law—based on a further and more persuasive showing of "its impact on those whose conduct it affects." Something like this is what the joint opinion (that is, Justice O'Connor) said about the twenty-four-hour wait. The district court's findings, she said, "are troubling in some respects, but they do not demonstrate that the waiting period constitutes an undue burden"—because the district judge was not applying the undue burden standard, and so did not specifically decide that the delay was a "substantial obstacle" to exercise of the right of choice. Rather, the district court had fallen into the error of applying *Roe*'s strict scrutiny.[266] "Hence, *on this*

---

[265] Id at 895.

[266] Id at 886.

record, we cannot say that the waiting period imposes a real health risk."[267]

This line of explanation may seem less than compelling to you, as it does to me. But, as a way to assure Justice Kennedy's continued support, and at the same time to keep the issue alive for the future, it serves as well as the average judicial device for avoidance. In an attempted salvage operation, Planned Parenthood went back to the district court. They got the desired findings, and then faced stone walls in the Third Circuit and the Supreme Court. Justice Souter, as Circuit Justice, put the final stone in the final wall, denying a stay of the court of appeals's mandate. His brief opinion expressed doubt that the Court would grant certiorari or that Planned Parenthood would ultimately prevail on the issue. He read Justice O'Connor's reference to "this record" to be no more than a statement that other litigants, in other cases, might put together a more convincing record.[268] To round out my speculation, a more plainspoken version of the final message might have been, "We've exhausted our capacity for maintaining a united front. Don't push your luck."

In the years since *Casey*, the Supreme Court has chosen not to decide many cases on abortion choice regulation. The two chief cases that they have decided both serve as illustrations of the principle that a case of small scale can be the occasion for high emotion—precisely because the dimensions of the case emphasize its symbolic importance. Symbolism is what was mainly at stake in both cases. But—let no one underemphasize the importance of symbolism in the politics of cultural counterrevolution. It is no exaggeration to say that this brand of politics takes its importance because of its focus on symbols of group identity and status.

The first of these cases was *Mazurek v Armstrong*.[269] In Montana there is no surplus of doctors available to perform abortions. However, Susan Cahill, a physician's assistant, was the one non-doctor in the state authorized to perform abortions; the state did not argue that she lacked the competence or training to perform them successfully. The Montana legislature, with the specific purpose to

---

[267] Id (emphasis added).

[268] If you were to tell me that Justice Souter ran this one by Justice O'Connor and Justice Kennedy before acting, I wouldn't be shocked.

[269] 520 US 968 (1997).

disqualify Ms. Cahill—she was pointed out by name in the legislative debate—adopted a law limiting the performance of abortions to doctors. Forty other states had such laws, and in the absence of a legislative purpose to burden the right of choice, the law would likely be upheld under *Casey*. But Justice O'Connor had written in *Casey* that a purpose to interfere with exercise of the right of choice would, of itself, invalidate a law. Here, in a per curiam opinion, six Justices (including Justices O'Connor, Kennedy, and Souter) concluded that there was no basis for finding such a purpose, saying that any such purpose "is positively contradicted by the fact that only a single practitioner is affected."[270] With respect, that particular assertion strains credulity, given the law's legislative history.[271] But the case's procedural posture gave the majority another reason to reject the claim: the Ninth Circuit had intervened improperly, ordering an injunction before trial.[272] Perhaps there was a further concern that a contrary decision might send the wrong message about the validity of other doctors-only laws. In any event, Ms. Cahill, who formerly was allowed to perform an abortion only under the supervision of a doctor who was physically present, now must limit her ministrations to assisting the doctor who is performing the abortion. Depending on how one defines "assisting" and "performing," it is possible for a non-physician to wonder how much has changed.

Abortion-choice politics takes no holidays. Those who would mobilize constituencies around anti-abortion-choice themes are on the lookout for opportunities to propose restrictive laws. One purpose, of course, is to recruit new citizens to the anti-abortion-choice cause. In part, the politics of status domination concerns the group identity of the constituent. The political operative regularly offers the constituent not only the chance to *do* something (cast a vote, or contribute time or money), but, by taking that action, to *be* someone whose identity is validated by the state. So,

---

[270] Id at 973.

[271] An additional indicator of the legislature's purpose was that this law was one of a package of three anti-abortion-choice laws. The other two required second-trimester abortions to be performed in hospitals, and forbade advertising of abortion services. Both of these provisions had been held unconstitutional at the federal district court level. On the import of such omnibus packages, see the text at note 294.

[272] The same procedural posture caused the dissenters to say the Supreme Court's own intervention was improper at this stage.

among its other consequences, the enactment of a law restricting abortion choice can symbolize a status gain, reassuring the supporting constituents that this is Our state. But another purpose emphasizes the identity of the politician, reassuring the existing anti-abortion-choice constituency of the politicians' loyalty to the "pro-life" position. Enacting a law restricting abortion choice is politically productive, even when the law is unconstitutional and never takes effect, for it allows the legislator to show that he is one of Us—a true believer in the cause.[273] In the 1990s, anti-abortion-choice activists found a new way to dramatize their case: to propose and enact laws forbidding what they named "partial birth abortion." Legislators around the country rushed to enact these laws, and litigation proliferated to challenge the laws' validity.[274]

"Partial birth abortion" is not a medical term; it is a designedly incendiary metaphor for an infrequently used procedure called intact dilation and extraction (or D & X), mainly used after the fifteenth week of gestation. Doctors who use D & X say they do so only when, in their opinion, it is safer for the woman than would be the more common (at that stage) method of dilation and extraction (or D & E).[275] There is no dispute that, under *Casey* (as formerly under *Roe*), a law prohibiting the use of D & E before the stage of viability would be unconstitutional. In *Stenberg v Carhart*,[276] the Supreme Court, 5–4, held Nebraska's law unconstitutional on two grounds. First, it did not provide an exception for an abortion necessary to preserve the life or health of the pregnant woman. Second, by extending beyond forbidding D & X to prohibit some forms of D & E, it imposed an undue burden on use of the latter, constitutionally protected, procedure.

---

[273] I explored this theme of group status politics (that "futility can be an advantage") in Karst, *Socialization of Children* at 1022 (cited in note 179).

[274] Some 30 states adopted such laws, mainly in the South and the Midwest. The volume of litigation justified an ALR annotation. See Carolyn Bower, *Annotation: Validity, Construction, and Application of Statutory Restrictions on Partial Birth Abortions*, 76 ALR 5th 637 (2000). A large majority of these cases produced rulings that the laws were unconstitutional, even before the Supreme Court acted.

[275] In any abortion as late as the fifteenth week of gestation, the skull of the fetus must be collapsed. In D & E, the fetus is extracted head first, with the skull collapsed before extraction. In D & X, the fetus is extracted feet first, with the skull collapsed after part of the fetus has been extracted. Hence the coinage by anti-abortion choice advocates of the nonmedical but politically potent term, "partial birth abortion." Just why D & E does not carry the same label is presumably not a medical question. Perhaps, however, this is to be the next step for the politics of status.

[276] 530 US 914 (2000).

Justice O'Connor concurred in Justice Stephen G. Breyer's opinion of the Court, but added an opinion of her own. She pointed out that Nebraska would present a constitutional question "quite different from the one we face today" if it were (1) to add an exception (paralleling its exception to the general law prohibiting post-viability abortions) allowing the procedure when it is necessary to preserve the life or health of the woman who is the patient, and (2) to define the prohibited D & X more narrowly (as other state laws had done), to exclude the danger that the law might be applied to the more commonly used methods of abortion, including D & E.[277]

Even defenders of these laws forbidding D & X refer to the procedure as rare.[278] And, concededly, such a law contributes not at all to the two interests identified—by Justices on both sides of abortion choice controversies from *Roe* to *Casey*—as justifications for regulating abortion choice: protection of fetal life and protection of women's health.[279] The dissents in *Stenberg* urge that government has legitimate and powerful interests beyond the protection of fetal life and a woman's health, and they take note that these interests lie in the realm of symbolism—that is, expressing the state's official moral views to the doctor and to the woman. Justice Kennedy suggests that one such state interest is to preserve doctors' self-images as healers, by nurturing their respect for life. The idea is that D & X, by "using the natural delivery process to kill the fetus,"[280] more strongly resembles infanticide than does

---

[277] Id at 950. She provided examples of such laws in Kansas and Montana.

[278] An example is Judge Daniel Manion, dissenting in *Planned Parenthood of Wisconsin v Doyle*, 162 F3d 463, 471 (7th Cir 1998) ("very rare"). This decision invalidating the Wisconsin law was consolidated with a case challenging a similar Illinois law, and reversed en banc (5–4) sub nom. *Hope Clinic v Ryan*, 195 F3d 857 (7th Cir 1999). On remand after *Stenberg*, the Seventh Circuit held the Wisconsin law and the Illinois law invalid. 245 F3d 603 (7th Cir 2001). Abortions in the United States are running at an annual rate well over a million. In *Stenberg*, the Court said there were no reliable data on the number of D & X procedures per year, which had been estimated at a low of 640 and a high of 5,000. (These estimates appear to have come, respectively, from an opponent and a proponent of laws prohibiting D & X.)

[279] As Judge Richard Posner said, "The only fetuses whom the statute will save are those whose mothers are afraid for reasons of health to undergo an alternative procedure to a partial birth abortion." *Planned Parenthood of Wisconsin v Doyle*, 162 F2d at 471 (cited in note 278).

[280] This characterization appears to draw a distinction between D & E, which causes fetal death in the womb, and D & X, which causes death a moment later in the birth canal. See id at 470.

D & E. Another such interest, he says, is the moral construction of a woman's self-definition, by telling her that one procedure is more immoral than another.[281] Justice Thomas further suggests that "respect for fetal life" is such a state's interest.[282]

Here we can see a close parallel with the symbolic politics of abortion choice restriction. What is at stake, for the *Stenberg* dissenters, is the creation and maintenance of a symbolic world, in which personal identities are negotiated. The symbolic negotiation of identity plays a vital role in the lives of all of us, and I hope it is not disrespectful to suggest that Justices may be included in this generalization. The vehemence of an opinion may intensify if a Justice thinks that he or she is not merely *doing* something, but *being* a particular sort of person.

As an illustration, consider the question whether D & X is—or can be in some patients' cases—safer than D & E. Medical witnesses and medical groups (as amici curiae) showed up on both sides of *Stenberg*, differing as to the morality of D & X and as to its degree of safety relative to D & E. The *Stenberg* majority emphasizes a respectable medical view that D & X may be safer for some patients[283]—a point supported by the district court's findings. The state, and the dissenters, claiming support from other medical authority, conclude that this safety factor is trivial. Justice Thomas says, "it is not clear that *any* woman would be deprived of a safe abortion by her inability to obtain a partial birth abortion."[284] Let us assume that, on this issue, as on the number of D & X abortions actually performed, the available sources of data are in dispute. What does a Justice do, confronting such uncertainty?

A Justice does what you (or I) would do: decide on the basis of your own worldview about the area of experience under consideration (here, regulations of abortion choice) and your own sense of self—and then write an opinion maximizing the evidence supporting your view, and minimizing the evidence on the other side. If you think *Roe v Wade* was "grievously wrong," and "the *Casey* joint opinion was constructed by its authors out of whole cloth,"[285]

---

[281] 530 US at 962–64.

[282] Id at 1020.

[283] Id at 937.

[284] 503 US at 1020 (emphasis in original).

[285] Id at 980, 981 (Thomas dissenting).

surely you will place your trust in the state legislature's medical judgment. Alternatively, you may believe that "Courts are ill-equipped to evaluate the relative worth of particular surgical procedures."[286] If, however, you are committed to a woman's right of reproductive choice, and you strongly suspect that this is just another law designed "to chip away at the private choice shielded by *Roe v Wade*,"[287] you will be inclined to think that a physician's professional judgment about the safety of a surgical procedure in a particular patient's case is more trustworthy than the wholesale medical judgment of a legislator who votes for this law with his[288] mind on scoring points with a particular constituency.[289] You will also be concerned about any potential for reduced safety when D & X is banned. Beyond that, you will fear that upholding this law may well lead to further restrictive legislation and further erosion of the woman's constitutional right. Whichever way you come down—on the factual issue of the relative safety of D & X for some women, or on the broader constitutional issue—you may sense that the underlying symbolic struggle has implications for your own identity. For ordinary citizens as well as public servants, doing and being are not sharply differentiated. A major element of who we *are* consists of what we choose to *do*. With this in mind, a fresh reading of Justice O'Connor's concurrence in *Stenberg* is worth while.

---

[286] Id at 968 (Kennedy dissenting), citing similar language in Justice O'Connor's *Akron* dissent, 462 US at 452 (cited in note 34).

[287] Judge Posner, dissenting in *Hope Clinic v Ryan*, 195 F3d at 881 (cited in note 278), quoted by Justice Ginsburg in her *Stenberg* concurrence (joined by Justice Stevens), 530 US at 952.

[288] Again, I do mean *his*. On a related theme, I have looked at circuit court opinions written before *Stenberg*, see Bower, *Annotation*, 76 ALR 5th 637 (cited in note 275) (on laws prohibiting D & X), to see how women judges voted. All of the four women circuit judges who heard such cases agreed with the position later taken by Justices O'Connor and Ginsburg in *Stenberg*. A sample of six would not satisfy any social scientist, but I doubt that this unanimity is accidental.

[289] Judge Richard Posner had this to say about the laws prohibiting D & X:

These statutes, remember, are not concerned with saving fetuses, with protecting fetuses from a particularly cruel death, with protecting the health of women, with protecting viable fetuses, or with increasing the Wisconsin population (as intimated, surely not seriously, by Wisconsin's counsel). They are concerned with making a statement in an ongoing war for public opinion, though an incidental effect may be to discourage some late-term abortions. The statement is that fetal life is more valuable than women's health.

Hope Clinic v Ryan, note 278 above, 195 F3d at 880–81 (Posner, J, dissenting).

Recall that Justice O'Connor supports both of the majority's grounds: the Nebraska law's failure to allow an exception where D & X is necessary to preserve the life or health of the pregnant woman, and the prohibition's overly broad coverage, extending to the constitutionally protected D & E procedure. But—and here I am reminded of her affirmative action opinions from *Wygant* to *Adarand*—she goes on to commend a path along which Nebraska's legislators can achieve a legitimate objective without endangering the constitutional right of reproductive choice. She does not associate herself with the skeptical belief (which I share) that Nebraska's law is first and foremost a salvo in the politics of group status. Nor, on the other hand, does she think there is any disrespect for Nebraska in a judicial insistence that the state protect a doctor's judgment of medical necessity and explicitly sever its punishment of a doctor who uses D & X from the threat to a doctor who uses D & E. If any sense of personal identity is to be found here, I think it is the self-image of a judge who listens—and pays sympathetic attention—to the concerns expressed on both sides of a constitutional dispute.

So, have Rachael Pine and Sylvia Law been confirmed in their prediction about *Casey?*[290] Does it effectively overrule *Roe*, or undermine it? *Stenberg* is a counterexample, but in this field, decisions (especially 5–4 decisions) can readily succumb to changes in the Supreme Court's personnel. One vital issue remains to be considered seriously by the Court: whether birth control clinics—today indispensable to the right of reproductive choice—are to be protected against legislative attack.[291] Specifically, will the Court defend the clinics against laws requiring abortions to be performed in hospitals? The *Akron* Justice O'Connor voted to uphold such a law, but what will the *Casey* Justice O'Connor think? Don't you have a hunch? If the Court fails to protect the clinics, it will have abandoned the right of choice reaffirmed in *Casey.*

---

[290] See note 250 supra.

[291] The Court has upheld injunctions offering considerable protection against anti-abortion picketers' harassment of patients and others who seek to enter clinics. Justice O'Connor has joined in those opinions, from *Madsen v Women's Health Center, Inc.*, 512 US 753 (1994), through *Hill v Colorado*, 530 US 703 (2000). She also joined in *National Organization for Women v Scheidler*, 510 US 249 (1994), in which the Court applied the damages provision of the federal Racketeer Influenced and Corrupt Organizations Act (RICO) against repeated unlawful blocking of entrances to clinics. That same year, Congress provided damages and injunctive remedies against such tactics in the Freedom of Access to Clinic Entrances Act (FACE), upheld in *United States v Scott*, 187 F3d 282 (2d Cir 1999).

One common feature of anti-choice lawmaking, from *Akron* to the present, is the tendency to wrap a number of different restrictions in a single legislative package. Surely this feature of the *Akron* case had some influence on Justice Powell's skepticism, expressed in his statement that portions of the package of restrictions "supposedly" were motivated by a concern to inform a woman's decision to undergo an abortion.[292] A hospital requirement, in 2003 as in 1983, is not just burdensome because it drastically increases the cost of abortions; it is almost certainly *designed* to undermine abortion choice by that very means.[293] This motivation is not a sometime thing; it is ever-present in these omnibus compilations of abortion choice restrictions.[294] When a court is asked to rule on the constitutionality of a law that limits women's access to reproductive health services, the legislative context of today's anti-abortion-choice politics strongly suggests that Judge Posner's skepticism[295] is justified. A judge's usual deference to legislative judgments deserves reappraisal, given the high probability that a purpose other than protecting women's interests is driving the legislative process.

3. *Sexual orientation.* The political program of gay rights advocates has had considerable success in recent years, and by 2003 had secured the repeal or judicial invalidation of sodomy laws in three-quarters of the states, along with the enactment of antidiscrimination legislation in a modest number of states and a large number of cities.[296] Public and private institutions by the hundreds

---

[292] See note 32 and accompanying text. Justice Powell was similarly receptive to realism in *Edwards v Aguillard*, 482 US 578, 597 (1987) (Powell, J, concurring), in evaluating the politics that converted the Book of Genesis into "Creation Science." Justice O'Connor joined that opinion.

[293] A similar purpose to increase costs and deter the exercise of a right of choice is conspicuously visible in South Carolina's extraordinarily exacting regulations of outpatient abortions in clinics and doctors' offices. *Greenville Women's Clinic v Bryant*, 222 F3d 157 (4th Cir 2000). You will get no inkling of the facts of this case from the Fourth Circuit majority; to understand these regulations for what they are, you have to read the district court's opinion, 66 F Supp 2d 691 (DCSC 1999), or Judge Hamilton's dissent in the court of appeals, 222 F3d at 175. Surprisingly, the Supreme Court denied certiorari, 531 US 1191 (2001). It is conceivable that the Justices felt they needed a break from the subject of abortion after the discord of the *Stenberg* case, 530 US 914 (cited in note 276).

[294] It was present in *Casey*, for that matter, but, as we have seen, Justice O'Connor had her work cut out for her in getting a majority for her position invalidating the husband-notice provision.

[295] Quoted in note 289.

[296] See William N. Eskridge, Jr., *Gaylaw: Challenging the Apartheid of the Closet* 356–71 (Harvard, 1999), for a chart of such laws as they were then.

have made health insurance and other employment benefits available to gay and lesbian couples.[297] Some states have adopted laws offering some benefits to gay and lesbian couples, and Hawaii, Vermont, and California have adopted domestic partnership laws authorizing unions that are similar in legal effects to marriage. All these changes reflect the movement's more fundamental success in persuading millions of gay and lesbian Americans[298] to "come out," acknowledging this aspect of their self-definition. By the dawn of this century, public attitudes toward homosexuality had become far more generous than they were a generation ago.[299] As one would expect, so conspicuous a cultural change has produced a political backlash of considerable intensity.

In two ways, this backlash is a politics centered on group identity and group status: First, it frequently touches a strand of nervousness (especially male nervousness) about the constituent's own identity.[300] Second, the central question that it raises overtly is whether a gay identity is acceptable—and, for the practitioners of backlash politics, the answer is No. Senator Helms's 1990 campaign statement[301] is just one example. The very idea of a gay identity, of course, is immensely complicated. Humans just do not fit into neat categories of sexuality, but live their lives and define themselves in endless variety.[302] All the identity labels are just that: labels, constructs of the mind, myths.[303] But this is precisely where identity politics takes a hand, imposing on political strategy—and

---

[297] Lisa Fackler, *In Gay Rights, Private Sector Is "Unlikely Hero," Survey Finds*, LA Times A30 (Aug 14, 2002).

[298] To avoid awkwardness in writing, I say "gay and lesbian," or sometimes just "gay," in the hope that the reader will supplement the terms with others such as bisexual or transgendered where that may be appropriate.

[299] See, e.g., Jeni Loftus, *America's Liberalization in Attitudes Toward Homosexuality, 1973 to 1998*, 66 Am Soc Rev 762 (2001).

[300] I examined this subject at length in Kenneth L. Karst, *The Pursuit of Manhood and the Desegregation of the Armed Forces*, 38 UCLA L Rev 499, 502–10, 549–63 (1991).

[301] Quoted in text at note 177.

[302] The most interesting modern source on the kaleidoscopic varieties of sexual identity is Eve Kosofsky Sedgwick, *Epistemology of the Closet* (California, 1990). My favorite epigram along these lines comes from James Baldwin: "Homosexual is not a noun." Richard Goldstein, *"Go the Way Your Blood Beats": An Interview with James Baldwin*, in William B. Rubenstein, *Cases and Materials on Sexual Orientation and the Law* 71, 77 (West, 2d ed 1997).

[303] On the myths of gay identity, and their uses and abuses in politics and law, see Kenneth L. Karst, *Myths of Identity: Individual and Group Portraits of Race and Sexual Orientation*, 43 UCLA L Rev 263, 275–79, 284–86, 302–05, 308–11, 318–21, 353–64 (1995).

even on law—a binary system of categories: gay or straight. Gay rights activists necessarily mobilize much of their support around the self-categorization of gay identity, and their political antagonists seek to vilify gay identity as a way of portraying an Enemy[304] that threatens Our group's values and status dominance. As for law, the very antidiscrimination legislation that promotes the inclusion of gay and lesbian Americans as equal citizens has the unavoidable effect of reinforcing the labels of sexual orientation. At the same time, law (in the form of prohibitions and exclusions) has been a preferred tool for demonizing gay identity.[305] Politics and law keep pulling us back to the same question, and it is a question that makes identity central in a question about inclusion: Is it OK to be gay?

One feature of the backlash against gay rights successes was a national movement to repeal the new antidiscrimination laws. That movement, coordinated by the Christian Coalition, culminated in a 1992 ballot proposition (Amendment 2) to amend Colorado's state constitution, repealing all laws and policies of state agencies and local governments that forbade discrimination on the basis of sexual orientation, and prohibiting any such laws or policies for the future. The campaign for Amendment 2 laid bare the sponsors' purpose to pronounce an official anathema on homosexual orientation. A group called Colorado for Family Values distributed an eight-page pamphlet to some 750,000 homes. The pamphlet's main message was the asserted evil of homosexuality (enticement of children, destruction of the family, forcing churches to perform gay marriages, and the like).[306] The campaign also included distribution of 4,000 copies of a lurid fifteen-minute video, "The Gay Agenda," produced by the Springs of Life Ministries of Antelope Valley, California.[307] The video was later featured on the 700

---

[304] On the utility of an Enemy in political mobilization, see Murray J. Edelman, *Constructing the Political Spectacle* 66–89 (Chicago, 1988); James D. Hunter, *Culture Wars: The Struggle to Define America* 144–47 (Basic, 1991). The technique is an old one. See Richard Hofstadter, *The Paranoid Style in American Politics and Other Essays* 2–141 (1965; Chicago Reprint Phoenix ed, 1979).

[305] See Eskridge, *Gaylaw* at 205–38 (cited in note 296).

[306] The pamphlet is printed as an appendix to Robert F. Nagel, *Playing Defense*, 6 Wm & Mary Bill of Rts J 167, 192–99 (1997). The figure 750,000 comes from his article. Andrew Koppelman, *The Gay Rights Question in Contemporary American Law* 23 (Chicago, 2002), places the figure at 800,000.

[307] The same video reappeared when President Clinton was proposing to lift the ban on gay and lesbian service members. The Commandant of the Marine Corps gave copies to

Club, Rev. Pat Robertson's nationwide television program, and by 1993 the video's producers and the Christian Coalition had distributed some 25,000 copies nationally.[308] Colorado was to have been the proving ground for similar legislation in other states. But the Supreme Court called at least a temporary halt in *Romer v Evans*.[309]

Before we examine the opinions in *Romer*, let us take a look at the way the case was argued. We have seen that Justice O'Connor had joined the majority in *Bowers v Hardwick*, upholding Georgia's sodomy law in application to homosexual sex.[310] One argument in *Romer*, persuasive to three (but only three) Justices, was that *Hardwick* had settled the question: if the state could prohibit homosexual sex, then surely it could express its disapproval of that conduct, and thus refuse to protect the conduct's practitioners against discrimination. The scornful majority opinion in *Bowers v Hardwick*, which validated Georgia's (assumed) purpose to declare homosexual conduct immoral, invited interpretation as an acceptance of antigay sentiment, discrediting a gay identity.[311] This argument is far from a logical necessity,[312] but it expresses a social reality, just as prominent among those who self-identify as gay or lesbian as among those who despise homosexuality and all its works. So, those who challenged the constitutionality of Colorado's Amendment 2 had their work cut out for them, and they saw Justice O'Connor's vote in *Hardwick* as a part of their problem.

Led by Laurence Tribe, five law teachers filed a brief as amici curiae, calling for invalidation of Amendment 2 on a ground that did not require overruling *Hardwick*. In Einsteinian physics, light bends as it passes a major gravitational source. If the light of the law teachers' brief was bent, one reason was Justice O'Connor's

---

members of the Joint Chiefs of Staff, and uniformed servicemen distributed it to members of Congress. Karst, *Law's Promise* at 129 and n 113 (cited in note 87).

[308] David Colker, *Anti-Gay Video Highlights Church's Agenda*, LA Times (Feb 22, 1993), A1.

[309] 517 US 620 (1996).

[310] 478 US 186 (cited in note 41).

[311] The Burger concurrence expressed the Chief Justice's own stigmatizing sentiment even more directly. 478 US at 196.

[312] The logical flaw is that the argument lumps homosexual conduct and homosexual identity together. Yet, this is exactly what the majority opinion in *Hardwick* had done, without pausing to take notice. See Janet E. Halley, *Reasoning about Sodomy: Act and Identity In and After Bowers v Hardwick*, 79 Va L Rev 1721 (1993).

gravitational pull.[313] They argued that Amendment 2 had singled out gay and lesbian Coloradans as ineligible for protection against discrimination—a denial of equal protection of the laws in its simplest form. At the oral argument in *Romer*, Justice O'Connor asked several questions exploring this argument. For example:

> Does the amendment mean that gays are not covered by Colorado's laws of general applicability?, O'Connor asked. The literal language suggests that, for example, a public library could actively discriminate against homosexual patrons, who would be unable to find relief without garnering enough support to enact an amendment repealing Amendment 2, O'Connor said.[314]

Colorado's supreme court, anticipating this concern, had tried to give a more limited interpretation of the broad language of Amendment 2, but Justice O'Connor's question highlighted the sweeping coverage of the amendment. That effect, together with the amendment's narrow targeting of persons with homosexual identity, was crucial in the Supreme Court's eventual opinion. Justice Kennedy, writing for the Court, expressed doubt that the Colorado court's interpretation would be sufficient to block the application of Amendment 2 as a more general limit on gay Coloradans' right to invoke general antidiscrimination laws. But, he went on, the law's singling out of homosexual orientation, and its breadth of application, could be explained only by animus toward the group constituted by gay and lesbian citizens—a basis for the law that failed the test of rationality.[315] Animus there may have been, but much of the motivation for Yes voters on Amendment 2 surely was fear—the very kind of fear that had fed the Social Issues Agenda of the 1980s. Surely many voters thought they were defending their way of life and their cherished values (and their social status) against an incom-

---

[313] One sensible strategy, given Justice O'Connor's likely pivotal role, was to present the brief on behalf of teachers across a fairly wide spectrum of views about substantive due process and judicial activism. The amici, in addition to Tribe, were Kathleen Sullivan (like Tribe, seen as a constitutional liberal), John Hart Ely (critic of *Roe v Wade*), Gerald Gunther (rock-solid lawyer's-law expert and well-known admirer of the second Justice Harlan), and Philip Kurland (trenchant critic of the Warren Court).

[314] *Arguments Before the Court*, 64 US L Week 3279 (1995).

[315] At the oral argument, Justice Kennedy had commented that the classification in Amendment 2 seemed to have been adopted "just for its own sake"; as a justification, "it just doesn't work." 64 US L Week at 3279.

ing tide of irreligion and sexual permissiveness.[316] Fear and animus may overlap, but they are not identical. Yet Justice Kennedy, when he wrote of animus, was not making a factual finding that half a million Coloradans voted for Amendment 2 because they hated their gay and lesbian co-citizens. Rather, he was drawing a legal conclusion that a state cannot subject a group to a disqualification from equal citizenship—a grave harm—with no purpose but maintaining the group's subordination. Animus may not be a perfect word to express this legal conclusion, but it will do.

After the decision, commentators on the *Romer* opinion focused on Justice Kennedy's reference to animus: How did that concept differ from the moral disapproval that had been articulated as the basis for upholding the law in *Hardwick?*[317] This seeming inconsistency was the central point of Justice Scalia's acid dissent, and he pointed out that Justice Kennedy had not even mentioned *Hardwick*.[318] One answer, uttered in private, might itself have recognized Justice O'Connor's gravitational pull: "Yes, there is plenty of tension here. But let's wait a while before we press her to take a fresh view of that subject." For me, the most impressive statement in Justice Kennedy's opinion is one that resonates with a number of Justice O'Connor's decisions and opinions in other fields:[319]

> We find nothing special in the protections Amendment 2 withholds. These are protections taken for granted by most people either because they already have them or do not need them; these are protections against exclusion from an almost limitless number of transactions and endeavors that constitute ordinary civil life in a free society.[320]

Here Justice Kennedy is expressing the nation's aspiration to an inclusive public world. In doctrinal terms, he is talking the language of equal citizenship.[321]

---

[316] This complicating factor is effectively expounded in Nagel, 66 Wm & Mary Bill of Rts J 167 (cited in note 306).

[317] I have provided citations to this extensive commentary in Kenneth L. Karst, *Constitutional Equality as a Cultural Form: The Courts and the Meanings of Sex and Gender*, 38 Wake Forest L Rev 513, 548–49 nn 201–07 (2003).

[318] 517 US at 640.

[319] At this point Justice Kennedy is responding to the argument in the dissent—echoing one of the more respectable slogans in the political campaign for Amendment 2—that Amendment 2 merely denies "special rights" to gay and lesbian Coloradans.

[320] 517 US at 631.

[321] See Joseph S. Jackson, *Persons of Equal Worth: Romer v Evans and the Politics of Equal Protection*, 45 UCLA L Rev 453 (1997).

Last Term, when *Lawrence v Texas*[322] came to the Supreme Court, raising a challenge to the Texas law that criminalized homosexual sodomy, a great many briefs amici curiae were filed. One such brief was especially notable: that of the American Bar Association (ABA). As early as 1973, the ABA had adopted a policy urging the repeal of sodomy laws, and since that time it had adopted various policies urging elimination of discrimination based on sexual orientation. The brief was well crafted. It urged, on due process liberty grounds, that *Hardwick* be overruled, and also urged that the Texas law violated the Equal Protection Clause. But perhaps the most important fact about the brief was that the ABA had weighed in so strongly against the Texas law. The brief contained an appendix listing the names of eighty-one out of the Nation's one hundred largest law firms that had told a national survey that they had policies specifically forbidding discrimination based on sexual orientation.[323] (The brief noted that several additional firms among the hundred largest also had such policies, advertised on their web sites.) One could hardly wish for a more persuasive demonstration that time had passed *Hardwick* by.[324] Other briefs seeking invalidation of the Texas law seemed concerned to speak directly to Justice O'Connor. No one could know whether she would be amenable to an overruling of *Hardwick*, and so—while arguing for just such an overruling—some advocates directed their main arguments to the equal protection claim, in the *Romer* vocabulary.[325] On the last day of the 2002 Term, the Court provided a second pillar (the first being *Romer*) supporting the edifice of equal citizenship for lesbians and gay men.

---

[322] 123 S Ct 2472 (2003).

[323] For many of the firms, a policy of discrimination would violate state law. For all of them, discrimination would violate the rules for on-campus interviewing issued by the Association of American Law Schools.

[324] "Romer did not overrule Bowers. But America did." Jay Michaelson, *On Listening to the Kulturkampf, or, How America Overruled Bowers v Hardwick, Even Though Romer v Evans Didn't*, 49 Duke L J 1559, 1607 (2000).

[325] One brief, written by Pamela Karlan and William Rubenstein, was filed on behalf of 18 law teachers as amici curiae. (I was one of the amici.) The brief began by agreeing with the Petitioners that *Hardwick* should be overruled, but from that point forward it was devoted to a demonstration that, under the Equal Protection Clause, the discrimination in the Texas law was invalid because it was "not related to the achievement of a legitimate state interest." Justice O'Connor's opinion suggests that she was receptive to argument along these lines.

Now the Court squarely faces the issue of due process that *Romer* had avoided, and, in a remarkably strong opinion by Justice Kennedy, expounds a vigorous version of the freedom of intimate association. The right in question, he says, is not limited to sexual conduct. Sodomy laws, in their penalties and their purposes,

> have more far reaching consequences, touching upon the most private human conduct, sexual behavior, and in the most private of places, the home. The statutes do seek to control a personal relationship that, whether or not entitled to formal recognition in law, is within the liberty of persons to choose without being punished as criminals. . . . [A]dults may choose to enter upon this relationship or to set its boundaries absent injury to a person or abuse of an institution the law protects. When sexuality finds overt expression in intimate conduct with another person, the conduct can be but one element in a personal bond that is more enduring. The liberty protected by the Constitution allows homosexual persons to make this choice.[326]

As for *Bowers v Hardwick*, Justice Kennedy concludes a long historical and doctrinal examination by saying the decision "was not correct when it was decided, and it is not correct today"; therefore, it "should be and now is overruled."[327]

Justice O'Connor, concurring separately, begins with a statement that will take its place in the annals of lukewarm acceptance of precedent: "I joined *Bowers*, and do not join the Court in overruling it."[328] Instead, invoking *Romer* and other related decisions, she concludes that the Texas law violates the Equal Protection Clause:

> Texas' sodomy law brands all homosexuals as criminals, thereby making it more difficult for homosexuals to be treated in the same manner as everyone else. Indeed, Texas itself has previously acknowledged the collateral effects of the law, stipulating in a prior challenge to this action that the law "legally sanctions discrimination against [homosexuals] in a variety of ways unrelated to the criminal law," including in the areas of "employment, family issues, and housing." . . . While it is true that the law applies only to conduct, the conduct targeted by

---

[326] Id at 2478.

[327] Id at 2484.

[328] Id. She also says the issue whether a general sodomy law, not limited to homosexual sodomy, would violate the Due Process Clause "need not be decided today"—thus at least hinting that her attachment to the *Hardwick* precedent is not strong. Id at 2487.

this law is conduct that is closely correlated with being homosexual. Under such circumstances, Texas' sodomy law is targeted at more than conduct. It is instead directed toward gay persons as a class. . . . A legislative classification that threatens the creation of an underclass . . . cannot be reconciled with the Equal Protection Clause.[329]

Despite their different doctrinal paths to decision, the opinion of the Court and Justice O'Connor's concurrence have much in common, substantively speaking. Justice Kennedy explicitly remarks on the overlap of the two constitutional grounds:

Equality of treatment and the due process right to demand respect for conduct protected by the substantive guarantee of liberty are linked in important respects, and a decision on the latter point advances both interests. If protected conduct is made criminal and the law which does so remains unexamined for its substantive validity, its stigma might remain even if it were not enforceable as drawn for equal protection reasons. When homosexual conduct is made criminal by the law of the State, that declaration in and of itself is an invitation to subject homosexual persons to discrimination both in the public and in the private spheres. The central holding of Bowers has been brought in question by this case, and it should be addressed. Its continuance as precedent demeans the lives of homosexual persons.[330]

In the quoted passages, both of these opinions highlight the theme of equal citizenship.[331] Not surprisingly, both opinions dismiss Texas's argument that the law finds justification in the legislature's wish to express official moral disapproval of homosexuality. Justice Kennedy for the Court, and Justice O'Connor, too, find this argument inadequate to satisfy even the mere-rationality standard of review.[332] Surely they are right in concluding that the principle of equal citizenship trumps a legislative majority's determination to denigrate a group of citizens.

---

[329] Id at 2486–87 (citation and internal quotation marks omitted).

[330] Id at 2482.

[331] For a thoughtful assessment of due process liberty and equal protection strategies for minority advocates, see Eskridge, 47 UCLA L Rev 1183 (cited in note 261). The *Lawrence* opinions (Justice Kennedy's for the Court, and Justice O'Connor's concurrence) strike me as confirmations of Eskridge's theses.

[332] At the relevant point in her opinion, Justice O'Connor says, "*Bowers* did not hold that moral disapproval of a group is a rational basis under the Equal Protection Clause to criminalize homosexual sodomy when heterosexual sodomy is not punished." 123 S Ct 2486.

For gay rights advocates, the combination of these two opinions has an attraction all its own. With Justice O'Connor's opinion resting squarely on the Equal Protection Clause, and Justice Kennedy's discussion of equality as both a source and a product of the freedom of intimate association, the stage is now set for a more rigorous judicial scrutiny of official discrimination founded on sexual orientation. Both Justice Kennedy and Justice O'Connor are careful to reserve the question of gay marriage for another day. Justice Scalia, dissenting, suggests that the equal protection ground leaves "on pretty shaky grounds" a state law limiting marriage to a man and a woman.[333] On principle, of course, he is right; yet there can be little doubt that a decision invalidating such a legal limit lies some distance in the future. Surely, though, that decision will arrive, one day.[334] In the meanwhile, all sorts of discriminations on grounds of sexual orientation are suspect—not yet "suspect classifications" in the conventional doctrinal sense, but at the very least requiring substantial justification in the manner of *Plyler v Doe*[335] and *Cleburne v Cleburne Living Center*,[336] both cited by Justice O'Connor and both applying rationality review with rigor.[337] In a single remarkable week, the Court has given us two landmark decisions fostering the constitutional principle of equal citizenship and the ideal of an inclusive public world.

III. State Sovereignty, Equal Citizenship, and the Limits of Trust

Of the constitutional subjects that might be said to be close to Justice O'Connor's heart, surely one of the closest is state sovereignty. During the Burger Court years, we saw her arguing for a robust form of state autonomy, invulnerable to intrusions by Congress. Her view eventually prevailed in cases of the kind presented

---

[333] Id at 2496.

[334] I am assuming here that the Constitution will not be amended to ban any official recognition of gay marriage. But see Elizabeth Shogren, *Foes of Gay Marriage Find New Momentum*, LA Times A1 (Aug 1, 2003).

[335] 457 US 202 (1982).

[336] 473 US 432 (1985).

[337] On the irrationality of statutes and judicial decisions disqualifying gay and lesbian candidates to be adoptive parents, see Karst, *Socialization of Children* at 971–82 (cited in note 179).

in *FERC v Mississippi*,[338] now called "commandeering" cases.[339] In such a case, concerns about maintaining an inclusive society, or defending the constitutional right of equal citizenship, typically are marginal.[340] But in another doctrinal context, limitations on congressional power in the name of state sovereignty do present those concerns. I refer, of course, to congressional efforts to protect civil rights. The fifth section of the Fourteenth Amendment (Section 5) broadly authorizes Congress to "enforce" the amendment's provisions. The Supreme Court, with Justice O'Connor a regular participant, has recently given Section 5 a series of restrictive interpretations. In this section I do not offer a full analysis of any of those decisions. Instead, I focus on Justice O'Connor, seeking to highlight the potential for tension when her views of state sovereignty come into contact with Congress's efforts to strengthen the principle of equal citizenship through the medium of federal civil rights laws.

We begin with the power of Congress to protect civil rights through laws governing the behavior of private (nongovernmental) individuals, and then turn to another question: Assuming that Congress has the power to regulate behavior by the states, can it abrogate the states' sovereign immunity, subjecting them to liability for money damages? The Rehnquist Court's response to these issues has been largely unreceptive to congressional power. Alas for Congress's power to protect civil rights, today's "new federalism" bears an uncomfortably strong resemblance to the unlamented "dual federalisms" of the American past.

The first dual federalism was summed up by a member of the Court in these terms:

> In my judgment the power over this subject is exclusively with the several states . . . and the action of the several states upon this subject, cannot be controlled by congress, either by virtue of its power to regulate commerce, or by virtue of any other power . . . .

---

[338] 456 US 742 (cited in note 26).

[339] *New York v United States*, 505 US 144 (1992); *Printz v United States*, 521 US 898 (1997).

[340] An exceptional case was *EEOC v Wyoming*, 460 US 226 (1983), upholding application of the Age Discrimination in Employment Act to a state as employer. Justice O'Connor was in dissent, and her views won back a portion of that ground in *Kimel v Florida Board of Regents*, 528 US 62 (2000), mentioned in the text at note 371.

The writer was Chief Justice Roger B. Taney, and the subject was slavery.[341]

The second dual federalism, both a political and doctrinal heir of the first one, is illustrated by this quotation from a well-known 1944 book:

> Bills against lynching have been introduced in Congress many times since 1922, but none of them has come close to passage. Southern congressmen center their strategy against anti-lynching legislation by claiming that it would be unconstitutional and an infringement upon states' rights.[342]

Lynching, of course, was private violence, in which state and local government officials typically had no immediate role. This is not to say that those officials had no responsibility in the matter. Indeed, one tragic feature of lynching was that, in one instance after another, state and local officials turned a blind eye. This state inaction systematically denied the protection of the laws.

In pre-Civil War America, and in the America that turned its back on the Fourteenth Amendment's promise of equal citizenship for three generations, the doctrine of dual federalism was in full flower. But, in the era from the New Deal to the Warren Court, judicial attitudes were markedly more receptive to congressional power in general and to Congress's protection of civil rights in particular. In the words of Inspector Clouseau, not any more.[343]

A. CONGRESS AND PRIVATE INVASIONS OF CIVIL RIGHTS

Violence against women—and especially domestic battering—has reached "epidemic proportions" in our nation.[344] *Domestic vio-*

---

[341] *Groves v Slaughter*, 40 US (15 Pet) 449, 508 (1841) (Taney, CJ, concurring).

[342] Gunnar Myrdal, *An American Dilemma: The Negro Problem and Modern Democracy* 565 note a (Harper & Brothers, 1944).

[343] The inspector was portrayed by Peter Sellers in the *Pink Panther* movie series. When, during a chase, he sprawled over a grand piano, reducing it to splinters, his hostess exclaimed, "*That* is a four thousand dollar piano!" Calmly, the inspector replied, "Not any more."

[344] Neil S. Jacobson and John M. Gottman, *When Men Batter Women: New Insights into Ending Abusive Relationships* 267 (Simon & Schuster, 1998). Low estimates of battering are in the neighborhood of 12 percent of all marriages, with some estimates reaching as high as 50 percent. "Battering" here means repeated hitting or beating. See Christine A. Littleton, *Women's Experiences and the Problem of Transition: Perspectives on Male Battering of Women*, 56 U Chi L Rev 23, 28 (1989); Martha R. Mahoney, *Legal Images of Battered Women: Redefining the Issue of Separation*, 90 Mich L Rev 1, 10–11 (1991). For further statistical confirmation of continuing widespread violence against women, especially pregnant women, see Reva B. Siegel, *"The Rule of Love": Wife Beating as Prerogative and Privacy*, 105 Yale L J 2117, 2172–73 (1996).

lence is an exercise of power and a divestment of power, and its effects are not limited to its individual women victims. In the aggregate, battering is a major source of the subordination of women. The analogy to lynching in the early twentieth century is uncomfortably apt: a persistent pattern of private violence, with state law enforcement officials and state judges systematically disinclined to intervene. This disinclination is largely founded in the view that government should not intrude into the "private" sphere of domestic life.[345] The result is a massive disempowerment of women as a group, not only denying them liberty but excluding them from the fundamentals of equal citizenship. A woman thus battered, and turned away from official avenues of protection, has no individual equal protection claim unless she can get over a barrier that is well-nigh insurmountable. She must prove that some state actor (for example, the maker of a policy that sharply limits police intervention in domestic battering, or the police officer who decides not to intervene, or the judge who responds to the woman's case with a hands-off attitude) was motivated by a purpose to discriminate against women.[346] In sum, we confront a condition in which large numbers of women are beaten, and state protective laws are effectively neutralized by the systematic laxity of their administration. Yet, this condition finds no legal recourse in the form of a remedy for a constitutional violation. In other contexts, such as employment and housing discrimination, federal civil rights legislation has been adopted to fill similar gaps in the protection of citizens against private wrongdoing. Perhaps a federal statutory remedy could help here.

State law enforcement officials certainly thought so. Starting in 1990, the National Association of Attorneys General supported a series of bills in Congress to involve the United States in the solution of a nationwide increase in violence against women. In 1993 the attorneys general of thirty-six states and the District of Columbia wrote a letter to Congress expressing support for the bill that became the Violence Against Woman Act (VAWA); soon after-

---

[345] On the roots of this attitude in the women-subordinating traditions of the common law, see Siegel, 105 Yale L J passim (cited in note 344).

[346] This is not just a reference to the general rule in *Personnel Administrator v Feeney,* 442 US 256 (1979), but the explicit conclusion of the First Circuit in the case of a real, live domestic violence victim—whereupon the Supreme Court denied review. *Soto v Flores,* 103 F3d 1056 (1st Cir 1997), cert denied, 522 US 819 (1997).

ward, four more states' attorneys general added their names to the letter.[347] The Act became law in 1994, creating civil remedies (damages, injunction) against batterers for victims of violence motivated by gender.[348]

The Rehnquist Court, protecting the states' sovereignty against the expressed wishes of their own highest law enforcement officers, held VAWA unconstitutional as an invasion of states' rights. The case was *United States v Morrison;*[349] the vote was 5–4; Justice O'Connor joined the opinion of the Court by Chief Justice Rehnquist. This opinion briefly states the facts of the case in six flat sentences, and for the next twenty-six pages treats the reader to an exercise in formal logic, cut loose from the facts of life.[350] (One simply cannot imagine Justice O'Connor's *writing* an opinion so abstract, so relentless in its avoidance of real-life contexts.) The Court concluded that Congress lacked power to enact this federal remedy, either under the Commerce Clause or under Section 5 of the Fourteenth Amendment. As to the commerce power: Congress had made extensive findings about the serious impact of domestic violence on women's employment, and thus on the national economy. The Court simply waved those findings away, saying that Congress can regulate local activities on the basis of their aggregate impacts on interstate commerce—but only when the regulated activity is economic. Gender-motivated violence *itself,* the majority declares, is not economic activity. Given this abstract categorical exclusion of congressional power, the real-life effects of domestic violence on production, earnings, and other elements of the economy are irrelevant. As to Section 5, the Court said that Congress's elaborate findings of pervasive bias in state justice systems against real-life victims of gender-motivated violence might justify "corrective" congressional action against discrimination by

---

[347] Letter of July 22, 1993, to Hon. Jack Brooks from Robert Abrams, Attorney General of New York, et al, in *Crimes of Violence Against Women,* Hearing before the Subcommittee on Civil and Constitutional Rights, Comm on Judiciary, HR, 103d Cong, 1st Sess 34–36 (1994) (hereafter "Hearing").

[348] The negotiations in Congress about the bill's terms are recounted and analyzed in Siegel, 105 Yale L J at 2196–2206 (cited in note 344).

[349] 529 US 598 (2000).

[350] Catharine MacKinnon has ably shredded the entire *Morrison* opinion, but her discussion of the triumph of abstraction over life is a gem that should not be missed. Catharine A. MacKinnon, *The Supreme Court, 1999 Term—Comment: Disputing Male Sovereignty: On United States v Morrison,* 114 Harv L Rev 135, 145–72 and passim (2000).

state officials,[351] but VAWA is directed at the individuals who commit the violence—and so is not "congruent" with unconstitutional state action. Nor is the VAWA remedy "proportional"[352] to state gender discrimination, for it applies throughout the nation—while (says the majority) Congress's findings were based on task force reports from only twenty-one states. The latter point is dubious in the extreme,[353] but put it aside for now. Let us turn to the "state action" limitation, beginning at the beginning.

As the large body of congressional civil rights legislation in the Reconstruction era testifies, private violence and intimidation were central features of southern resistance to the recognition of black Americans' equal citizenship. The Fourteenth Amendment does not speak of "action"; it forbids a state to "deny" the equal protection of the laws. In May 1871, Judge William Woods, sitting in the circuit court in Alabama, decided a case in which private individuals were accused of a federal crime: conspiring to deny citizens the freedom of speech and association. There had been no showing of any participation by a state or local officer, but Judge Woods was concerned with the substance of protection: "Denying includes inaction as well as action, and denying the equal protection of the laws includes the omission to protect . . . . [To guard the citizen's rights,] as well against state legislation as state inaction, or incompetency, the amendment gives Congress the power to enforce its

---

[351] Take a moment to think about what those corrective measures might be. Imagine the battered woman, wondering how she will prove that the system was unresponsive. If she were to seek legal advice, would not the lawyer also have some heavy wondering to do? Who is the appropriate defendant? Is failure to arrest "action"? What about a failure to recommend a prosecution, or to provide a judicial remedy theoretically available according to the law in books?

[352] Today the terms "congruent" and "proportional" are part of the obligatory vocabulary of Section 5; they are the now-hardened exudates of *City of Boerne v Flores*, 521 US 507 (1997).

[353] The suggestion unjustly minimizes the bases for Congress's finding of widespread failure of state law enforcement—and it ignores entirely the request for federal aid in the form of this very law, joined by the highest law enforcement officers of more than 40 states. More dishearteningly, it treats the factual basis for an exercise of Congress's Section 5 power as if legislation were a prosecution in court, with each state individually in the dock and "innocent" unless proved "guilty" beyond a reasonable doubt. Furthermore, it is wholly inconsistent with a major precedent, *Oregon v Mitchell*, 400 US 112 (1970), where the Court upheld a nationwide congressional prohibition on literacy tests as a condition on voting, on the basis of evidence of abuse in some, but not all, states. For full and persuasive articulation of all these points, see Robert C. Post and Reva B. Siegel, *Equal Protection by Law: Federal Antidiscrimination Legislation After Morrison and Kimel*, 110 Yale L J 441, 476–81 (2000).

provisions by appropriate legislation."[354] The opinion is very much in the spirit of the Fourteenth Amendment, but Judge Woods did not originate the quoted words. He borrowed them from a letter he had received two months earlier from Justice Joseph Bradley, responding to his request for advice.[355] Woods later became a Justice, and was in the majority that joined in Justice Bradley's opinion of the Court in the *Civil Rights Cases*,[356] which invented the "state action" doctrine as a limitation on the Fourteenth Amendment.

Why this turnaround? The "state action" doctrine was the 1883 coinage of post-Reconstruction judges who had become inhospitable to the Reconstruction civil rights laws. The Justices were bent on reconciling North and South—or, to be more precise, northern whites and southern whites. For them, the Compromise of 1877[357] loomed larger than the principle of equal citizenship.[358] In modern lingo, we can imagine them saying, "Reconstruction? Civil rights? That's so 1860s."[359]

In the current season of civil rights deregulation, the precedent of the *Civil Rights Cases* has played a starring role. The *Morrison* opinion is a prime example, citing with approval not only the *Civil Rights Cases* but also *United States v Harris*.[360] Both of those opinions held unconstitutional acts of Congress that directly regulated private conduct. But even in those cases of post-Reconstruction retrenchment, the Supreme Court was careful to point out (i) the availability of state law remedies, and (ii) the lack of evidence of

---

[354] *United States v Hall*, 26 Fed Cas 79, 81–82 (Cir CSD Ala 1871). Judge Woods rested the decision on Congress's Section 5 power to enforce both the Privileges and Immunities Clause and the Equal Protection Clause.

[355] See Harold M. Hyman and William M. Wiecek, *Equal Justice Under Law: Constitutional Development, 1835–1875* 436 n 90 (Harper & Row, 1982).

[356] 109 US 3 (1883).

[357] In that compromise, the Republicans traded the turnover of southern race relations to Democratic "redeemer" (white) legislators in exchange for the Hayes presidency. See generally C. Vann Woodward, *Reunion and Reaction: The Compromise of 1877 and the End of Reconstruction* (Little, Brown, 1966). Justice Bradley was a member of the electoral commission that adopted the compromise—just six years before he wrote for the Court in the *Civil Rights Cases*.

[358] See John Anthony Scott, *Justice Bradley's Evolving Concept of the Fourteenth Amendment from the Slaughterhouse Cases to the Civil Rights Cases*, 25 Rutgers L Rev 552 (1971).

[359] It is not impossible to imagine a parallel reaction by some of today's judges to the civil rights heritage of the 1960s.

[360] 106 US 129 (1883). The opinion was by Justice Woods. Like Bradley, he had changed his view after the Compromise of 1877.

any official misconduct that would justify extending federal power to private individuals. In dramatic contrast, the Congress that enacted VAWA had explicitly found a widespread failure of state officers to provide the remedies theoretically provided by state law in cases of private violence—or, to say it more pointedly, widespread denial by state officers of equal protection under state laws.[361] In this circumstance, application of the state action doctrine as a bar to congressional remedy stands the Fourteenth Amendment on its head.

For some of those who had given a careful reading to Justice O'Connor's *Casey* opinion, with its concern about wife battering at the heart of her reasoning that the husband-notice provision was invalid, this vote came as a surprise.[362] Her *Bray* dissent, too, had suggested not only a readiness to apply a federal civil rights law against private wrongdoers, but a concern for protecting women against intimidation—even describing that intimidation as gender-based.[363] Surely she must have been torn by the *Morrison* case. Surely she did not regard the epidemic of domestic violence as trivial, or as unrelated to the status of women. Here, once again, I am about to commit acts of blatant speculation.

Perhaps Justice O'Connor simply agreed with Chief Justice Rehnquist, who had publicly announced, before VAWA was enacted, that he opposed its adoption because its "broad definition of criminal [*sic*] conduct" was "so open-ended, and the new private right so sweeping, that [VAWA] could involve the federal courts in a whole host of domestic relations disputes."[364] (A corollary to this concern about expanding federal jurisdiction, as the Chief Justice intimated, is that conduct leading to civil relief under VAWA

---

[361] For elaboration of this point, see Post and Siegel, 110 Yale L J at 474–76 (cited in note 353).

[362] I admit to my own surprise. Before *Morrison* came down, I opined to a friend that Justice O'Connor would likely see this case as an important one for women's equal citizenship. My friend said, "Well, don't be too sure. She likes women, but she also likes states."

[363] 506 US at 345–56 (cited in note 244).

[364] William H. Rehnquist, *Chief Justice's 1991 Year-End Report on the Federal Judiciary, Third Branch,* Jan 1, 1992, at 1, 3. Most citizens, after opposing the enactment of a bill, lack the power to invalidate the law that results. The Chief Justice did not think it necessary to recuse himself in this 5–4 case. A similar opposition was registered by the Committee on State-Federal Relations of the Conference of [state] Chief Justices. See Hearing at 77–79 (cited in note 347). Here we might recall Justice O'Connor's article, written while she was a state appellate judge, criticizing federal intervention into various local legal affairs. O'Connor, 22 Wm & Mary L Rev 801 (cited in note 25).

would, indeed, amount to crime—an area that the recent version of dual federalism tends to assign to the sphere of the states.) Or perhaps, for Justice O'Connor, the difference between *Morrison* and *Bray* came down to this: she was unpersuaded of the need for federal intervention to protect women at home.[365] These speculations are (barely) plausible, but, after the *Casey* opinion, they do not seem wholly satisfying. For me, however, another speculation has greater persuasive power. It raises an issue of trust.

I think Justice O'Connor retains, from the time of the *FERC* case[366] and even before, a deeply felt suspicion that Congress will, if left unchecked, barge in on areas of traditional state and local concern and responsibility, displacing state laws, fastening a "straitjacket" on the states,[367] converting state governments into the equivalent of departments in France—"field offices of the national bureaucracy."[368] That sort of skepticism might suggest the *Morrison* technique of requiring Congress to pass a form of strict scrutiny in order to exercise its Section 5 power. In *Morrison*, remember, the Congress in adopting VAWA had taken a page from the strategy that worked in the civil rights era, relying partly on the commerce power. In the year following VAWA's enactment, the Supreme Court had announced a new and restrictive Commerce Clause standard for such laws.[369] One who is distrustful of the congressional octopus may be disinclined to let the Section 5 power take over where an appeal to the commerce power no longer works.[370] And this distrust may well reach to the factual underpinning of VAWA's justification under Section 5: Perhaps, given Justice O'Connor's own experience in state government, it is hard for her to accept that state police officers and judges, affected by gender stereotypes, are often inclined to treat domestic violence as a private matter into which the state should not intrude. End of speculation, for the moment.

---

[365] Christy Brzonkala, the victim of violence in Morrison, was not at home; to put the facts in a manner generous to the defendant, this was a date rape.

[366] 456 US 742 (cited in note 26).

[367] See her *Thornburgh* dissent, 476 US at 814–33 (cited in note 40).

[368] *FERC v Mississippi*, 456 US at 777 (O'Connor, J, dissenting) (cited in note 26).

[369] *United States v López*, 514 US 549 (1995).

[370] On the centrality of "pretext review" to test "congressional good faith" in the recent decisions on both the commerce power and the Section 5 power, see J. Randy Beck, *The Heart of Federalism: Pretext Review of Means-End Relationships*, 36 UC Davis L Rev 407 (2003).

B. CONGRESS AND THE ABROGATION OF STATE SOVEREIGN
   IMMUNITY

Starting in the late 1990s, a 5–4 majority—the lineup that has become so familiar in the last decade as to need no listing—has made the states' sovereign immunity into a formidable bar to private suits against the states for damages. Repeatedly, this majority has rebuffed attempts by Congress to abrogate the states' immunity, even in cases where it is conceded that Congress has the power to require the states to comply with its laws. Two of the cases involved federal civil rights laws. In *Kimel v Florida Board of Regents*,[371] Justice O'Connor wrote for the Court, holding that Section 5 did not authorize Congress to allow a suit for money damages against a state employer under the Age Discrimination in Employment Act. In order to justify its abrogation of the state's sovereign immunity under Section 5, the Court said, Congress must find a practice of unconstitutional state action and show that the damages remedy is appropriate to remedy or prevent such behavior. Congress had not specified any such pattern of unconstitutional state age discrimination—mainly because, under the Supreme Court's interpretation, a state's age discrimination is unconstitutional only in the extreme (and rare) case when it is irrational. Absent a showing of unconstitutional state action, says the Court, Congress's claim of power under Section 5 must fail. The dissenting Justices did not reach the issue of Section 5 power; they argued only that Congress could abrogate the state's immunity under the commerce power—a claim the majority readily rejected, following recent precedent.[372]

The following year, in *Board of Trustees of the University of Alabama v Garrett*,[373] the same majority reached the same result as to the Americans with Disabilities Act. The Court agreed that the state as employer was subject to the ADA, but Congress had no power under Section 5 to enforce that obligation by allowing an individual harmed by the state's violation to sue for damages against the state. This time Justice Breyer, in dissent, did articulate

[371] 528 US 62 (2000).

[372] The decision that inaugurated the New Era of State Sovereign Immunity was *Seminole Tribe of Florida v Florida*, 517 US 44 (1996); See Daniel J. Meltzer, *The Seminole Decision and State Sovereign Immunity*, 1996 Supreme Court Review 1.

[373] 531 US 356 (2001).

the claim that Congress's Section 5 power authorized abrogation of the states' immunity. He offered a mountain of examples of governmental discrimination against the disabled as proof that abrogation was appropriate as a prophylaxis against further discrimination. The majority's bland opinion, by Chief Justice Rehnquist, characterized the mountain as "anecdotal" and said that Congress had not satisfied its obligation of convincing proof of unconstitutional state action. After all, discrimination by the state against the disabled, like official age discrimination, was constitutionally valid so long as it was not irrational. After *Garrett*, civil rights advocates began to wonder whether any congressional showing would satisfy the new strict scrutiny test imposed by this majority. For example, would a state employee, subjected to sex discrimination on the job, now lose her right to sue the state for damages under Title VII of the 1964 Civil Rights Act?

Then, just last Term, a ray of light shone on the civil rights world. The Chief Justice and Justice O'Connor joined the four Justices who had been dissenting all along in the "new sovereign immunity" cases. A 6–3 majority upheld Congress's power under Section 5 to abrogate state sovereign immunity in actions for damages under the Family and Medical Leave Act. The case was *Nevada Department of Human Resources v Hibbs*.[374] Several points are common ground, shared by the majority and dissenting opinions. First, Congress can compel the states to provide their employees with the family and medical leave requirements of FMLA.[375] Second, Congress can rely on the Section 5 power only to remedy a state's violation of the Fourteenth Amendment, and the federal law must satisfy the tests of congruence and proportionality.

So far, so agreed. But the latter multifactored point divides the Justices when they apply it to this law. The principal dissenting opinion, by Justice Kennedy, reads very much like the majority opinions in *Kimel* and *Garrett*—two opinions that he cites repeatedly. He criticizes the majority's reliance on (*a*) studies showing widespread discrimination in private employers' leave policies, supplemented only by one survey's general conclusion that the states as employers tend to follow private employers' practices, and (*b*)

---

[374] 123 S Ct at 1972.

[375] The Commerce Clause is said to justify the act. Presumably, the entire Court is now reconciled to *García v San Antonio Met. Transit Auth.*, 469 US 528 (cited in note 28).

another unsupported assertion about state discrimination that had been addressed to Congress. (Both of the latter statements were made in support of an earlier bill, limited to parental leave, that Congress did not pass.) Justice Kennedy has no trouble demonstrating that this showing is thin, when compared to the Court's recent impositions on Congress of an extremely demanding standard of proof of constitutional violations by the states. Many states already have family leave policies, some of them more generous than the policy required by FMLA. Perhaps state leave policies have had disparate impacts on women and men, but to find a pattern of equal protection violation, he argues, it would be necessary to show intentional sex discrimination. Even assuming a pattern of state violation, Justice Kennedy concludes that FMLA fails the test of "congruence." If the constitutional violation be sex discrimination, all Congress need do is forbid the states to have different leave policies for women and men. True, that would leave it open for the states to provide no family leave at all—but, he says, such a policy would not violate the Equal Protection Clause.

Chief Justice Rehnquist, for the majority (including Justice O'Connor), responds that sex discrimination is doctrinally different from discrimination based on age or disability. Given the heightened scrutiny required when a state engages in sex discrimination, as a matter of logic it will be easier for Congress to prove a pattern of state constitutional violations in this field. The heart of the pattern, as identified by the Court, is the effect of traditional sex-role stereotypes on employer leave policies. Women have long been seen as the caregivers in their families, and that assumption has influenced a number of states-as-employers to focus on allowing leaves to women who are parents or who have other family care responsibilities. The stereotype of Woman as Nurturer is especially likely to produce sex discrimination when states give their supervisors wide discretion in allowing leaves.

If anyone cares, I fully support the majority's decision in *Hibbs*, and its reasoning, too. Still, Justice Kennedy is right in saying that the Court's standard for Congress's justification for exercising the Section 5 power is manifestly softer here than it was in all the earlier Section 5 cases. Indeed, the majority here agrees that it is giving Congress more latitude for "prophylactic" enforcement of the equal protection clause than it has tolerated in the earlier cases. FMLA, after all, is a remedy for sex discrimination. But *Morrison* also involved an act of Congress aimed at remedying sex discrimination, and the majority in *Hibbs* relies on inferences about state "constitutional violations" of a kind that the *Morrison* opinion derided as insufficient. Neither the majority nor Justice Kennedy cites *Morrison*.[376] Given our purposes here, however, it is worth our attention in comparison with *Hibbs*. Warning: We are reentering the speculation zone.

We can begin by noting that there may be a different "feel" to the Section 5 issue when it is presented in the two contexts of these cases. In *Hibbs*, unlike *Morrison*, it is conceded that Congress can regulate the states; the only matter in issue is the availability of damages in a private lawsuit. In other words, the congressional octopus has already intruded; validating damages on a Section 5 theory adds only an incremental strain, of uncertain degree, on the general principle of dual federalism. In *Morrison*, on the other hand, the Court had the opportunity to play Horatius at the bridge, to keep Congress out of the states' bailiwick altogether. There may be a second difference in the feel of the two laws— the feel, that is, to the Chief Justice and to Justice O'Connor. Perhaps FMLA feels like a true civil rights statute; as the Chief Justice says, it is "narrowly targeted at the fault line between work and family—precisely where sex-based overgeneralization has been and remains strongest."[377] To reach the opposite result would be to endanger Title VII's damages remedy when states are the employers. Now, you may say, VAWA was itself a civil rights law—and besides, the stereotype of women as sex objects is surely as pervasive and deep-seated as the stereotype identifying women as caregivers. If you said that, you would get no disagreement from me. But—and this is not merely a question of "feel," but a doctrinal distinction—finding "congruence" in VAWA's application to private conduct would raise concerns at the heart of the current majority's version of dual federalism, concerns going far beyond sex discrimination. For the *Morrison* majority, those concerns simply outweighed the argument that widespread domestic violence, widely condoned by officials, is a major contributor to group subordination.[378] In an era of civil rights deregulation, perhaps it

---

[376] In a separate dissent, Justice Scalia does cite *Morrison*, but not for its requirements on Congress to justify its exercise of the Section 5 power.

[377] 123 S Ct at 1983.

[378] 529 US 598, discussed in the text at note 349.

would be too much to expect for the majority—you know, the usual five—to break ranks on so fundamental a question.

C. WHOM DO YOU TRUST?

Racial classifications are "suspect";[379] sex classifications need "exceedingly persuasive justification" because they are likely to result from archaic stereotypes;[380] legislative-style democracy should rule unless there is reason for judicial distrust because some people are systematically underrepresented.[381] These are statements about trust. In theory, any standard of review—from the most relaxed rationality standard to the strictest strict scrutiny—is to be determined at the outset of reasoning about the case, and then applied, with the case's result turning on the application. I hope it is not too cynical to suggest that, from time to time, it appears that a judge has decided a case on the basis of some generalized notion of fairness, and only then selected a standard of review. My point here is that this sense of fairness is—properly—influenced by the judge's sense of trust or distrust in the process that has produced the government action that is being challenged in court. So, when I have opined in this article about Justice O'Connor's distrust of Congress,[382] or her willingness to consider the realities of group status politics as a basis for distrust of legislative motive,[383] I have not been suggesting any impropriety. Far from it.

To make this point by reference to a relatively neutral bit of judicial subject matter, consider the question of "undue burden" when it is raised in the context of a state regulation of interstate commerce. Suppose the judge thinks the law in question is designed to create an advantage for local interests, and a corresponding disadvantage for out-of-state interests. The judge might declare that the law discriminates against interstate commerce, and is thus invalid. An alternative, arguably gentler, opinion would

---

[379] The 100 percent ironic citation here is *Korematsu v United States*, 323 US 214, 216 (1944).

[380] *United States v Virginia* (note 189 above), 518 US at 524 and passim.

[381] A book-length treatment is John Hart Ely, *Democracy and Distrust: A Theory of Judicial Review* (Harvard, 1980). Ely takes "Footnote 4" as one starting point. *United States v Carolene Products Co.*, 304 US 144, 152 n 4 (1938).

[382] See, for example, *FERC*, 529 US 598, discussed in the text at notes 26, 366.

[383] As in *Rogers*, 458 US 613 (cited in note 70).

note that the law's burden on interstate commerce is considerable, while the state's legitimate (that is, nondiscriminatory) interests are marginal; hence, an undue burden; hence, an invalid law. It is not a giant step to see similar possibilities in the treatment by judges of social issues that are of great importance in group status conflicts.

Taking an example that is far from random, consider the subject of sex-role preservation, in the context of a law that requires abortions to be in a hospital or a surgical center. A judge may suspect—even know—that the law is designed to appeal to a particular constituency's interest in making abortion costly, perhaps as part of the constituency's larger status concern to obtain state endorsement of the image of women as maternal objects. If that is the judge's view, he or she may—in all propriety—distrust legislators' assertions about the need for hospitalization as a way to protect the health and safety of pregnant women. So, too, with South Carolina's extremely burdensome regulations of abortions in clinics and doctors' offices, which the Supreme Court declined to review.[384] Here, too, "undue burden" would be a nonaccusing way of expressing the conclusion that the law is invalid.

Justice O'Connor did show her distrust of the Pennsylvania legislature's law requiring a woman to notify her husband of her intent to have an abortion—and her *Casey* opinion made clear that the distrust was based on the law's foundation in traditional sex-role stereotyping about women's subordinate relation to their husbands. But there is something notable about the idea of stereotypes as a basis for distrust. *Hibbs* expresses the idea that a constitutional violation may lurk in a formally sex-neutral law when the legislature has been influenced by a sex-based stereotype. This idea is now well understood—thanks in good measure to the insights that can be seen in Justice O'Connor's *Hogan* opinion.[385] But the idea is in some tension with the Court's conclusion in *Personnel Administrator v Feeney*[386] that a finding of sex discrimination, when the text of the law is not explicitly discriminatory, requires a showing of a purpose to discriminate on the basis of sex.[387] If pressed to

---

[384] See note 293.

[385] 458 US 718 (cited in note 14).

[386] 442 US 256 (cited in note 346).

[387] Justice Kennedy raises this point in his *Hibbs* dissent, 123 S Ct at 1989, citing not *Feeney* but *Washington v Davis* (cited in note 65).

choose, I shall choose *Hibbs*, which is in tune with the principle of equal citizenship under the Fourteenth Amendment, and let *Feeney* shift for itself.

Moving to the recent *Grutter* decision, Chief Justice Rehnquist makes explicit his distrust of the University of Michigan's law faculty when he says the school's diversity admissions program has been misrepresented: "Stripped of its 'critical mass' veil, [the program] is revealed as a naked effort to achieve racial balancing."[388] Justice O'Connor, in contrast, recounts the testimony of various faculty members, and makes clear that she believes in the sincerity of their motives. She refuses to call the program a quota, disguised or otherwise, and notes that Justice Powell, in his *Bakke* opinion, had accepted the good faith of university officials. It is evident that each of these Justices has approached the record in the case with a general view of the relevance of race to university admissions today. Their different conclusions, we may confidently assume, grow out of their different attitudes toward the problem at hand. I leave it to others to discuss the Chief Justice's attitudes. Justice O'Connor's starting point, let me suggest, is plain enough on the surface of her *Grutter* opinion. She believes strongly in an America where the public world is characterized by trust—and by inclusion. After all these years of keeping the door open, last Term, in affirmative action's most important test ever, she provided the door with a "welcome" mat.

IV. CLOSING THOUGHTS

In her memoir, Justice O'Connor wryly notes that she has been called "the most powerful woman in the United States."[389] The observation appears in a chapter reflecting on "Women in Power," where she urges women to take their place in the public world as equal citizens, with "equal voices and equal responsibilities."[390] On the question whether women as a group may differ from men as a group in the way they exercise power, she suggests that if there are any differences, they are subtle. Whatever we may

---

[388] 123 S Ct at 2365.

[389] O'Connor, *The Majesty of the Law* at 195 (cited in note 85).

[390] Id at 201.

think about that question,[391] it may be useful for our present purposes to envision the idea of power along a continuum, with Power as Control ("I am in charge") at one pole, and Power as Capacity ("I am in a position to make a contribution") at the other. After some months of intensive review of Justice O'Connor's decisions and opinions on the subject of equal citizenship, I have no doubt that she sees her power as a Justice from the perspective of the latter pole.

For Justice O'Connor, we have repeatedly seen, context matters. The business of a judge is not to operate as a justice machine, but to exercise judgment. In the course of these twenty-two Terms, she has paid careful attention to detail, listening and learning. During an oral argument, when she asks a question, it is a *question*, not a bit of rhetoric designed to instruct counsel or the other Justices. It is this receptivity to new data and new points of view, I believe, that has contributed the most to her broadened views on such constitutional subjects as a woman's reproductive choice or discrimination on the basis of sexual orientation. She still deserves the label "moderate conservative"; what has changed is her awareness of what needs conserving if we are to be a nation.

Devotion to the principle of equal citizenship implies a way of thinking about the Constitution that keeps in mind the connections among individuals and peoples—the inevitable interdependence of Americans. The harm of stigma is, in its most immediate sense, the hurt of severance from connection. But the harm is not limited to the individual who is stigmatized; the whole community suffers from public policies of exclusion. From the early 1980s (her *Hogan* opinion for the Court and her concurrence in *Lynch*) to last Term's decisions (her opinion for the Court in *Grutter* and her concurrence in *Lawrence*), Justice O'Connor has perceived the importance of a broadly inclusive public world. This is not noblesse oblige; it is patriotism, the love of a whole country. In giving life to the constitutional principle of equal citizenship, she has served not only the interests of individual claimants to inclusion, but the nation's larger interest in the moral and material strength of an integrated polity.

---

[391] See Carol Gilligan, *In a Different Voice: Psychological Theory and Women's Development* (1982); Sherry, 72 Va L Rev 543 (cited in note 11); Karst, *Woman's Constitution* at 447 (cited in note 222).